Palgrave Studies in Disaster Science and Emergency Management provides state-of-the-art summaries of the field of disaster science and emergency management. The series aims to transfer evidence-based scholarship that enables researchers, practitioners, and students to impact science, practice, and policies. Each volume addresses social and global inequalities in an effort to reduce human suffering. The series sets an agenda for future research, policy, and practice interventions needed to move scholarship and emergency management forward.

The series editors and editorial board welcome proposals for short volumes (25,000–50,000 words) or authored monographs and edited collections (80,000–120,000 words) that address critical topics of concern worldwide.

Subhasis Bhadra • C. Jayakumar
Sanjeev Kumar Manikappa
Ajay Kumar Goyal
Dinakaran Damodharan • Kasi Sekar
Editors

Psychosocial and Mental Health Support for Disaster Management in India

palgrave
macmillan

Editors
Subhasis Bhadra
National Institute of Mental Health and Neurosciences (NIMHANS)
Bengaluru, Karnataka, India

C. Jayakumar
National Institute of Mental Health and Neurosciences (NIMHANS)
Bengaluru, Karnataka, India

Sanjeev Kumar Manikappa
National Institute of Mental Health and Neurosciences (NIMHANS)
Bengaluru, Karnataka, India

Ajay Kumar Goyal
National Institute of Mental Health and Neurosciences (NIMHANS)
Bengaluru, Karnataka, India

Dinakaran Damodharan
National Institute of Mental Health and Neurosciences (NIMHANS)
Bengaluru, Karnataka, India

Kasi Sekar
National Institute of Mental Health and Neurosciences (NIMHANS)
Bengaluru, Karnataka, India

ISSN 3059-2097 ISSN 3059-2100 (electronic)
Palgrave Studies in Disaster Science and Emergency Management
ISBN 978-3-032-02510-4 ISBN 978-3-032-02511-1 (eBook)
https://doi.org/10.1007/978-3-032-02511-1

Cover credit: DrAfter123

This Palgrave Macmillan imprint is published by the registered company Springer Nature Switzerland AG.
The registered company address is: Gewerbestrasse 11, 6330 Cham, Switzerland

Foreword

Disasters, whether natural or human-made, are more than ruptures in the earth or breaches in civil peace—they are emotional and psychological cataclysms that impact individuals, families, and communities long after physical wounds have healed. The psychosocial dimension of disaster response and recovery, therefore, is not peripheral—it is central. It is with a deep sense of commitment and urgency that I commend this timely and scholarly contribution, *Psychosocial and Mental Health Support for Disaster Management in India*, to all stakeholders engaged in the field of disaster preparedness, response, recovery, and resilience building.

The evolution of psychosocial support (PSS) as a critical and integral part of disaster management in India has been a journey marked by responsiveness, innovation, and interdisciplinary collaboration. From the early days of the 1981 circus fire tragedy in Bangalore—where civil society and government first worked in concert to address the psychosocial needs of survivors—to the institutionalization of PSS interventions after the 2004 Indian Ocean tsunami, India's experience stands as a unique and compelling case study. It is this trajectory, rich in learning, challenge, and triumph, that this book captures with commendable depth and clarity.

NIMHANS, as an institute of national importance under the Ministry of Health and Family Welfare, Government of India, has been at the forefront of this journey. Our institute has long upheld the importance of integrating mental health into primary and public health systems. Following the Indian Ocean tsunami of 2004, the Government of India designated NIMHANS as the nodal center for psychosocial support in disaster situations. Since then, our institute has actively developed and implemented models of care, trained thousands of mental health professionals and disaster responders, and contributed to policy formulation and capacity building at multiple levels. Many faculty, staff, and students from multidisciplinary backgrounds have helped to shape timely and appropriate responses to disasters.

The book rightly highlights how the experience of disasters like the 1981 Venus circus fire tragedy, the 1984 Bhopal gas tragedy, 1993 Marathwada earthquake, the 1999 Odisha super cyclone, the 2001 Gujarat earthquake, and the 2004 South Asian Tsunami, not only tested the nation's response systems but also exposed the long shadow that psychological trauma can cast over generations. These disasters forced a national reckoning with the importance of mental health and psychosocial well-being—not merely as afterthoughts, but as essential components of comprehensive disaster response and recovery.

Perhaps one of the most profound outcomes of these collective experiences was the formulation of the Disaster Management Act in 2005 and the subsequent creation of the National Disaster Management Authority (NDMA). These milestones laid the groundwork for institutional frameworks that explicitly recognized the psychosocial consequences of disasters. In 2009, the first-ever National Guidelines on Psychosocial Support and Mental Health Services (PSSMHS) were released—a watershed moment in India's disaster risk reduction and mental health narrative.

Since being declared a Centre of Excellence in PSSMHS by NDMA in 2010, NIMHANS has worked diligently to operationalize and expand the reach of psychosocial services across disaster-affected zones in the country. From providing emergency psychological first aid to training local primary healthcare workers, our efforts have embraced the principle of building disaster-resilient communities through mental health promotion, community mobilization, and stakeholder engagement.

In August 2019, the creation of the *Centre for Psychosocial Support in Disaster Management* at NIMHANS marked yet another pivotal point in institutionalizing disaster mental health. This was further upgraded in

2022 as the *Department of Psychosocial Support in Disaster Management*—a national-level nodal department that now leads psychosocial interventions across a wide range of disaster contexts, including pandemics, such as COVID-19.

This book emerges at a critical juncture, where the lessons of the past must inform and shape the policies of the future. It is comprehensive in scope, covering various models of psychosocial intervention, risk reduction strategies, capacity-building mechanisms, and the integration of mental health into emergency and disaster response frameworks. It provides rich case studies and offers grounded strategies that are informed by decades of fieldwork and research. Moreover, it underscores the necessity of multi-stakeholder collaboration and community engagement—a cornerstone of sustainable recovery.

I am particularly heartened by the academic utility of this book. Its content is immensely relevant for students of social work, psychology, psychiatry, nursing, disaster management, and public health. At NIMHANS and across many academic institutions in India, undergraduate and postgraduate programs have increasingly adopted interdisciplinary approaches to understanding trauma, crisis intervention, and disaster mental health. This book will serve as a core text and a practical guide in such modules and courses.

It will also be of significant value to civil society actors, government officials, first responders, and policy-makers. The strategic guidance provided in the book can inform real-time decision-making and long-term planning alike. Practitioners engaged in emergency response, rehabilitation, and peacebuilding will find this volume a critical resource in addressing both visible and invisible wounds of disaster.

As a nation that continues to face multifaceted disaster risks due to its geography, climate, and social-political landscape, India requires a proactive and sustained commitment to psychosocial resilience. This book helps illuminate a path forward. It does not merely look back at what has been done; it invites readers to think about what more can be achieved through evidence-based policy, inclusive programming, and human-centric planning.

The integration of psychosocial support into India's disaster management framework has not been a linear journey—it has been forged through real-world crises, shaped by the dedication of countless professionals, and driven by the indomitable spirit of communities. This book honors that journey. It is a testament to the vision that mental health is not a luxury in disaster management—it is a necessity. It is also a tribute to the resilience of individuals and communities in the face of disasters, as well as evidence that with support, they can emerge successfully out of crisis.

I congratulate the authors and editors for producing a scholarly and accessible work that bridges practice, research, and policy. As we move toward a future where resilience is measured not just by infrastructure but by emotional and social well-being, this book will remain a vital companion and a beacon of guidance.

Let this book inspire continued learning, collaborative action, and, above all, a deepened commitment to caring for the human mind and spirit—especially when tested by the extraordinary circumstances of disaster.

National Institute of Mental Health
and Neurosciences (NIMHANS)
Bengaluru, India

Pratima Murthy

Editorial Preface

It is with great honor and commitment that we present this edited volume, *Psychosocial and Mental Health Support for Disaster Management in India*, a significant and timely contribution to the expanding field of disaster mental health and psychosocial support (PSSMHS). This book is a product of collective wisdom, field-based knowledge, and academic engagement, brought together by the editorial team comprising Dr. Subhasis Bhadra, Dr. Jayakumar C, Dr. Sanjeev Kumar Manikappa, Dr. Ajay Kumar Goyal, Dr. Dinakaran Damodaran, and Senior Professor Dr Kasi Sekar, along with a committed team of doctoral and fellowship scholars from the Department of Psychosocial Support in Disaster Management at the National Institute of Mental Health and Neurosciences (NIMHANS), Bengaluru.

India, with its vast geographical spread, diverse ecological zones, dense population, and sociopolitical complexities, stands as one of the most disaster-prone nations in the world. It is not uncommon for India to experience multiple disasters—natural or human-made—within a single calendar year. This has made the country a global case study in both vulnerability and resilience. The scale and frequency of these events have long called for a robust and inclusive disaster management strategy that integrates psychosocial and mental health considerations as core components. In this context, the mental health and psychosocial well-being of both affected populations and disaster intervention workers have emerged as critical concerns.

This book captures the journey of psychosocial support in disaster management in India—an evolution that has spanned over five decades and has seen a gradual, yet purposeful shift from micro-level, immediate crisis response to macro-level, policy-influenced, sustainable mental health interventions. The National Institute of Mental Health and Neurosciences (NIMHANS), as a premier mental health institution in India, has played a pivotal role in this developmental trajectory. Through its research, training, and field-based action, NIMHANS has influenced not only direct disaster response practices but also broader public health and disaster policy frameworks at the national and international levels.

The distinct feature of this book is its specific focus on disaster intervention workers—those who are on the frontline, offering aid, relief, medical care, psychological first aid (PFA), and emotional support. While the community impact of disasters is often at the forefront of public discourse, the mental health of intervention workers is often neglected. These professionals, whether they are healthcare providers, humanitarian aid workers, first responders, or psychosocial counselors, face enormous emotional and psychological stress in disaster settings. This book attempts to bring their experiences, needs, and care practices into focus. By doing so, it offers a lens that is rarely highlighted in disaster literature but is fundamentally necessary for effective and humane disaster response systems.

The book is also a response to the changing academic landscape in India. With the increasing recognition of the importance of disaster management, many institutions of higher learning have introduced courses in disaster preparedness, response, and recovery. The University Grants Commission (UGC) has also mandated a two-credit course in disaster management for all undergraduate students, which includes a dedicated unit on psychosocial support. As a result, there is a growing need for well-researched, evidence-informed, and contextually relevant academic resources that can inform and guide this education. This book fulfills that need. It is tailored for students of social work, psychology, psychiatry, nursing, disaster management, and related disciplines, and will serve as a critical reference point in their learning journey.

The chapters in this volume are written by scholars, practitioners, and researchers who bring both depth of field experience and academic rigor. Collectively, the 19 chapters address a wide range of disaster types and mental health challenges, from the infamous Bangalore cirsus fire tragedy to the more recent COVID-19 pandemic. These chapters draw from disasters that are both natural (cyclones, earthquakes, floods) and human-induced (industrial accidents, communal violence), and address vulnerable populations, including children, persons with disabilities, and marginalized communities. These case studies are not only narrations of past events but also analyses of the psychosocial strategies that were applied, refined, or evolved in response to them.

The global nature of disaster vulnerability and resilience is acknowledged through comparative insights drawn from other continents. The Indian experience is situated within a global understanding of PSSMHS, allowing readers to appreciate the universal principles of psychosocial care in disasters while also recognizing the importance of context-specific adaptations. This global-local (glocal) approach makes the book relevant not just to readers in India, but also to international scholars, practitioners, and humanitarian organizations interested in South Asian models of intervention.

One of the book's significant strengths is its emphasis on evidence-based practices and field-validated modules that can be replicated or adapted in various settings. The chapters highlighted strong theoretical underpinnings in various interventions that are crucial for establishing scientific evidence. Several chapters introduce and elaborate on intervention modules that have been developed and applied in real-time disasters, such as:

- Safe School Protocols for disaster preparedness
- Hospital preparedness and psychosocial response
- Community-based disaster mental health models
- Specialized interventions for children and disabled persons
- CBRN (Chemical, Biological, Radiological, and Nuclear) disaster psychosocial modules
- Peace initiatives through psychosocial support
- Self-care frameworks for intervention workers

These modules provide a valuable toolkit for government agencies, NGOs, academic institutions, and frontline workers alike. Organizations such as Oxfam India, CARE India, UNICEF, ActionAid, and EveryChild UK, among many others, have historically played crucial roles in these intervention efforts. Their partnership with mental health institutions, including NIMHANS, has made it possible to develop scalable, contextually appropriate psychosocial interventions. This book captures many such collaborations and offers practical lessons for future partnerships and practice.

The volume also contributes to the ongoing discourse on Disaster Risk Reduction (DRR) by emphasizing the integration of psychosocial support into preparedness and mitigation strategies, rather than treating it merely as a post-disaster response. By doing so, it strengthens the bridge between mental health and public health, and between humanitarian response and development policy. With the United Nations' Sustainable Development Goals (SDGs) placing emphasis on mental health and well-being (Goal 3), this book offers a timely contribution to the intersection of mental health, disaster response, and sustainable development.

From a pedagogical standpoint, the book is structured to serve as both a reference text and a classroom companion. Educators can use it to design courses, training programs, and simulation exercises. For students and early-career professionals, it provides a foundational understanding as well as advanced insights into the real-world application of psychosocial support principles.

As editors, we take pride in the collaborative spirit that underpins this publication. The contributors—doctoral and fellowship scholars at NIMHANS—have brought in perspectives grounded in contemporary research, field immersion, and policy engagement. Their voices reflect the next generation of leaders in disaster mental health, and their contributions ensure that this volume remains rooted in both experience and inquiry.

In closing, we envision this book not just as a compilation of past experiences, but as a living document that will inspire ongoing dialogue, reflection, research, and innovation in the field of psychosocial support in disaster contexts. We hope it will become a go-to resource for students, teachers, researchers, planners, policy influencers, and, above all, disaster intervention workers whose service to humanity continues to be a beacon of courage and compassion in times of crisis.

We extend our sincere gratitude to all contributors, partners, and institutions who have shared their knowledge, experiences, and wisdom in shaping this work. May this book contribute meaningfully to building more resilient individuals, institutions, and societies.

We express our heartfelt gratitude to the Director of NIMHANS for her kind approval and encouragement in undertaking this important project. Our sincere thanks to Palgrave Macmillan for their continued support and cooperation throughout the publication process. We acknowledge the dedication of the doctoral and fellowship scholars from the Department of Psychosocial Support in Disaster Management (DPSSDM), NIMHANS, for their commitment to writing, reviewing, and incorporating feedback alongside their academic responsibilities. We also extend our appreciation to all the staff of DPSSDM for their direct and indirect contributions and unwavering support in bringing this book to fruition.

The Editorial Team

Bengaluru, Karnataka, India	Subhasis Bhadra
Bengaluru, Karnataka, India	C. Jayakumar
Bengaluru, Karnataka, India	Sanjeev Kumar Manikappa
Bengaluru, Karnataka, India	Ajay Kumar Goyal
Bengaluru, Karnataka, India	Dinakaran Damodharan
Bengaluru, Karnataka, India	Kasi Sekar

Acknowledgement

Bringing together the experience and expertise in the field of psychosocial support and disaster management in India has been a deeply thought-out initiative. This work has taken shape with the tireless efforts of many individuals committed to sharing their knowledge to help the world better understand the concepts and practices of psychosocial care and support in disaster settings, as well as in disaster risk reduction to live in a sustainable world with the concept of 'build-back-better' to 'build-better-before'.

Our immense gratitude to the senior Professor of Psychiatry, Dr. Pratima Murthy, Director of NIMHANS, for her support. The work in disaster mental health in India began in the decade of 1980s, led by Dr. H.S. Narayanan, and subsequently by Dr. R.S. Murthy, Dr. M.K. Isaac, Dr. R. Parthasarathy, Dr. Srikala Bharath, Dr. K.V.K. Kishore Kumar, and other professionals from different departments at NIMHANS who built a strong foundation in this area.

Government bodies such as NDMA, NIDM, and the State Disaster Management Authorities have collaborated closely. NGOs, including ActionAid, Oxfam, CARE India, USAID, EveryChild, Terre des hommes—India, and grassroots organizations like Unnathi, Saath, Samarth, Hath Milao, and many others have supported the field-level work. Different social work, psychology, and psychiatry departments at various institutes have supported the endeavor to work with the survivors of disaster. We humbly recognize their unconditional support and contribution.

We are deeply indebted to the survivors, whose trust, participation, and consent formed the foundation of all our initiatives. Their cooperation made it possible to reach and support affected communities meaningfully. Community members, Panchayat Raj Institutions, teachers, ICDS teams, Anganwadi workers, health workers, and community-level volunteers contributed to training and outreach efforts, helping to reach the individuals, families, and communities effectively.

We appreciate the valuable insights and suggestions provided by the reviewers, in both the internal and external review processes. Their feedback helped us refine and strengthen the overall structure of the book, and the necessary revisions were made accordingly.

Special thanks to Prof. Allen Dyer for his contributions, along with the support of other contributors, faculty members, senior professors, research scholars, students, administrators, project teams, the Registrar, and the publication team at Palgrave, who helped take this initiative forward across India and globally.

Dr. Subhasis Bhadra

On behalf of the Editorial Team

Contents

Notes on Contributors

V. R. Akhila is a UGC-NET-qualified PhD scholar in the Department of Psychosocial Support in Disaster Management at the National Institute of Mental Health and Neuro Sciences (NIMHANS), Bangalore. She holds a Bachelor's degree in Physics and a Master's degree in Social Work with a specialization in Medical and Psychiatry from the Central University of Kerala. She earned the Achiever of the Year Award (2019–20) from the Central University of Kerala and the Best All-Rounder Award (2016–19) from Providence Women's College, Kerala. She completed her MPhil. in Psychiatric Social Work at the Central Institute of Psychiatry, Ranchi. She has also worked at the Mental Health Action Trust, which provides comprehensive and recovery-oriented mental health care to those members of the poorest sections of the population who are suffering from severe mental disorders. Her academic and professional interests center on psychosocial support, mental health in disaster management, and capacity building. Currently, her PhD area of research focuses on the biopsychosocial dimensions of landslides on first responders and caregivers, reflecting her broader passion for understanding and mitigating the human impact of disasters.

S. Bala Shanthi Nikketha is currently a psychosocial consultant for The Asia Foundation, India on the Tridep initiative. With an MPhil and a PhD in Psychiatric Social Work from NIMHANS, she has vast experience in research, teaching, and practice in the area of psychosocial care and support. She has served as a consultant for the UNDP, coordinated the COVID-19 psychosocial program, and has worked with several civil society organizations, including Oxfam, India, UNICEF, and USAID. Her areas of interest include addressing the mental health needs of the vulnerable population, interventions for substance use disorders, and stress and well-being.

Urmila Bamney is a PhD scholar in the Department of Psychosocial Support in Disaster Management, NIMHANS. She has a BA degree in Psychology, Economics, and Sociology (2012) from Mount Carmel College, a Master of Social Work (MSW) specializing in Medical and Psychiatric Social Work from Bangalore University and received gold medal for securing 1st place among 11 affiliated colleges in 2014, a PGDHRM from KSOU, Mysore (2015), and an MPhil. in Psychiatric Social Work from Central University of Karnataka, Kalaburagi (2021). Her research interests involve the mental health of children, neuro-palliative care counselling, psychosocial interventions for disaster-affected populations, counseling, and psychotherapy. She has been actively involved in organizing and facilitating a wide range of training programs for children and adolescents, caregivers, educators, and professionals across sectors. She has also been engaged in training central and state government officers on topics, including mental health and emotional well-being, psychosocial support, and disaster psychosocial preparedness, contributing to systemic capacity building in public service.

Subhasis Bhadra is a Professor of Psychiatric Social Work in the Department of Psychosocial Support in Disaster Management at NIMHANS. Dr. Bhadra holds an MPhil. and a PhD in Psychiatric Social Work from NIMHANS. He started teaching in 2009 at Assam Central University and subsequently taught at Gautam Buddha University, and the Central University of Rajasthan. Dr. Bhadra worked in various disaster-affected areas in India and other Asian countries (Indonesia, Sri Lanka, Myanmar, Mongolia, Japan, and China) through different organizations, namely, Care India, the American Red Cross, ActionAid, and the International Medical Corps. He has completed a number of research and consultancy projects supported by NCW, SILF, International

Federation of Red Cross (IFRC), Discipleship Center, etc. His research interests include peacebuilding, psychosocial support, disaster mental health, and sustainable development. A total of five candidates have completed PhD research under his supervision. His publications include 45 academic articles, 48 book chapters, two books and one edited volume.

Ateev Sudhir Chandna is an experienced psychiatrist with a special interest in community psychiatry, psychosocial support in disaster management, and telepsychiatry. He has a proven track record in delivering comprehensive care, conducting research, and training healthcare professionals and is skilled in academic instruction, policy development, and community outreach. He has been recognized for excellence in psychiatry and psychotherapy with multiple awards and honours and is adept in managing diverse clinical settings and collaborating with multidisciplinary teams.

Allen Christopher is a PhD scholar at the Department of Psychosocial Support in Disaster Management, NIMHANS, studying geriatric mental health during the COVID-19 pandemic. He has an MA in Social Work and a fellowship degree in Psychosocial Support in Disaster Management. During this time, he was a part of the national psychosocial support helpline during the COVID-19 pandemic. His areas of interest include exploring the issues of the various vulnerable population in disasters and the role and effectiveness of tele-based interventions for mental health issues.

Dinakaran Damodharan Achieved an MBBS from Govt Stanley Medical College, Chennai (2005–2011). He then completed an MD Psychiatry from NIMHANS, Bengaluru with a Gold medal (2013–2016) He is currently working as an Assistant Professor of Psychiatry at NIMHANS. His research interests include biological psychiatry, trauma and resilience, and brain stimulation. He has published more than 50 research papers and 20 book chapters. He is a co-Investigator in the Tamil Nadu Police well-being program, Karnataka TeleMANAS project.

Anil Hemanna Doddamani is currently working as a research officer in the project titled "Health Sector Disaster Preparedness and Management" funded by MoH&FW, GoI. He is also pursuing his PhD in Psychosocial Support in Disaster Management at the Department of Psychosocial

Support in Disaster Management (DPSSDM), National Institute of Mental Health and Neurosciences (NIMHANS), Bengaluru. He is involved in the National Psychosocial Support Helpline services for disaster survivors and has more than five years of experience in the field of mental health. His area of interest is helping disaster survivors with psychosocial interventions.

Allen R. Dyer, MD, PhD is Professor of Psychiatry and Behavioral Sciences and Vice Chair for Education at the George Washington University in Washington, DC. Previously, he was Senior Health Advisor at the International Medical Corps. He is a graduate of Brown University and received MD and PhD degrees from Duke University. He has designed education programs to help communities heal after a number of disasters and conflicts. He is the recipient of a number of awards, including the Bruno Lima Award of the American Psychiatric Association and an Award and Recognition for service to the people of Iraq. He is the author of a number of books, including *Ethics and Psychiatry: Toward Professional Definition*, and is Editor of the *Textbook of Global Mental Health: Ethical Principles and Best Practices*.

Sona Francis is a PhD scholar in the Department of Psychosocial Support in Disaster Management at NIMHANS. She holds a BSc. in Chemistry from St. Joseph's College, Calicut, and a Master's in Social Work (MSW) with a specialization in Clinical and Community Practice from CHRIST University, Bangalore. She has qualified for the UGC NET-JRF (2022) in Social Work. Her research interests include disaster mental health, community disaster resilience, the psychosocial well-being of vulnerable populations, climate change-induced disaster threats, and disaster governance.

Ajay Kumar Goyal started his career in the year 2000 after achieving a PG in applied psychology. He worked in an ICMR project at the Institute of Human Behaviour and Allied Sciences, Delhi. Subsequently, earned an MPhil. in clinical psychology from NIMHANS and a Doctoral in "Collective Intelligence" from Indian Institute of Science, Bengaluru. He worked as a consultant in Training, Assessment, and Leadership Development divisions at 'Wipro Ltd' and 'Infosys Ltd.' He taught at

'Christ University' and Alliance University, Bengaluru for five years. Since October 2020, he has been working as an Assistant Professor of Clinical Psychology at the Department of Psycho-Social Support in Disaster Management, NIMHANS.

S. Harshavardhini is currently pursuing a Fellowship in Psychosocial Support in Disaster Management at the National Institute of Mental Health and Neurosciences. She holds a Master of Arts degree in Applied Psychology (Clinical and Counselling Practice) from the Tata Institute of Social Sciences. Her areas of interest lie in community mental health and supporting populations affected by disasters and conflicts. She is eager to develop expertise in mental health interventions for trauma survivors and trauma-informed approaches.

C. Jayakumar earned a PhD in Psychiatric Social Work from NIMHANS. He has more than 23 years of experience in the area of psychosocial care and disaster mental health and worked as a senior consultant for psychosocial care in NDMA. He also worked as Director of Operations for the American Red Cross in India. His contribution as coordinator of psychosocial care in tsunami-affected states enabled him to design, develop, and implement psychosocial care in the communities. He is also the Principal Investigator of 13 national and international projects. Dr. Jayakumar's areas of research interest are psychosocial care in disasters, disaster mental health, stress and well-being of marginalized communities (LGBTIQA, PWD), care for first responders, disaster preparedness, risk reduction, climate change and mental health.

Patrick Jude Lucas completed his MPhil. in Clinical Social Work from Government Stanley Medical College and Hospital, Chennai (2012–2014) and his PhD from the Department of Psychiatric Social Work, National Institute of Mental Health and Social Sciences (NIMHANS), Bengaluru (2014–2019). He is currently working as Assistant Professor in Psychiatric Social Work at the Department of Psychology, CHRIST (Deemed to be University), Bengaluru. His areas of interest are school mental health, psychosocial support in disasters, stress management for teaching communities and uniformed personnel, promotive mental health, psychosocial interventions, service learning, and peace education.

Sanjeev Kumar Manikappa, a qualified mental health professional trained at the Central Institute of Psychiatry and National Institute of Mental Health and Neurosciences, is currently working as an Associate Professor in the Department of Psychosocial Support in Disaster Management, NIMHANS where he is involved in clinical, academic, research, and training activities in the field of disaster mental health. His areas of interest are working with disaster survivors, especially children and adolescents, and mentally ill persons and their families by using curative, preventive, and promotive approaches. As a national trainer, he has carried more than 1000 capacity-building programs across India.

Chaitali Mendon is currently pursuing her PhD with the Department of Psychosocial Support in Disaster Management, NIMHANS. She holds a Master's degree in Counselling Psychology from CHRIST (Deemed to be University), Bengaluru. She has previously worked as a counsellor with Doctors Without Borders (MSF), India's sexual violence treatment center, and Tata Institute of Social Sciences' Sukoon project. She is interested in working as a practitioner and researcher with community-based mental health projects in humanitarian settings.

Bhavya Muniraju is a Fellow in the Department of Psychosocial Support in Disaster Management, NIMHANS. She has a BA degree in Psychology, Economics, and Sociology (2017) from NMKRV College for women, and an MSc degree in psychology from St. Francis De Sales college affiliated with Bangalore University. Her research interests involve life skills among adolescents, mental health of media personnel, and Indigenous practices of people vulnerable or affected by disasters. She has also carried out various capacity-building programs for children, students, Indian Railway officers, teachers, NGO workers, and healthcare professionals on subjects such as life skills education, mental health awareness, stress management, psychosocial care in disaster management, and student enrichment.

Lipika Pradhan is currently working as a Clinical Psychologist in the Department of Psychosocial Support in Disaster Management, NIMHANS, Bengaluru. She has earned a Bachelor's degree in Psychology from Utkal University and a Master's degree in Psychology from Ravenshaw University, Odisha. She has also earned an MPhil. degree in

Clinical Psychology from the Mental Health Institute (COE), SCBMCH, Cuttack, Odisha. Ms. Lipika has about four years of clinical experience as a Child Psychologist at NHM, Odisha, and subsequently worked as Clinical Psychologist in Adolescent Psychiatry at NISER, Bhubaneswar & and Telemanas, Cuttack, Odisha. Her areas of interest are psychological perspectives of disaster and intervention related to traumatic life events. Ms. Lipika's prospective areas of research are child and adolescent psychology in disaster preparedness and recovery, neurocognitive interventions, and rehabilitation for stress and traumatic experiences in disaster.

N. Sathana is a PhD Scholar at NIMHANS, Bengaluru, specializing in psychosocial support in disaster management. She holds a BSc. in Chemistry from Alagappa University (2019) and a Master of Social Work (MSW) with a specialization in Medical and Psychiatric Social Work from Madurai Kamaraj University, both awarded with Gold Medals for Academic Excellence at the University Level. Her academic and research interests lie at the intersection of climate change and mental health, with a particular emphasis on disaster governance. With a fervent commitment to scholarly inquiry, she seeks to advance understanding of the nuanced dynamics of disaster management, particularly within the framework of psychosocial support systems. Through her research, she aspires to contribute significantly to the discourse on mitigating the adverse psychosocial impacts of climate change-induced disasters, especially among vulnerable communities.

Kasi Sekar is presently a consultant with the Ministry of Health and Family Welfare and closely associated with central and state governments in the formulation of policies for PSSMHS in disaster management. He has an MSW from Madurai Kamaraj University, and a PhD in Psychiatric Social Work from NIMHANS, Bangalore. He is former Professor and Head of PSW and Head, Department for Psychosocial Support in Disaster Management, and Registrar at the NIMHANS. He was associated with NIMHANS for the past four decades. His areas of interest are disaster psychosocial support and mental health services (PSSMHS), strength-based social work, children in difficult circumstances, and community mental health. He has developed more than 250 national/international publications, and a number of training manuals and Information, Education, Communication (IEC) materials to be used by different target groups. Dr. Kasi Sekar has received many prestigious awards. He has worked in major disasters in India and abroad during the past three and a half decades.

K. A. Tansa is a mental health professional with more than ten years of experience. She completed her PhD in DPSSDM, NIMHANS, Bengaluru in 2025. She has developed and implemented various psychosocial care modules for schoolchildren across the state of Karnataka in collaboration with the education department and NGOs. She has also worked with more than 60 government schools in Bengaluru, Karnataka. As a national trainer, she has carried out various capacity-building activities. She has participated in various national and international conferences and has published a lot of research work. Her areas of interest are children, adolescents, and women.

Shubham Tiwari is currently pursuing a DM in Geriatric Psychiatry at the National Institute of Mental Health and Neurosciences (NIMHANS), Bengaluru. He completed his MBBS in 2019 from King George's Medical University (KGMU), Lucknow, where he was awarded a Bronze Medal in Forensic Medicine. He obtained his MD in Psychiatry from the Postgraduate Institute of Medical Education and Research (PGIMER), Chandigarh, in 2023. Following his MD, he briefly worked as a Senior Resident in the Department of Psychosocial Support in Disaster Management at NIMHANS for one month. His clinical and academic interests include psychiatric disorders in old age and policy-making, psychopharmacology, and psychotherapy.

List of Figures

List of Diagrams

List of Tables

Part I

Outlining the Trajectory of PSSMHS and Stakeholders in Disaster Interventions

1

Evolution of Psychosocial Support in Disaster Management in India; Mapping the Trajectory

Kasi Sekar and Subhasis Bhadra

Introduction

Over the years, psychosocial support (PSS) in disaster management has emerged as the core theme of disaster intervention in India. Since 1981, the National Institute of Mental Health and Neuro Sciences (NIMHANS), the premier mental health institute in India, has been involved in providing PSS to the survivors of disasters and it has played a significant role in developing the policies and programs in this regard. In the twenty-first century, the threat of disasters has substantially increased, and dealing with the events of disasters is always a challenge. Every such incident leaves a long trail of suffering that restricts development and pushes back hard-earned achievements. The disasters are not just nature's fury, but rather an outcome of various human actions and inactions as well. It is proved that there is no disaster without a human hand (Steinberg, 2000).

K. Sekar • S. Bhadra (✉)
Department of Psychosocial Support in Disaster Management, NIMHANS, Bengaluru, Karnataka, India

S. Bhadra et al. (eds.), *Psychosocial and Mental Health Support for Disaster Management in India*, Palgrave Studies in Disaster Science and Emergency Management,
https://doi.org/10.1007/978-3-032-02511-1_1

Earthquakes do not kill. It is the falling of a building that kills. Similarly, global warming, war, and refugee situations are outcomes of excessive consumption or aggression. Issues related to climate change and global warming are becoming the major reasons for these disasters. In the twenty-first century, almost 90% of disasters are classified as being weather- and climate-related. The accumulated loss to the world economy is estimated to be 520 billion USD each year, while 26 million people across the globe are pushed into poverty as a result (UN, 2020). Gradually, disasters are becoming grave and frequent, and climate change is working as a risk multiplier. Individuals, families, groups, communities, and nations are affected in multiple directions at multiple levels. Rescue, relief, rehabilitation, and resettlements are becoming increasingly challenging. Over the years, disaster intervention has been extended with the concepts of resiliency, "build-back-better," and sustainable development, and the strengthening of local solutions to global problems. In all the efforts of disaster management and intervention, one of the core strategies of intervention is PSS, which cuts across all the domains. In various national and international guidelines, PSS has been considered a cross-cutting theme for ensuring effective outcomes on any intervention. Hence, every humanitarian service provider working at different levels, starting from community-level workers to policy planners, is required to be trained to gain knowledge, attitude, and practical skills of intervention. The approach of PSS support has now taken shape towards "build-better-before" for disaster risk reduction (DRR) and "build-back-better" after any disaster (Diaz, 2004), Throughout the cycle of disaster, effective intervention is most crucial for enhancing the well-being of the people. This book aims to give a comprehensive understanding of the practice and integration of psychosocial support at different periods in the cycles of disaster management. This chapter captures, in brief, the trajectory of changes in disaster management and psychosocial support interventions in India.

In India, a book titled *Disaster Mental Health in India* was published in 2004. Subsequently, disaster management interventions, policies, and programs have developed substantially. The Disaster Management Act, of 2005, is an important milestone in this regard. Further, in 2024, the revisions in the act are proposed in the Indian Parliament with few modifications. Disaster management systems have evolved as an institutional response with a systematic approach and continuous engagement for DRR. Psychosocial support and mental health services (PSSMHS) have gradually taken central stage in disaster management intervention and DRR efforts. The development of Information, Education, Communication (IEC) materials, continuous capacity building for different cadres of staff and volunteers in various sectors, academic courses on disaster management, and research are among the important dimensions of development for strengthening PSSMHS interventions across the nation.

PSSMHS Interventions in Different Disasters in India

In India, PSSMHS in disasters became a mainstream intervention following the tsunami which struck the Indian subcontinent in 2004. The psychological and mental health consequences of disaster were taken as the subject of intervention and study since 1981, when Bangalore city, in Karnataka state, South India, witnessed a horrific circus fire tragedy in 1981, which killed 70 victims, of which were 53 schoolchildren. This intervention, for the first time, came in the form of an outreach service to the families of victims, focusing on individual pathological development and facilitating individual coping and family-based mental health care for recovery. In 1984, on a winter night in December, the people of Bhopal City, of Madhya Pradesh state, woke up with severe choking and breathing trouble as a result of a chemical leak. The disaster of the Bhopal Gas tragedy unfolded after the severe leakage of methyl isocyanide gas from a pesticide plant. That incident killed more than 8000 people over a period of two weeks, and the severe health consequences persisted for decades. The intervention to support mental health was initiated when there was no psychiatrist in Bhopal with the primary health care (PHC) doctors who were trained in mental health care. Long-term studies have revealed the need for intensive PSS to prevent long-term disabilities and illnesses that are closely linked to the psychological trauma of disaster.

The PSS interventions in the Marthawada earthquake, Maharashtra (1993), were at the community level by involving PHC healthcare workers and medical officers. Later, a super cyclone battered three coastal districts of Orisha in 1999, killing more than 10,000 and resulting in an equal number of missing. To deal with the severe trauma, a whole robust PSS model was developed to work with the community, institutions, and, specifically, with each family of survivors and various vulnerable groups. Here, civil society organizations and the State Government worked in collaboration to facilitate immediate and long-term PSSMHS. Two years later, in 2001, the western state of India Gujarat was jolted by an earthquake with a magnitude of 8.6 which killed about 13,800 people, and 1,67,000 suffered injuries. About 13,800 people died and 1,67,000 suffered injury (BHADA, 2011). In the next year, a few districts of the state were ripped apart by severe communal conflict and riots. The intervention in the earthquake focused similarly on the whole-community approach with a special focus on high-risk groups such as schoolchildren, women, the elderly, and survivors with severe spinal cord injuries and amputation. The intervention in riots was PSS for conflict resolution and peacebuilding at the individual, group, family, and community levels by engaging multiple stakeholders. The intervention with the survivors of communal conflict clearly showed the psychosocial needs of the disaster intervention or humanitarian workers. The referral services for mental health care needs, developing a specific model to work with women of sexual violence, and facilitating healing through community engagements were important highlights for building harmony between the communities that followed the principles of restorative justice.

In December 2004, when the Indian subcontinent was battered by the waves of the tsunami, the PSS intervention was extensively implemented in all the affected communities, taking the shape of state-level intervention. Since 2004, in several disasters (as with the earthquake in Jammu and Kashmir, 2005 (Mathew 2009); the Kandhmal riots in Odisha, 2008; floods, cyclones, landslides in different states; major air/rail/road accidents; and COVID-19), both PSS and MHS have been provided at the community and institutional level as a multi-stakeholder engagement model. During the COVID-19 pandemic, psychosocial and mental health issues surfaced across sections of the population as the random infection, and lockdown measures took a huge toll on the mental health of the nation. Fear, feelings of loneliness, personal losses, family issues, income insecurity, educational crisis, and professional challenges were all crippling the life of the people around the country. At this time a nationwide 24-hour hour helpline for psychosocial support was initiated by the Department of Psychosocial Support in Disaster Management at NIMHANS. This initiative turned into a nationwide program of Tele MANAS, a dedicated helpline for mental health support. The learning from each of the interventions was captured through several scientific studies, monographs, and reports that reflected the importance of psychosocial support for effective recovery, strengthening resiliency, and long-term sustainable development at multiple levels. Table 1.1 represents the major psychosocial interventions in different disasters and the key outcomes of each of these interventions.

Table 1.1 Major psychosocial interventions in disasters in India to track the trajectory

Event of Disaster: Venus Circus Fire Tragedy, Bangaluru, February 7, 1981 (Narayanan, 2004)
Damage: 70 persons belonging to 58 families, died. 40% of the victims died due to burn injuries. Th other 60% died due to stampede, shock, asphyxia, and other causes such as boulders falling on them, etc.
PSSMHS interventions:
• Family-based intervention at the home of the survivors started six months after the incident. Home visits by mental health professionals to provide emotional support to deal with grief, depression, negative coping, and loss. Referral of a few cases for therapeutic and pharmacological support to NIMHANS.
Key learning outcomes:
• Reaching out to the survivors at their doorstep is most crucial. Often, survivors are reluctant to seek psychiatric help. Home-based support using community resources is feasible.
• Reactions of survivors are reflections of social, cultural, and personal factors. Cultural contextualization of service is important.
• Survivors have multiple psychosocial needs, that need to be addressed comprehensively; psychosocial support is an essential component in post-disaster intervention for all survivors.

(continued)

Table 1.1 (continued)

Event of Disaster: Bhopal Gas leak (Chemical) Disaster, Bhopal, December 2/3, 1984 (Murthy, 2014)

Damage: About 40 tons of methyl isocyanate (MIC), an extremely hazardous chemical gas, leaked and spread about 7 km around the plant in the city of Bhopal, Madhya Pradesh. This leak occurred over a short span of a few hours, killing more than 2000 people and directly affecting about 200,000 people.

PSSMHS interventions:

- After eight weeks of the incident, mental health intervention began. Psychiatrists from NIMHANS worked to prepare clinical vignettes of patients to sensitize medical professionals and administrators. The symptoms were perceived by medical officers' administrators as fake complaints to get financial compensation. Misconception was corrected by demonstrating the real nature of the symptoms.
- Teams of psychiatrists, clinical psychologists, and psychiatric social workers were posted in the hospitals for periods of four weeks to provide mental health care.
- Training for the medical officers posted in the affected area to enhance their sensitivity to the emotional needs of individuals and to provide the skills to recognize, diagnose, and treat (and refer when required) mental health problems.
- A manual for mental health care was prepared and distributed to all the doctors working with the gas-affected population.

Key learning outcomes:

- Need for comprehensive mental health care, both hospital-based and community-based, with good linkages, after any disasters and immediate and long-term emotional problems have intensive disability impact on the survivors.
- Integration of mental health care with general health care and capacity building of the physicians to diagnose, treat, and refer the mental health problems.
- Continuous dialog with the survivors and develop community support systems, to understand their perceptions and needs, as well as for wide use of "self-care" measures for mental health.

(continued)

Event of Disaster: Marathwada earthquake, September 30, 1993. (Agashe, 2004)
Damage: Earthquake of 6.4 on the Richter scale in which approximately 8000 people died and 14,000 were injured; over 34,000 buildings suffered some degree of damage.
PSSMHS interventions:
- The short-term plan of mental health care comprised immediate intervention in the first month for hospitalized injured survivors, survivors sheltered in relief camps, and outreach counseling services from the second to sixth months for survivors in the high-impact zone.
- Training of health personnel and NGO workers was carried out. Creating a permanent mental health care infrastructure locally in a region was considered.
- The Indian Council of Medical Research (ICMR) established Advanced Research on Mental Health Consequences of earthquake for a period of five years at the Maharashtra Institute of Mental Health (MIMH), Pune, and study reported mental health morbidity among the survivors was double.

Key learning outcomes:
- Emotional trauma and rebuilding of the individuals' psyche has to be considered as the center point of interventions after any disaster.
- The poorest survivors and other marginalized groups are more vulnerable and need more care and support during recovery. Developing local leadership should be carried out.
- Community participation for empowerment should be done by engaging community volunteers in the process of decision-making and implementation.

Event of Disaster: Orissa Super Cyclone, October 29, 1999 (Sekar, Orissa Super cyclone, 2004)
Damage: With a wind speed of nearly 300 km and incessant rains for about 48 hours, the tidal waves from the sea rose to 10 meters and struck the Orissa coast. Sea weaves came almost 15 km inland. There was a massive loss of life (10,000 and many missing) and damage to houses, vegetation, livelihood, and the environment.
PSSMHS interventions:
- A community-based psychosocial care model *Sneha Abhiyan*, "a campaign of love," was initiated to ensure the rehabilitation of the most vulnerable among the survivors.
- Intensive participatory, experiential learning-oriented training was conducted through a cascading model (mental health professionals trained master trainers; they, in turn, trained community-level helpers [CLW]).
- Manuals for CLWs and individual care were developed on psychosocial support. Focused intervention for orphans/semi-orphan children and widowed women was conducted.

Key learning outcomes:
- CLWs can provide psychosocial support with handholding support by professionals and are found to be most effective in providing support to the whole community.
- Psychosocial support significantly reduces psychological morbidity and functional disabilities and improves the quality of life among the survivors.
- Engagement of the NGOs and government agencies with the community in the reconstruction of community life is crucial for psychosocial rehabilitation.

(continued)

Table 1.1 (continued)

Event of Disaster: Gujarat Earthquake, January 26, 2001. (Ramappa & Bhadra, 2004) **Damage**: An earthquake measuring 7.7 magnitude occurred in the state of Gujarat, western India. The earthquake and its aftershocks affected nearly 15.9 million people, resulting in more than 20,000 deaths, 167,000 injuries, and the destruction of over 1 million homes. **PSSMHS interventions:** • Community-based intervention with survivors at individuals, families, groups, and community levels. Focused intervention with vulnerable populations (widowed women, orphan children, persons with spinal injuries, amputees, and persons with disabilities [PWD]). • Psychosocial rehabilitation in the temporary relief shelters and in the communities in rural and urban areas. • Capacity building of the community volunteers, NGO staff, teachers and healthcare professionals engaged in the rehabilitation of the PWD and persons with spinal cord injuries and amputation. • Development of psychosocial support with manuals for community-level workers/volunteers. **Key learning outcomes:** • Families with multiple losses require continuous support. • The vulnerable population requires intensive PSSMHS support. • The health professionals (physiotherapists, occupational therapists, nurses) working with persons with spinal cord injuries and amputations must be trained in PSSMHS issues to provide effective intervention. • The longer duration of stay in a temporary shelter is often a major cause of distress. • Capacity building and handholding support to the trained volunteers and staff by the mental health professional is essential for effective PSSMHS.

(continued)

Table 1.1 (continued)

Event of Disaster: Gujarat Riots, February 27, 2002 and continued for six to eight months sporadically across the state. (Bhadra & Allen, 2011)

Damage: Following an attack and the burning of a train, the communal conflict between two communities unfolds all across the state. Some areas (Ahmedabad, Vadodara) were severely affected by communal clashes. About 2000 people were killed in different incidences of rioting that continued for six to eight months. Over lakhs of people were displaced and lived in relief camps

PSSMHS interventions:

- Psychosocial support to deal with the survivors of communal violence in the relief camps and in the affected areas, with the displaced communities with both communities.
- Conflict resolution and peacebuilding through psychosocial support activities to facilitate reconciliation at the individual, group, and community levels.
- Facilitated community-based models of peacebuilding (Aman Samudaya Community of Peace; Gujarat Harmony Project) with the support of national and local NGOs.
- Capacity building, and the development of four manuals (psychosocial care for individuals, children, women, and community volunteers) for the community volunteers to use and work for peacebuilding.

Key learning outcomes:

- Psychosocial support for peacebuilding in the community is most crucial for harmonious living among the people. Individual reconciliation and community initiatives for peacebuilding are possible through psychosocial support.
- The model of psychosocial support for destigmatizing the issues of sexual violence is crucial for recovery. Working through restorative justice is essential for peacebuilding at the community level.
- Integrated model of support and mainstreaming of psychosocial support in all sector interventions (housing, livelihood, micro-finance, education, youth empowerment) is essential for holistic recovery.

(continued)

Table 1.1 (continued)

Event of Disaster: Indian Ocean Tsunami, December 26, 2004 (Bhadra, 2014)
Damage: The coastal districts of four states (Andhra Pradesh, Kerala, Tamil Nadu, Andaman Nicobar) and one union territory (Puducherry) of India were severely battered by the waves of the tsunami. About 10,000 people died, and 6000 were missing. In total, it impacted a total of 37 million people.
PSSMHS interventions:
- Major focus by the central and state governments to ensure psychosocial support to all the survivors at the relief camps and affected communities.
- Extensive capacity building for government and NGO staff and community volunteers following the cascading model. A large number of trainings for the master trainers (health workers, child-care workers, SHG leaders, elected representatives of villages, teachers, and primary healthcare center [PHC] doctors) were conducted across the states.
- Adaptation and contextualization of IEC materials in multiple local languages (Tamil, Malayalam, Telegu, Hindi).
- Long-term interventions and mainstreaming of psychosocial support components as part of disaster risk reduction strategies.

Key learning outcomes:
- Psychosocial support is a cross-cutting theme for any intervention to facilitate well-being. Disaster preparedness, resiliency building, and psychosocial support components must be included in training and implementation.
- Need for specific research to establish scientific evidence of psychosocial support intervention in improving various conditions of the survivors.
- Psychosocial support at the individual, group, and community level as a whole helps in developing, positive coping and facilitates rebuilding resiliency.

Event of Disaster: North Karnataka flood, October 2009. (Vranda & Sekar, 2011)
Damage: Heavy rainfall from September 28 to October 2, 2009 and subsequent flooding killed 246 people and caused massive destruction of property infrastructure and damaged crops.
PSSMHS interventions:
- Psychosocial support for the people in the relief camps and for the bereaved families in the immediate and long term.
- Capacity building for the government and NGOs staff, and community volunteers to work for the survivors with a specific focus on the vulnerable population.
- Intervention for psychological preparedness for the community people and schoolchildren to facilitate the resiliency in the long term.

Key learning outcomes:
- Developing resiliency through safe community, safe institution, safe hospital, and safe school practices and adequate disaster preparedness through psychosocial intervention is crucial for dealing with such perennial disasters (heavy rain, flood, cyclone, etc.).
- Adequate implementation of psychosocial support guidelines is important.
- Scientific research and documentation of the psychosocial aspect is essential for resiliency building and preparedness as part of DRR and mitigation activities.

(continued)

Table 1.1 (continued)

Event of Disaster: Mangalore Flight Crash, May 22, 2010. (Shekhar & Sekar, 2011)
Damage: Air India Express flight IX-812, Boeing 737-800, overran the airport runway and crashed into a gorge, killing 2 pilots, 4 cabin crew, and 152 passengers. Only 8 passengers survived with injuries.
PSSMHS interventions:
- Psychosocial support for the families of all diseases and surviving passengers.
- Home-based psychosocial support to deal with grief, severe traumatic experiences, referral, and follow-up.
- Home visits and establishing connections with the different agencies to deal with local and compensation issues and the promotion of support groups.

Key learning outcomes:
- The trauma was very severe among the family members, as hope turned into despair all of a sudden in a very unexpected manner. Reactions of disbelief and grief reactions were widespread.
- Intensive support, psychiatric referral, connecting with insurance agencies were done for holistic care provisions.
- Loss of earning members at home was highly stressful and required intensive care to support the practical issues of the families.

Event of Disaster: Uttarakhand Flood, Landslide and Cloud Blast, June 17, 2013. (Bhadra, 2018)
Damage: This area is known for pilgrimage and there are five important holy places located on the difficult terrain of the Himalayas which are visited by Hindus (Kedarnath, Badrinath, Gangotri, Yamunotri) and Sikhs (Hemkund). All the roads and connected bridges were washed away and more than one lakh tourists were rescued. The disaster killed about 6000 people, including around 1000 local residents. The distressed families from outside the state were spread across the whole of India. Residential settlements near the rivers, and hotels and business establishments dependent on tourism, faced severe losses.
PSSMHS interventions:
- The team of multidisciplinary mental health professionals were deployed and reached the relief camps where the local villagers were sheltering.
- Specific focus on children, women, and the geriatric population as they had major issues due to the uncertainties and the ongoing difficulties.
- Capacity building of the health workers, child-care workers, medical officers, and NGO staff of the affected areas to provide psychosocial support, and to promote group activities for healing and pharmacological intervention is required.

Key learning outcomes:
- Reaching out to the survivors from across the nation was difficult due to the lack of a database immediately after the disaster.
- Local survivors were often difficult to leach as families of the deceased or missing persons were living in remote villages.
- Difficult terrain was a major issue to facilitate immediate support.
- Preparedness of all systems (health, education, child care, etc.) at the local level is essential to provide psychosocial support. Nationwide capacity building on psychosocial support is crucial.

(continued)

Table 1.1 (continued)

Event of Disaster: COVID-19 pandemic, March 2020 and the next two years. (Sadh et al., 2021)
Damage: Nationwide spread of the virus and lockdown and subsequent difficulties crippled the whole nation and the life of the people. Medical facilities were in a crisis in dealing with the spread of the virus. Serious mental health consequences impacted everyone.
PSSMHS interventions:
• Large-scale capacity building through online mode for different categories of professionals and various webinars to spread knowledge about the psychological issues due to the pandemic and the subsequent psychosocial support for well-being at individual, family, and community levels. Specific focus on psychosocial care for healthcare professionals
• 24/7 helpline managed by the healthcare professionals started to provide psychosocial support across the nation in different languages under the "Samasraya Program" (equal service/safe shelter for all).
• More than 6 lakh calls were received and various interventions (giving information to clarify doubts, giving information about available support, referral for medical care, online counseling to deal with distress, psychological first aid., etc.) were provided.
Key learning outcomes:
• Mass awareness about psychosocial issues in a disaster/crisis is essential for reducing the vulnerabilities at individual, family, and community levels.
• Need of mental health support and care through telephonic service is the need of the hour. The TeleMANAS program was initiated based on these experiences.
• Broad-based hospital preparedness programs are essential to deal with various disasters.
• No one is immune to disaster; hence psychosocial preparedness with DRR is crucial for the health sector. During disasters, the health sector always plays a major role in providing service.
• Multidisciplinary professional approach is crucial for dealing with disaster interventions for disaster preparedness.

The table importantly captured four dimensions of development in the trajectory of psychosocial support and mental health services in disaster management. There are: (a) micro-level interventions to multifaceted national-level programs for psychosocial support in disaster interventions; (b) establishing the standardized model of practice with different stakeholders; (c) the development of a number of IEC materials for capacity building and information sharing; and (d) technology integration in the extension of service and the gradual move from disaster response to management to disaster risk reduction. During the phase of disaster mitigation, the disaster intervention strategies were largely governed by the drive of "build-back-better." Further, psychosocial support in disaster management is considered for building resiliency with the philosophy of "build-better-before." These developments have shaped a better understanding of the importance of PSSMHS, which has further pushed the development of academic courses, research, the extension of the PSSMHS beyond the national boundaries, and new areas of exploration with biological variables to establish the relationship between mind, brain, and body in the context of disasters, crisis, and increasing climactic conditions.

Evolution of the Institutional Structure for PSSMHS at NIMHANS

After the tsunami in 2004, the PSS intervention was considered one of the mainstream interventions in any disaster (Murthy, 2004). NIMHANS was declared the nodal center for PSS in disasters by the Ministry of Health and Family Welfare, Government of India in 2005. Subsequently, the Central Government framed the Disaster Management Act (2005), policies, institutional mechanisms like NDMA (National Disaster Management Authority), and various guidelines pertaining to disaster management. The first ever National Guidelines on PSSMHS was released in 2009. In 2010, NIMHANS was considered the "Centre of Excellence in Psychosocial Support and Mental Health Services (PSSMHS)" by the NDMA. Further, the Centre for Psychosocial Support in Disaster Management was established at the National level at NIMHANS, Bengaluru in August 2019. This was later, in 2020, considered a nodal center for providing psychosocial support during COVID-19. In 2022, the center was institutionalized and upgraded as a Department of Psychosocial Support in Disaster Management (DPSDM).

Theoretical Understanding of PSSMHS

Psychology of Place

The work of the PSS and the MHS is a "normalization model," considering the disaster reactions to be "normal reactions to an abnormal situation" that require specific intervention to normalize the emotional, behavioral, and physical reactions. The disaster alters the attachments with the place, which is explained in terms of the attachment theory given by M.T. Fullilove (Fullilove, 1996). The psychology of place explains the need for belonging in a place thriving for betterment. As a basic nature, humans strive to achieve a sense of belonging to a place. This sense of belonging to a place is also associated with community life, the ability to move freely with a feeling of safety, to develop relationships, enjoy, participate, and to gain connectedness for attaining satisfaction. Everyone strives to have a "good enough" place to live. There are three psychological dimensions in this psychological process of attaining a "sense of place": familiarity, attachment, and identity. Attachment is about a sense of mutually trusting caretaking bond between the individuals and the place. It derives the feeling of safety, love, and satisfaction. Familiarity gives a feeling of comfort and it is about detailed cognitive knowledge of the place of living. It encourages free movement, forming associations, and making collective decisions for shared goals. Identity is fundamental to human existence. The place of living gives a specific spatial memory, imagery, ideas, and aspirations. A sense of self is derived from the place in which one passes one's life. Thus, attachment, familiarity, and identity create a complete sense of place. Disasters cause death, destruction, displacement, and distortion of the living environment. The emotional connectedness gets ruptured. The familiarity turns into disorientation, attachments become nostalgia, and identity tunes into alienation. This situation causes a sense of loss of attachment, familiarity, and identity and people feel disheartened about their place of living. The individuals in the community become survivors. The "good-enough" place of living becomes worrisome after a disaster. Diagram 1.1 explains the changes that occur from the normal context to a disaster situation. In

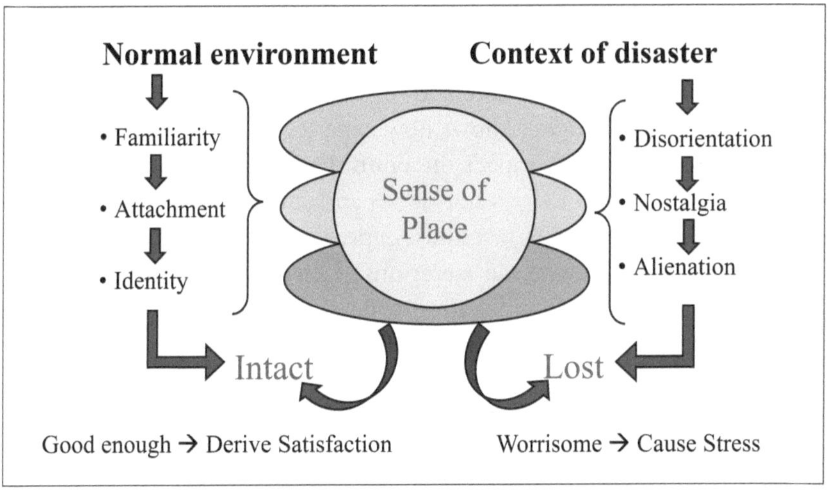

Diagram 1.1 A "good enough place" turned into worrisome following a disaster causes psychosocial stress

such a context providing psychosocial support becomes essential to regain normalcy, by promoting individual initiatives, family and group unity, and mobilizing social support. The concept of psychosocial support is explained in detail in the chapter 5. The PSS and MHS at NIMHANS have always been practiced as an interdisciplinary team approach with the engagement of mental health professionals from psychiatric social work, clinical psychology, psychiatric nursing, and psychiatry. Through the community engagement model of practice, the participation of multiple stakeholders from government departments (healthcare, child care, education, first responders, police, disaster management authorities, etc.), civil society organizations (international & national non-governmental organizations, United Nations agencies, Red Cross movements, etc.), community representatives (elected members, informal leaders, school teachers, SHG members, priests and significant others), corporate and business sectors (corporate social responsibility representatives, banking and financing sectors, media houses, etc.), and community people (women, men, youths, children, representatives of vulnerable & excluded sections, etc.) is pertinent.

Brian and Behavior

Similarly, there is a strong connection between the brain and behavior. Multiple research evidence shows how experiences of living or surviving through stressful events impact the brain, its functioning, and its structure. Disasters produce stress hormones and impact biological functioning, which produces stress reactions, depression, or post-traumatic stress disorder (PTSD) in extreme situations. Disasters, whether natural or human-made, can profoundly affect the neurobiology of the brain, triggering a cascade of physiological and psychological responses. These impacts can be observed across various brain regions and neurotransmitter systems, influencing emotions, cognition, and stress regulation. Investigating the neurobiological changes brought on by great stress and trauma is necessary to comprehend the distinctions between a normal brain and a brain affected by disaster. In a normal situation, the brain structure helps to maintain well-being and functionality. Generally, steady volumes and functional connections are maintained by brain areas like the hippocampus, prefrontal cortex, and amygdala in a normal brain. This helps in maintaining higher cognitive functioning and comprehending a situation with an appropriate response. These areas of the brain may undergo structural alterations/plasticity after a disaster, or stressful situation. For example, extended stress exposure might cause the hippocampus to shrink and become less connected. The amygdala can become hyperactivated, which would raise emotional reactions. Additionally, prefrontal brain changes may impact executive processes, including controlling emotions and making decisions (McEwen et al., 2012; Shin & Liberzon, 2010). Severe climatic conditions or climate-induced disasters are gradually imposing serious threats to human well-being. Disaster exposure highly impacts the mental processes involved in memory, learning, thinking, and reasoning. Direct exposure, or being a disaster survivor, has a more disabling impact. A study by Mishra (Mishra, 2023) reported that the survivors with direct exposure to the wildfire had higher frontal lobe activity while dealing with distractions. The frontal lobe deals with higher-order cognitive functions. Higher frontal brain activity suggests that people exposed to wild fires (disaster experiences) may be having more difficulty processing distractions and compensating by exerting more effort. This causes more anxiety, inability to rest, impaired logical thinking, etc. Thus, strategies of psychosocial support (being with family, volunteering in community activities, working with peer groups, initiating livelihood activities, developing strong social support and trusting bonds, etc.) and self-care (regular sleep, exercise, positive lifestyle, relaxation, mindfulness, etc.) become very crucial to recovery and maintain well-being (Deb & Gerrard, 2022). Consequently, the PSS and MHS facilitate a change that helps to reduce stress reactions on the body and mind, reassure well-being, and promote the possibility of post-traumatic growth. Psychosocial support activities encourage an individual to be engaged and be responsible for her/his own progress and changes. At the group level, it facilitates bonding and mutual support. At the community level, it promotes cohesion and compassion to work together for betterment.

Psychosocial Preparedness for Disaster Risk Reduction (DRR)

Disaster risk reduction includes all the activities that effectively reduce vulnerabilities and increase the capacities of the stakeholders and environment. The United Nations International Strategy for Disaster Risk Reduction (UNISDR) defines preparedness as the knowledge and capacities developed by governments, response and recovery organizations, communities, and individuals to effectively anticipate, respond to, and recover from the impacts of likely, imminent, or current disasters (UNDRR, 2015). This definition alludes to the need for knowledge and capability development. Based on different research, seven important functional categories can be identified. (1) Structural (e.g., seismic retrofitting, creating a defensible space), (2) Survival (e.g., storing food and water), (3) Planning and functional (evacuation, family preparedness, information access), (4) Psychological (enhance self, learning skills, positive coping, lifestyle choices, and family coping), (5) Community/capacity building (work with neighbors to confront local issues), (6) Livelihood (meet employment needs), and (7) Community-agency components (collaborate with response agencies, businesses, NGOs, etc., during recovery and rebuilding). All these categories of preparedness activities support each other and build overall resiliency where the psychological aspect plays a crucial role in facilitating the attitude toward change and adapting to the practice of understanding the risk communication and skills of responding effectively at the individual, family, group, or community levels. While a risk is communicated to the people, not everyone adopts a similar level of preparedness measures; the majority of them tend to take a few steps or no action towards preparedness, while a few take adequate required measures (Marti et al., 2018). Often unrealistic optimism, and risk rejection, cause fatalistic consequences. In the context of DRR, social capital and social engagement are important in facilitating effective psychosocial preparedness. Social capital is about having strong social networks, trusting relationships, and effective communication that support working together, to cultivate collective resiliency. Bonding, bridging, and linking capital are three important components of social capital. The bond between the family, groups, and community members facilitates effective risk communication and timely preparedness activities. Bridging between diverse groups, multiple stakeholders, and removing social barriers, facilitates adequate information flow and cooperation to deal with challenges before, during, and after the disasters. Linking capital is about developing adequate policies, programs, and inclusive, integrated approaches for risk reduction. In strengthening social capital, community engagement and participation in a systematic approach is the most crucial aspect. Community engagement leads to an augmenting sense of community participation, the spirit of civic and voluntary engagements, collective efficacy, and empowerment (Paton, Co-existing with Natural Hazards and their Consequences, 2017). Social capital and community engagement effectively combine psychosocial support preparedness in DRR initiatives and activities. Psychological preparedness contributes to increasing perceived control, and appropriate decision-making. Thus, it enables the creation of a psychological state conducive to people's risk acceptance and the progressive development of their preparedness. This preparedness at all levels i.e. individual, family, community, and social/agency levels works together to adopt the practice of disaster risk reduction (Paton, 2019). The NIMHANS model of psychosocial support strengthens the psychosocial components of disaster risk

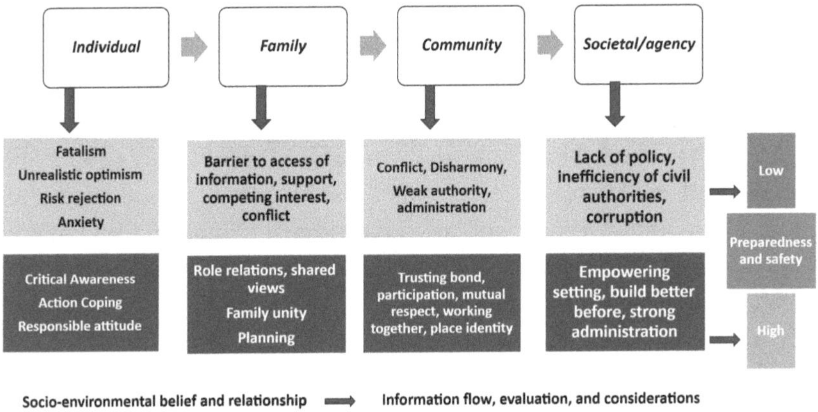

Diagram 1.2 Factors contributing to psychosocial preparedness

reduction preparedness and promotes capacity building for a sustainable resilient future. Diagram 1.2, shows the factors that contribute to low or high psychosocial preparedness.

Extension of Psychosocial Support in Disaster Management

The psychosocial support in disaster management has been extended to different fields for the purpose of effective preparedness. Psychosocial preparedness is the key to sustainable development as the intensity and frequency of disasters are increasing all over the globe. Climatic disasters are taking precedence that require substantial preparedness while other forms of natural and human-made disasters are becoming more frequent. Given below are some of the important programs for disaster risk reduction pioneered by NIMHANS and taken up by different institutions.

Health Sector Disaster Preparedness and Response The health sector plays a very significant role in rehabilitating disaster survivors, in preparing communities to face future disasters, and in building coping and resilience among them to overcome any emergencies caused by disasters.

Therefore, PSSMHS capacity building is incorporated within the healthcare systems to develop trained human resources (doctors, nurses, social workers, psychologists, paramedic professionals) at all levels (state, district, block, and village) for successful inclusion and integration of PSS with health programs before, during, and after disasters. It is a collaborative work of the Directorate General of Health Services, Government of India, and the Department of Psychosocial Support in Disaster Management, NIMHANS, Bengaluru with active support from the respective States.

International Training on PSSMHS in Disaster Management NIMHANS envisages sharing the Indian model of psychosocial care in disaster management with some of the most vulnerable island nations of the Asia Pacific region. Through this initiative, the stakeholders from the Government of Fiji and the Government of the Philippines were trained on PSSMHS, at NIMHANS. These nations, with the support of NIMHANS, are designing policies and effective programs to deal with various disasters and emergencies specific to the geo-political-cultural context. The Ministry of External Affairs, Government of India, facilitated this program and exchange of professional knowledge, skills, and expertise.

Integration of PSSMHS in different disaster management protocols and capacity building Hospital preparedness to deal with public health emergencies is a major task for developing resilient and effective health services. The management of psychosocial issues in hospital disasters is included as one of the components. Similarly, the National Institute of Disaster Management (NIDM) has included the PSSMHS components, in the safe-school program, in the training of the disaster response forces, first responders, and in various other capacity-building modules. In the basic training course on CBRN emergency management, "Medical Aspect and Psychosocial Impact of CBRM Emergency" is a module that has included psychological first aid (PFA) as an important component in handling disasters and emergencies. Similarly, railway disaster management, and emergency handling at airports, have included modules of PSS. Various courses on disaster management at the university system and the model course for undergraduate and postgraduate students developed by NIDM included the PSSMHS as a unit of the syllabus.

Development of IEC (information, education, communication) materials on PSSMHS Developing standard manuals and training modules was one of the needs that has been achieved by NIMHANS through continuous engagement, research, field testing, and reuse. There are four important information manuals (1-Psychosocial Care For Individuals; 2-Psychosocial Care by Community Level Workers; 3-Psychosocial Care for Children; 4-Psychosocial Care for Women), one Training of Trainers Manual (Facilitation Manual For Trainers of Trainees In Natural Disasters) and two workbooks for the capacity-building program (Psychosocial Care in Disaster Management: My Work Book, Harmonizing Personal, Familial And Professional Life—Stress Management Workbook). Further, with NIDM four manuals are developed on PFA (National Disaster Management Training Module-1 Psychosocial First Aid, 2 Psychosocial Care in Disasters, 3 Psychosocial Preparedness, 4 Disaster Mental Health Services). There are 12 pamphlets on PSSMHS that are being widely circulated and used across the nation and internationally:

1. Understanding disaster
2. Impact of disaster
3. Dos and don'ts in disaster
4. Emotional reactions of survivors
5. Principles of emotional support
6. Psychosocial care techniques
7. Psychosocial referral
8. Children in disaster
9. Women in disaster
10. Person with disability and elderly in disaster
11. Dealing with marginalized groups
12. Self-care management strategies in disaster

Framing Policy Guidelines for PSSMHS

The first policy document, "Psychosocial Support and Mental Health Service in Disaster" (NDMA, 2009), was published by the National Disaster Management Authority in 2009. This is the most important guideline for dealing with PSSMHS as an integrated service provision before, during, and after disasters. Three core aspects of this guideline: (1) Preparedness: including proper planning and resource mapping at all levels, along with capacity development and upgrading of infrastructure; (2) Response: explaining the role of various ministries, departments, stake stakeholders at national, state and district levels, and role of community institutions, and community as a stakeholder; and (3) Implementations: elaborating the framework of action. NIMHANS took the lead in designing this guideline. In 2023, the same guidelines were updated.

Conclusion

PSSMHS evolved over the decades as one of the core areas of interventions, study, and research (Sekar et al., 2007). The wide extension of PSSMHS is important for dealing with disaster vulnerabilities and for augmenting the capacity of the different stakeholders. Toward this direction, the DPSDM has started online courses through NIMHANS Digital Academy, which is benefiting professionals across different parts of the nation and the globe. The DPSDM at NIMHANS is also focusing on cutting-edge research to gain a more scientific understanding of climate change-induced disasters and the biological interphase with the psychosocial sphere. Living under the threat of disasters, the impact of pollution on the cognitive abilities of children, the efficacy of telephonic services during the pandemic, enhancing resiliency through school, and community-based interventions, and such scientific studies are conducted in the department to build various models of intervention that supports sustainable development, and a safe future. The focus is on understanding post-traumatic growth and "building-better-before" to promote inclusion and well-being for all.

References

Agashe, M. (2004). Mental health aspects of Marathwada earthquake. In J. O. Diaz, R. Murthy, & R. N. Lakshminarayan (Eds.), *Disaster mental health in India* (pp. 102–109). Indian Red Cross Society.

BHADA. (2011). Earthquake 2001, Bhuj Area Development Authority, Assessed on 21/12/2024 source: https://bhujada.com/earthquake-2001/#:~:text=The%20earthquake%20in%20Bhuj%20on%20January%2026%2C,infrastructures%20like%20water%20supply%2C%20electricity%2C%20and%20telecommunications

Bhadra, S. (2014). Community as the key for disaster recovery—A case of long-term intervention in Kanyakumari District. In S. Bhatt & N. Agnimitra (Eds.), *Social work response to environment and disaster* (pp. 133–148). Shipra.

Bhadra, S. (2018). A man-made, so called natural disaster and resiliency of hill community: Himalayan Tsunami in India. *Integrated Journal of Social Sciences, 5*(1), 1–6.

Bhadra, S., & Allen, R. D. (2011). Psychosocial support for communal harmony and peace building. In HiPeC (Ed.), *Peace from disaster—Indigenous initiatives across communities, countries and continents* (pp. 103–109). HiPeC, Hiroshima University.

Deb, S., & Gerrard, B. A. (2022). *Handbook of health and well-being: Challenges, strategies and future trends*. Springer Singapore.

Diaz, J. P. (2004). The cycle of disasters: From disaster mental health to psychosocial care. In J. P. Diaz, S. R. Murthy, & R. N. Lakshminarayan (Eds.), *Disaster mental health in India* (pp. 38–55). Indian Red Cross Society.

Fullilove, M. T. (1996). Psychiatric implication of displacement: Contribution from the psychology of place. *American Journal of Psychiatry, 152*(12), 1516–1523. https://doi.org/10.1176/ajp.153.12.1516

Marti, M., Stauffacher, M., Matthes, J., & Wiemer, S. (2018). Communicating earthquake preparedness: The influence of induced mood, perceived risk, and gain or loss frames on homeowners' attitudes toward general precautionary measures for earthquakes. *Risk Analysis, 38*(4), 710–723. https://doi.org/10.1111/risa.12875

Mathew, V., Arafat, Y. S., Bhadra, S., & Sekar, K. (2009). Psychosocial care capacity building program for GOs and NGOs of Kashmir earthquake survivors. In NDMC (Ed.), *National disaster management congress, national disaster management authority* (p. 201). NDMA.

McEwen, B. S., Eiland, L., Hunter, R. G., & Miller, M. (2012). Stress and anxiety: Structural plasticity and epigenetic regulation as a consequence of stress. *Neuropharmacology, 62*(1), 3–12. https://doi.org/10.1016/j.neuropharm.2011.07.014

Mishra, J. (2023, January 26). *Wellbeing and mental health: Here's what the trauma of extreme weather events does to our brains—Study*. Retrieved from World Economic Forum: https://www.weforum.org/stories/2023/01/climate-change-trauma-impacts-cognition-brain-study/

Murthy, S. R. (2004). Evolution of disaster mental health in India. In J. P. Diaz, S. R. Murthy, & R. N. Lakshminarayan (Eds.), *Disaster mental health in India* (pp. 56–69). Indian Red Cross Society.

Murthy, R. (2014). Mental health of survivors of 1984 Bhopal disaster: A continuing challenge. *Indian Journal of Psychiatry, 23*(2), 86–93. https://doi.org/10.4103/0972-6748.151668

Narayanan, H. S. (2004). Bangalore circus tragedy-home care for disaster survivors. In J. P. Diaz, R. S. Murthy, & R. Lakshminarayana (Eds.), *Disaster mental health in India* (pp. 84–90). Indian Red Cross Society.

NDMA. (2009). *Psychosocial support and mental health services in disaster—National guidelines*. National Disaster Management Authority, Government of India.

Paton, D. (2017). Co-existing with natural hazards and their consequences. In D. Paton & D. M. Johnston (Eds.), *Disaster resilience: An integrated approach* (2nd ed., pp. 3–17). Charles C. Thomas.

Paton, D. (2019). Disaster risk reduction: Psychological perspectives on preparedness. *Australian Journal of Psychology, 71*(4), 327–341. https://doi.org/10.1111/ajpy.12237

Ramappa, G., & Bhadra, S. (2004). Institutional responses—Oxfam (India): Psychosocial support programme for survivors of the earthquake. In J. O. Diaz, R. Murthy, & R. L. Lakshminarayan (Eds.), *Disaster mental health in India* (pp. 140–150). Indian Red Cross Society.

Sadh, K. P., Reddy, B., George, S., Christopher, A., Mosale, A., Gupta, N., et al. (2021). An initiative to address the COVID-19 and pandemic-related psychosocial and mental health concerns in India. *Indian Journal of Psychological Medicine, 43*(2), 181–183.

Sekar, K. (2004). Orissa supecycole. In J. P. Diaz, R. Murthy, & R. L. Lakshminarayan (Eds.), *Disaster mental health in India* (pp. 110–118). Indian Red Cross Society.

Sekar, K., Bhadra, S., & Dyer, A. (2007). A decade of disasters: Lessons from the Indian experience. *Southern Medical Journal, Special Section: Spirituality/Medicine Interface Project, 100*(9), 929–931.

Shekhar, R., & Sekar, K. (2011). *A study on psycho social support for survivors and families of the victims of Mangalore air crash 22nd May 2010*. School of Social Work, Roshni Nilaya, Managlore and NIMHANS Bangalore (unpublished).

Shin, L., & Liberzon, I. (2010). The neurocircuitry of fear, stress, and anxiety disorders. *Neuropsychopharmacology, 35*(1), 169–191. https://doi.org/10.1038/npp.2009.83

Steinberg, T. (2000). *The acts of God: The unnatural history of disasters in America*. Oxford University Press.

UN. (2020, September 30). *The climate crisis—A race we can win*. Retrieved from United Nations—UN25; 2020 and Beyond—Shaping our future together: https://www.un.org/en/un75/climate-crisis-race-we-can-win#:~:text=90%20per%20cent%20of%20disasters,and%20create%20a%20cleaner%20world

UNDRR. (2015, January 23). *Preparedness*. Retrieved from Sendai Framework Terminology on Disaster Risk Reduction: https://www.undrr.org/terminology/preparedness

Vranda, M. N., & Sekar, K. (2011). Psychosocial impact of flood on children: A qualitative study. *The Odisha Journal of Psychiatry, 11*(4), 29–37.

2

Crossroads Between Disaster and Disability: Psychosocial Support and Mental Health Services for the Empowerment of Persons with Disability

Subhasis Bhadra and Kasi Sekar

Introduction

Disasters devastate and push back development efforts for years, particularly if post-disaster interventions are unplanned or delayed, or if they are not appropriately integrated with disaster risk reduction approaches and sustainable development. Disasters leave a long trail of mortality, morbidity, and disability. Deaths, devastation, and disabilities punctuate every disaster, varying according to its nature, intensity, duration, and doctrine. The nature of the disaster refers to the causative factor of the disaster and the human issues which arise. In a natural disaster such as a flood, drowning is common, whereas in an earthquake, complicated injuries due to the falling of heavy objects and fractures are frequent. In

S. Bhadra • K. Sekar (✉)
Department of Psychosocial Support in Disaster Management, NIMHANS, Bengaluru, Karnataka, India

S. Bhadra et al. (eds.), *Psychosocial and Mental Health Support for Disaster Management in India*, Palgrave Studies in Disaster Science and Emergency Management,
https://doi.org/10.1007/978-3-032-02511-1_2

communal conflicts, the injuries are usually the result of burns, being struck by bullets, or receiving cuts from sharp weapons. In the case of an accident, bomb blasts, burn injuries, and bruises occur more. The intensity of a disaster relates to the force of hazardous events such as the magnitude of an earthquake, the wind speed of a cyclones, or the strength of the flow of water in a flood/tsunami, etc. The higher the intensity of the hazardous event, the greater the level of the impact on the survivors. Duration relates to the length of the hazardous events. A long-duration flood, war situation, or any hazardous event causes more problems for the various rescue, relief, and rehabilitation interventions. Finally, the doctrine refers to the specific beliefs and practices, and the level of preparedness of the communities and authorities to deal with disasters at various levels, including policies, guidelines, and administrative clearance. Therefore, a disaster and its aftermaths, which cause suffering and disabilities among the survivors, can be seen as a combined product of the geo-climatic and social context.

In the first two decades of the millennium (2000–2019), the number of disasters has increased sharply, with the recorded number of disaster events being 7348 (Centre for Research on the Epidemiology of Disaster Emergency Events Database). These disasters claimed approximately 1.23 million lives, an average of 60,000 per annum, and affected a total of more than 4 billion people (many on more than one occasion). Theye resulted in a calculated global loss of approximately US$2.97 trillion (CRED-UNDRR, 2020). More recently, 2023 experienced a high level of disaster mortality, with a total of 86,473 deaths. Within these figures, India is one of the top 10 most affected countries, and in 2023, an estimated 4.4 million people were affected by disasters, principally tropical floods, heatwaves, and cyclones (UCLouven CRED USAID, 2024). Persons with disabilities (PWDs) are one of the most vulnerable groups in any community, and every disaster adds to the number, who continue to suffer from extreme marginalization in the absence of coordinated efforts of disaster response. About 16% of the world's population lives with some form of disability, and 80% of these are living in the Global South. These groups are frequently the worst affected by natural hazards, climate-induced disasters, and global health emergencies. A report published by the United Nations Office for Disaster Risk Reduction (UNDRR, 2023) revealed that over the past ten years (2013 to 2023), there has been little progress made in disability inclusion in Disaster Risk Reduction (DRR). Despite some progress in policy frameworks in various countries regarding the inclusion of PWD in disaster response, there has been very slow implementation, and there is a dearth of widely coordinated efforts at a state level. Accordingly, the participation of PWD in DRR planning and capacity building is negligible. UNDRR report has highlighted the following critical findings that are now essential to consider for the holistic recovery and rehabilitation of PWD.

Key Findings of the 2023 Global Survey Report on PWDs and Disasters

1. No personal preparedness plan for disaster was reported by 84% of the respondents.
2. Evacuation during the disaster was a major issue, even though, in a few cases, early warning was issued. Some of them need support for evacuation.
3. More than half did not have access to disaster risk-related information in their communities.
4. Awareness about the DRR plan is a major lacuna among PWDs.
5. More than 90% of the local DRR plan had no consideration of the specific needs of PWD.
6. Though more than half of the PWDs are willing to participate in the DRR planning, only 14% had a chance to participate in community-level DRR planning
7. In any community, issues of accessibility, lack of awareness, acceptance, poverty, and other barriers continue to limit the participation of PWDs in DRR planning in the community.
8. Often, the personnel with disability expertise are not assigned leadership roles that have specific demands for disability inclusion in governance structures.

Source: (UNDRR, 2023)

The Disaster Vulnerability Profile of India (NDMA, 2022) clearly shows that India has multiple disaster threats, and that every place has more than one issue of vulnerability. Hence, no place is immune to disasters, and social situations such as poverty, lack of health service facilities, inadequate DRR infrastructure, and preparedness constantly add risk factors for PWD during disasters. The disaster risk profile of India showed that 27 states out of 36 are disaster-prone. The country's 58.6% landmass is prone to moderate to high-intensity earthquakes, and 12% of the land is prone to flood and river erosion. Drought is a slow-onset disaster, and 68% of the cultivable land is vulnerable. The coastal line also has a high risk of cyclones (7516 km) and tsunamis (5700 km). The risk of landslides and avalanches is high in all hill areas, with about 15% of the landmass is prone to such issues. Urban floods, another major disaster, have occurred more frequently over the years; at present, some 5161 urban local bodies are prone to disaster. Each urban area has a complex infrastructure, overcrowding, unauthorized buildings, slums, and the usual maintenance problems of drainage that complicate the issue. Industrial accidents, road accidents, the incidence of fire (particularly in summer) accidents, and various threats involving the storage and handling of chemical, biological, and radioactive materials have all increased the risk of disasters. Further, political unrest, communal rift, and insurgency issues are currently posing a threat to the lives of the common people.

PWDs During Disasters and Persons with Disaster-Induced Disabilities

In every disaster, people with disabilities are at a higher risk of marginalization. Their pre-existing vulnerabilities such as poverty, lack of employment, lack of education, social security benefits, and the lack of access to adequate assistive devices cause major limitations in pre-disaster situations. During disasters, such vulnerabilities become quite evident, increasing their sufferings and delaying recovery. Often, they fail to get the basic facilities in relief camps or assistive devices and suffer from a lack of support services. Similarly, during the rehabilitation phase, PWD need additional support to restart their livelihood and regain normalcy and confidence. Medical attention is often an essential requirement for persons with disabilities. The interphase between disaster and disability clearly established various facts in the different incidences of disasters across India and around the globe (Villeneuve & Chang, 2023): (1) people with disabilities are two to four times more likely to die in a disaster than the general population; (2) they experience more loss of their possessions; (3) dependency on others for rescue and evacuation cause a huge amount of stress; (4) often the shelters provided and the arrangements in the relief camp do not have special provisions for the PWD and they encounter higher stress during the period of displacement; (5) low levels of access to information usually continue from the pre-disaster period, and they are unable to access support services unless specially focused on the care for the persons with disabilities; (6) often people lose their assistive devices (wheelchair, walker, hearing aid, spectacles etc) during a disaster. Regaining the assistive devices after the disaster presents another, bigger challenge as such items might be in short supply; (7) PWD sustain more physical injuries and are more susceptible to communicable diseases after the disaster; (8) the caregivers of the persons with visual impairments encounter higher stress during the disaster to provide adequate support to their family members; (9) PWD in disaster loses their existing social support networks. They fail to reconnect with other fellows in times of crisis; and (10) disasters become far more disabling for the person with disability, with intersectionality issues becoming apparent. For example, a widowed woman living with disability, who has issues of poverty and belongs to a lower caste, or one who lives in a remote village, has many more problems in disaster situations than others who live in privileged situations.

Further, disaster-induced disabilities are another major issue in every disaster while working for the well-being of the survivors through the different phases of disaster. Survivors who sustain major injuries often develop permanent disabilities and subsequent problems in their personal, familial, or societal lives which impose a number of livelihood challenges and present problems in terms of accessing services. In the Gujarat earthquake in 2001, for example, more than 1000 people became permanently disabled because of the amputation of a limb or a sustained spinal cord injury, leading to paraplegia or quadriplegia (Ramappa & Bhadra, 2004). Head injuries, chest injuries, and abdominal injuries also cause long-term health issues among survivors. Similarly, in fire disasters and accidents, survivors also develop physical disabilities. In communal conflicts, many people have also sustained grave injuries, bullet injuries, and complicated bone fractures, causing permanent disabilities. During landslides, survivors rescued from the rubble often developed grave injuries. Injury is a common outcome of disasters, and, often, delays in rescues, poor medical attention, and a lack of medicine and surgical facilities cause permanent disabilities in such situations. Disaster-induced disabilities have a number of critical factors that call for special consideration during rehabilitation: (1) The survivors who develop permanent disability following disaster often have high adjustment issues with the changes in circumstances of life. (2) Often, the survivors have high expectations for recovery to regain full physical abilities, causing a lot of psychological stress, manifested in the form of depression, anxiety, and post-traumatic stress disorder (PTSD) in the long term. (3) In the case of amputation, 'phantom limb' symptoms are common problems with the survivors. (4) The changed physical status alters their role, status, and position in familial and social life. For example, after amputation, a driver or tailor may be unable to continue their profession. (5) With disabilities, often women face higher rejection from close family members and suffer from family violence. (6) Family members too often have very high expectations of recovery and bargain with the treating team for the best care; they have difficulty accepting the changed status. (7) The medical cost for the care of the injured family member often becomes a source of financial stress. (8) The life planning of these survivors is completely altered following the disaster and the infliction of disabilities. For example, a young man or woman who is supposed to get married soon may now be unable to do so, or a person's career plan to travel abroad for their job will no longer be possible. Such situations, of which there may be many, cause severe distress. (9) The survivors find problems in accessing support services, as they have no prior knowledge about what is available. (10) The survivors develop a very high dependency on the caregivers and often become too demanding.

Thus, a disaster intervention program needs to be sensitive and appropriate for the two groups of persons with disabilities. In both cases, the psychological problems are higher, and they need specialized care during the different phases and disaster intervention. An inclusive approach for PWDs in DRR programs is essential to bring about the long-term changes necessary to build sustainable response strategies.

Understanding Disability in the Context of Disaster

According to WHO (1992), a disaster is "a severe disruption of ecological and psychosocial which greatly exceeds the coping capacity of the affected community". This definition exclusively denoted the need for external help to rejuvenate the lives of the survivors as the impact of the disaster events is beyond the coping capacity of the affected community. Disasters impact the whole social equilibrium and pattern of normal functioning of the affected survivors. Coping with the situation for the survivors becomes difficult, and there is a need for support from agencies outside the affected community. Government departments and civil society organizations become primarily responsible for responding to the situation with the rescue, relief, and rehabilitation of the survivors. The definition given by UNDRR (2016a, 2016b) "A serious disruption of the functioning of a community or a society at any scale due to hazardous events interacting with conditions of exposure, vulnerability, and capacity, leading to one or more of the following: human, material, economic, and environmental losses and impacts." A disaster tests the capacity of the community. A well-prepared community is able to handle the impact better than a community with a number of vulnerabilities. The disaster impacts are multi-dimensional and complex, and they impact the person with disabilities disproportionately due to the number of pre-existing vulnerabilities and the lack of effective response strategies. Often, in post-disaster situations, the vulnerabilities are aggravated and continue to impose barriers and restrictions on their movement, life chances, and opportunities for development. The post-disaster situation demands specific rehabilitation strategies and policies to ensure holistic recovery. For the disabled survivors and the persons with injuries who develop disabilities, the situation becomes even more challenging as their increased vulnerability also causes marginalization in the rehabilitation phase (Schaffer, 2023).

In the different types of disasters, the suffering of the survivors of disability also differs. Within the scope of the Sendai Framework for Disaster

Risk Reduction 2015–2030 (para. 15) (UNDRR, 2016a, 2016b) the following types of situations are highlighted.

- Small-scale disasters only affect local communities which require assistance beyond the affected community. Here, the disaster impact is usually not widely spread, and impacts can be managed within the available support system of the state or federal government and organizations. It may be a flash flood in a locality, an incident of fire in a market, the collapse of one building, a bridge collapse, a ferry accident, etc. In all such situations, if the person with a disability is a resident of the building or locality, will have less chance to escape.
- Large-scale disasters are affecting a society and require national or international assistance. Such disasters are widespread, with huge deaths, destruction, and losses, and require long-term interventions during rehabilitation. Revival of the infrastructure becomes quite challenging, and also regaining the normal level of functioning requires a multi-dimensional integrated approach. Incidents like tsunamis, earthquakes, severe cyclones, wars, and refugee situations usually turn out to be large-scale disasters. Here, disaster-induced disability becomes obvious as many injuries cause permanent disabilities. The PWD who survive such large-scale disasters usually face serious issues of marginalization, and they receive less customized services and low attention in disaster interventions as children, women, and other vulnerable groups become high-priority groups.
- Frequent disasters are understood based on the probability of the event occurring within a certain period, the presence of hazards within the environment, and their impacts on human life, ecology, and the environment. The impact of frequent disasters could be cumulative, or become chronic for a community or a society. For example, certain areas are considered highly flood-prone or prone to soil erosion that imposes threats on the community people during the rainy season almost every year. Such disasters are also called perennial disasters. The riverbank erosion gradually pushes many communities to leave their houses, and every year, the situation becomes worse. The river bank erosion of Ganga, Brahmaputra, and Narmada is constantly a reason

for suffering for many communities in this erosion-prone region. Loss of land ownership, houses, social isolation, and anxiety become common issues of suffering among internally displaced people due to river erosion, as reported in a study from Bangladesh (Kaiser, 2023). The areas affected by perennial disasters suffer from poor economic opportunities and often lack development, and high levels of poverty is a feature of community life. PWD living in such poverty-stricken communities are often the worst victims of the disaster. They lack opportunities to live with basic amenities and face a number of stigmas and marginalization in the communities.

- A slow-onset disaster is, by nature, slow in its unfolding to appear with its severity as a disaster that starts crippling the life of the people and causes severe resource crunches in the society. Examples of slow-onset disasters could be drought, dzud (severe winter conditions), desertification, sea-level rise, and epidemic disease. Initially, the community people expect that the situation will improve and try to adjust. As the situation becomes severe, the suffering of the people starts causing a number of disabling impacts. The individuals, families, and communities need external help for basic supplies like food, water, medicine, facilities for new housing, education, and healthcare. The drought has a severe impact on the food chain and leads to malnutrition. The PWD living in such situations often get a low priority to receive the support that they require. The issues of poverty and marginalization strike them very hard. The deterioration in their life happens faster than others, and they also suffer from higher morbidity.
- A sudden-onset disaster is more common. The disaster is triggered by a hazardous event that emerges quickly or unexpectedly and deeply impacts the lives of the people. Examples of such disasters are earthquakes, volcanic eruptions, flash floods, chemical explosions, bomb blasts, and transport accidents. Sudden-onset disasters disproportionately impact the PWD. With a low level of disaster preparedness, the persons with disabilities become the worst sufferers. The sudden onset of disasters also causes more physical injuries that cause more permanent disabilities.

The nature, intensity, and duration of disaster are closely linked to the severity of the physical injuries and subsequent complexities in a social atmosphere and the rehabilitation of the survivors. A disaster of a higher magnitude leads to a higher number of injuries which causes different types of permanent disabilities (amputation, paraplegia, quadriplegia, disfiguration, brain injury, secondary mental retardation, neurological issues, etc.). The equilibrium of society and social cohesion, harmony, and functioning after a severe disaster is greatly disturbed, and it takes a longer period to regain normalcy. In such a situation, disabled survivors need continuous support to secure a comfortable space in a relief camp, temporary shelter, and within the family, community, and socioeconomic spheres. Adjustment and coping is a process that applies not only to the survivors who become disabled but also all family members, community people, and others around him/her. The traditional or existing service delivery mechanism is usually unable to cope with the problems and needs a lot of external and additional support to ensure a better living for the survivors with disability. Survivors with severe permanent disabilities face a number of problems during rehabilitation, and specific rehabilitation strategies need to be developed for PWD in a disaster setting. PWD in disasters face multiple layers of victimization, and the different variables that denote poor living conditions and delay in recovery are quite often highly concentrated on them.

Disaster and Disability as a Public Health Concern

Public health in an emergency is a major concern, as the health crisis increases after any disaster and imposes a severe impairing impact on the survivors. The central goal of public health is the reduction and prevention of disease through the improvement of the health of the community, thereby prolonging life. It relies on a combination of scientific knowledge and social approaches. Organized community efforts, the development of social machinery, health education awareness, early detection prevention, and the management of disease in order to ensure adequate standards of living for every individual in the community are essential components of public health. Thereby, such measures should also include all efforts targeted at the prevention of climate-induced health emergencies, pandemics, natural disasters, bioterrorism, and any threat to human health. Thus, population-based and clinical preventive activities to improve community health are equally important (Novic & Morrow, 2015). Disaster is a threat to health, totally destroying the well-being of healthy living of the survivors. Accordingly, every disaster is also invariably a public health crisis. Disability is a major concern within the public health fold that increases the suffering of the survivors in a number of different ways. Migration, the refugee situation, civil unrest, the threat of genocide, and civil war will continue to threaten the well-being of the people and the public health services and infrastructure. Hence, public health preparedness is most crucial in helping those with disabilities (Tulchinsky & Varavikova, 2015).

There are several factors that influence and trigger the impact of disasters, including lack of adequate disaster management policy, the response system, a defunct public health system, inadequate development of infrastructure, absence of disaster preparedness programs, government inertia, lack of a sense of direction among the voluntary sector, geographical challenges (e.g., hilly terrain, flood zones, remote location, etc.), and the overarching issues of global warming and climatic changes. As mentioned earlier, disasters leave many people disabled, whether by landmines, earthquakes, or in a huge range of other events, both natural and man-made. Many children, adolescents, and adult survivors in every war zone suffer injuries and become permanently disabled. Often, they become amputees. Neurological damage from head injuries and inaccessibility to prostheses, wheelchairs, and other needs make their rehabilitation a distant reality. The future of many war-torn countries is punctuated by the unending and inhumane legacy of landmines.

Typically, earthquakes are one of the major natural disasters that cause a wider range of disabilities among the survivors and leave a large number of people with long-term/permanent disabilities with severe impairing effects, specifically amputees and people with spinal cord injury (SCI) (Bhadra, 2015). The delayed response after the Latur (Maharashtra) earthquake in 1993 resulted in a manifold increase in stress and trauma. In the earthquake-hit areas, there are many paraplegics awaiting a humane response, even after a period of eight years. The earthquake in Gujarat was a relatively severe on, with the number of reported cases of injuries standing at 166,836 (Mistry et al., 2001), and with a total of 5029 being provided with supportive devices (Chatterjee, 2002). More than 100 survivors became either paraplegic or quadriplegic (The Indian People's Tribunal on Environmental and Human Rights (IPT), December 2001). In the Gujarat riots also, a number of people were injured, with many suffering permanent disabilities (Medico Friend Circle, 2002). This emphasized the strong need to deal with human-made eventualities (Engineer, 2003). A review of the situation of the injured and disabled survivors of the Boxing Day tsunami 2004 indicated that "some individuals who survive a disaster may become disabled due to injuries sustained in emergency situations. Causes could be the lack of access to medical aid, mobility aids, and/or preventative care following the disaster. After the Asian tsunami in 2004, the number of persons with disabilities in the affected areas has increased by an estimated 20 percent" (Oosters, 2005). Similarly, a review showed that the survivors of Hurricane Katrina in August 2005 and the Asian tsunami of December 2004, two disasters that occurred on different continents thousands of miles apart, disabled people were adversely affected in terms of their physical safety and access to immediate aid, shelter, evacuation, and relief. Subsequently, they faced a number of difficulties in striving to regain normalcy. In the Mumbai train blast (2006), the number of injured persons was more than eight hundred, and many of them developed a permanent disability. However, there is a lack of exact data from these disaster incidents.

Flood is almost a regular event in different parts of India. Each of these events causes injuries, and the person with disabilities faces the worst challenges. On July 30, 2024, three villages in the Wayanad districts of Kerala state in south India were severely devastated and washed away by a huge landslide and flood. In this event, 397 people were injured, and about 400 people were either dead or reported missing. Most of the injured survivors recovered; being displaced, however, they remain in a state of trauma and shock (Disaster Management Division, 2024).

Cyclone Michaung battered the east coast of India on December 3, 2023, in en event which also severely impacted the lives of the survivors, and the persons with disabilities faced a number of issues, from rescue to relief. Many of them stayed in their homes as there was not enough support for them to move to relief camps (Sphere India, 2023). Health, hygiene, nutrition, medical care, and safety issues always become the major public health concerns in maintaining the well-being of PWD, both during disasters and subsequently (Kelman & Stough, 2015).

Conventions, Declarations, Acts, and Policies on Disability in Disaster

There are several policy documents and guidelines for the purpose of ensuring equity and inclusion of PWD in the context of disasters and in the phase of disaster risk reduction for preparedness. The Convention of the Rights of Persons with Disabilities (United Nations, 2007), passed by the United Nations Ad Hoc Committee on Disability in 2007, under Article 11 proposes that "State parties shall take, in accordance with their obligations under international law, including international humanitarian law and international human rights necessary measures to ensure protection and safety of persons with disabilities in situations of risk, including situations of armed conflict, humanitarian emergencies and the occurrence of natural disasters." The Convention has been signed by more than 100 nations, including India. Hence, the rehabilitation of persons with disabilities and survivors who have developed permanent disabilities is now an important subject for disaster response programs. The Sphere Project (Humanitarian Charter and Minimum Standards in Humanitarian Response, 2011), mentioned that disability is one of the cross-cutting issues that should be considered in every sector (health, housing, water sanitation, food security, etc.) of disaster response programmes. To further such aims, the United Nations Office for Disaster Risk Reduction (UNDRR) was created in December 1999 to ensure the implementation of the International Strategy for Disaster Reduction. Subsequently, within the commitment of Sendai Framework of Disaster

Risk Reduction, 2015, disability inclusion in disaster risk reduction becomes a key element. UNDRR has taken multiple steps to fully comply with United Nations Disability Inclusion Strategy (UNDIS) requirements. In this context, persons with disabilities are given a special focus such that governments can actively implement disability-inclusive disaster management policies, strategies, and programs. Emphasis is given to increased leadership and advocacy on disability-inclusive DRR, the availability of disaggregated data in different aspects, and ensuring the participation of PWD in the stakeholder group to ensure inclusion in all aspects of DRR (UNDRR, 2021). The "Disability Inclusion in Climate Finance" initiative, which aims to integrate disability-inclusive principles in climate investment, has highlighted the need for targeted action for the inclusion of PWD in every program in order to ensure mitigation of climate change impacts on the life of PWD (CIF, 2024).

India considers disaster management to be one of the core components of strengthening sustainable development efforts. Therefore, over the past three decades, significant developments have been made by the country in mainstreaming and strengthening disaster management in various sectors. The inclusion of marginalized communities is an important consideration in various disaster management guidelines and policies that specifically include children, women, persons with disabilities, the geriatric population, and other specific vulnerable minority groups. There are three important acts that address the concerns and empowerment of persons with disabilities: (a) Rights of the Persons with Disabilities Act 2016; (b) National Trust for the Welfare of the Persons with Autism, Cerebral Palsy, Mental Retardation, and Multiple Disability Act, 1999; and (c) Rehabilitation Council of Disability Act 1992. The Rights of the Persons with Disabilities Act 2016 contains an important passage about the context of disaster: "The persons with disabilities shall have equal protection and safety in situations of risk, armed conflict, humanitarian emergencies, and natural disasters" (GOI, 2016, p. 6) and subsequently underscored the provisions that should be made by the Disaster Management Authorities and other responsible bodies during the different phases of disasters. The accountability of the authorities for the care and protection of PWD in disaster is also about protecting their human rights in times of crisis, ensuring dignity in response. However, the other two Acts do not have any specific mention of the disaster and emergency situations, although they do have a close link to the welfare and empowerment of PWD.

In 2009, the National Policy on Disaster Management (NDMA, 2009) became a key document in planning disaster management for the whole nation. This document considered differently-abled persons to be one of the special vulnerable sections that need special care and attention before, during, and after disasters. The MHPSS guidelines (NDMA, 2023) explain that disability includes "people who have a visual impairment, hearing impairment, locomotor disabilities, developmental disabilities (including autism, intellectual disability, speech, and language impairments), muscular and neurological disabilities and mental illness". National Guidelines on Temporary Shelters for Disaster-Affected Families (NDMA, 2019b) has mentioned special consideration of the needs of PWD and ensuring th establishment of a disabled-friendly infrastructure. Various other guidelines by NDMA[1] on disaster management have considered PWD/differently abled as one of the vulnerable sections of society, and stipulated that there must be special provisions for them during the rescue, rehabilitation, disaster management, and risk reduction programs. Maintaining appropriate data about this group is crucial for effective programming.

National Disaster Management Guidelines on Disability-Inclusive Disaster Risk Reduction, (NDMA, 2019a) is a milestone document, mainstreaming the issues of PWD in the context of disaster management and risk reduction. India is the first country to develop such a comprehensive set of guidelines on disability-inclusive disaster risk reduction (DiDRR). Among the most important action points given in this guideline are (NDMA, 2020): (1) effective data management and resource mapping; (2) adoption of universal design principles to support the needs of PWD, facilitation of accessibility and access to assistive technology; (3) preparedness and mitigation strategies, early warning system, search, rescue and evacuation at the time disaster; (4) access to services during relief rehabilitation and reconstruction; (5) addressing of needs of PWD with other vulnerable factors, such as women and girls with disabilities,

[1] https://ndma.gov.in/Governance/Guidelines

children with disabilities, elderly persons, Scheduled Castes (SC), Scheduled Tribes (ST), LGBT persons with disabilities, persons with psychosocial disabilities, etc.; (6) active participation of persons with disabilities and their organizations in decision-making; and (7) program for capacity building for caregivers with appropriate, timely information. This guideline is for use by government officials, all the persons responsible for dealing with disaster management, organizations working in the area of disability, caregivers, teachers in schools, media houses, and other relevant stakeholders.

Inter-Sectoral Support for PWDs Towards Holistic Recovery

During disaster rehabilitation, long-term planning for resiliency building is crucial for the holistic recovery (Busapathumrong, 2017) of PWDs to ensure independent living and adequate quality of life. This is also about an integrated model of recovery involving individuals, groups, and communities. A community-based approach aiming at developing a caring community is crucial for the well-being of the PWDs. The approach of a holistic model of recovery includes aspects of vulnerability and resiliency. The reduction of factors of vulnerability in disasters and improving the capacity with a target of resiliency building ensures holistic recovery. This is an interdisciplinary subject with multisectoral engagement in the context of disaster management. Protection, human rights fulfillment, human development with cultural integrity, and restoring value systems become crucial.

The multidimensional grave impact of a disaster on PWDs needs to be tackled by adopting a holistic model of recovery. The different guidelines mentioned the multisectoral needs of the PWDSs, which should be addressed in a coordinated manner to facilitate relief and recovery. The following table presents the usual problems in different sectors of intervention and the actual response that is required to be designed for holistic recovery. The table highlighted the different issues of the PWDs under six different sectors that are crucial for ensuring integrated support and holistic recovery. The key sectors for intervention are as follows: (1) Housing and infrastructure; (2) Water and sanitation; (3) Livelihood; (4) Medical facilities; (5) Psychosocial support; and (6) Rights and protections (Table 2.1).

The table depicted the needs and highlighted the need for multisectoral engagement with professional engagement from different disciplines, particularly social work, mental health, livelihood, water and sanitation, housing, legal, and particularly medical (doctors, nurses, physiotherapists, occupational therapists), and paramedical professionals (health care workers, technicians). Engagement and empowerment are crucial needs for holistic recovery. Engagement of the PWDs, organization, family members, caregivers, local leaders, and school teachers is extremely important for developing a community-based approach where neighborhood groups, local organizations, self-help groups, and other local community groups (prayer groups, advocacy groups) become part of the caring community. Similarly, strengthening the response system from the grassroots level to higher-ups is essential to ensure risk reduction. This includes health, education, livelihood, and governance systems, specifically of all the different sectors. This would ensure the building of resilient structures, access for the PWDs, adequate capacity building of the staff in different sectors, provision of an emergency budget, and a disabled-friendly empowering attitude that ensures dignity and protection of rights.

Proposed Model of Empowerment for the PWDs

In the proposed empowerment model, the PWDs, the survivors who become permanently disabled, are at the center. The individual, family, and community are in sequence to strengthen the community-driven process of holistic recovery with the participation of the stakeholders. The focus is on sustainable development and disaster risk reduction, which ultimately constructs the continuum from build-better-before to build-back-better. Family empowerment and community-based care are

Table 2.1 Inter-sectoral support for the PWDs for holistic recovery

	Rescue		Relief		Rehabilitation		Rebuilding with DRR	
	Usual issues	Desirable situation	Usual issues	Desirable situation	Usual issues	Desirable situation	Usual issues	Desirable situation
Housing and infrastructure	No/little special support for evacuation, dependency on caregivers	Evacuation plan, and support to ensure safe rescue	No/less special facility for disabled survivors at relief camp Inaccessible facility (place of sleeping, toilet, etc)	Disabled friendly shelter/ Compound/ accessible infrastructure	Houses are designed considering other family needs. Need for the PWDs often ignored/less prioritised	Provision of Disabled-friendly houses and permanent housing. Ensure mobility, enhancing functionality of the PWDs	Confinement within the home. Lack of access to community facilities. No special capacity-building training. Lack of engagement of caregivers	Maintenance and facilities for disabled to ensure well-being, mobility/ functionality at home & community (road/park/ institutions) Resilient infrastructure
Water and Sanitation	Sanitation issues are ignored. Women face higher issues	Immediate needs to meet at per with others. Adequate supply of drinking water and sanitation facilities	No special facility for PWDs to ensure safe water supply and hygiene facility	Provision of safe water. Disabled-friendly sanitation facilities in temporary shelter/relief camps	Lack of disabled-friendly baths and toilets. High dependency for daily needs	Households with disabled family members to construct disabled-friendly homes with facilities for safe sanitation	Lack of maintenance, needs of the disabled were less prioritized gradually	Commitment to facilitate disabled friendly conditions, barrier-free access to toilet, bathroom. Safe facility to prevent infection

Livelihood	Inability to save the livelihood assets/capital	Adequate preparedness to save the livelihood assets and financial assets	Delay/inability to restart the livelihood activity and high dependency on others	Support for financial security and to initiate the livelihood venture for strengthening financial abilities	Support mainly to cater to the needs of family, less intervention to empower the disabled survivors	Disabled survivors to be focused based on his/her skills by capacity building/ vocational training that socio-economically empower	Unable to cope with livelihood option chosen immediately. Little focus on sustainable livelihood. Inability to regain confidence No independent livelihood	Sustainable livelihood pattern of continuous engagement. Access to loan, subsidiary, capacity building, and insurance
Medical Facilities	Susceptibility to severe injuries, infection Reduced capacity of medical facility Low priority in medical care	Trained First Aider, immediate mobilization of services, immediate medical care to prevent future ailment. Adequate	Less medical care/facilities in remote areas. High treatment cost. Lack of institutional care for PWDs	Adequate supply of medicine/ equipment, visit by professionals Institutional care in case of need and for training for basic skills of living	Supplies of medical equipment/ services limited to town areas Poor care leads to infection. Gradual decrease in services. Lack of health care professional	Adequate supply of medical care & equipment. Capacity building of local professionals, institutional arrangements for services. Strengthening local manpower/ institution	Free supplies of medicine reduces. Institutional care for medical needs became costly. Poor maintenance of supportive equipment, almost no opportunity to replace in free of cost	Established Institutional system to provide continuous care in sustainable basis to ensure maintenance of equipment, medical care, professional interventions for wellbeing Institutional provisions for medical care

(continued)

Table 2.1 (continued)

	Rescue		Relief		Rehabilitation		Rebuilding with DRR	
	Usual issues	Desirable situation	Usual issues	Desirable situation	Usual issues	Desirable situation	Usual issues	Desirable situation
Psychosocial Support (PSS)	No/limited provision of Psychological First Aid (PFA). Overcrowding. Violence abuse, denial of basic facilities	Immediate attention to the traumatic experiences through PFA. Referral in case of need. Ensuring basic care, support group with empathy	Few trained local professionals/ volunteers to provide PFA. Inability to provide PFA and PSS. Relieving trauma and living with stress	Trained people to provide PFA and initiate PSS activities to encourage community participation and stakeholdership	Sporadic PSS activities and no organized mechanisms for the disabled survivors, by and large	PSS to be integrated in every disaster intervention. Initiate community process of recovery at individual/ family/ community levels. Empowering caregivers/ family members of PWDs	PSS trained volunteers organized activities lead by few organization. No designed long-term intervention to ensure community well-being in integration with the disabled survivors	Structured intervention for PSS that the disabled can participate in community life with dignity and ensure well-being. Integration of the PWDs with different issues of vulnerabilities (gender, socio-economic, caste issues)

Rights and protections	No access to Information, No knowledge/ skill for personal safety. Lack of food. At times face abuse	Access to information on time, support for rescue Provision of adequate food, nutrition/ assistive devices	Lack of special provisions, assistive devices. Abuse in relief camps. Lack of access to basic services	Institutional mechanisms for setting PWDs in priority list. Surveillance for prevention of abuse. Mobilize volunteers/ para-professionals to support	Low priority, lack of funds, Decline in support. Special needs are ignored. Face/chance of abuse from close members	Capacity building of volunteers, professionals to ensure services for PWDs. Data surveillance. Regular monitoring Legal support to assess compensations	Low priority to PWDs. Lack of long-term committed funding. Lack of engagement of PWDs/ organizations/ advocacy/ regular monitoring/ updated information	Capacity building for safety, personal care Participation of PWD representatives in decision-making. Developing resilient mechanisms. Strong database to respond in times of crisis Technology integration to empower

crucial approaches for holistic recovery. With all anticipation of the disaster, an adequate DRR mechanism for PWDs is crucial. The proposed model is arranged in four domains, and each domain has four subfunctions (Diagram 2.1).

Domain -A: Common function.

A-1: Coordination and continuous assessment
A-2: Protection of human rights
A-3: Human resource development
A-4: M&E (Monitoring & evaluation) of interventions (Rescue, Relief, Rehabilitation, Reconstruction)

Domain -B: Core MHPSS.

B-1: PFA-PSS
B-2: Social engagements
B-3: Access to information
B-4: Health services,

Domain -C: Inter-sector services

C-1: Nutrition & sanitation
C-2: Disabled-friendly infrastructure
C-3: Social security schemes
C-4: Skill development livelihood promotion

Domain -D: Mainstreaming disability:

D-1: Innovation, technology integration
D-2: Legal and policy framework
D-3: Inclusive disaster preparedness
D-4: Multidisciplinary collaboration for service and research

The common functions are the cross-sectional factors that should be considered throughout the disaster interventions and DRR process. Coordinated efforts, developing networks, and sharing of data are

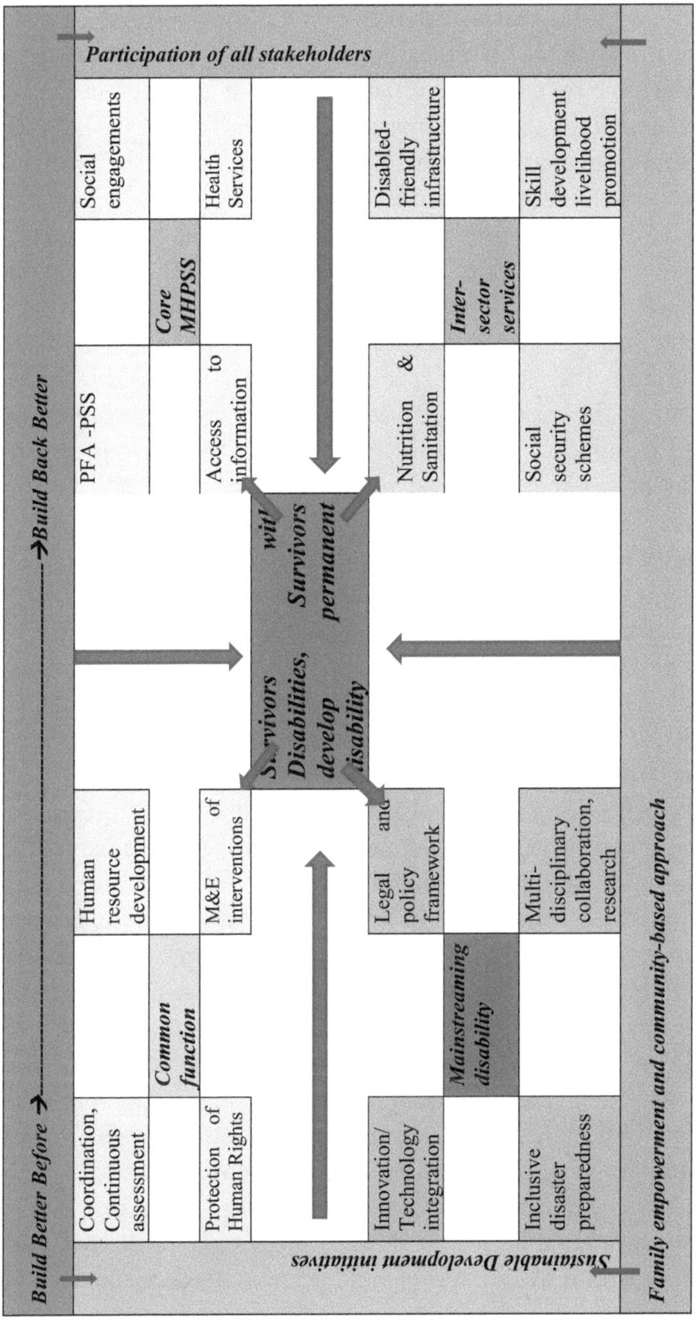

Diagram 2.1 Model of empowerment of PWDs in disaster management and disaster risk reduction

essential for ensuring adequate participation of the stakeholders. The protection of human rights is crucial for well-being. This is to ensure a system of vigilance by community networks about the prevention of any abuse and ensuring safety, security, and living with dignity (Sekar, 2008). Ensuring no stigmatization or marginalization due to disability should be a regular check. Continuous assessment of the mental health and psychosocial situation of these groups of survivors should be built into the process of interventions to assess the changes and fulfill the emerging needs for empowerment and well-being. For effective monitoring and evaluation, identifying and fixing the indicators agreed upon by all stakeholders, including the survivors, is essential for sustainable, effective programming. Human resource development would include capacity building for the local staff (healthcare workers, teachers, micro-finance disbursement workers, etc.) and volunteers from the local community. Developing the capacity of the caregivers is equally important to reduce the caregiver's burden.

The second dimension, on 'Core mental health and psychosocial support,' includes the factors that are crucial for overall well-being. Proving psychological first aid and organizing psychosocial support to develop adequate social groups, community networks, and positive relationships with others all fall into this category. Gradually, social engagement with the PWDs helps mainstream the issue within the community to work together to establish effective, inclusive programs. The consultative process, cooperation, and sharing of knowledge resources between the organizations at the community level are important. Access to the right information on time helps reduce distress, receive support, and allow availing safety measures in times of crisis. Developing appropriate information dissemination systems, like mobile-based applications, dedicated helplines, and volunteer networks, are some methods to facilitate the same. Health services for PWD are essential to provide a basic quality of life and to enhance the standards of living. The health service must include both physical and mental health aspects of the survivors. The physical aspect of health denotes provisions of treatment, surgical intervention, providing helping aids (wheelchair, walker, prosthesis, etc.), and regular medical follow-up. In the case of mental health provision, regular visits of the community-level workers and provision for referral in case of need should be made.

Inter-sector services are essential for a holistic recovery. Skill development and livelihood promotion with adequate technical and financial support help PWDs and their caregivers earn a decent living. The livelihood venture should be planned based on the experience, capacity, orientation, educational background, economic capacity, and social and cultural background of survivors. Engaging livelihood experts and coordination with business schools and banks, as well as access to subsidiaries, are essential for effective implementation. The construction of disabled-friendly infrastructure is equally important in homes and in public places for promoting accessibility for PWDs. Fulfillment of nutritional needs, adequate water, sanitation, and hygiene facilities are important interventions for the prevention of disease infection and maintaining well-being. Social security schemes (pension, scholarship, free helping aid) create a safety network for the PWDs.

Mainstreaming disability in development is a clarion call for all stakeholders. Both Effective policy acts and program implementation are crucial. Innovation and technology integration can help in designing new ways to remove barriers and ensure higher functionality for the PWDs. This requires a continuous engagement of professionals from different disciplines and research to improve the lives of PWDs in crisis situations and otherwise.

Conclusion

The rehabilitation of PWDS is a long-drawn-out process that needs a well-designed program approach with intensive investment in an integrated manner with the involvement of professionals from different disciplines. The proposed model highlighted the possibility of empowering survivors with disability by adopting a holistic recovery approach that is empowering and engaging. Mental health and psychosocial well-being are crucial, integral parts of their rehabilitation that determine the best outcome of the disaster intervention program and disaster risk reduction measures. Similarly, the family as a unit of care, and considering the well-being of the caregiver and the family members at par with the persons with disability, should be considered throughout the empowerment model of rehabilitation.

References

Bhadra, S. (2015). Failure and hope: Living or not with disability after the 2001 Gujarat earthquake. In I. Kelman & L. Stough (Eds.), *Disability and disaster* (pp. 61–68). Palgrave Macmillan.

Busapathumrong, P. (2017). Models for holistic recovery. In P. Busapathumrong (Ed.), *Handbook of disaster risk reduction & management* (pp. 677–695). Nanyang Technological University.

Chatterjee, P. (2002, January 26). One year after the Gujarat earthquake. *The Lancet, 359*, 327.

CIF. (2024). *Disability inclusion in climate finance.* Climate Investment Funds. Retrieved from https://cif.org/knowledge-documents/disability-inclusion-climate-finance#

CRED-UNDRR. (2020). *The human cost of disasters: An overview of the last 20 years (2000–2019).* Centre for Research on the Epidemiology of Disasters (CRED). Retrieved from https://www.undrr.org/media/48008/download?startDownload=20240923

Disaster Management Division. (2024). *Situation report regarding flood/heavy rainfall in the country as on 14.08.2024.* National Emergency Response Center, Disaster Management Division Ministry of Home Affairs.

GOI. (2016). *The rights of the persons with disabilities act.* Ministry of Law and Justice, Government of India.

Kaiser, A. Z. (2023). Analysis of the livelihood and health of internally displaced persons due to riverbank erosion in Bangladesh. *Journal of Migration and Health, 7*(2), 1–11. https://doi.org/10.1016/j.jmh.2023.100157

Kelman, I., & Stough, L. M. (2015). *Disability and disaster: Explorations and exchanges.* Palgrave Macmillan.

Medico Friend Circle. (2002). *Carnage in Gujarat—A public health crisis. Report of the investigation by Medico Friend Circle.* Medico Friend Circle.

Mistry, R., Dong, W., & Shah, H. (2001). *Interdisciplinary observation on the January 2001, Bhuj, Gujarat Earthquake.* World Seismic Sofety Initiatives.

NDMA. (2009). *National policy on disaster management.* National Disaster Management Authority, Government of India.

NDMA. (2019a). *National disaster management guidelines on disability-inclusive disaster risk reduction*. National Disaster Management Authority, Government of India.

NDMA. (2019b). *National guidelines on temporary shelters for disaster-affected families*. National Disaster Management Authority, Government of India.

NDMA. (2020). *Disability-inclusive disaster risk reduction—Transformative journey towards a disability-inclusive society*. National Institute of Disaster Management.

NDMA. (2022). *Annual report 2021–22*. National Disaster Management Authority, Government of India. Retrieved from https://ndma.gov.in/sites/default/files/PDF/Reports/NDMA_Annual_Report_2021-22.pdf

NDMA. (2023). *National disaster management guidelines, mental health and psychosocial support services in disasters*. National Disaster Management Authority, Government of India.

Novic, L. F., & Morrow, C. B. (2015). *Defining public health: Historical and contemporary development*. Jones and Bartlett.

Oosters, B. (2005). *Looking with a disability lens at the disaster caused by the Tsunami in South-East Asia*. CBM International.

Ramappa, G., & Bhadra, S. (2004). Institutional response—Oxfam (India): Psychosocial support programme for survivors of earthquake. In S. R. Murthy, J. Prewitt-Diaz, & R. Lakshminarayan (Eds.), *Disaster mental health in India* (pp. 140–150). Indian Red Cross Society.

Schaffer, D. (2023). Disabilities in disaster situations: How a rescuer handles what they encounter. *Review of Disability Studies: An International Journal, 18*(3), 11–22.

Sekar, K. (2008). Human rights and disaster: Psychosocial support and mental health services. In D. Nagaraja & P. Murthy (Eds.), *Mental health care and human rights* (pp. 243–266). National Human Rights Commission.

Sphere India. (2023). *Joint rapid needs assessment—Cyclone Michaung*. Sphere India. Retrieved from https://www.sphereindia.org.in/sites/default/files/2023-12/TN_Cyclone%20Michaung_JRNA%20Report.pdf

The Indian People's Tribunal on Environmental and Human Rights (IPT). (2001, December). *No foresight no follow up*. The Indian People's Tribunal.

The Sphere Project. (2011). *Humanitarian charter and minimum standards in humanitarian response*. The Sphere Project.

Tulchinsky, T. H., & Varavikova, E. A. (2015). A history of public health. In T. H. Tulchinsky & E. A. Varavikova (Eds.), *The new public health* (pp. 1–42). Academic Press.

UCLouven CRED USAID. (2024). *2023 disasters in numbers—A significant year in number*. Centre for Research on the Epidemiology of Disasters (CRED). Retrieved from https://files.emdat.be/reports/2023_EMDAT_report.pdf

UNDRR. (2016a, March 27). *Disaster*. Retrieved from Sendai Framework Terminology on Disaster Risk Reduction: https://www.undrr.org/terminology/disaster#:~:text=For%20the%20purpose%20of%20the,critical%20infrastructure%20failure%2C%20transport%20accident

UNDRR. (2016b, January 5). *Sendai framework terminology on disaster risk reduction*. Retrieved from United Nations Office of Disaster Risk Reduction: https://www.undrr.org/terminology/disaster

UNDRR. (2021). *UNDRR strategic framework 2022–25*. United Nations Office for Disaster Risk Reduction. Retrieved from https://www.undrr.org/publication/undrr-strategic-framework-2022-2025

UNDRR. (2023). *2023 global survey report on persons with disabilities and disasters*. United Nations Office for Disaster Risk Reduction. Retrieved from https://www.undrr.org/report/2023-gobal-survey-report-on-persons-with-disabilities-and-disasters

United Nations. (2007). *Convention of the rights of persons with disabilities*. United Nations.

WHO. (1992). *Psychosocial Consequences of Disasters*: Prevention and Management (WHO/MNH/PSF/ 93.1 Rev.1), Division of Mental Health, World Health Organization, Geneva.

Villeneuve, M., & Chang, J. (2023). *Emergency management capabilities for Disability Inclusive Disaster Risk Reduction (DIDRR): A scoping study*. Impact Centre for Disability Research and Policy. The University of Sydney.

3

Psychosocial Support and Mental Health Services (PSSMHS): Policy and Institutional Framework in Disaster Management—An Indian Experience

C. Jayakumar and Patrick Jude Lucas

Disasters can impact any country's natural, psychosocial, economic, and political landscapes. Climate change, for example, has posed an immense global challenge that calls for joint constructive efforts aimed at preparedness, resulting in prompt and adequate responses to disasters. The geographical location of India increases its hazards, risks, and vulnerability to disasters, and, since time immemorial, the country has witnessed large-scale major and minor disasters. Given the risks associated with rapid climate change, the vulnerability has scaled up, and the frequency and

C. Jayakumar (✉)
Department of Psychosocial Support in Disaster Management, NIMHANS, Bengaluru, Karnataka, India

P. J. Lucas
Department of Psychology, CHRIST (Deemed to be University), Bengaluru, Karnataka, India
e-mail: patrick.jude@christuniversity.in

S. Bhadra et al. (eds.), *Psychosocial and Mental Health Support for Disaster Management in India*, Palgrave Studies in Disaster Science and Emergency Management,
https://doi.org/10.1007/978-3-032-02511-1_3

intensity of disasters are now greater than in decades before. This chapter will discuss the history of psychosocial support services in India, orient the readers on the evolution of the international and national policies and frameworks leading to psychosocial support service inclusion, and highlight the response created by our team to heighten capacity in relation to psychosocial care service provision and drive psychosocial care machinery at different levels.

Evolution of Psychosocial Care Initiatives in India

Different stakeholders have been instrumental in catering to the psychosocial needs of disaster-affected communities at various times. The first documented evidence for psychosocial care post-disasters in India came after **the Venus Circus Tragedy** (1981), Bengaluru. The psychosocial care for the parents of victims of a fire accident employed a person-centered approach. Mental health professionals from the National Institute of Mental Health and Neuro Sciences (NIMHANS) assessed the psychosocial impact of the disaster and provided individual therapy aiming at grief reduction. The program highlighted for governing bodies and professionals on the need for psychosocial assistance programs in post-disaster situations (Narayan et al., 1987; Narayan, 2004). **The Bhopal gas tragedy** (1984) was the next platform on which the service providers staged a psychosocial plan integration. As there was a dearth of mental health professionals in the nearby medical colleges at this time, trained medical officers helped to identify mental health problems and providing mental healthcare for the affected communities (Srinivasamurthy & Issac, 1987). This experience emphasized the importance of putting in place mechanisms to create a workforce in mental healthcare and to make them available to the local community. This model created an understanding that non-mental health professionals can dispense psychosocial care services if they are trained in aspects of psychosocial care.

The **Latur Earthquake** (1993) was the first disaster in which programs focusing on psychosocial support were implemented almost immediately, just one week after the natural calamity. The government budgeted psychosocial support for the state plan. Mental health professionals from the Maharashtra Institute of Mental Health trained health workers and volunteers from non-governmental organizations (NGOs) to provide individual and group counseling. Lessons learnt from the previous experiences developed an understanding that the integration of psychosocial care should shift from individual to community-centered practices (Kar, 2000). The **Mumbai riots** (1993) enabled the installation of psychosocial services through individual and group counseling with collaborative efforts of professionals from the Tata Institute of Social Sciences (TISS) to heal the troubled minds and promote communal harmony. This event was the first example of psychosocial support being implemented after a man-made, rather than a natural disaster (Joseph, 2000; Joseph & Jaswal, 2023). The psychosocial needs of the victims became prominent during the **Orissa Super Cyclone** (1999), with support from the state and central governments and also NGOs. The focus in this situation was on assessing the individual, family, and community capacities and promoting resilience. One of the hallmark features was the involvement of large numbers of laypersons in the provision of psychosocial care (Murthy, 2018). As the work progressed with a significant focus for the community, in the community, and with the community, the experiences of Gujarat during both **the earthquake** (2001) and the **riots** (2002) enabled a special emphasis on children affected by disasters. On these occasions, UNICEF and the Indian Red Cross Society played a crucial role in dealing with the psychosocial issues of children in the affected communities. In the riot situation, collaboration was sought from civil society organizations to instill peace and harmony and to build trust among the community members. Community-level workers (CLWs), who were volunteers from the community, managed the large-scale psychosocial needs of the disaster-affected communities. These CLWs, who were trained in psychological first aid, facilitated referrals, and helped in networking with the local resources. Parallel sensitization of the mental health professionals with the regard to psychosocial care during disasters also took place.

An elaborate review of case studies from the Bhopal Tragedy and experiences from the intensive rehabilitation efforts in three districts of Orissa and the Bhuj and Anjar districts of Gujarat emphasized the need to focus on issues relating to women and also persons with disabilities during disaster. During the same period, NIMHANS finalized the facilitator manual and workbook on psychosocial care (Kasi et al., 2002). The capacity-building resource on psychosocial care during disasters disseminated understanding on disasters and psychosocial care, the psychosocial needs of victims, techniques of psychosocial care, and working with vulnerable groups (women, children, persons with disabilities, and older adults). During the same time, there were instances of care providers reporting vicarious stress-related issues. The need to preserve the mental health of care providers/first responders and community-level workers evolved. This phenomenon led to the development of the workbook on harmonizing personal, familial, and professional life (Kasi et al., 2005).

The hallmark opportunity for experimenting with new avenues in psychosocial care and implementing psychosocial care activities was during the aftermath of the **Tsunami** (2004). On this occasion, the psychosocial paradigm focused on the larger community development with the involvement of multiple stakeholders, ranging from the central and state governments to international and local NGOs, and other bodies. By involving multiple stakeholders, a spectrum of care was tailored. NIMHANS, along with other mental health agencies in the affected areas and international and local NGOs, spearheaded the provision of psychosocial care in three Southern States and two Union Territories. The NIMHANS team developed Information, Education and Communication (IEC) materials and Tsunami disaster-specific manuals, exclusively for CLWs, psychosocial mediums for children, caring for women, persons with disability, older adults, and self-care for CLWs. Post-Tsunami rehabilitation efforts continued for five to six years with multisectoral acceptance from the Departments of Health, Women and Child Development, Social Welfare, Education, and Revenue, and other line departments (Bhugra & van Ommeren, 2006; Chandra et al., 2006).

States like Gujarat and Odisha had a State Disaster Management Plan immediately after their respective states' natural and artificial disasters. The aftermath of the Tsunami, or the giant killer wave, alarmed the nation sufficiently to devise and strategize a pan-nation disaster management strategy. The central government passed the Disaster Management Act in 2005, which included directives and provisions to streamline disaster management activities across the country. Though psychosocial services were carried out predominantly during this time (especially post-Tsunami), the act was badly informed about psychosocial services.

Prelude to Strengthening Psychosocial Care

As described above, every disaster unveiled new arenas for experimenting with psychosocial care. The **Kashmir Earthquake** (2005) provided an opportunity to implement psychosocial care in one of the richest, and most conflict-laden, parts of the country. Psychosocial work focused on individuals, families, and communities with special attention on children and other vulnerable groups in the sensitive areas. Along with managing the impact of the natural disaster, the team responded to the stress caused by the long-standing strife as a result of border tension. After the **Kandhamal violence** (2006) in Odisha, psychosocial care was rendered to tribal communities, with the intention of promoting peace and harmony. Hence, psychosocial support, which was initially more centered toward the distribution of relief and an individual-centered approach, through years of experimentation, evolved as a community empowerment model with the appropriate participation of the local community. This approach sought the collaboration of multiple stakeholders, starting from the central/state governments, INGOs/NGOs, and the local community, and with the aim of promoting resilience. The lessons learnt over the three decades led to the instrumentation of National Guidelines on Psychosocial Support and Mental Health Services in Disasters (NDMA, 2009). The guidelines discuss the existing systems, gaps, and integration of psychosocial care in the preparedness, mitigation, relief, rescue, and rehabilitation phases. Since then, NIMHANS, along with other key players in mental health service delivery in the country and with the support from the central government, various state governments, and INGOs/NGOs, has carried out the tried-and-tested model for the implementation of psychosocial care services in different parts of the country. The national guidelines on psychosocial support (PSS) strengthened activities across the country. They helped implement the same during the disasters that hit communities, henceforth with the trusted PSS model. Given all these developments in PSS, when floods inundated the plains of **North Karnataka** (2009), the psychosocial support team assessed the survivors' psychosocial needs, delivered comprehensive psychosocial interventions, and built up the local community's capacity to respond to the psychosocial needs in advance.

The **Mangalore Air Crash** (2010) was the first time on which schools of social work were involved in adapting psychosocial care to the needs of the families of victims and the survivors. Through this initiative, the social work students trained on psychosocial care provided sustainable PSS care in the affected communities during their fieldwork and block placement. Each of these disasters was unique and provided opportunities for new experimentation on PSS based on the area, culture, and resource predisposition. Along with routine psychosocial care, the team provided information to the hard-to-reach communities in the hilly terrain through local newspapers and the use of an SMS service in the local language during the **Sikkim earthquake** (2011). NIMHANS and the Institute of Human Behaviour and Allied Sciences (IHBAS) sensitized the entire administrative machinery on PSS and facilitated the localization of psychosocial care. In the **Uttarakhand Cloudburst disaster** (2013), mental health professionals delivered services based on the psychosocial needs of pilgrims from different parts of the country and the local people during the initial months. Later, ASHA workers continued to localize services and facilitated referrals (Bhadra, 2018). **Kashmir floods** (2014) again provided an opportunity to implement PSS among the survivors who were also victims of the long-lasting armed conflict (Hassan et al., 2018). During **Cyclone Phailin** (2014), which shook the coastal belts of Odisha, the team sensitized the affected communities to PSS and bolstered their capacity to respond to the cyclical needs. Technical support on PSS was rendered not only within the country but also to other neighboring countries like Sri Lanka (post-Tsunami), Nepal (earthquake, 2015), and Bangladesh (cyclone,

2019). During the **Chennai floods** (2015), a team visited the affected communities, assessed their psychosocial needs, and educated administrators about PSS. Training staff and students at Social Work Colleges and within NGOs enabled the localization of PSS. PSS was implemented in 11 districts during the **Kerala floods** (2018) using multisectoral collaboration. The expert team trained more than 5000 volunteers, including school and college teachers, counsellors, social workers, psychologists, NGO staff, and health workers. Services principally focused on children, older adults, and families with breadwinners who were living abroad, along with routine psychosocial care for the affected survivors. With handholding support from NIMHANS, the same-trained human resources continued PSS services during floods that hit the region the following year.

Similar implementation, along with the District Mental Health Programme (DMHP) in 10 districts of **Karnataka,** was followed during the floods that badly inundated the region in 2019. PSS, predominantly utilizing technological devices, were also tested in the most recent biological disaster, COVID-19. A pan-India helpline to render psychosocial care was set up in NIMHANS, and local mental health resources were linked through the country's premier institutes like Institute of Human Behaviour and Allied Sciences (IHBAS), Central Institute of Psychiatry (CIP), and Lokapriya Gopinath Bordoloi Regional Institute of Mental Health (LGBRIMH). A total of more than three and a half lakh distress calls were registered. The team provided policy-level integration to facilitate rapid mitigation response to the government of India. The services focused on various marginalized groups and the general population through webinars on enhancing mental health during the pandemic situation, caring for the infected and those in isolation, and mental health service delivery amidst the COVID situation. The capacity building of stakeholders with regard to psychosocial care during biological hazards and the development of guidelines/IEC materials for the same were also carried out (Joshi, 2021; Ravindran et al., 2020).

COVID-19 was an eye-opener as it unveiled avenues that initiated and continued the talk on the importance of PSS/MHS services across the country, and the public's reception toward psychosocial services had an improved outlook. PSS services that began as an individual-centered work have now grown into community resilience-focused programmes.

International Chronicles on Psychosocial Focus in Disaster Management

Under resolution 44/326, the United Nations General Assembly declared 1990 to 2000 to be the International Decade for Natural Disaster Reduction (IDNDR). This declaration urged all nations to fully implement the International Framework of Action with the aim of achieving natural disaster reduction during this tenure through the establishment of national committees and to reaffirm the need of the decade to work in close co-operation with the United Nations Disaster Relief Organization (Hays, 1992). This call for action followed the development of guidelines (prioritizing vulnerable groups, reinforcing international cooperation, fostering risk assessment, and mitigation by integrating technology and local knowledge on disaster management) for Natural Disaster Prevention, Preparedness and Mitigation with an action plan agreed at the First World Conference on Natural Disasters held in Yokohama, 1994. Later, the Johannesburg Plan of Implementation highlighted an integrated multi-hazard inclusive approach to address vulnerability, risk assessment, and disaster management, including prevention, mitigation, preparedness, response, and recovery in order to create a safer world in the twenty-first century (Hens & Nath, 2003). Then, in its eleventh session, the Commission for Sustainable Development (CSD) identified, for its 2014/2015 cycle, 'Disaster Management and Vulnerability' as a thematic cluster and adopted the CSD's multi-year programme work for the period 2004–2017 (Mensah, 2017).

From 2005 to 2015, the Hyogo Framework acted as the global blueprint to tailor efforts to reduce disaster risk. It also considered the role of psychosocial support services. This period was the first time on which the initial integration of psychosocial support services in disaster management occurred. The main goal of this ten-year framework was to decrease disaster losses by 2015 and to build resilience and coping mechanisms in the affected communities. It outlined principles to deal with disasters and promote a strategic and systemic approach, thereby reducing vulnerabilities and hazard risks (Nagaishi, 2006). Though the Hyogo framework recognised the importance of psychosocial support services, PSS was not given a central role in this framework. Despite highlighting the need to focus on psychosocial recovery after disasters, the primary focus was on physical and institutional mechanisms rather than psychosocial coverage. Additionally, the framework had multiple gaps with the lack of measurable indicators, and it was mostly a response-based model rather than a preventive approach.

Meanwhile, the Interagency Standing Committee (IASC) in 2007 issued guidelines on the mental health and psychosocial support in times of emergency in the areas of coordination of all sectors applying sharing systems in monitoring and evaluation, giving legal protection, and providing IEC materials, and enhancing humanitarian resources. The guidelines outlined interventions across a layered system of care, from basic needs and security to specialized services, highlighting the importance of cultural sensitivity, community-based approaches, and the protection of human rights to foster resilience and recovery. Then, the Sphere Guidelines (2011), an offshoot of the Sphere Project initiated by different international humanitarian organizations, provided regulations to encourage care standards for the worldwide community affected by disasters. It emphasized the purpose of the right to life, dignity, and the right to assistance for the people affected by disaster. One of the core standards of the Sphere Guidelines was to provide help providers with training to enhance their knowledge, attitude, and skills, their behavior in handling psychosocial care, and their support in the planning and implementation of effective humanitarian responses in disaster management phase. This called for action among policy-makers to train staff on psychosocial support services at different fields and levels (Mathbor & Bourassa, 2012).

There were multiple gaps in the Hyogo Framework. The Sendai Framework, which replaced it, fleshed this out with measures to promote extensive disaster risk reduction, to alleviate life losses, and to ameliorate livelihoods and health in the social-cultural, economic, physical, and environmental resources of persons, communities, and nations from 2015 to 2030. It was also based on the person-centered approach

(Aitsi-Selmi et al., 2015). The Sendai Framework emphasized psychosocial support integration at all phases of disaster management, focusing on building resilience, enabling recovery, and managing mental health conditions that emerge in post-disaster settings. As a response to disaster risk reduction, the Sustainable Development Goals majorly governed the 2015–2030 Agenda of the Sendai Framework. SDG target 11.5 states that by 2030, there should be significant efforts to reduce the number of deaths and people affected in the context of disaster, focusing on poor and vulnerable populations. At the same time, target 11.5b aims to integrate plans and policies to include preparedness, resilience, and adaptation to climate change in all cities with an adequate workforce. SDG target 13.1 states the necessity to strengthen resilience and adaptive capacity to all nations' climate-related hazards and natural disasters (Valente et al., 2022; Wen et al., 2023).

The path shown by the international and national guidelines on integrating PSS services in Disaster Management and experiences gained in carrying out PSS in different states led to the percolation of the same into India's National Disaster Management Plan (2019). This document elaborates on the importance of capacity building of stakeholders ranging from bureaucrats to community dwellers, the provisions for catering/strengthening Psychosocial Support Services (PSS)/Mental Health Services (MHS), and the responsibilities of the state and other organizations while rendering PSS/MHS and building PSS/MHS in different phases of the disaster.

Review of Disaster Management Guidelines Given by National Disaster Management Authority (NDMA)

To understand the inclusion and emphasis of PSS/MHS in the NDMA's disaster management guidelines, we reviewed all 34 guidelines proposed from 2007 to 2020. Of the 34 guidelines, 12 did not mention any themes related to psychosocial support or mental health services. Table 3.1

Table 3.1 Psychosocial themes identified in the NDMA's disaster management guidelines

Themes	Description
Psychosocial trauma	The psychosocial issues faced by community members post any disaster, and the mental health consequences
Psychosocial counselling	Provision of psychosocial first aid services during disaster rescue and response phases
Psychosocial teams	Trained partners who work together in the affected areas to render psychosocial support services
Psychosocial support in medical preparedness	Teams responsible and psychosocial support services to be carried out as a part of medical preparedness
Post-disaster psychosocial support	Psychosocial support activities that need to be carried out following any disaster
Mental health services	Ensuring the availability of mental health services during different phases of disaster
Psychosocial support in community preparedness	Partnering with the community in building resilience by using community resources, even before the impact of disasters
Capacity building	Building the capacity of multiple stakeholders in dispensing psychosocial support and mental health services in different phases of disaster
Intersectoral collaboration	The need for multisectoral collaboration during disasters
Vulnerable groups	The groups that need special attention during any disaster situation
Psychosocial support for first responders	The need for caring for the carers

presents the identified psychosocial themes from the 22 disaster management guidelines, which include psychosocial and mental health services.

State- and District-Wise Mapping to Identify Psychosocial Services During Disasters

The team also searched strategically to identify the inclusion of PSS/MHS in the state/district disaster management plans by visiting the websites of all the Disaster Management Authorities of Indian States and Union Territories. The review aimed to identify the provisions for including psychosocial care in the State/District Disaster Management Plans, projects undertaken, and resources available. State Disaster Management Plans (SDMPs) and District Disaster Management Plans (DDMPs) available only in English constituted the review sample. The list of documents reviewed was:

1. SDMPs of all 28 States and 8 Union Territories
2. DDMPs of 728 Districts

We have tabulated the findings in Tables 3.2 and 3.3.
The review revealed the following key issues:

- More than half (59.45%) of the SDMPs have spoken about psychological first aid after disasters, and only 34.6% of the DDMPs have mentioned providing psychological first aid services.
- Almost 64.8% of the SDMPs have guidelines on providing psychosocial support during disasters, and only 37.7% of the DDMPs have included integrating PSS services.

Table 3.2 Integration of psychosocial support in state disaster management plans

S. no	Identified themes	States		Union Territories (UTs)		States and UTs	
		Yes	No	Yes	No	Yes	No
1	PSS in rehabilitation & reconstruction	10	18	3	5	13	23
2	Psychosocial response teams	13	15	2	6	15	21
3	Support for PSS services	3	25	2	6	5	31
4	Establishing trauma counselling desks	4	24	3	5	7	29
5	PSS during disaster	20	8	4	4	24	12
6	PSS in schools	2	26	0	8	2	34
7	PSS preparedness	7	21	2	6	9	27
8	PSS capacity building	15	13	4	4	19	17
9	Designating hospitals to cover PSS/ MHS	3	25	2	6	5	31
10	Provision of mental health services	14	14	4	4	18	18
11	PSS in disaster risk reduction	1	27	1	7	2	34
12	PSS for vulnerable groups	3	25	3	5	6	30
13	PSS mitigation plan	0	28	1	7	1	35
14	Institutional framework and functionaries for PSS	0	28	1	7	1	35

Table 3.3 Integration of psychosocial support in district disaster management plans

S. no	Identified themes	State				Union Territories				States and UTs			
		Y	N	NA	RL	Y	N	NA	RL	Y	N	NA	RL
1	Trauma counselling/ psychosocial first aid	241	105	244	93	11	16	18	0	252	121	262	93
2	PSS needs assessment	41	305	244	93	18	9	18	0	59	314	262	93
3	Preparation of PSS teams	145	201	244	93	5	22	18	0	150	223	262	93
4	Building capacity on PSS	149	197	244	93	9	18	18	0	158	215	262	93
5	Developing systems for PSS	63	283	244	93	3	24	18	0	66	307	262	93
6	Mental health services	74	272	244	88	6	21	18	0	80	293	262	88
7	Intersectoral collaboration	133	213	244	93	3	24	18	0	136	237	262	93
8	Resource mobilization in PSS	15	331	244	93	3	24	18	0	18	355	262	93
9	Community-based preparedness	15	331	244	93	8	19	18	0	23	350	262	93
10	PSS in DRR and mitigation	20	326	244	93	3	24	18	0	23	350	262	93
11	PSS in long-term recovery	211	135	244	93	10	17	18	0	221	152	262	93
12	PSS for vulnerable groups	0	0	0	0	0	0	0	0	0	0	0	0
12a	PSS for children	42	292	244	93	4	23	18	0	46	315	262	93
12b	PSS for women	21	325	244	93	3	24	18	0	24	349	262	93
12c	PSS for elderly	6	340	244	93	3	24	18	0	9	364	262	93
12d	PSS for PWD	8	338	244	93	3	24	18	0	11	362	262	93
12e	PSS for farmers	1	345	244	93	3	24	18	0	4	369	262	93
13	PSS in disaster management information system	1	345	244	93	3	24	18	0	4	369	262	93

Y Yes, *N* No, *NA* Not Available, *RL* Regional Language, *DRR* Disaster Risk Reduction, *PWD* Persons with Disabilities

- Half of the SDMPs have included capacity building on PSS/MHS, whereas almost three-quarters of the DDMPs have not included the same.
- 35.13% of the SDMPs and 30.35% of the DDMPs have spoken about including psychosocial care services in rehabilitation and restoration phases.
- SDMPs (32.4%) and DDMPs (6.31%) have mentioned PSS integration in the Preparedness Phase of Disaster Management.
- Only 16.2% of the SDMPs have highlighted the need to deliver PSS/MHS to vulnerable groups, and 12.9% of the DDMPs have emphasized PSS/MHS to vulnerable populations (women, children, elderly, persons with disability, and farmers).

Guidelines on Mental Health and Psychosocial Support Services (MHPSS)

The Guidelines on MHPSS is the governing document that guides all PSS/MHS services in the country. NDMA brought the initial document in 2009, which was updated in 2023. Table 3.4 presents the comparisons in the contents of the two documents.

Gaps Identified from the Review

Though the revised MHPSS policy document has brought a lot of path-breaking emphasis to the disaster management machinery for the inclusion of MHPSS, it would take time to institutionalize the framework. Below are some challenges the nation is currently experiencing, including MHPSS.

Planning and Coordination There exists a lack of planning and coordination between stakeholders. Psychosocial support is generally taken as a one-time activity immediately after any disaster and is not followed up or taken for preparedness action. An integrated and intersectoral approach is needed to address the preparedness and long-term rehabilitation plan in the spectrum of PSSMHS in all areas of disasters.

Table 3.4 Thematic comparison on the major changes in the guidelines on MHPSS

Theme	2009 guidelines	2023 guidelines
Chapters	7 chapters	12 chapters
Focus	Primarily focused on initiating services post-disaster	Includes MHPSS across the disaster management cycle
Capacity building	Information provided on capacity building (who, what)	Presents detailed content on capacity building (who, how, what)
Priority	Prioritized psychosocial first aid and basic mental health services	Prioritized community-based psychosocial interventions that build community resilience even before the impact
Collaboration	Operationalization of MHPSS included with minimal emphasis on multi- and intersectoral collaboration	Multi- and intersectoral collaboration and integration with national programmes operationalized
Monitoring and feedback	Mentioning of monitoring and feedback mechanisms	Well-structured monitoring and feedback mechanisms with checklists that are more practical
Vulnerable groups	Included vulnerable groups	Expanded vulnerable groups

Assessment Assessment measures are not uniform. Mostly, assessment initiatives for a country with a large population and limited human resources make it challenging to carry on. Based on the Geographical Information System, vulnerability assessment must be initiated as a part of preparedness programmes, ensuring comprehensive implementation of PSSMHS.

Staffing Service providers skilled in psychosocial care are in short supply in delivering PSSMHS. Lack of training in psychosocial care is a massive drawback for implementation. In most cases, details about the trained personnel and available workforce are absent.

Service Delivery Existing models of PSSMHS focus mainly on immediate disaster relief, and no preference is given for programs that focus on long-term rehabilitation and preparedness.

Integration A permanent public–private partnership (PPP) is lacking in integrating government, non-government, and other private organizations to perform activities with a common agenda to uplift the affected community.

Planning It must include a bio-psychosocial care model focusing on all types of disasters and affected populations.

Ethical Considerations Given PSSMHS, the necessary ethical guidelines are not made available.

Monitoring and Evaluation There is a need for protocols and mechanisms to evaluate and monitor the programs about PSSMHS.

Human Resource Development Inadequate training and the availability of skilled professionals are barriers to building the capacity in PSSMHS.

Implementation and Coordination Lack of regional- and central-level coordination in implementing the programmes of PSSMHS for the affected population in the disaster area.

Research and Development In all phases of disaster, inadequate research resources, tools, and structure are available, given PSSMHS.

Documentation Protocol for documentation of the services delivered during different phases of the disaster need to be created and followed rigorously.

Modules on Psychosocial Care and Preparedness for Multiple Stakeholders

Active absorption and utilization of Guidelines on MHPSS (2023) would resolve most of these issues. Based on the review and the consultative discussion with multiple stakeholders ranging from administrators, policymakers, first responders, international and national NGO representatives'

Module 1: Psychosocial First Aid

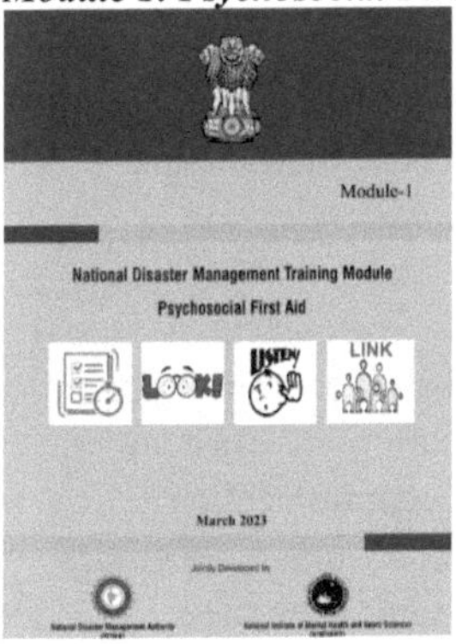

1. Introduction to Disaster
2. Psychosocial First Aid (PSFA)
3. Prepare
4. Look
5. Listen
6. Link
7. PSFA strategies with vulnerable group
8. Caring for the Carers

The Module orients participants on the essentials of psychosocial first aid and how to conduct PSFA training.

Fig. 3.1 Module 1: Psychosocial first aid (Sekar et al., 2023a)

Module 2: Psychosocial Care

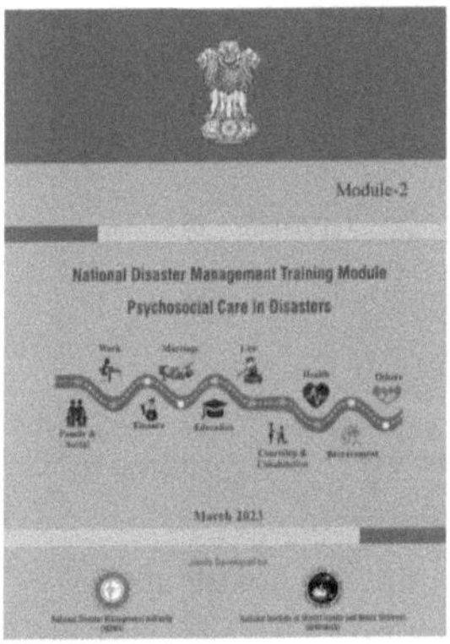

1. Introduction to Disaster and PSFA
2. Psychosocial Triage
3. Psychosocial Support in disasters
4. Psychosocial needs assessment
5. Stress during disasters
6. Mental Health issues among disaster survivors
7. Life events, family life cycle and disaster
8. Psychosocial support techniques
9. Referrals and follow-up
10. Vulnerable groups in disasters
11. Impact of disasters on vulnerable groups
12. Strategies for working with vulnerable groups
13. Roles of psychosocial caregivers
14. Disaster related work and mental health complications
15. Mental health preservation strategies

Fig. 3.2 Module 2: Psychosocial care (Sekar et al., 2023b)

feedback we were able to develop four modules which aimed at the capacity building of different personnel on psychosocial support and mental health services using a trainer of trainers (ToT) model (Figs. 3.1, 3.2, 3.3, and 3.4).

Module 3: Psychosocial Preparedness

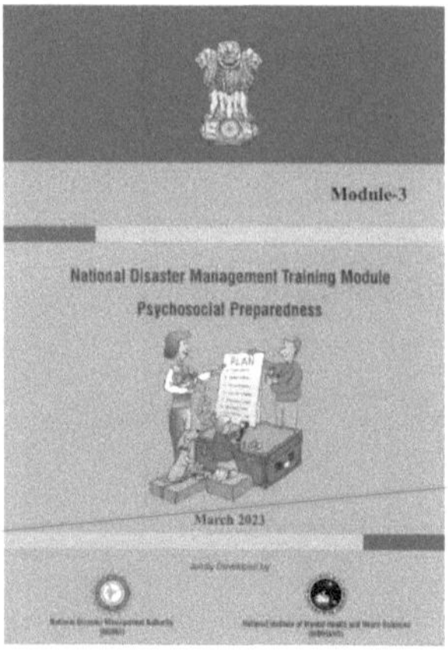

1. Preparedness in disasters
2. Psychosocial Hazard, Risk and Vulnerability Analysis
3. Resource Mapping
4. Psychosocial competency
5. Psychosocial skill demonstration
6. Cultural sensitivity in disasters
7. Disaster risk communication
8. Preparedness for vulnerable groups
9. Caregivers and preparedness
10. Community resilience building
11. Multisectoral collaboration in disasters
12. Ethics in disaster management
13. Documentation in emergencies
14. Developing action plan

Fig. 3.3 Module 3: Psychosocial preparedness (Sekar et al., 2023c)

Module 4: Disaster Mental Health Services

1. Introduction to disasters
2. Introduction to mental health and psychosocial support
3. Mental health impact of disasters
4. Vulnerable groups in disasters
5. Triaging and Psychosocial First Aid
6. Interview and assessment methods
7. Psychosocial management
8. Medical management
9. Primary Care Doctor as an administrator

Fig. 3.4 Module 4: Disaster mental health services (Dinakaran et al., 2023)

All modules have three sections

Section A – Reading materials for the participants (course content)
Section B – Facilitator module (ToT training)
Section C – Workbook (assessment and worksheets)

Since the translation of psychosocial and mental health services into multiple systems in the country is essential and is a long way off, we also propose a model (Fig. 3.5) for the institutionalization of PSSMHS services.

Conclusion

The overall experience evidently revealed that Psychosocial Support and Mental Health Services (PSSMHS) in India have undergone rapid evolution, progressing from individual-centric services to approaches that now focus on building community resilience. What initially began as relief efforts has now expanded to include preparedness and mitigation measures. The revised guidelines offer clear instructions for strengthening the institutionalization of PSSMHS across the country. The four modules developed by the team aim to orient stakeholders toward the creation of a Psychosocial Grid (PSG), which will outline the process of establishing a national infrastructure for initiating and implementing psychosocial care and preparedness activities at national, state, and district levels. Key players, including nodal departments/ministries, state and line departments, State Disaster Management Authorities (SDMAs), District Disaster Management Authorities (DDMAs), Schools of Social Work and Psychology, NGOs, faith-based organizations, and community volunteers must be enlisted and adequately trained to ensure the quality and continuity of services.

Future measures must also be strengthened to enhance coordination among stakeholders. In addition to facilitating the seamless flow of activities, there is a need to create an accreditation mechanism to ensure the proper training, certification, and effective utilization of human resources during emergencies. The journey ahead may seem overwhelming,

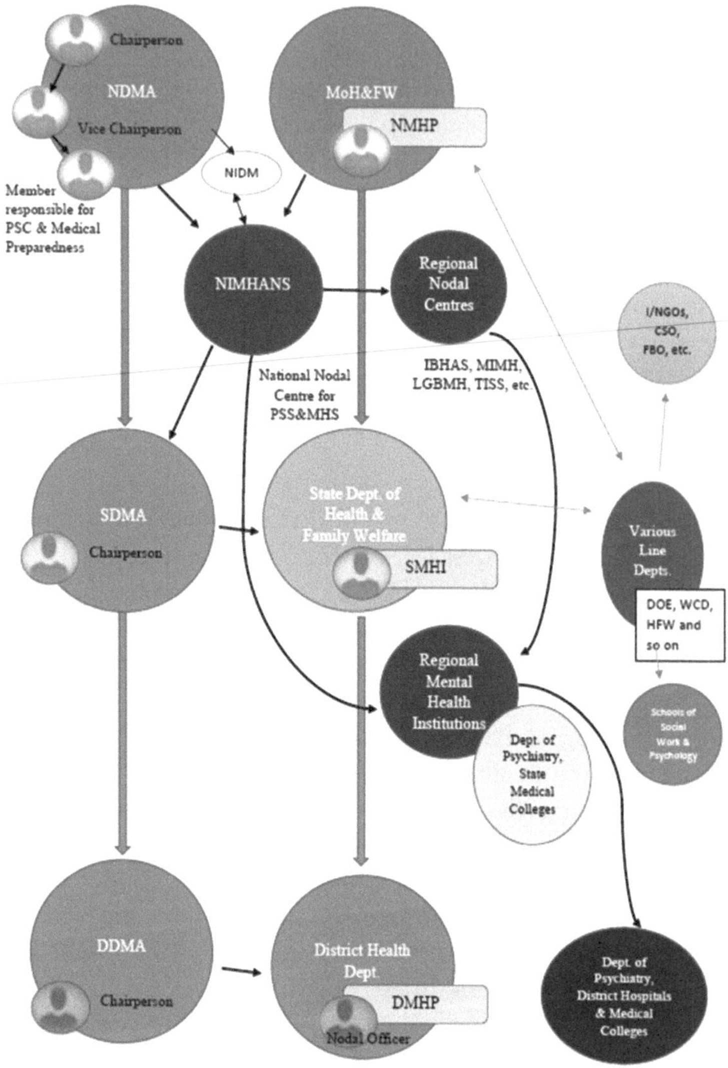

Fig. 3.5 Model for institutionalization of PSSMHS

especially considering the evolving challenges posed by climate change. However, statutory guidelines from international, national, and state agencies designed to safeguard populations and promote community resilience offer hope for the future. Coordinated efforts, from local to national to global levels, are urgently needed to create resilient communities through the strategic and integrated application of psychosocial support and mental health services across curative, preventive, and promotive domains.

References

Aitsi-Selmi, A., Egawa, S., Sasaki, H., Wannous, C., & Murray, V. (2015). The Sendai framework for disaster risk reduction: Renewing the global commitment to people's resilience, health, and well-being. *International Journal of Disaster Risk Science, 6*(2), 164–176. https://doi.org/10.1007/s13753-015-0050-9

Bhadra, S. (2018). A man-made, so-called natural disaster and resiliency of hill community: Himalayan tsunami in India. *Integrated Journal of Social Sciences, 5*(1), 1–6.

Bhugra, D., & van Ommeren, M. (2006). Mental health, psychosocial support and the tsunami. *International Review of Psychiatry, 18*(3), 213–216. https://doi.org/10.1080/09540260600746560

Chandra, V., Pandav, R., & Bhugra, D. (2006). Mental health and psychosocial support after the tsunami: Observations across affected nations. *International Review of Psychiatry, 18*(3), 205–211. https://doi.org/10.1080/09540260600746545

Dinakaran, D., Sekar, K., Jayakumar, C., & Patrick Jude, L. (2023). *National disaster management training module 4: Disaster mental health services*. National Disaster Management Authority (NDMA) and National Institute of Mental Health and Neuro Sciences (NIMHANS).

Hassan, F. U., Singh, G., & Sekar, K. (2018). Children's reactions to flood disaster in Kashmir. *Indian Journal of Psychological Medicine, 40*(5), 414–419. https://doi.org/10.4103/IJPSYM.IJPSYM_137_18

Hays, W. W. (1992). For natural disaster reduction. In *Natural and technological disasters: Causes, effects, and preventive measures* (Vol. 16, pp. 1–10).

Hens, L., & Nath, B. (2003). The Johannesburg conference. *Environment, Development and Sustainability, 5*, 7–39. https://doi.org/10.1023/A:1025376326537

Joseph, H. S. (2000). A response to communal riots—A social disaster (Case studies). *Indian Journal of Social Work, 61*, 664–674.

Joseph, J., & Jaswal, S. (2023). *Centrifugal disasters: Trajectories of vulnerability, recovery and resilience*. Taylor & Francis.

Joshi, A. (2021). COVID-19 pandemic in India: Through psycho-social lens. *Journal of Social and Economic Development, 23*(Suppl 2), 414–437. https://doi.org/10.1007/s40847-021-00163-z

Kar, G. C. (2000). Disaster and mental health. *Indian Journal of Psychiatry, 42*(1), 3–13.

Kasi, S., Sen Dave, A., Bhadra, S., & Jayakumar, C. (2002). *Harmony: Psychosocial care for individuals*: Information manual 1. National Institute of Mental Health and Neurosciences (NIMHANS).

Kasi, S., Bhadra, S., Jayakumar, C., & Kishore Kumar, K. V. (2005). *Harmonizing personal, professional and family life: Stress management work book*. National Institute of Mental Health and Neurosciences (NIMHANS).

Mathbor, G., & Bourassa, J. (2012). Disaster management and humanitarian action. In K. Lyons, T. Hokenstad, M. Pawar, N. Huegler, & H. Hall (Eds.), *The SAGE handbook of international social work* (pp. 294–310). SAGE Publications.

Mensah, C. (2017). The United Nations Commission on Sustainable Development. In T. E. Downie (Ed.), *Greening international institutions* (pp. 21–37). Routledge.

Murthy, R. S. (2018). Disaster mental health and social psychiatry: Challenges and opportunities. *Indian Journal of Social Psychiatry, 34*(4), 323–327. https://doi.org/10.4103/ijsp.ijsp_44_18

Nagaishi, M. (2006). Report on the UN World Conference on Disaster Reduction—JICA's cooperation for disaster reduction in developing countries. *Technology and Development (Tokyo—English Edition), 19*, 86–90.

Narayan, H. S. (2004). Bangalore circus tragedy—Home care for disaster survivors. In J. Prewitt Diaz et al. (Eds.), *Disaster mental health in India* (pp. 191–204). Indian Red Cross Society.

Narayan, H. S., Sathyavathi, K., Nardev, G., & Thakur, S. (1987). Grief reaction among bereaved relatives following a fire disaster in a circus. *NIMHANS Journal, 5*, 13–21.

National Disaster Management Authority. (2009). *National guidelines on psychosocial support and mental health services in disasters*. Government of India. https://nidm.gov.in/PDF/pubs/NDMA/8.pdf

National Disaster Management Authority. (2023). *National guidelines on mental health and psychosocial support services in disasters*. Government of India.

https://ndma.gov.in/sites/default/files/PDF/Guidelines/Guidelines_Mental_Health_Psychosocial_Support_Dec23.pdf

Ravindran, S., Channaveerachari, N. K., Seshadri, S. P., Kasi, S., Manikappa, S. K., Cherian, A. V., et al. (2020). Crossing barriers: Role of a tele-outreach program addressing psychosocial needs in the midst of COVID-19 pandemic. *Asian Journal of Psychiatry, 53*, 102351. https://doi.org/10.1016/j.ajp.2020.102351

Sekar, K., Bhadra, S., Jayakumar, C., & Kishorekumar, K. V. (2002). *Facilitator manual and workbook on psychosocial care in disasters*. National Institute of Mental Health and Neuro Sciences (NIMHANS).

Sekar, K., Bhadra, S., Jayakumar, C., & Kishorekumar, K. V. (2005). *Workbook on harmonising personal, familial, and professional life*. NIMHANS—CITRAP.

Sekar, K., Jayakumar, C., & Patrick Jude, L. (2023a). *National disaster management training module 1: Psychosocial first aid*. National Disaster Management Authority (NDMA) and National Institute of Mental Health and Neuro Sciences (NIMHANS).

Sekar, K., Jayakumar, C., & Patrick Jude, L. (2023b). *National disaster management training module 2: Psychosocial care in disasters*. National Disaster Management Authority (NDMA) and National Institute of Mental Health and Neuro Sciences (NIMHANS).

Sekar, K., Jayakumar, C., & Patrick Jude, L. (2023c). *National disaster management training module 3: Psychosocial preparedness*. National Disaster Management Authority (NDMA) and National Institute of Mental Health and Neuro Sciences (NIMHANS).

Srinivasamurthy, R., & Issac, M. K. (1987). Mental health needs of Bhopal gas disaster victims and training of medical officers in mental health aspects. *Indian Journal of Medical Research, 86*(Suppl), 51–58.

Valente, M., Trentin, M., Ragazzoni, L., & Barone-Adesi, F. (2022). Aligning disaster risk reduction and climate change adaptation in the post-COP26 era. *The Lancet Planetary Health, 6*(2), e76–e77. https://doi.org/10.1016/S2542-5196(22)00001-2

Wen, J., Wan, C., Ye, Q., Yan, J., & Li, W. (2023). Disaster risk reduction, climate change adaptation and their linkages with sustainable development over the past 30 years: A review. *International Journal of Disaster Risk Science, 14*(1), 1–13. https://doi.org/10.1007/s13753-023-00449-8

4

Humanitarian Organizations in Disaster Management: Exploring Role, Function, and Scope

C. Jayakumar, Bala Shanthi Nikketha Selvaraj, Allen Daniel Christopher, and Akhila Vijayaraj

Introduction

"The true measure of any society can be found in how it treats its most vulnerable members"

—Mahatma Gandhi

Humanitarian crises, often resulting from natural disasters, armed conflicts, or other emergencies, can have far-reaching impacts on affected populations and the broader society. These crises can lead to significant loss of life, widespread displacement, and immense suffering for those caught in their wake. These ramifications extend beyond immediate

C. Jayakumar (✉) • B. S. N. Selvaraj • A. D. Christopher • A. Vijayaraj
Department of Psychosocial Support in Disaster Management, NIMHANS, Bengaluru, Karnataka, India

S. Bhadra et al. (eds.), *Psychosocial and Mental Health Support for Disaster Management in India*, Palgrave Studies in Disaster Science and Emergency Management,
https://doi.org/10.1007/978-3-032-02511-1_4

physical needs, profoundly affecting mental health, social structures, and economic stability.

The psychosocial consequences of humanitarian crises are particularly overwhelming. Affected individuals often experience trauma, grief, and a sense of loss that can persist long after the immediate danger has passed. Children may face disrupted education, while families may be torn apart, exacerbating the emotional toll. The long-term impacts can include chronic stress, anxiety, and depression, which necessitate comprehensive support systems to aid recovery.

Humanitarian organizations play a critical role in addressing these impacts. These can be broadly defined as non-profit organizations that are independent of governments, whose main mission is to help vulnerable populations. These include international, foreign or local non-governmental organizations. They have different structures, cover diverse geographical regions, and conduct a wide range of activities. Their efforts encompass providing essential services such as food, water, shelter, and medical care, as well as offering psychological support to help individuals cope with their experiences. These organizations also work to rebuild communities, restore livelihoods, and promote resilience in the face of future disasters. By fostering collaborative efforts between the public and private sectors, India can enhance its disaster response capabilities, ultimately leading to a more proactive and effective management strategy in the face of natural calamities (Hanspal & Behera, 2024).

In India, the importance of integrating psychosocial care into disaster response has become increasingly recognized. The evolution of humanitarian aid in disaster response has highlighted the need for a holistic approach that encompasses both physical and psychological well-being. Humanitarian organizations have been at the forefront of these efforts, contributing to the development of frameworks and practices that address the multifaceted needs of disaster-affected populations. This chapter is an attempt to outline the role of humanitarian organizations in disaster management in the context of psychosocial support and mental health services (PSSMHS) for disaster-affected individuals, families and communities.

History of Disaster Management in India

Humanitarian organizations play an essential role in providing psychosocial care and support during disasters. Their role encompasses service delivery, capacity building, and research to enhance their effectiveness. In India, these organizations have been integrating psychosocial care into disaster response, recognizing its critical importance alongside physical aid.

Historically, India's approach to disaster management has evolved significantly. Initially focused on basic relief efforts, it has now adopted a more holistic approach. Significant events, such as the Odisha super cyclone, the Gujarat earthquake, and the South Indian tsunami, have highlighted the crucial role of non-governmental organizations (NGOs) in providing comprehensive support, including mental health services.

Natural disasters in the 1960s and 1970s marked the first time the government actively focused on rehabilitating affected communities. Efforts included providing compensation, allocating shelters to displaced populations, and implementing other rehabilitation measures.

Many international organizations began collaborating with local NGOs and the government, contributing resources, best practices, technology, and human resource development. This marked the beginning of a shift from merely providing basic material aid to addressing specialized areas of support, such as education, health, livelihood, and skill building.

The 1999 Odisha super cyclone marked a turning point for disaster management (Odisha's Turnaround in Disaster Management Has Lessons for the World, 2023), highlighting the indispensable resourcefulness of NGOs in providing holistic and sustained support. NGOs began to bring in expertise in various sectors to address the diverse needs of different population groups. Subsequent mega-disasters, such as the Gujarat earthquake and the South Indian tsunami, reaffirmed the significant role of NGOs in providing multidimensional support, including psychosocial care to affected communities. These disasters underscored the need for convergence in disaster management.

India's disaster management structure operates at three levels: national, state, and district. The National Disaster Management Authority

(NDMA), under the Prime Minister's leadership, coordinates efforts across central ministries. Similarly, State Disaster Management Authorities (SDMAs) and District Disaster Management Authorities (DDMAs) handle regional and local initiatives. These bodies are essentially responsible for ensuring coordinated and proportionate disaster management efforts across the country (NDMA, GoI).

The Disaster Management Act of 2005 formalized this three-tier system and established the National Disaster Response Fund (NDRF) to provide financial support to states affected by disasters. The establishment of the NDRF created a specialized rescue force to aid in disaster relief operations, transforming India's approach from simple relief efforts to a comprehensive, community-focused framework.

As disaster management in India continues to evolve, the focus remains on addressing both physical and psychosocial needs, ensuring a holistic recovery for affected communities.

The Advent of Psychosocial Support and Mental Health Framework in Disaster Management

Disasters, whether natural or human-made, are harbingers of death and destruction, leaving enormous mental trauma that incapacitates individuals, families, and communities, in their ability not only to recover but also to cope. If this traumatic experience of loss is not addressed, it may lead to dysfunction, disorders, and various other mental health issues in the future. Hence, psychosocial support has been recognized to be one of the primary interventions in disasters worldwide, focusing on both short-term and long-term care and services for affected communities.

In the past, post-traumatic stress disorder (PTSD) was regarded as the primary consequence of disasters, with most interventions targeting these specific symptoms. However, subsequent studies on the long-term psychosocial effects of events like the Bhopal disaster, the Orissa super cyclone, the Gujarat earthquake, and the South Indian tsunami have highlighted significant negative impacts on survivors' mental health, behavior, and overall functioning. These findings underscore the short- and long-term effects of psychosocial factors on communities, emphasizing the need for comprehensive guidelines to deliver holistic psychosocial support and mental health services (PSSMHS). Epidemiological studies in populations unaffected by disasters estimate that approximately 8–10% of individuals require mental health services. Following disasters, this number is expected to increase two- to threefold, necessitating greater focus on psychosocial and mental health interventions (*National Disaster Management Guidelines: Psycho-Social Support and Mental Health Services in Disasters*, 2009).

Since the Bhopal gas tragedy, PSSMHS in the aftermath of disasters have been provided by mental health professionals, institutions, and the Ministry of Health and Family Welfare (MoH&FW), albeit on a limited scale. These efforts became more pronounced during the Gujarat earthquake, and the government's recognition of the importance of PSSMHS gained greater clarity and prominence following the tsunami. In response to the tsunami, the MoH&FW, the National Institute of Mental Health and Neurosciences (NIMHANS), numerous NGOs, international organizations, and community-based social workers collaboratively addressed the short- and long-term psychosocial effects on affected communities.

Over the past two decades, the field of disaster mental health has evolved significantly. Initially focused on a mental disorder-based approach adopted after the Bhopal disaster, it shifted to integrating mental health with public health following the Latur earthquake. This approach further expanded to include comprehensive psychosocial and mental health care during events such as the Orissa super cyclone, the Gujarat earthquake, the tsunami, and the Kashmir earthquake.

The traditional clinic- or hospital-based delivery of services has transitioned to community-based models that actively utilize local resources. This shift has also changed the composition of the workforce providing these services. Previously dominated by psychiatrists, service delivery now involves a broader range of mental health professionals, including clinical psychologists, psychiatric social workers, para-professionals, trained community-level workers (CLWs), and volunteers.

However, existing resources, such as private medical practitioners, NGOs working within communities, schools of social work, departments of clinical psychology, nursing colleges, family counselling centers, the

Indian Medical Association, the Indian Psychiatric Society, the Nursing Council of India, and other professional bodies, remain underutilized. Leveraging these resources more effectively could help address deficiencies in the provision of PSSMHS (*National Disaster Management Guidelines: Psycho-Social Support and Mental Health Services in Disasters*, 2009).

The Evolution of Humanitarian Aid in Disaster Response over the Years

Historical Overview

The evolution of humanitarian aid in the Indian context can be traced through various significant historical events and shifts in approach to disaster response. This development reflects broader trends in humanitarianism globally, as well as unique regional dynamics.

Early Humanitarian Responses Humanitarian assistance has a long history in India, characterized by responses to the natural disasters and famines that have plagued the region. Historical records indicate that relief efforts were often mobilized during catastrophic events, such as famines and floods, where food and material aid were provided to the affected populations (Ranjan, 2024). The great famine of 1876–1878, which led to millions of deaths, is a poignant example demonstrating the urgent need for organized humanitarian efforts, highlighting the gap in immediate assistance mechanisms (Ganaie, 2020).

Partition and Refugee Crises The Partition of British India in 1947 marked a significant turning point in the history of humanitarian aid in the region. With nearly 14 million refugees crossing borders, the need for relief and rehabilitation was paramount. However, the international community's involvement during this crisis was limited due to legal frameworks excluding Partition's displaced populations from receiving aid under the Refugee Convention 1951. This scenario showcased the challenges of mobilizing humanitarian assistance without international legal protections.

Cold War and Changing Dynamics The end of the Cold War in the late twentieth century brought about transformative changes like humanitarian assistance in India. The rising prevalence of armed and ethnic conflicts necessitated a shift toward more comprehensive approaches, in which humanitarian aid began intertwining with long-term development and peacebuilding efforts. This period saw an increase in foreign assistance, although initially met with ambivalence, as the Indian government weighed the benefits of aid against concerns over sovereignty and dependency (Ganaie, 2020).

Contemporary Challenges and Innovations In recent decades, disaster risk reduction (DRR) challenges have become increasingly complex, prompting a re-evaluation of humanitarian strategies. Major disasters, such as the Bhola cyclone in 1970 and the Orissa super cyclone in 1999, underscored the need for improved disaster management frameworks and highlighted the importance of community involvement in resilience-building efforts (Ganaie, 2020). Technological advancements in data management and geo-information have begun to play a pivotal role in enhancing disaster response capabilities. However, many opportunities remain underutilized in the context of humanitarian aid (Hanspal & Behera, 2024).

The Inclusion of Psychosocial Facets in Frameworks and Policies

National Disaster Management Authority (NDMA) The establishment of the National Disaster Management Authority (NDMA) in 2005 marked a significant evolution in India's approach to disaster management. The NDMA serves as the principal agency for coordinating disaster response and preparedness efforts at the national level. Following its establishment, the National Policy on Disaster Management (NPDM) was introduced in 2009, outlining critical guidelines for executing domestic relief measures. Although international relief is not a direct mandate of the NDMA, it frequently collaborates with foreign entities for capacity building and resource deployment abroad (Parmar, 2012b).

Institutional Framework and Guidelines The enactment of the Disaster Management Act of 2005 created a comprehensive legal framework for disaster preparedness, mitigation, and response across India. This legislation led to the decentralization of disaster management, with the formation of state-level disaster management authorities tailored to address local vulnerabilities (Paulmann, 2013). Furthermore, the Minimum Standards of Relief document, last revised in 2016, is intended to provide essential guidance on relief entitlements and operational guidelines, emphasizing timeliness, adequacy, quality, and transparency in disaster response (Parmar, 2012a).

Humanitarian Assistance and Disaster Relief (HADR) Humanitarian Assistance and Disaster Relief (HAD*R*) missions are essential operations executed by the Indian Armed Forces to provide immediate support during humanitarian crises. These missions include search and rescue operations, medical assistance, and community engagement (Paulmann, 2013; Stephan et al., 2017). Although India lacks a formal HADR policy, the Development Partnership Administration (DPA) of the Ministry of External Affairs (MEA) manages external HADR efforts, coordinating with the Ministry of Defence and various governmental and non-governmental entities.

Coordination and Collaboration Effective disaster response relies heavily on established standard operating procedures and inter-agency coordination. To manage relief efforts, the NDMA works closely with multiple stakeholders, including state governments, civil society organizations, and the Armed Forces. Clear guidelines and a well-defined chain of command are critical to streamlining these processes, especially during emergencies (Shanbog & Kevlihan, 2022; WFP India, 2023). The integration of military and civilian agencies in disaster management has been underscored by joint exercises and collaborative frameworks that enhance overall readiness and operational effectiveness (Paulmann, 2013).

Key Players in Humanitarian Aid

It is essential to understand the key players in the domain of humanitarian aid during emergencies and disasters. The following is a note on some of the prominent organizations that have a global presence.

The Role of the United Nations The United Nations (UN) plays a crucial and leading role in the field of humanitarian assistance globally, coordinating efforts among various actors to respond to crises effectively. The UN facilitates funding, resources, and expertise for humanitarian responses, engaging with governmental and non-governmental organizations to maximize impact during emergencies. Through agencies such as the United Nations Office for the Coordination of Humanitarian Affairs (UNOCHA), the UN helps establish humanitarian spaces in conflict zones and advocates for the protection of civilians during crises (Parmar, 2012a).

Indian Government Agencies In the Indian context, the government plays a central role in disaster response through the Development Partnership Administration (DPA) within the Ministry of External Affairs (MEA). The DPA coordinates humanitarian aid and disaster relief (HADR) efforts with other government agencies, such as the Ministry of Defence and the National Disaster Response Force (NDRF), to ensure a cohesive approach during emergencies. Although the Indian government primarily channels assistance through government-to-government arrangements, there are occasional opportunities for local non-governmental organizations (NGOs) to receive support via Indian embassies abroad, particularly in regions affected by natural disasters or conflicts (WFP India, 2023).

Non-Governmental Organizations (NGOs) and Civil Society Civil society organizations and NGOs are pivotal in providing disaster relief in

India, primarily due to the country's vast and diverse population. Many prominent NGOs with religious affiliations and cross-border ethnic linkages have historically mobilized to provide on-ground relief during emergencies, such as the 2015 Nepal earthquake. These organizations assist in immediate relief efforts and play a significant role in community education and preparedness initiatives to enhance resilience against future disasters (Pal et al., 2023).

International Collaboration and Regional Institutions India has been encouraged to leverage regional institutions for HADR, including the Indian Ocean Rim Association (IORA) and the South Asian Association for Regional Cooperation (SAARC). These platforms offer mechanisms for enhancing cooperation among member states, thereby improving preparedness and response capabilities in humanitarian emergencies throughout the Indo-Pacific region. Furthermore, engaging more with international organizations such as the International Federation of the Red Cross and Red Crescent Societies (IFRC) could help India enhance its global humanitarian presence and effectiveness (WFP India, 2023).

Humanitarian Aid and Foreign Relations India's humanitarian response during crises, including the COVID-19 pandemic, illustrates the complexities of balancing domestic needs with international aid commitments. Despite significant internal challenges, India extended support to multiple countries, providing medical supplies and assistance to nations like Afghanistan and Myanmar. This paradoxical scenario emphasizes the need for strategic disaster response planning to ensure that national and international obligations are met effectively. The role of the Ministry of External Affairs in coordinating these efforts has been critical in showcasing India's commitment to global humanitarian aid (Hasnain, 2024).

Types of Humanitarian Organizations

Humanitarian organizations are critical in providing psychosocial care and support during disasters, particularly in the Indian context. These organizations can be broadly categorized based on their operational focus and geographic reach.

By Operational Focus

Direct Service NGOs These organizations prioritize the immediate needs of communities affected by disasters. They run programs in essential areas such as healthcare, education, food distribution, and housing. Direct service NGOs aim to solve pressing problems by providing necessary resources and support. For example, the Smile Foundation operates across India, delivering medical care and educational support to disadvantaged people (Abiddin et al., 2022; Jagannathan, 2001; Sharma, 2022).

Advocacy NGOs Focused on creating systemic change, advocacy NGOs work to influence policies and raise awareness about specific issues such as human rights, environmental protection, and labor rights. Their efforts often include lobbying, organizing campaigns, and offering legal aid to marginalized groups. The Centre for Environment and Development is an example of an advocacy NGO that collaborates with communities and policy-makers to promote sustainable development (Abiddin et al., 2022; Jagannathan, 2001; Sharma, 2022).

Charity-Based NGOs These organizations provide relief and charitable aid, typically through monetary support, goods, or temporary assistance. Charity-based NGOs concentrate on humanitarian challenges like poverty alleviation and disaster recovery. Goonj, for instance, addresses urban–rural disparities by repurposing urban waste as essential resources for rural communities (Abiddin et al., 2022; Jagannathan, 2001; Sharma, 2022).

By Geographic Reach

National NGOs These organizations operate within India, addressing domestic humanitarian needs and engaging with local communities. Their efforts often focus on tailoring interventions to meet specific cultural and regional contexts, which is essential for adequate support during disasters (WFP India, 2023).

International NGOs International NGOs operate across national borders and frequently address global issues such as climate change, human rights, and public health crises. They often collaborate with local partners to implement culturally relevant programs. Oxfam India is an example, as it works on poverty alleviation and social justice while engaging in grassroots advocacy for women's rights and economic development (Abiddin et al., 2022; Jagannathan, 2001; Sharma, 2022).

By Focus Areas

Humanitarian organizations may also be categorized based on their target social or environmental issues.

Educational NGOs These NGOs aim to enhance access to education and improve learning outcomes for underprivileged children, particularly in disaster-affected areas. Addressing educational disparities contributes to long-term recovery and resilience (Abiddin et al., 2022; Jagannathan, 2001; Sharma, 2022).

Mental Health and Psychosocial Support NGOs These organizations focus on addressing the mental health needs of individuals affected by humanitarian crises. They provide tailored interventions, such as community-based programs and counselling services, that are sensitive to the sociocultural contexts of the communities they serve. Local NGOs are crucial in delivering adequate mental health support, as they can quickly mobilize resources and build trust within the community (Tol et al., 2015).

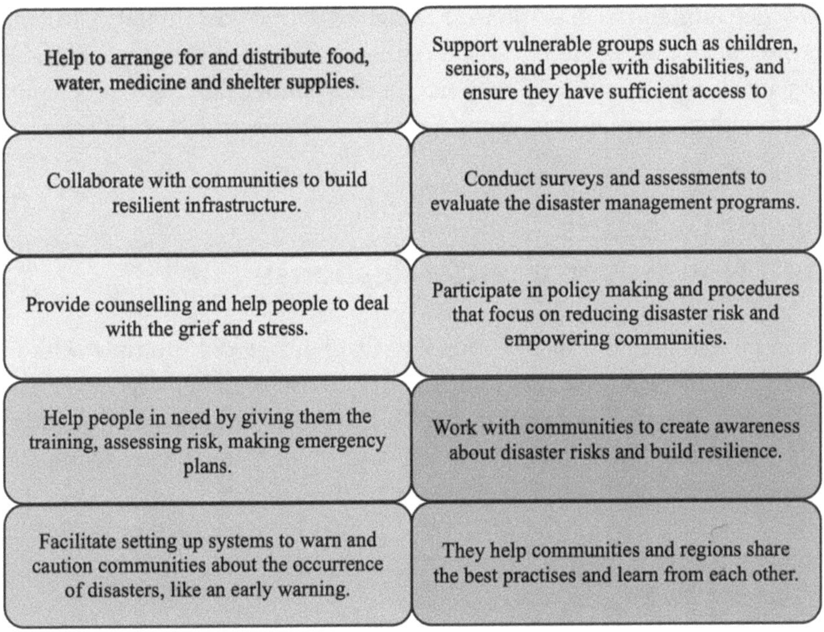

Illustration depicting role of humanitarian organizations

In times of crisis, NGOs play a pivotal role in delivering mental health and psychosocial support to affected populations. Psychosocial support (PSS) is a critical component in disaster response, addressing the emotional and psychological challenges faced by the individuals and communities affected by emergencies. Their efforts are vital in addressing the psychological and emotional needs of individuals who have experienced trauma due to disasters. Psychosocial support (PSS) is a critical component in disaster response, addressing the emotional and psychological challenges faced by individuals and communities affected by emergencies. NGOs often implement community-based programs and provide counselling services that are culturally sensitive and tailored to the specific needs of the community. These organizations are crucial in bridging the gap between immediate relief efforts and long-term mental health care.

NGOs not only offer direct support but also engage in advocacy to raise awareness about the importance of mental health during and after crises. They work to ensure that mental health care is integrated into broader humanitarian responses, recognizing that emotional well-being is essential for overall recovery and resilience. The expertise of local NGOs is particularly valuable, as they have a deep understanding of the community dynamics and can quickly mobilize resources and build trust.

Major Disasters and Non-Governmental Response

Non-governmental organizations (NGOs) have played multiple roles in providing humanitarian assistance during disasters and emergencies. The following case studies pertaining to India further elaborate on the interplay between governmental bodies and NGOs in the psychosocial response to disaster.

Gujarat Earthquake, 2001

The Gujarat earthquake of January 26, 2001 recorded a magnitude of 7.7 and primarily affected the Bhuj district. It led to the deaths of over 20,000 individuals and left countless others injured and homeless. This disaster highlighted the critical importance of coordination among various government agencies and NGOs to provide timely assistance and support to affected populations. The response involved significant international aid and showcased India's capability to mobilize resources rapidly in the face of catastrophe (Jaishankar & Godbole, 2022).

Uttarakhand Floods, 2013

In June 2013, Uttarakhand faced one of the worst floods in its history, triggered by a cloudburst that led to devastating flash floods and landslides. The floods affected key religious sites and left over 100,000 people stranded, with an estimated 4094 fatalities and more than 5700 individuals reported missing (Jaishankar & Godbole, 2022). Immediate rescue operations and subsequent assessments characterized the government's response to rebuild infrastructure and restore livelihoods in the affected areas. This incident underscored the need for adaptive planning and stakeholder involvement in disaster management processes (Stephan et al., 2017).

Humanitarian Organizations as Significant Actors in Psychosocial Care and Support During Disasters

Humanitarian organizations have played a crucial role in providing psychosocial care and support during disasters in India, evolving significantly over time to address the complex needs of affected populations. The evolution of humanitarian aid can be traced back to the informal community support systems that emerged in response to local disasters, transitioning into more structured efforts in the nineteenth century by establishing organizations like the International Committee of the Red Cross in 1863. This marked a pivotal shift toward organized humanitarian responses that emphasized principles of neutrality and impartiality, which are still central to humanitarian missions today (Hugelius, 2022). India's humanitarian system has developed substantially following significant crises such as the Bhopal gas tragedy in 1984 and the Orissa super cyclone in 1999. These events highlighted the need for integrating mental health services within primary healthcare, leading to the incorporation of psychosocial support mechanisms in disaster response strategies. For instance, community-level workers who were survivors became instrumental in providing support during the aftermath of these disasters (Sekar, 2011). As awareness of the psychological impacts of disasters grew, India shifted its focus from merely addressing physical health needs to incorporating mental health interventions, thereby establishing a more holistic approach to disaster management (Sekar, 2011). The humanitarian landscape in India has also been enriched by a diverse array of NGOs dedicated to disaster management. These NGOs have evolved from providing charity-based aid to adopting a rights-based approach, facilitating innovations and good practices at local levels. The involvement of voluntary and philanthropic organizations has fostered a collaborative environment essential for effective humanitarian response (WFP India, 2023). By engaging with local populations and understanding their unique cultural contexts, these organizations ensure that psychosocial care is relevant and impactful (Greene et al., 2017).

Role of Humanitarian Organizations in Providing Psychosocial Support and Mental Health Services in Disasters and Emergencies

The Hyogo Framework of Action (2005–2015), which aimed to help nations and communities to become disaster-resilient, underscores the importance of involving civil societies, non-governmental organizations, community organizations, and voluntary groups in the disaster risk reduction process. There is a need to mainstream DRR into developmental sectors, making the role of NGOs pivotal in building community resilience.

Role of the Humanitarian Sector

Disaster psychosocial response The contributions of the humanitarian sector to disaster rescue, relief, and response initiatives are innumerable. In the immediate response phase, where there is loss of lives, property, and disruption of systems, NGOs and voluntary organizations play a critical role in physical rescue, coordination, first aid, providing relief, and organization of physical and structural support. Similarly, the humanitarian sector also plays a big part in addressing the psychosocial needs of the disaster survivors through different phases of the disaster using diverse methods and approaches. NGOs offer psychosocial support services to help survivors cope with the emotional and psychological impact of disasters at individual, family, and community levels. They organize counselling, support groups and mental health services to the survivors experiencing distress and trauma in addition to several other measures during the rehabilitation and preparedness phase.

Raising awareness and sensitization The non-governmental sector plays a critical role in increasing knowledge and awareness regarding the impact of disasters. In the emergency response phase, survivors who have witnessed disasters exhibit various psychosocial and mental health issues. Reactions like shock, denial, anger, confusion and the disruption of biological rhythm may be common. NGOs, along with support from mental health professionals, play a critical role in increasing awareness and identifying them in the community. Since organizations and personnel working in the geographical area have a greater understanding of the local community, their ability to reach and network with stakeholders and survivors is **better.**

Engagement in psychosocial care and support initiatives The incapacitated social support systems during the occurrence of a disasters are often realigned through psychosocial support and mental health services (PSSMHS) in the aftermath of the disasters. NGOs often play a vital role in this. NGOs and community-based organizations (CBOs) have resources that can establish a supportive caring community (National Disaster Management guidelines, 2009). The integration of the PSSMHS framework into the already existing disaster relief and rescue work and, consequently, the rehabilitation and other developmental activities results in this. Care and service provision of PSSMH by NGOs may range from providing psychological first aid, addressing disaster-related grief and trauma, individual- and group-based counselling services, networking, referral and long-term handholding support and follow-up with survivors.

Capacity-building activities NGO and CBO workers are from diverse backgrounds, and hence they require appropriate professional training to provide better standards of care to the survivors of disasters (National Disaster Management guidelines, 2009). Training and capacity building on skills and knowledge required to address needs of disaster-affected individuals, families, and communities are critical for NGOs. The Training of Trainers (ToT) model is adopted commonly to attain this end. Additionally NGOs, along with technical support from institutions (governmental and private), engage in capacity-building activities on PSSMHS for diverse actors like government functionaries, community frontliners, uniformed first responders, etc. An illustration of the same would be the virtual ToT capacity building initiatives undertaken by UNDP, India, along with the Department of Psychosocial Support in Disaster Management, NIMHANS, India, during the COVID-19 pandemic between 2020 and 2021.

Networking and coordination with government systems Coordination with central and state governments is an essential function that NGOs play during emergencies. The national, regional, and international non-profit organizations network constantly with regional bodies like the State Disaster Management Authority (SDMA) and District Disaster Management Authority (DDMAs) and also with National Disaster Management Authority (NDMA) and National Institute of Disaster Management (NIDM). The objective of coordination and networking is usually to plan and implement Psychosocial care (PSC) and PSS for disaster-affected communities, to avail financial resources, for training and capacity building. NGOs also collect themselves as networks for effective service delivery and coordination. Examples of these include Orissa disaster mitigation mission (Orissa super cyclone, 1999), Abhiyan (Gujarat earthquake, 2001), NGO coordination and resource centre (Indian Ocean tsunami, 2004).

Social media engagement for psychosocial care As social media is deeply embedded in our contemporary society, it becomes an integral part of our day-to-day living. During emergencies and disasters, there exists a dearth of human resources. Under these circumstances, the successful employment of media platforms can enable effective service delivery. For instance, during the COVID-19 pandemic between 2020 and 2023, the Indian state of Kerala was also hit by severe floods. In response, organizations such as Goonj, Smile Foundation lead social media campaigns to help survivors living in remote locations and who were affected by the floods (Shinde et al., 2019; International Strategy for Disaster Reduction, 2006; Sawant, 2023). Social media has been widely used by NGOs to spread awareness and sensitize people regarding the psychosocial and mental health impact of disasters. They use panel discussions, short films and advertisements to do the same. It has also been used to provide immediate support and care, where NGOs connect with survivors and facilitate reaching out to resources. Thus making effective linkages between the community and resources.

Disaster Risk Reduction

Disaster risk reduction strategies are focused on minimizing damage to lives and livelihoods due to natural and human-made disasters. In order to successfully implement risk reduction community engagement with awareness of local knowledge and cultural practices is necessary. Local people and organizations are the main actors during natural disasters in disaster response and preparedness. On occasions where governmental capacities are limited, these functions are primarily carried out by the voluntary sectors. NGOs can operate at the grassroots level and they can mobilize communities and local organizations as partners. They can employ participatory approach for planning and implementation. Their operational flexibility further enables them to overlook systems and structures, making them respond promptly to disaster scenarios.

NGO initiatives toward DRR may be grouped as participation as policy changes, and advocacy for mainstreaming DRR into developmental planning. The Minimum Services Package (MSP) for MHPSS developed by WHO, UNHRC, UNICEF, and UNFPA is an illustration of this. The program outlines high-priority activities to address critical needs in emergencies. Building on existing MHPSS standards and tools in regions. The same has been tested in five countries.

Knowledge and education, to facilitate awareness about disaster prevention and resilience. Many NGOs have played a key role in this through their tailored programs and projects. Educating the local community about the potential nature of hazards and address them through collective action. One such example is the *Gujarat school safety initiative program* conceived and implemented by Gujarat State Disaster Management Authority, India, and SEEDS (a national NGO), post the 2001 Gujarat earthquake in India. The program aimed at enhancing awareness and preparedness among school students, teachers, and parents to reduce disaster risk in schools and prepare to act appropriately in an emergency.

Community-based vulnerability and risk assessment, pinned on the assumption that communities know their situations adequately and risks asessment should be done locally emerging from communities perspecctive. The output from these exercises can further inform the national and international risk reduction framework. An example for the same would be assessment *Community risk assessment tool kits* developed by NGOs, that look at hazard, vulnerability and capacity assessment.

Community-based mitigation and preparedness, NGOs play a significant role in disaster mitigation and preparedness. The demonstrable result of community-based disaster mitigation and preparedness programs may be attributed to the voluntary sector's initiative. Their engagement in the planning, implementation, and evaluation of programs engaging the local community's knowledge and skill sets needs mention. This includes applying best-practice methods of community risk and vulnerability assessments, building community capacities by training local stakeholders like leaders, volunteers, and community front liners, and involving traditional organizational structures present in the community.

Exploring Challenges and Opportunities for the Engagement of Humanitarian Organizations in Disaster PSSMHS

Challenges Faced by Humanitarian Organizations Humanitarian organizations face numerous challenges in delivering mental health and psychosocial support (MHPSS) during disasters and crisis. These challenges are exacerbated by the complex nature of humanitarian emergencies, which can disrupt existing health services and surge demand for mental health interventions among affected populations. Some of the challenges that Humanitarian organisations encounter are detailed below

Disruption of Services Humanitarian crises, such as armed conflicts and natural disasters, often lead to the erosion of health facilities and reduced staff and medical supplies (Troup et al., 2021). This disruption can hinder the timely delivery of MHPSS services, as humanitarian agencies may establish new services that operate parallel to existing systems, leading to a lack of coordination among stakeholders (Troup et al., 2021). Consequently, integrating psychological support into broader health systems remains a critical concern, as fragmented services may not meet the diverse needs of crisis-affected individuals and communities (Tol et al., 2020).

Increased Demand for Mental Health Support The psychological impact of crises is significant, with research indicating that approximately one in five people affected by humanitarian situations experiences moderate to severe mental health conditions, including depression and post-traumatic stress disorder (PTSD) (Ndlovu et al., 2024). This heightened need for support can overwhelm existing resources, particularly when access to care is further impeded by barriers such as stigma, discrimination, and the cultural inappropriateness of treatments (Troup et al., 2021). Organizations must navigate these barriers while ensuring that their interventions are sensitive to the local context and the unique needs of vulnerable populations.

Limited Resources and Funding One substantial barrier to the sustainability of MHPSS initiatives is the reliance on short-term, grant-based funding (Battey et al., 2023). This funding model can hinder long-term planning and community engagement, as organizations often focus on securing new grants rather than building enduring relationships within the communities they serve. There is a pressing need for a shift toward more stable, long-term investments that empower organizations to address complex issues effectively and foster community trust (Battey et al., 2023).

Need for Multisectoral Integration Despite the growing recognition of the importance of integrating mental health into various sectors, challenges remain in achieving effective multisectoral collaboration. Calls for integration have intensified since the World Health Report in 2001 highlighted the neglect of mental health within health systems (Tol et al., 2020). Although there is evidence that integrated interventions can enhance access and acceptability, implementing these approaches often varies, and certain aspects remain undetermined (Ndlovu et al., 2024). Key facilitators of successful integration include adequate training for implementing staff and establishing strong interdisciplinary partnerships (Ndlovu et al., 2024).

Cultural and Contextual Sensitivity Humanitarian organizations must also prioritize cultural and contextual sensitivity in their interventions. Recommendations from international guidelines emphasize the importance of understanding local capacities and preferences and advocating for multilayered support that respects the affected populations' dignity and rights (Tol et al., 2020). Failure to address these considerations can lead to ineffective or even harmful interventions, underscoring the need for research and adaptation of best practices to align with the diverse needs of communities in crisis.

Role of Community Community plays a vital role in the Atmiyata model, emphasizing local engagement for effective psychosocial care. These village-based volunteers are selected for their familiarity with the community's culture and dynamics, essential for building trust and facilitating interventions. They are trained through village mapping to ensure that demographic information and community needs are accurately assessed. This participatory approach empowers champions and enhances the sustainability of programs by fostering a sense of ownership within the community (Battey et al., 2023).

Integrated Interventions Implementing integrated interventions is crucial for addressing the multifaceted challenges target populations face. Research indicates that tailoring interventions to align with local cultural contexts significantly improves their acceptability and effectiveness. Organizations can enhance the relevance of their programs by involving local stakeholders in designing and adapting interventions, leading to better implementation outcomes (Ndlovu et al., 2024). Furthermore, ongoing stakeholder engagement throughout the project cycle ensures that interventions remain aligned with community needs and preferences (Lee et al., 2019).

Monitoring and Evaluation Effective monitoring and evaluation systems are essential for the sustainability of humanitarian interventions. Challenges in this area often stem from inconsistencies in activity reporting and inadequate data collection methods. Successful strategies include establishing comprehensive information systems that track staff performance and program impact. Regular visits by community facilitators for supervision and support, combined with real-time data collection through tools like the Atmiyata application, ensure that champions (psychosocial support providers) receive the necessary guidance and that programs can adapt to emerging challenges (Troup et al., 2021).

Multisectoral Partnerships Developing multisectoral partnerships is critical for the success of integrated interventions. Collaborative efforts among various stakeholders, including academic institutions, local organizations, and government bodies, can enhance resource mobilization and expand the reach of programs. However, challenges remain in sustaining these partnerships, mainly when discrepancies in priorities exist between research and practice. Engaging stakeholders early in the intervention design process fosters a shared understanding and commitment, which is vital for overcoming barriers to collaboration (Troup et al., 2021).

Training and Capacity Building Continuous training and capacity building for community facilitators and champions are essential for maintaining momentum in psychosocial care initiatives. By employing practice-based approaches, such as role-plays, these programs ensure facilitators and volunteers develop the necessary skills to navigate complex community dynamics effectively. Consistent support and mentorship from community facilitators help champions address early performance issues, enhancing the legitimacy and perceived value of interventions within their communities (Battey et al., 2023).

Conclusion and Way Forward

Protecting and improving mental health and psychosocial well-being is a priority, requiring coordinated action among humanitarian assistance providers such as governmental agencies, NGOs, and civil society groups involved in MHPSS. The pivotal role of civil society organizations, particularly NGOs, in disaster management underscores their enduring commitment to fostering psychosocial resilience, addressing vulnerabilities, and promoting sustainable development, reflecting a collective endeavor toward a more resilient and inclusive society. In fragile environments, they are often the sole actors capable of reaching contested areas (Vaughan & Hillier, 2019). Disrupted unprepared health systems compromised primary care, limited resources, and lack of integration of MHPSS into the regular health system makes delivery of MHPSS a challenge during disasters and emergencies. Despite their extraordinary efforts in bridging the gap between MHPSS needs and service delivery, the humanitarian sector often faces challenges and limitations during disaster situations. The spectrum of care approach of integrating psychosocial care encompassing various areas such as legal aid, livelihood support, shelter, psychosocial care, education, medical assistance, and aid in accessing compensations, among others, has been well received by the communities (Kilby, 2007; Barhate et al., 2021). Going forward, humanitarian organizations can benefit greatly by structured coordinated efforts with regional governments, by developing systems for action in the wake of disasters prior to the occurrence of the disasters in the preparedness phase. Standard operating procedures (SoPs) that would be set in prompt motion as soon as the disasters occur are necessary. The effective service delivery by organizations can be enhanced by using technology for gathering and analysing vital information related to the PSSMHS needs of the affected population. Additionally, technology may also be employed for communication across geographical regions that are disaster-hit. There is also a pressing need for the humanitarian sector to participate in action research that is community-led and sensitive to cultural contexts. This would warrant evidence-based, inclusive practices and policies for PSSMHS during disasters (Shinde et al., 2019; International Strategy for Disaster Reduction, 2006; Sawant, 2023).

References

Abiddin, N. Z., Ibrahim, I., & Abdul Aziz, S. A. (2022). Non-governmental organisations (NGOs) and their part towards Sustainable Community Development. *Sustainability, 14*(8), 4386. https://doi.org/10.3390/su14084386

Barhate, B., Hirudayaraj, M., Gunasekara, N., Ibrahim, G., Alizadeh, A., & Abadi, M. (2021). Crisis within a crisis: Migrant workers' predicament during COVID-19 lockdown and the role of non-profit organizations in India. *Indian Journal of Human Development, 15*(1), 151–164. https://doi.org/10.1177/0973703021997624

Battey, J., Garcia, A., Mahita, A. N., Moudgil, T., Tjangdjaja, L., & Fisher, S. (2023). *Atmiyata: Addressing mental distress in India. Reach Alliance, Munk School of Global Affairs and Public Policy.*

Ganaie, A. H. (2020). An introduction to Humanitarian assistance: India's policy and practice for humanitarian aid. *Purakala (UGC Care Listed Journal), 31*(16), 200–210. https://doi.org/10.5281/zenodo.6547876

Greene, M. C., Jordans, M. J. D., Kohrt, B. A., Ventevogel, P., Kirmayer, L. J., Hassan, G., Chiumento, A., van Ommeren, M., & Tol, W. A. (2017). Addressing culture and context in humanitarian response: Preparing desk reviews to inform mental health and psychosocial support. *Conflict and Health, 11*(1), 21. https://doi.org/10.1186/s13031-017-0123-z

Hanspal, M., & Behera, B. (2024). Role of emerging technology in disaster management in India: An overview. *International Journal of Disaster Risk Management, 6*, 133–148. https://doi.org/10.18485/ijdrm.2024.6.2.9

Hasnain, S. A. (2024). 20 years after Indian Ocean Tsunami, India is better prepared. *The Indian Express.* https://indianexpress.com/article/opinion/columns/20-years-after-indian-ocean-tsunami-india-is-better-prepared-9744359/

Hugelius, K. (2022). Measurement of perceived needs in humanitarian contexts using the HESPER scale: A scoping study with reflections on the collaboration between researchers and humanitarian actors. *Conflict and Health, 16*(1), 44. https://doi.org/10.1186/s13031-022-00478-6

International Strategy for Disaster Reduction. (2006). *NGOs & disaster risk reduction: A preliminary review of initiatives and progress made background paper for a consultative meeting on a "Global Network of NGOs for Community Resilience to Disasters."* http://www.unisdr.org/eng/isdr-system/In-a-nutshell.htm

Jagannathan, S. (2001). *The role of nongovernmental organizations in primary education: A study of six NGOs in India.* www.worldbank.org/research/workingpapers

Jaishankar, D., & Godbole, S. (2022). *Aid wars: US–Soviet competition in India.* Brookings. https://www.brookings.edu/articles/aid-wars-u-s-soviet-competition-in-india/

Kilby, P. (2007). The strength of networks: The local NGO response to the tsunami in India. *Disasters, 32*(1), 120–130. https://doi.org/10.1111/j.1467-7717.2007.01030.x

Lee, C., Nguyen, A. J., Haroz, E., Tol, W., Aules, Y., & Bolton, P. (2019). Identifying research priorities for psychosocial support programs in humanitarian settings. *Global Mental Health (Cambridge, England), 6*, e23. https://doi.org/10.1017/gmh.2019.19

National Disaster Management Guidelines: Psycho-Social Support and Mental Health Services in Disasters. (2009). www.springer.com/13753

Ndlovu, J. N., Lind, J., Patlán, A. B., Upadhaya, N., Leku, M. R., Akellot, J., Skovdal, M., Augustinavicius, J. L., & Tol, W. A. (2024). Integration of psychological interventions in multi-sectoral humanitarian programmes: A systematic review. *BMC Health Services Research, 24*(1), 1528. https://doi.org/10.1186/s12913-024-11704-7

Odisha's Turnaround in Disaster Management Has Lessons for the World. (2023). Retrieved December 30, 2024, from https://www.worldbank.org/en/news/opinion/2023/11/03/odisha-s-turnaround-in-disaster-management-has-lessons-for-the-world

Pal, I., Ghosh, S., Dash, I., & Mukhopadhyay, A. (2023). Review of Tsunami early warning system and coastal resilience with a focus on Indian Ocean. *International Journal of Disaster Resilience in the Built Environment, 14*(5), 593–610.

Parmar, S. (2012a). Humanitarian assistance and disaster relief (HADR) in India's national strategy focus. *Journal of Defence Studies, 6*, 91.

Parmar, S. S. (2012b). Humanitarian assistance and disaster relief (HADR) in India's national strategy. *Journal of Defence Studies, 6*(1), 91–101. https://idsa.in/system/files/jds_6_1_SarabjeetParmar.pdf

Paulmann, J. (2013). Conjunctures in the history of international humanitarian aid during the twentieth century. *Humanity—An International Journal of Human Rights Humanitarianism and Development, 4*(2), 215–238.

Ranjan, R. (2024). Understanding the historical trajectory of disasters: Lessons from India and the world. *Times of India*, March 16, 2024.

Sawant, R. K. (2023). Role of NGOs in disaster management and sustainability. *Epitome: International Journal of Multidisciplinary Research, 9*(3), 12–22.

Sekar, K. (2011). (A14) Psychosocial support services in disasters—Indian experiences. *Prehospital and Disaster Medicine, 26*(S1), s3–s4. https://doi.org/10.1017/S1049023X11000276

Shanbog, R., & Kevlihan, R. (2022, November). *India's humanitarian assistance abroad: A domestic and foreign policy issue*. Alternatives Humanitaires.
Sharma, N. (2022). *NGO impact on India's development process*. https://doi.org/10.13140/RG.2.2.31972.24963
Shinde, H. T., Kendre, T., & Ghute, B. (2019). Role of non-governmental organization in disaster management. *International Journal of Management and Economics, 1*(29), 234–236.
Stephan, C., Norf, C., & Fekete, A. (2017). How "sustainable" are post-disaster measures? Lessons to be learned a decade after the 2004 tsunami in the Indian ocean. *International Journal of Disaster Risk Science, 8*(1), 33–45.
Tol, W. A., Purgato, M., Bass, J. K., Galappatti, A., & Eaton, W. (2015). Mental health and psychosocial support in humanitarian settings: A public mental health perspective. *Epidemiology and Psychiatric Sciences, 24*(6), 484–494.
Tol, W. A., Ager, A., Bizouerne, C., Bryant, R., El Chammay, R., Colebunders, R., García-Moreno, C., Hamdani, S. U., James, L. E., Jansen, S. C. J., Leku, M. R., Likindikoki, S., Panter-Brick, C., Pluess, M., Robinson, C., Ruttenberg, L., Savage, K., Welton-Mitchell, C., Hall, B. J., et al. (2020). Improving mental health and psychosocial wellbeing in humanitarian settings: Reflections on research funded through R2HC. *Conflict and Health, 14*(1), 71. https://doi.org/10.1186/s13031-020-00317-6
Troup, J., Fuhr, D. C., Woodward, A., Sondorp, E., & Roberts, B. (2021). Barriers and facilitators for scaling up mental health and psychosocial support interventions in low- and middle-income countries for populations affected by humanitarian crises: A systematic review. *International Journal of Mental Health Systems, 15*(1), 5. https://doi.org/10.1186/s13033-020-00431-1
Vaughan, A., & Hillier, D. (2019). *Ensuring impact: The role of civil society organisations in strengthening World Bank disaster risk financing*. Centre for Disaster Protection. https://reliefweb.int/report/world/ensuring-impact-role-civil-society-organisations-strengthening-world-bank-disaster-risk
WFP India. (2023). *Strengthening the humanitarian system in India*. https://www.wfp.org/publications/strengthening-humanitarian-system-india-0

5

Psychosocial Support and Mental Health Services in The Disaster Management Paradigm: Concepts and Theoretical Perspectives

Sona Francis, Subhasis Bhadra, and C. Jayakumar

Introduction

India is prone to many disasters due to its unique geo-climatic conditions. According to the 2022–2023 report of the National Disaster Management Authority, out of 36 states and union territories, 27 have been identified as disaster-prone ones. Of the total landmass, 58.6% is prone to moderate to very high-intensity earthquakes. Out of 7516 km of coastline, 5700 km are vulnerable to cyclones and tsunamis; 68% of cultivable land is vulnerable to drought; hilly areas are at risk from landslides and avalanches; and 15% of the landmass is prone to landslides (National Disaster Management Authority, 2023). In addition to natural disasters, India also experiences several human-induced disasters

S. Francis • S. Bhadra (✉) • C. Jayakumar
Department of Psychosocial Support in Disaster Management, NIMHANS, Bengaluru, Karnataka, India

S. Bhadra et al. (eds.), *Psychosocial and Mental Health Support for Disaster Management in India*, Palgrave Studies in Disaster Science and Emergency Management,
https://doi.org/10.1007/978-3-032-02511-1_5

including technological disasters, terrorist activities, communal violence, and accidents, making the country "a theatre of disasters" (Sekar, 2005). Environmental degradation-related disasters that result from the degradation of the environment, such as climate change, loss of biodiversity, pollution, and the depletion of natural resources, are also issues from which India is not exempt.

According to the National Disaster Management Act of 2005, disaster means "a catastrophe, mishap, calamity, or grave occurrence in any area, arising from natural or man-made causes, or by accident or negligence which results in substantial loss of life or human suffering or damage to, and destruction of, property, or damage to, or degradation of, environment and is of such a nature or magnitude as to be beyond the coping capacity of the community of the affected area" (NDMA, 2005). The above concept of disasters that it is either natural, which means driven by natural forces that man has no control over, or man-made, which means some human actions have directly caused it, has changed to an understanding that all disasters have some human-induced causes behind them or that simply no disasters are completely natural. Disasters are highly destructive and devastating and no one who experiences a disaster remains unaffected. This understanding calls for more effective and timely disaster management in all phases, from prevention to reconstruction. The Disaster Management Act defines disaster management as "a continuous and integrated process of planning, organizing, coordinating, and implementing measures that are necessary or expedient for the prevention of danger or threat of any disaster, mitigation or reduction of risk of any disaster or its severity or consequences, capacity-building, preparedness to deal with any disaster, prompt response to any threatening disaster situation or disaster, and for assessing the severity or magnitude of effects of any disaster" (NDMA, 2005).

Disasters affect different aspects of human life, including physical, emotional, social, and economic. The physical impacts include deaths, loss, injury, amputations, and illness. The distress and trauma from experiencing and witnessing disasters will contribute to several mental health consequences which manifest in various forms such as e anxiety, depression, substance abuse, post-traumatic stress disorder (PTSD), and violence (Manning & Clayton, 2018). Disasters not only impact physical and mental health but also disrupt livelihoods, financial stability, and access to essential services. They disturb family dynamics, weaken social support systems, and fracture community networks. All these social situations, along with decreased perceived social and emotional support, also add to psychiatric symptomology, including anxiety, substance use, depression, and PTSD (Solomon et al., 1993). Vulnerable groups, such as women, children, the elderly, persons with disabilities (PWD), people with chronic illness, newborns, pregnant and lactating women, and the LGBTQI+ population, have higher chances of serious mental health consequences from disasters. The physical and mobility challenges, limited access to resources, increased caregiver burden, pre-existing health conditions, social isolation, stigma and discrimination, socioeconomic vulnerabilities, and the risks of neglect, abuse, violence, harassment, and exploitation in such situations add to the challenges faced by vulnerable groups during disasters.

Psychosocial support and mental health services are integral components of the disaster management process as disasters cause severe threats to the mental health and the psychosocial well-being of individuals. These services include a range of care, support, and interventions that aim to address the mental, emotional, and psychosocial needs of individuals. While mental health services in disasters primarily focus on diagnosing, treating, and preventing mental health issues and disorders arising from the stress and trauma associated with such events, the psychosocial component focuses on addressing the immediate needs which includes psychological first aid (PFA), extending emotional support, strengthening social support networks, providing education and awareness, advocacy, training and capacity building, as well as livelihood support. The combination of these services becomes crucial in disaster management initiatives for mitigating the long-term psychological impacts of disasters.

The current chapter, therefore, will offer a detailed understanding of the concepts of psychosocial support and mental health services in disaster management, their importance, and the theoretical perspectives, effective intervention strategies, possible challenges, and associated policy framework.

PSSMH: Conceptual Understanding

"Mental health is a state of mental well-being that enables people to cope with the stresses of life, realize their abilities, learn well and work well, and contribute to their community" (World Health Organization, 2022). According to the World Health Origanization (WHO), mental health is a basic human right and a crucial aspect of health and well-being which impacts our ability to make decisions, form relationships, and influence the world around us. Disasters can be a traumatic experience for the individuals and communities affected by them. The unpredictability, unexpectedness, and sudden occurrence intensify the emotional and psychological impacts. These impacts usually manifest as immediate emotional responses such as feelings of fear, stress, anxiety, anger, disbelief, shock, numbness, disorientation, helplessness, grief, and loss of control, which can lead to long-term mental health concerns if not addressed. Disasters also cause collective trauma, where the psychological impacts extend beyond the individuals and affect the whole community. In such cases, the community's identity and cohesion may be altered as members collectively process the disaster's aftermath, while the shared experience of loss, fear, and destruction creates a deep sense of grief and disrupts the social equilibrium. Individual and collective trauma from disasters can create significant imbalances in the mental health of affected individuals and create a social environment that hinders recovery and well-being. Studies have reported a high prevalence of mental health and psychosocial problems in humanitarian settings, several emergency situations, armed conflicts, and natural and human-induced disasters (Tol et al., 2011).

The concept of 'Psychosocial Health' highlights the dynamic relationship between psychological factors such as thoughts, emotions, feelings, and behavior, and the broader social factors such as relationships, values, traditions, culture, etc. (Hansen, 2009). Disasters have a profound impact on the psychosocial well-being of individuals and communities as they shatter the social structure, support systems, social relationships, and community well-being. Individuals experience feelings of isolation and helplessness, while they struggle to cope with the loss and distress arising from it. These will affect an individual's sense of belonging and security and impact their ability to meet their social roles. The breakdown of traditional family structures, routines, cultural norms, and community networks can make communities more vulnerable to social issues such as fragmentation, displacement, marginalization, and disintegration. This creates an environment where mental health issues are developed and exacerbated, disproportionately affecting the overall recovery of the community.

Individuals' mental and psychosocial health are important for their overall health, their well-being, and their community. Moreover, from the perspective of human rights, mental health services and psychosocial support are basic rights of disaster survivors, allowing them to live with dignity and receive empathy from others (Sekar, 2005). The Inter-Agency Standing Committee (IASC) has provided a framework for understanding the psychosocial and mental health consequences of disasters. This framework divides the consequences into psychological and social, which can be exacerbated by disasters, induced by disasters, or caused by disaster management or response-related issues. While disasters can induce social problems like family separation, internal displacements, disrupted social networks, communal tensions, and increased gender-based violence, and can also exacerbate re-existing social problems like poverty and marginalization, disaster management initiatives can sometimes affect the established community structures and traditional support systems. On the psychological front, while disasters induce new psychological issues such as emotional distress, grief, depression, anxiety, PTSD, etc. they can also worsen pre-existing mental health issues like severe mental disorders or substance use disorders. Poor disaster management responses also increase psychological distress and disturbances (Inter-Agency Standing Committee, 2007).

Before the middle of the twentieth century, search and rescue operations, as well as the provision of basic supplies, were the primary focus of disaster management and the psychosocial side was almost neglected. But it was becoming increasingly clear that the stress that survivors suffered extended beyond wounds and material losses. India saw multiple catastrophic events in the years since its Independence, including the partition in 1947, the Bengaluru circus tragedy in 1981, the Bhopal gas tragedy in 1984, the Marathwada earthquake in 1993, the Orrisa super cyclone in 199, the Gujarat earthquake in 2001, the Gujarat riots in 2002, and the Indian Ocean tsunami in 2004, etc., which reported mass trauma and mental health concerns on the part of the affected population. It brought attention to the importance of comprehensive psychosocial support and mental healthcare in disasters and emergencies. Recognizing the importance of Mental Health and Psychosocial Support (MHPSS), these initiatives are increasingly integrated into humanitarian aid programs (Tol et al., 2011).

Timeline of National and International Initiatives Focusing on Disaster Mental Health

As defined by the Inter-Agency Standing Committee, mental health and psychosocial support include "any type of local or outside support that aims to protect or promote psychosocial well-being and/or prevent or treat mental disorder" (Inter-Agency Standing Committee, 2007). In the context of disasters, psychosocial support refers to comprehensive interventions meant to address different psychosocial issues that may arise in the wake of a disaster. This includes addressing essential needs, enhancing individual and community capacity, improving social support systems and community networks, and recognizing the impact of value systems, culture, and other social factors that influence mental health. Psychosocial support will include broad initiatives associated with greater demands for relief work, social support, and harmony to support or safeguard the survivors' psychosocial well-being. Mental health services in disaster management encompass the interventions for the treatment or prevention of psychological disorders or symptoms associated with disasters.

The general goals of MHPSS services are to enhance well-being, reduce trauma and emotional distress, and prevent, treat, or mitigate mental disorders that arise from, or become worse due to, disasters or disaster management processes. Moreover, these initiatives will preserve rights and dignity, and support people, families, and groups in re-establishing social connection and infrastructure. While mental health issues and the need for psychosocial support require different methods, they are closely

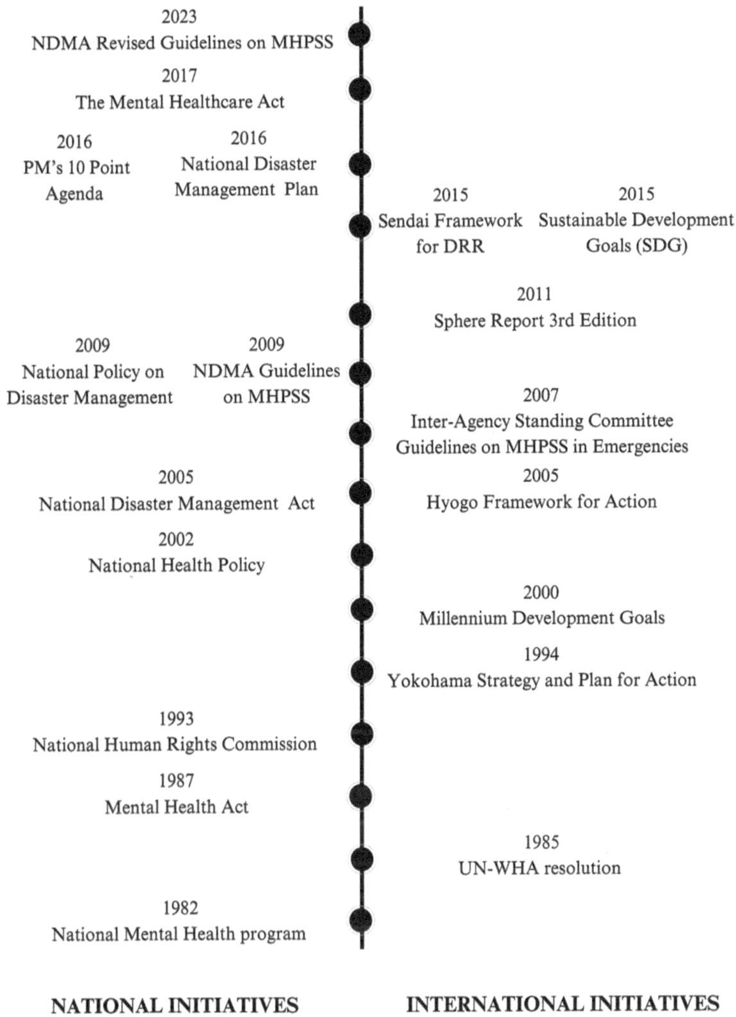

connected (Hansen, 2009). Mild, moderate, or even severe mental health issues can arise as a result of psychosocial issues that are either extremely severe, or last for a long time without any form of intervention. Similarly, psychosocial issues are also common among individuals with mental health issues.

Why Do Disasters Affect Mental Health?

Disasters impact the physical, mental, emotional, social, and economic aspects of life for the affected population. They cause severe distress among the survivors due to the devastating experiences and resulting trauma, which can lead to long-term mental health problems.

The table below outlines some of the impacts of disaster on individuals, families, and communities that can cause distress and trauma.

Individuals	Families	Communities
Physical injuries and disabilities	Disruption of family structure and roles	Loss of social cohesion
Loss of loved ones	Disruption of family routine	Lack of trust in existing systems
Loss of employment or income and livelihood	Separation of family members	Lack of support networks
Loss of shelter and displacement	Forced displacements	Damage to infrastructure and basic services
Lack of sense of security	Relationship strains	Increase in marginalization, stigmatization, and social inequalities
Grief from losses	Lack of social support systems	Corruption and injustice
Emotional distress and trauma	Financial instability and debts	Challenges in accessing food, clean water, and basic healthcare
Uncertainty about future	Disruption in children's education	Disaster induced migration
Increased vulnerability to substance use	Increased caregiving responsibilities	Collapse of the local economy
	Increased domestic violence	Collective trauma
		Increased vulnerability to social conflicts

Phases of Disaster Management and Mental Health Concerns

Disaster management is a systematic approach to effectively respond to, recover from, and prepare for disasters to mitigate the impacts and losses caused by them. The phase includes pre-disaster, during-disaster, and post-disaster measures which aim to manage risks, reduce vulnerability, and enhance resilience. Each phase requires specialized psychosocial and mental health initiatives and interventions that address the population's specific needs of the population.

Mitigation Phase

This phase of disaster management, which occurs before the disaster event, primarily aims at mitigating the negative impacts and consequences of potential hazards. It involves identifying potential hazards and assessing the vulnerabilities and risks. Mitigating the mental health impact of potential hazards is the key area of focus of the psychosocial activities and mental health services during the mitigation phase. Any underlying psychosocial vulnerabilities that could elevate the impacts of disasters, if any, are identified and appropriate measures are taken to address those. Raising public awareness about the importance of incorporating mental health considerations into disaster management activities is important here. The understanding that effective strategies will reduce the prevalence and severity of mental health concerns among the disaster-affected population is important in establishing an inclusive, collaborative, and multi-level approach that includes administration, policy-makers, mental health professionals, responders, volunteers, local governance, civil society, and the community.

Preparedness Phase

The preparedness phase is the period of planning, organizing, and preparing individuals, communities, and organizations to effectively manage the impact of potential disasters. Emergency plans encompassing comprehensive disaster response plans at local, regional, and national levels, evacuation routes, shelter locations, and relief distribution places are prepared. Several measures must be implemented in this phase in the context of mental health and psychosocial support. Primarily mental health and psychosocial support have to be incorporated into the preparedness plan. Planning for the availability of mental health resources and professionals, training for first responders and volunteers on psychosocial first aid (PFA) and related skills, strengthening the community support system and network, educating the public about effective coping strategies, and other culturally sensitive pre-disaster interventions can improve communities' emotional and mental resilience towards disaster.

Response Phase

The response phase is characterized by search and rescue operations, relief distribution, evacuating individuals at risk to safe locations, setting up temporary shelters and camps, providing emergency medical care to the affected ones, deploying mobile medical units, facilitating communication among government, public, civil society and other stakeholders, etc. Also, ensuring the safety and security of the affected areas, providing accurate and timely information, addressing rumors, and conducting rapid assessments to understand the extent of damage and needs are part of the interventions of the response phase. Providing immediate psychosocial support through PFAs, need-based training for first responders, professionals, and volunteers, establishing crisis counseling services, identifying individuals exhibiting signs of acute stress, anxiety, trauma, or other conditions, implementing mental health interventions, creating safe spaces and providing specialized care for women, children, elderly and other vulnerable groups, informing public about available services and how and where to access those, and educating the public about the long-term mental health impacts and need for sustained mental health-care, etc. are some of the psychosocial and pro-mental health activities during the response phase.

Recovery Phase

The recovery phase begins after the immediate response phase. This phase continues until the affected population returns to a functional state. In the recovery phase, the focus shifts from immediate relief efforts to long-term rehabilitation and reconstruction. The utmost goal of the recovery phase initiatives is to rebuild stronger and more resilient communities to disasters. The phase ensures that essential services are restored and the community becomes functional in the necessary aspects. Ensuring emotional and mental health is a major focus in the recovery phase is important for the long-term mental well-being of the survivors of disasters. Programs in the recovery phase focus on rebuilding social connections, reducing isolation, and enhancing community resilience. Trauma-focused interventions that recognize the affected population's psychological and emotional needs are promoted. The recovery efforts should ensure that the initiatives and interventions are inclusive and address the special needs of different groups and vulnerable populations in the community. More focus is given to community-led initiatives which are culturally and contextually sensitive, and effective in enhancing the community's psychosocial resilience and minimizing the long-term mental health issues.

MHPSS Activities in Disasters

Pre-disaster	Mental health and psychosocial risk assessments Vulnerability mapping Capacity building and training Resilience building Research and awareness generation (identified risks, vulnerabilities, capacities, and efficacy of programs conducted) Planning and policy development

(continued)

(continued)

During disaster	Rapid and extended need assessments Early identification and support Psychosocial interventions (PFA, ensuring basic needs, providing necessary, accurate information, etc.) and referral Mental health interventions (emotion, cognition, and behavioural focused) and referral Community-based interventions (organizing support groups, engaging local leaders and healers, mobilizing, and optimally utilizing local resources, etc.)
Post-disaster	Proving long-term mental health services Rehabilitation and psychosocial reintegration Monitoring, evaluation, and follow-up Research and dissemination of information (mental health and psychosocial impacts of the disaster, interventions done and their efficacy, the extent of preparedness, response mechanisms, the resilience of the population, adequacy of existing policies, systems, and practices, limitation in disaster risk reduction in terms of psychosocial and mental health, etc.) Advocacy for recovery and '*build back better*'

MHPSS Pyramid in Disasters

The Mental Health and Psychosocial Support (MHPSS) Pyramid, proposed by IASC, has been adapted to the Indian context in the 2023 MHPSS guidelines by the NDMA to address the diverse population, cultural variations, and unique challenges of the country in disaster situations. This pyramid offers a multilayered model designed to provide different levels of support to affected communities. It ensures both immediate and long-term care by providing scalable and flexible services at each level, based on the community's needs and priorities. It also recognizes the importance of family- and community-based interventions in parallel with individual ones. Ranging from basic needs and security to specialized mental healthcare, the interventions are arranged into four levels (Inter-Agency Standing Committee, 2007).

Level 1: Basic Service and Security The foundation level of the pyramid is focused on meeting basic and essential needs like food, water, shelter, safety, etc. This level ensures the basic protection and well-being of the affected population by providing services that are sensitive and appropriate to their emotional and cultural needs. Everyone affected by disaster needs psychosocial support. This includes the primary survivors (directly affected) as well as the secondary survivors. The secondary survivors may be neighboring communities, friends, relatives, and primary responders of the disasters.

Level 2: Family and Community-Based Care At this level, support is offered to those who need it to restore a sense of normality or to reestablish functionality. This includes addressing the needs of those who are at risk of developing mental health issues. Re-establishing and reuniting family and community systems, creating social connections, facilitating community healing, and providing access to available resources are some of the focuses of this level. This includes all the primary survivors in the affected region who have experienced, witnessed the loss, or faced the threat of the disaster intensively being in the same location.

Level 3: Focused, Non-Specialized Services At this level, the ones who develop mild to moderate mental health disorders receive focused psychosocial care. Individual, family, or group interventions are provided by non-specialists like trained and supervised staff or volunteers. This level aims to assist people to recover from distress and prevent it from worsening to more serious mental health problems. A vulnerability mapping through a participatory process is crucial to identify the people who require specialized services for the next level of interventions.

Level 4: Specialized Care This level focuses on specialized and professional care for individuals with severe distress or mental health disorders. This includes professional psychiatric or psychological support such as therapies, medication, in-patient care, and referral. Individuals with pre-existing mental health problems are given special focus. Further including them in the process of community rehabilitation during the phase of rehabilitation and rebuilding is very much essential for integration and recovery. Alongside individual intervention, the support at this level may need detailed social interventions.

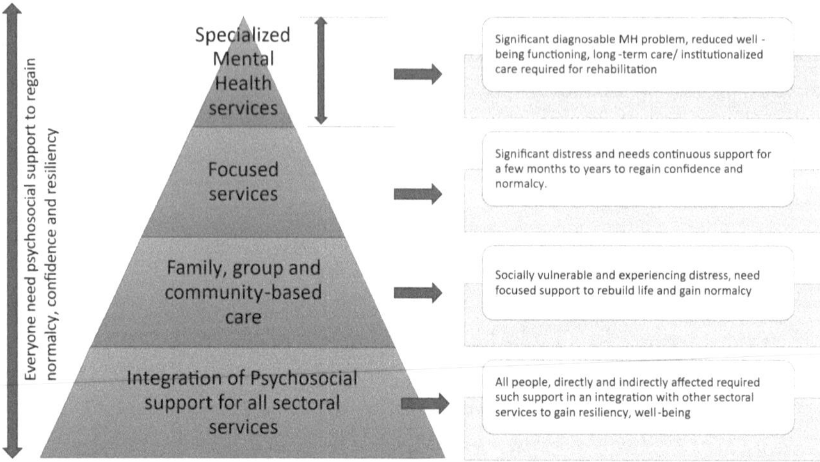

Adopted from IASC-MHPSS Guidelines (2007)

Who Can Provide MHPSS?

MHPSS activities require coordinated efforts from various sectors and departments, including civil society. This collaborative approach is necessary for delivering effective care and support at different levels of MHPSS interventions, during different stages of the disaster and disaster management process. This mandates an adequate group of trained and skilled human resources to coordinate and perform the essential tasks in the field. MHPSS service providers need to be aware of various ways that individuals and communities express their distress to provide appropriate and immediate help.

MHPSS initiatives can be done by both professional and trained non-professionals in mental health depending on the level of care needed. The first three levels of MHPSS interventions of the pyramid, which are basic service and security, family and community-based care, and focused, non-specialized care, can be carried out by first responders, trained staff, or skilled volunteers who have received appropriate training in psychosocial care. They can help the affected population with immediate emotional needs, restore social connections, establish support systems, and provide basic PFA. The fourth level, which involves specialized care for those who experience severe mental health problems, needs professional support. These professionals can include psychiatrists, psychologists, social workers, and other mental health professionals who are qualified to provide specialized therapies and medical interventions.

The Guiding Principle of MHPSS Delivery

To maintain the quality and effectiveness of services when modified based on contextual realities, resource constraints, and logistical concerns, NDMA, in its MHPSS guidelines, has proposed the guiding principles in service delivery.

1. Stepped care approach—This method emphasizes delivering care at different levels, starting from the least resource-intensive, immediate, and non-specialized care, and progressing to the specialized interventions, based on the needs of individuals.
2. Social justice-informed—This approach focuses on ensuring equity, access, safety, and dignity for the affected population at all levels of care and intervention and employing a participatory approach.
3. Sensitivity of culture and context—This method prioritizes providing tailor-made interventions that align with the cultural and local values, customs, traditions, and practices to respect diversity and promote inclusivity.
4. Recognizing strength—This approach focuses on leveraging the strengths and capacities of individuals and communities as a primary resource for building resilience and facilitating disaster recovery. It empowers people to recognize and build upon their strengths to better prepare for and overcome disasters.
5. Protecting dignity—This approach highlights the importance of treating individuals with respect and assuring their dignity and self-worth. It includes ensuring confidentiality and privacy, obtaining informed consent, and honoring individual's rights and safety.
6. Increasing access—This principle focuses on increasing the availability and accessibility of mental health and psychosocial services for all, particularly vulnerable populations, by addressing the challenges and barriers to access.

7. Continuity of care—This principle promotes sustained and long-term service and support by ensuring that they are not limited to the immediate aftermath of disasters.
8. Promoting participation—This approach emphasizes involving individuals and communities at every stage of the disaster intervention framework, from planning and decision-making to the evaluation of services. It helps in achieving the goal of 'holistic care' by making interventions participatory.
9. Facilitating safety—This principle ensures the creation of a safe and supportive environment for individuals who seek help, addressing both their physical and emotional well-being. It also involves measures to prevent violence, exploitation, and harm and ensures the help-seekers feel secure and protected.
10. Upholding accountability—This principle advocates for transparency and responsibility in service delivery to ensure that the interventions are effective, relevant, ethical, and just. It includes establishing monitoring and evaluation systems with feedback mechanisms to keep goals and outcomes on track.

NDMA (2023)

PSSMH Triage

Psychosocial triaging is a method for assessing and categorizing people affected by disasters based on their mental health and psychosocial needs. It is a technique that helps care providers prioritize care by identifying the neediest and those who require immediate care and support.

Key components of psychosocial triaging:

1. Systematic assessments—Caregivers assess and evaluate the mental health conditions of the survivors based on their physical closeness to disaster-affected sites, expressive closeness with the disaster-affected ones, individual vulnerabilities, environmental vulnerabilities, their instant reaction during the disaster, then ongoing reactions, and coping mechanisms (Sekar et al., 2023a).
2. Prioritizing care—Based on the assessment, individuals are classified into low, medium, or high levels of risk. This classification helps in determining the type of support to be given, whether it is immediate and professional mental health treatment, psychological care, or ongoing monitoring (Fig. 2.1 of the NDMA Training Module on Psychosocial Care in Disaster-Module 2), (Sekar et al., 2023a).
3. Resource optimization—Triaging helps to provide more organized and coordinated mental health care in disaster-affected communities. By prioritizing the needs, the limited mental health resources can be effectively planned and utilized.
4. Ensuring quality of service and enhanced support—Psychosocial triaging in disasters aims to mitigate the adverse mental health impacts of disasters among the survivors. It ensures a need-based level of care and support and thereby ensures the quality of service provided.

Vulnerable Populations in Disasters

Disasters and vulnerability are related in two ways. First, disasters cause physical, mental, and social vulnerabilities among the affected population. Second, disasters exacerbate the existing vulnerabilities and make the life and survival of the vulnerable even more difficult.

Disasters elevate the socioeconomic vulnerabilities of individuals, families, and communities. The lack of financial stability and resilience among the affected population worsens their struggles and disrupts their recovery process. Studies report that the poor are more vulnerable to disasters, in terms of loss of both human and economic capital (Rentschler, 2013). Structural issues such as poverty, unemployment, exploitation, and corruption, which are exacerbated during disasters, further increase the vulnerabilities of economically weaker populations (Bhadra, 2021). Social vulnerabilities such as marginalization, stigmatization, and discrimination based on gender, sexuality, ethnicity, caste, and social class are compounded in the aftermath of disasters. These social vulnerabilities weaken the social support systems of affected populations, hindering both recovery and reintegration.

Women face the most risk in disasters due to physical and sexual abuse, violence, exploitation, harassment, and neglect. The atrocities against women are increased during disasters, which undermines their physical, mental, and psychosocial well-being. Children and adolescents are primary concerns in disasters and emergencies as they are highly vulnerable to trafficking, abuse, and neglect. A lot of children are lost, orphaned, and abandoned in the aftermath of disasters which puts them at risk of abuse, violence, exploitation, and forced beggary (Rao, 2006). Elderly people are particularly vulnerable to the immediate and long-term impacts of disasters due to their physical and cognitive disabilities. They are often neglected in emergencies and crises. People with disabilities and chronic illnesses face unique challenges in disasters. The barriers to accessing information, resources, relief, and safety measures make them vulnerable in such situations. Also, discrimination toward disabled individuals is often increased in the aftermath of disasters (Alexander, 2012). Another population that is highly vulnerable to disasters is individuals from the LGBTQI+ community. The stigma prevailing in the societies, the discrimination and harassment toward them, their limited access to resources, and the poor social support they receive worsen their challenges and add to their struggles throughout the recovery process.

Techniques of Providing Psychosocial Support

In the NDMA training module 2 on Psychosocial Care in Disasters, NDMA and NIMHANS have developed ten basic techniques for providing psychosocial support effectively in disasters (Sekar et al., 2023a). Anyone seeking to help people affected by disasters can follow these techniques to mitigate the negative psychosocial impacts and facilitate recovery. These techniques, when applied with culturally sensitive methods in a supportive environment, can effectively promote the psychosocial and mental well-being of disaster survivors.

- Be empathetic
- Encourage ventilation of emotions
- Practice active listening
- Help maintain routines
- Promote adaptive coping strategies
- Foster social support
- Introduce yoga and relaxation exercises
- Encourage recreational activities
- Incorporate spirituality
- Encourage externalization of interests

Spectrum of Care: An Integrated Model

Psychosocial care encompasses different types and levels of care in a disaster-affected population. The spectrum of care model, which uses an integrated approach, views psychosocial support as an entry point to other support platforms and aims to provide a holistic 'umbrella of support' to the affected individuals and communities. Under the umbrella of care, seven basic areas affected by a disaster must be addressed with a comprehensive psychosocial intervention plan.

While working with the disaster-affected communities it is essential to work for 'build-back-better' (BBB). This ensures communities become stronger to deal with future crises and eventualities that can cause

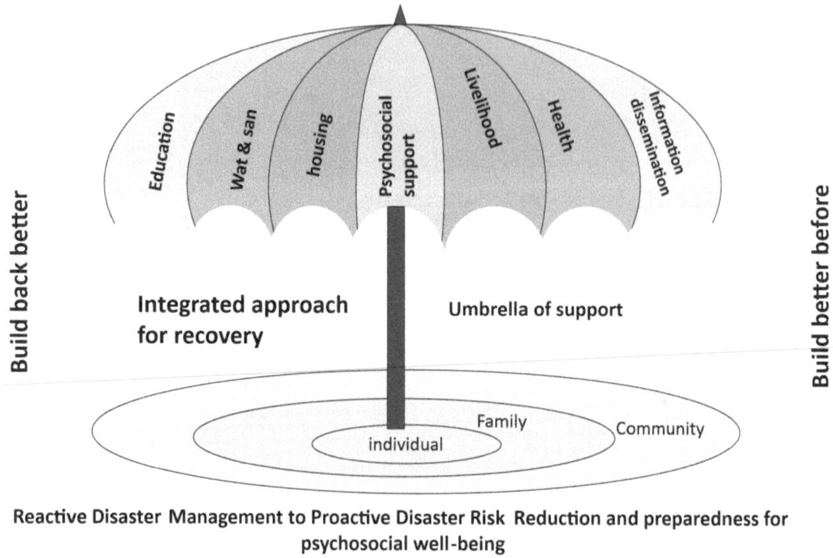

disaster. Further, as a whole disaster management is now proactive and guided for disaster risk reduction. Therefore, working to 'build-better-before' became more crucial. In such a situation, disaster risk reduction becomes an integrated part of every developmental initiative that makes the whole system sustainable.

Community-Based MHPSS Interventions

Disasters impact large populations at a time and cause widespread distress and disruption. The high number of populations affected, and the lack of adequate mental health professionals, hinder effective and timely mental health and psychosocial support services. In such situations, community-based interventions, which can reach more people within limited resources, prove to be more effective than individual-focused interventions.

Community-based MHPSS interventions emphasize a participatory approach that incorporates local resources, capacities, cultural systems, and indigenous knowledge and practices for promoting holistic psychosocial care. While addressing mental health concerns, these interventions also foster resilience, trust, and cohesion in the community and strengthen social networks. In such interventions, community members are the active participants and the strengths and capacities of the local communities are the key resources. They are encouraged to be responsible for overcoming the challenges. Community members are involved in all the phases of an intervention starting from need assessment, planning activities, drafting proposals, mobilizing resources, and implementing activities, to monitoring and evaluation (Hansen, 2009). These interventions are based on local realities and involve indigenous knowledge, values, and coping strategies that are culturally sensitive and suitable to the context. All the community structures such as family, religious institutions, traditional healers, local leaders, democratic and statutory bodies, non-governmental organizations, and the broader civil society play significant roles in the formulation and implementation of community-based interventions.

Significance of community-based MHPSS interventions in disasters

- Wider reach
- More accessible
- Culturally sensitive
- Sustainable
- Strength-based
- Promote community resilience

Among the key components of community-based interventions that proved to be effective in disasters and emergencies are:

- Forming inclusive and representative tract committees within communities (including local representatives, community leaders, women, youth, children and adolescents, elderly, spiritual leaders, teachers, and other influential community members). These committees are involved in the planning, designing, implementing, and monitoring programs in the community. They can also coordinate and facilitate the implementation and integration of psychosocial interventions in the communities.

- For example: Village Tract Committees which were formed in Myanmar during Cyclone Nargis in 2008, and Community Committees formed in Kanyakumari, after the Indian Ocean Tsunami in 2004.
- Establishing community centers in disaster-affected communities that serve as a place for them to come together and engage in community activities and initiatives has proven effective. These community centers can be used for community meetings, support groups, and other activities like art classes, training programs, sports, and other recreational activities.
- For example: Community centers that were set up in Indonesia following the Indian Ocean Tsunami, in 2004.
- Promoting volunteerism in disaster-affected communities is an impactful method in facilitating rebuilding and rehabilitative initiatives. Volunteers are usually the members of the communities themselves. Their familiarity with the local situations and the trust the communities have for them are key benefits of such interventions. Along with providing and coordinating immediate needs supplies, they can also help with emotional and psychosocial support. They can be trained and encouraged to ensure the proper reach of interventions at the grassroots level. Volunteerism can improve social cohesion, community strengths, and a collective spirit, as community members come together for each other. Also, volunteerism enhances the feeling of self-worth and satisfaction among the volunteers (Bhadra & Pulla, 2014). These volunteers act as voices of the affected community to ensure their needs are addressed. This strategy was found successful in the psychosocial interventions at Kanyakumari in 2004, post-tsunami.
- Awareness generation and psychoeducation are highly impactful in promoting mental health and psychosocial well-being in disasters. This helps in reducing stigma and increases the understanding of addressing mental health problems and seeking help. The understanding of early signs and warnings of mental health problems can help in providing early interventions. Having essential information on positive adaptive mechanisms can help in managing stress, anxiety, and distress related to disasters. Awareness about available mental health services and resources will increase access to such services.

Psychoeducation is also helpful in understanding and differentiating the normal (sadness, confusion, fear, denial, anxiousness, irritability, etc.) and abnormal emotional reactions (feeling overwhelmed, acute stress, severe anxiety, panic attacks, extreme avoidance, psychosomatic responses, suicidal thoughts, etc.) to disasters. Awareness about mental health needs and problems in disasters will improve communities' preparedness and empower them to manage and overcome the challenges.

- School-based programs are effective community-based interventions as schools provide an ideal entry point to a community. They are usually set up in accessible locations and are highly valued. School-based programs can reach to different types of populations such as students, parents, teachers, and other stakeholders. These programs help in mitigating the emotional and psychological impacts of disasters on children and reduce symptoms. Initiatives such as Safe School Projects, which aim at improving the preparedness of children and schools for potential disasters, are impactful. Encouraging children to return to school in the aftermath of disasters is an important element of the normalization of routine in communities. This comeback provides students, teachers, and other non-teaching workers in a school with a space to restore predictability and daily routines and also to process their experiences (Hansen, 2009).
- Capacity building and training are important strategies, both before and after disasters. Providing structured training using standardized modules will effectively empower the communities in dealing with diseases in the preparedness, response, and recovery phases of disasters. Training can be given for different community groups who are associated with different departments such as education, health, transport, safety and rescue, etc. on basic skills like PFA and the administration of screening tools, referral, etc. This ensures a smooth task-shifting process where mental health and psychosocial care can reach the grassroots levels through the community itself. WHO's mhGAP training, which is aimed at equipping non-specialist healthcare workers with the skills to manage mental health concerns and increase the capacity of healthcare systems for responding to mental health needs, is an example of task shifting for promoting mental well-being. Several training programs conducted by NIMHANS for different government

departments such as police, fire services, railways, healthcare workers, and non-government entities on basic psychosocial support skills have been found effective.

- Establishing support groups in communities is an influential method for many reasons. Support groups will have members who have similar backgrounds and had similar experiences. These groups provide a safe and supportive space, where individuals can share their feelings and experiences, and receive a sense of belonging. This will reduce the feeling of isolation and helplessness. Peer learning will be facilitated as they exchange their coping strategies and problem-solving methods among the ones who face similar challenges. Support groups are rather sustainable and are potential support for long-term positive mental health outcomes. They also empower the communities by fostering collective problem-solving, reducing stigma, and increasing resilience.
- Place-based psychosocial interventions are impactful community-based interventions in disaster-affected communities. The concept of 'place' acts as a cornerstone of community identity. There are strong emotional ties attached to the place in which communities foster. The environment, culture, social capital, collective memories, etc. are components of a 'place.' Disasters can disrupt these familiar places of communities which causes a sense of loss, instability, and insecurity in the community members. The loss of secure places even increases vulnerabilities and helplessness. This loss of place results in displacement and can cause 'root shock' (the trauma experienced by individuals and communities when they are forcefully displaced), which can, in turn, contribute to mental health problems like anxiety, depression, and PTSD among disaster survivors. While individuals and communities struggle to adjust to the new environments, place-based psychosocial interventions are effective in re-establishing a 'place attachment' and 'sense of place' with the new place. These interventions are participatory and provide a space for communities to identify their needs for rebuilding the social capital (Diaz, 2018).
- Among the place-based psychosocial activities suggested by Prewitt Diaz are:

- Enhancing the capacity of disaster-affected communities to create their own place development plans and implementation strategies.
- Gathering information by mapping areas to understand their environmental features, infrastructure, available support systems, and social and environmental resources.
- Supporting in improving communities' decision-making skills by involving all groups in the community.
- Improving communities' ability to resolve conflicts and negotiate effectively.
- Encouraging the participation of various external organizations or groups to improve the psychosocial, cultural, ecological, legal, and economic environments within the community.
- Creating and carrying out projects related to adaptive resilience.

Assessment Tools

In disaster-prone areas, it is important to have tools for assessment and disaster risk reduction (DRR) tools that will help identify vulnerability, risks, and strengthen preparedness. These include hazard mapping, vulnerability assessments, risk analysis structures, community resilience assessment, etc. These will serve as the key insights for the policy-makers, emergency responders, and the communities to take proactive steps in DRR. These tools help in informed decision-making, allocating resources effectively, enhancing resilience and making optimum development of effective disaster management strategies through systematic evaluation of potential threats and their impacts. Below are some tools which assess aspects such as vulnerabilities, risks, resilience, etc.

1. Psychosocial Hazard, Risk, Vulnerability (PS-HRV) Analysis (Sekar et al., 2023b)
2. Psychosocial Vulnerability in Disaster-Prone areas (Zacharias et al., 2024)
3. Resource Mapping (Sekar et al., 2023b)
4. Psychosocial Adaptation Instrument (Zacharias et al., 2022)
5. Disaster Preparedness Index (Rohith et al., 2018)
6. Community Advanced Resilience Toolkit (Pfefferbaum et al., 2015).

Theoretical Framework

Various theoretical perspectives highlight the emotional and mental health impacts of disasters and the importance of MHPSS in the recovery and healing process. These theoretical frameworks underscore the need for tailored interventions that address the holistic needs of individuals and communities in disasters.

Trauma-Informed Care

Individuals who have experienced traumatic life events such as disasters will have emotional trauma and physiological distress in the aftermath, which can lead to chronic disorders like PTSD (van der Kolk, 1994). Trauma-informed care which is unique to their individual needs can be beneficial for such individuals. Trauma theory is the foundation of trauma-informed care. Classic neuroscience research on trauma supports the early psychologists' hypothesis that traumatic memories are stored as physiological reactions to stimuli, situations, or states of arousal that recall the traumatic experience if they cannot be verbally or symbolically processed (Reeves, 2015).

To be "trauma-informed" means to be aware of how the majority of people who seek mental health, drug abuse, and other such services have experienced violence and victimization in the past and to apply this knowledge to the design of services and the provision of care to meet the needs and vulnerabilities of trauma survivors and encourage their involvement in their care. A trauma-informed approach to care views trauma as a formative experience that may have influenced an individual's current condition rather than simply a past event. Understanding individuals and their symptoms considering their past experiences and cultural background, and acknowledging that some symptoms can be a form of coping, is essential. Rather than "what is wrong with the person," this approach focuses on "what happened to the person." Also, measures are taken to minimize the chances of traumatization during the care or treatment to prevent further harm (Butler et al., 2011).

Butler et al. (2011) provided ten principles of trauma-informed services, which were adapted from Elliott et al. (2005). Trauma-informed services:

- Acknowledge how victimization and violence affect coping mechanisms and development
- Prioritize trauma recovery.
- Use an empowerment model.
- Aim to optimize the client's decisions and autonomy over her or his recovery.
- Are founded on a cooperative relationship.
- Establish a setting that respects the needs of the survivor for acceptance, safety, and respect.
- Acknowledge the client's strengths and accomplishments.
- Aim to reduce the likelihood of re-traumatization.
- Seek to be culturally aware and considerate of your client's cultural heritage and life experiences.
- Involve clients in designing and evaluating services.

Crisis Intervention

Crisis theory is based on the relationship and homeostatic balance between the coping processes and psychological functioning. An emotion crisis occurs when an individual experiences an emotionally hazardous situation and is unable to utilize previously learned coping mechanisms or new problem-solving strategies to reduce stress. When an individual fails to cope effectively, an emotional hazard can escalate into an emotional crisis (Baldwin, 1979). The concept of crisis intervention originated with Lindemann, who worked on unresolved and pathological grief following the Cocoanut Grove Field Fire in 1943 (Baldwin, 1979; Lindemann, 1944). The general goal of crisis intervention is to support the individual in crisis in returning to at least their pre-crisis level of functioning as quickly as possible. It also helps prevent the individual in crisis from learning or using maladaptive coping strategies, while encouraging learning adaptive ones, resolving the underlying conflicts, and integrating the positive changes from adaptive coping strategies to cognitive and affective levels (Baldwin, 1979).

Disasters are usually sudden, strong, external, uncontrolled, and mostly unexpected and, therefore, can be potentially emotionally hazardous situations that can cause emotional crises in affected ones. Crisis interventions during disasters are largely acknowledged for reducing psychological distress and preventing its escalation into long-term mental health problems. This type of intervention is referred to as 'psychological first aid' (PFA).

Psychological First Aid (PFA)

Psychological first aid (PFA) is an important component of MHPSS in disasters and emergencies. It is an early disaster response intervention that is aimed at reducing the immediate distress caused by traumatic events, promoting a sense of safety and security among the survivors, and connecting them to necessary services and resources. Although it is not a long-term intervention, it is a crucial immediate step toward improving mental health outcomes. PFA is usually administered at the first point of contact with the individual in distress and can be provided to both children and adults. The major aspects of PFA include assessing needs, offering comfort, providing access to services and information, ensuring social support, and thereby protecting individuals from further harm or the worsening of the distress experienced. The IASC describes PFA as a "humane and supportive response to a fellow human being who is suffering and who may need support" (Inter-Agency Standing Committee, 2007).

PFA encompasses the following:

- Listen patiently, without judgment.
- Show genuine compassion.
- Identify and meet basic practical needs.
- Ask about concerns and try to address them.
- Allow survivors to talk about their experience without pressure, and respect their choice if they do not want to share.

- Inform survivors of their right to refuse to speak with aid workers or journalists.
- Protect individuals from further harm, especially when they may make risky decisions due to distress.
- Discourage negative coping, like using alcohol or drugs, especially in times of severe distress.
- Encourage involvement in daily routines and positive coping methods, such as relaxation techniques or cultural and spiritual supports.
- Suggest being in the company of family or friends, but do not force it.
- Offer the option for follow-up support if needed.
- Refer to local support systems or trained clinicians when appropriate.

There are several recognized PFA training programs, including online courses offered by Johns Hopkins University, the World Health Organization's PFA guide for field-level workers (developed by WHO, War Trauma Foundation, and World Vision International), and the National Disaster Management Training Module developed by NDMA and NIMHANS. Also, trauma-informed PFA training, such as the one developed by the National Child Traumatic Stress Network, provides the responders with the basic necessary skills to offer immediate care and support in the aftermath of disasters (NDMA, 2023).

WHO model of PFA, with the action principles 'Look, Listen, Link,' offers an effective method for delivering PFA in crises and emergencies. The first step, 'Look,' is to look for individuals who need care and support. This includes observing verbal and non-verbal signals, emotional and behavioral cues, and other signs of distress among the affected individuals. The responders can quickly recognize and identify the individuals who require support and interventions by actively looking for such signs of distress. Once such individuals are identified, the responders must actively 'Listen' to their feelings, concerns, and experiences without prejudice, judgment, or interruption. The responder should demonstrate empathy, respect, validation, and acceptance toward the individuals and ensure a safe and supportive environment for individuals to express themselves and share their concerns. The final step is to 'Link' the individuals who need further help or support to appropriate resources, services, or social networks that can help them address their needs and provide necessary information. This may include referring them to professional care like mental health professionals, community organizations, related institutions, or other services (World Health Organization, 2011).

Resilience Theory

The ability of an entity, such as an asset, organization, community, or region, to foresee, resist, absorb, respond to, adapt to, and recover from an adverse impact is known as resilience. A community's or region's resilience is determined by the resilience of its subsystems, which include its economy, civil society, essential infrastructures, government (including emergency services), supply chains, and dependencies (Carlson et al., 2012). In a community context, resilience is the capacity of a community to absorb an adverse change while maintaining its basic functions (Longstaff et al., 2010). In the cases of disasters, Diaz and Agarwal (2018) emphasize that to improve the resilience of communities in disasters, a multi-level approach that includes individuals, families, places, and communities is important. This points out the need for comprehensive and holistic care for disaster-affected populations taking into account their diverse needs and problems. The integrated model of care (umbrella of care), PFA, and community-based psychosocial support activities are effective ways to reach out to the different psychosocial and mental health of individuals and communities to facilitate recovery and promote their disaster resilience.

Challenges and Barriers to MHPSS Delivery in India

- Stigma related to mental health—Stigma surrounding mental health prevents individuals from reporting mental health problems and seeking and accepting mental health services.
- Social and cultural barriers—In a diverse country like India, having populations with varied cultures and social backgrounds, it is often found difficult to implement a standard approach across the commu-

nities, due to the differing languages, beliefs, traditions, and attitudes toward mental health.

- Resource limitation—Limited human, financial, and material resources often hinder MHPSS delivery. The lack of trained professionals to cater to the wide mental health needs of a huge population, especially in the context of disasters is a significant barrier to effective mental health promotion and service delivery.
- Coordination among agencies—In disaster situations, governmental, non-governmental, and inter-governmental agencies offer and deliver MHPSS. But often there is a visible gap in coordination between these agencies, resulting in unplanned distribution of resources, duplication of services, gaps in care, and reduced quality of services.
- Well-being of MHPSS providers—The lack of adequate human resources and skilled professionals adds to the burden of available ones, especially in emergencies. MHPSS providers often experience stress, burnout, secondary trauma, and compassion fatigue, which affects their physical and mental health. Additionally, the lack of guidelines and protocols ensuring the safety, security, and well-being of MHPSS workers, in situations such as social conflicts and communal violence, is a limitation in providing quality services while safeguarding the well-being of workers.

Ethical Consideration in Disaster Mental Health Services

Ethics are moral judgments or standards of behavior that are employed in determining what is appropriate or inappropriate in a particular social setting. Working in disasters and emergencies will have unique ethical challenges, which need careful efforts to uphold dignity, respect, cultural sensitivity, and justice. Understanding the ethical standards that need to be adhered to before, during, and following disasters will assist caregivers in enhancing service quality (Sekar et al., 2023b). The principle of "do no harm" is basic to psychosocial services. Autonomy and consent, privacy, confidentiality, cultural sensitivity, competence, and non-discrimination are among the major ethical concerns while working in disasters. Among the ethical dilemmas for psychosocial caregivers in disasters are balancing individual and collective needs, prioritizing vulnerable populations, the equitable distribution of resources, and cultural conflicts.

In the NDMA and NIMHANS training modules on disaster preparedness, Sekar et al. (2023b) has outlined the following general ethical principles for working with disaster-affected populations.

- Collective responsibility—Ensure that all the stakeholders, including governments, organizations, and communities, work together to protect and support the affected population.
- Prevention—Take active steps to prevent disasters, reduce risks and the harm that disasters cause.
- Sovereignty—Join with the authority and leadership of national and local governments in disaster response and recovery efforts.
- Humanity—Prioritize compassion, dignity, and the well-being of affected individuals while providing aid and support.
- Neutrality—Prevent political, religious or ideological bias in humanitarian actions and operations solely on need.
- Non-discrimination—Helping without bias of race, gender, religion, nationality, or socioeconomic status.
- Cooperation—Facilitating collaboration and coordination among different stakeholders to ensure effective disaster risk reduction measures.

Considering the high chances of facing ethically challenging situations, there should be clear strategies employed for addressing these issues. There should be clear-cut ethical guidelines that align with the social and cultural background of the population while adhering to national and international standards. Psychosocial caregivers should be trained in ethics in service delivery, which includes confidentiality, informed consent, cultural sensitivity, etc. The beneficiaries of services (individuals, groups, families, and communities) should be involved in the planning, implementation, and evaluation to ensure the appropriateness and adequacy of the services. This will improve communication, trust, and acceptance of caregivers in the communities. Continuous monitoring and regular evaluation of interventions must be done to ensure that interventions are effective and are not causing further harm or distress.

Conclusion

In the current scenario of increasing natural disasters, the threat of climate change, and ongoing social conflicts, disaster mental health should be a primary concern worldwide. Psychosocial and mental health interventions in the right manner at the right time are imperative in mitigating or preventing the adverse mental health impacts of disasters. Standardized and structured interventions that do not compromise the culture and social background of the affected population should be promoted. A multisectoral approach that includes different stakeholders should be followed to provide integrated MHPSS services to disaster-affected individuals, families, and communities. Efforts to empower communities by making them physically, emotionally, mentally, economically, and socially resilient to disasters should be promoted.

References

Alexander, D. (2012). Disability and disaster. In *Handbook of hazards and disaster risk reduction* (pp. 413–423). Routledge.

Baldwin, B. A. (1979). Crisis intervention: An overview of theory and practice. *The Counseling Psychologist, 8*(2), 43–52.

Bhadra, S. (2021). Vulnerabilities of the Rural Poor in India during pandemic COVID-19: Social Work perspective for designing sustainable emergency response. *Asian Social Work and Policy Review, 15*(3), 221–233. https://doi.org/10.1111/aswp.12236

Bhadra, S., & Pulla, V. (2014). *Community interventions in disasters.* https://research.usc.edu.au

Butler, L. D., Critelli, F. M., & Rinfrette, E. S. (2011). Trauma-informed care and mental health. *Directions in Psychiatry, 31*(3), 197–212.

Carlson, J. L., Haffenden, R. A., Bassett, G. W., Buehring, W. A., Collins, M. J., III, Folga, S. M., Petit, F. D., Phillips, J. A., Verner, D. R., & Whitfield,

R. G. (2012). *Resilience: Theory and application*. Argonne National Lab. (ANL), Argonne, IL (United States).

Diaz, J. O. P. (2018). Place-based psychosocial interventions in the aftermath of Hurricane Maria in Puerto Rico. In J. O. P. Diaz (Ed.), *Disaster recovery* (1st ed., pp. 307–320). Apple Academic Press.

Diaz, J. O. P., & Agarwal, S. P. (2018). Theoretical building blocks for community-based psychosocial support. In *Disaster recovery* (pp. 3–34). Apple Academic Press.

Elliott, D. E., Bjelajac, P., Fallot, R. D., Markoff, L. S., & Reed, B. G. (2005). Trauma-informed or trauma-denied: Principles and implementation of trauma-informed services for women. *Journal of Community Psychology, 33*(4), 461–477. https://doi.org/10.1002/jcop.20063

Hansen, P. (2009). In W. Ager (Ed.), *Psychosocial interventions: A handbook*. International Federation Reference Centre for Psychosocial Support.

Inter-Agency Standing Committee. (2007). *IASC guidelines on mental health and psychosocial support in emergency settings*. https://interagencystanding-committee.org/sites/default/files/migrated/2020-11/IASC%20Guidelines%20on%20Mental%20Health%20and%20Psychosocial%20Support%20in%20Emergency%20Settings%20%28English%29.pdf

Lindemann, E. (1944). Symptomatology and management of acute of acute grief. *American Journal of Psychiatry, 101*(2), 141–148. https://doi.org/10.1176/ajp.101.2.141

Longstaff, P. H., Armstrong, N. J., Perrin, K., Parker, W. M., & Hidek, M. A. (2010). Building resilient communities: A preliminary framework for assessment. *Homeland Security Affairs, 6*(3), 1–23.

Manning, C., & Clayton, S. (2018). Threats to mental health and wellbeing associated with climate change. In *Psychology and climate change* (pp. 217–244). Elsevier. https://doi.org/10.1016/B978-0-12-813130-5.00009-6

National Disaster Management Authority. (2023). *Annual report 2022–2023*. https://ndma.gov.in/sites/default/files/PDF/Reports/NDMA-Annual-Report_20-21.pdf

NDMA. (2005). *Disaster Management Act*. National Disaster Management Authority, Government of India.

NDMA. (2023). *National disaster management guidelines: mental health and psychosocial support services in disasters*. National Disaster Management Authority, Government of India.

Pfefferbaum, R. L., Pfefferbaum, B., Nitiéma, P., Houston, J. B., & Van Horn, R. L. (2015). Assessing community resilience: An application of the expanded CART survey instrument with affiliated volunteer responders. *American Behavioral Scientist, 59*(2), 181–199. https://doi.org/10.1177/0002764214550295

Rao, K. (2006). Lessons learnt in mental health and psychosocial care in India after disasters. *International Review of Psychiatry, 18*(6), 547–552. https://doi.org/10.1080/09540260601037961

Reeves, E. (2015). A synthesis of the literature on trauma-informed care. *Issues in Mental Health Nursing, 36*(9), 698–709. https://doi.org/10.3109/01612840.2015.1025319

Rentschler, J. E. (2013). *Why resilience matters—The poverty impacts of disasters.*

Rohith, V. R., Kolathayar, S., Priyatham, K., Kumar, V. K., & Nikil, S. (2018). Disaster preparedness index: A valid and reliable tool to comprehend disaster preparedness in India. In *Urbanization challenges in emerging economies* (pp. 156–163). https://doi.org/10.1061/9780784482032.017

Sekar, K. (2005). Human rights and disaster: Psychosocial support and mental health services. In D. Nagaraja & P. Murthy (Eds.), *Mental health care and human rights* (p. 243). National Human Rights Commission.

Sekar, K., Jayakumar, C., & Jude, P. (2023a). *National disaster management training module-2, psychosocial care in disasters* (1st ed.). NDMA, NIMHANS.

Sekar, K., Jayakumar, C., & Jude, P. (2023b). *National disaster management training module-3, psychosocial preparedness* (1st ed.). NDMA, NIMHANS.

Solomon, S. D., Bravo, M., Rubio-Stipec, M., & Canino, G. (1993). Effect of family role on response to disaster. *Journal of Traumatic Stress, 6*(2), 255–269. https://doi.org/10.1002/jts.2490060208

Tol, W. A., Barbui, C., Galappatti, A., Silove, D., Betancourt, T. S., Souza, R., Golaz, A., & van Ommeren, M. (2011). Mental health and psychosocial support in humanitarian settings: Linking practice and research. *The Lancet, 378*(9802), 1581–1591. https://doi.org/10.1016/S0140-6736(11)61094-5

van der Kolk, B. A. (1994). The body keeps the score: Memory and the evolving psychobiology of posttraumatic stress. *Harvard Review of Psychiatry, 1*(5), 253–265. https://doi.org/10.3109/10673229409017088

World Health Organization. (2011). *Psychological first aid: Guide for field workers.* World Health Organization, War Trauma Foundation and World Vision International.

World Health Organization. (2022). *World mental health report: Transforming mental health for all.Geneva: World Health Organization.*

Zacharias, L., Christy, J., Roopesh, B. N., Binu, V. S., Das, S. K., & Sekar, K. (2022). Development of an instrument on psychosocial adaptation for people living in a disaster-prone area. *International Journal of Disaster Risk Reduction, 68*, 102716. https://doi.org/10.1016/j.ijdrr.2021.102716

Zacharias, L., Christy, J., Roopesh, B. N., Binu, V. S., & Kasi, S. (2024). Development of a scale for measuring psychosocial vulnerability in disaster-prone areas. *International Journal of Disaster Risk Reduction, 113*, 104761. https://doi.org/10.1016/j.ijdrr.2024.104761

6

Social Psychology of Riots: Clash of Collective Minds

Ajay Kumar Goyal

Introduction

Human groups have been involved in violent clashes for thousands of years, leading to incalculable losses and suffering. Riots involve an assault on persons and property simply because they are part of a given subgroup of the community. Race riots are usually sparked by a provocation involving members of two races. Life and property are treated with indifference and recklessness, *contrary to the basic values* held in society, and thus involving an acute *breakdown of social control*. The losses and suffering caused by events of riots across the globe are extensive, with consequences that ripple through societies for years. The immediate impacts include the loss of life, injury, destruction of property, displacement, and psychological trauma. However, the longer-term effects include economic

A. K. Goyal (✉)
Department of Psychosocial Support in Disaster Management, NIMHANS, Bengaluru, Karnataka, India

S. Bhadra et al. (eds.), *Psychosocial and Mental Health Support for Disaster Management in India*, Palgrave Studies in Disaster Science and Emergency Management,
https://doi.org/10.1007/978-3-032-02511-1_6

destabilization, social fragmentation, and challenges in rebuilding communities.

India has a long history of communal strife, with one of the first recorded riots occurring in Benares in August 1809 (Visuvalingam & Chalier-Visuvalingam, 2016). A number of the major communal clashes that have occurred in India have claimed very heavy death tolls and widespread human suffering (e.g. Time, 1946, October 28; Brass, 2011, January 18; Ramakrishnan, 2016, October 8; Mishra, 2012, March 14). According to the database of the Uppsala Conflict Data Program (UCDP), 32 events of organized violence have occurred over a period of 34 years (1989–2023), in India alone, each claiming at least 25 lives (Hegre et al., 2020)). Many dyads of social groups involved in these conflicts have had repetitive incidents of clashes, e.g., the National Socialist Council of Nagaland-IM versus the National Socialist Council of Nagaland-Khaplang, Kuki versus Naga, and Hindus versus Muslims. The most recent instance of communal clashes between Kuki and Meitei began in May 2023 and has not yet completely ceased. These events have claimed more than 5000 lives and left millions displaced from their native land. Globally, the count of similar events, involving no organized armed groups as a party, according to the same database is 1632 in the same period, claiming a total 0f 371,933 lives to date. Again, in most cases, the incidents of violence had occurred repetitively between the same dyads (parties).

If we account for the events of violence, in which at least one party involved was either an organized armed group (rebels, separatists etc.) or the state itself, then the available data on losses provide an extremely grim picture. The Rwanda Genocide, of 1994, went on for a hundred days, with 800,000 persons (largely from the Tutsi community) being killed (BBC News, 2014, April 4) and approximately two million Rwandans fleeing the country (Encyclopaedia Britannica (n.d.). *Rwanda genocide of 1994*). According to BBC News, the communal violence of 2017, in Myanmar, involving Myanmar's army (backed by local Buddhist mobs) and Rohingya Muslims led to at least 6700 deaths and 600,000 displaced to Bangladesh alone (BBC News, 2017b, September 25). A recent incident in India where there are multiple claims and allegations of the covert involvement of the state have been advanced in media involves the

Manipur clashes between Kukis and Meities, which started in May 2023. At the time of writing, this event has claimed at least 258 lives and caused 60,000 people to be displaced (Reuters, 2024, September 7).

Other than human losses, if we take into account the losses in terms of damage to property, losses of livelihood, the losses in political stability, displacement and refugee crises, and the psychological trauma that occurs as a result of exposure to violence, the sheer magnitude would suggest that the management of riots should be the top priority of any nation's actions and conscience. The systematic study of conflict has been a comparatively recent development in social and behavioral sciences. In this chapter the author aims to develop a set of theoretical propositions from the perspective of social psychology to add to existing knowledge about social conflicts in general, and riots in particular.

Psychosocial Processes in Social Conflicts

Understanding the psychology of social conflict requires an examination of the intricate interplay of individual motivations, group dynamics, societal factors, and situational triggers that contribute to the onset and escalation of social conflict. Existing theoretical ideas point to various possible social psychological processes describing and explaining individual behavior during riots. This section introduces some of the main psychological theories and concepts in this area. The concept of normative social influence (Asch, 1955) highlights the role of social norms in shaping behavior, as individuals conform to perceived group expectations. Social identity theory (Tajfel & Turner, 1979) posits that individuals derive a sense of self from their membership in social groups, and that conflicts between groups can lead to intergroup dynamics, such as in-group favoritism and out-group hostility. The concept of 'deindividuation' refers to the loss of self-awareness and personal accountability which occurs when individuals are part of a large crowd. Individuals may feel that their actions are justified as part of the collective movement. Relative deprivation theory (Gurr, 1970), by contrast, emphasizes the role of perceived injustice and inequality in fuelling collective unrest. Emergent norm theory (Turner & Killian, 1987) explores how norms emerge and evolve within rioting crowds, shaping behavior in unpredictable ways. Emotional contagion and arousal can spread rapidly within rioting crowds, leading to heightened aggression and violence (Le Bon, 1895). Social learning and observational modelling play a role in transmitting rioting behaviors within social networks (Bandura & Walters, 1977). Cognitive biases such as group polarization can reinforce extremist attitudes and escalate conflict (Moscovici & Zavalloni, 1969). *Groupthink* and group polarization can reinforce extremist attitudes and suppress dissent within rioting crowds (Janis, 1972). *Identity fusion* can lead individuals to engage in extreme pro-group behavior, including violence, in defense of their group identity (Swann Jr. et al., 2012). Perceived injustice and social norms play critical roles in fuelling collective unrest. Grievance narratives and perceptions of inequality can mobilize individuals to participate in riots (Stott & Drury, 2000). Media framing and social discourse can shape perceptions of the legitimacy of rioting behavior (Reicher & Stott, 2011). Perceived social norms regarding the acceptability of violence and protest can influence individuals' decisions to engage in rioting behavior (Cialdini & Goldstein, 2004).

Though the above conceptual ideas have been widely supported by objective evidence, all of these theories focus upon what is known as psychosocial processes involving either events within the individual minds—cognitions, feelings, and behaviors—or the interindividual processes e.g. contagion of emotions in groups. These theoretical ideas do not explicitly recognize or conceive the existence and influence of 'collective minds' of various subgroups (particularly racial and ethnic groups) that operate at the collective levels and are primary causes of the above psychosocial processes. It is quite apparent that riots represent events of conflict and violence among groups rather than individuals. Individual qualities, except those related to their membership in a group (e.g. race, ethnicity, religion etc), are of little significance with regard to how they behave toward others nor in how others behave toward them during riots. All that matters is the group to which they belong. The individuals who are enacting the rioting behaviors generally are not behaving according to their private interests, cognitions, and beliefs. It is the collective interests, ideologies, and feelings that are primarily leading their actions, ideations, and feelings during the incidence of communal violence.

The Collective Mind

Sigmund Freud, one of the earliest proponents of the idea of the collective mind, has stated, “If a Psychology, concerned with exploring the predispositions, the instincts, the motives and the aims of an individual man down to his actions and his relations with those who are nearest to him, had completely achieved its task, and had cleared up the whole of these matters with their inter-connections, it would then suddenly find itself confronted by a new task which would lie before it unachieved. It would be obliged to explain the surprising fact that under a certain condition this individual whom it had come to understand thought, felt, and acted in quite a different way from what would have been expected. *And this condition is his insertion into a collection of people* which has acquired the characteristic of a ‘psychological group’.”. In this statement, there is a clear implication that a collective mind (‘psychological group’) determines individual thoughts, feeling, and behaviors and which cannot be explained by their individual characteristics alone.

According to Le Bon (1895): ‘The most striking peculiarity presented by a psychological crowd is the following: Whoever be the individuals that compose it, however like or unlike be their mode of life, their occupations, their character, or their intelligence, the fact that they have been transformed into a crowd puts them in possession of a sort of collective mind which makes them feel, think, and act in a manner quite different from that in which each individual of them would feel, think, and act were he in a state of isolation.. There are certain ideas and feelings which do not come into being, or do not transform themselves into acts except in the case of individuals forming a group. The psychological group is a provisional being formed of heterogeneous elements, which for a moment are combined, exactly as the cells which constitute a living body form by their reunion a new being which displays characteristics very different from those possessed by each of the cells singly.’ (p. 29)

After observing the collective behaviors of various birds and animals involving synchronous and coherent movements, e.g. circling, wheeling, rending, darting of tens of thousands of starlings, naturalists have espoused theories of collective mind for more than a century. Edmund

Selous (1905) suggested that somehow a *connectivity of individual minds and transference of thoughts must underlie such behavior*. Such synchronous behaviors arising out of collective minds have the function of enhancing survival among animals e.g. the identification of the location of resources (nutrition) or predators (defense). *Close behavioral coupling* among near neighbors allows a localized change in direction to be amplified, creating a rapidly growing and propagating wave of turning across the group. This positive feedback results from the *ability of individuals to influence and be influenced by others*, and *allows them to experience an 'effective range' of perception much larger than their actual sensory range*. Establishing how this collective mind comes into existence is not the purpose of this chapter; the basic aim is to highlight the fact that the phenomenon of collective minds does exists and directs the behaviors of its individual constituent, thus leading to synchronized group actions.

Thus, the phenomenon of emergence of a collective mind, leading to a synchronous behavior as a whole group, in spite of its individual differences, has been observed among birds and animals, as well as human collectives.

Aggression Among Collectives

Many animal collectives live as colonies (or societies), can clearly discriminate members from non-members, and behave aggressively toward members coming from another colony or society. For example, huge communities of social insects (ants, termites, bees), comprising millions of individuals may form a single clan and recognize members by the characteristic smell of their hive or nest. If members of a different clan enter the wrong nest, this leads to conflict (Lorenz, 1966).

The human social group is an organism that is entirely different from any other, and unlike any of its parts. Accordingly, its nature cannot be inferred from their nature; rather, the nature of the individual is more likely to be influenced by it (Gumplowicz, 1899). Every political organization, and hence every developing civilization, begins at the moment when one group permanently subjects another. The subjection of some to others is the source of political organization, which, in turn, is the essential condition for social growth. Gumplowicz outlined three sets of relations between unlike groups: *those between the differentiating parts of a whole that was before time strictly homogeneous*; *those between the parts of a whole which is tending toward homogeneity by assimilation and amalgamation of its parts*; and *finally, those between independent wholes which exhibit antagonism and conflict whenever their spheres of influence overlap* (p. 10). A study of the relations of several classes to each other will show a logical sequence from the conflict of independent wholes through the subjection of one to the other, even up to the complete homogeneity of the new whole through assimilation or amalgamation. *Social distinctions* continue the antagonism between groups which began with ethnical differences. Some social groups, like the ruling, subject, and merchant classes, are original, primary, ethnical and hereditary. Others, like the priestly and professional classes, are secondary and evolutionary and arise by differentiation. Nevertheless, all social groups, whatever their origin, are alike active as *social elements* tend to strengthen their coherence with the help of *group-making factors*—material, economic, and moral. These groups struggle for their interests as collectives, and their conduct as a group shows utter disregard for individual members. The influence of the social environment on the individual is strong enough to change his mind, thus producing social types whose tenacity is directly related to the solidarity of the group (p. 16).

When two distinct groups come together, the natural tendency of each is to exploit the other—a primary impulse in the social process. This tendency is so inherent in every human group—so natural and indomitable—that it is impossible to conceive of groups coming together without displaying it, without generating the social process (Gumplowicz, 1899, p. 85). However, nature has also laid the foundation for ethnically composite states in human necessities and sentiments. Given the necessity of human labor, sympathy with kindred and tribe, combined with a deadly hatred of strangers, led to foreign wars. Thus, conquest and the satisfaction of needs through the labor of the conquered—essentially the same phenomenon, though differing in form—represent a central theme in human history, from prehistoric times up to the most recent plans for a Congo state. One party commands; the other labors and accommodates itself to superior force. As every war must eventually cease, and the weaker party must abandon fruitless opposition, nature facilitates the emergence of a peaceful and lasting situation. Peace and permanence are the foundations of order, from which arise habit, custom, and rights. The hostile contact between social elements of unequal strength constitutes the primary condition for the creation of rights; conditions established by force and accepted in weakness, if peaceably continued, eventually become rightful. Inequality of power is essential, since contestants of equal strength would exhaust themselves in mutual conflict or, more likely, would unite to subjugate a weaker group (Gumplowicz, 1899, p. 121).

Evolution is both founded upon, and promoted by, organized sovereignty. Equality prevails only in the most primitive hordes. The subjection of some to the service of others stands in opposition to the sentiments of equality, solidarity, and consanguineous relationships. Developmental stagnation is prevented by the steady growth of the desires of both rulers and subjects, for the principle that wants increase with the opportunity to satisfy them is universal (Gumplowicz, 1899, p. 125). Peace is as necessary as occasional war, for both arise from the natural law of strife. Thus, the establishment of states became possible, since otherwise the more powerful would have had to exterminate the weaker. However, peace is meaningless without the opportunity to satisfy the desires that war was undertaken to secure. Ultimately, only one party can emerge as victor: one secures better satisfaction of its needs, while the other becomes constrained and oppressed. Force is necessary to maintain the unequal condition during peacetime; suitable institutions must therefore be established and diligently sustained. Thus, apparent peace is merely a continuous, latent struggle (p. 126).

Studies of riots across the globe have underlined the frequent complicity of police, courts, and other government institutions with the dominant group, as supported by credible information. Attempts to search for and identify the culprits of riots, assign blame, seek a trial in a court of law, and analyse the immediate antecedents triggering communal violence are common social and institutional processes following a riot. However, for the scholarly community, attempting to explain a social event like a riot solely in terms of the behaviors of individual political actors, institutions, and law enforcement agencies may not be the most theoretically sound approach. Political blame games, the unjust treatment of one social group by community institutions, and the over-attribution of responsibility to existing governments are all common phenomena across nations. This is not to discount the observed facts supporting these accusations, but rather to develop a theoretical rationale based on the observed consistency of these patterns across nations, governments, and riot events. This chapter undertakes an in-depth exploration of core social-psychological factors embedded in the psychosocial fabric of a community (the 'collective minds'), which are proposed as primary determinants of riots. The idea proposed in this chapter is neither to discount the importance of facilitating justice and establishing social order nor to suggest that certain acts or behaviors by individuals or groups that instigate violence bear no responsibility for triggering it. Rather, the aim is to focus solely on the theoretically relevant categories of phenomena that help us understand how a clash of collective minds contributes objectively to the causation of riots.

The primary purpose of this chapter is to emphasize objective social-psychological processes by mapping them onto the idea of a clash of collective minds and demonstrating the causal links between these psychosocial processes and the triggering, maintenance, and recurrence of violent conflicts. This, in turn, can help shift the focus away from more subjective and debatable causal attributions to the actions of individual or institutional actors, and instead explore deeper causal processes embedded within the collective psychologies of society that render it more or less vulnerable to social conflict. These attributions are sometimes politically motivated blame games, while at other times the allegations may appear genuine; in either case, however, they involve an overestimation of presumed rationality on the part of the actors involved. This presumption of rationality among actors during riots contrasts with the well-known theory of crowd behavior espoused by the French polymath Gustave Le Bon (1895). Le Bon clearly highlighted the substitution of unconscious crowd action for the conscious (rational) activity of individuals as a fundamental cause of various types of socially violent events, such as riots, revolutions, and wars.

Many of our aggressive behaviors at the individual level have been explained by the concept of an aggressive instinct; as, for example, with Sigmund Freud's idea of *Thanatos*. Konrad Lorenz (1966) outlined a systematic exposition of aggressive behavior as instinctively elicited by various environmental stimuli. According to him, a significant proportion of aggressive behavior has evolutionary roots. Such behaviors are triggered by simple stimuli, such as, among others, a stranger's intrusion into one's perceived territory, close proximity between two strangers, competition for the same resources, or being cornered. These and similar stimuli reliably elicit aggressive behaviors across species and are largely hard-wired into individual minds.

According to Sigmund Freud, civilization is a process in the service of *Eros*, whose purpose is to unite individuals, then families, and eventually tribes, peoples, and nations into one great unit—humanity. However, the tendency toward aggression is an original, autonomous disposition—a descendant and principal representative of the death drive in humans—and it constitutes the greatest obstacle to civilization. Civilizations employ various means to inhibit this impulse, render it harmless, or possibly eliminate it altogether. These efforts result in the introjection and internalization of aggression, which is subsequently directed against the individual's own ego (Freud, 1930, pp. 52–54).

From the above discussion, we can conclude that aggression represents a basic drive present in both animals and humans. There are certain fundamental stimuli that invariably elicit aggressive reactions—such as the infringement of one's subjective territory, being cornered, or coming into close proximity with a stranger. If such aggressive impulses are left unchecked, societies are unlikely to develop, and human existence may not differ significantly from that of animals. However, civilizations do grow and evolve, primarily by reshaping basic drives to ensure that the survival functions of aggression are preserved, while simultaneously rendering natural aggressive reactions harmless to society. This transformation enables the coexistence of diverse groups within shared social spaces.

The products of civilization used to regulate aggression include various normative ideas and social institutions—such as moral codes, systems of law and order, and educational structures. Moreover, as different races and social groups begin to live together under socially constructed regulatory frameworks, the basic drive of aggression acquires new meanings. Territory is no longer limited to physical space; in more advanced civilizations, it increasingly takes on psychosocial dimensions—such as occupational domains, organizational membership, or politically sanctioned rights and privileges. It may also encompass culturally significant objects that symbolize a group's history, beliefs, sentiments, and shared narratives. These objects might be represented by an animal, a book, a building or architectural site, or a statue of a revered leader or historical figure.

Therefore, the "collective mind" of a social group and its concept of territory may include not only political and economic rights and privileges but also culturally and spiritually significant symbols, customs, languages, practices, and ideas.

Social Psychology of Riots: Clash of Collective Mind

To understand the complex social phenomenon of riots within any society or community, we propose a set of conceptual propositions that may warrant empirical investigation. Drawing on five historical cases of communal riots in India, we formulate these propositions to conceptualize the idea of a "clash of collective minds" as a key social-psychological determinant of such violent events. The five cases include:

1. The **1984 anti-Sikh riots**, between Hindus and Sikhs, which occurred across multiple states of India.
2. The **1989 Bhagalpur violence**, between Hindus and Muslims in Bhagalpur district, Bihar, beginning on October 24 and continuing for two months.
3. The **2002 Gujarat riots**, between Hindus and Muslims.
4. The **2008 Kandhamal violence**, between Hindus and Christians, in Kandhamal district, Odisha.
5. The ongoing **Manipur violence (2023–2025)**, between the Kuki and Meitei communities in Manipur, India.

Each proposition is framed as a tentative theoretical claim, supported by evidence from these events, and serves to outline the psychological underpinnings of intergroup violence.

The nature of the collective mind The *collective mind* refers to a shared cognitive representation of a group's common history—expressed through stories, myths, architecture, literature, and cultural objects such as symbols, traditions, rituals, and belief systems. When a group coexists in a shared environment of language, cultural experience, social interactions, common habits, and religious faiths, a collective mind inevitably emerges. This mind functions to bind individuals into a unified social entity. The strength of this unification is contingent on the number and salience of "group-making" factors. A key marker of a strong collective mind is that individuals are primarily perceived through the lens of their group identity—by both in-group and out-group members—rather than in terms of their personal, individual characteristics. This perception becomes especially powerful when the collective identity is made psychologically salient. For example, during the 1984 anti-Sikh riots, violence against individual Sikhs was triggered solely by information or visible signs of their group membership. No evidence of direct or indirect involvement in the assassination of Prime Minister Indira Gandhi—an event that served as the catalyst for the violence—was necessary to provoke attack. The mobs were not seeking revenge for personal grievances; rather, they were expressing collective anger over an attack on a national symbol, the prime minister of India. Similarly, prior events such as *Operation Blue Star* were perceived by the Sikh community as a direct assault on their religious identity, reinforcing the salience of the collective mind and its symbolic territories.

The Manipur riots, which began in May 2023, exemplify how communal identities, historical grievances, and psychological dynamics can fuel violent intergroup conflict. At the core of the Manipur conflict lies the clash of ethnic identities among its three major communities: the Meitei, Kuki, and Naga populations. The conflict often manifests as a struggle to protect "us" against "them," giving rise to a pervasive in-group versus out-group mentality. When these identities are perceived as threatened, group members become more prone to violence in defense of their collective interests. The perception that one's community is perpetually under threat or marginalized fosters collective defensiveness, which can escalate into violent outbursts. The collective mind of each community in Manipur is shaped by its unique history, culture, and relationship with state institutions. The Meiteis, concentrated primarily in the Imphal Valley, have historically held political and cultural dominance. In contrast, the Kuki and Naga communities, largely located in the hill regions, often perceive themselves as marginalized by both the state and the dominant Meitei population. This dissonance in worldview contributes to deep-seated mistrust and alienation, which, when amplified, can erupt into violent conflict.

Narratives of Victimhood and Empowerment

Each community holds distinct narratives of victimhood or empowerment, often resulting in the demonization of the "other." The Meiteis may regard themselves as guardians of the state's territorial integrity, while the Kuki and Naga communities may see themselves as defenders of ancestral lands and cultural autonomy. These competing narratives reinforce the belief that the survival and future of each group depend on the defeat or subjugation of the other, escalating tensions in a self-reinforcing cycle of conflict. A comparable dynamic was observed during the 2002 Gujarat riots, when the burning of a train carrying Hindu pilgrims was widely perceived as an attack on Hindu identity. In response, large-scale violence—primarily targeting Muslims—was unleashed. As the violence escalated, both communities mobilized around their collective identities, transforming the conflict into a brutal struggle over religious and cultural preservation. This clash was not solely physical but also ideological, driven by historical tensions and religious divides that shaped a binary opposition between "us" and "them." This type of identity-driven conflict is a recurrent feature in communal riots, where a shared sense of marginalization and collective grievance often culminates in violent collective action.

Why Are Social Groups Divided on Racial, Ethnic, or Other Grounds?

If two or more groups have different historical trajectories, they are likely to have developed distinct collective minds. These collective minds manifest in differences in perceived individual identities, sentiments, beliefs, and general ways of living. Once a group forms a collective mind, it begins to shape the thoughts, emotions, and behaviors of its individual members, rendering the group relatively uniform in its worldview and actions. These shared patterns of thought and behavior become the basis for distinguishing members from non-members.

Over time, the collective begins to behave like a unitary entity, reacting to external stimuli—particularly perceived threats—with coordinated responses. The presence of a non-member in close proximity may automatically trigger an aggressive reaction. For instance, the Naga conflict in Northeast India represents one of the longest-running separatist movements in the country (Karmakar, S, 2024, August 14). Despite repeated attempts by the Indian government since the 1950s to resolve the issue, Naga representative organizations, such as the National Socialist Council of Nagaland (NSCN), have persistently sought a separate territory, flag, and constitution—grounded in claims of a distinct history and tradition. After the formation of the Naga National Council (NNC) in 1946, the initial demand was for autonomy within India, but this later escalated into a call for full independence (Chaube, 1999, p. 105). The NSCN was founded with the explicit goal of creating a sovereign Naga nation, or "Nagalim," by integrating all Naga-inhabited areas across Northeast India and parts of Myanmar (Dholabhai, 2011, February 18).

Similar patterns are evident in other collectivities. The Sikh community, with its distinct religion, cultural practices, and spiritual leadership, has advocated for a separate state—Khalistan (Land of the Khalsa)—for over a century (Axel, 2001). Although periods of peace have alternated with conflict, the demand for Khalistan has persisted. Likewise, movements such as the Jammu and Kashmir Liberation Front (JKLF) have advanced comparable demands for autonomy or independence based on the assertion of a separate collective identity. The call for a separate

"Kukiland," dating back to the late 1980s, has also resurfaced periodically (Roy, 2023, August 27).

In any large and complex national society, various subgroups inevitably develop a collective mind (or consciousness) along fault lines such as race, ethnicity, language, and religion. National governments often struggle to maintain integration among these subgroups. The fact that these collectives have evolved significantly into distinct collective minds—characterized by unified ways of thinking, feeling, and behaving—is evident from the strong support their representatives receive from within their communities. These representatives are frequently involved in confrontations with national governments and military forces.

Organizing social events and activities around common issues and involving members from different collectives may help reduce the salience of divisions along racial and ethnic lines. During peacebuilding efforts in the aftermath of the 2002 Gujarat riots, aimed at promoting intergroup harmony, teams from National Institute of Mental Health & Neuro Sciences (NIMHANS) and various community organizations encouraged Hindu workers to visit and work in camps located in minority areas. Participation from both communities was made mandatory in every program. For instance, in livelihood promotion initiatives, beneficiaries were selected from both communities, and micro-financing, self-help, and savings-credit groups were established with active participation from both Hindu and Muslim members (Bhadra, 2011). These efforts contributed to reducing perceived divisions between Hindus and Muslims.

Why Do Different Social Groups So Often Engage in Violent Interactions?

If aggression is the natural first reaction when distinct social groups come into proximity, then why do we also witness numerous examples of racial, ethnic, and social groups coexisting harmoniously within the same regions or states? The tendency to aggress and exploit is indeed a natural reaction when two or more distinct social groups come into close contact. If these groups differ significantly in terms of their historical trajectories, racial characteristics, religious or ethnic practices, and general lifestyles—and if they come to inhabit a shared space—then violence is a highly probable outcome, unless other social forces intervene to regulate intergroup aggression.

For instance, immediately after the 2002 Gujarat riots, the continued physical proximity of Hindus and Muslims exacerbated mutual apprehension (Bhadra & Dyer, 2011). However, violence cannot persist indefinitely. Eventually, one of three outcomes typically occurs: one group may exterminate the other; the groups may segregate; or, most commonly, they may learn to coexist by regulating their aggressive impulses. Following the Gujarat riots, efforts were made to foster such coexistence. The NIMHANS team facilitated this process by creating a shared platform and organizing psychosocial interventions aimed at dismantling mental, social, and political barriers between the communities. Activities included child and youth engagement programs, women-focused gatherings, cultural events, and life skills education initiatives to promote social harmony. These events were intentionally held in non-threatening, inclusive, and safe environments, targeting areas where both Hindu and Muslim communities lived in close proximity (Bhadra & Dyer, 2011).

This intergroup learning primarily involves the establishment of both physical and psychosocial boundaries, alongside the development of hierarchical structures that enable the dominant group to benefit at the expense of the subjugated collective. Physical boundaries are reflected in the spatial segregation of communities within a region. For example, in Manipur (India), the Kuki communities have historically inhabited the hilly regions, whereas the Meitei population predominantly resides in the valleys.

Psychological boundaries refer to the mental and emotional distancing individuals maintain from others, often constructed through perceptions of threat, historical antagonism, and identity-based differentiation. A salient example is the portrayal of Muslims as a threat to Hindu identity—an idea deeply embedded in dominant narratives and media representations (Jaffrelot, 2003). Muslims are often depicted as a monolithic and threatening presence, which perpetuates psychological distance and reinforces intergroup boundaries (Zein, 2005). Psychosocial boundaries manifest in the form of segregated social institutions, cultural practices, languages, occupational niches, and unequal access to rights and privileges—such as exclusive land ownership rights, job reservations, or targeted welfare schemes. For instance, the Kuki and Meitei communities have maintained distinct ethnic identities that are often linked to territorial claims and historical grievances. The conversion of the Kuki population to Christianity has created an additional religious divide, further accentuating social separation from the predominantly Hindu Meitei community. This divide manifests in restricted intergroup participation in religious and cultural events, thereby reinforcing psychological distance (Sengupta, 2005).

Education, a critical integrative institution, is also implicated in this segregation. Schools and colleges often cater exclusively to either Kuki or Meitei students, limiting opportunities for cross-community interaction and fostering parallel systems of socialization (Singh, 2012). Similar patterns are evident in economic domains: certain markets are dominated by Meitei vendors, while others are run by Kuki traders. Such physical separation extends into public spaces, where members of each group may consciously avoid areas where they form a minority (Panda, 2010).

A comparable example is the Dravidian movement in Tamil Nadu, led by figures such as E.V. Ramasamy (Periyar), which emphasized Tamil identity in opposition to perceived North Indian (particularly Hindi-speaking) hegemony. Political parties such as the Dravida Munnetra Kazhagam (DMK) and the All-India Anna Dravida Munnetra Kazhagam (AIADMK) have reinforced this cultural and psychological separation by promoting Tamil linguistic and regional pride (Teltumbde, 2007).

Segregation of social interaction implies that intergroup encounters are often limited, formal, and task-specific, in contrast to intragroup interactions, which tend to be more frequent, intimate, and emotionally meaningful. Practices such as strict endogamy and exclusion from religious and cultural institutions further institutionalize these boundaries. In order to regulate aggression, societies construct moral codes, which are then codified into legal frameworks. While these systems serve to curtail violence to an extent, the more effective containment of aggression is achieved through territorial (both physical and psychosocial) segregation and differentiated resource distribution.

What Explains the Recurrent Alternation Between Peace and Riots?

The segregation of physical and psychosocial boundaries, along with the establishment of moral and legal regulations, does not eliminate the aggressive instinct inherent in human collectives; rather, it functions to manage the triggering of these instincts and to contain expressions of aggression within certain limits of intensity and extent. As long as these regulatory mechanisms remain effective, multiple collectives can coexist peacefully within their allocated rights and privileges. However, society is a dynamic organism—its psychological, economic, political, and environmental conditions are in constant flux.

The apparent peace in such societies is a negotiated settlement, based on established boundaries, regulations, and the division of rights and privileges. This negotiated arrangement must be actively maintained against ongoing demands from all collectives for readjustments. Moreover, such settlements are seldom equitable; one group typically receives more favorable terms than others. As a result, the disadvantaged collective is often engaged in continuous efforts to renegotiate for improved rights and recognition. Simultaneously, dominant groups may seek to further consolidate or enhance their privileges.

When these bargaining processes encounter resistance or deadlock, they may evoke frustration and heightened aggression—often exceeding the containment capacity of formal regulations and segregated boundaries. Social peace becomes precarious, vulnerable to shifts in power dynamics and unmet collective aspirations. Empirical evidence supports this pattern. When civil society institutions promote shared civic life at the local level, intergroup violence becomes less likely (Varshney, 2002). For instance, economic interdependence between Hindus and Muslims in urban centers of Gujarat, where they frequently functioned as business partners, helped maintain peace prior to the 2002 riots (Bajpai, 2003). However, this stability proved fragile. Following the Godhra incident—when the Sabarmati Express train, returning from Ayodhya to Ahmedabad, was set on fire, resulting in the deaths of 59 Hindu pilgrims—violence erupted across Gujarat. Revenge attacks specifically targeted Muslims.

Media outlets described these acts as expressions of injury to the Hindu collective conscience.

For many Muslims, the 2002 violence was perceived as part of a broader pattern of marginalization and systemic subjugation (Pandey, 2001). The Godhra attack was interpreted by many Hindus as a symbolic assault on their communal identity, sparking collective outrage and a retaliatory urge (Engineer, 2005).

If such aggressive actions by one group are not swiftly curtailed, they often provoke counterattacks from the opposing collective. This retaliation is typically accompanied by a series of cascading social-psychological processes: the increased salience of group identities, deindividuation, emotional contagion, and moral disengagement—ultimately transforming the conflict into a chain of escalating attacks and counterattacks.

What Can Be the Role of Community Organizations and Leaders in Such Contexts?

Politicians and community leaders can play varied roles during episodes of intergroup conflict. Those in government bear the critical responsibility for impartially exercising the authority of regulatory agencies, enforcing law and order during immediate crises, and facilitating processes of renegotiation between conflicting community representatives both before and after violent events.

Prior to the 2002 Gujarat riots, several local initiatives were led by religious and community leaders from both Hindu and Muslim communities to reduce communal tensions. These included interfaith dialogues, grassroots peacebuilding activities, and cultural initiatives aimed at fostering tolerance (Jaffrelot, 2003). Festivals such as Uttarayan (the kite-flying festival), Diwali, and Eid often served as occasions for shared celebration, where members of both communities exchanged gifts, participated in each other's cultural practices, and cohabited social spaces. These acts of cultural exchange promoted a superficial sense of social integration and contributed to the suppression of overt animosity (Siddiqui, 2000).

Civil society organizations also played a pivotal role. Initiatives such as the Gujarat Unity Forum and Sabrang Trust undertook peacebuilding efforts and organized interfaith forums to reduce communal tensions. Activities included peace marches, intercommunal meetings, and support networks for survivors of violence (The Guardian, 2001). One of the major forums established in the aftermath of the riots was *Aman Samudaya* ("Community for Peace"), which focused on relief, rehabilitation, and justice. Its interventions ranged from providing basic supplies and legal aid to campaigning against human rights violations and offering psychosocial support to traumatized individuals, especially women and children.

Another significant initiative was the Gujarat Harmony Project (GHP), launched by CARE India. GHP was designed to promote pluralism, tolerance, and peaceful coexistence in the wake of widespread fear, misinformation, and intercommunal mistrust. The project ensured that all its community-based programs explicitly served the goal of communal harmony by facilitating shared dialogue, collaborative problem solving, and mutual support (Bhadra & Dyer, 2011, p. 97).

In communal conflicts, actors both within and outside the government may play pivotal roles in shaping public perception. Some individuals—whether holding formal authority or not—may deliberately distort information or offer biased interpretations of events, thereby intensifying the perception of collective injury. The media, too, can significantly influence public discourse. A newspaper, for example, may either misrepresent facts or present them in a manner that frames the incident as an assault on the collective identity of a group, thus provoking strong emotional and aggressive reactions.

In such contexts, the rising tide of group-based aggression can overwhelm the state's regulatory agencies, even when efforts to contain the violence are initially planned. A further complication arises when the formal instruments of power are predominantly controlled by members of the dominant community. This asymmetry may result in an unequal perception of loss and suffering between groups, thereby introducing bias in the evaluation of actions taken by each side.

If violence is not contained at the onset and crosses a critical threshold, regulatory authorities themselves may begin to act as partisan agents. At this stage, the intensity of group conflict can override professional norms and ethical guidelines. The psychological processes of **deindividuation** and the **heightened salience of group identity** may affect not only ordinary citizens but also individuals within state institutions. Their cognitive processing may become dominated by in-group biases, making it difficult for state agencies to enforce laws impartially.

Community leaders, in this context, can play a dual role. They may either strengthen regulatory mechanisms and containment strategies or, conversely, escalate tensions by promoting provocative narratives. In the latter case, such narratives can bypass existing regulations and incite further intergroup aggression.

Toward a Theoretical Model for Predicting and Mitigating Intergroup Violence

Yes, the development of a theoretical and testable model for explaining, predicting, preventing, and mitigating communal violence is the overarching objective of this chapter. When two or more distinct groups cohabit the same space—whether physically or psychologically—the emergence of violent conflict is not an aberration, but a likely and natural outcome, rooted in competing collective identities and historical antagonisms. The core question is not *whether* collective minds will engage in aggression, but *under what conditions* such aggression can be anticipated, regulated, or transformed.

This leads us to focus on the conditions of cohabitation that either contain or exacerbate aggressive interactions. These conditions may include the establishment of boundaries (physical, psychological, and social), the formation of regulatory arrangements (both informal and institutionalized by the state), or the systemic subjugation or assimilation of one group by another. In some cases, homogenization efforts are employed to reduce the salience of differences between groups.

Yet, violence is inherently unsustainable. Prolonged conflict often leads to exhaustion, destruction, and eventual negotiation. More often than not, the group that is relatively weaker ends up accepting a less favorable settlement, paying a higher premium for peace. The outcome of such negotiated settlements frequently includes the delineation of boundaries and a regulatory framework that defines differentiated rights and privileges—thus minimizing direct conflict under normal conditions.

This post-conflict equilibrium can be analogized to celestial bodies revolving in distinct orbits: they remain in proximity without collision due to the delineation of space and roles. Similarly, social groups maintain distinct identities defined by unique symbols, practices, deities, songs, leaders, narratives, flags, and rituals—all contributing to the construction of collective consciousness. These shared elements form the foundation of in-group sentiments and identities, which do not translate across group lines.

The risk of renewed conflict emerges when members of one group, intentionally or unintentionally, violate or denigrate the symbolic elements of another group. Such boundary violations are perceived as assaults on group dignity and may trigger emotional, retaliatory responses. If not immediately addressed—through apology, restitution, or mediation—the conflict may escalate. Where conciliatory leadership is absent, the responsibility shifts to state regulatory agencies such as the police or military to intervene decisively and restore order.

Given this framework, a testable theoretical model (Fig. 6.1) can be developed—potentially operationalized as a regression model—that identifies and quantifies key variables influencing the probability and intensity of communal violence.

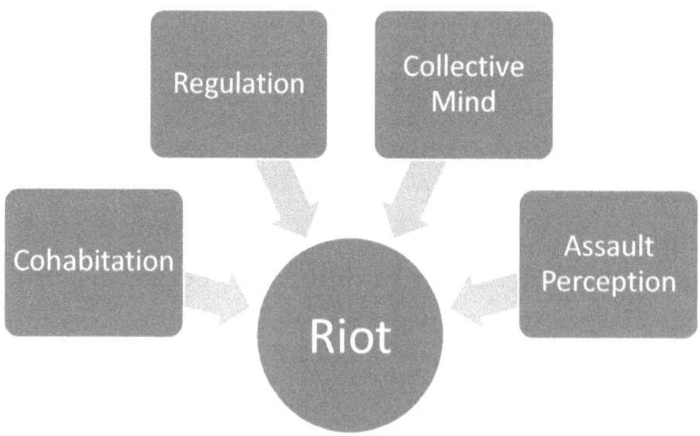

Fig. 6.1 Theoretical model of social conflict

$$\textbf{Social Conflict}\left(\textbf{R}\right) = \textbf{Cohabitation} \times \textbf{Regulation} \times \textbf{Collective Mind} \times \textbf{Assault Perception}$$

This model posits that the emergence and dynamics of intergroup social conflict (R)—such as communal riots—are determined by the interaction of four primary social-psychological and structural variables: Cohabitation, Regulation, Collective Mind, and Assault Perception. These variables interact multiplicatively, suggesting that the risk of conflict is significantly heightened when all four factors co-occur at elevated levels.

1. **Riot**—The dependent variable, *Riot*, refers to the onset, intensity, duration, and geographic spread of communal violence. Each of these aspects may be analyzed independently or in aggregate, depending on the specific aims of the research. The model seeks to identify the conditions under which the likelihood or severity of riots increases.
2. **Independent Variables (Predictors):**
   - **Cohabitation**—This refers to the extent to which two or more distinct social groups share a common space—whether physical, psychological, or social.
     - **Physical cohabitation** entails geographical proximity (e.g., living in the same neighborhood, town, or region).
     - **Psychological and social cohabitation** refers to mutual awareness, familiarity with each other's beliefs and behaviors, and regular interaction in professional, civic, or social contexts. Indicators may include intergroup friendships, participation in shared festivals or rituals, and cross-group institutional membership.
   - **Regulation**—This variable captures the presence and effectiveness of mechanisms designed to restrain collective aggression, including both **moral codes** and **legal institutions**.
     - **Moral regulation** includes socialization into values of tolerance, pluralism, and mutual respect, which are transmitted through education, religion, and civil society.

  - **Legal regulation** involves impartial enforcement of laws by professionalized institutions (e.g., police, judiciary), and mechanisms for peacefully resolving intergroup disputes.
- **Collective Mind**—This refers to the degree to which a group has developed a shared identity based on common history, symbols, customs, and social practices.
  - A strong collective mind is evidenced by high investment in cultural and religious events, emotional salience of group symbols, and alignment of personal decisions (e.g., marriage, residence, occupation) with group identity.
  - Indicators may include frequency of communal celebrations, levels of volunteerism in group activities, and exclusivity in social affiliations.
- **Assault Perception**—This variable reflects the extent to which members of one group perceive that the actions of another group threaten their **symbolic** or **material** interests.
  - **Symbolic assaults** include perceived violations of sacred symbols, revered figures, religious texts, or traditions.
  - **Material assaults** involve perceived encroachments on collective resources such as territory, legal rights, or institutional access.
  - Even unintended or ambiguous acts can be interpreted as assaults if group identities are highly salient, making perception itself a central construct.

Implications for Action

Communal violence represents an extraordinarily complex phenomenon. The onset, duration, geographic spread, and overall socioeconomic impact of riots vary significantly across events. This complexity—further compounded by political blame games, deep-rooted social polarization, and enduring psychological and material consequences—necessitates a more systematic, institutionalized approach to the study and regulation of communal conflict.

Given the recurring politicization of such incidents, even democratic institutions—such as the rule of law, law enforcement bodies, and justice delivery mechanisms—are frequently undermined. This reinforces the urgent need to institutionalize rigorous, objective research and analysis of communal violence, focused on prediction, prevention, mitigation, and long-term recovery. The proposed model has important implications for policy-making and institutional administration. These implications can be better understood through the lens of India's current policy framework for managing communal harmony.

At present, the Government of India has issued advisory "Guidelines for Promoting Communal Harmony" (Ministry of Home Affairs, 2022, Report No. 1234), which lack the legal enforceability of statutory provisions. In contrast to the Disaster Management Act (2005), these guidelines impose no penalties for non-compliance, and their implementation largely depends on voluntary cooperation from local authorities and community stakeholders.

However, the cumulative damage caused by communal riots—both tangible and intangible—can rival, and often exceed, the impact of natural disasters. In addition to economic losses and displacement, communal violence results in prolonged psychological trauma, social disintegration, reputational damage in the international arena, and broader political destabilization. These factors collectively justify the formulation of a comprehensive National Law for the Regulation of Communal Violence, supported by parallel institutional structures at both the central and state levels—comparable to those introduced under the Disaster Management Act (2005).

The proposed law could draw upon the theoretical model articulated earlier in this chapter. For instance, a centralized research and monitoring body could be tasked with:

- mapping regions where communal cohabitation is pronounced,
- assessing the strength of group identities and "collective minds,"
- evaluating intergroup boundaries (physical, social, psychological), and
- issuing early warnings based on predictive indicators.

The law could also mandate the creation of standard operating procedures (SOPs) for institutional neutrality and intervention at different stages of a conflict. Provisions may include compulsory consultation with community leaders during periods of high tension, the use of counternarratives to disrupt disinformation, and psychologically-informed protocols for reducing group-based fear and hostility.

By grounding state responses in the empirical social psychology of intergroup conflict, such a law could offer a more proactive and preventive framework for mitigating communal violence and supporting societal recovery. This approach represents a necessary shift—from reactive containment to strategic regulation—of these avoidable, human-made disasters.

Conclusion

Social conflict has been a near-universal phenomenon throughout human history. These conflicts may involve unorganized groups, organized armed factions, or highly institutionalized state actors—appearing as one or both parties to the conflict. Depending on the configuration of actors involved, such events may be characterized as riots, genocides, or wars. Regardless of their specific form, the consequences of these conflicts—in terms of fatalities, injuries, property destruction, displacement, psychological trauma, and broader social and economic instability—are often so severe that they can reverse decades of developmental progress within a matter of weeks.

Systematic understandings of social conflict have been accumulating in the social and behavioral sciences for over a century. In this chapter, the author has attempted to develop a coherent framework for understanding riot events by integrating existing theoretical perspectives from various disciplines with empirical insights drawn from publicly available accounts of actual riots in India. Through the theoretical lens of the *clash of collective minds*, a conceptual model of riots has been proposed. It is hoped that this model will serve as a meaningful step toward the development of a more systematic approach to understanding, predicting, and preventing communal violence in the future.

Acknowledgment I would like to express my sincere gratitude to Dr. Subhasis Bhadra from DPSSDM, NIMHANS, for his valuable contributions to this work. His insightful feedback, especially regarding the inclusion of policy actions, significantly enriched the content. I am also thankful for the relevant writings he generously shared, and for his timely support in reviewing and proofreading the document.

References

Asch, S. E. (1955). Opinions and social pressure. *Scientific American, 193*(5), 31–35.

Axel, B. K. (2001). *The nation's tortured body: Violence, representation, and the formation of a Sikh "diaspora"*. Duke University Press.

Bajpai, N. (2003). Understanding the Gujarat riots: The role of political and social movements. *Economic and Political Weekly, 38*(14), 1437–1447.

Bandura, A., & Walters, R. H. (1977). *Social learning theory* (Vol. 1, pp. 141–154). Prentice Hall.

BBC News. (2014, April 4). *Rwanda genocide: 100 days of slaughter*. https://www.bbc.com/news/world-africa-26875506

BBC News. (2017b, September 25). *Rohingya crisis: The 'race against time' for refugees*. https://www.bbc.com/news/world-asia-41566561

Bhadra, S. (2011). Livelihood promotion for peacebuilding in communities affected by human-made disasters. *Jharkhand Journal of Development and Management Studies, 9*(1), 4291–4301.

Bhadra, S., & Dyer, A. R. (2011). Psychosocial support for harmony and peacebuilding: Rebuilding community in Gujarat. In *Peace from disasters—Indigenous initiatives across communities, countries and continents* (pp. 97–104). Hiroshima: Hiroshima University. http://hipec.hiroshima-u.ac.jp/oldhipec/ja/products/report/international_peacebuilding_conference_2011.pdf. Accessed 19 May 2017

Brass, P. R. (2011, January 18). *Hindu-Muslim communal riots in India II (1986–2011)*. Sciences Po. https://www.sciencespo.fr/

Chaube, S. K. (1999). *Hill politics in Northeast India*. Orient Longman.

Cialdini, R. B., & Goldstein, N. J. (2004). Social influence: Compliance and conformity. *Annual Review of Psychology, 55*(1), 591–621. https://doi.org/10.1146/annurev.psych.55.090902.142015

Dholabhai, N. (2011, February 18). NSCN wants swift solution. *The Telegraph*. https://www.telegraphindia.com/india/nscn-wants-swift-solution/cid/419828.

Encyclopaedia Britannica. (n.d.). Rwanda genocide of 1994. In *Encyclopaedia Britannica*. https://www.britannica.com/event/Rwanda-genocide-of-1994
Engineer, A. (2005). *The Gujarat carnage: A report*. South Asia Human Rights Documentation Centre.
Freud, S. (1930). Civilization and its discontents (J. Riviere, Trans.). London: Hogarth Press
Gumplowicz, L. (1899). *Outlines of sociology*. Publications of the American Academy of Political and Social Science.
Gurr, T. R. (1970). *Why men rebel*. Princeton University Press.
Hegre, H., Croicu, M., Eck, K., & Högbladh, S. (2020, July). Introducing the UCDP candidate events dataset. *Research & Politics, 7*(3). https://doi.org/10.1177/2053168020935257
Jaffrelot, C. (2003). *India's silent revolution: The rise of the lower castes*. Columbia University Press.
Janis, I. L. (1972). *Victims of groupthink: A psychological study of foreign-policy decisions and fiascoes*. Houghton Mifflin.
Karmakar, S. (2024, August 14). Naga conflict remains unresolved for 77 years, NSCN-IM targets PM Narendra Modi again over 2015 "Framework Agreement". Deccan Herald. Retrieved from https://www.deccanherald.com/india/nagaland/naga-conflict-remains-unresolvedfor-77-years-nscn-im-targets-pmnarendra-modi-again-over-2015-framework-agreement-3150723
Le Bon, G. (1895). *The psychology of the crowd*. T. Fisher Unwin.
Lorenz, K. (1966). *On aggression*. Methuen.
Ministry of Home Affairs. (2022). *Guidelines for maintaining communal harmony and public order* (Report No. 1234). Government of India. https://www.mha.gov.in/documents
Mishra, P. (2012, March 14). The Gujarat massacre: New India's blood rite. *The Guardian*. https://www.theguardian.com
Moscovici, S., & Zavalloni, M. (1969). The group as a polarizer of attitudes. *Journal of Personality and Social Psychology, 12*(2), 125–135.
Panda, S. K. (2010). Social segregation in urban Manipur: The Kuki–Meitei divide. *Urban Anthropology and Studies of Cultural Systems and World Economic Development, 39*(3), 354–371.
Pandey, G. (2001). *Remembering partition: Violence, nationalism and history in India*. Cambridge University Press.
Pettersson, T. (2024). *UCDP non-state conflict codebook v.24.1*. Uppsala Conflict Data Program. https://ucdp.uu.se/downloads/

Ramakrishnan, S. (2016, October 8). 1984 anti-Sikh riots: Calls for justice in India. *Al Jazeera*. https://www.aljazeera.com

Reicher, S., & Stott, C. J. T. (2011). *Mad mobs and Englishmen: Myths and realities of the 2011 riots*. Constable & Robinson.

Reuters. (2024, September 7). Ethnic violence in India's Manipur escalates; six killed. *Reuters*. https://www.reuters.com/world/india/ethnic-violence-indias-manipur-escalates-six-killed-2024-09-07

Roy, E. (2023, August 27). The demand for a Kuki homeland, its history and rationale. *The Indian Express*. https://indianexpress.com/article/explained/explained-culture/the-demand-for-a-kuki-homeland-its-history-and-rationale-8613096/

Selous, E. (1905). *Bird life glimpses*. George Allen.

Sengupta, R. (2005). Christianity, ethnicity, and identity: The Kuki in Manipur. *Modern Asian Studies, 39*(1), 111–134. https://doi.org/10.1017/S0026749X04001692

Siddiqui, M. (2000). Festivals of Gujarat: Celebrations across communities. *South Asian Studies Journal, 15*(2), 101–115.

Singh, T. N. (2012). Educational disparities and social segregation in Manipur. *Journal of Social Issues, 37*(4), 238–253.

Stott, C., & Drury, J. (2000). Crowds, context and identity: Dynamic categorization processes in the 'poll tax riot'. *Human Relations, 53*(2), 247–273.

Swann, W. B., Jr., Jetten, J., Gómez, Á., Whitehouse, H., & Bastian, B. (2012). When group membership gets personal: A theory of identity fusion. *Psychological Review, 119*(3), 441–456. https://doi.org/10.1037/a0028589

Tajfel, H., & Turner, J. C. (1979). An integrative theory of intergroup conflict. In W. G. Austin & S. Worchel (Eds.), *The social psychology of intergroup relations* (pp. 33–47). Brooks/Cole.

Teltumbde, A. (2007). Dravidian politics and Tamil nationalism. *Economic and Political Weekly, 42*(31), 3074–3081.

The Guardian. (2001, November 22). NGOs promote peace in Gujarat amid growing tensions. *The Guardian*.

Time. (1946, October 28). India: Written in blood. *Time, 42*, 28.

Turner, R. H., & Killian, L. M. (1987). *Collective behavior* (3rd ed.). Prentice-Hall.

Varshney, A. (2002). *Ethnic conflict and civic life: Hindus and Muslims in India*. Yale University Press.

Visuvalingam, S., & Chalier-Visuvalingam, E. (2016). Violence and the other in Hinduism and Islam: 1809 Lat Bhairon riots of Banaras. In *Perspectives on violence and othering in India* (pp. 85–127).

Zein, M. (2005). Muslims in the Indian media: Stereotyping, identity, and marginalization. In *The Hindu nationalist movement and Indian politics: The perils of the majority* (pp. 215–240). Oxford University Press.

7

Addressing Psychosocial Challenges and Building The Resilience of Families in Disasters: Insights from a Longitudinal Qualitative Study

Sona Francis and Subhasis Bhadra

Introduction

The family is the primary unit of human life, providing a nurturing, caring, and protective environment for all members across all ages. Disaster threatens this basic equilibrium of the family unit; thus, its ability to perform the critical caring role becomes jeopardized. Each family, within its members, internal emotional connectedness, shared roles, and responsibilities, achieves a homeostasis of functionality, and regaining the same post-disaster is a crucial task. Because of its size, population, and several vulnerabilities, India accounts for a significant percentage of disaster-related emergencies in Asia (CRED, 2024). India experiences a wide range of natural disasters because of its distinct topography and climate (Patankar, 2019). Approximately 12% of India is vulnerable to floods, while 60% of the country is prone to earthquakes. Some 7500 kilometers

S. Francis • S. Bhadra (✉)
Department of Psychosocial Support in Disaster Management, NIMHANS, Bengaluru, Karnataka, India

S. Bhadra et al. (eds.), *Psychosocial and Mental Health Support for Disaster Management in India*, Palgrave Studies in Disaster Science and Emergency Management,
https://doi.org/10.1007/978-3-032-02511-1_7

of coastline of the country are vulnerable to tropical cyclones, and 68% of its land is at risk of drought (Chari, 2010; National Disaster Management Authority, 2023; Sandhu & Kaur, 2013). Apart from natural disasters, the country experiences several human-induced ones, such as border conflicts, communal conflicts, mass violence, and accidents. With the increasing threat of climate change and political instability, the frequency and intensity of these disasters are constantly increasing. Further, each of such events is exacerbating the pre-existing vulnerabilities and challenging the coping strategies of individuals, families, and communities. Over time, it has been understood that every disaster has human hands and impacts on human life, and social ecology is a large concern for survival. Thus, the family, as the primary unit for the survival of human beings, needs to be protected and strengthened to be resilient and maintain the ethos of disaster risk reduction in the sustainable development paradigm.

Disasters, whether natural or human-induced, cause huge hardship and loss to individuals as well as their families and communities. During and post-disaster, psychosocial distress is a combined outcome of deaths, destruction, injuries, and losses that severely impact the life, livelihood, and socioeconomic function of the affected families and communities. Severe distress caused by disasters is manifested in various traumatic stress reactions like anxiety, depression, substance abuse, post-traumatic stress disorder (PTSD), and violence among individuals, which also impact their family life (Manning & Clayton, 2018). Apart from causing immediate physical suffering, disasters disrupt family dynamics, disturb daily routines, and strain social support systems, leaving individuals and families suffering from psychosocial stress and economic hardships. In the face of such adversity, families need aid and assistance to emerge as a vital source of support, protection, and nurturing for individuals. Strong family resilience, characterized by close family bonds, positive parenting, and strong support from extended and immediate family members, plays a major role in overcoming disaster-induced challenges (Basu et al., 2022). All these factors make it important to address the familial outcomes of trauma in any disaster intervention or approach, focusing on its strengths and resilience.

Family is equally an important unit for recovery during the disaster response and recovery program. Family and community-based support is suggested as the second level of care according to the Mental Health and Psychosocial Support (MHPSS) pyramid suggested by the 2023 MHPSS guidelines of NDMA (2023). During the rescue phase, it becomes essential to keep the family together and encourage family reunions as soon as possible. Similarly, during the relief phase, the family units are considered for the distribution of various household items like tents, kitchen utensils, hygiene kits, etc. In many such situations, the average family size is usually taken into consideration. In the disbursal of disaster compensation, the family becomes the unit of the count. While planning for housing resettlements, livelihood restoration, or providing water and sanitation facilities, the family is taken as the basic unit of the beneficiary to ensure support for all the members. Considering all these, exploring the specific vulnerabilities of the families (e.g., women, young adults, elderly-headed families, families with injured, disabled survivors, families with severe traumatic loss, etc.) becomes crucial to facilitate adequate support provision during relief or rehabilitation. Though families are mentioned sporadically in different guidelines, a family-empowering strategy for disaster management and disaster risk reduction is not available. Further, this point is explored under the policy dimension in this article.

Resiliency as a psychological variable has been studied widely (Masten & Obradovic, 2006), highlighting the ability to withstand the face of adversity and the capacity to revive, recover, and bounce back after an event of threat or disaster. Resilient families are essentially the stronger units with close emotional connections among the members and also have extended formal and informal support systems to cultivate positive strength. Mental health problems and issues of deviance are found to be higher in broken families with weak ties and relationships among the members, with enmeshed family boundaries, with poor planning and execution of caring and protective roles for each other (An et al., 2024; Luvira et al., 2023). Stronger family support and emotional bonding are major protective factors from psychological distress faced by any member. After a disaster, while multiple difficulties are imposed on the families and the members fail to function as a unit, it becomes essential to support the family in regaining its ability to function as a unit. Thus, resiliency building of the family is essential for hastening the recovery and rebuilding the social system. Various formal and informal community mechanisms, like self-help groups, livelihood groups, youth groups, geriatric support groups, child care centers, health services, and educational support, are provided to rebuild adequate family and community life in the disaster-affected areas as well as to strengthen disaster risk reduction efforts. Thus, family resiliency building as part of disaster intervention needs further scientific planning and focus during disaster interventions and subsequently.

Systemic Perspective on Family Dynamics

Family is an indivisible, fundamental, and universal social institution that is inherent to human life (Chakravorty et al., 2021; Sonawat, 2001). Family dynamics are the complex interactions and relationships that govern a family unit and have a major effect on its overall functioning and well-being (Jabbari et al., 2023). These relationships are shaped by individual personalities, cultural norms, and other external factors. Comprehending these interactions is essential in understanding how families respond to challenges and overcome them. From a systemic perspective, the family is a multidimensional social system with interrelated components and subsystems such as parent–child, sibling, and marital units, that influence and are influenced by one another (McGinnis & Wright, 2023). Developed by Ludwig von Bertalanffy in the 1920s, General Systems Theory (GST) emphasizes the dynamic interactions between a system and the individual components within it. Introduced by Wiener in 1948, cybernetics investigates how self-regulating systems, such as families, use feedback mechanisms to maintain stability and develop adaptation mechanisms in changing conditions. Family Systems Theory (FST), which explains the interactions within families and their embedded settings, is built on these earlier concepts (Thomas & Priest, 2016; Watson, 2012). Several other theories, which explain the development, nature, and functioning of families as well as the roles, relationships, mutual learning, and emotional dynamics within families, can be better understood in the context of disasters through a systemic perspective.

Duval classifies the family life cycle into eight stages, from married couples without children to aging families (Duvall, 1988). Each stage has its own natural changes, demands, and challenges and there are some developmental tasks, roles, and responsibilities for every family member. Disasters significantly impact family life, causing loss of livelihood, employment, and habitat. They affect the normally expected family life cycle, creating imbalances such as preventing the completion of stages, altering their sequence, and disturbing the fulfillment and stability of each stage. For example, the loss of family members leads to severe psychological distress and disturbed family systems. The consequent role reversals, increased role expectations, and multiplicity of roles lead to poor adaptive patterns and coping strategies among the survivors. These will increase the burden on family members, making them vulnerable to psychosocial issues. Disasters often uproot families from familiar neighborhoods, affecting primary social support (Sekar et al., 2023).

Given the importance of families in disasters, the current study explores the multidimensional impacts of disasters on families in India, their needs, the challenges they face during disaster situations and in disaster management, the feasible effective interventions, and the gaps in existing policies and practices, and advances recommendations for developing a holistic approach prioritizing familial well-being in disaster management and recovery efforts.

Methodology

The authors are trained to provide psychosocial support in disasters; the corresponding author has over two decades of experience in disaster management across India and South Asia. His firsthand involvement in disaster response and intervention activities across multiple disaster-affected regions in India is the source of the qualitative method used for this study. He worked on several disasters, including the Gujarat earthquake (2001) and communal riots (2002), the South Asian tsunami (2004), the Kashmir earthquake (2005), the Uttarakhand floods (2013), the COVID-19 pandemic, and the Wayanad Landslide (2024) providing psychosocial support and services. The first author also has about two years of experience working in recent disasters.

This study is based on the author's longitudinal, participatory observations, and experiences from various research studies, projects, and intervention initiatives conducted in India. These engagements included providing psychosocial support and services integrated with programs for livelihood development, water and sanitation, micro-finance, housing, disaster preparedness, peacebuilding, and other health interventions, with families as a core focus (Table 7.1). At least one hundred families

Table 7.1 Areas of interventions in various disasters

Disaster	Focuses of PSS interventions with families
Gujarat earthquake (2001)	Psychosocial rehabilitation for strengthening family coping to deal with different losses among widowed women, orphaned children, injured, disabled
	Psychosocial support (PSS) and capacity building for families in temporary shelters, and villages
Gujarat riots (2002)	PSS for families in relief camps
	PSS for survivors of rape and violence
	Conflict resolution, peacebuilding, and livelihood restoration
South Asian tsunami (2004)	Psychosocial rehabilitation and support for women, men, and the elderly at individual, family, and community levels
	School-based PSS interventions for the well-being of children and adolescents
Kashmir earthquake (2005)	PSS for children and their mothers
	Strengthening family units to deal with ongoing stress due to conflict and emerging issues of the earthquake
	Capacity building for health workers, teachers, and medical professionals
Uttarakhand floods (2013)	Psychosocial intervention for displaced families
	Community-based PSS interventions
COVID-19 pandemic	Awareness and education on self-care, family unity, and maintaining a healthy lifestyle
	PSS for patient and family members during quarantine and subsequently
	Psychosocial preparedness and telecounseling
Wayanad Landslide (2024)	Providing family-based interventions in relief camps for transition to new settlements
	Capacity building, training, and education through trained staff and volunteers
	Awareness and education through IEC

received psychosocial support as part of each disaster intervention, which combined culturally sensitive methods with family-centered intervention models specifically adapted to each situation. The authors worked closely with various groups within families, including women, children, adolescents, the elderly, youth, and third-gender population, as well as families who experienced severe vulnerabilities including economic struggles and social stigma. Specialized and tailored interventions such as need assessments, home visits, and group sessions were initiated to ensure sustained psychosocial recovery. All interventions adhered to ethical standards and guidelines.

Qualitative evaluation based on regular field visits and systematic documentation captured the real challenges of families during disasters and highlighted the need to build resilience and empowerment. The longitudinal approach highlights the importance of understanding families' experiences from emergencies in the long run. It also reduces bias and obstacles while providing a comprehensive understanding of family resilience and recovery. The study emphasizes the importance of effective family-centered disaster management in achieving India's development goals by recognizing families as the cornerstone of resilience and progress.

Families in Disasters

The profound impact of disasters on individuals disturbs the whole family's functioning. Every member suffers from the collective family trauma. During such events, the family often gets disjointed, apart, and disconnected due to several devastating impacts of the disaster. Survivors of disasters mostly try to be together with their families. Immediately after the disaster, the safety and security of loved ones become the priority. It is seen that some family members took extreme risks and risked their lives to save their children, parents, spouses, or others. Thus, tension within the family system becomes an obvious feature of the family unit in disasters. Based on the structure, the nuclear or joint family encounters different types of stress and undergoes several changes to which each member strives to adjust. Individual choices and collective efforts within the family drive the settlement of the family situations, which may take several years. Based on the experiences of disaster interventions, the typical family issues in disasters and conflicts are explained across five dimensions:

(a) The structural and functional alterations due to disasters within the families.
(b) Physical and mental health challenges of the families during and after disasters.
(c) Issues of pre-existing vulnerabilities of the families and exaggerated impact of the disaster.
(d) Vulnerable members within families during disasters.
(e) Exploring specific impacts on families in different phases of disaster.

Structural and Functional Alterations Due to Disaster

Family structures are significantly impacted by disasters because of the death, displacement, and separation of family members (Inter-Agency Standing Committee, 2007). The defined roles and status of the members get altered as the family fails to function as a unit and becomes dependent on external help for survival needs. Natural disasters like floods, cyclones, and earthquakes, as well as human-induced ones like accidents and incidents of communal violence, commonly lead to higher death rates, injuries, separation, loss of belongings, and destruction of houses, which challenge the foundation of a stable family unit. Additionally, following disasters, both short-term and long-term displacement, often involuntary or forced, overturn conventional family living patterns. In general, a higher rate of internal displacement is observed post-disasters. Also, the movement of family members in search of better possibilities for livelihoods puts more stress on family structures, frequently resulting in broken kinship networks and heightened vulnerability for those left behind. As a result of changes in the existing family structure, role shifting or task shifting occurs within families. As individuals prioritize survival and recovery post-disasters, the traditional and practiced roles and responsibilities of individuals in families are altered to re-establish stability and regain the functioning of the families. To support their families, women who had never worked outside the home were forced to take up these jobs, challenging the traditional gender roles. Children who have lost parents may find themselves taking care of their younger siblings. In some cases, the aged grandparents become the primary support for children who have lost their parents. In all these situations, sudden and demanded changes in the roles within the family can cause distress and added burden, which affects the family's functioning.

Marriage, widowhood, and remarriage become some of the typical issues in the post-disaster phase. Loss of spouses and the breakdown of marital units happen among many surviving families. According to cultural norms, the remarriage of men is quite acceptable in India. It was observed in Gujarat, Tamil Nadu, Andhra Pradesh, Odisha, and other states that the widower received support from the family members and remarried mostly within a year of the disaster. For widowed women, however, this is not the case as they face a lot of socio-cultural and economic restrictions. It is found that sometimes the widowed woman is either abandoned by the in-laws' family, or they are denied property rights. In such situations, she is often left with limited choices and faces hardship in dealing with her daily needs and dependent children. A widowed woman with paraplegia was living with her young daughter in the temporary shelter of Anjar Town of Gujarat, India, following the earthquake of 2001, as she was marked as unlucky by her in-laws' family. Her only subsistence for living was the disability pension from the government. Her neighbors and local non-governmental organizations were her main sources of support during such difficult times. She explained that her family life was ruined, and she had to live only for her daughter. In a subsequent field visit after about 12 years, it was revealed that her daughter got married at an early age, as she expired due to infections with a lack of medical attention. Lack of family support becomes a major issue for survival for many young widows in the post-disaster period. On many occasions, women are forbidden from remarrying while they are in receipt of monetary compensation because of the death of their husband or children (Rao, 2006). In such situations, the in-laws' family was found to keep a close watch on the woman in order to secure the compensation.

Another concern in the post-disaster family situation is the higher rates of child marriages, particularly among girls, when families are in a hurry to get their daughters married off in order to reduce the financial burden. Usually, after a disaster, the dowry ranges are reduced as families find themselves in difficulties. Also, the need to rebuild families following cultural customs has resulted in these young girls, at times, being married to widowers who lost their partners in disasters, or young boys not being financially independent in their careers. Such marriages were of financial benefit in times of crisis. The newlywed couple often encountered multiple difficulties in starting their family life in cramped living conditions. The couple becomes dependent on their parents for support, and, often, the girl faces family pressures to perform various household chores. In such situations, the family relationship starts with strain, and the couple falls into conflict. In Gujarat and different states of South India, the rates of separation among newlywed couples following a disaster was found to be high.

Disasters cause disturbances in family rituals, routines that bring them together and are an important aspect of family functioning. Traditional practices like family prayers, meal times, and other quality time they spend together were entirely interrupted by disasters. For example, families accustomed to cooking and eating together find difficulties in maintaining this routine in crowded relief camps, where community kitchens are used and family members are housed separately. Also, the privacy issues in a community setting become a concern for family members. Children and the elderly are more likely to experience severe stress because of these sudden changes in their normal routines and rituals.

Physical and Mental Health Challenges of the Families During and After Disasters

Disasters have profound impacts on the physical and mental health of the affected population. In cases of traumatic loss like death, cultural and spiritual practices offer individuals a sense of solace (Walsh, 2007). The disaster situation often hinders traditional mourning and bereavement practices, which leads to psychosocial distress among family members. The loss and missing of family members without evidence of death or survival, missing dead bodies, the difficulty in identification, and the large number of deaths in the community make disaster deaths more tragic. Consequent mass graves or improper burials and unresolved legal and administrative issues cause distress among loved ones. The limitation in practicing conventional rituals, such as burial services and prayers, because of restrictions or the overwhelming of facilities during events such as the Tsunami, earthquakes, and the COVID-19 pandemic exacerbates grief and complicates the mourning process. In such situations of disaster, the grieving period becomes prolonged, and healing is hindered because of an absence of closure, which results from not being able to bid a proper farewell to the loved ones.

Such ambiguous losses are very common in disaster situations, meaning that the suffering of the surviving family members is prolonged. In such situations, the loss is unclear without any official verification of life or death. Since there is no resolution of the situation, ambiguous loss is the most stressful kind of loss (Boss, 2017). In the case of ambiguous losses, grieving and coping mechanisms are frozen, decisions are postponed, and grief is exacerbated (Betz & Thorngren, 2006; Boss, 2017). During disasters, when many individuals are missing, but the resources for locating them are limited or non-functional, the sense of ambiguity escalates. Also, the lack of information and support systems in place increases uncertainty. This may create many other problems within the family, which cause additional stress. For instance, in the aftermath of the Indian Ocean Tsunami 2004, many couples lost their children and faced high trauma. The women were then pressured to undergo recanalization (surgical intervention to conceive a child again, after tubectomy), which led to many physical and mental health problems. These medical interventions elevated their emotional distress, including heightened anxiety, depression, and feelings of guilt. The women were under pressure to give birth to a male child, and they often faced family pressure from in-laws and husbands. In many cases, this led to disrupted family dynamics and spousal relationships. Similar incidents were also reported in the aftermath of the Marthwada earthquake in the state of Maharashtra in 1993 (Kedare & Dhavale, 2002).

The physical injuries or illnesses of family members after disasters cause distress and trauma for the families. For example, the loss of limbs from injuries or amputation has severe physical and psychological consequences for the survivors (Sahu et al., 2016). Adjusting to living with an amputation involves a lot of struggle and requires immense effort in relearning the basic tasks and rehabilitation, which can be overwhelming for them. These struggles, along with the fear of stigma and societal perceptions, often lead to a range of distressing emotional reactions like anger, grief, frustration, depression, etc. The sudden changes in their life plans, such as education, marriage, career goals, etc., cause severe stress and feelings of hopelessness to them. Also, in some cases, amputation and paraplegia affect their sexual performance, which impacts their family life and is a cause of concern for them. In Gujarat, there were a few male paraplegic patients who became highly suspicious and abusive of their wives after losing their sexual abilities. A very systematic intervention by engaging their peer groups and helping the women to join women's self-help groups (SHGs) for livelihood and regular family visits helped them to regain family cohesion (Ramappa & Bhadra, 2004). These sufferings extended beyond individuals to their families, who often played a crucial role in caregiving and providing support and assistance. The sudden onset of a disability among a family member severely strains familial relationships, caregiving dynamics, and even family resources. The family also experiences stress and caregiver burden when they go through the challenges of taking care of their loved ones while simultaneously coping with their emotional reactions to the disasters. Furthermore, the cost of medical bills, rehabilitation, and assistive devices strains the family's finances and increases stress.

In a developing country such as India, where economic stability and financial security in disasters, such as disaster insurance, are not very profound, the loss of property and livelihood in disasters severely impacts individuals and families, leaving them in economic hardship. Moreover, in India, many hold a sentimental connection with houses and property. Hence, losing these makes them highly distressed and traumatized. Also, families feel a sense of insecurity and instability in cases of the loss of houses and shelters. Households' ability to generate income was severely compromised by the negative effects of disasters on human capital, specifically in relation to nutrition, education, and health (Rentschler, 2013). The families in a few of the villages located on the cliff of the hill of Uttarakhand were under severe stress as the erosion continued after the flash flood in 2013, and the villages were gradually endangered by the risk of landslides. So, families had to leave the houses that they had been living in for generations or that they had constructed with their life savings (Bhadra, 2018). The loss of their livelihood and means of income pushes the families into poverty, debt, and uncertainty. In many cases, the financial crises resulting from disaster loss may cause limited access to basic needs like food, clean water, healthcare, and shelter. This situation was further worsened when there were individuals with special needs such as people with illnesses, pregnant women, infants, children, the elderly, or people with disabilities (PWD). The stress of rebuilding lives and homes in the struggles of unemployment and livelihood loss causes psychological issues and long-term financial struggles. The social manifestations of financial crises were evident in the form of increased school dropout rates and child labor among children, lack of nutrition leading to related diseases, inadequate access to medical care, increased poverty levels, and strained social support systems. These further disrupted the family dynamics and functioning. Another complicated aspect during the post-disaster phase was the legal systems, documentation, and certifications. Often, filling up forms for compensation claims and reissuing basic certificates (e.g., birth certificates, legal papers of land, driving license school certificates, etc.) required long persuasion for days together in government offices. The tasks of dead body identification, completing formalities for death certificates, instances of multiple families claiming the same body for completing the compensation procedures, feeling that the received body is not of their loved ones, etc., were highly emotionally exhausting in different disaster situations (Rao, 2006).

Disasters also disturb the social support networks of a family which elevates the challenges faced by them. The threats faced due to disasters, forced displacements, violence, and poverty not only contribute to immediate suffering but also obstruct the rebuilding of social networks which are imperative for regaining psychosocial well-being (Inter-Agency Standing Committee, 2007). The disruption of larger social support systems such as friends, extended families, neighbors, healthcare systems, and community organizations further complicates the challenges faced by the survivors and brings uncertainty to their everyday lives. Declined perceived social and emotional support received also adds to psychiatric symptomology, including anxiety, substance use, depression, and PTSD. Also, the burden of providing support to others may worsen these psychiatric symptoms, indicating a complicated relationship between social support and psychosocial well-being in the aftermath of disasters (Solomon et al., 1993).

Despite all the challenges, sometimes disasters also catalyze growth and resilience in families. Studies indicate that post-disaster, some families go through a phase of post-traumatic growth marked by improved connection, emotional resilience, and gratitude for life (Tedeschi & Calhoun, 2004). Several positive changes are included in this growth, such as new opportunities, more meaningful connections, heightened spirituality, improved resilience, and reordered priorities. Strong connection with others and trust in their support reduce feelings of helplessness and insecurity, and facilitate resilience and post-traumatic growth (Walsh, 2007).

Issues of Pre-existing Vulnerabilities of the Families

The pre-existing socioeconomic vulnerabilities of the families significantly impact their lives during disasters. When families already struggle with existing economic instability, limited access to resources, and marginalized social status, the effects of disaster become more intense. The lack of financial resilience is a fundamental aspect of socioeconomic vulnerability. Evidence indicates that the poor are more vulnerable to losses of both human and economic capital during disasters (Rentschler, 2013). Families suffering from poverty or unemployment would not have any savings or insurance, which leaves them highly vulnerable to the financial destruction of disasters such as the loss of houses, livelihood, and possessions. Lack of awareness about provisions that can be claimed, as well as available resources and aids like loans, government schemes, and other benefits, adds to the economic vulnerability. These economic instabilities lead to limited healthcare access, educational opportunities, nutrition, and basic facilities like power supply, clean water, etc. Limited access to healthcare services, especially in rural and tribal areas, affects family decision-making, caregiving responsibilities, and financial stability

(Balarajan et al., 2011). In addition, structural issues such as lack of income opportunities, exploitation, and corruption are exacerbated during disasters, further deepening the vulnerability of these communities (Bhadra, 2021).

The pre-existing social vulnerabilities in families include marginalization and discrimination based on race, ethnicity, gender, sexuality, disability, and social class. Inequalities and discrimination can limit a family's access to basic needs, and, thereby, they face additional hurdles in coping and recovering from disasters. For example, post-Tsunami in 2004, the small-scale fishing communities, particularly the Irula tribal communities which were settled far from the shore, were mostly unreached. Similarly, in Gujarat, remote village residents, whose houses were made of loose rocks, were not only physically injured but also often overlooked in disaster relief efforts. In the cases of urban riots, those in slum areas faced heightened risks as they were disproportionately targeted by rioters. Among the most vulnerable to disasters are low-income and poor homes, households headed by a single parent, and households that are socially isolated. Also, those who have recently moved in, such as immigrants, undocumented residents, refugees, Indigenous populations, marginalized ethnic groups, institutionalized populations, and homeless people, are extremely vulnerable (Bradshaw, 2004).

Vulnerable Members Within Families During Disasters

During disasters and emergencies, women are the group that faces the most risk due to neglect, physical and sexual abuse, domestic violence, harassment, exploitation, etc. (Alam & Rahman, 2014; Enarson & Fordham, 2001; Thurston et al., 2021). Still, they are expected to play the role of caregivers and support providers for children, spouses, and dependent elders in the family, at times of loss, relocation, injury, death, and trauma. When it comes to non-traditional family structures with widowed women or women-led single-parent households, such families suffer the most in terms of loss and access to resources because of several socioeconomic limitations faced by women. Compared to single women running houses, women in traditional relationships with men received greater support in preparing for and recovering from disasters (Enarson & Morrow, 1998). When long-standing, male-dominated social control systems are disrupted, women and their children are most often neglected or affected, and women are less likely to organize because they are more likely to be alone, less educated, or directly threatened (Wiest et al., 1994).

Families with children are a primary concern during disasters as they are vulnerable to trafficking, abuse, and neglect. Such families face more difficulties at every stage of the disaster. For example, during the evacuation phase, children with impairments and their families may be less likely to leave the threatened area, even in cases where it is feasible to do so (Alexander, 2012). During disasters, the usual support system of children, which includes adults and families, often struggles or fails to help them respond to and recover from disasters. Even extended support systems like schools, community centers, etc., will be dysfunctional due to the destruction of infrastructure. This puts them in severe distress and problems. Children and adolescents who face the death or loss of family members, displacement, or separation from families might develop risks of improper development or maladaptive coping behaviors. The impact of disasters on children primarily depends on how their families and caregivers handle the stress and trauma. In situations where families experience extreme stress due to events like loss of homes and belongings, relocation, loss of jobs, and temporary living conditions with constant arguments and fights, young children are likely to exhibit behaviors and emotions that are indicative of this unstable family atmosphere. Also, children, especially adolescent girls, face severe struggles such as exposure to deviant behavior from their co-inhabitants in relief camps or temporary shelters. There is a higher risk of them engaging in sexual activities and, therefore, a higher risk of unwanted pregnancies. Their families face significant psychological and emotional turmoil because of this. However, such instances are usually hidden and not reported by family members. A lot of children are orphaned in the aftermath of disasters. These children are highly vulnerable as the lost, abandoned, and orphaned are at risk of exploitation, sexual abuse, violence, and forced beggary (Rao, 2006).

Elderly people are often a group that is particularly vulnerable to the effects of disasters, in terms of both immediate and long-term impacts (Ngo, 2001). Physical disabilities in hearing, sight, mobility, and communication, cognitive disabilities, less access to resources and social support, high dependency on caregivers, etc., make the aged population more vulnerable (Maltais, 2019). Older adults often depend on family members for their daily needs, such as doing daily routines, healthcare, and emotional support. This system is affected by disasters, meaning that they are often neglected or abused in such situations. In the phases of response and rescue, they are usually the least considered or prioritized. When families are struggling to rebuild their lives, find livelihoods, manage temporary housing, and deal with economic loss, the needs of elderly family members can sometimes be overlooked. Additionally, when the primary caregivers in the family are overwhelmed or distressed, the elderly find it difficult to meet their basic needs, resulting in a reduced quality of life. In some cases, the powers the elderly have in their families will be compromised or undermined during disasters, making them feel weak or powerless. All these difficult situations can lead to increased feelings of isolation, anxiety, and depression among the elderly.

During disasters, families with people with disability (PWD) face unique challenges, making it more difficult for them to react, evacuate, and recover. The effects of disasters are disproportionately felt by PWD because of several barriers faced by them in receiving early warnings, accessing evacuation routes, lack of assistive devices, non-inclusive response and recovery measures, and discrimination in relief distribution. They are more likely to suffer fatalities, be injured, or lose their property after a disaster than those without impairments. The degree of discrimination toward disabled individuals often rises in the aftermath of disasters (Alexander, 2012). The needs of those with mobility disabilities are frequently overlooked in traditional evacuation preparations, which makes it challenging for these families to get to safety. Furthermore, individuals who have hearing or vision disabilities miss out on important information regarding early warnings, evacuation, and relief distribution, due to challenges with communication. This puts more responsibilities and burdens on their family members and caregivers. Because of all these, in some cases, families with PWD are forced to choose between either staying in unsafe conditions or finding other means to evacuate, which can be riskier sometimes. Also, families will have to make sure they have a sufficient supply of medical equipment, medicines, and assistive devices, which can be difficult to do during a crisis. Families with individuals who have chronic illnesses face similar difficulties due to the breakdown of the healthcare system, and their dependency on medical equipment, which adds to the challenges in evacuation and transportation, medicine shortages, financial constraints, and communication barriers.

Individuals from the LGBTQI+ community are highly vulnerable to disasters due to the stigma, discrimination, harassment, and abuse they face. Primarily, they may have fear or challenges in disclosing their gender identities in such situations, which leads to mental health crises such as increased anxiety, stress, and depression. The relief shelter facilities where basic needs such as sanitation and toilets are often unsuitable for their needs, make them feel insecure and unsafe. The inequitable resource allocation and distribution, limited access to LGBTQI+-friendly medical services, difficulties in meeting their special needs, evacuation challenges, and documentation issues due to gender identity are some of the common challenges they face. The limited social and community support further worsens these challenges. Not only do such individuals struggle with stigma, bias, and prejudice, but their families also face these challenges along with legal and policy barriers. In some cases, LGBTQI+ individuals have left or been forced to leave home due to the lack of acceptance in their families. However, during a disaster when everyone seeks emotional support and help, and families long to be together, both these individuals and their families suffer.

Exploring Specific Impacts on Families in Different Phases of Disaster

Families face extensive difficulties throughout disasters and disaster management processes. At the onset of a disaster, starting from response and rescue, to the preparation and mitigation of potential future ones, families are at high risk and are severely impacted due to several social, economic, political, and cultural factors. Table 7.2 outlines the major challenges of families in each disaster management phase and the feasible, effective solutions for them.

Table 7.2 Challenges and solutions for families in disasters

	Issues faced by families during different phases of disaster	Possible solutions and interventions
Response and rescue	• Violence, abuse, and insecurity • Neglect • Individuals with special needs • Lack of proper instructions • Improper communication system • Psychosocial trauma • Death, injuries, illness, amputation • Spread of diseases • Ambiguous loss • Loss of property and possessions • Separation of family members	• Prompt administrative response • Just and equitable responses • Special attention to the vulnerable population • Ensuring the safety and protection of women and children • Training of individuals who are involved in search and rescue operations • Establishing a proper system for tracking and updating information about lost and missing individuals • Respect the dignity and worth of individuals
Relief	• Unjust and inequitable division of resources • Corruption and exploitation • Special needs of vulnerable populations within families (children, the elderly, newborns, lactating mothers, PWD, ill ones) • Limited supply of relief measures • Disorganized relief supply • Cultural insensitivity in the relief materials supplied • Separation of family members • Disruption of family routines • Adjusting to communal living arrangements • Difficulty in sanitation and hygiene • Lack of family privacy	• Establishing and practicing minimum standards in relief provisions • Following SOPs • Equitable relief distribution • Coordination of relief supply • Keep families together in relief facilities like camps • Normalizing family routines • Psychosocial first aid (PFA) • Gender-sensitive facilities • Culturally sensitive relief materials • Considering individuals with special needs • Psychosocial support like counseling in camps for families

(continued)

Table 7.2 (continued)

	Issues faced by families during different phases of disaster	Possible solutions and interventions
Reconstruction and rehabilitation	• Family disintegration • Financial struggles, no savings or insurance • Lack of social and emotional support • Social stigma • Lack of awareness about claims and provisions • Lack of access to resources • Lack of closure, disrupted mourning and bereavement practices, complicated grief • Legal procedures • Dependence on the disaster relief system	• Promote the reintegration of families into society • Establishing support systems • Connecting to resources and services • Educating about claims and provisions • Establishing clear guidelines for legal procedures • Proper data management of survivors and their loss • Speeding up certification procedures • Establishing a proper disaster victim identification system • Establishing a proper system to monitor the claims, compensations, and benefits • Vocational training for skill development and income generation • Following up on physical and mental health needs
Preparedness and mitigation	• Socioeconomic disparity and isolation • Poverty and financial instability • Unemployment • Lack of resources • Single-parent households • Women-headed households • Lack of access to early warning signals and information systems • Lack of facilities for evacuation • Lack of awareness and education	• Inclusive and participatory approach in disaster management • Family-inclusive policies • Hazard Risk Vulnerability (HRV) analysis with families' participation • Generating awareness and education • Capacity building and skill development • Promoting financial resilience • Mock drills • Establishing proper and inclusive early warning systems • Building proper crisis communication networks

Rao (2006); Wiest et al. (1994)

Psychosocial Interventions for Families in Disasters

Appropriate interventions among disaster-affected families are important in facilitating their recovery, resilience, and coping mechanisms post-disaster. Disaster interventions involve reestablishing functional family dynamics, providing needed resources and services, restoring social support, and empowering individuals and families to recover physically and mentally from the traumatic experience.

Family-centered disaster risk reduction which involves families in disaster preparedness, planning, response, and decision-making should be practiced. The families themselves should be seen as active agents of resilience and change. This model should integrate different interventions and approaches for promoting empowerment, collaboration, and collective action among families. The family-centered disaster risk reduction approaches must have inclusive and sustainable strategies that support families in recovery and reintegration into society. More focus should be given to vulnerable groups like women, people with disability, the elderly, ethnic minorities, the indigenous population, the poor, etc. Through a participatory and inclusive approach, their needs, concerns, and specific issues should be considered in all steps of disaster management and policy development. Family resilience should be the primary focus of this approach as it empowers families to rebound from difficulties. This includes making them capable of identifying their own needs, resources, and vulnerabilities. Family resilience works on the foundation of shared experience and collective problem solving. Awareness about disasters, early warning systems, emergency and rescue plans, relief materials, and available and accessible resources must be known by the families. Such awareness generation and educational interventions are effective in building family resilience. In a wider view, communities must also be equipped with efficient local leadership, networks, resources, and self-resilience to face future challenges.

Employing strength-based approaches, which are centered on identifying and building on the existing strengths, resources, and resilience of the families is crucial while working with disaster-affected families. Focusing more on what they have rather than their deficits instils confidence in them to build upon their inherent strengths and develop effective coping strategies for overcoming challenges. Mental health professionals are the most appropriate ones to employ strength-based principles through their consultations and therapies while working with families. Disaster mental health-sensitized therapies like Trauma-Focused Cognitive Behavioural Therapy (TF-CBT) are evidence-based treatments designed to address the psychological impact of trauma. By integrating cognitive restructuring, exposure therapies, and relaxation techniques, TF-CBT helps individuals and families manage distress and build resilience. Mindfulness-based interventions and techniques like meditation, breathing exercises, and grounding techniques, are effective in developing greater emotional regulation and reducing stress by generating present-moment awareness, acceptance, and self-compassion. Family therapies that focus on strengthening familial bonds, improving communication, and addressing familial conflicts are effective ways to build family strengths and resilience. Crisis counseling and other emergency supports that are strength-based and solution-focused should be prioritized while working with families in disasters.

Psychoeducation involves providing families with knowledge, skills, and resources to better understand and manage the psychosocial and practical challenges related to disasters. By educating and generating awareness about normal reactions to disasters, difficulties of different survivor groups, coping strategies, seeking support, safety planning, available resources, parenting in crisis, and family resilience, families can be empowered to make informed decisions, access appropriate care and resources, and recover better. Better knowledge about disasters and their management improves families' self-efficacy in dealing with difficulties and trauma.

Support groups work well with families in disasters. Support groups and peer groups allow families to come together, share their stories, and provide mutual support. This will reduce feelings of isolation, create a sense of belongingness, and develop an atmosphere of empathy. Interventions that align with the cultural and spiritual healing practices of the community which bring together culturally sensitive and spiritually informed practices should be promoted. By leveraging the traditional practices rooted in Indian culture, these culturally sensitive practices develop a sense of collective strength. Social support groups, community-based organizations, and local leaders play an important role in mobilizing resources. The training of community volunteers with the knowledge, skills, and awareness needed to engage with the local community has proven effective.

Economic empowerment programs and financial resilience are to be promoted for building disaster-resilient families. These interventions are significant both during the preparedness phase and the post-impact phase when families struggle with their financial loss and destruction. Programs such as vocational training, skill building, and micro-finance initiatives for youth and women will enhance the financial resilience of the overall family and offer livelihood support. By providing opportunities for livelihood support, income generation, and financial stability, such programs can contribute to long-term recovery and self-sufficiency.

Leveraging technology in disasters has more potential to be explored. There is a clear scope for using technological interventions among individuals and families across the disaster management phases, from preparedness to rehabilitation and reconstruction. Digital platforms like mobile apps, online support groups, teletherapy, and teleconsultation services can deliver both mental health support and other assistance to the affected ones. These interventions can create accessible, cost-effective, and stigma-free platforms for seeking support and assistance. For this to be worked out effectively, engaging families in the preparedness phase to train them in accessing and using these technological platforms has to be done, particularly those in remote or underserved areas. These pre-interventions will help reduce the digital divide in post-service delivery and access.

Another effective way to reach out to families affected by disasters is through their communities. Community-based organizations and local leaders play an important role in this. Therefore, community interventions, like training of community volunteers, field-level workers, and other grassroots-level people, will help in providing help and assistance to the families. Such volunteers should be trained to equip them with the knowledge, skills, and awareness needed to work with the unique needs and preferences of families. As the volunteers are themselves from the community, it is easier for them to identify and reach out to the needy as well as to provide culturally sensitive interventions and support. Post-tsunami community interventions in the Kanyakumari district of Tamil Nadu, which included community organization and mobilization, community engagement programs, promoting volunteerism among community members, and capacity building of the community, were proven effective in facilitating subjective well-being among the community members.

Administrative Responses and Policies

The Sphere Handbook is a globally recognized and accepted reference for humanitarian response during emergencies. The handbook includes guidelines and standards for policy and practice. These comprehensive guidelines and standards extend beyond individuals as the focus and encompass families and communities affected by crises and emergencies. The handbook directly impacts the resilience and stability of families by addressing key areas such as health, food, shelter, and livelihood. The guidelines ensure that families have access to safe and dignified shelters with at least the minimum standards that safeguard their well-being and respect the family system by proper measures such as keeping them together, ensuring privacy, and addressing their special needs. The guidelines also mention food security and nutrition which support the vulnerable populations within the families like children, newborns, pregnant and lactating women, and the elderly, etc. By emphasizing education, protection, and livelihood support, the handbook looks to support and aid the rehabilitation and long-term recovery of the affected individuals post-disasters. Through its holistic, participatory, and inclusive approach, the Sphere Handbook holds a vital position in promoting the resilience and well-being of families in the humanitarian context (The Sphere Project, 2011).

In its guidelines of 2007, the Inter-Agency Standing Committee provides recommendations for emergency response and management and specifically addresses the needs of families (Inter-Agency Standing Committee, 2007). The guidelines signify the importance of involving women, children, and others who are affected in the decision-making process regarding resources, site planning, shelter, etc. Encouraging the participation of families in the process will reduce the disorganization and lack of coordination in disaster management activities which directly affect them. Moreover, the guidelines highlight the importance of the participation of women in planning emergency shelters to address the existing gaps in gender-sensitive needs like privacy and protection. Recognizing the impact on mental health and psychosocial well-being of families in crisis, the guidelines set a special focus on reducing conflicts over resources and fostering social cohesiveness in emergency settings.

According to the National Disaster Management Authority (NDMA) guidelines on Mental Health and Psychosocial Support of 2023, families are given particular recognition during disasters and emergencies in India. The guidelines recognize the vulnerabilities that exist within family units, such as households headed by women, single parents, and those with several dependents, as well as those with caregiving responsibilities. This classification of vulnerabilities according to family structures allows for the development of focused interventions that successfully address particular requirements. The guidelines also recognize the collective trauma experienced by the families and communities facing disasters, thereby advocating for strategies for rebuilding familial and social support systems. These strategies include addressing concerns regarding changes in child-rearing and relationship patterns, reducing issues such as displacement and fragmentation of families, and restoration of familial and communal support systems (NDMA, 2023). However, it would be more effective if the guidelines could explicitly recognize the special needs and roles of families in disaster resilience and recovery, rather than combining them with the larger community. Under the NDMA guidelines of 2023, the resilience of families and well-being can be effectively enhanced by advocating for tailored interventions that specifically address their unique challenges, independent of community considerations. This will make sure that their unique concerns are adequately addressed.

Gaps and Recommendations

Disaster management planning in the conventional approaches generally treats the traditional family as the basic unit and thereby fails to recognize family diversity and changes in family compositions and structures in contemporary society. A more inclusive approach that recognizes, accepts, and integrates the diverse types of households in the current society is important so that disaster management efforts can better understand the unique social dynamics and vulnerabilities within the families.

The 2023 guidelines of NDMA on Mental Health and Psychosocial Support (MHPSS) in disasters emphasize the significance of focusing on several vulnerable populations, many of which are components of families (NDMA, 2023). However, the distinct functions and roles of families in the context of disaster resilience and recovery, apart from those of larger communities, are not recognized and clearly stated. This gap can lead to a lack of targeted and tailored interventions that address the needs of families, thereby leaving them vulnerable and underserved during disasters. This can be rectified by making clear and focused family-centric guidelines and protocols, ensuring safety, security, and targeted service to families in disasters. Also, in India, there exists a significant gap in understanding the family demography as such. This lack of knowledge sources limits the scope of studying the pressing contemporary family issues, such as domestic violence and separation, and current dynamics, such as same-sex relationships and living in relationships. Without comprehensive data on family structure and dynamics, it becomes challenging for policy-makers and practitioners to develop policies and interventions that address the diverse needs of families across the country.

In India, the absence of an efficient system for tracking and updating information about lost and missing individuals during disasters induces distress and prolonged anxiety for families and caregivers. A reliable tracking system utilizing technological support and innovation is needed to facilitate the relief and closure that families require in the aftermath of disasters. Addressing the lack of regionally validated tools for quantitatively measuring family resilience is also crucial. Existing scales, mostly validated for Western populations, may not accurately capture the unique challenges and strengths of Indian familial structures. Developing regionally valid scales tailored to the sociocultural context of Indian families is important for accurately assessing and enhancing family resilience. These scales should consider the diverse range of challenges faced by diverse families in India and facilitate more targeted and effective resilience-building initiatives.

Conclusion

The different and varied impacts of disasters on families highlight the importance of family-centered disaster risk reduction in all phases of disasters, from preparedness and response to recovery and reconstruction. Prioritizing family well-being helps ensure that the most vulnerable people in society receive the support and help they need to manage and overcome the challenges posed by disasters. Equity and inclusivity must be considered while developing policies and standards, considering the various requirements of families with varying socioeconomic backgrounds, cultural contexts, resources, and capacities. With a holistic approach focused on families as central to the disaster management efforts, we will have more resilient communities and less impact of disasters on individuals, their families, and society in the long term (Fig. 7.1).

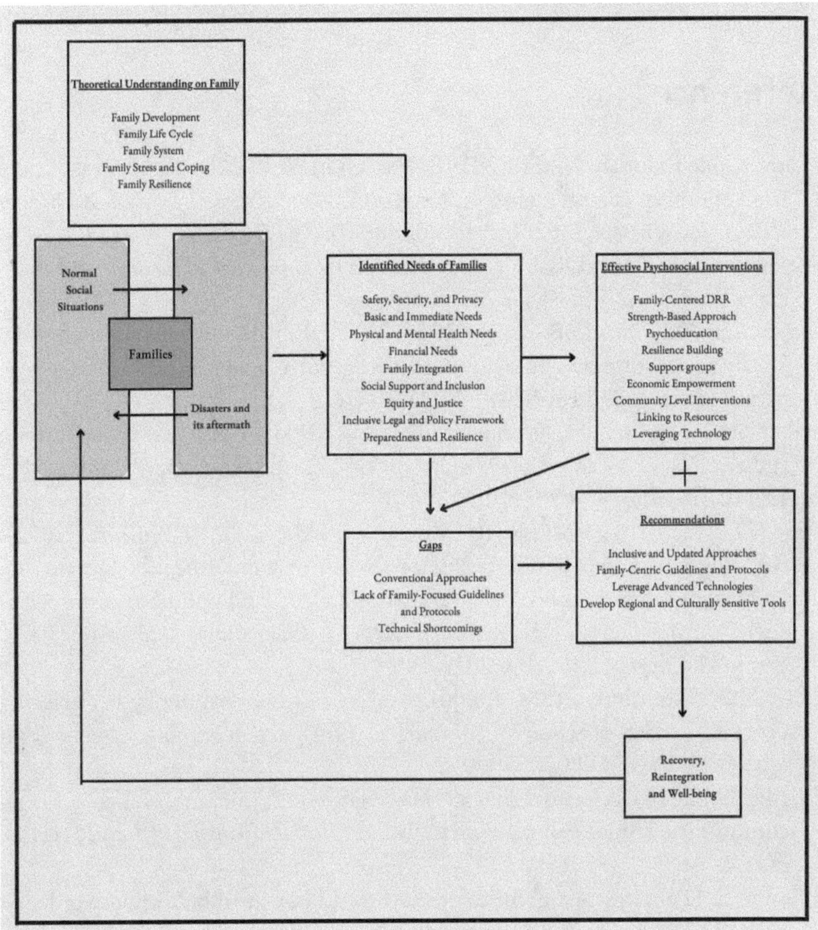

Fig. 7.1 Families in disasters: A conceptual model

Ethics Committee Approval and Informed Consent This study does not require ethical approval as it is based solely on the author's personal observations and experiences. The research does not involve the direct participation of any human participants. Instead, the study draws conclusions from the author's reflections and analyses. Therefore, no ethical review or approval or informed consent is required for this chapter. Conflict of Interest The authors declare that there is no potential conflict of interest concerning the research and publication of this article.

References

Alam, K., & Rahman, M. H. (2014). Women in natural disasters: A case study from southern coastal region of Bangladesh. *International Journal of Disaster Risk Reduction, 8*, 68–82. https://doi.org/10.1016/j.ijdrr.2014.01.003

Alexander, D. (2012). Disability and disaster. In *Handbook of hazards and disaster risk reduction* (pp. 413–423). Routledge.

An, J., Zhu, X., Shi, Z., & An, J. (2024). A serial mediating effect of perceived family support on psychological well-being. *BMC Public Health, 24*(1), 940. https://doi.org/10.1186/s12889-024-18476-z

Balarajan, Y., Selvaraj, S., & Subramanian, S. (2011). Health care and equity in India. *The Lancet, 377*(9764), 505–515. Elsevier B.V. https://doi.org/10.1016/S0140-6736(10)61894-6

Basu, D., Nagpal, S., Pillai, R. R., Mutiso, V., Ndetei, D., & Bhui, K. (2022). Building youth and family resilience for better mental health: Developing and testing a hybrid model of intervention in low- and middle-income countries. *British Journal of Psychiatry, 220*(1). Cambridge University Press. https://doi.org/10.1192/bjp.2021.129

Betz, G., & Thorngren, J. M. (2006). Ambiguous loss and the family grieving process. *The Family Journal, 14*(4), 359–365. https://doi.org/10.1177/1066480706290052

Bhadra, S. (2018). A man-made, so called natural disaster and resiliency of hill community: Himalayan tsunami in India. *Integrated Journal of Social Sciences, 5*(1), 1–6.

Bhadra, S. (2021). Vulnerabilities of the Rural Poor in India during pandemic COVID-19: Social Work perspective for designing sustainable emergency response. *Asian Social Work and Policy Review, 15*(3), 221–233. https://doi.org/10.1111/aswp.12236

Boss, P. (2017). Families of the missing: Psychosocial effects and therapeutic approaches. *International Review of the Red Cross, 99*(905), 519–534. https://doi.org/10.1017/S1816383118000140

Bradshaw, S. (2004). *Socio-economic impacts of natural disasters: A gender analysis*. ECLAC.

Chakravorty, S., Goli, S., & James, K. S. (2021). Family demography in India: Emerging patterns and its challenges. *SAGE Open, 11*(2), 215824402110081. https://doi.org/10.1177/21582440211008178

Chari, P. R. (2010). India and natural disasters. In *Global warming and climate change* (pp. 145–158). Palgrave Macmillan UK. https://doi.org/10.1057/9780230281257_9

Centre for Research on the Epidemiology of Disasters. (2024). *2023 disasters in numbers: A significant year of disaster impact.* Centre for Research on the Epidemiology of Disasters. Retrieved from https://www.un-spider.org/news-and-events/news/cred-publication-2023-disasters-numbers-significant-year-disaster-impact

Duvall, E. M. (1988). Family development's first forty years. *Family Relations, 37*, 127–134.

Enarson, E., & Fordham, M. (2001). From women's needs to women's rights in disasters. *Environmental Hazards, 3*(3), 133–136. https://doi.org/10.3763/ehaz.2001.0314

Enarson, E., & Morrow, B. H. (1998). Why gender? Why women? An introduction to women and disaster. In *The gendered terrain of disaster: Through women's eyes* (pp. 1–8).

Inter-Agency Standing Committee. (2007). *IASC guidelines on mental health and psychosocial support in emergency settings.* Geneva: Inter-Agency Standing Committee.

Jabbari, B., Schoo, C., & Rouster, A. S. (2023). Family Dynamics. In StatPearls. StatPearls Publishing.

Kedare, J., & Dhavale, H. S. (2002). Effects of the Marathwada Earthquake on widows and married women. *Indian Journal of Social Work, 63*, 182–193.

Luvira, V., Nonjui, P., Butsathon, N., Deenok, P., & Aunruean, W. (2023). Family background issues as predictors of mental health problems for university students. *Healthcare, 11*(3), 316. https://doi.org/10.3390/healthcare11030316

Maltais, D. (2019). Elderly people with disabilities and natural disasters: Vulnerability of seniors and post trauma. *Gerontology & Geriatric Medicine, 5*(4), 1–7. https://doi.org/10.24966/GGM-8662/100041

Manning, C., & Clayton, S. (2018). Threats to mental health and wellbeing associated with climate change. In *Psychology and climate change* (pp. 217–244). Elsevier. https://doi.org/10.1016/B978-0-12-813130-5.00009-6

Masten, A. S., & Obradovic, J. (2006). Competence and resilience in development. *Annals of the New York Academy of Sciences, 1094*(1), 13–27. https://doi.org/10.1196/annals.1376.003

McGinnis, H. A., & Wright, A. W. (2023). Adoption and child health and psychosocial well-being. In *Encyclopedia of child and adolescent health* (pp. 582–598). Elsevier. https://doi.org/10.1016/B978-0-12-818872-9.00115-1

National Disaster Management Authority. (2023). *Annual report 2022–2023.* https://ndma.gov.in/sites/default/files/PDF/Reports/NDMA-Annual-Report_20-21.pdf

NDMA. (2023). *National disaster management guidelines mental health and psychosocial support services in disasters.* National Disaster Management Authority, Government of India.

Ngo, E. B. (2001). When disasters and age collide: Reviewing vulnerability of the elderly. *Natural Hazards Review, 2*(2), 80–89. https://doi.org/10.1061/(ASCE)1527-6988(2001)2:2(80)

Patankar, A. (2019). Impacts of natural disasters on households and small businesses in India. In *ADB economics working paper series, no. 603.* Asian Development Bank (ADB).

Ramappa, G., & Bhadra, S. (2004). Institutional responses—Oxfam (India): Psycho social support programme for survivors of the earthquake. *Disaster Mental Health in India*, 140–150.

Rao, K. (2006). Lessons learnt in mental health and psychosocial care in India after disasters. *International Review of Psychiatry, 18*(6), 547–552. https://doi.org/10.1080/09540260601037961

Rentschler, J. E. (2013). *Why resilience matters—The poverty impacts of disasters.*

Sahu, A., Sagar, R., Sarkar, S., & Sagar, S. (2016). Psychological effects of amputation: A review of studies from India. *Industrial Psychiatry Journal, 25*(1), 4. https://doi.org/10.4103/0972-6748.196041

Sandhu, D., & Kaur, S. (2013). Psychological impacts of natural disasters. *Indian Journal of Health and Wellbeing, 4*(6), 1317–1319.

Sekar, K., Jayakumar, C., & Jude, P. (2023). *National disaster management training module-2, psychosocial care in disasters* (First). NDMA, NIMHANS.

Solomon, S. D., Bravo, M., Rubio-Stipec, M., & Canino, G. (1993). Effect of family role on response to disaster. *Journal of Traumatic Stress, 6*(2), 255–269. https://doi.org/10.1002/jts.2490060208

Sonawat, R. (2001). Understanding families in India: A reflection of societal changes. *Psicologia: Teoria e Pesquisa, 17*(2), 177–186. https://doi.org/10.1590/S0102-37722001000200010

Tedeschi, R. G., & Calhoun, L. G. (2004). Posttraumatic growth: Conceptual foundations and empirical evidence. *Psychological Inquiry, 15*(1), 1–18. Routledge. https://doi.org/10.1207/s15327965pli1501_01

The Sphere Project. (2011). *The Sphere Project, Sphere handbook: Humanitarian charter and minimum standards in disaster response*. The Sphere Project.

Thomas, V., & Priest, J. B. (2016). Family therapy. In *Encyclopedia of mental health: Second edition* (pp. 235–239). https://doi.org/10.1016/B978-0-12-397045-9.00179-8

Thurston, A. M., Stöckl, H., & Ranganathan, M. (2021). Natural hazards, disasters and violence against women and girls: A global mixed-methods systematic review. *BMJ Global Health, 6*(4). https://doi.org/10.1136/bmjgh-2020-004377

Walsh, F. (2007). Traumatic loss and major disasters: Strengthening family and community resilience. *Family Process, 46*(2), 207–227. https://doi.org/10.1111/j.1545-5300.2007.00205.x

Watson, W. H. (2012). Family systems. In *Encyclopedia of human behavior: Second edition* (pp. 84–193). https://doi.org/10.1016/B978-0-12-375000-6.00169-5

Wiest, R. E., Mocellin, J. S. P., & Thandiwe Motsisi, D. (1994). *The needs of women in disasters and emergencies*. Disaster Research Institute, University of Manitoba.

Part II

Learning from PSSMHS Interventions in Different Disasters

8

Learnings from Bhopal Gas Tragedy: Psychosocial Impacts and Interventions

S. Harshavardhini and Subhasis Bhadra

Introduction

The Bhopal gas tragedy has been classified as one of the worst industrial disasters in the world due to the staggering loss of life and enduring, visible consequences it inflicted upon the affected individuals and their community. The fatal evening of December 2, 1984 witnessed the abrupt end of thousands of lives, as a noxious plume of methyl isocyanate (MIC) gas emanated from the Union Carbide India Limited plant, enshrouding adjacent communities in a suffocating veil. Immediately following the catastrophic event, approximately 3800 individuals succumbed to its lethal effects, while reports indicate that the total death toll due to the exposure to the toxic gas has since climbed to around 20,000 over the years (Broughton, 2005). Furthermore, an estimated 200,000 individuals continue to grapple with the toxic aftermath of the exposure. While

S. Harshavardhini • S. Bhadra (✉)
Department of Psychosocial Support in Disaster Management, NIMHANS, Bengaluru, Karnataka, India

S. Bhadra et al. (eds.), *Psychosocial and Mental Health Support for Disaster Management in India*, Palgrave Studies in Disaster Science and Emergency Management,
https://doi.org/10.1007/978-3-032-02511-1_8

the physical health impacts, including those on anatomy and physiological functioning, have garnered significant attention and study, the tragedy's repercussions extend far beyond the realm of bodily harm. It has profoundly eroded the sociocultural fabric of the region and inflicted profound mental health and psychosocial distress upon those affected. Moreover, the Bhopal gas tragedy has starkly illuminated the pre-existing societal inequalities, exposed deficiencies in government post-disaster management and compensation protocols, and underscored the inadequacies in professional preparedness and mental health awareness within relevant sectors.

Unpacking the Tragedy

The Union Carbide Plant in Bhopal, established in 1969, was its fourteenth. The Union Carbide Company (UCC), with encouragement from the Indian Government to establish and invest in local industries, set up a plant to manufacture Sevin, a pesticide. Union Carbide India Limited (UCIL), a subsidiary of UCC, was established in which the Indian government also had a 22% stake (Broughton, 2005). The Bhopal plant was originally established to import, package, and distribute raw fertilizers and pesticides in India and other East Asian countries. In 1980, the company decided to convert it into a manufacturing unit because of financial concerns and planned to build a production unit within it for aforementioned reasons (Riddle, 2002; Broughton, 2005). While local officials expressed their objections upon hearing the news, many in the area were anticipating the employment opportunities that would arise from the expansion of the plant. By 11:00 PM on December 2, 1984, a plant operator had detected a minor leakage of MIC gas and noted a rise in pressure within a storage tank. This leakage occurred as UCIL made plans to dismantle key production units of the facility, intending to relocate them to another country due to declining profitability, and thereby leading to the substandard operation of safety procedures and equipment. Safety mechanisms, including the vent-gas scrubber to neutralize toxic discharges and the refrigeration unit to cool the storage tank, as well as the gas flare safety system, were not operational (Srivastava, 1987 &

Fortun, 2001 as mentioned in Broughton, 2005; Bowonder, 1987). Compounding the situation, a faulty valve allowed approximately one ton of water, used for cleaning pipes, to mix with over forty tons of MIC.

Prior to the chemical leak incident, recommendations had been made by the safety inspection team and safety experts to establish a warning system that would alert the communities in the vicinity in the event of a chemical leak, and an evacuation plan to evacuate the local residents in the event of a mishap. However, these recommendations were not conveyed to the local officials and necessary steps were not taken to put them into action (Riddle, 2002). It should be noted that the plant officials implemented many of the changes suggested by the safety inspection team, and the plant did not experience any notable chemical leaks at the time. However, with increasing economic strain on the company and growing competition, the officials began to cut costs in areas that they deemed safe, such as patching leaky pipes rather than replacing them (Riddle, 2002). Key positions in the plant were filled by underqualified individuals. It is reported that employees also demonstrated strikes in response to how safety issues concerning the employees were handled (Riddle, 2002). Reports of negligence to safety concerns and the lack of prompt response to, and stringent investigations of, leaks by plant workers, officials and the company are also documented (Diamond, 1985; Riddle, 2002; Bowonder, 1987). Amidst the process of industrialization and the encouraging foreign investments in local industries, the Indian Government did not put in place adequate laws and policies that rigorously regulate and monitor industries and concerned safety issues (Broughton, 2005).

Around 1 AM, the safety valve failed, releasing a plume of MIC gas into the air. Almost 3800 individuals reportedly succumbed immediately, predominantly comprising residents of the impoverished slum colony nearby the plant. Local hospitals found themselves inundated with affected individuals, exacerbated by limited understanding of the gas and its consequences (Broughton, 2005). More than 500,000 people were impacted by the toxic gas leak, with subsequent studies revealing the severity of its effects. In March 1985, the Indian government passed the Bhopal Gas Leak Disaster Act to expedite the fair resolution of accident-related claims. The act designated the government as the victims' primary advocate in courts both domestically and internationally. Gradually, all legal matters related to the disaster were transferred completely to the Indian jurisdiction from the American legal system. Ultimately, Union Carbide Corporation (UCC) acknowledged moral responsibility for the incident, agreeing to pay $470 million to the Indian government for distribution as compensation. This amount was agreed on based on the claim that only 3000 individuals died and around 1 lakh individuals experienced permanent disabilities. By late October 2003, the Bhopal Gas Tragedy Relief and Rehabilitation Department reported compensating 554,895 individuals for injuries and 15,310 survivors of the deceased. The average compensation granted to families of the deceased totaled $2200 (Kumar, 2004). However, this figure may not accurately reflect the true extent of those affected, as narratives from individuals reveal that those without proper documentation, or who had lost their documents, were unable to access compensation despite being impacted. Moreover, the amount paid by the UCC is also thought to be inadequate and meager given the extensive damage suffered by those surrounding the plant (Kumar, 2004).

Risk Perception and Safety Negligence

Risk perception, within the disaster management context, includes awareness, beliefs, and attitudes regarding the likelihood and seriousness of the threat. An individual's attitude reflects how the individual perceives the threat (Bodas et al., 2022). Literature has shown that risk perception is a key element of safety (Zhao et al., 2021). In addition to the attitude toward the threat, attitude toward the safety of others and oneself also plays a crucial role in ensuring preparedness for any incident. Research shows that safety attitude, safety knowledge, and leadership all have an impact on the risk perception, particularly among industrial workers (Zhao et al., 2021). In the events preceding the accident, it was evident that the safety of the equipment and workers were not taken seriously enough (Riddle, 2002). Despite multiple warnings from safety inspections, there was a lack of action, and substandard operations resulted from cost-cutting measures implemented by plant officials and the company. These cost-cutting measures also led to the hiring of unqualified individuals for important positions, indicating that there may have been a lack of training and awareness about safety concerns and protocols among the employees. Accounts also reveal a lax attitude on the part of the workers, supervisors and the company toward potential safety threats. An analysis of the Bhopal gas tragedy revealed failures at multiple levels. It identified management, technical, operator, and government failures. The basic causes of these failures included poor perception of the risk involved, poor risk assessment practices, poor safety concern at a corporate level, poor training, failure to equip the plant for the required level of safety, and failing to perceive the seriousness of the risk. This indicates that the risk perception was low at multiple levels, particularly at the corporate level, where there was negligence in addressing safety concerns even after being made aware of them.

This negligence of safety concerns and operation of the plant at substandard conditions compared to its American counterparts can be discussed in the context of regulatory arbitrage. Regulatory arbitrage includes organizing practices by the corporate or firm to profit from gaps or loopholes in regulations or laws (Pollman, 2019). The company allowed the plant to function at substandard conditions, taking into advantage the underdeveloped and weak regulatory environment in India, a developing nation. When the UCC was taken to court by the Government of India, they paid a meager settlement compared to the damage caused. Broughton (2005) compared this result to a similar incident in the US, where UCC faced legal action related to asbestos mining. He noted that if the Bhopal victims had been compensated at the same rate as the asbestosis victims in the US, total compensation would have exceeded 10 billion dollars, compared to the 470 million dollars that was actually paid out. Furthermore, after UCC ceased operations at the Bhopal plant following the tragedy, they did not clean up the site completely (Broughton, 2005). This highlights how developing nations, laws, and their people are exploited in such situations. In this context, the concepts of environmental justice and environmental racism are relevant to the Bhopal gas tragedy. Environmental racism refers to the disproportionate burden and the impact of environmental hazards on communities of color, often due to disadvantageous laws and regulations. The principle of environmental justice asserts that all individuals and communities are entitled to the same environmental protections and benefits (Mohai et al., 2009). It is evident that the Bhopal gas tragedy and its aftermath was plagued with environmental injustices, with various violations apparent.

Bhopal Gas Tragedy: a Complex Emergency

Complex emergencies are crises that follow a disaster or conflict that are human-made, resulting from social, medical, and political circumstances. These crises may include mass displacement, food insecurity, public health crisis, increased incidence of communicable diseases, such as diarrhea, malaria, respiratory illnesses, etc., and non-communicable diseases, such as mental health problems and reproductive issues (Bartels et al., 2016). Bhopal gas tragedy, although initially a chemical leak incident, led to various complications and crisis. The overwhelming of the public healthcare system and the uncertainty of the chemical leaked, led to numerous individuals not being able to access healthcare and receive timely treatment. Malnutrition was also observed in the weeks following the tragedy (ICMR, 2004). The disposal of chemical waste, even prior to the disaster, had left the water contaminated, requiring government intervention even two decades after the incident (*Water Contamination Crisis—Bhopal's Second Disaster*, n.d.). Additionally, food insecurity may have been prevalent, especially among the poor, who were disproportionately affected. Many were unable to work and had the burden of healthcare expenses (Sourav, 2019; Riddle, 2002).

Various studies have been conducted over the years to comprehend the impact of the MIC gas leak. These studies have consistently identified issues affecting the respiratory, cardiovascular, gastrointestinal, and musculoskeletal systems of those affected. Furthermore, research indicates the prevalence of mental health issues and psychosocial challenges as a consequence of this disaster. Long-term studies have also been undertaken to investigate the lasting health and mental health effects on individuals affected by the tragedy. These findings underscore the profound and multifaceted repercussions of the tragedy.

Impact of the Tragedy

Health Impacts

The health impact of the Bhopal gas tragedy represents one of the most extensively studied areas post-disaster, characterized by its visibility and profound effects. This encompasses a spectrum of both short-term and long-term health consequences. Various studies have documented the health impacts in the acute and subacute phases, occurring within one to six months post-disaster, as well as those observed in the chronic phase. A technical report on the health effects caused due to the disaster was published by the Indian Council of Medical Research for the period of 1984–1994. The report presented that the mortality rate in the most severely affected area was highest across all age groups compared to other affected regions (ICMR, 2004). It is reported that about 75% of the deaths occurred within the first two or three days. Across the affected region, regardless of the severity of exposure, most deaths were accounted to unknown causes in 1986. Individuals exposed experienced acute toxic gas inhalation injury leading to acute ocular symptoms, including intense irritation, burning, swelling, and blurred vision (ICMR, 2004). Autopsies revealed that the acute toxic gas inhalation had also resulted in damages in multiple organ systems (ICMR, 2004). Respiratory symptoms encompassed breathlessness, chest pain, severe dry cough, pulmonary edema, distress, and pneumonitis (ICMR, 2004). Gastrointestinal symptoms consisted of persistent diarrhea, anorexia, and abdominal pain, while immunological effects and reproductive issues ranged from spontaneous miscarriages and perinatal mortality to menstrual irregularities (Andersson et al., 1988; Dhara, 1994). Furthermore, it is reported that the abortion rate rose to about 50% in the severely affected area immediately after the disaster in 1984. General symptoms, such as muscle weakness, sleepiness, loss of appetite, nausea, vomiting, and fever, were also reported. Radiological studies also suggested that old pathologies in individuals were aggravated post the gas exposure (Gupta et al., 1988). Additionally, acute psychological and neurological symptoms, detailed in the subsequent paragraphs, were noted (Mishra et al., 2009).

A review paper examined clinical and experimental findings spanning a 25-year period following the disaster. Along with the acute health issues experienced, it also documented studies conducted six months after the gas-exposure tragedy. Chronic ocular effects included damage to the posterior ocular chamber, corneal opacity, conjunctivitis, chronic lesions, and deficiency of tear secretion (Mishra et al., 2009). Respiratory complications encompassed cough, chest pain, wheezing, lowered lung functions, obstructions in airways, and acute bronchio-alveolitis (Cullinan et al., 1997; Kamat et al., 1987; De, 2012). Chronic reproductive issues consisted of increased pregnancy loss, infant mortality, and decreased placental/fetal weight. The post-accident pregnancy loss rate of 43% in Bhopal is three to four times higher than the average rate of spontaneous abortion (Varma, 1987). Immunological changes led to hyper-responsiveness of the immune system in in-utero-exposed individuals. Additionally, there was a marginal increase in oropharynx cancer and growth retardation in exposed adolescent males (Dikshit & Kanhere, 1999; Mishra et al., 2009). Chronic psychological and neurological impairments, such as defective cognitive function, motor speed precision, and muscle aches, were also reported (Gupta et al., 1988). While mental health and psychosocial impacts did not receive immediate attention, there was a recognition of the urgent need to address these issues, leading to subsequent studies in the field of mental health.

Mental Impacts

When the Advisory Committee on Mental Health of the ICMR convened in mid-December 1984, they deliberated on the various mental health needs arising from the recent disaster in Bhopal. The committee recognized the necessity to address both short-term and long-term service needs and research initiatives. The immediate aftermath of a disaster demanded urgent attention to manage confusion, anxiety, and grief. But the journey to recovery extended far beyond, requiring long-term support for those facing chronic impacts, future uncertainties, and the fragmented social fabric (Murthy & Isaac, 1987). Following the recommendations advanced by the Advisory Committee, initial assessments were conducted eight weeks after the disaster, in the first week of February 1985, by Prof. R. Srinivasa Murthy from NIMHANS, Bangalore, and Prof. B.B. Sethi from KG Medical College, Lucknow. It estimated that mental health issues affected approximately 50% of the community and about 20% of clinic attendees. These assessments involved visiting affected individuals in their homes and examining those seeking care at medical facilities (Murthy, 1990).

Subsequently, a team of psychiatrists, led by Dr Srinivasa Murthy from NIMHANS, Bangalore, and Dr B.B. Sethi from KG Medical College, Lucknow, embarked on a study to understand the acute mental health needs and the provision of mental health services (Murthy & Isaac, 1987). The team identified four categories of mental health needs among the victims of the gas leak: post-traumatic stress disorder (PTSD), pathological grief reactions, emotional reactions to physical problems, and pre-existing psychiatric issues. Within the PTSD category, individuals experienced a range of issues, including anxiety, depression, panic, re-experiencing the disaster, fear, insecurity, changes in sleep and appetite, somatic complaints, impaired cognitive functions such as forgetfulness and difficulty concentrating, as well as general fatigue and weakness. Pathological grief reactions were identified as the most severe emotional consequences for individuals who lost loved ones. These reactions were marked by intense feelings of depression and grief, accompanied by symptoms such as sleep disturbances, suicidal ideation, lack of interest in daily activities, a pessimistic view of the future, and impairments in personal, social, and vocational functioning. Emotional reactions to physical disability resulting from gas exposure were also noted, with individuals experiencing greater emotional distress, including depression, hostility, helplessness, and fear for the future, corresponding to the severity of their physical problems. Additionally, individuals with pre-existing psychiatric conditions exhibited an exacerbation of their pre-existing symptoms. To address these acute mental health needs, a training module was developed to educate medical officers on mental health needs and interventions, as discussed in the subsequent section.

Building upon the initial investigation by Murthy and Isaac (1987), which delineated the acute mental health needs of the gas leak survivors, Sethi et al. (1987) further delved into the longitudinal psychiatric morbidity among those seeking medical care, providing a comprehensive understanding of the evolving mental health challenges over a three-month period. The study conducted by Sethi et al. (1987) aimed to comprehend the psychiatric morbidity among affected individuals seeking medical care over a three-month period. It revealed a spectrum of mental health challenges, including depression, anxiety, and adjustment reactions, experienced by survivors of the tragedy. Data collection occurred through two methods: firstly, a randomized screening of patients at ten government clinics on three occasions to identify psychiatric morbidity among incoming patients, and secondly, through psychiatric services provided at a government clinic—Chhola Road Polyclinic, situated in one of the severely affected areas—where all patients underwent mental health screening. The randomized assessment of outpatients across the ten clinics showed that 22.6% of the screened population grappled with mental health issues. Of these, approximately 37.3% were diagnosed with neurotic depression, 24.9% exhibited symptoms of anxiety, and about 35.2% manifested adjustment reactions. The authors also observed that psychosis was uncommon among the general population. The data obtained from the Chhola Road Polyclinic similarly revealed mental health issues being experienced by survivors. Out of the 208 patients who visited the clinic, 94 were identified as having mental health disorders. Of these, 45.2% were diagnosed with neurotic depression, 34.7% with anxiety states, 9.2% with adjustment reactions, and 2.4% with hysteria. The majority of patients in this study were female (73.6%) and under the age of 45 (78.8%). However, the authors themselves note that this finding does not accurately represent the true morbidity of the population, as only clinic-based data was utilized and only severely ill individuals would seek medical attention at hospitals. Additionally, the narratives of individuals who had lost trust and hope in government healthcare institutions at that time further underscore this limitation (Kapoor, 1992; Amnesty International, 2004). These narratives revealed that some individuals preferred not to seek care at government hospitals.

The researchers also highlight the atypical symptom profiles observed in the diagnosed conditions. These include nighttime sleep disturbances, distinct from daytime patterns, as well as feelings of grief and despair. Patients presented with a variety of somatic symptoms, particularly related to breathing difficulties and eye complaints, along with general listlessness and fatigue. Many expressed constant fear regarding potential organ damage. Additionally, patients exhibited symptoms indicative of re-experiencing the traumatic event, including recurrent intrusive recollections, nightmares, and apprehension of another disaster. The authors attributed the breadth of mental health issues to various psychosocial factors, such as distress stemming from actual and perceived physical disabilities, uncertainty about the future, fractured social support networks, and the grief and loss associated with reduced capacity to work and earn. They emphasized the need for long-term studies, as they would be vital in ascertaining the course and the outcomes of the mental health issues experienced by the survivors.

In 1985, Gupta et al. (1988) conducted comprehensive clinical, radiological, and behavioral studies involving 1109 affected individuals. A team of specialists conducted thorough history-taking, clinical examinations, and radiological assessments, while also administering behavioral tests to evaluate various cognitive and personality aspects, such as auditory and visual memory retention, perceptual motor speed and coordination and non-intellectual personality disturbances. Clinical examinations unveiled prevalent symptoms pertaining to the respiratory, cardiovascular, gastrointestinal, and musculoskeletal systems among the subjects. Additionally, findings indicated a significantly higher incidence of respiratory and gastrointestinal issues among those residing within four kilometers of the plant. In radiological examinations, 10% of the subjects displayed radiological alterations indicative of distinct pathological conditions, encompassing pulmonary tuberculosis, pneumonitis, and emphysema. However, radiological findings in 17 subjects indicated evidence of pre-existing conditions, which were further exacerbated by exposure to the gas.

The behavioral tests uncovered severe impairment in memory, visual perception, attention/response speed, and attention/vigilance among the exposed population. Further examination revealed that memory deficits were more pronounced in females than in males; however, immediate memory was found to be lower in males compared to females in tests of visual memory. Overall, the exposed group exhibited significantly poorer performance compared to the control group, with attention/vigilance and attention response being notably impaired in the affected population.

Commencing in June 1985, a subsequent extensive community-level epidemiological study spanned five years, focusing on the assessment and monitoring of survivors. Prior to its initiation, a new census of the total population was conducted. The study encompassed populations exposed to the disaster to varying degrees, including a control group situated far from the affected area but within the same city. Household heads were interviewed annually to identify symptoms using a standardized checklist, and a qualified psychiatrist then assessed and diagnosed the symptoms using the ICD-9 criteria. Each year, a new set of families was included in the sample, alongside follow-up assessments of patients diagnosed in the preceding years. Findings from the first year of the survey, which involved approximately 4098 adults from 1201 households, revealed that approximately 94 individuals per 1000 were diagnosed with mental health disorders. The majority of the population comprised females (71%) and individuals aged between 16 and 45 (83%). In alignment with findings from other mental health studies, the majority of the population (94%) received a diagnosis of neurosis, with neurotic depression at 51%, anxiety state at 41%, and hysteria at 2%, and demonstrated a temporal correlation. The study highlighted a significantly higher prevalence of psychiatric disorders in the affected population compared to the general population. This relationship between higher rates of psychiatric morbidity and the severity of exposure to the poisonous gas persisted throughout the five years of the survey period. Nevertheless, by the conclusion of the five-year period, only a small number had fully recovered, while a substantial portion continued to endure symptoms alongside significant disability in functioning (Basu & Murthy, 2003). The narratives provided by individuals quoted in the paper unveiled accounts of various behavioral changes, memory difficulties, irritability, aggressive behavior, anxiety, mild episodic depression, apprehension about the future, functional aphonia, incoherent speech, and behaviors resembling disconnection from reality (possibly including delusions) following the gas leak. The authors observed a lack of instances where individuals received proper and continuous treatment. None of the narratives indicated that, despite ongoing issues, individuals were met with empathy and care, which they likely anticipated. Additionally, the authors noted widespread psychosocial isolation among families affected by the tragedy. After reviewing all the recordings, the researchers felt as if "Bhopal is suffering from a kind of emotional bluntness toward the survivors affected by mental illnesses" (Basu & Murthy, 2003, p. 1080).

Long-Term Mental Health Impacts

In January 1994, a study conducted nine years after the disaster involved 474 subjects, with 76 undergoing comprehensive neurological examinations, including assessments for short-term memory, vestibular function, and peripheral sensory function. A significant portion of the subjects exhibited various neuropsychiatric symptoms, such as abnormal smell, taste, dizziness, headaches, drowsiness, and impaired balance. Headaches were reported by 80% of the subjects, compared to 50% in the control group. Neurological examinations revealed a considerable number of individuals displaying clinical signs of central, peripheral, or vestibular neurological disorders. Furthermore, heavily exposed individuals exhibited the lowest mean scores for short-term memory and demonstrated evidence of impaired extrapyramidal functions. Abnormalities were also observed in vertical drawing tests among the exposed group. Reported psychological symptoms encompassed fatigue (88%), anxiety (65%), difficulty maintaining focus (64%), and challenges in decision-making (80%), while irritability was reported by 33% of the subjects, in contrast to none in the control group. A consistent trend was evident across various exposure groups for all symptoms except depression, with around 25% experiencing depressive symptoms (Cullinan et al., 1996).

Although the focus on the victims of the Bhopal gas tragedy gradually diminished during the late 1990s and 2000s, some initiatives and activities persisted, albeit at a reduced scale compared to the extensive efforts seen in the 1980s and 1990s (Murthy, 2014). The National Institute for Research in Environmental Health (NIREH) was established in Bhopal in 2010. The institute's mental health studies aimed to comprehend the ongoing mental health requirements of the population and develop a training program and manual to educate general medical officers in mental healthcare. Their mental health initiatives included a follow-up assessment of psychiatric patients from 1985 to 1994, revealing the chronic nature of mental disorders in many patients and the limited mental healthcare they received. Additionally, a study conducted in 2012 aimed to ascertain the prevalence of mental disorders, involving 500 families. Utilizing a two-stage screening approach for mental disorders, the study revealed that around 20% of participants exhibited indications of potential mental disorders. Moreover, elevated rates were noted among individuals confronting socioeconomic hardships and those with underlying medical conditions (Murthy, 2014).

According to Murthy (2014), the mental health needs identified in 2014 encompass several categories: (1) Individuals experiencing post-disaster mental health conditions, such as anxiety, depression, adjustment disorder conditions, and PTSD, that is directly linked to the 1984 disaster; (2) Individuals with psychiatric disorders stemming from various life changes, familial, and occupational disruptions directly and indirectly related to the disaster experiences; (3) Individuals grappling with chronic physical ailments which may lead to associated psychiatric conditions; and (4) Individuals contending with psychiatric disorders unrelated to the disaster.

Psychosocial Impacts

The repercussions of a disaster are particularly harsh on marginalized communities, with women bearing a disproportionate burden due to longstanding social inequalities (Kapoor, 1992). The health and mental health impacts of the events were accompanied by significant sociocultural challenges, further exacerbating the mental distress experienced by individuals. Documented narratives reveal that those affected often incurred substantial debts due to healthcare expenses (Sourav, 2019; Riddle, 2002). It is important to note that the poorest were most severely affected by the disaster due to the position of the plant and the wind direction (Amnesty International, 2004). The most severely hit locality, J.P. Colony, was reportedly home to many Muslim and lower-caste Hindu families (Khare, 1987). According to the report released by ICMR on the studies conducted (2004), between 68 and 86% of the population were from "very depressed socio-economic status," and more than 70% of the population lived in poor-quality houses. After the tragedy, many individuals lost their livelihood and suffered reduced income due to the inability to work. According to a survey, about 65% of the individuals experienced a reduction in their income by 20–100% (Medico Friend Circle, 1985).

These financial burdens not only detrimentally affected current living standards but also jeopardized the future prospects of families, particularly regarding children's education and subsequent opportunities. Additionally, accounts highlight the pervasive issue of gender-based and domestic violence within households. Women who were unable to conceive or bear children following the gas exposure encountered various social obstacles, including explicit instances of domestic abuse perpetrated by their husbands and hostility from in-laws. Narratives depict scenarios where husbands blamed their wives for the loss of their sons or engaged in conflicts due to misconceptions regarding infertility, further contributing to women's mental distress. While the narratives may not explicitly delineate the mental health condition of women in these circumstances, it is reasonable to infer that such experiences induced significant distress, particularly stemming from the inability to conceive.

The shift from the expected maternal role to one of loss, coupled with sociocultural norms emphasizing women's identity as mothers and nurturers, likely intensified the stress experienced by these women. Accounts also detail women's desires to reverse sterilization procedures and their insecurities regarding future spousal roles, underscoring the societal significance attached to their identities as mothers and nurturers. Additionally, the mistreatment endured from husbands and in-laws likely exacerbated their psychological burden. Stories from women highlighted challenges related to reproductive health, miscarriage, and infertility, yet their struggles were dismissed with a mere certification of well-being (certificate B), depriving them of their rightful compensation and exacerbating their vulnerability to hostility and ostracization from their in-laws (Kapoor, 1992). Furthermore, some individuals grappled with the absence of partners and prolonged separation from family members and children before eventual reunification. Remarriages among women were also noted, primarily driven by considerations of social security and the welfare of their children (Kapoor, 1992; Basu & Murthy, 2003).

Children also faced a profound and multifaceted impact, as they endured the trauma of separation from loved ones, witnessed death and destruction, and were thrust into roles as caretakers for surviving siblings (Sourav, 2019). Many lost access to education due to both financial constraints and health issues caused by the disaster, leaving a lasting sense of regret and longing for opportunities lost (Riddle, 2002).

Therefore, it becomes evident that these health and mental health impacts should not be perceived in isolation, but rather as factors that generate psychosocial dysfunctions in an individual's life. The World Health Organisation Disability Assessment Schedule 2.0 (WHODAS) (Üstün et al., 2010) assesses disability in seven domains—Understanding and Communicating, Getting Around, Self-Care, Getting Along with People, Life activities— Household, Life activities—School/Work, and Participation in Life. Although the studies undertaken post Bhopal gas tragedy did not directly assess the functional disability of individuals, findings from the abovementioned studies indicate the individuals would have fulfilled criteria for items under each of the sections of WHODAS 2.0. Studies conducted by Gupta et al. (1988) and Cullinan et al. (1996) have elucidated that populations exposed to toxic gas experienced cognitive deficits, including impairment in memory, difficulties in maintaining focus, and compromised decision-making abilities. Likewise, a multitude of narratives have been documented demonstrating memory challenges and an inability to recall, which significantly impact their day-to-day lives, work, and education (Basu & Murthy, 2003). Physical ailments resulting from gas exposure, such as hypotonia and weakness of limbs, particularly among children, would likely have contributed to functional difficulties in mobility (Sourav, 2019). Studies have also identified instances and narratives of loss of self-care as a result of the mental health challenges and disorders that individuals experienced (Basu & Murthy, 2003). Narratives also illustrate that the Bhopal gas tragedy led to a breakdown of the social fabric, causing individuals to lose their understanding of social obligations, roles, and responsibilities within their families and communities. This breakdown also created difficulties in their relationships (Kapoor, 1992; Basu & Murthy, 2003).

Accounts of individuals' household activities, livelihood and educational activities being affected due to physical health, mental health, and economic consequences of gas exposure have been documented (Riddle, 2002; Basu & Murthy, 2003; Sourav, 2019). Likewise, narratives detailing compromised self-esteem and confidence resulting from physical ailments shed light on the challenges individuals encountered due to the attitudes and actions of others, thereby exposing impediments to their participation in and integration into society (Kapoor, 1992). Additionally, numerous accounts attest to the significant economic and emotional ramifications of individuals' physical health, which may have hindered their ability to engage in societal activities (Sourav, 2019). Hence, although explicit studies have not been conducted to assess the functional disability of individuals during that period, it is reasonable to presume that individuals would have experienced functional disability, considering the indicators outlined in WHODAS 2.0.

Social Trauma

The Bhopal gas tragedy not only inflicted individual pain, both physical and psychological, but also shattered the fabric of the society. Social institutions were disrupted, and the healthcare system was overwhelmed, uncertain of the cause and treatment for the pain individuals were experiencing. There was a destruction of the social infrastructure, leading to an array of psychosocial issues. Social trauma is of two types: Collective and Cultural (Abrutyn, 2023). Collective trauma occurs when a group of individuals collectively endure or hold a collective memory of a horrific event that leaves a lasting mark (Abrutyn, 2023; Hirschberger, 2018). These events that result in social trauma can be assessed based on the magnitude, intensity or extent, temporality, and material, social, psychological and cultural resources that are available (Abrutyn, 2023). It also results in a crisis of meaning and involves reconstruction of the incident to understand and make some sense of it (Hirschberger, 2018). Cultural trauma goes a step further to address the "collective identity," encompassing collective traumas that fundamentally alter the future identity of the group (Abrutyn, 2023; Alexander et al., 2004). The survivors of the

Bhopal gas tragedy have a shared experience of fear, loss, and suffering, both from the disaster and from the injustices that ensued. The event had a lasting impact on the affected, with its effects still visible today. The event altered the identity of the individuals affected and of the city itself. Individual identities were altered with loss and shifting roles and transformed their social identities due to their inability to work and losing livelihoods. Bhopal, an industrial center, is now associated with the tragic incident and industrial accident (Khare, 1987). The Bhopal gas tragedy is a defining moment in the city's history. Survivors and their descendants hold a collective memory of the incident, remembering the disaster through memorials, protests, arts, and writings.

The enduring repercussions of the disaster and ongoing efforts to advocate for justice on behalf of those affected persist. Mandal and Rahman (2021) draw attention to the ongoing struggles faced by survivors of the Bhopal gas tragedy amidst the backdrop of the COVID-19 pandemic in their article. In line with the injustice faced by the Bhopal gas tragedy survivors in subsequent years of the disasters, the authors bring to the forefront the lack of attention paid to the Bhopal gas tragedy survivors amidst the COVID-19 pandemic. The majority of deaths reported in Bhopal due to COVID-19 were of Bhopal gas tragedy survivors. Survivors of the tragedy were already suffering from a range of physical issues, especially respiratory issues, making them more vulnerable to the coronavirus. They also highlight the possible psychological distress experienced by the survivors who were experiencing yet another catastrophe, emphasizing on the feelings of anxiety, helplessness, uncertainty, and fear of death that survivors may be experiencing.

Psychosocial Interventions

Addressing the critical mental health and psychosocial repercussions of the Bhopal gas tragedy required concerted interventions, yet the immediate response was hindered by a shortage of mental health professionals in the region. The direct participation of psychiatrists and neurologists at the field level did not commence until approximately eight weeks following the disaster. According to Basu and Murthy (2003), this delay occurred despite the early acknowledgment, within the first fortnight, of the crucial significance of addressing the mental health effects resulting from the catastrophe. A primary contributing factor to this delay was the scarcity of mental health professionals in Madhya Pradesh and Bhopal. Notably, during that period, none of the five medical colleges boasted a psychiatrist among their faculty.

Mental Health Initiatives

Initial interventions began as a part of research studies to understand the mental health concerns of the affected population. One of the initial interventions provided was part of Sethi et al.'s (1987) research. This study utilized data gathered from an outpatient clinic service provided for mental health. The outpatient clinic service, overseen by a psychiatrist and two social workers, implemented an intake procedure involving the screening of all visiting patients for mental health disorders. However, as the program and its services became more familiar to the community, it was no longer deemed necessary to screen all patients, as individuals began seeking advice from the mental health team proactively (Sethi et al., 1987). Additionally, ten other government outpatient clinics were included in the study. These clinics were randomly visited on three separate occasions by a team consisting of a psychiatrist, a clinical psychologist, and a social worker. The team screened all newly registered patients using the Self-Reporting Questionnaire (SRQ) developed by Harding et al. (1980), and individuals showing signs of probable psychiatric issues were subjected to further evaluation and diagnosis based on the ICD-9 criteria.

The study conducted as part of the follow-up from the ICMR mental health advisory committee meeting aimed to address the shortage of mental health professionals available to meet the extensive mental health needs within communities. It was recognized that medical officers lacked awareness of the emotional needs of disaster victims, resulting in unaddressed psychological impacts (Murthy & Isaac, 1987). Conversations with medical professionals revealed a perception that emotional and psychological issues were attributed to government aid rather than being acknowledged as legitimate concerns. Furthermore, medical officers had not received formal mental health training as part of their initial education. Thus, the training initiative sought to sensitize medical officers to individuals' emotional needs, equipping them with skills to recognize, diagnose, and treat mental health issues, and facilitate appropriate referrals.

The training program consisted of a six-day interactive and practical session, limiting each batch to 20 participants to enhance engagement and personalized attention. Adult learning principles were integrated, utilizing methodologies like lectures and group discussions supported by audio-visual materials. Two consultant psychiatrists, Dr. Srinivasa Murthy and Dr. Mohan K Isaac, led the training, drawing from their experience at NIMHANS, Bangalore. A draft version of the training manual on Counselling for Doctors was developed by Sriram et al. (1990). It covered topics such as emotional responses to severe stress, children's reactions to stress, and emotional reactions to physical ailments. Video presentations assessed participants' psychiatric knowledge before training, featuring interviews with disaster-affected individuals and those with psychiatric disorders.

The psychiatrists conducted hands-on training at healthcare facilities, focusing on interview skills and counseling techniques. Initial sessions included sharing trainees' experiences, followed by discussions on mental health issues in affected communities and distinguishing normal from abnormal behavior. Techniques for interacting with emotionally distressed individuals and conducting mental examinations were taught using audio and video materials. Crucially, trainees discussed challenges faced in outpatient clinics, aided by patient audio and video materials (Murthy & Isaac, 1987). Sessions also addressed children's emotional reactions and responses to physical disabilities and chronic illnesses, incorporating role-plays and recordings of psychotherapy sessions with local patients. Pre- and post-training evaluations were also conducted.

Epidemiological studies conducted to assess the prevalence of mental health issues and disorders can also be seen as interventions aimed at understanding and addressing the mental health of affected populations. For instance, a five-year-long epidemiological study included interviews and diagnoses. Each year, a new set of families was sampled and followed up, along with previous patients. Such studies, which assessed and diagnosed individuals for mental health disorders, also provided interventions within their capacity or referred participants for further care (Basu & Murthy, 2003).

Governmental and Non-governmental Psychosocial Interventions

Following the gas tragedy, non-governmental organizations stepped up to provide support to the affected population. In conjunction with these efforts, the government of Madhya Pradesh also initiated various measures for medical, economic, social, and environmental rehabilitation. The Bhopal Gas Tragedy Relief and Rehabilitation website launched by the Madhya Pradesh government provides information related to the various services that have been delivered to the victims of the tragedy, as well as current services that are being dispatched. The Medical Rehabilitation Programme aimed to provide free medical relief to gas victims. The allocated budget covered construction, equipping, staffing, and the provision of free medicines and medical treatment through super-specialty, specialty, and general medical facilities, as well as dispensaries.

In addition to medical rehabilitation, efforts were made to ensure the economic rehabilitation of the victims from lower socio-economic strata, who constituted a significant portion of the survivors. An Industrial Training Institute was established to provide training to unemployed gas victims, and approximately 152 industrial sheds were constructed to increase employment and provide livelihoods to gas-affected individuals. Various non-governmental organizations have taken over these workshops, offering employment opportunities to gas victims through diverse training and production activities. Additionally, the government allocated four crores for a specialized Economic Rehabilitation Programme aimed at training individuals in traditional art forms such as Zari, Zardoji, Paper Pulp Work, etc. Accounts further illustrate that initiatives like offering employment opportunities, particularly geared toward women, not only offer economic support but also enhance their standing within the family, granting them greater agency in financial matters and increased autonomy over their own bodies (Kapoor, 1992).

The Madhya Pradesh Hasth Shilpa Vikas Nigam Initiative was established for training and skill development purposes. The programme identified four NGOs to provide training to gas victims: Manav Vikas Seva Sangh, Bhopal; Seva Bharati, Madhya Bharat, Bhopal; Rajiv Smriti Gas Peedith Punarwas Kendra, Bhopal; and Gyanoday Educational Society, Bhopal. Following the completion of basic training, a six-month skill development program was launched through the aforementioned organizations, with each center tasked with training 20 gas-affected beneficiaries. Additionally, the initiative identified ten NGOs to provide training in tailoring and Kashidakari. The Madhya Pradesh Women Financial Development Corporation offered training in paper napkin/sanitary napkin production to 600 women gas victims. The Center for Entrepreneurship Development Madhya Pradesh, Bhopal (CEDMAP) was also involved in conducting job-oriented training programs in various trades.

Furthermore, 10 NGOs, already associated with gas relief efforts, were selected for training purposes. In the Second Action Plan for Economic Rehabilitation, Rs. 104 crores were allocated for subsidies to entrepreneurs to establish ventures. However, this plan faced challenges as no organizations or entrepreneurs came forward within the allotted schedules. Responding to the preference of victims for employment over entrepreneurship training, the department issued a call for Expressions of Interest for a "Training cum Employment/Placement" program.

In a similar vein, various measures were introduced for social rehabilitation, including providing pensions of about Rs. 200 per month to widows. Educational facilities and institutions were established, with 11 schools constructed (comprising 5 primary and 6 middle schools) and 6 schools repaired and upgraded. To ensure education for children affected by the gas tragedy, the department repurposed Claims Court Buildings into educational and social institutes, resulting in the establishment of 15 such institutes. Additionally, in 2001, following a decision by the State Advisory Committee for Bhopal gas victims, other vacated Claim Courts were allocated for use by schools, colleges, and other government organizations.

Expectant and nursing mothers, along with children up to 6 years old, received free milk (150 ml per person per day) through 5 Integrated Child Development Services (ICDS) projects, covering 792 Anganwadis in the town. From 1984 to 2000, support was provided to 27 orphans, and two houses were allocated to orphaned children affected by the gas tragedy. A total of 2486 houses were built and distributed to families of gas victims, who perished due to gas exposure.

Under the second action plan for social rehabilitation, widow pensions were increased to Rs. 1000 per month. Budgets were allocated to improve physical fitness through yoga, construct and upgrade sewage systems in gas-affected areas, and build schools in gas-affected regions, among other initiatives.

In parallel, the gas-affected areas have endured significant environmental losses and ecological degradation. Therefore, to address these issues and to enhance the ecological conditions of these areas, various activities were undertaken for environmental rehabilitation. Some of the initiatives implemented included ensuring the provision of safe drinking water, planting trees, developing green belts and open areas, constructing children's parks, covering and constructing nullahs, paving streets, laying roads, building sewerage/drainage lines, improving water supply schemes, lighting streets, constructing smokeless chulhas, converting dry/open latrines into water flush latrines, and constructing Sulabh Sauchalayas.

In summary, the coordinated efforts of various stakeholders, including governmental bodies, NGOs, and healthcare professionals, were instrumental in addressing the challenges posed by the gas tragedy in Bhopal. These efforts encompassed medical, mental health, economic, social, and environmental rehabilitation initiatives, although they were not implemented in an integrative manner. Upon reflection on the interventions implemented and their resultant outcomes, it is apparent that collaborative efforts and comprehensive planning play vital roles in addressing and mitigating the enduring effects of such calamities and cultivating resilience within communities.

Key Learnings

Necessity for a Strengthened Legal Framework

- Following the tragedy, India enacted various laws to ensure the protection of the environment. After the events of December 3, 1984, there was a notable surge in environmental consciousness and activism across India. The Indian government also aimed to put into action the declaration of the UN Conference on Human Environment of 1972, held in Stockholm. This led to the enactment of the Environment Protection Act (EPA) in 1986, which led to the establishment of the Ministry of Environment and Forests (MoEF) (Broughton, 2005). The MoEF assumed the pivotal role of overseeing the implementation and enforcement of environmental regulations and policies. The EPA, 1986, bolstered the regulations concerning pollution control and environmental protection for hazardous industries by including rules pertaining to the discharge of pollutants, smoke emission, etc. The "Hazardous Waste (Management and Handling) Rules, 1989" was enacted soon after under the EPA, 1986, which details information on the categories of waste and places accountability for proper management and handling of waste.
- The Bhopal gas tragedy emphasized the critical importance of robust disaster preparedness policies. Despite prior safety inspections indicating the necessity for disaster and evacuation plans, the lack of implementation underscored the vulnerability of communities to industrial accidents (Riddle, 2002). This highlighted the imperative for proactive policy development and enforcement to ensure the safety and protection of citizens in the face of potential hazards. The Environment Impact Assessment Notification of 1994 also mandated carrying out an environmental impact assessment of any project before passing them. It instituted "right to know," enabling public hearing where any individual who might be impacted by the project is given the opportunity to be informed about the project and voice any concerns. The National Environment Appellate Authority Act was enacted in 1997 which established an appellate authority tasked with reviewing appeals

on restrictions on areas where the operation of industries or processes are prohibited. Subsequently, the National Green Tribunal was established in 2010, under the National Green Tribunal Act, to ensure efficient and timely resolution of cases pertaining to environment protection and forest conservation.

- Laws to protect the rights of the employees were also established. To protect the welfare and rights of the workers, communities and victims of such industrial accidents, the Indian government enacted and amended deficient laws. The first act passed immediately following the gas tragedy was the Bhopal Gas Leak (Processing of Claims) Act, 1985, which gave central government the power to handle claims stemming from or linked to the Bhopal gas tragedy. It was legislated to ensure the prompt and fair resolution of claims. The Factories Act, 1948, was amended in 1987 to expand the scope from only covering workers to including the public and individuals in the vicinity. Changes to the permissible quantity of hazardous materials, clearly defining responsibilities, revised penalties in case of non-compliance were also addressed during the amendment. In 1991, the Public Liability Insurance Act was passed to introduce an insurance mechanism, aimed at providing assistance to individuals affected by accidents from handling hazardous substances. In 2020, the Occupational Safety, Health, and Working Conditions Code was enacted to modify and subsume laws related to occupational safety, health, and working conditions. This code has subsumed about 13 laws, including the Factories Act, 1948.

A Paradigm Shift Toward Community-Based Care

- The Bhopal gas tragedy underscored a critical need for immediate mental health support for survivors, revealing a significant shortage of mental health professionals. Recognizing this gap, it became evident that existing healthcare professionals could play a vital role if adequately trained in mental health and psychiatric care. Consequently, initiatives were launched to develop training programs tailored to equip healthcare providers with the essential competencies to address mental health challenges among survivors. This incident also marked a pivotal moment in involving first responders, who are not mental health professionals, in disseminating mental health services. In the decades that followed, community-level workers, such as Accredited Social Health Activists (ASHAs), Anganwadi workers, auxiliary nurses and midwives would also be trained in a similar manner to provide psychosocial support to affected community.

- The efforts taken in the aftermath of the tragedy marked an essential step toward extending mental health services to the affected community, acknowledging the imperative to integrate psychological support into disaster response frameworks. Guidelines related to the management of various hazards now also include a section on psychosocial support and mental health. The manual for "Basic Training Course on CBRN Emergency Management for Airport Emergency Handlers" includes a chapter on the medical aspects and psychosocial impact of CBRN Emergency. The chapter includes the various psychological reactions that individuals may experience, and steps to provide psychosocial first aid. Though incremental, it represents progress toward a more comprehensive approach.
- One crucial learning from the Bhopal gas tragedy is the necessity to bring treatment centers to the communities. Thus can be seen as a watershed moment in providing mental healthcare following a disaster. Establishing robust community support systems and rehabilitation programs can significantly improve the lives of affected individuals. By shifting the focus from centralized or tertiary treatment facilities to community-based care, survivors gain access to the ongoing support, resources, and social networks crucial for their recovery. This approach fosters a sense of belonging, empowerment, and resilience within the affected community, promoting long-term healing and holistic well-being. While vulnerable groups did not receive specialized attention at this stage. it laid the groundwork for providing specialized attention to vulnerable groups after a disaster in the years to come.
- The Bhopal gas tragedy underscored the importance of holistic care for survivors' recovery, emphasizing the need to address not only physical but also mental and social well-being. This approach necessitated the collaboration between government agencies and non-governmental organizations to provide a range of support services. This tragedy

stands out as one of the early instances where partnerships between NGOs and government bodies emerged in disaster response and recovery efforts, laying the groundwork for more coordinated and impactful collaborations in subsequent disasters.

Conclusion

In reflecting on the Bhopal gas tragedy, it becomes evident that the aftermath yielded crucial lessons that spurred significant changes in both regulatory frameworks and mental health support systems. The aftermath of the Bhopal gas tragedy highlighted the need to broaden the scope of mental health support beyond traditional medical channels. While mental healthcare during the aftermath of the tragedy focused on identifying mental health issues through medical professionals, the lessons learned paved the way for the development of more comprehensive mechanisms to disseminate psychosocial support and mental health care. These advancements involved engaging various stakeholders beyond healthcare professionals in addressing the psychosocial challenges inherent in disasters and crisis situations, thereby laying the groundwork for more integrative and effective responses to disasters that were to come. Furthermore, the catastrophic nature of the Bhopal gas tragedy underscores the imperative for special regulations and disaster preparedness tailored specifically for chemical disasters. This includes stringent safety protocols, community awareness programs, and emergency response plans designed to mitigate the risks and minimize the impact of such events on both human health and the environment.

References

Abrutyn, S. (2023). The roots of social trauma: Collective, cultural pain and its consequences. *Society and Mental Health/Society and Mental Health*. https://doi.org/10.1177/21568693231213088

Alexander, J. C., Eyerman, R., Giesen, B., Smelser, N. J., & Sztompka, P. (2004). *Cultural trauma and collective identity*. University of California Press.

Amnesty International. (2004). *Clouds of injustice Bhopal disaster 20 years on.* Amnesty International Publications. https://www.amnesty.org/en/documents/asa20/015/2004/en/

Andersson, N., Muir, M. K., Mehra, V., & Salmon, A. G. (1988). Exposure and response to methyl isocyanate: Results of a community based survey in Bhopal. *Occupational and Environmental Medicine, 45*(7), 469–475. https://doi.org/10.1136/oem.45.7.469

Bartels, S., Hall, M., Burkle, F., & Greenough, P. (2016). Complex emergencies. https://doi.org/10.1016/B978-0-323-28665-7.00007-8

Basu, A. R., & Murthy, R. S. (2003). Disaster and mental health: Revisiting Bhopal. *Economic and Political Weekly, 38*(11), 1074–1082. http://www.jstor.org/stable/4413345.

Bodas, M., Peleg, K., Stolero, N., & Adini, B. (2022). Risk Perception of Natural and Human-Made Disasters—CROSS sectional study in eight countries in Europe and beyond. *Frontiers in Public Health, 10*. https://doi.org/10.3389/fpubh.2022.825985

Bowonder, B. (1987). An analysis of the Bhopal accident. *Project Appraisal, 2*(3), 157–168. https://doi.org/10.1080/02688867.1987.9726622

Broughton, E. (2005). The Bhopal disaster and its aftermath: A review. *Environmental Health, 4*(1). https://doi.org/10.1186/1476-069x-4-6

Cullinan, P., Acquilla, S. D., & Dhara, V. R. (1996). Long term morbidity in survivors of the 1984 Bhopal gas leak. *The National Medical Journal of India, 9*(1), 5–10.

Cullinan, P., Acquilla, S., & Dhara, V. R. (1997). Respiratory morbidity 10 years after the Union Carbide gas leak at Bhopal: A cross sectional survey. *BMJ. British Medical Journal, 314*(7077), 338. https://doi.org/10.1136/bmj.314.7077.338

De, S. (2012). Retrospective analysis of lung function abnormalities of Bhopal gas tragedy affected population. *PubMed*. https://pubmed.ncbi.nlm.nih.gov/22446861

Dhara, R. (1994). Health effects of the Bhopal gas leak: A review. *NEW SOLUTIONS: A Journal of Environmental and Occupational Health Policy, 4*(3), 35–48. https://doi.org/10.2190/NS4.3.g

Diamond, S. (1985, January 28). The Bhopal disaster: How it happened. *The New York Times*. https://www.nytimes.com/1985/01/28/world/the-bhopal-disaster-how-it-happened.html

Dikshit, R. P., & Kanhere, S. (1999). Cancer patterns of lung, oropharynx and oral cavity cancer in relation to gas exposure at Bhopal. *Cancer Causes & Control: CCC, 10*(6), 627–636. https://doi.org/10.1023/a:100893022030

Gupta, B. N., Rastogi, S., Chandra, H., Mathur, A., Mathur, N., Mahendra, P. N., Pangtey, B. S., Kumar, S., Kumar, P., & Seth, R. (1988). Effect of exposure to toxic gas on the population of Bhopal: Part I—Epidemiological, clinical, radiological & behavioral studies. *PubMed, 26*(3), 149–160. https://pubmed.ncbi.nlm.nih.gov/3397117

Harding, T., De Arango, V., Baltazar, J. C., Climent, C. E., Ibrahim, H. H. A., Ladrido-Ignacio, L., & Nn, W. (1980). Mental disorders in primary health care: A study of their frequency and diagnosis in four developing countries. *Psychological Medicine, 10*(2), 231–241. https://doi.org/10.1017/s0033291700043993

Hirschberger, G. (2018). Collective trauma and the social construction of meaning. *Frontiers in Psychology, 9*. https://doi.org/10.3389/fpsyg.2018.01441

ICMR. (2004). *Health effects of the toxic gas leak from the union carbide methyl isocyanate plant in Bhopal, technical report on population based long-term clinical studies (1985–1994)*. Indian Council of Medical Research. https://main.icmr.nic.in/sites/default/files/reports/tech_rep_clinical.pdf

Kamat, S. R., Patel, M. H., Kolhatkar, V. P., Dave, A. A., & Mahashur, A. A. (1987). Sequential respiratory changes in those exposed to the gas leak at Bhopal. *The Indian Journal of Medical Research, 86*(Suppl), 20–38.

Kapoor, R. (1992). The psychosocial consequences of an environmental disaster: Selected case studies of the Bhopal gas tragedy. *Population and Environment, 13*(3), 209–215. https://doi.org/10.1007/bf01256416

Khare, R. (1987). The Bhopal Industrial Accident: Anthropological and civic issues. *Anthropology Today, 3*(4), 4. https://doi.org/10.2307/3033214

Kumar, S. (2004). Victims of gas leak in Bhopal seek redress on compensation. *BMJ (Clinical Research ed.), 329*(7462), 366. https://doi.org/10.1136/bmj.329.7462.366-b

Mandal, M., & Rahman, R. (2021). Bhopal disaster gas victims': Trauma before & during the COVID-19 pandemic. *Problemy Ekorozwoju, 16*(2), 51–57. https://doi.org/10.35784/pe.2021.2.06

Medico Friend Circle. (1985). *The Bhopal Disaster Aftermath: An epidemiology and socio-medical survey*. https://mfcindia.org/wp-content/uploads/2023/02/The-Bhopal-Disaster-Aftermath.pdf

Mishra, P. K., Samarth, R. M., Pathak, N., Jain, S. K., Banerjee, S., & Maudar, K. K. (2009). Bhopal Gas Tragedy: Review of clinical and experimental findings after 25 years. *International Journal of Occupational Medicine and Environmental Health, 22*(3). https://doi.org/10.2478/v10001-009-0028-1

Mohai, P., Pellow, D., & Roberts, J. T. (2009). Environmental justice. *Annual Review of Environment and Resources, 34*(1), 405–430. https://doi.org/10.1146/annurev-environ-082508-094348

Murthy, R. S. (1990). Bhopal. *International Journal of Mental Health, 19*(2), 30–35. https://doi.org/10.1080/00207411.1990.11449160

Murthy, R. S. (2014). Mental health of survivors of 1984 Bhopal disaster: A continuing challenge. *Industrial Psychiatry Journal, 23*(2), 86. https://doi.org/10.4103/0972-6748.151668

Murthy, R. S., & Isaac, M. K. (1987). Mental health needs of Bhopal disaster victims & training of medical officers in mental health aspects. *The Indian Journal of Medical Research, 86*(Suppl), 51–58.

Pollman, E. (2019). Tech, regulatory arbitrage, and limits. *European Business Organization Law Review, 20*(3), 567–590. https://doi.org/10.1007/s40804-019-00155-x

Riddle, J. (2002). *Bhopal: Great disasters, reforms and ramifications*. Chelsea House Publishers. https://www.scribd.com/document/457310097/Bhopal-Great-Disasters-Reforms-and-Ramifications

Sethi, B. B., Sharma, M., Trivedi, J. K., & Singh, H. (1987). Psychiatric morbidity in patients attending clinics in gas affected areas in Bhopal. *The Indian Journal of Medical Research, 86*(Suppl), 45–50.

Sourav, S. (2019). Children and disaster: A case of Bhopal gas tragedy. *Indian Anthropologist, 49*(1), 51–65. https://www.jstor.org/stable/26855091.

Sriram, T. G., Chandrashekar, C. R., Isaac, M. K., & Murthy, R. S. (1990). *Manual of counselling for doctors*. National Institute of Mental Health and Neuro Sciences.

Üstün, T. B., Kostanjsek, N., Chatterji, S., & Rehm, J. (2010). *Measuring health and disability: Manual for WHO disability assessment schedule WHODAS 2.0*. World Health Organization.

Varma, D. R. (1987). Epidemiological and experimental studies on the effects of methyl isocyanate on the course of pregnancy. *Environmental Health Perspectives, 72*, 153–157. https://doi.org/10.1289/ehp.8772153

Water Contamination Crisis—Bhopal's Second Disaster. (n.d.). The Bhopal Medical Appeal. https://www.bhopal.org/continuing-disaster/second-poisoning/bhopal-second-poisoning/water-contamination-briefing-paper/

Zhao, Y., Zhang, M., Liu, T., & Mebarki, A. (2021). Impact of safety attitude, safety knowledge and safety leadership on chemical industry workers' risk perception based on Structural Equation Modelling and System Dynamics. *Journal of Loss Prevention in the Process Industries, 72*, 104542. https://doi.org/10.1016/j.jlp.2021.104542

9

Devastation to Recovery: Psychosocial Support and Mental Health Care in the Wake of the 1993 Marathwada Earthquake

Bhavya Muniraju, Anil Hemanna Doddamani, Sanjeev Kumar Manikappa, K. A. Tansa, Urmila Bamney, and Kasi Sekar

Background

India is one of the most disaster-prone countries in the world and faces a lot of natural disasters every year due to climate change, including floods, landslides, earthquakes, droughts, and cyclones. Earthquakes are among the most devastating natural disasters in terms of both human and economic impact, often resulting in widespread physical and psychological consequences (WHO, 1992). Earthquakes bring sudden devastation, aftershock risks, and long-term rebuilding, often triggering mental health problems like depression, anxiety, post-traumatic stress disorder (PTSD),

B. Muniraju • A. H. Doddamani • S. K. Manikappa (✉) • K. A. Tansa • U. Bamney • K. Sekar
Department of Psychosocial Support in Disaster Management, NIMHANS, Bengaluru, Karnataka, India

S. Bhadra et al. (eds.), *Psychosocial and Mental Health Support for Disaster Management in India*, Palgrave Studies in Disaster Science and Emergency Management,
https://doi.org/10.1007/978-3-032-02511-1_9

insomnia, and even substance abuse (Akram et al., 2024). A powerful earthquake (6.4 magnitude) struck Latur, India on September 30, 1993 at 3:56 AM, devastating the Marathwada region of Maharashtra state in India. The epicenter was located near the village of Killari in Latur District. The early morning timing coincided with religious celebrations for the Hindu deity Shiva, resulting in some residents already being awake. The earthquake caused widespread devastation and significant loss of life (Jigyasu, 2001): there were 1220 deaths in Killari alone, over 7500 total fatalities, and 30,000 families were displaced (Comfort, 1995). Latur and Osmanabad districts faced a challenging disaster response due to widespread poverty and illiteracy in the region, resulting in low preparedness at both the community and administrative levels (Comfort, 1995). In many natural or human-induced disasters, psychosocial aspects are often overlooked, which can hinder survivors' ability to recover effectively. Therefore, it is essential to address psychosocial issues in the aftermath of disasters to facilitate healing and resilience.

The National Disaster Management Authority (NDMA) has recognized the importance of psychosocial support and mental health services in disaster management. According to the NDMA, psychosocial support can be defined as a comprehensive intervention aimed at addressing a wide range of psychosocial and mental health problems arising in the aftermath of disasters. These interventions help individuals, families, and groups to build human capacities and restore social cohesion and infrastructure, in addition to maintaining their independence, dignity, and cultural integrity. Psychosocial support helps to reduce the level of actual and perceived stress and to prevent adverse psychological and social consequences amongst disaster-affected communities. Mental health services in disaster interventions are aimed at the identification and management of stress-related psychological signs and symptoms or mental disorders among disaster-affected persons and persons with pre-existing mental health problems. In addition, psychosocial support interventions are aimed at promoting mental health and psychological well-being, and the promotion and prevention of psychological and psychiatric symptoms.

The Psycho-Social Support and Mental Health Services (PSSMHS) can be considered a continuum of the interventions as an important component of general health services in disaster situations. Psychosocial support will comprise of the general interventions related to the larger issues of promoting or protecting psychosocial well-being through relief work, meeting essential needs, restoring social relationships, enhancing coping capacities, and promoting harmony among survivors. The mental health services will comprise of interventions aimed at the prevention or treatment of psychological and psychiatric symptoms or disorders. The overall goal of psychosocial support and mental health services is the restoration of well-being within the disaster-affected community.

Latest Evidence/Situation Analysis

Recent studies have deepened our understanding of the long-term psychological impact of the 1993 Marathwada earthquake, especially in relation to mental health care responses. Although the immediate aftermath involved considerable relief and rehabilitation, it is the mental health consequences and responses that are now receiving greater attention. New data highlight how, over the decades, such disasters leave lasting scars on both individuals and communities. Furthermore, the significance of mental health interventions during such calamities is becoming a growing priority, driven by ongoing humanitarian and public health research (Akram et al., 2024).

In the immediate aftermath of the Latur earthquake, mental health concerns were overshadowed by the overwhelming focus on physical health and material recovery. However, the mental health impact was also profound. Studies indicate increased levels of depression, anxiety, PTSD, and other psychological conditions following the disaster. Research by Akram et al. (2024) suggests that survivors who experienced displacement, loss of life, and property destruction have displayed persistent psychological trauma, further worsened by inadequate long-term care.

Moreover, resource constraints and a lack of culturally appropriate responses were also significant challenges to mental health care at the time (Pande et al., 2000a, 2000b). Recent analyses emphasize the necessity of integrating psychosocial care within the overall disaster response framework, as the gap between physical recovery and mental health restoration remains a pressing issue.

The establishment of the Maharashtra Institute of Mental Health (MIMH) in 1991, prior to the earthquake, proved crucial in addressing these emerging needs. However, despite the state's investment in mental health, gaps persisted. Many professionals lacked the capacity to deliver comprehensive care to the earthquake-affected population due to inadequate resources and training, and a poor outreach infrastructure (Pande et al., 2000a, 2000b). Contemporary studies highlight these gaps, suggesting that mental health care responses, though initiated, were not sustained effectively. Today, researchers and policy-makers advocate for continuous care models, capable of addressing both immediate and long-term mental health needs.

The Marathwada earthquake response demonstrated an early attempt at integrating mental health care into disaster management. Nevertheless, despite the advances made, there remains a critical need for modernized, scalable interventions, particularly those that address cultural sensitivities and promote community-level preparedness. Galson (2009) emphasized the importance of ongoing mental health programs and training for local personnel as critical components of long-term recovery and resilience.

Issues and Concerns

Despite commendable efforts during the 1993 Marathwada earthquake, significant issues and concerns in delivering psychosocial support and mental health care were evident. The following sections detail the key concerns identified, ranging from institutional weaknesses to community-level challenges that affected recovery and resilience in the years following the disaster.

The mental health infrastructure in Maharashtra, although bolstered by the MIMH, was insufficient to meet the needs of the earthquake survivors. One major concern was the lack of mental health professionals with disaster-specific training. Most of the initial responders were untrained in trauma care, leaving many survivors without the appropriate psychosocial support (Pande et al., 2000a, 2000b). Further, healthcare centers were ill-equipped to handle the sheer volume of mental health issues that arose during the crisis.

Resource shortages exacerbated the problems. Limited access to psychiatric medication, therapy services, and psychological first aid hampered the relief efforts. Although international agencies and NGOs provided temporary support, the local health systems lacked the sustainable resources required for long-term care. These resource limitations, along with insufficient outreach, meant that many victims, especially in remote areas, did not receive timely or adequate care (Comfort, 1995).

Cultural insensitivity in mental health service delivery further hindered the effectiveness of care. Many communities in Latur and Osmanabad were unfamiliar with, or reluctant to engage in, modern psychological treatment methods. The social stigma associated with mental health issues created barriers, discouraging people from seeking help (Pande et al., 2000a, 2000b). This issue highlights the need for more culturally sensitive interventions in future disaster responses, including awareness programs and community-based mental health support models.

There was a lack of coordination between governmental agencies, NGOs, and mental health institutions. The state's mental health strategy was not fully integrated into the broader disaster response plan, which led to a fragmentation in services. This disorganization resulted in missed opportunities to provide effective early interventions, which are crucial in minimizing long-term psychological trauma (Comfort, 1995).

Another significant concern was the failure to implement long-term mental health care strategies. Once the initial relief phase ended, mental health services were largely withdrawn. The discontinuity of care left many survivors vulnerable to chronic psychological conditions, with little follow-up to assess their recovery or address ongoing mental health needs (Jigyasu, 2001).

Mental Health Services and Interventions

In the aftermath of the 1993 Marathwada earthquake, mental health and psychosocial interventions were crucial to help communities recover from the invisible wounds of disaster. Recognizing this, several mental health institutions, prominently the Tata Institute of Social Sciences

(TISS), partnered with local organizations to offer a structured, multi-level support system.

1. **Three-Tiered Mental Health Approach:**
   Mental health professionals implemented a three-tiered framework:

   - **General awareness sessions:** These were public talks or community gatherings aimed at educating people about common psychological reactions to disasters. The goal was to normalize distress and reduce stigma.
   - **Group counseling:** Small groups, often based on shared experiences (e.g., women, children, families), were formed to process trauma collectively, facilitating peer support and emotional sharing.
   - **Individual therapy:** Those showing signs of severe distress, such as prolonged grief, PTSD, or depression, were offered one-on-one sessions with trained counselors or psychologists.

   This tiered model allowed for broad coverage while ensuring intensive care for those most in need.
2. **Culturally Sensitive, Trauma-Informed Outreach:**
   Counseling efforts were tailored to local cultures and community dynamics. Special attention was given to women and children, who are often more vulnerable in disaster contexts. Techniques used included:

   - **Storytelling:** A familiar and culturally resonant way to share experiences and emotions.
   - **Art-based expression:** Drawing or painting allowed participants, especially children, to externalize feelings they couldn't verbalize.
   - **Community theatre:** This collective form of expression helped communities reenact, reflect, and process their trauma in a shared space.

   These methods restored normalcy, encouraged grieving, and promoted psychological healing through non-threatening, familiar mediums.

3. **Community-Led Coping Mechanisms:**

   Over time, self-organization among community members played a pivotal role in long-term recovery. Even after the withdrawal of external agencies, informal support networks emerged:

   - **Peer support groups:** Neighbors and relatives met regularly to share, vent, and offer mutual support.
   - **Cooperative rebuilding efforts:** Communities came together to rebuild homes and infrastructure, fostering a sense of purpose and unity.

   This bottom-up approach to recovery is known as community resilience and is often more sustainable than external interventions alone.

Psychosocial Support and Mental Health Services

The Maharashtra Institute of Mental Health, Pune, played a very crucial role in providing psychosocial support and mental services to disaster survivors of the Marathwada earthquake. It initially needed an assessment and understood the situation better, then later came with one proper care plan like short-term and long-term services. The short-term plan aimed to deploy human resources to provide affected individuals with rapid access to comprehensive mental health care on their doorstep. In order to guarantee the community's ongoing access to services, the long-term plan sought to establish a permanent mental health care infrastructure locally. Here's an overview of the services typically provided:

1. **Basic Needs Support**: Basic essentials like food, housing, and healthcare were provided.
2. **Immediate Psychological First Aid (PFA):** PFA was put into place to help survivors with their urgent emotional and psychological needs. Support was given by qualified volunteers and mental health professionals such as social workers, psychologists, psychiatrists, and nurses.

3. **Counseling Services:** Individual and group counseling sessions were offered to help survivors cope with grief, anxiety, and post-traumatic stress.
4. **Community-Based Interventions:** Community workshops and support groups were organized to foster social support networks, encouraging survivors to share their experiences and feelings in a safe environment.
5. **Awareness Programs:** Educational programs aimed at reducing stigma around mental health issues were conducted, helping communities recognize symptoms of distress and the importance of seeking help.
6. **Collaboration with NGOs:** Various non-governmental organizations played a key role in delivering psychosocial support. They provided training for local volunteers and mental health professionals to effectively address the needs of the affected populations.

Here are key elements of long-term interventions:

1. **Establishment of Mental Health:** Dedicated rehabilitation centers were set up to provide ongoing mental health services, including therapy and support groups. Mental health services were integrated into existing healthcare facilities to ensure accessibility and reduce stigma.
2. **Training of Local Health Workers:** Capacity-building training programs for local health professionals, community workers, and volunteers were implemented to equip them with skills in PFA and trauma-informed care. Encouraging local participation in mental health initiatives fostered a sense of ownership and increased community resilience.
3. **Continuous Counseling and Support Groups:** Ongoing support groups were established to provide safe spaces for survivors to share experiences, promoting mutual support and healing. Continued access to mental health professionals for one-on-one therapy was essential for those experiencing prolonged distress.
4. **Public Awareness Campaigns:** Campaigns aimed at reducing stigma around mental health were vital. Education on recognizing mental health issues and encouraging help-seeking behavior was prioritized.

Regular workshops were held in communities to educate residents about mental health, coping mechanisms, and available services.

5. **Monitoring and Evaluation:** Ongoing assessments helped identify the evolving needs of the community, ensuring that mental health services remained relevant and effective. Gathering feedback from survivors and community members informed the improvement of services and interventions.
6. **Holistic Approaches: Integration of Psychosocial and Economic Support**: Programs that combined mental health services with economic rehabilitation, such as skills training and job placement, addressed both psychological and practical needs. Interventions were designed to be culturally appropriate, taking into account local beliefs and practices related to mental health.
7. **Research and Policy Advocacy:** Research initiatives documented the psychological impact of the earthquake, providing evidence for future interventions and policies. Advocacy for mental health policy changes at local and national levels aimed to improve resource allocation and support for mental health services.
8. **Collaboration with NGOs and International Bodies:** Collaborating with non-governmental organizations and international agencies ensured a coordinated response and pooled resources for mental health initiatives. Efforts were made to secure funding and support for long-term mental health programs from various stakeholders.

Discussion The mental health response to the Marathwada earthquake, though groundbreaking in some respects, was limited by various systemic flaws. While the establishment of the MIMH and the early mobilization of resources were notable, the lack of a disaster-focused mental health infrastructure meant that many survivors did not receive adequate care. This raises a broader question about the preparedness of mental health systems in disaster-prone areas. Efforts must be made to ensure that mental health services are not only available during the relief phase but also continue as part of the long-term rehabilitation process. One key takeaway from the Marathwada experience is the importance of building resilient health systems that integrate mental health care into the overall disaster response framework. Training and capacity building at the community level are crucial in closing the gaps identified. Had local health workers been equipped with the necessary psychosocial skills, they could have provided timely and culturally sensitive interventions. This points to the need for future disaster management strategies to emphasize training programs for local personnel, ensuring that mental health care is embedded into local health systems and community networks (Akram et al., 2024). Another important lesson is the significance of cultural sensitivity in mental health interventions. Communities in disaster-affected areas often have unique cultural contexts, and any mental health response must consider these factors. Going forward, it is essential that disaster management policies incorporate mental health services that are tailored to local social and cultural norms. Community engagement programs and public awareness campaigns could reduce the stigma associated with mental health and encourage people to seek care.

Finally, this discussion underscores the need for stronger, more cohesive policy frameworks that integrate mental health into the disaster management process. Mental health should be treated not as an afterthought but as a core component of disaster preparedness and response. Coordinated efforts between government bodies, health institutions, and NGOs will be essential in ensuring that mental health care is prioritized in future disaster scenarios.

Conclusion The response to the 1993 Marathwada earthquake highlighted the critical importance of psychosocial support and mental health services in disaster recovery. The psychosocial initiatives implemented in the aftermath demonstrated significant effectiveness in addressing the emotional and psychological needs of survivors. By providing immediate and long-term support, these interventions not only helped individuals cope with acute distress but also fostered a sense of community resilience. The training of local health workers and awareness campaigns played a crucial role in breaking down stigma surrounding mental health, encouraging survivors to seek help and engage in the healing process. The lessons learned from this disaster emphasize the need for a holistic approach to disaster preparedness and response. Future disaster management plans must integrate mental health services as a fundamental component, ensuring that psychosocial support is readily available in the wake of any disaster. By prioritizing mental health and community engagement, we can enhance the recovery journey for individuals and communities affected by trauma, ultimately promoting resilience and long-term well-being. In moving forward, it is essential to continue developing and refining these support systems, leveraging technology and local resources to provide sustainable mental health care. By doing so, we can better equip communities to face the challenges of future disasters and facilitate their recovery in a more comprehensive and effective manner.

References

Akram, S., Baloch, M. Y. J., Alrefaei, A. F., Almutairi, M. H., Idrees, M., & Al-Kubaisi, H. A. R. A. (2024). Interface between mental health and the earthquake: Considering humanitarian endeavor. *Frontiers in Public Health, 12*, 1326407. https://doi.org/10.3389/fpubh.2024.1326407

Comfort, L. K. (1995). *Self-organization in disaster response and recovery: The Maharashtra, India earthquake of September 30, 1993* (Vol. 42). FMHI Publications. https://digitalcommons.usf.edu/fmhi_pub/42

Galson, S. K. (2009). Mental health matters. *Public Health Reports, 124*(2), 189–191. https://doi.org/10.1177/003335490912400202

Jigyasu, R. (2001). From natural to cultural disaster: Consequences of the post-earthquake rehabilitation process on the cultural heritage in Marathwada region, India. *Bulletin of the New Zealand Society for Earthquake Engineering, 34*(3), 237–242.

Pande, N. R., Phadke, S. S., Dalal, M. S., & Agashe, M. M. (2000a). Mental health care in Marathwada earthquake disaster—1: Organisation of services. *Indian Journal of Social Work, 61*, 631–639.

Pande, N. R., Phadke, S. S., Dalal, M. S., Gadkari, P. J., Nagapurkar, U. S., & Agashe, M. M. (2000b). Mental health care in Marathwada earthquake disaster—2: Short-term outreach counselling. *Indian Journal of Social Work, 61*, 640–651.

World Health Organization. (1992). *Psychosocial consequences of disasters: Prevention and management (No. WHO/MNH/PSF/91.3 Rev. 1)*. World Health Organization.

10

Cyclone Disasters of Odisha: Learning and Achievements over Decades of Psychosocial Support Mental Services (PSSMHS) Interventions

Lipika Pradhan and Kasi Sekar

Introduction

A natural catastrophe can be defined as a significant disturbance of a community's or society's ability to function at any scale brought on by dangerous occurrences interacting with exposure, vulnerability and capacity conditions, and resulting in losses and effects on people, the economy and the environment (UNDRR, 2009). In addition to having a substantial impact on people's bodily and mental health, it also significantly alters society and communities. Some studies have suggested that in 2015 global natural disasters caused around 98 million people to be impacted and cost US$66.5 billion in economic damages (Patel et al., 2020). Due to its distinct geo-climatic conditions, India has historically been susceptible to catastrophic disaster. Reports on disaster management indicate that around 58.6% of the country's territory is vulnerable to earthquakes of different magnitudes, 12% to floods and river erosion,

L. Pradhan • K. Sekar (✉)
Department of Psychosocial Support in Disaster Management, NIMHANS, Bengaluru, Karnataka, India

S. Bhadra et al. (eds.), *Psychosocial and Mental Health Support for Disaster Management in India*, Palgrave Studies in Disaster Science and Emergency Management,
https://doi.org/10.1007/978-3-032-02511-1_10

and 15% to 1% landslides, 68% of the land is vulnerable to drought, while 8% of the entire region is vulnerable to cyclones (NDMA, 2021). During the 1990s and 2000s, disasters affected approximately 30 million people yearly and claimed an average of 4344 lives (Ministry of Home Affairs, 2004). World Bank research from 2003 found that natural disasters constituted a significant barrier to India's progress, with some reports claiming that between 1996 and 2001, it cost the country some 2.5% of its GDP (Satapathy, 2012). The super cyclonic Storm Amphan struck eastern India on May 21, 2020, causing extensive devastation, particularly in west Bengal, Odisha, and Bangladesh, and resulting in approximately $14 billion in damages and 128 fatalities (O'connor et al., 2021). Similarly, on May 19, 2021, another cyclonic storm hit Gujarat, causing 185 fatalities, 81 missing, and $2.87 billion of damages (Verma & Kumar Gupta, 2021). Then, on October 25, 2024, Cyclone Dana struck Odisha, affecting 14 districts and causing damage of $72 million, with an estimated 41 lakh people impacted (Barua, 2024). There has also been an enormous loss of government, private, and community assets.

Odisha & Disaster

Odisha's coastline comprises only 17% of the Indian east coast, an area which experiences roughly 35% of all cyclonic and severe cyclonic storms worldwide. Large areas of coastal districts have frequently been impacted by storm surges. Every year, between five and six tropical cyclones of varying intensities, from light to severe, occur in the Bay of Bengal. In comparison with the other eastern states, Odisha is reportedly almost twice as susceptible to storms, whatever the intensity (OSDMA, 2023).

Numerous natural hazards pose a threat to the state of Odisha. The state's coastline is 480 km long, and the coastal areas have a far higher population density than the interior. According to the 2011 census, there were 41 million people living in Odisha at the time, with the majority of them living on the plains of its river systems. Heavy silt deposits in the rivers in these regions significantly lower their carrying capacity, causing frequent floods that are occasionally worsened by breaches of the embankment. Between 1996 and 2021, Odisha endured 13 years of flooding,

8 years of drought and 7 years of cyclones (Sethi, 2019). The objective of this chapter is to understand the major severe cyclones (Super cyclone 1999, Phailin 2013, Fani 2019) faced by the people of the state of Odisha, and to assess their psychosocial requirements and mental health following such a disaster. In addition, this chapter explores the psychosocial support (PSS) interventions carried out by NIMHANS and the institutionalization of the PSS by the Odisha State Government through disaster management initiatives to promote efforts for Disaster Risk Reduction (DRR).

The Super Cyclone, 1999

The super cyclone that hit Odisha on October 29, 1999, is arguably one of the most destructive natural disasters in India in the last hundred years. It reached a maximum wind speed of almost 300 km/h, and there were continuous rains for a period of 48 hours, with a total rainfall of 447 to 995 mm. Tidal waves up to 10 meters high hit the Orissa coast and moved nearly 15 kilometers inland, washing away everything in its path. Houses, vegetation, livelihoods, and the environment were all severely damaged. Over 15 million people were impacted in the 12 districts, and more than 10,000 individuals were killed (ActionAid India, 2002). The State Government's Revenue Department reports that there were 9885 fatalities, with 8386 of those deaths occurring in the district of Jagatsinghpur alone, of which 8119 occurred in Erasama Block. The typhoon and the subsequent water caused damage to a total of about 1,650,086 dwellings. The estimated damages total led 39,680 million Indian rupees. (around one billion USD) (Kar et al., 1999).

The Phailin, 2013

Around 2230 hours IST on October 12, 2013, the extremely powerful cyclonic Storm "Phailin" passed over Odisha and the nearby coast of north Andhra Pradesh near Gopalpur (Odisha), with a sustained maximum surface wind speed of 200 km/ph. Strong gale winds and extremely heavy rains across Odisha resulted in floods, extensive structural damage, and storm surges that caused widespread coastal inundation. In Odisha, 18 of the 30 districts were impacted by the cyclone and the ensuing flooding. In addition to destroying 256,600 homes and killing 44 persons, the storm impacted 13.2 million people across more than 18,370 localities. Even though there were fewer fatalities than during the super cyclone in October 1999, the cyclonic storm and flooding caused more than 50% of the 1,292,967 hectares of agricultural, horticultural, and perennial crops to be lost. Some 44,806 families of coastal fishermen and 1564 houses of artisans were impacted by the hurricane and floods. In one of the biggest evacuations ever carried out by disaster management, around one million people were moved into shelter homes. The water supply pipes, power supply, telecommunications, and all surface communication networks were completely disrupted (OSDMA, 2013).

The Fani, 2019

On May 3, 2019, at around 8.30 AM, Cyclone "Fani," an exceptionally powerful cyclonic storm, made landfall between Satapada and Puri. The maximum sustained surface wind speed recorded during landfall was 205 km/h, according to India Meteorological Department (IMD). After making landfall, the cyclone largely maintained its ferocity for the next six hours. This was the strongest cyclone to ever hit Odisha, being, according to IMD statistics, the first time a cyclone of this magnitude had passed across India in April since 1976. The cyclone's destruction was mostly caused by the wind's gusts and the intense rains. An estimated 159.85 lakh persons in 159 Blocks, 51 Urban Local Bodies, and 20,367 villages were impacted, according to a report that the collectors provided. In addition, 5,08,467 homes in 14 districts sustained damage, 64 people died as a result of the typhoon, and 1.49 lakh hectares of horticultural and agricultural crops, including orchards, have been damaged. The significant loss of boats and nets has also had a serious negative impact on the fishing community, and the loss of looms, tools, accessories, and raw materials used by handloom and handicraft craftsmen has greatly impacted the artisan community. In addition, livestock and poultry farmers have also suffered significant losses, and significant harm has been done to public properties (OSDMA, 2019).

Impact of Disaster and Psychological Reactions

When a disaster occurs, it not only has a physical and economic effect on the wider society but also impacts the emotional, behavioral, and psychological states of individuals, families, and community members. Developing nations are more affected by disasters because of their high population density, the borderline economic condition of the vulnerable population, and the lack of resources for disaster preparedness and recovery (Juvva & Rajendran, 2000). Studies show that, on average, the prevalence of psychopathology rises by 17% after a disaster compared to the pre-disaster period (Rubonis & Bickman, 1991). Disaster survivors experience a range of psychological symptoms following traumatic events, including extreme stress, overwhelming emotions, psychosomatic problems, and protracted sadness and bereavement. The functioning of individuals and the community is impacted by common psychological problems such as depression, anxiety, dissociation, adjustment difficulties, and substance abuse. This leads to relational strain and disputes in families and communities. A feeling of emotional shock and sadness is brought on by such disasters. For survivors, this traumatic event causes loss for themselves, their families, and their communities. It also interferes with their psychological functioning. Families affected by natural disasters deal with a loss of identity as a result of their roles in the community being disrupted and the work they have been doing being lost. This can lead to an absence of optimism. One study found that, in such circumstances, elevated levels of acute psychological distress were linked to resources being lost, daily routines being disrupted, personal property being lost, and a decrease in the levels of social support (Hackbarth et al., 2012).

The 1999 Odisha super cyclone was one of the most destructive cyclonic storms ever reported, causing several mental health problems in addition to the loss of lives and property (Kar et al., 1999). According to research reports done by Sneha Abhiyan in partnership with ActionAid and NIMHANS, the psychological impact of the super cyclone was more catastrophic nationally than any other disaster in this century. The psychological reactions are more severe in the first three months, which include symptoms such as crying, sobbing, stupefaction, numbness, talking excessively, sometimes irrelevantly, forgetfulness, and strange behaviors. Approximately 30–40%t of women were regularly losing consciousness, and victims such as widows and mothers who had lost their children were hearing the voices of their deceased family members, particularly spouses and children (Sekar et al., 2004). Depressive symptoms such as low mood, sadness, helplessness and hopelessness about the future, irritability, guilt, suicidal ideation and attempts, negative thoughts, fear of death, etc., were witnessed among many of the survivors. Some of the victims were unable to accept the reality and were still in a dilemma. In a few of the fishing communities, women wait for 12 years if their husband is not back from the sea to accept widowhood. Such a cultural belief was also a reason for some women to accept the death of their husbands.

The psychological impact of the super cyclone on children was also highly traumatic. After losing their parents and family members, most children were in shock and crying out for basic amenities. Some of them became mute, refusing to take food, and showing social withdrawal behaviors. Children experienced nightmares, and a few had symptoms of somnambulism. It has been seen that children were unable to express their emotional states, decreasing their self-esteem and developing a range of depressive traits. There have also been reports of orphans and teenage females being sexually, physically, and emotionally abused by their carers. The majority of the children were mostly sad, crying frequently and remembering their parents (ActionAid India, 2002). Some of the victims remained traumatized for longer periods of time. Victims were also reported as feeling sad and crying during the time of festivals and there was a notable number of reported school dropouts. According to figures provided by *Sneha kermis* (psychosocial carers), some 5% of children reported depressive symptoms (Yadav et al., 2023).

Victims with significant distress and pre-existing psychiatric problems became more vulnerable some weeks after the disaster. Psychological issues like dissociative convulsions, an inability to respond, death wishes, suicidal thoughts (and attempts), self-harming behaviors, low self-esteem, poor self-care, a decline in taking care of children and family members, and a decrease in sleep and appetite were all commonly observed (Murthy et al., 2003). According to studies, 80.4% of the individuals had probable psychiatric conditions after a few months of the super cyclone, 44.3% had post-traumatic stress disorder (PTSD), 57.5% had an anxiety disorder, and 52.5% had depression. Some 63.4% of cases exhibited comorbid psychiatric disorders. Most of the survivors with significant psychiatric problems came from vulnerable groups, such as women, children, the elderly, people with a lower socioeconomic status, the less educated, the unemployed, the physically hurt, people exposed to more danger, people under a lot of stress before the disaster, people with a history of mental health problems, etc. The report shows higher rates of suicide after disaster (Kar et al., 1999).

Women's lives were more severely impacted by the super storm. After a calamity, there were many reports of child weddings, elopements, remarriages, and even marriages to men who had been previously married to another person. Widow's lives became more difficult; they felt insecure and needed help for basic survival. In such instances, the relationship grew and soon led to sexual interactions. However, it has been observed that women were used for sexual gratification and many of the women needed money, as well as having sexual needs. Cases of unwanted pregnancies were reported. After the cyclone, men who suffered severe losses adopted various negative coping and negative lifestyle choices. Alcohol consumption among men increased substantially and most of them were ignoring family responsibilities and staying away from family members for longer periods (Sekar et al., 2005).

People in the state of Odisha began experiencing to mental health problems after twenty years as a result of the impact of the "Extremely Severe Cyclonic Storm Fani.". The loss of livelihood and property caused by this cyclone has had an effect on people's mental health. One month after the cyclone, research found that the prevalence of PTSD was 42.9%, the figure for severe anxiety was 36.7%, that for moderate to severe depression was 16.5%, that for severe depression was 3.8%, and the levels for suicidal thoughts increased by 14%. Significant correlations were found between PTSD, depression, and anxiety and the experience of evacuation and displacement (Kar, 2022).

PSS-MHS Interventions in Disasters

Natural disasters such as cyclones have a profound effect on people's and their families' emotional and mental health. Psychosocial support and mental health services (PSSMHS) aim to offer mental health care and support to disaster survivors in order to address their psychological issues and psychosocial well-being (Dückers et al., 2022). As part of the Sneha Abhyan project, which was funded and carried out by Action Aid India in technical cooperation with NIMHANS, trained community-level workers, named *Sneha Karmi*, delivered PSSMHS on a mass scale in the community during the 1999 super cyclone. The recovery and restoration of the survivors' mental health and well-being were greatly aided by this initiative by community-based psychosocial carers. Twenty trainers of trainees (ToT) participated in a seven-day training program led by mental health professionals (psychiatrists and psychiatry social workers) as part of the intervention. The program included field-oriented observation, internalization, and hands-on demonstration on how to understand mental health issues and provide psychosocial intervention at the individual, family, and community levels by interacting with survivors and other stakeholders. The final training session focused on volunteer self-care and debriefing, outlining duties and responsibilities (Sekar, 2004). Similarly, for children, a special intervention training program was carried out for the counsellor, who spent a month teaching the group play therapy and psychosocial counselling. Psychiatrists trained the Gram Panchayat (village Committee) coordinators and *Sneha Karmis* for two days, equipping them to address the mental health issues faced by women, specifically those who lost their husbands in the cyclone (Sekar et al., 2004). Further training programs were repeated to create a large number of trained community-based psychosocial support workers.

Additionally, the NIMHANS team created guides for "Community-level helpers" (Kumar et al., 2000) and "Individuals" (Murthy et. al., 2000) with assistance from ActionAid India. The manuals helped the *Shena Karmis* and other volunteers and NGO staff to better understand the physical difficulties, psychological reactions, and socioeconomic issues in the aftermath of the cyclone. This manual provided information about how to reorganize, rebuild, and rehabilitate the lives of survivors and their families. After receiving appropriate counselling and being given the opportunity to express their feelings on the cyclone, trained volunteers were assigned to the 35 Sneha Abhiyan intervention villages to carry out the psychological support program in a systematic way. In Erasama Block, the state government built 35 shelter homes for the most vulnerable groups immediately after the disaster, and ActionAid India took the responsibility of managing them. These shelter homes were named *Mamta Gruhas* (homes of love). Further, the intervention was extended to other selected areas (Patra, 2024). Covering a large population with lay volunteers with limited professional involvement is a unique aspect of this Odisha disaster relief, rehabilitation, and reconstruction program. The "community-level helpers" handbook included a variety of topics, including civil defense personnel, National Social Service volunteers, lay volunteers, local workers, Anganwadi (child care) workers, and *Grama sevakas* (village volunteers). Understanding the effects of the super cyclone, different types of emotional reactions to disasters, phases of disaster responses, and emotional support in terms of practical guidelines for psychosocial interventions with the general public and special groups like women, children, the elderly, and people with special needs were all covered in the handbook (Sekar, 2004).

Post-Disaster Psychosocial Care at Different Stages During the Super Cyclone 1999 by Sneha Karmis

In the initial few months, the counsellors used few techniques to provide psychosocial support to survivors to cope with grief. By listening, the counsellors helped the victims in ventilation, facilitated relaxation, and encouraged them to adopt positive coping. In order to provide emotional support, counsellors usually stayed with victims in *Mamata Gruhas* and conducted a series of meetings with community members, allowing the victims to share their stories of bravery, which helped to build rapport and cope with the situation. Counsellors deliberately provided activities to some of the survivors to support their sense of responsibility. Engagement in some activities in *Mamata Gruhas* such as helping in cooking, storytelling and playing with children, helping in the distribution of clothes, etc. helped a lot to cope with the situation. The *Sneha Karmis* mostly used distraction methods to encourage the victims to be self-dependent. "*Mass Shradhanjali*" was arranged at the community level as mourning rituals (grieving procedure) for all those who died in the cyclone to re-establishing faith facilitated the healing. Religious activities like bhajans, '*Arti praharis*,' *Saraswati puja*, and *Gayatri japa* (different types of prayers) were continued which gave hope that God will take care (Murthy, 2004).

Over the course of 3–12 months, the *Sneha Karmis* became more focused on the education and information about the realities, rights, and duties of the survivors. **Assertiveness** was taught to victims, which helped them to engage in their **daily living activities** independently and reminded them of their capabilities before the disaster. Local peoples were able to show their resilience, and productivity was increased in their daily life. Different Sneha committees and self-help groups were formed to identify and address the needs of the community by organizing community meetings and awareness and development programs. Self-help groups specifically helped people to deal with legal procedures to get compensation and other documents (identity cards, ration cards, documents for banking/property, etc.) to restart their lives. Counsellors organized a 'School Chlo rally' (Let us go to the school) for children to take them back to school and initiate plays (street plays), often with mythological content, to support healing and rebuild hope. Different role-plays were conducted to teach them assertive techniques and coping mechanisms at the school level (Murthy et al., 2003).

Psychosocial care and support were continued until some three or four years after the super cyclone. After long-term counselling and support by PSSMHS, the survivors were gradually weaned out of their dependency on relief. Communication and cohesion level between individuals in families and communities improved. People started to adopt the situation and moved on. Some victims were helped by community members to get married and start a new life. Counsellors focused a lot on **spreading awareness** among the parents and caregivers about the needs of the children under care, emphasizing their need for education, play, and other recreational activities, etc. Assertiveness training programs continued for people; they were made aware of their rights and helped them to understand how to achieve them. Annual *Shradhanjali* (death anniversaries and prayers to homage) were conducted in communities as acts of remembrance for the dead. *Mahila Samiti* (women groups), *Shishu Sangha* (groups for children), and other organizations continued to work for the betterment of the community (Murthy et al., 2003).

Post-Disaster Psychosocial Care During Cyclone Fani (2019)

Cyclone Fani affected the psychological and emotional well-being of the people of coastal Odisha. During Cyclone Fani, the Odisha government did an excellent job in evacuation, relief, and restoration. However, the post-disaster situation was marked by a serious risk to life due to injury, trauma, and the possibilities of infection. In order to address the mental health issues, psychosocial support training programs were conducted by the Youth Council for Development Alternatives (YCDA) with the support of NIMHANS and Basic Needs India (BNI). A total of 50 volunteers were trained to handle the mental health strain in the community. Mental health professionals from different District Mental Health Programs (DMHP) and volunteers were appointed in different locations of coastal districts to counsel the children and vulnerable groups and to support the community. Thes programs help the communities to cope better with the psychological trauma they have encountered during and after the disaster. It has been observed, as mentioned earlier, that many people (including children) develop different psychological symptoms such as a lack of interest in activities, restlessness, sleep disturbances, low energy, etc. Those who showed severe levels of distress were referred for further higher-level treatment. It has also been reported that volunteers referred a total of 640 persons to district mental health units to access mental health and psychosocial care & support. After counselling, most of the people were able to cope with the condition and resumed their daily living activities (YCDA, 2019).

Intervention with Specific Vulnerable/ Marginalized Groups

According to the World Health Organization (WHO), vulnerability is defined as "the circumstances resulting from physical, social, economic, and environmental factors or processes that make a person, a community, assets, or systems more susceptible to the effects of hazards" (WHO, 2022). Certain groups are deemed to be more vulnerable than others, including those who are impoverished, women, children and young people, the elderly, those with disabilities, those who have underlying medical issues or chronic illnesses, migrants, members of ethnic minorities, Indigenous people, and sexual minorities because of their underlying condition in the pre-disaster period in the society (Newnham et al., 2022). It has been observed that these groups are more vulnerable to developed physical and psychological symptoms at an early stage than other groups (Marshall et al., 2020). This, special attention should be given to these populations, especially with regard to their mental health, psychosocial needs, psychosocial care, support, intervention and rehabilitation (Sekar et al., 2023).

Children

During Super Cyclone 1999, it was reported that the highest percentages of symptoms elicited among the children e.g., slow learning, fear, sleep problems, and wetting the clothes. Within these overall figures, girls developed more psychological symptoms than boys, And young children within the age group of 5–10 years reported a proportionately larger number of symptoms than children in the age group of 11–15 years (Sekar, 2004). Children's minds and emotional states are not developed enough to deal with problems in the same way as adults. Thus, they often display behavioral issues and cannot articulate their feelings. It is necessary for the parents/caregivers to understand these changes and take certain measures to help children get over the stress. The goal of the caregivers/parents was to improve the feeling of security and bonding between them. Children require **expressive mediums** that enable them to unconsciously express their feelings and inner experiences. Psychosocial caregivers assessed the psychological and social impact of the disaster and planned for intervention strategies accordingly. Both the group mode of interaction and intervention help to facilitate the healing process (Sekar et al., 2023).

Basic strategies that psychosocial caregivers/parents used while dealing with children were leaving children with known adults, i.e. mother, siblings, and known neighbors, and allowing them to interact with other children. Caregivers focused more on daily living activities and initiated regular routines such as eating, playing, studying, sleeping, etc. Such involvement and activities helped the child to develop a sense of security. Physical closeness with young children, such as touching and hugging the child often (in an appropriate manner), reassuring them verbally, giving them favorite toys, using pieces of cloth (mother's sari) which the child used earlier as a soother, keeping a small light while the child is sleeping, etc. were encouraged to practice, in order to help to the better recovery of the children. These actions allowed them to participate in activities that provided a sense of control over the situation, such as allowing the children to talk about the incident and listening without offering advice, and encouraging play activities that were related to the incident. (For example, children would make paper boats and put them in water. The boats might rock, creating turbulence in the water, and the difficulties of people in the boat might then be discussed.) Children were encouraged to participate in different types of play, like story-telling, singing songs, drawing, etc. Approval might be given of different coping behavior too, like praising him/her for going back to school and following a routine, etc. Liaison with the teacher also helped in the recovery of the children. Paying more attention and spending more time with them on their studies was also helpful in developing positive coping abilities (Murthy et al., 1999).

Women

Iin India's patriarchal society, women are more prone to developing psychological and emotional issues. Most of them are economically dependent on men, poorly educated, culturally deprived of rights, and vulnerable to being abused (physically, sexually, and emotionally). The multiple losses, especially the loss of husbands or male members of the households, push women toward increased vulnerability and make their livelihood and safety harder. These pre-existing social vulnerabilities, along with physical and social conditions, make them more vulnerable both during and after disasters. Such conditions deprive them of access to psychosocial care and support services or resources. It has been observed that women who were young, single, widowed, orphaned, disabled, or who had lost children needed specific attention in the aftermath of the disaster. The caregivers initially focused more on the privacy and safety of the female members in the shelter homes. Services were provided to meet the specific requirements of women, such as dealing with domestic violence, substance abuse, abuse of children, high-risk pregnancy, etc. Vulnerable groups among women, such as those who were single or widowed or pregnant, were closely monitored and given appropriate support. The *Sneha Karmis* allowed them to be involved in various activities of social relevance, like the maintenance of cleanliness, helping in the preparation of making, and taking care of children, the old and the sick, which gave them a sense of responsibility, self-respect, and the opportunity for better coping (Sekar et al., 2005).

Older Adults

Elderly people with pre-existing health complications, such as age-related deficiencies in eyesight, hearing abilities, memory, lower levels of physical strength and a higher risk of infection, are more susceptible to disasters. Further, the lack of adequate social support causes the development of psychological issues like helplessness, hopelessness, feelings of loneliness, death wishes, and difficulties in accessing the resources and support that are available, etc. Often elderly people are unable to recognize and access disaster-related warnings and important information related to safety (Sekar et al., 2023). Therefore, caregivers need to make detailed assessments of the needs of older adults, in terms of medicine, assistive devices, psychological support, and family support. Under the Senha Abhyan Program, caregivers encouraged the elderly survivors to express their emotions and thoughts related to the disaster and repeatedly conveyed any positive to them news (Murthy et al., 2000). Such reassurance helped the elderly survivors to regain confidence and lead a better-adjusted life in the post-disaster context.

Disabled People

Persons with disabilities (PWD) are those who are physically or mentally dependent on others for their daily living activities and who have restrictions on mobility or in relation to living an independent life in normal circumstances. So, natural disasters like cyclones not only worsen their conditions but also increase the factors contributing to disability. Their pre-existing conditions, and the lack of awareness and support from society, make them more vulnerable during times of disaster. So, caregivers focused more on the rights and needs of PWD and minimized their limitations in getting psychosocial support and care during and after the disaster (Sekar et al., 2023). The major role of psychosocial caregivers was to update them on the situation, giving PWD a feeling of being involved rather than ignored. There was also a focus on specific tasks that they could perform within the limitations and available circumstances. It is better to have groups comprising differently abled people and some PWD to facilitate inclusion in rescue and recovery (Murthy et al., 2000).

Interventions at the Community Level

A community is an independent entity with its own resources, capabilities, interests, and preferences (Brennan et al., 2005). Local volunteers, governance systems, and community-based organizations are important parts of an organized community in terms of dealing with the situation before, during, and after disasters. Adequate preparedness is essential to reduce the damage due to disaster and to rebuild the lives of the people during and after the disaster. Community-based preparedness and action are essential components of disaster risk reduction (Patterson et al., 2010). In Odisha, community-level psychosocial interventions became one of the most effective intervention approaches for disaster risk reduction. During the super cyclone (1999), ActionAid implemented *Sneha Abhiyan* (local volunteers) in partnership with the Government of India, the Government of Orissa, Open Learning Systems, Nature's Club, UNICEF, and local community-based organizations. In addition to protecting the survivors from exploitation, they planned their long-term rehabilitation, offered emotional support, and tended to their basic needs while they were in shelter houses. The community care workers (*Sneha Karmis*) were trained by NIMHANS at the village level in play therapies, basic skills in personal psychological care, basic counselling skills, and recreational activities as encouragement for foster families and identification of those with mental illnesses for appropriate referral (Chachra, 2004). These forms of community-based solutions made the communities more robust to calamities and other difficulties.

In Odisha, psychosocial caregivers organized mass group mourning at the community level to address the grief of the survivors toward their deceased family members and relatives after the disaster. It offers the bereaved communities solidarity and promotes cooperation and group effort. Similarly, village-level group meetings organized by the local volunteers enabled the community to function as a whole, which assisted the community not only in accepting the reality of loss and emptiness but also in starting collective action and getting life restarted (Sekar et al., 2005). Psychosocial caregivers (*Sneha Karmis*) organized various cultural and spiritual programs, such as singing folk songs and bhajans/hymns (religious prayers), where survivors can participate in expressing their emotions related to tragedy, and also organized rallies to sensitize the administration and hasten restoration, rebuilding, relocation, compensation, etc. *Mamtha Gruha* was also established where children without parents and women who have lost their families can stay safely. '*Shramadhan*' (voluntary labour) was organized by psychosocial caregivers, where volunteers participated in rebuilding houses, schools, medical facilities, and other services for the survivors (ActionAid India, 2002). It has been reported that after the introduction of community-level care and intervention, there was a reduction in the severity level of emotional distress, trauma, negative thoughts, and suicidal ideations among survivors (Chachra, 2004).

Working with the Humanitarian Service Providers

A joint UN evaluation framework was created following the super cyclone at the request of the Odisha by the government of Odisha (Sinha, 2009). The United Nations Development Programme (UNDP), the United Nations International Children's Emergency Fund (UNICEF), the Food and Agriculture Organization (FAO), the WHO, and the World Food Program (WFP) conducted an immediate assessment to determine the amount of damage inflicted on various sectors during the cyclone. Several UN missions, including the (FAO), WHO, the United Nations Educational, Cultural and Social Organization (UNESCO), and the International Labour Organization (ILO), visited Orissa in November and December 1999 to assess the cyclone's effects and the long-term rehabilitation needs in agriculture, livelihood, health, and education. In order to address new challenges that arose during the relief, rehabilitation, and reconstruction phases, thematic workshops were organized. There were workshops on food security (FAO) and shelter (UNDP) in February and March 2000 and on education (UNESCO) and health (WHO) in April and May 2000. A senior World Bank team visited the hurricane-affected state to assess the damage. For the twenty members of the team, determining the resources required to restore the state's economy was the main task. The UNICEF state representative in Bhubaneswar convened daily coordination meetings with state and local government officials and high-level representatives from national and international relief organizations. According to Sinha (2009), the relief efforts engaged more than 25 foreign NGOs. The *Senha Karmis*, and other community volunteers who had received psychosocial support training, actively worked to support the survivors' overall recovery by integrating a variety of sectoral supports (such as livelihood, housing, water sanitation, education, etc.) during the reconstruction phase in the impacted villages. Additionally, they were crucial in developing collaboration among many authorities.

Over the past few decades, it has been noted that, in addition to the government, NGOs have played a crucial role in disaster planning, response, and mitigation initiatives in various regions of Odisha. Many international NGOs specifically focused on providing humanitarian aid to disaster-affected people. Local NGOs in Odisha have also played a dynamic role in disaster management in the last decade and during Cyclone Phailin, Hudhud & Fani (OSDMA, 2023).

Outcome and Learning from PSSMHS Interventions

According to the United Nations International Strategy for Disaster Reduction (UNISDR), the term "preparedness" refers to the ability and knowledge that governments, response and recovery organizations, communities, and individuals have gained to successfully foresee, respond to, and recover from the effects of likely, imminent, or existing catastrophes (UNISDR, 2009). There are many factors that can affect individuals' psychological state in disasters. It can be physical injuries, financial crisis, excessive burden, lack of support from family or society, lack of emotional support, lack of awareness/knowledge, etc. "Psychological preparedness can lower the likelihood of developing any kind of significant psychological stress or trauma because it encompasses a number of interconnected elements within individual processes and capacities, including awareness, knowledge, anticipation, concern, thinking, feelings, experienced stress, motivation, intentions, and decision making, as well as management of or coping with one's thoughts, feelings, and actions" (Zulch, 2019). There are numerous psychological preparedness theories that back up the idea that being prepared in advance can lessen the intensity of a disaster's detrimental effects on a person's mental health and also help survivors cope and become more resilient. Some of the disaster preparedness theories that increase people's ability to deal with disasters more effectively are explained in the following table.

Theories of Psychological Preparedness in Disaster (Paton, 2019)

- Health belief model: This model explains how people's perceptions of their vulnerability to danger, their assessments of the threat's seriousness, and their assessments of the costs and rewards of taking action all affected their readiness for disasters.
- Protection motivation theory: This theory helps determine how people's perceptions of the efficacy of preparedness measures and their capacity to carry them out connect with their acceptance and personalization of risk in order to forecast readiness.
- Transcortical model: People's transition from a pre-contemplation to a contemplation stage was primarily influenced by perceived vulnerability and response efficacy, while the most significant predictors of their transition from contemplation to action were subjective hazard knowledge, response efficacy, information about the seriousness of the consequences, and the costs of protective measures. Perception of the internal and external advantages of hazard readiness turned out to be a significant predictor of the transition from action to maintenance.
- Person related to event theory: People's beliefs about event characteristics (e.g., severity) and preparedness are mediated by perceived resource availability and personal traits (self-efficacy, outcome efficacy, coping assessment).
- Theory of planned behavior: The relationship among people's readiness attitudes, subjective preparedness norms, and views about their degree of behavioural control over the adoption of preparedness measures is described by the Theory of Planned Behaviour (TPB).

Disaster preparedness at the community level is also crucial. Community resilience not only helps in developing the capacity to prepare but also supports the recovery, restoration, and rehabilitation phases of a disaster. Resilience and improved coping during and after emergencies are also facilitated by community-based interventions and strategies. The nine main components of community resilience are divided into 19 smaller components, including local language, community networks and relationships, communication, health, leadership and governance, resources, financial investment, readiness, and mental attitude, according to research (Patel et al., 2017). In disasters, resilience-building interventions are mostly carried out at the community level, which strengthens the community-based adaptation approach. According to the conceptual dimension of resilience in the risk management approach, it is essential to transform the resources and power (social, economic, etc.) in different phases, which enable the community for effective management in an emergency. Diagram 10.1 describes the conceptual dimensions of community resiliency in different phases of disaster; preparation (build better before) helps the community to respond (be ready) and recover (build back better), which leads to developing a better prevention strategy and building capacity in an emergency.

During the super cyclone, 1999, due to a lack of warning systems and preparation, huge devastation occurred, which marked a turning point in Odisha's development. In the wake of the super cyclone, Odisha became the first state in India to establish a disaster management authority (OSDMA) immediately after the disaster, doing so on December 28, 1999. During cyclones Phailin (2013) and Fani (2019), Odisha set a

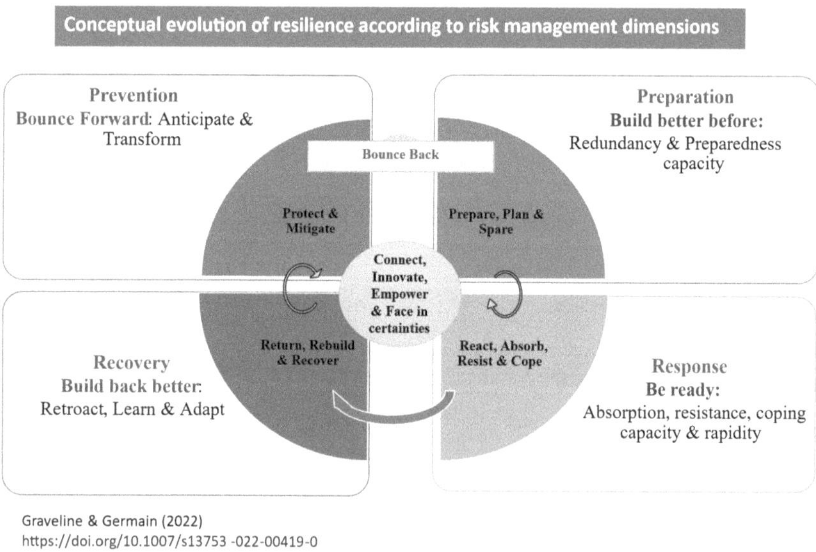

Diagram 10.1 Conceptual evolution of resilience (Gravelin & Germain, 2022; https://doi.org/10.1007/s13753-022-00419-0)

global benchmark in handling disasters by leveraging technology, strengthening institutional capacities, and building resilient measures. Odisha's years of planning and preparation in disaster management paid off as fatalities from powerful cyclones reduced significantly. The state government activates all the government departments, national, and international organizations and NGO facilities during emergencies. The most important conventional approach in disaster management by OSDMA is empowering the local community members and volunteers. Training programs and mock drills were conducted each year twice by state disaster management for local community members such as Gram panchayat members, women's self-help groups, and the cadre of volunteers to reduce the disaster risk and manage rescue and relief operations (Jena & Kouame, 2023). The disaster-specific targets of Sustainable Development Goals (SDG) 2030 and the short- and long-term targets of Odisha Vision Document 2036 for Disaster Management, along with the Sendai Framework for Disaster Risk Reduction (SFDRR) 2015–2030, as well as the Honorable Prime Minister's ten-point agenda for disaster risk reduction (DRR) have been taken into active consideration for the preparation of the State Disaster Management Plan (OSDMA, 2023).

In order to handle mental health concerns following a disaster and offer psychological support, care, and rehabilitation, OSDMA worked in conjunction with NIMHANS and other state and federal organizations. The active participation of mental health professionals during the super cyclone and Cyclone Fani helps a lot of the people of Odisha to cope with the disaster effectively. Several psychosocial care & support manuals at both the individual and community levels were developed by the NIMHANS team in collaboration with ActionAid and OXFAM to manage the psychological, emotional, and behavioral issues during the disaster (Sekar et al., 2023). Diagram 10.2 shows the collaboration of OSDMA with NIMHANS in the context of psychosocial care at each phase of the disaster. NIMHANS has been working to help the people of Odisha since the 1999 super cyclone.

Some studies found that after receiving various forms of community-level training, there has been an increase in Odisha residents' levels of coping and resilience. According to a study report, Fani survivors' higher levels of hope, self-efficacy, cognitive flexibility, collective efficacy, social

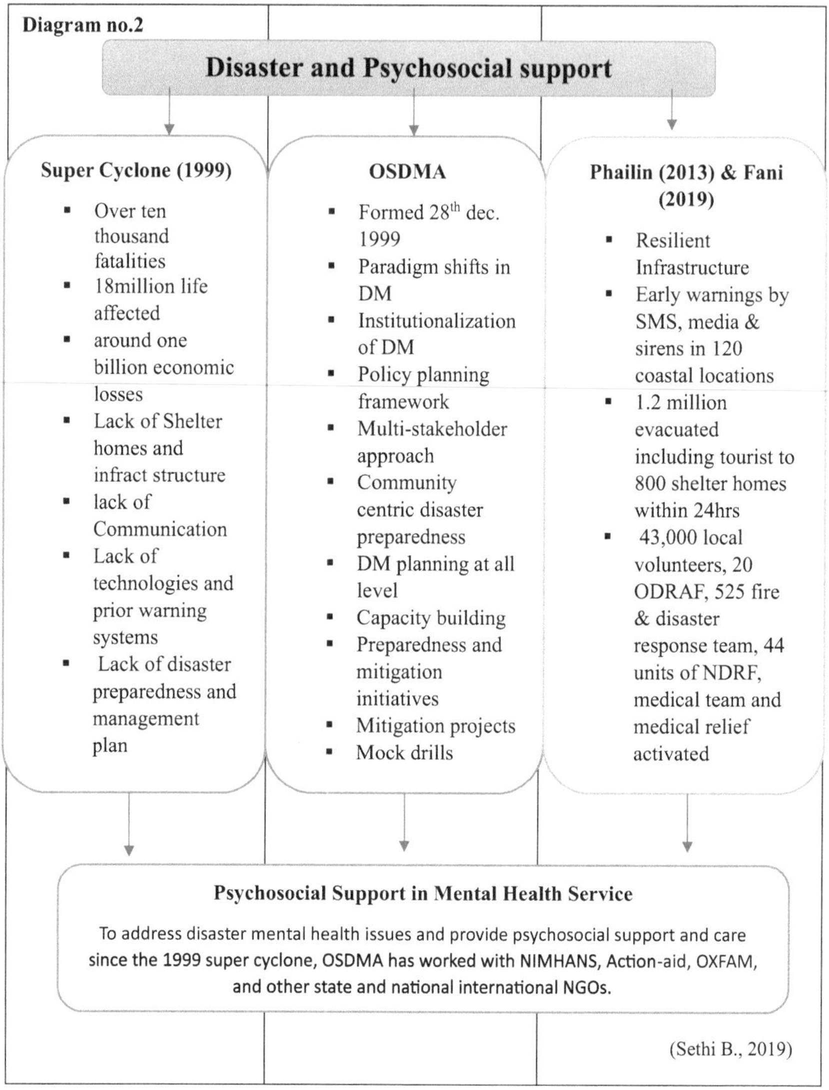

Diagram 10.2 Events of disasters and psychosocial support interventions (Sethi, 2019)

support, and health are all associated with their increased resilience. A greater degree of resilience promotes the post-traumatic growth and well-being of survivors in terms of meaning, purpose, life satisfaction, self-worth, and a sense of success. The relationship between antecedents and consequences is mediated by the resilience of survivors. Disaster survivors can flourish and experience post-traumatic growth if their antecedent resources and resilience are improved (Panigrahi & Suar, 2023). Presently, India has included mental health services and psychosocial support into its disaster management framework. The National Guidelines for Psychosocial Support and Mental Health Services (PSSMHS) were released in December 2009. They serve as a comprehensive guide for effective and efficient qualitative services for survivors before, during, and after a disaster.

Conclusion

Natural disasters are common in the state of Odisha. The state government believed that it was essential to have a specific disaster management policy and to provide the necessary guidelines on all aspects of emergency management in light of the International Decade for Natural Disaster Reduction (IDNDR), national initiatives, and the state's own experience during the 1999 cyclone. By improving the physical infrastructure and the biophysical, psychological, social, and economic well-being of the people, the Disaster Management Policy will concentrate on reducing vulnerability and managing risks overall. It will also make the populace more robust to disasters (OSDMA, 2005).

As a cyclone-prone state, Odisha learned from its own experience. After the 1999 cyclone, Odisha's disaster risk reduction and community resilience strategy successfully endeavored as per the Sendai Framework. An important part of successful disaster management is the model of preparedness set by Odisha. By developing appropriate relief infrastructure, relief distribution protocol, highly trained manpower, community-centric standard operating procedures, accurate early warning systems, the effective coordination of various stakeholders, and above all, proactive governance, Odisha set an example for others. This state has conducted several workshops and training programs for individuals, families, and community members at the state and district levels to address mental health issues and provide psychosocial care and support (PSSMHS) in emergencies, in collaboration with the NIMHANS and other national and international organizations. By offering psychological first aid, emotional and social support, putting the needs of the most vulnerable members of society first, and emphasizing rehabilitation, psychosocial support and care (PSS) helps the people of Odisha accept and cope with the traumatic and stressful events of Super Cyclone Fani. A study (Jena & Kouame, 2023) reported that, by strengthening the capacity of people at the community level with better infrastructure, technology, and communication, nowadays people of Odisha have become more resilient and more capable of handling disaster situations like any other developed country.

References

Barua, K. (2024). List of cyclones that hit India from 2019 to 2024. Jagran Josh, Bhubaneswar, https://www.jagranjosh.com/general-knowledge/list-of-cyclones-in-india-1591178815-1

Brennan, M. A., Barnett, R. V., & Flint, C. G. (2005). Community volunteers: the front line of disaster response. *The International Journal of Volunteer Administration, XXIV*(4), 52–56.

Chachra, S. (2004). Disasters and mental health in India: An institutional response. In *Disaster mental health in India* (2004 ed.). ActionAid India.

Dückers, M., van Hoof, W., Willems, A., & te Brake, H. (2022). Appraising evidence-based mental health and psychosocial support (MHPSS) guidelines—PART II: A content analysis with implications for disaster risk reduction. *International Journal of Environmental Research and Public Health, 19*(13), 7798. https://doi.org/10.3390/ijerph19137798

Graveline, M. H., & Germain, D. (2022). Disaster Risk Resilience: Conceptual Evolution, Key Issues, and Opportunities. *International Journal of Disaster Risk Science, 13*(3), 330–341. https://doi.org/10.1007/s13753-022-00419-0

Hackbarth, M., Pavkov, T., Wetchler, J., & Flannery, M. (2012). Natural disasters: An assessment of family resiliency following hurricane Katrina. *Journal of Marital and Family Therapy, 38*(2), 340–351. https://doi.org/10.1111/j.1752-0606.2011.00227.x

Jena, P., & Kouame, A. (2023). *Odisha's turnaround in disaster management has lessons for the world*. www.worldbank.org

Juvva, S., & Rajendran, P. (2000). *Disaster mental health: A current perspective.* https://www.researchgate.net/publication/297851748

Kar, N. (2022). *Disaster mental health in India: A long journey ahead.*https://www.researchgate.net/publication/359370104

Kar, N., Sharma, P., Murali, N., & Mehrotra, S. (1999). Mental health consequences of the trauma of super-cyclone. *Indian Journal of Psychiatry, 46*(3).

Marshall, J., Wiltshire, J., Delva, J., Bello, T., & Masys, A. J. (2020). Natural and manmade disasters: Vulnerable populations. In *Global health security* (pp. 143–161). Springer. https://doi.org/10.1007/978-3-030-23491-1_7

Murthy et al., (2003). *Evaluation report on psychosocial care of survivors of super cyclone in Orissa.*ActionAid India.https://www.researchgate.net/publication/259892051

Murthy, RS., Kar, N., Sekar, K., Swain, S., Mishra, V., Daniel, U. (2003). *Psychosocial care for survivors of Orissa supercyclone*. Bhubaneshwar, Orissa: Action Aid India.

Murthy RS., Sekar, K, Bharat, S., Kumar KVK., Chandrashekar CR., Chawdhary P., Parthasarathy R., Girimji S, (2000); *Psychosocial care for individuals- Super cyclone, Information Manual-1*. Action Aid and NIMHANS, Bengaluru, www.booksforchange.net,

Murthy, S. (2004). Contributions of the National Institute of Mental Health and Neuroscience (NIMHANS), Bangalore, to disaster and mental health care (1981–2002). In *Disaster mental health in India* (2004 ed.). Action Aid India.

Murthy, et al. (1999). *Psychosocial care for individuals*. www.booksforchange.net

NDMA. (2021). *Annual report (2020–2021).*https://ndma.gov.in/sites/default/files/PDF/Reports/NDMA_Annual_Report_2021-22.pdf

Newnham et al.,(2022). *WHO guidance on research methods for health emergency and disaster risk management*. https://iris.who.int

O'connor, J., Eberle, C., Newsom, A., & Sebesvari, Z. (2021). *Cyclone Amphan.* https://s3.eu-central-1.amazonaws.com

OSDMA. (2005). *State Disaster Management Policy*. https://www.osdma.org/

OSDMA (2013). *Cyclone Phailin in Odisha: Rapid damage and needs assessment* https://documents1.worldbank.org/curated/en/168471468257979992/pdf/838860WP0P14880Box382116B00PUBLIC0.pdf

OSDMA. (2019). *Memorandum: Extremely severe cyclonic storm "Fani."*
OSDMA. (2023). *State disaster management plan.* https://www.osdma.org/state-dm-plan
Panigrahi, G. S., & Suar, D. (2023). Antecedents and consequences of resilience among survivors of Cyclone Fani. *Current Psychology, 42*(31), 27203–27216. https://doi.org/10.1007/s12144-022-03835-z
Patel, S. K., Mathew, B., Nanda, A., Mohanty, B., & Saggurti, N. (2020). Voices of rural people: Community-level assessment of effects and resilience to natural disasters in Odisha, India. *International Journal of Population Studies, 6*(1), 3–15. https://doi.org/10.18063/ijps.v6i1.1042
Patel SS, Rogers MB, Amlôt R, Rubin GJ (2017). What Do We Mean by 'Community Resilience'? A Systematic Literature Review of How It Is Defined in the Literature. *PLoS Curr.* 2017 Feb 1;9:ecurrents.dis.db775aff25efc5ac4f0660ad9c9f7db2. doi: 10.1371/currents.dis.db775aff25efc5ac4f0660ad9c9f7db2. PMID: 29188132; PMCID: PMC5693357
Paton, D. (2019). Disaster risk reduction: Psychological perspectives on preparedness. *Australian Journal of Psychology, 71*(4), 327–341. https://doi.org/10.1111/ajpy.12237
Patra, D. (2024). Odisha Super Cyclone: Why disaster response should focus on both preventing casualties and minimising trauma to rebuild livelihood. Down to Earth https://www.downtoearth.org
Patterson, O., Weil, F., & Patel, K. (2010). The role of community in disaster response: Conceptual models. *Population Research and Policy Review, 29*(2), 127–141. https://doi.org/10.1007/s11113-009-9133-x
Rubonis, A. V., & Bickman, L. (1991). Psychological impairment in the wake of disaster: The disaster-psychopathology relationship. *Psychological Bulletin, 109*(3), 384–399. https://doi.org/10.1037/0033-2909.109.3.384
Satapathy, S. (2012). *Mental health impact of disasters in India: Ex-ante and ex-post analysis* (pp. 425–461). ERIA.
Sekar, K. (2004). Orissa super cyclone. *Disaster mental health in India.* Indian Red Cross Society. ISBN 81-89113-00-3
Sekar, K., Jayakumar, C., & Jude, P. (2004). *National disaster management training psychosocial care in disasters national disaster management training module-2 psychosocial care in disasters III.* www.nimhans.ac.in
Sekar, K., Bhadra, S., Jayakumar, C., Aravindraj, E., Grace, H., & Kumar, K. (2005). *Psychosocial care in disaster management: Facilitation manual for trainers of trainees in natural disaster.*

Sekar, K., Jayakumar, C., & Jude, P. (2023). *National disaster management training module-2 psychosocial care in disasters*. www.nimhans.ac.in

Sethi, B. (2019). *Disaster Preparedness in Odisha*. Commissioner-cum-Secretary, Disaster Management, Special Relief Commissioner and Managing Director, Odisha State Disaster Management Authority, Government of Odisha.

Sinha, A. (2009). Report on Recovery and Reconstruction Following the Orissa Super Cyclone in October 1999. *Asian Disaster Reduction Center*, http://www.osdma.org/

UNDRR. (2009). *Sendai framework terminology on disaster risk reduction*.

UNISDR. (2009). *International strategy for disaster reduction*. www.preventionweb.net

Verma, K., & Kumar Gupta, A. (2021). *Cyclone Tauktae: Cyclones, their impacts and disasters risk management*. https://www.researchgate.net/publication/354450767

WHO. (2022). *Guidance on research methods for health emergency and disaster risk management*. https://iris.who.int

Yadav, P. K., Dubey, D., & Mishra, M. (2023). A study and analysis of earthquake in India. *Indian Journal of Science Research*.https://www.ijsronline.org/issue/20230315-015248.822.pdf

YCDA. (2019). *Report of cyclone "Fani" affected communities in Odisha*. https://www.globalgiving.org/pfil/39999/Report_of_Fani_.pdf

Zulch, H. (2019). *Psychological preparedness for natural hazards—Improving disaster preparedness policy and practice*. https://www.undrr.org

11

Psychosocial Support for the Survivors of the Gujarat Earthquake (2001) with Specific Focuses on the Vulnerable Survivors of the Disaster

Subhasis Bhadra and Lipika Pradhan

Introduction

Earthquakes are one of the most destructive and unpredictable natural hazards faced by human beings all over the world. Studies reported that over the past century, more than 1100 destructive earthquakes occurred, causing around 1.5 million deaths worldwide (Jena et al., 2021). According to the Long Short-Term Memory (LSTM) model (a Geographic Information System [GIS] technique to assess earthquake vulnerability across the whole of India), reported that the areas around Delhi, the north-eastern region of India, major parts of Gujarat, and the West Bengal Plain exhibit very-high seismic vulnerability (Jena et al., 2021). India experiences about 200–250 mild earthquakes every year in different regions, of which only a few are noticeable to people. Over the past half-century, earthquakes have caused significant loss of life and

S. Bhadra (✉) • L. Pradhan
Department of Psychosocial Support in Disaster Management, NIMHANS, Bengaluru, Karnataka, India

S. Bhadra et al. (eds.), *Psychosocial and Mental Health Support for Disaster Management in India*, Palgrave Studies in Disaster Science and Emergency Management,
https://doi.org/10.1007/978-3-032-02511-1_11

property damage in India (Dubey & Mishra, 2023). It not only damages physical infrastructure, resulting in human deaths and injuries, but also has substantial direct and indirect effects on the mental health as well as the social and economic conditions of the individuals and society (Bertinelli et al., 2023).

According to geologists, 80% of the planet's earthquakes occur due to the geological and geotechnical effects in certain regions like the rim of the Pacific Ocean and mostly occur around fault zones, where tectonic plates collide or slide against each other (Mckeever & Vergano, 2019). However, some other reports suggest that certain man-made activities also contribute to natural disasters such as earthquakes and other climate-induced disasters (Gibbens, 2017). According to the report of the human-induced earthquake database (HiQuake) by the Seismological Society of America (2017), 730 earthquakes have been triggered by human-induced activities (Shivni, 2017). According to Wilson, one of the geophysicists suggested that among the major causes behind the earthquakes contributed by humans are mining projects (37%), water impounded behind dams (23%), unconventional oil and gas extraction, and nuclear explosions (Wilson et al., 2017). According to reports in 2008, an estimated 80,000 people died or went missing following a 7.9 earthquake in China's Sichuan province and scientists viewed that the earthquake was triggered by the weight of 320 million tons of water that had been collected in the Zipingpu Reservoir (Foulger et al., 2017). Another example in Nepal in 2015, a 7.8 magnitude earthquake, was likely caused by groundwater extraction (Gibbens, 2017). Thus, it is not only geological conditions but also the structural design, economic conditions, and social behavior of human beings becoming the major contributing factors to increased vulnerability in disasters such as earthquakes (Pradhan et al., 2021).

Gujarat Earthquake (2001)

Gujarat is the fifth-largest Indian state by area, covering some 196,024 km^2 (75,685 sq. miles), and the ninth most populous state, with a population of 6.03 crores according to the 2011 census report. Its coastline, of about 1600 km (990 miles), is the longest in the country. The Kachchh region in the state of Gujarat is highly prone to earthquakes due to its location on the boundary of the Indian and Eurasian plates (Gujarat State Disaster Management Authority [GSDMA], 2023). On January 26, 2001, the 51st Republic Day, at 08:46 AM IST, a massive earthquake, measuring 7.7 on the Richter Scale, occurred in the state of Gujarat, western India. The epicenter was about 9 km south-southwest of the village of Chobari in Bhachau Taluka of Kutch (Kachchh) District of Gujarat, India. Over 37.8 million people were affected as the devastating earthquake destroyed homes, schools, roads, communication systems, industries, public infrastructures, and power lines. The earthquake was followed by several aftershocks over the next few days (WHO, 2021). According to the Indian Metrological Department report, more than 500 aftershocks of magnitude 3.0 and above continued through the month of March. According to reports from the Government of Gujarat, 20,086 died and 166,000 were injured; of these, 20,000 were severely injured in the earthquake. The number of people still missing is 233 in Kutch (Vatsa, 2001). About 600,000 people were left homeless, 348,000 houses were destroyed and an additional 844,000 were partially damaged. The Indian State Department estimates that the earthquake affected, directly or indirectly, some 15.9 million people out of a total state population of 37.8 million. More than 20,000 cattle are reported to have died. Government estimates place the direct economic losses at $1.3 billion. Other estimates indicated that the losses may be as high as $5 billion (Sinha, 2001). According to reports, more than 3000 health facilities were destroyed, including a 281-bed district hospital, a 16-bed mental hospital at Bhuj, and 239 health centers (Sharma, 2002).

Impact of Disaster and Psychological Reactions

Earthquakes are one of the most destructive and frequently occurring natural disasters. According to Strobl et al. (2023), people who are exposed to earthquakes are likely to increase their propensity toward developing mental and behavioral disorders by directly inducing fear, anxiety, depression, or causing post-traumatic stress disorder (PTSD) and indirectly sustained psychological injuries, including the deaths of loved ones, or losing belongings or their employment following an earthquake (Bertinelli et al., 2023). These life-threatening events generate stress and sadness, resulting in 'Psychological traps.' Psarros et al. (2002) observed the psychological effects one month after the earthquake and found that psychological suffering was not restricted solely to the initial damage, but also included the long-standing effect on survivors (Bhadra, 2011a, 2011b). According to the assessment report carried out done by Indian Council of Medical Research(ICMR) in collaboration with Institute of Human Behaviour & Allied Sciences (IHBAS) (2005) following the Gujarat earthquake, found that 70–90% of the population in the affected area had transient psychological disturbances four to five weeks after the earthquake, and 30–50% of the population was expected to have moderate to severe psychological/psychiatric signs and symptoms, subsyndromal problems and acute stress-related disorders three to six months after the earthquake and also that 5–15% of the survivors were expected to have long-term mental health morbidity (Shah et al., 2005).

In this devastating earthquake in Gujarat, specifically, it was the cities of Bhuj, Bachhau, Anjar, Rapar, and Gandhidham that were the worst-affected settlements in the district of Kutch, and some portions of Ahmedabad, Rajkot, Jamnagar, and Patan districts were also severely affected. To address the mental health needs of the survivors, one team of health professionals from government hospitals in Gujarat visited affected health facilities and shelter homes and communities (Vankar & Mehta, 2004). According to the World Health Organization (WHO), 13 meetings of health sector group coordination were held during the initial period of 6 months and it continued for the next couple of months to focus on health promotion, rehabilitation, psychosocial support, reproductive and child health, etc. (WHO, 2002). Temporary health centers were set up in different places of Bhuj cities to facilitate the health services and the continuity of disease surveillance (WHO, 2021). A team of mental health professionals from ActionAid India, in collaboration with the National Institute of Mental Health in Neuro Sciences (NIMHANS) and Oxfam India Trust also visited the survivors and injured to understand their psychological distress after the earthquake at institutions and communities. According to studies, in the initial phase of assessment, it has been reported that 45.5% of patients attending primary health centers showed higher levels of psychological distress and disability related to earthquakes (Vankar & Mehta, 2004). A study carried out by a non-governmental organization (NGO) also found that 80% of people with paraplegia and amputation showed high psychological morbidity, which was mostly associated with high family burden and responsibility (Ramappa & Bhadra, 2004). According to Oxfam India, psychosocial disability was high among the survivors of young adolescent to middle-aged group people (15 to 35 years), which indicates that the working-age group was largely affected by the socioeconomic difficulties of the families in this earthquake. Looking at the income level of the families, it was seen that about half of the persons with disability were from the lower-income group, which became an added burden for family members following the earthquake. Another study found that in the Kutch district, out of 507 teachers, 171 (33.6%) met the criteria for PTSD, and the risk factors were the death of the schoolchildren, injuries to students, or the death of family members. Considering the gender perspective, it has been reported that 40% of women, compared with 27.8% of men, had met the criteria for PTSD. The United Nations International Children's Emergency Fund (UNICEF) conducted one study with children and adolescent survivors and reported that 19.8% of adolescents had clinically significant features of PTSD, which means that, out of 126 cases, one in five adolescents experienced post-traumatic stress disorder (Gupta, 2004). The most common type of psychological symptoms found in 40% of adolescent groups with PTSD were impaired attention and concentration, lack of pleasure in activities, being easily startled, avoidance of trauma reminders, survivor guilt, apprehension of recurrence, regressive behavior, difficulties in sleep and appetite, etc. (Vankar & Mehta, 2004).

According to Government of Gujarat reports, 17,000 people were operated on for various injuries immediately or within a few weeks after the earthquake, and some 167,000 were treated at various makeshift facilities in the affected areas (Sharma, 2002). Some follow-up reports from various organizations suggested that lack of post-operative care after injuries leads many people to develop gangrene out of infections and required amputation. According to Oxfam, India, increased disability load also increased the psychosocial distress within the individuals and their family members each passing day after the earthquake (Unnikrishnan,

2002). In the Gujarat earthquake, it has been observed that immediately after the disaster, huge numbers of injured people came for medical help, but the number of healthcare staff, medical equipment, and medicines was completely inadequate. According to one study report, unsafe blood transfusions and instances of surgeons using a single instrument on many patients without disinfecting (due to lack of time and medical supplies) were increasing threats of another HIV disaster in Gujarat (Sharma, 2002).

The World Health Organization Disability Assessment Schedule-2 (WHO-DAS-2) showed that disability is higher among those who had a higher score in Self Reporting Questionnaire (SRQ). The psychological stress among people who became disabled due to injury was high, which signifies the likelihood of having diagnosable mental health problems (Bhadra, 2011a, 2011b). According to reports from the Indian People's Tribunal on Environmental and Human Rights (2001), there are many cases of permanent disabilities due to either amputation or spinal cord injury (SCI), and more than 100 survivors became either paraplegic or quadriplegic (Bhadra, 2015). According to studies, it has also been reported that the prevalence of mental health problems in rural areas was 36.1% in the most severely affected villages and 23% in moderately affected villages. Similarly, in urban areas, the level of mental health morbidity was 81.7%, and populations who had lost family members accounted for 90.9% of mental health problems (Ramappa & Bhadra, 2004). Studies reported that exposure to repeated earthquake and house damage can lead to long-term negative psychological and physical health (psychosomatic) consequences (Stroebe et al., 2021). According to studies, it has also been reported that the long-term impact of the Gujarat earthquake induced psychological distress such as trauma and adjustment issues in children (Kumar et al., 2016). Studies also reported that the impact of natural disasters can induce both internalizing (depression, anxiety, etc.) and externalizing (conduct and other behavioral issues) problems in youth (Rubens et al., 2018).

PSS-MHS Interventions in Disasters

In order to address mental health problems and psychosocial needs, ActionAid India, in collaboration with NIMHANS, Oxfam (India), and many other NGOs, worked together to provide psychosocial care and support to the survivors of the Gujarat earthquake. The major program was organized through ActionAid India under the *Sneha Samudaya* (Community of love/affection) program (community level) in collaboration with eight local-level organizations. The aim of the program was to support women and children, more specifically single women (Ekalnari), orphans, disabled, and children with single parents (Ramappa & Bhadra, 2004). The rehabilitation and well-being of the vulnerable groups was a major intervention under the *Sneha Samudaya* program. In the earthquake, a total of 146 villages were affected and 164 community volunteers (called *Senhakarmi*, workers for spreading love/affection) were trained on different aspects of psychosocial care and support. Under the psychosocial care and support program, 1553 disabled persons, 4979 single women, 244 orphans, 1544 children with a single parent, and 789 aged persons were directly provided with long-term interventions (Chachra, 2004). Oxfam India carried out a major project for the rehabilitation of persons with spinal cord injuries or amputations. A team of physiotherapists and social workers would visit the patients in their homes to provide treatment and care. At this time, the social workers played a major role in establishing rapport with the patient, the primary caregivers, and their families. It was seen that after corrective surgery, while the persons with paraplegia did return home, they required continuous medical care. Further, the patients and family members had very high expectations about recovery. Most of them expected that with physiotherapy intervention, they would be able to walk. Thus, at this point, establishing rapport with the patients was crucial for setting realistic expectations and helping them develop the necessary skills for daily living. Thus, social workers provided psychosocial support to individuals who were in the community. Working with the cases of amputations was equally important as often they were unhappy with the prosthesis and did not use the same. The psychosocial support intervention was organized at the individual, family, group, and community levels through capacity building among the community volunteers. Psychosocial support and mental health awareness training were also organized for the physiotherapists and nurses so that they could understand the feelings and explain the treatment outcome gradually and help the patient to choose a livelihood option or regain confidence in the household activities within their new physical and social limitations. About six months after the earthquake, Oxfam India started a residential care facility providing intensive physiotherapy training for persons with paraplegia with 20 beds. The facility was a temporary structure, constructed of bamboo and wood, and a tin roof, but with no concrete walls that could have made it earthquake-proof. It was constructed quickly and at low cost to address an immediate need. In this institutional facility, persons with paraplegia were involved in a number of exercise and sports activities, group meetings and individual sessions to facilitate both physical and psychological healing. Initially, the inmates reported substantial level of depression and other psychological problems such as anxiety, distress, adjustment, anger, frustration, hopelessness, helplessness, lack of interest, and lack of sexual capacity, which leads to different patterns of sexual behavior, suicidal wishes, and substance cravings. Some of them now experienced feelings of shame because of their physical dependence on others for their daily living activities. The psychosocial interventions, activity scheduling, individual sessions, and group meetings with the inmates and family and others helped in the gradual recovery. Each patient stayed for about two or three months before they returned to their families. Additionally, a few of them were provided financial support, livelihood training, compensation (from the government), and other legal and paralegal help as part of the community-based rehabilitation (Ramappa & Bhadra, 2004). The disabled-friendly houses for persons with paraplegia and amputation were provided by organizations that worked on housing projects.

The NIMHANS team, in collaboration with Action Aid India, and Oxfam India, developed training manuals for volunteers, teachers, and health professionals to provide psychosocial care and support to survivors of the earthquakes in Gujarat (Murthy, 2004). Manual number 1 was to provide psychosocial support to the individuals so that survivors can understand their emotional reactions and adopt various strategies to deal with the stress reaction in order to regain normalcy. The second manual was for families to help the surviving families understand various stressful situations and reactions on their physical and psychological journey and further develop healthy coping to rebuild the family unit with adequate emotional bonds, responsibilities, and mutual cooperation. Coordination with others, reaching out for support, restarting livelihood initiatives, and working as community volunteers were among the techniques that were described in detail. The third manual was concerned with psychosocial support for children and adolescents, which became very important for teachers who worked in the school. These manuals highlighted the normalization of reactions, adopting self-care strategies, community participation, and gaining well-being in the aftermath of disaster. These were translated and published in Gujarati by Sneha Samudaya as well as the Gujarat Council for Educational Research and Training (GCERT) for various training programs and subsequent use. UNICEF focused on psychosocial care provided by teachers through GCERT. Various so-called Training of Trainers (TOT) programs were organized to facilitate the cascading model of knowledge and skill transfer to the teachers, community-level volunteers, NGO staff, and other grassroots-level workers. Following the TOT program, mental health professionals from the Health and Family Welfare Department and educators from the Education Department were identified as facilitators of training programs. The sessions comprised of the sharing of individual experiences related to the earthquake, the psychosocial effects of disaster on children, effective communication skills to deal with survivors, basic counseling skills, the recognition and identification of severe emotional problems and referral, self-care and classroom-based activities for healing, etc. (Vankar & Mehta, 2004). Many such training programs with community volunteers were conducted in the affected areas, focusing on the specific issues of the different vulnerable groups such as survivors of injury, orphan and semi-orphan children, widowed women, elderly survivors, youths, and others. Community-based psychosocial support by engaging the community-level volunteers through the involvement of the local NGOs was the main strategy employed to reach out and sustain the intervention. Close contact with the Bhuj Mental Hospital was made to deal with the cases that needed medication for higher levels of distress. Medical outreach camps for mental health screening were conducted initially for the first six to eight months in collaboration with the mental hospital, local hospitals, and NGOs to facilitate screening and referral.

Intervention with Specific Vulnerable/ Marginalized Group

A vulnerable group can be defined as a population within a country that has specific characteristics that make it at a higher risk of needing humanitarian assistance than others or being excluded from financial and social services. In a crisis, such groups (the elderly, children, women, and physically and mentally disabled) would need extra assistance, which appeals to additional measures such as extra capacity and resources as part of the emergency response during a disaster (Kuran et al., 2020). In the Gujarat earthquake (2001), it was reported that children who lost their parents, single women, widows, people who developed permanent disabilities due to injuries, older adults, people from the *Dalit* communities, and other marginalized people in the society were more prone to developing psychological symptoms in comparison with others in the aftermath of the earthquake.

Children

According to UNICEF, in the Gujarat earthquake, 12,000 buildings were destroyed; as a result, 400,000 children were affected by the closure of schools. About five million children under the age of 14 have been affected, including young people who lost their homes, their schools, and also their sense of security. Some three million children also lost family members or friends in the quake. Studies reported that 100% of school students and 75% of teachers reported a psychological problem. Symptoms of depression, anxiety, sleeplessness, avoidance of contact with the outside world, and suicidal tendencies were among the manifestations of psychological problems (Sharma, 2002). According to studies, it has been reported that natural disasters have a long-term and negative effect on the psychological well-being of children. Children exposed to natural disasters have often developed significant attachment and adjustment issues following disasters (Kumar et al., 2016). Studies showed that prolonged exposure to traumatic experiences and violence can negatively affect the psychological well-being of children and increase the chances of developing psychological distress/disorders like PTSD, adjustment, etc. (Target et al., 2016).

To provide psychosocial care and support to children, Oxfam India, in collaboration with ActionAid (India) under the banner of *Sneha Samudaya*, started working for them, specifically orphans & children with single parents, by reaching out to families in the community at large. In villages, a center for children (*Sneha Center*) was established where the children could come and spend time with the *Senhakarme* to talk about disaster situations and plan for the future. The caregivers and the other community members also visited the center to plan the children's future. Those extended family members who became the primary caregivers were supported in various other livelihood programs to facilitate adequate family relationships. *Senhakarmi* used to visit these children in their homes. They have also conducted small-group-level interaction (*Bal Melas*) to understand their feeling and needs. The *Bal Melas* were conducted in various age groups of children (Ramappa & Bhadra, 2004). In 2001, considering the needs of the uncared children without family support, SOS Children's Village started a center at Gandhidham, which then shifted to Bhuj. This provided alternative family homes to a number of the affected children (SOS Children's Village, 2001).

UNICEF started a project to train teachers and service providers to develop and strengthen the capacities for the psychosocial care of children and families in the communities, to strengthen the specialized psychosocial services for traumatized children, and to develop disaster preparedness plans and policies for children (Gupta, 2004). In schools, teachers conducted various psychosocial support activities for supporting ventilation, open discussion, and strengthening positive coping and hope. "Worry Box" was one activity that helped students to write about their worries, and teachers also addressed those concerns. Similarly, there were several activities of drawing, writing, and storytelling in the schools to facilitate the psychosocial healing of the students and bring normalcy to the classroom activities. Life skills education was initiated for both children and adolescents. It was observed that after a few sessions, young children were able to express their feelings, such as fear, emotions toward their parents, and their longing to be with their nearest and dearest became a prominent issue. Specific sessions were arranged for those who had high post-traumatic stress reactions and other related psychological issues. Some of them also complained about the foster parents for not giving them care and emotional support; some of them also wanted to start working to help their family instead of going to school. Children above 14 years of age mostly spoke about their insecurity and the lack of care and support. Many of these issues were gradually handled through the *Sneha Samudaya* program (Ramappa & Bhadra, 2004).

Women

Women in disaster are often the most vulnerable group because of preexisting conditions such as age, lack of education, financial dependence on male members of the family, social boundaries, and restrictions (Bhadra, 2017). In the Gujarat earthquake, it has been reported that women, especially single women and widows, were affected more by the disaster. Many women lost their husbands and children, and their homes. Some of the women sustained severe injuries and had additional physical and psychological issues. Many widowed women had reported psychological symptoms such as feelings of guilt, being overburdened, low self-esteem, and a lack of decision-making capability, which is mostly related to their family, their socioeconomic status, their financial dependency, and their additional family responsibilities after the disaster. Many of the widowed women were discriminated against by other family members. Most of their movements outside the family home were restricted by family members, and they were fearful of losing their rights. They also developed identity crises in their new status as widows. It was reported that widowed women were denied the right to control the compensations that they had received because of the death of their husbands or the loss of their house, which made them more vulnerable. In some families, it has been seen that girls were not allowed to study, and that boys were forced to take up some work to support the family after the death of their father. The early marriage of young girls became more prevalent. The caste system also became one of the major barriers for females during disasters. In some of the caste-based communities, women were always forced to be within the family and had the practice of the *parda* system (covering their face while in public) imposed on them. The widowed women from many communities were either not allowed or were discouraged from taking up any livelihood activities outside the home following the disaster. Single women did not receive enough (or regular) medical care and suffered higher disabilities following the earthquake. They have also developed other physical problems, such as abnormal blood pressure, headache, giddiness, sleep disturbances, poor nutrition etc. Single women more frequently reported feelings of deprivation, dissatisfaction, loneliness, anger, etc. Constant feelings of pressure imposed by in-laws and society after the death of their husbands made them more stressed and vulnerable (Ramappa & Bhadra, 2004).

To address the psychosocial needs of women (particularly those who were single or widowed), ActionAid India, in collaboration with NIMHANS and Oxfam, developed a community-based holistic care approach. Through this intervention model, they met each of the women and their family members in turn, provided medical care and support, and referred some of them for further necessary action. A few women from target villages were trained (these were known as *Ekalnari Sangini*—friend of single women) on psychosocial support, precisely the issues of women in their personal, family, and community life. In the training, a holistic care model was introduced which includes the integration of available services, such as healthcare, livelihood support, housing, microfinance and finance support, community support groups, etc. Through the psychosocial support program, the women were encouraged to form self-help groups and neighborhood groups, which allowed them to express their feelings and emotions and explore new opportunities. Under the holistic care model, economic, housing, medical, and legal aid support were also mobilized by the team members. One group was organized (*Sangathan*) at each village level to facilitate psychosocial intervention and awareness among the general population. About 4500 single women (*Ekalnaries*) were provided with interventions by NGOs, and 1200 were referred for other sectoral interventions under the holistic care approach (Ramappa & Bhadra, 2004).

Disabled

Disability leads to marginalization, even when society is functioning normally, and disaster causes additional challenges for this section of the population (Nanjunda et al., 2016). Disabled people are much more vulnerable in disaster situations compared to all other human beings in society. Pre-existing health conditions, physical dependency, and low socio-economic status often make them more dependent and helpless, while they are not being empowered with adequate training in the pre-disaster phase. It has been recorded in the Gujarat earthquake that a total of 104 paraplegics and 270 amputees were present in the 100 villages in Kutch, where Oxfam started to make an intervention for the rehabilitation of people with injuries. According to Oxfam (India), the disability rate was high among young adolescents, and this was the major reason why they developed psychological distress and trauma after the earthquake. The people who became disabled after sustaining severe injuries and subsequent amputation showed very high levels of distress, and some of them developed phantom limb syndrome. There was continuous resistance to accepting the reality of a wheelchair-bound life or living with assistive devices. They had developed psychological symptoms like anger outbursts toward family members, repeated vague complaints of body pain (somatization), sleep disturbances, frequent headaches, hopelessness, lack of interest, feelings of shame due to dependence on others, substance abuse, and loss of sexual capacity, which led to the development of a different pattern of abusive sexual behaviors (Ramappa & Bhadra, 2004).

The psychosocial support team of expert members closely observed the conditions of the injured, provided psychosocial support, and conducted different training programs for community-level volunteers, health support staff (physiotherapists, occupational therapists, nurses), and awareness generation for the family members at individual and community levels. The community-level helpers (called *Vikalanga Bandhu*—friends of people with disabilities) played an important role in providing support and care to people with disabilities on doorsteps on a regular basis. They helped them to accept and adjust to the situation. Injured paraplegics and amputees were admitted under institutional care run by Oxfam (India), where, along with physiotherapy, mental health care was also provided. There was continuous individual and group interaction with the patients, which helped the survivors to express their emotions and learn new skills of coping and activities for daily living and self-care techniques. In order to provide institutional care, Oxfam (India) made a rehabilitation center for paraplegics and amputees where they helped people with disabilities to accept the changed lifestyle and develop positive coping abilities and opportunities to plan their other livelihood options. The families of people suffering from spinal cord injuries and amputation were also engaged in self-help group activities and livelihood support so that they could maintain their basic life support. Oxfam India and Action Aid India, in coordination with the local NGOs, took major initiatives to ensure legal rights to people with disabilities and injured and a monthly disability pension for persons with spinal cord injuries was initiated (Bhadra, 2011b).

Seven years after the earthquake, it was observed that 20% of the population who sustained spinal cord injuries or undergone amputation also had several physical complications (frequent infection, pain, inability to adjust with artificial limbs, inability to continue self-care activities etc.) and associated psychological issues due to lack of medical attention, and other community support. Among the survivors, women survivors have better coping abilities as they are able to resume their household work in wheelchairs (Bhadra, 2011b). Another study revealed that independence in the area of Activities of Daily Living (ADL) plays a vital role in reducing the complications for survivors who sustained spinal cord injuries in the Gujarat earthquake and helped to improve their quality of life (Rosalin et al., 2009).

Other Marginalized Communities

A number of sections of our society were marginalized due to various sociocultural factors, and, during disaster, failure to recognize the psychosocial needs of those groups, and barriers to getting equal access to appropriate vital services and support make them more vulnerable (sphere 2004). In the Gujarat earthquake, it was seen that the relief materials were not equally distributed in *Dalit* (the lowest communities in the caste hierarchy) communities such as the *Kolis*, the *Rabaris*, and the Muslim communities, which made them more vulnerable to developed psychological distress and trauma following the earthquake (Louis, 2001). In the *Darbar* and *Rajput* castes, the widow women were under various restrictions because of caste-based practices. 'Ekalanari Sangathna' was established at the community level by the trained CLW to support those groups of women who were marginalized in the aftermath of the disaster, such as: widows, physically tortured, mentally tortured, physically disabled, psychologically depressed, totally controlled by in-laws, financially dependent on others (Bhadra, 2017). Similarly, the LGBTQ community was another marginalized section of society, who had a greater chance of developing psychological morbidity following a disaster. In Bhuj and Anjar Town, there are remote areas near the hill where a few members of the LGBTQ community were living, and they were supported during the rehabilitation. They had problems in obtaining temporary shelter as other community members had raised objections to their presence. It was often difficult to reach out to these community members because of the high levels of stigma associated with them. Another major vulnerable community was those families who were living as tenants in the towns of Bhuj, Anjar, and Bachua. They had lost their belongings, sustained injuries, and lost family members. These families were not eligible to receive compensation for the damage to the house as they were not the owners. This aspect was one major reason for distress. Further, legal support was provided to settle the aspects, and a few NGOs took active initiatives to provide independent houses to some of these families. Following the earthquake, while villages started housing projects and reconstruction, in the town areas, these were delayed for more than three years, as the planning for reconstruction took a lot of time in the absence of a town planning policy in the post-disaster scenario (Mukherji, 2015). Such situations often caused psychological distress and extended the period of suffering for the families. Even after more than twenty years of such a housing project, some of the families are yet to receive the legal documents about the ownership of their houses (Dahiya, 2022).

Interventions at the Community Level

In the Gujarat earthquake, CLW played a vital role in the rescue and rehabilitation of survivors in the post-disaster phase. The community care project, which was financially supported by Action Aid, was named "*Sneha Samudaya*," which means a caring community (community of love/affection). This community project was a replication of the psychosocial rehabilitation project "*Sanha Abhyan*" (campaign of love) which ActionAid, in partnership with NIMHANS, developed in Odisha following the super cyclone in 1999. This project was a collective response by ActionAid India, and eight local NGOs, namely Behavioral Science Center, Gantar, Unnati, Praya-Gujarat, Marga, Saath, Prayas-Delhi, and Hath Milao, to ensure psychosocial care and rehabilitation within families and communities with a specific emphasis on the vulnerable groups within society. The *Snehakarmis* (community-level workers) in the initial phases of disaster principally focused on physical rebuilding and mental health care. Remarkable changes appeared in the conditions of the most vulnerable survivors of the earthquake as a result of the collective efforts of *Sneha Samudaya*, in which all different sectors of community volunteer workers (*Ekalnari Sangini, Vikalang Bandhu*) were engaged together (Chachra, 2004). Various training programs were conducted by mental health professionals to train the community-level workers in aspects of mental health and emotional well-being of the survivors in the aftermath of disasters and to ensure an improved level of functioning and quality of life. The CLW (*Snehakarmis*), through regular community visits and engagement with the survivors, helped to identify the psychosocial needs of the survivors and were able to mobilize services. They were further trained on various legal issues like filling out the forms for compensation, enrolling in social security benefit schemes (disability, widow, old age pensions), reissuing certificates, etc. The volunteers enrolled many children back into the formal schools after the relocation or the reopening of the schools in the villages. Regular community engagement activities like *Bal Melas* (Children's Fair), community picnics, and community prayers were organized at the villages that helped the survivors to regain normalcy and facilitated community connections (Chachra, 2004). Another major area Oxfam India worked in was ensuring proper compensation for the affected people, helping to organize the people to avail themselves of the benefits, and ensuring the rights of vulnerable sections of society such as the injured, paraplegics, amputees, widows, orphans, elderly, etc. (Ramappa & Bhadra, 2004). An Indian People's Tribunal was organized to document the various demands of the survivors and to process them so that they could receive adequate compensation (Sukumaran, 2001).

Humanitarian Service Providers

The Gujarat earthquake broke down individuals, families, and society both physically and emotionally. During such conditions, numerous humanitarian NGOs, national, international and local organizations participated in rescue and relief operations and, subsequently, in the rehabilitation process. According to the Asian Disaster Center Report (2001), the Gujarat State Disaster Management Authority (GSDMA) implemented the reconstruction and rehabilitation with support from various other agencies in the quake-hit area (Shina, 2001). The World Bank and the Asian Development Bank, in association with other bilateral agencies, such as the European Union (EU), the Department for International Development (DFID), the United States Agency for International Development (USAID), and the Canadian International Development Agency (CIDA), provided financial assistance for the rehabilitation program. The Housing and Urban Development Corporation (HUDCO) and the National Housing Bank (NHB), two major public sector institutions in India, provide support to rebuild houses. Other commercial organizations, such as Reliance, VSNL, TATA, ESSAR, Videocon, Wipro etc., also contributed to the long-term rehabilitation of earthquake survivors. The American Red Cross, the International Federation of Red Cross with the Indian Red Cross Branch, CARE (India), Help Age India, Handicapped International, Caritas India, and many other organizations participated in immediate rescue and long-term rehabilitation operations such as providing shelter, water, sanitation, medical facilities, clothes, etc., in rural areas. The Red Cross Society (India), Oxfam (India), and Action Aid India, in collaboration with NIMHANS, Bangalore, principally focused on the mental health aspects and provided psychosocial care and support to individuals, families, communities and vulnerable populations in the post-earthquake situation (Murthy, 2004). The World Health Organization (WHO) responded to the earthquake by placing experts in emergency and humanitarian action in Ahmedabad and Bhuj on the morning after the earthquake and providing various technical support. The WHO mainly focused on the health sector coordination, the containment of disease outbreaks, the enhancement of capacity/capability of disease surveillance practices, and water quality assurance. Other health challenges include addressing psychological first aid (PFA), trauma counseling, maternity health, emergency care, etc., also managed by both national and international organizations (Shina, 2001). The Government of Gujarat and the United Nations Office for the Coordination of Humanitarian Affairs (OCHA) coordinated relief operations from Ahmedabad and Bhuj airport, which became the focal point for the collection and dissemination of assessment information. In addition, the UNICEF, the UN Population Fund (UNFPA), the International Labor Organization (ILO), and the Food and Agriculture Organization (FAO) were involved in the rescue, relief and rehabilitation phases of disaster in India (USAID, 2001). While the international organizations started moving out of the area after three to five years, the local NGOs continued working toward developing a more resilient community.

Outcome of the PSSMHS Intervention: A Theoretical Underpinning

In a disaster context, the term vulnerability is associated not only with physical conditions and social scarcity but also the individuals' and community's mental health status. Research studies viewed the psychological effects of earthquakes or any other disaster on human beings as a combined effect of multiple variables, including the level of exposure, experiences of loss, pre-disaster vulnerabilities, post-disaster support, community mechanisms, family relationships, and individual sociodemographic and psychological factors. All these factors support insight into individuals' capacities that affect their ability to prepare for, respond to, and recover from disastrous events, as well as assist them in avoiding or reducing risks that make them susceptible to disaster (Jean et al., 2023). Broadly, the effects can be two types: one is short-term, which depends more on the intensity of the events, but in which its level of suffering depends on the individual's mental health status; and long-term effects, which mainly depend on the duration, support provided, and the recovery efforts by internal and external agencies. But the disaster impacts lead to the development of different psychological disorders like PTSD, anxiety, depression, etc. (Gokhale et al., 2004).

The dependency on the earth's ecosystem for the survival of human beings is unquestionable. All materialistic and non-materialistic requirements are supported by the existing ecology. Therefore, maintaining ecological balance is pivotal for survival and a sustainable future. The increasing threat and risk of disasters need a clear focus on a shift of the developmental paradigm to ensure a safe and secure environment for living and growing with full potential (DesMarais et al., 2016). Over the past half-century or so, various conscious and unconscious human activities have negatively altered global ecosystems more rapidly and extensively, which is going to have long-term impacts on human survival (Rouse, 2014). The vast and detrimental changes to the Earth's ecosystems have increased the severity and number of disasters.

In this context, the mental health impact of disaster and psychosocial support at the individual and community level could be understood from the ecological systems theory propagated by Bronfenbrenner. Human development is explained through the relationship between the individual and the environment. There are at least four levels to explore the development and context of disaster. In the microsystem, individuals interact with persons and objectives in the school, family, neighborhood, peer groups, workplace, etc. While the disaster stuck in the community, the whole environment became scary, dangerous, and unsafe. In this context, people, as survivors of disaster, develop psychological problems as they experience traumatic events. The next level is the mesosystem, where the relationship between settings in which the person's interactions become crucial. For example, what happens in family life, in the working life, or at school also influences development and leads to satisfaction or dissatisfaction. After the disaster, the family and community life are equally disturbed. The families could not follow the regular routine as the home was destroyed, and, similarly, the community people could not support each other as the whole community suffered the impact of the disaster (earthquake). Above this is the exosystem, where people get affected by other events surrounding them. After the disaster, all of the people living in the affected area suffered. Some had higher losses than others, but no one was untouched. Finally, the macrosystem is about widely shared cultural values, beliefs, laws, and practices that influence everyone. While rescue and relief are mobilized, the people join together to help each other. Subsequently, the recovery efforts started to shape the community life. Thus, people suffer from the impact of disaster as they are living in an environment that determines their well-being and suffering. Over time, as the rehabilitation efforts become stronger, the survivors regain confidence and develop greater satisfaction with the new, altered environment. Diagram 11.1 explains how a normal development and disaster interphase cause traumatic suffering and, subsequently, how psychosocial support facilitates well-being and recovery in building new relationships between individuals and the environment.

The intensity of the Gujarat earthquake was extremely traumatic. It not only damaged the economic bone of the state but also left people with a life full of traumatic experiences and memories. The mental health care and psychosocial support provided by numerous humanitarian organizations brought hope for people of the state to restart their lives. The psychosocial support and mental health (PSSMH) interventions with the community volunteers, medical practitioners, and NGO workers showed the need and potential of PSSMH services for normalizing the stress reactions and for improving the quality of life among the survivors by following a holistic model of services termed the "umbrella of care." Along with PSSMHS, there were several advocacy campaigns to establish the rights

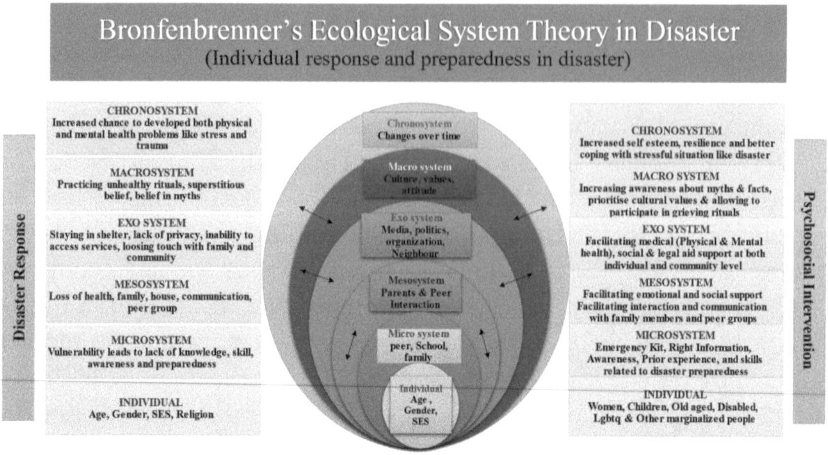

Diagram 11.1 Ecological system theory in disaster

of the survivors of disasters that added an important dimension regarding the protection of the human rights of the survivors of disasters.

Policy and Institutional Framework

The state of Gujarat, located in the western part of India, is the fifth-largest state by area and the ninth-most populous, with a population of 6.3 crores, which is around 5% of the country's population. Gujarat has the longest coastline in India (about 1600 km), which makes it vulnerable to numerous hydro-metrological disasters, viz. cyclones, storm surges, gusty winds, heavy rainfall, etc. (GSDMA, 2023). Geologically it is one of the earthquake-prone states with a high vulnerability. Immediately after the earthquake, the Government of Gujarat took initiatives and established the Gujarat State Disaster Management Authority (GSDMA). This was registered as a "Society" under the provisions of the Societies Registration Act and the Bombay Public Trust Act on February 8, 2001. GSDMA was initially mandated to implement the gigantic task of rehabilitation and reconstruction program in the earthquake-affected areas of the state and simultaneously to act as a nodal agency to plan and implement pre-disaster preparedness and mitigation activities, including the training and capacity building of all the stakeholders involved in disaster management (gsdma.org).

The aim of the Gujarat State Disaster Management Policy is to establish the necessary systems, structures, programs, resources, capabilities, and guiding principles for reducing disaster risks and preparing for and responding to disasters and threats of disasters in the state of Gujarat in order to save lives and property, avoid disruption of economic activity and damage to the environment, and ensure the continuity and sustainability of development (gsdmp.org).

Conclusion

The well-documented intensive psychosocial support and mental health service interventions for the survivors of the Gujarat earthquake by NIMHANS gave three important learnings. First, community-based psychosocial support is most crucial for recovery by engaging the local community volunteers who assumed equal stakeholders in the rehabilitation efforts. Second, capacity building on psychosocial support for the community volunteers and other intervention workers (nurses, physiotherapists, healthcare workers, child-care workers, etc.) is particularly crucial and needs to be simple, skill-based, and regular with adequate field-based supervision by mental health professionals. Third, a holistic model of support and integration of psychosocial support and mental health services with other sectoral interventions is crucial for strengthening the recovery and well-being of the survivors of disaster. The Gujarat earthquake intervention also set the priority for different authorities of national and state governments to develop and implement a systematic disaster response and rehabilitation program. Further, it called for a focused approach to integrating disaster risk reduction practices within the sustainable development paradigm.

References

Bertinelli, L., Mahé, C., & Strobl, E. (2023). Earthquakes and mental health. *World Development, 169*, 106283. https://doi.org/10.1016/j.worlddev.2023.106283

Bhadra, S. (2011a). *Psychological distress among the survivors of natural and human made disaster*. Prasad Psycho Corporation. ISSN: 09760709.

Bhadra, S. (2011b). Social work intervention for rehabilitation of disabled survivors of disaster in Gujarat Earthquake. *Jharkhand Journal of Development and Management Studies*, Vol-9, No.4 (October to December). Pp 4563–4577. (ISSN: 0973-8444).

Bhadra, S. (2017). Women in disasters and conflicts in India: Interventions in view of the millennium development goals. *International Journal of Disaster Risk Science, 8*(2), 196–207. https://doi.org/10.1007/s13753-017-0124-y

Bronfenbrenner, U. (1989). Ecological system theory. In R Vasta (Ed.) *Annals of Child Development: Vol.6. Six theories of child development: Revised formulation and current issues* (pp187–249). Greenwish, CT: JAI Press

Chachra, S. (2004). Disasters and mental health in India: An institutional response: Action Aid India. In *Disaster mental health of India* (2004th ed.). Indian Red Cross Society. ISBN-81-89113-00-3.

Dubey, D. K., & Mishra, M. (2023). A study and analysis of earthquake in India. *Indian Journal of Science Research*. www.ijsronline.org

Gibbens, S. (2017, October). How humans are causing deadly earthquakes. *Nationalgeographic.Com*, Accessed on 29 June 2023, url: https://www.nationalgeographic.com/science/article/human-induced-earthquakesfracking-mining-video-spd.

Gokhale, V. A., Joshi, D. R., & Abhayankar, A. (2004). *3rd World Conference on Earthquake Engineering: The Psychological and socioeconomic aspects of earthquake occurrence*, 13th World Conference on Earthquake Engineering, Paper No. 2927, (Conference proceeding) Vancouver, British Columbia, Canada, from August 1–6, 2004.

Gujarat State Disaster Management Authority (GSDMA). (2023).

Gupta, S. S. (2004). Psychosocial assistance after an earthquake: A case study of UNICEF support in Gujarat. In *Disaster mental health of India* (2004 ed.). Indian Red Cross Society. ISBN-81-89113-00-3.

Jean, C., Hall, T. E., & Vickery, J. (2023). Intersectionality as a forward-thinking approach in disaster research. In *Oxford research encyclopedia of natural hazard science*. Oxford University Press. https://doi.org/10.1093/acrefore/9780199389407.013.425

Jena, R., Naik, S. P., Pradhan, B., Beydoun, G., Park, H.-J., & Alamri, A. (2021). Earthquake vulnerability assessment for the Indian subcontinent using the Long Short-Term Memory model (LSTM). *International Journal of Disaster Risk Reduction, 66*, 102642. https://doi.org/10.1016/j.ijdrr.2021.102642

Kumar, M., Fonagy, P., & Target, M. (2016). Long term impact of disasters' trauma on the psychosocial adjustment of children in Gujarat, India. *African Journal of Traumatic Stress, 5*. https://www.researchgate.net/publication/318641289

Kuran, C. H. A., Morsut, C., Kruke, B. I., Krüger, M., Segnestam, L., Orru, K., Nævestad, T. O., Airola, M., Keränen, J., Gabel, F., Hansson, S., & Torpan, S. (2020). Vulnerability and vulnerable groups from an intersectionality perspective. *International Journal of Disaster Risk Reduction, 50*. https://doi.org/10.1016/j.ijdrr.2020.101826

Louis, P. (2001). Earthquake and after. *Economic and Political Weekly, 36*, 908–910. http://www.Jstor.Org/Stable/4410394

Murthy, D. R. S. (2004). Contributions of the National Institute of Mental Health and Neuro Sciences (NIMHANS), Bangalore, to disaster and mental health care (1981–2002). In *Disaster mental health of India* (2004 ed.). Indian Red Cross Society. ISBN-81-89113-00-3.

Ramappa, G., & Bhadra, S. (2004). Institutional responses—Oxfam (India): Psychosocial support programme for survivors of the earthquake. In *Disaster mental health of India* (2004th ed.). Indian Red Cross Society. ISBN-81-89113-00-3.

Rouse, A. (2014). *Living Planet Report 2014 Species and spaces, people and places.* WWF. www.livingplanetindex.org

Rubens, S. L., Felix, E. D., & Hambrick, E. P. (2018). A meta-analysis of the impact of natural disasters on internalizing and externalizing problems in youth. *Journal of Traumatic Stress, 31*(3), 332–341. https://doi.org/10.1002/jts.22292

Shah, B., Parhee, R., Kumar, N., Khanna, T., & Singh, R. (2005). *Mental health research in India Mental health research mental health research in India (Technical monograph on ICMR mental health studies)*. Division of Noncommunicable Diseases, Indian Council of Medical Research, New Delhi.

Sharma, R. (2002). Gujarat earthquake causes major mental health problems. *BMJ, 324*(7332), 259. https://doi.org/10.1136/bmj.324.7332.259c

Shina, A. K. (2001). *The Gujarat Earthquake 2001 Asian Disaster Reduction Center*, Kobe, Hyogo prefecture, Japan

Shivni, R. (2017). Human activity can trigger earthquakes, but how many? This number might surprise you. *Pbs.Org* assessed on 27th June 2023, url: https://www.pbs.org/newshour/science/human-activity-can-triggerearthquakes-many-number-might-surprise.

Stroebe, K., Kanis, B., Richardson, J., Oldersma, F., Broer, J., Greven, F., & Postmes, T. (2021). Chronic disaster impact: The long-term psychological and physical health consequences of housing damage due to induced earthquakes. *BMJ Open, 11*(5). https://doi.org/10.1136/bmjopen-2020-040710

Vankar, G. K., & Mehta, K. (2004). Gujarat earthquake. In J. O. Prewitt Diaz, R. S. Murthy, & R. Lakshminarayana (Eds.), *Disaster mental health of India* (2004 ed.). Indian Red Cross Society of India. ISBN-81-89113-00-3.

Vatsa, K. S. (2001). *The Bhuj Earthquake District of Kutch, State of Gujarat (India) A reconnaissance report identification of priority issues prepared for DRM-World Institute for Disaster Risk Management.* http://gujarat-earthquake.gov.in/final/indiaeq.html

WHO. (2002). *Gujarat Earthquake Relief Mission: Third Report of WHO Activities following the Earthquake.* World Health Organization. Gandhinagar, Gujarat

WHO. (2021). *Resilient reconstruction: 20 years after Gujarat earthquake*, WHO, Gandhinagar, Gujarat, (url: https://www.who.int/india/news-room/feature-stories/detail/resilient-reconstruction-20-years-after-gujaratearthquake) assessed on 21st June 2023.

Wilson, M. P., Foulger, G. R., Gluyas, J. G., Davies, R. J., & Julian, B. R. (2017). The human-induced earthquake database. *Seismological Research Letters, 88*(6), 1560–1565. https://doi.org/10.1785/0220170112

12

From Tragedy to Transformation: Psychosocial Responses and Mental Health Strategies in the Wake of the 2004 Indian Ocean Tsunami

C. Jayakumar, Subhasis Bhadra, N. Sathana, and Kasi Sekar

Introduction

On December 26, 2004, the Indian Ocean was struck by one of the most severe earthquakes ever recorded, triggering a devastating tsunami that caused widespread destruction along the coastal regions of Indonesia, Sri Lanka, India, and Thailand. The incident had led to extensive casualties, which shockingly stood at over 230,000 deaths across the 14 affected countries, and the location of the disaster greatly hindered the status of property, lives, and means of livelihood in the impacted countries. India's southeastern state of Tamil Nadu was one that was most badly affected by the tsunami.

C. Jayakumar (✉) • S. Bhadra • N. Sathana • K. Sekar
Department of Psychosocial Support in Disaster Management, NIMHANS, Bengaluru, Karnataka, India

S. Bhadra et al. (eds.), *Psychosocial and Mental Health Support for Disaster Management in India*, Palgrave Studies in Disaster Science and Emergency Management,
https://doi.org/10.1007/978-3-032-02511-1_12

This 2004 disaster marked a watershed moment in disaster management. It can be admitted that the basic preconditions that regulate the functioning of coastal communities were revealed, as well as the need for proper psychosocial support as an aspect of disaster management intervention. Alongside the medical issues and physical impairments, however, the survivors experienced great emotional distress, loss, and grieving. This chapter will focus on the disaster profile of India in general and state of Tamil Nadu in particular, with details being taken of its vulnerability to different natural disasters, especially cyclones. Such vulnerabilities will be examined in relation to the 2004 tsunami and the psychosocial care that developed in response to the catastrophe.

Disaster Profile of India

An Overview of Disasters in India

India has a very large geographical area at its disposal, with mountains, plains, deserts and large coastlines. Although this landscape does contribute to cultural and ecological diversity, it makes India particularly vulnerable to natural calamities. Earthquakes, floods, drought, landslides, and cyclones are among the major disasters that have been witnessed in the Indian subcontinent. All of these disasters endanger lives, property and environment in different ways.

It has been observed by the country's National Disaster Management Authority (NDMA) that India is hit by an average of about twenty major disasters every year (Government of India, 2009). They incur not only a heavy human toll but also come at a substantial financial cost. The impacts of the major natural disasters that struck India between 2001 and 2019 are given in Table 12.1. These disasters have become more frequent and intense due to the effects of climate change and improved standards of urbanization, population growth, and insufficient infrastructure, which all add to the development of struggling communities.

Table 12.1 Major natural disasters in India (2001–2019) and their impact

Year	Disaster type	Affected states	Fatalities	Economic loss (in billion USD)
2001	Earthquake	Gujarat	20,000	5.5
2004	Tsunami	Tamil Nadu	12,405	1.5
2013	Flood	Uttarakhand	5700	0.8
2019	Cyclone	Odisha	64	0.2

Note: The data are adapted from Ministry of Finance, Government of India (2001, 2004, 2013, & 2020). *Economic survey of India*

Cyclones in India: A Focus on Vulnerability

Of all the types of natural calamities, the cyclone is the most frequent and most damaging to India, particularly within the coastal areas of the states of Tamil Nadu, Andhra Pradesh, and Odisha. The places most affected with these natural phenomena are the Bay of Bengal and the Arabian Sea, and the Indian Meteorological Department (IMD) is responsible for both forecasting and tracking cyclones. These storms cause great winds, storm surges and very heavy rains, leading to floods and landslides. The impact of cyclones is exacerbated by several factors, including:

- **Geographical Location:** India follows significant water channels, extending to approximately 7500 kilometers of sea frontage to the Indian Ocean, bordering on the Bay of Bengal and the Arabian Sea.
- **Population Density:** There is high population density in the coastal regions, resulting in high incidence of loss of life and property during cyclones.
- **Socioeconomic Disparities:** Cyclones interfere with agriculture and fishing, two of the key industries for several coastal districts. When disasters occur, such communities are those whose ability to put in place structures for disaster management and response is often lacking. Additionally, they rarely have access to resources to which they could turn in the event of disaster.

Table 12.2 Major cyclone and tsunami events in Tamil Nadu: Impact on affected districts

Year	Cyclone name	Affected districts	Fatalities	Economic loss (in billion USD)
1999	Odisha Super Cyclone	Tamil Nadu (coastal areas)	10,000+	4.5
2004	Tsunami	Nagapattinam, Kanyakumari	12,405	1.5
2018	Gaja	Thanjavur, Nagapattinam	64	0.2

Note: The above data are adapted from Government of India, Ministry of Home Affairs (2005). *Disaster impact assessment report on cyclones and tsunamis in Tamil Nadu*. National Disaster Management Authority

Tamil Nadu: One of the Cyclone Capitals of India

Tamil Nadu has been historically vulnerable to cyclones and is therefore known as the "Cyclone Capital" of India. The state has suffered so many cyclonic natural disasters, principally affecting its coastal region. Table 12.2 presents the major cyclone and tsunami events in Tamil Nadu, outlining their respective impacts on the affected districts. The vulnerabilities in Tamil Nadu can be attributed to a combination of geographical, socioeconomic, and infrastructural factors:

- **Coastal Geography:** The coastline of Tamil Nadu is approximately 1076 kilometers long, accounting for 13–15% of India's total coastline. As a result, it is vulnerable to cyclones. The sea coastline areas such as Nagapattinam, Thanjavur and Kanyakumari are hit most frequently, and in the initial stages, when these natural calamities occur.
- **High Population Density:** Tamil Nadu coastal areas are highly populated due to the influx of people in radial settlements located in the low-altitude areas, which are easily flooded by storm surges. This high population density exacerbates the risk of casualties and challenges in the event of evacuation.

- **Socioeconomic Disparities:** A considerable number of people living in the coastal area of Tamil Nadu engage in fishing and farming activities. These sectors are very sensitive to cyclones, which cause widespread disruption, economic instability and high levels of poverty following disasters.
- **Inadequate Infrastructure:** The current conditions of many coastal regions are unable to provide adequate protection against the impact of cyclones. They are characterized by bad drainage, poor housing, and limited access to emergency services, among other limitations.

Analysing India's disaster profile, especially with regard to cyclones, it is evident that coastal states such as Tamil Nadu remain in a vulnerable position. Location, population density and distribution, cross-sectional poverty, and poor physical infrastructure put communities in a desperate situation, especially during natural calamities. Knowledge of these vulnerabilities is crucial for the elaboration of disaster relief and psychosocial support work and, in particular, the tragedy of mass disasters, such as the tsunami of 2004. The current chapter will aid the further analysis of these vulnerabilities along with the post-tsunami, psychosocial care developments that transpired.

The Tsunami of 2004: A Holistic Overview

The Event: Timeline and Geographic Impact

The tsunami, which occurred on December 26, 2004, originated from a subduction mega-thrust earthquake with an average magnitude of 9.1 to 9.3 on the west coast of northern Sumatra, Indonesia. This was the third-largest earthquake ever recorded and the largest in over forty years. The earthquake occurred at a depth of around 30 km, generating multiple disastrous tsunamis which affected more than one country within the Indian Ocean region.

Timeline of Key Events

On December 26, 2004, at 8:58 AM (UTC), a violent quake shook the Indian Ocean, giving rise to enormous tsunami waves ripping across the region (Lay et al., 2005). Thailand's western coast was struck by the first wave by 9:00 AM (UTC), followed by devastating impacts in Indonesia, Sri Lanka, India, and other nearby countries. Then, at 9:30 AM (UTC), the eastern coast of India, that is Tamil Nadu and the Andaman and Nicobar Islands, witnessed colossal destruction as the tsunami waves crashed ashore. Figure 12.1 illustrates the geographical distribution of the countries affected, providing a visual representation of the regional spread and the extent of impact across various nations involved in the disaster.

In the immediate aftermath, rescue and relief operations began within hours; however, the sheer magnitude of the disaster overwhelmed both the local and national agencies (Lay et al., 2005). To aggravate the

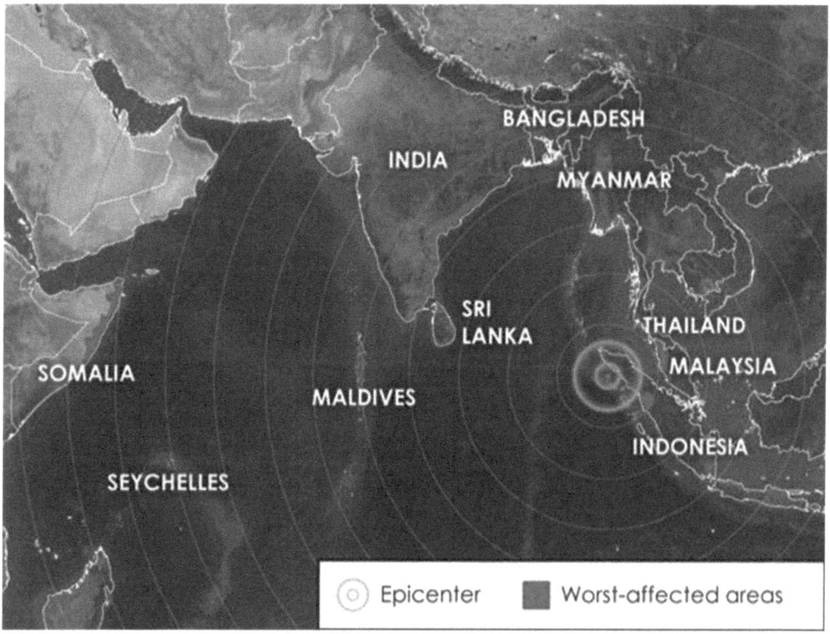

Fig. 12.1 Geographical distribution of countries affected and the epicenter of the 2004 tsunami. Credit: Kathleen Cantner, AGI

destruction, there was a severe breakdown of communication systems, making coordination in the response almost impossible. The tsunami affected 14 countries, with varying degrees of devastation. The geographic regions impacted include:

- **Indonesia:** Where schools and other structures were flattened, the worst-affected region, especially Aceh province. A tsunami hit with the wave height of about 30 meters and above with an estimated 167,000 deaths (Tsuji et al., 2006).
- **Sri Lanka:** The island nation got affected with the waves which flooded coastal zones in the region, resulting in more than 31,000 casualties and large-scale population displacement (Sabri et al., 2024).
- **India:** The southern states of Tamil Nadu and Andhra Pradesh were heavily affected by the calamity. Instances from different coastal locales, included the Chennai, Nagapattinam, Kanyakumari, and Thanjavur areas being devastated by fresh surges of tidal bore, with waves at a height of 10 meters (Narayan et al., 2006).
- **Andaman and Nicobar Islands:** The islands are utterly devastated. Some places have no houses, and large numbers of people have been killed (Bilham, 2005).
- **Other Countries:** Other countries, including Thailand, Maldives, Myanmar, Somalia and the rest, also did not escape the rise in sea level during the period, with effects ranging from loss of property to loss of lives. It therefore became evident that the effects of this natural calamity spread as far as the east coast of Africa (Okal, 2015).

Social, Economic, and Environmental Context

The disaster of 2004 escalated beyond physical loss and devastation. The tsunami also witnessed several social, economic, and even environmental impacts for the geographic areas affected.

Social Context According to the available records, **approximately 230,000 to 280,000 people** (United Nations Office for Disaster Risk Reduction [UNDRR], 2005) lost their loved ones in the disaster. There was social dissolution, with communities being split apart, and psychologically the effects were disastrous. Living through the suspension of life as it was, survivors also experienced trauma, loss, and anxiety for tomorrow. Loss of social relationships and harmonized community living aggravated the consequences for survivors and made the situation even worse. In many cases, these traditional support systems were eroded, or at least weakened, which in turn placed the affected groups in new conditions of heightened risk (Norris & Wind, 2009).

Economic Context The economic consequences of the tsunami were devastating. Fishing communities and beach-related businesses were more severely affected due to huge losses from these sectors. Houses, roads, and ports, as well as markets, were washed away, thereby affecting trade activities and people's sources of income. In the case of India alone, in the region of Tamil Nadu the impacts were severe, with extensive loss of boats and fishing equipment (Gupta & Sharma, 2006). The agricultural sector also suffered, as numerous tracts of land became swampy due to the invasion of salt water; similarly, fertile land turned to desert. Attempts were made to bring about relative calm, but the scope of damage was immense. This required large amounts of money and help from other countries (Adger et al., 2005).

The destruction of tourism infrastructure, including hotels, resorts, and local businesses, led to economic setbacks for both the tourism industry and the communities relying on it for employment and income. The long-term recovery included rebuilding these facilities and restoring confidence among travelers to ensure the sustainability of the region's tourism sector (Wilkinson et al., 2005).

Environmental Context Major coastal areas saw gross environmental disturbance as wildlife, plants, and other elements of nature were displaced or completely eliminated by the tsunami (Dahdouh-Guebas et al., 2005). The consequences for livelihoods and economic activity were particularly dire for those communities reliant upon coastal resources such as coral reefs, mangroves, and fisheries. The influx of saltwater affected local farming practices and contaminated freshwater sources, making daily survival even more challenging. Rescue operations not only focused on meeting the basic needs of the affected population but also included efforts to restore the land and ecosystem, ensuring that local communities could rebuild their lives and sustain their livelihoods.

Extent of Damage and Affected Communities

Damage Assessment in Tamil Nadu, the Andaman and Nicobar Islands, Indonesia, and Sri Lanka

Data on the extent of general damage were reported and the scale was alarming throughout the impacted areas. In Tamil Nadu alone, many houses were uprooted and scores of villages were subjected to forced evacuation. The worst-affected coastal districts were Nagapattinam and Kanyakumari in Tamil Nadu; reports suggest that over 6000 people were killed and millions of families were displaced. Infrastructure, including roads, schools and hospitals, were damaged, making rescue operations difficult and slow (UNDP, 2005).

The situation in the Andaman and Nicobar Islands was even more bleak as the majority of the islands suffered devastating losses, including the loss of all their structures. Thus, delivering relief was always a problem in these islands; the toll of lives lost is considered to be more than 3000 (Bilham, 2005). The ecology of the islands was also affected severely, giving rise to long-term environmental issues.

Elsewhere in Indonesia, and most especially in Aceh, the devastation was total. with many families being washed away and a death toll that angered the globe. The Indonesia government declared that the disaster had claimed more than 230,000 lives and made millions of people homeless (Tsuji et al., 2006). This tore the heart out of the infrastructure since roads, bridges, and public services became non-functional and required massive international support to rehabilitate (McAdoo et al., 2006).

Torrential rains on the coastline of Sri Lanka substantially affected the lives and properties of people. Some 31,000 residents died, and hundreds of thousands of residents were made homeless. Almost everything was destroyed by the tsunami, but the major impacts included residential places, schools, and hospitals in the southern and eastern regions of the afflicted country. The economic and social impact was alarming, mainly focusing on two important sectors: fishing and tourism (Athukorala & Resosudarmo, 2005).

Sociodemographic Profile of Affected Communities

The sociodemographic profile of the affected communities varied significantly across regions. Table 12.3 outlines the socioeconomic and demographic impact of the 2004 Indian Ocean tsunami in the affected regions, highlighting significant disruptions in livelihoods, the displacement of populations, changes in household structures, and the disproportionate effects on vulnerable groups such as women, children, and the elderly.

Overall, the tsunami of 2004 has had widespread and long-lasting implications on sociodemographic aspects in the zones it engulfed, with clear communication of the demand for targeted recovery work addressing the particular needs of diverse communities.

Psychosocial Care Post-Tsunami

Emergence of Psychosocial Needs

Referring back to those people with psychosocial needs post-December 2004 tsunami, it was shown that there was an immense need for psychosocial support for the survivors, encompassing their families, communities, and groups (World Health Organization [WHO], 2005). What was left behind was destruction, death, and a huge psychological fallout of trauma, grief, and loss. Those who survived were displaced from their homes; the trauma of losing loved ones and friends abruptly forced insecurity and anxiety about the future upon the survivors.

The emergence of psychosocial needs can be categorized into several key areas:

Table 12.3 Socioeconomic and demographic impact of the 2004 Indian Ocean Tsunami in affected regions

Region	Population affected	Key demographics	Economic activities	Impact
Tamil Nadu, India	Approximately 1.5 million	Predominantly fishing communities in coastal districts	Fishing as primary livelihood	Destroyed around 6000 fishing boats; over 100,000 fishermen displaced, leading to economic hardship and increased poverty
Andaman and Nicobar Islands, India	Approximately 380,000	Diverse population, including indigenous tribes	Traditional practices, limited external resources	Displaced about 20,000 individuals; loss of cultural heritage and traditional lifestyles, complicating recovery efforts
Aceh Province, Indonesia	Approximately 4.5 million	Mix of urban and rural communities	Urban: trade and services; Rural: agriculture and fishing	Approximately 170,000 deaths; urban poor faced severe recovery challenges due to pre-existing vulnerabilities and loss of livelihoods
Sri Lanka	Approximately 1 million	Diverse ethnic groups (Sinhalese, Tamils, Muslims)	Fishing and tourism	Around 31,000 lives lost; over 500,000 displaced; exacerbated ethnic tensions, increased poverty, and social instability

Note: The above information is adapted from World Bank (2006). *Rebuilding lives after the 2004 tsunami: Economic and social impacts in affected regions*. World Bank Publications

- **Trauma and Grief:** Many survivors described the common effects of post-traumatic Stress Disorder (PTSD), anxiety, and depression (Norris & Wind, 2009). For this reason, one of the common consequences of the disaster was that it left a lasting psychological effect that stemmed from the loss of loved ones and the traumatic character of the event.

- **Social Disruption:** These components reveal that the tsunami had negative impacts on social interactions and community unity. The individuals shown in this advertisement depicted dramatic examples of early victims who had no family or community to turn to for comfort or safety (Murthy & Lakshminarayana, 2006).
- **Economic Stress:** The loss of employment, especially in the fishing and agricultural sectors, resulted in changes in people's financial status. In addition, the economic pressure intensified the psychological pressure on everyone, including individuals and families (Ghodse & Galea, 2006).
- **Children and Vulnerable Populations:** This affected children in many ways, with complaints of feeling frightened, confused, and distressed being common. Grief resulting from the death of parents or caretakers and interruption of education had an enduring impact on their psychological well-being (Kar et al., 2013).

Realizing these psychosocial requirements, efforts to launch support programs to meet mental health and psychological wellness of the survivors were initiated by a range of different organizations.

Challenges in Rescue, Relief, and Recovery

The problems encountered during the rescue, relief, and recovery process remained complex and demanding.

- **Logistical Challenges**: Local and national agencies were not prepared for the size of the disaster. Some infrastructures were affected, specifically those linking the affected areas. This made it difficult for rescue teams to reach some areas. Due to the immediate impact, and the havoc caused, it was not easy to set up proper channels for social communication and cooperation among different relief organizations (Tsunami Evaluation Coalition [TEC], 2006).

- **Resource Allocation:** Such a situation meant confusion in the awarding of the various aids offered by different organizations or agencies. The commitment of the targeted amount was difficult because the aid had to reach the most vulnerable groups (Sphere Project, 2011).
- **Cultural Sensitivity:** The problem was that cultural competence was often missing from the disaster relief operations. Some of the psychosocial care interventions were initiated without taking into account the cultural beliefs of the people with asthma, which was an aspect that could have a negative impact on its outcome (Murthy & Lakshminarayana, 2006).
- **Long-Term Mental Health Support:** Despite giving the children emotional initial support, which included reassuring them, follow-up mental health care was rarely sought. The many people who were affected occasionally demanded sessions of therapy and counselling, which were in short supply in the visited zones (Math et al., 2008).

However, it was seen that there was the need for multisectoral collaboration to support Psycho-Social Functioning. It was understood by government bodies, NGOs and other members of the community that putting in effort into working as a team was critical in recovery.

Comprehensive Psychosocial Support Initiatives Post-Tsunami: Strategies, Impact, and Recognition

It was noted that following the December 2004 tsunami, the key player in providing psychosocial care to the affected communities was the NIMHANS. Acknowledging the potentially deep psychological effect of the disaster, NIMHANS put into practice of a set of specific measures that not only offered the initial amenity but also established the course for long-term mental health intervention.

PSSMHS Interventions in Different Phases of Tsunami Disaster Management

The destruction from the tsunami that struck several countries in the Indian Ocean in December 2004 caused widespread mortality and loss. Multisectoral psychosocial support (MHPSS) interventions were critical in tackling the mental health and psychosocial needs of the affected populations. A detailed overview of such interventions is provided below, with particular reference to the location, data, timeline, implementation, beneficiaries, and other agencies involved. The MHPSS interventions timeline following the tsunami will be outlined as follows:

In January 2005, a rapid needs assessment identified the psychosocial impact that required further evaluation within the affected populations. This fact-finding mission aimed to present the immediate mental health needs of survivors. In January through March of 2005, psychosocial first aid (PFA) was carried out among families and individuals in their temporary shelters. The immediate intervention provided psychological support to those families and assisted in dealing with acute emotional distress. Community support centers began to be set up in February 2005 for ongoing psychosocial support in the affected areas. These centers were to offer biomedical treatment and promote recreation and group therapy for survivors. From March to April of 2005, training was conducted for local counselors, local health services, and volunteers who were involved in the delivery of MHPSS. The referral system was established from 2005 in early January, allowing patients needing specialized mental health care to be referred to appropriate levels of services.

This helped implement these interventions through a collaboration of local and international NGOs with WHO and UNICEF. These NGOs have conducted rapid needs assessments to identify the mental care needs of the affected populations. PFA was offered to grieving families and individuals by trained volunteers and mental health professionals in communities and temporary shelters, thereby providing immediate psychological relief. NGOs such as Save the Children, in collaboration with local organizations, have opened support centers offering counseling, group therapy sessions, and psychosocial and recreational activities. Local counselors' training courses were held by experts from mental health organizations, such as Médecins Sans Frontières (MSF), in collaboration with local universities to foster a mental health response that is sustainable and grounded in the local milieu. These psychosocial support services included counseling and participation in community activities for close to 500,000 individuals. Special attention was paid to vulnerable groups, including women, children, the elderly, and persons with disabilities, to ensure interventions were tailored to address their specific needs.

Besides WHO, UNICEF, and International Organization for Migration, other organizations such as the Indian Red Cross, the American Red Cross, CARE India, and Save the Children played a major role in implementing and supporting community-based psychosocial support programs. These agencies cooperated by providing technical guidance to child protection, community reintegration support, and various other services to the affected population.

Phases of Disaster Management

MSPHSS interventions worked in immediate and longer-term psychosocial needs within affected populations during the tsunami disaster. These interventions followed a phased implementation to offer a rounded approach for disaster management. Table 12.4 details the phases of disaster response and corresponding intervention strategies, illustrating how relief efforts transition from immediate emergency response to recovery, rehabilitation, and long-term reconstruction, with each phase emphasizing specific goals such as rescue, psychosocial support, infrastructure rebuilding, and community resilience.

In the immediate response phase, all the needs assessments administered right after the tsunami focused on the psychosocial impact on survivors. This particular exercise has greatly influenced the identification of those immediate mental health and psychosocial support needs within the affected populations. Psychosocial first aid was provided to the

Table 12.4 Phases of disaster response and intervention strategies

Phase	Description	Intervention strategies
1. Occurrence of disaster	The tsunami strikes, causing immediate devastation and widespread impact on communities	Activate emergency response protocols and mobilize local disaster response teams
2. Immediate response phase	Addressing the immediate needs of survivors in the aftermath of the tsunami	Conduct rapid needs assessments, deliver psychosocial first aid (PFA), and establish temporary support centers
3. Search and rescue	Efforts to locate and assist individuals trapped or in need of urgent help	Coordinate search and rescue operations, provide first aid and medical care, and ensure safety of survivors
4. Recovery phase	Providing ongoing support to individuals and communities as they begin to heal and rebuild	Offer group sessions, recreational activities for children, and community healing workshops
5. Long-term rehabilitation	Focusing on rebuilding community infrastructure and enhancing resilience to future disasters	Implement community resilience initiatives, integrate psychosocial support into health systems, and provide training for local leaders
6. Evaluation and learning	Assessing the effectiveness of the response and identifying lessons learned for future preparedness	Conduct evaluations of psychosocial support interventions and disaster response efforts, and incorporate feedback into training and planning

affected people and families. In this regard, these people were most often offered emotional support, active listening, and help from trained volunteers for distressed individuals. Temporary support centers were established in the affected areas for survivors to have safe spaces to access psychosocial support, counseling, and community activities aimed at lightening their emotional load.

PFA was a fundamental component of the immediate response operation in support of those experiencing trauma, grief, and distress due to the 2004 tsunami. PFA was delivered to survivors using trained responders and incorporated strategies as varied as active listening, validation of emotions, and practical assistance. Active listening allowed the responders to join in with the survivors and encourage them to talk about how they were feeling and any concerns they might have. This was a crucial step in the recovery process (Kasi et al., 2007). By validating survivors' emotional experiences, responders helped survivors feel understood and supported, thus fostering their emotional resilience (Becker, 2009). Practical assistance included direct needs such as necessarily linking survivors with food, shelter, and medical attention.

From the immediate response phase to the recovery phase psychosocial support services were supplied which aimed to help survivors cope with any long-term needs experienced by those in the affected communities. In addition to individual support, group activities took place, which involved building community and peer support. Support groups created the venue where survivors can share their experiences as well as coping strategies, which then helped in the healing of psyche and spirit (Becker, 2009). Very special attention was given to children through art and play therapy, creating a safe space in which they could talk freely about their traumatic experiences. In the same way, community healing workshops focused on restoring social cohesion and resilience, thus enabling survivors to again come together as well as to develop collective coping strategies. Such functions were crucial in restoring channels of normalcy and emotional recovery in traumatized communities. Referral to specialized mental health care was also established for patients suffering severally from psychological distress.

Long-term rehabilitation work was focused on strengthening community resilience through training programs and workshops stressing mental health awareness and coping mechanisms. These served to empower the communities with information to guide them on their mental health in the aftermath of a disaster. Psychosocial support was thus integrated into existing health services for sustainability and continued access to mental health. The affected populations continued to receive support in order to rebuild their lives.

Capacity Building for Psychosocial Preparedness

Capacity building essentially enhances the ability of any community and responders to meet psychosocial needs in the wake of disasters. It entails training and developing resources, as well as promoting self-care among responders.

Training of Trainers Manual

The manuals were designed to teach local health personnel and volunteers enough about psychosocial support to come to the aid of disaster survivors. The manuals had to be comprehensive in nature. They range from core principles of psychosocial support and mental health care to more complicated themes such as providing trauma-informed care. They help give a complete understanding of the survivors' psychological needs after disasters and they emphasize the importance of trauma-informed care. Meanwhile, the intervention strategies offered practical guide concerning the provision of PFA, the conduct of group sessions, and the facilitation of community support activities to ensure effective service delivery. A salient element of the training was cultural sensitivity, which infused the premise that the mental health approaches for the implementers had to fit into the different cultures of the affected populations.

The training process employed a cascading model, where initial training sessions were for trainers who, in turn, would be disseminating their knowledge and imparting training to a wider group of community workers and volunteers. This was made to be obeyed by provisions of the service so as to maximize the effects that would reach the greatest number of affected individuals in the nation's.This trainer model trained key individuals to be able to create a multiplication effect by increasing the community-based qualified personnel providing mental health and psychosocial support.

Stress Management and Self-Care Strategies

Workshops for First Responders In addition to providing psychosocial support to disaster survivors, the well-being of first responders was to be addressed, this was seen as equally important, if not more so, than the help they gave to the survivors. Hence, training programs were developed to train responders in stress management and self-care techniques to suit their emotional needs while in disaster-affected areas. Mindfulness practices were introduced, with relaxation techniques for these responders to address their stress and emotional fatigue. This helped ground the responders in the present moment, and fostered emotional resilience in challenging environments.

Peer Support Networks To further promote the mental well-being of responders, peer support networks among them were formed. These were groupings where responders shared their experiences, coping strategies, and challenges. By regularly convening and checking in, peer groups provided a supportive place for responders to have conversations about the emotional impact of their work and celebrate moments of success. This initiative fostered a sense of community for those on the front lines, thereby alleviating feelings of isolation and burnout.

Resource Development In fostering ongoing support for self-care, first responders were also provided with pamphlets and web-based resources. These comprised articles to address mental health maintenance and signs of burnout, and how to get help from a professional. Equipping responders with easy-to-use self-care tools encouraged them to take preemptive, protective efforts toward their own mental well-being and ask for help when they needed it. These resources were an integral piece of the overall support for disaster responders.

The MSPHSS interventions during the tsunami disaster incorporated both the immediate and the long-term psychosocial needs of the affected communities. The phased approach to disaster management, psychosocial first aid, and a significant focus on capacity-building interventions aimed at enhancing community resilience and ensuring sustainable mental health support. The training and self-care for responders also added to the effectiveness of the support system, indicating the importance of preparedness for disaster responsive action in the future.

Networking and Collaboration in the Aftermath of the 2004 Tsunami

The 2004 Indian Ocean tsunami ranked as a historical global disaster that devastated millions of people residing in multiple nations, beginning with India. Many agencies, together with various organizations, swiftly assembled to offer psychosocial support and recovery assistance immediately following the incident. These combined entities demonstrated essential teamwork during response and recovery by sharing their expertise, their resources, and their familiarity with the local area.

Key Agencies Involved

Various organizations acted as essential forces in providing psychosocial support after the tsunami disaster and they assisted in the broader relief and recovery operation. The World Health Organization (WHO) effectively guided health responses by developing protocols for emergency mental health and psychosocial support (MHPSS) operations. During the recovery phase, WHO recommended primary healthcare systems should integrate mental health services at their core. Expert advice from these organizations formed the basis of mental healthcare strategies which established complete techniques for supporting survivor communities. Multiple states of India used their social welfare departments to serve as vital entities that directed relief response operations. They performed population vulnerability identification to allow psychosocial support services to access the most affected groups. Through partnerships with local NGOs, these departments set up psychological intervention programs which helped communities directly handle trauma exposure from the disaster.

Multiple organizations specialized in providing psychosocial care, including the Schizophrenia Research Foundation (SCARF). Through training initiatives, SCARF developed psychological capacity among volunteers and mental health professionals to provide support to tsunami survivors. The Banyan organization extended outreach programming which specifically reached women who suffered because of the disaster through their mental health care work. The organization provided counseling services together with rehabilitation programs that specifically targeted mental health needs of women recovering from the tsunami disaster.

A substantial role of UNICEF centered on providing relief to survivors who were children due to the impact of the tsunami. Making schools and communities part of their intervention programs, UNICEF provided psychosocial help that included play therapy and community activities for trauma recovery. Through their initiatives, UNICEF established protected locations in educational institutions so that affected children could safely share their emotions before starting recovery processes.

The American Red Cross provided paramount assistance toward both emergency crisis help and sustainable community-rebuilding initiatives. Local partners received support from the humanitarian organization to provide mental health resources which delivered essential psychosocial assistance to communities affected by the disaster during its recovery period. Tata Institute of Social Sciences emerged as an essential entity that led important research alongside delivering training initiatives. The assessment team determined the psychosocial impact of tsunami events through their studies before delivering specialized mental health training to both social workers and professionals who would provide care to the survivors according to their individual needs.

Multiple academic centers, including schools of social work and psychology and medicine and Allied Health Care, sent their students and professionals to support recovery activities. The institutions gave direct assistance while running training programs and research activities which strengthened collaboration between academic and local organizations. The recovery effort received essential service deliveries from a massive network of over 400 NGOs and spiritual organizations. The organizations provided comprehensive support, including food distribution services, together with mental health assistance at a local community level due to their existing trust with area members and deep knowledge about community needs.

Collaborative Efforts

The collaborative efforts among these agencies were characterized by several key initiatives:

- **Training and Capacity Building**: Organizations like SCARF and TISS conducted training programs for local mental health workers and volunteers, equipping them with skills to provide effective psychosocial support. This helped build a sustainable workforce capable of addressing ongoing mental health needs.
- **Community-Based Interventions**: Community-based interventions involved UNICEF together with local NGOs designing programs to provide survivors with recovery-based activities within their communities. The recovery activities included workshops, together with support groups and recreational programs which aimed to encourage social bonding and psychological recovery.
- **Research and Assessment**: Through their combined research and assessment work, TISS and WHO earned essential data about tsunami-related psychosocial effects that directed the development of targeted support programs. Through evaluation activities, the most vulnerable groups were identified together with their specific support requirements.
- **Integration of Services**: WHO emphasized primary health care services should integrate mental health services so survivors could access psychosocial support together with their physical health needs. By adopting this approach, mental health professionals acknowledged that physical and mental health recovery exists as a single interconnected system.
- **Spiritual and Cultural Support** Survivors needed spiritual and cultural support which came from spiritual organizations who provided them emotional and spiritual assistance. Through their leadership, the organizations scheduled spiritual ceremonies where grieving survivors gained emotional support and rebuilt their social bonds.

In conclusion, the decisive role of multiple agencies which collaborated networked together immediately following the 2004 tsunami served to tackle psychosocial challenges that affected communities faced. Joint coordination through the strengths of different organizations generated significant contributions toward community recovery and resilience after the disaster.

Challenges in Psychosocial Support Delivery

Inland vs. Island Challenges

The delivery of psychosocial support services varies significantly between inland and island regions, each presenting unique challenges (Paton, 2006). Table 12.5 summarizes the challenges in delivering psychosocial support services in inland and island scenarios.

This table highlights the distinct challenges faced in inland and island scenarios when delivering psychosocial support services in the aftermath of a disaster.

Table 12.5 Challenges in psychosocial support: Inland vs. island scenarios

Challenges	Inland scenario	Island scenario
Geographical accessibility	Limited infrastructure and transportation difficulties can hinder access to remote areas	Isolation and remoteness make it challenging to deliver services quickly
Resource allocation	High population density leads to competition for limited resources, straining service delivery	Limited resources and personnel due to geographical constraints
Logistical issues	Difficulty in mobilizing aid and professionals due to traffic congestion and damaged roads post-disaster	Transportation challenges due to reliance on boats or helicopters for aid delivery
Community engagement	Diverse population may lead to varying needs and difficulty in reaching all segments	Tight-knit communities that maintain close networks face increased challenges because they often display heightened scrutiny regarding mental health stigma

(continued)

Table 12.5 (continued)

Challenges	Inland scenario	Island scenario
Psychological impact	People who survive major catastrophes typically undergo severe shock because of event dimensions which heightens their anxiety levels and stress response	Feelings of abandonment and helplessness due to isolation from mainland support services
Coordination among agencies	Multiple organizations may operate without coordination, leading to overlapping services	Limited number of agencies present, which can lead to gaps in service provision
Cultural sensitivity	Need for culturally appropriate interventions that resonate with diverse inland communities	The requirement for localized cultural adaptation remains valid even though community practices show higher uniformity
Vulnerable populations	Increased challenges for vulnerable groups (e.g., women, children) due to socio-economic factors	People who are vulnerable experience additional dangers from being isolated such as children without parents and elderly persons
Training of professionals	Shortage of trained mental health professionals familiar with local contexts	Even fewer trained professionals available, making it difficult to provide adequate support
Linguistic barriers	Potential language diversity may hinder effective communication and support	Language barriers may also exist, but often fewer languages are spoken within island communities

The Issue of Biological Recanalization, Women's Remarriage, and Gendered Vulnerabilities in the Context of the 2004 Tsunami

The severity of disaster impacts on women exceeds that of men because sociocultural, economic, and political structures already create vulnerabilities for them. The traditional customs of purdah along with early marriage, together with patriarchal systems, work to maintain women's economic status at a disadvantage and restrict their access to options.

Studies of the Bhopal gas leak and Gujarat riots demonstrate enhanced mental health harm toward women during disaster situations, as shown by their increased exposure to trauma alongside violence-related injuries. Disaster events disrupt the roles that women perform in housework and their informal work networks, thus resulting in reduced resources and lost earnings. Restrictive clothing combined with maternal obligations and risky protective behaviors, including the fact that women tend to protect their families, results in higher disaster-caused deaths for women. Gender-based violence incidents rise during crisis times as women experience rising sexual violence throughout conflicts and disaster situations (Bhadra, 2017).

During the 2004 Indian Ocean tsunami, the state of Tamil Nadu experienced profound cultural as well as social changes that damaged its affected communities. The disaster caused severe suffering to women because they had previously experienced multiple challenges in their social structure as well as their economic situation. During the tsunami recovery period, two important gender-linked matters appeared as women experienced biological recanalization and widowed females chose to remarry due to cultural rules and societal standards which displayed intricate affiliations between traditional values and emergency response processes.

Biological Recanalization and Social Pressures

The surgical process known as biological recanalization allows women to regain their fertility after undergoing sterilization procedures. The desire for women to have children once again grew into an essential issue throughout Tamil Nadu's coastal regions because numerous women who had been sterilized now faced surgical reversals. The cultural belief regarding family structure, together with the tsunami's high death toll, compelled families to pressure women into expensive biological recanalization procedures. Table 12.6 highlights the gendered challenges and policy gaps in post-disaster recovery for women.

Table 12.6 Gendered challenges and policy gaps in post-disaster recovery for women

Aspect	Key points
Cultural and social implications	• Women blamed for child loss, coerced into recanalization • Responsibility for "rebuilding" families placed on women • Health risks and surgical complications ignored
Gendered impact	• Agency: Women lacked autonomy; decisions imposed by male relatives • Mental health: Significant trauma, anxiety, and depression due to loss and societal pressure
Policy gaps	• Neglect: Recovery programs ignored women's autonomy and mental health • Focus: Gender-insensitive interventions overlooked needs of widows and grieving mothers

The issues of biological recanalization and women's remarriage in the aftermath of the 2004 tsunami underscore the deeply entrenched gender norms that influence disaster recovery processes. Such solutions marketed for family rehabilitation simulated recovery efforts but did not prevent women from losing control of their decisions while making existing injustices even worse. Future disaster management plans require the adoption of gender-sensitive strategies which recognize women's leadership capacities and remove institutional barriers that increase their exposure to risks. True recovery, together with resilience, will become possible for all community members when these systems are eliminated from the recovery process.

Limitations in Service Provision

Cultural Appropriateness and Ethical Concerns

MHPSS services after the 2004 tsunami demonstrated multiple obstacles which hampered service capability in the affected area. These limitations included:

Lack of Culturally Appropriate Service Provision Western-style mental health interventions used following the tsunami failed to align with South Indian cultural customs, thereby inhibiting appropriate service delivery. Local culture did not accept or understand the therapeutic methods of cognitive behavioural therapy (CBT), along with other talk therapies, following their wide-scale introduction. The interventions using individual emotional expression as a focus failed to align with traditions where community and family support takes precedence over personal needs. The Tata Institute of Social Sciences (TISS) performed a study which showed survivors showed stronger preference for community-built support models that focused on family and social networks (TISS, 2006). Many implemented programs failed to respond properly to affected populations' preferences, meaning that several afflicted groups had a low level of involvement in these programs.

Replication and Duplication of Services The response to the tsunami led to the mobilization of more than 400 international organizations and NGOs who duplicated their services across overlapping service territories. The lack of coordination produced confusion among the people who received aid while weakening every support available. For instance, multiple organizations offered trauma counseling without a unified approach, resulting in beneficiaries receiving the same services from different providers without any additional benefit (Van der Velden et al., 2006).

Implementation of Western Strategies Not Validated in South Indian Context Many psychological interventions were adapted from Western frameworks without proper validation in the local context. For example, the use of Western-developed trauma assessment tools failed to adapt to South Indian cultural and social circumstances which otherwise needed evaluation. The misaligned practices produced wrong assessments and wrong interventions that could not properly resolve particular psychosocial requirements of survivors (Bryant & Njenga, 2006).

Unethical Practices The organizations chose unethical measures by valuing quantitative goals above meaningful achievements. Organizations measured success through beneficiary count statistics to the extent that they recorded inflated numbers of individuals served without a sufficient evaluation of program effectiveness. The reduction of healthcare quality along with weakened community trust in support services became the results of this organizational approach (Millar et al., 2013).

Lack of Trained Mental Health Professionals Effective mental health services faced barriers because the shortage of qualified mental health professionals in the region proved to be a major issue during service provision. Different organizations faced difficulties in recruiting staff who held knowledge of the local environment together with cultural particulars. The data showed that affected areas had only about 20% of their mental health professionals qualified to deliver trauma-informed care despite the noticeable shortage in such professionals (Raphael & Maguire, 2012).

Linguistic Barriers The diverse language landscape in South India became a major impediment when delivering useful psychosocial assistance. The inability to understand local community languages on the part of the mental health professionals limited their ability to build strong connections with the affected populations. Survivors from rural areas demonstrated communication problems because their local dialects were not comprehended by the city-trained professionals who delivered services (Padmavati et al., 2020). Best Practices in MHPSS

Evolution of Strategies Post-Tsunami

The response to the 2004 tsunami marked a watershed moment in the evolution of mental health and psychosocial support strategies in disaster management. Several best practices emerged from the lessons learned during this crisis:

Community-Based Approaches The emphasis on community involvement became a cornerstone of effective MHPSS strategies. Organizations like UNICEF and SCARF implemented community-based programs that engaged local leaders and volunteers to provide support. This approach recognized the strengths of communities in facilitating healing and recovery. For example, survivors developed community-run groups to exchange tsunami stories because they saw these networks as essential for social connection recovery following the disaster (UNICEF, 2006).

Integration of Services Primary healthcare systems received emphasis for mental health service incorporation according to WHO guidelines. The training of healthcare personnel in mental health identification created new possibilities for treating patients through comprehensive medical approaches in their recovery. This approach ensured that psychosocial support was accessible alongside physical health services. Health facilities across affected regions began incorporating mental health services into their services until they reached 60% coverage by 2006 (World Health Organization, 2008).

Culturally Sensitive Interventions Culturally adapted interventions were established as a highest priority. Health programs adapted their approaches to match local customs plus healthcare practices in each region. Traditional healing practices being combined with psychosocial support strategies permitted survivors to access familiar and trusted care methods that they already understood. This was particularly evident in programs developed by local NGOs that incorporated spiritual and community rituals into their support services (Tharoor & Thara, 2020).

Capacity Building and Training The need for training local professionals and volunteers was recognized as essential for sustainable recovery. Organizations like TISS and SCARF focused on building the capacity of local mental health workers through training programs that emphasized culturally relevant practices. This capacity-building approach ensured that communities had access to skilled professionals who understood their specific needs (TISS, 2006).

Understanding Bureaucratic and Executive Support MHPSS initiatives in the tsunami response required a full comprehension of both organizational support from bureaucrats and executive backing to succeed. National disaster management policies integrated psychosocial support as policy-makers hailed mental health importance for disaster recovery after major disasters. The establishment of new guidelines forced MHPSS integration as a mandatory component in emergency response plans to protect mental health during crises in future events (NDMA, 2009).

Data-Driven Approaches The analysis of disaster-related psychosocial data became essential for developing evidence-based interventions. The research activities at TISS and similar institutions generated essential data about population needs, which formed the basis for developing customized intervention programs. Through evidence-based approaches, organizations enhanced their strategy refinement process, which led to better outcomes of their intervention efforts (TISS, 2006).

Collaboration and Coordination Various stakeholders acknowledged the necessity to enhance coordination procedures for better organization of their efforts. The creation of networks that connected NGOs and government agencies with international organizations enabled collaborative work and the exchange of information. The coordinated efforts between organizations allowed them to minimize service overlaps while distributing resources properly to serve survivors effectively (International Federation of Red Cross, 2007).

The tsunami of 2004 became the foundational event which drove mental health and psychosocial support strategies toward modernization within the field of disaster management. The experiences from this disaster taught valuable lessons about implementing culture-focused community-oriented services that integrates different approaches while using trained specialists. Future disaster responses will provide improved psychosocial support to affected populations through addressing service limitations and implementing best strategies in provision.

Research and Evidence on Psychosocial Impacts

Overview of Research from NIMHANS

Through multiple research projects at the National Institute of Mental Health and Neurosciences (NIMHANS), scientists studied the psychosocial effects that hit survivors following the 2004 tsunami to determine mental health obstacles these groups encountered. The research conducted by NIMHANS about disaster-related mental health has led to the creation of effective psychosocial support strategies.

Key Studies and Findings

Psychosocial Impact of the Tsunami on Survivors in Tamil Nadu

Findings This study demonstrated that 35% of survey participants presented PTSD symptoms, and 25% displayed substantial depressive symptoms. Emotional distress, alongside anxiety symptoms, hit vulnerable individuals harder, particularly women and children who showed the highest rates of these conditions post-tsunami.

Implications These findings underscore the critical importance of implementing specialized emotional support systems for at-risk groups following disaster occurrences and validating disaster response strategies with mental health resources (James et al., 2020). Mental Health Needs Assessment Post-Tsunami

Findings The study documented that 60% of survivors showed significant psychological suffering from anxiety disorders and depression, alongside PTSD symptoms. Survivors were unaware of available mental health support options, which led to a reluctance to use the services.

Implications This study highlights the necessity of community awareness programs to educate populations about accessible mental health services that become available after disasters (Fazan Ahmad, 2024). Community-Based Mental Health Interventions Following the Tsunami

Findings Researchers found that community-directed psychosocial support programs led to a 40% decrease in PTSD symptoms and enhanced social functioning. Peer support and community engagement were crucial to survivors' emotional recovery and resilience.

Implications This study supports the enactment of community-based mental health intervention programs as critical components for disaster recovery. It also emphasizes the importance of providing psychosocial support training to community members to build local disaster response capabilities (Chakrapani & Bharat, 2023).

Research Gaps Identified

The valuable findings derived from these research studies show the existence of multiple significant gaps in knowledge:

Longitudinal Data The analysis of long-term psychological effects experienced by tsunami survivors depends on missing longitudinal research about their recovery outcomes. These unavailable data would display precise patterns of psychological recovery, together with information about intervention program endurance (Gosney & O'Connell, 2016).

Cultural Appropriateness The researchers emphasized the importance of conducting studies that develop interventions which meet local cultural norms and practices (Ranjan et al., 2008).

Barriers to Access Further research should identify precise access barriers that prevent different population groups, especially marginalized communities, from utilizing mental health services (Khan, 2012).

Standardized Evaluation Metrics A standardized assessment framework for community-based intervention success is absent, requiring the development of culturally sensitive evaluation metrics for better performance measurement (Patel et al., 2015).

Research Efforts, Evidence, and Implications from the Global Response to the Tsunami

The 2004 Indian Ocean tsunami was one of the worst natural disasters in contemporary history, prompting global research on the psychosocial effects caused by this catastrophic event. Research conducted in response to the 2004 tsunami generated essential evidence that drives universal disaster preparedness and recovery efforts. Table 12.7 presents the psychosocial impact of tsunamis by summarizing key research insights and proposing future strategies.

Conclusion

The 2004 tsunami established an important historical milestone for disaster management which drove essential changes in the development of response frameworks and policy frameworks to reduce the destructive forces of such massive disasters. Based on the impacts of the 2004 tsunami, the world needs to implement complete disaster preparedness systems with mental health-focused measures for disaster-affected individuals.

The tsunami disaster demonstrated to us that psychological help must involve culturally sensitive practices. Different cultural backgrounds of disaster-struck areas demanded suitable intervention strategies which honored local traditions along with native beliefs and rituals. Such integration enables disaster response teams to develop better-integrated

Table 12.7 Psychosocial impact of tsunamis: Research insights and future strategies

Research efforts	Key findings	Future disaster response implications
Global Collaborations: WHO and UNICEF, alongside international NGOs, conducted research across nations like Indonesia, Thailand, Sri Lanka, and India (World Health Organization, 2005)	**Mental Health Prevalence**: Significant rates of PTSD (30%–50%), anxiety, and depression, particularly among vulnerable groups (children, women, elderly)	**Incorporation of Mental Health**: Mental health services must be integral components of all disaster response plans (UNICEF, 2006)
Community Involvement: Community participation was key for valid and precise data collection operations	**Role of Community Support**: Community participation in local programs helped victims improve PTSD symptoms and promoted better emotional health (Gosney & O'Connell, 2016)	**Engagement of Communities**: Indigenous community members must be involved in implementing psychosocial support strategies for successful outcomes (Chandra et al., 2006)
Longitudinal Research: Investigating the long-term psychological effects on tsunami survivors	**Cultural Appropriateness**: Effective psychosocial support programs integrated local customs alongside traditional healing practices (Ahmad et al., 2014)	**Preparedness Strategies**: Developing rapid mental health response protocols is essential for emergency assessments after disasters (Patel et al., 2015)

trauma intervention programs which gain more acceptance from locals. When disaster response focuses on cultural sensitivity, it helps treat mental damage from disasters better while building stronger community resilience so people can recover better and reconstruct their existence after disasters.

Future disaster prevention strategies must include all knowledge gained from the 2004 tsunami between contemporary policy development initiatives. The process moves us ahead by taking advantage of learned lessons which guide our development of evidence-based disaster management plans for future incidents. The recovery process depends heavily on mental health services which policy-makers should establish as essential elements of planned disaster responses because psychological fitness plays an essential role in reaching full recovery.

The preparedness and response capabilities of disasters depend heavily upon enhanced connections between different sectors. Multiple sectors, together with local populations and education institutions, need to make combined efforts toward efficient disaster management throughout the entire process. Stakeholders who establish partnerships between different sectors can develop a comprehensive approach to disaster response which effectively tackles urgent requirements and sustained reconstruction.

In summary, the lessons derived from the 2004 tsunami emphasize the need for culturally sensitive psychosocial interventions and the importance of incorporating these insights into future disaster management policies. By strengthening collaborations across sectors and prioritizing mental health, we can build more resilient communities capable of withstanding and recovering from the challenges posed by natural disasters.

References

Adger, W. N., Hughes, T. P., Folke, C., Carpenter, S. R., & Rockström, J. (2005). Social-ecological resilience to coastal disasters. *Science, 309*(5737), 1036–1039. https://doi.org/10.1126/science.1112122

Ahmad, A., Mahmud, S., & O'Mathúna, D. (2014). Evidence and healthcare needs during disasters. In D. O'Mathúna, B. Gordijn, & M. Clarke (Eds.), *Disaster bioethics: Normative issues when nothing is normal* (pp. 111–130). Springer. https://doi.org/10.1007/978-94-007-3864-5_7

Athukorala, P. C., & Resosudarmo, B. P. (2005). The Indian Ocean tsunami: Economic impact, disaster management, and lessons. *Asian Economic Papers, 4*(1), 1–39. https://doi.org/10.1162/asep.2005.4.1.1

Becker, S. M. (2009). Psychosocial care for women survivors of the tsunami disaster in India. *American Journal of Public Health, 99*(4), 654–658. https://doi.org/10.2105/AJPH.2008.146571

Bhadra, S. (2017). Women in disasters and conflicts in India: Interventions in view of the Millennium Development Goals. *International Journal of Disaster Risk Science, 8*, 196–207. https://doi.org/10.1007/s13753-017-0124-y

Bilham, R., Engdahl, R., Feldl, N., & Satyabala, S. P. (2005). Partial and complete rupture of the Indo-Andaman plate boundary 1847–2004. *Seismological Research Letters, 76*(3), 299–311. https://doi.org/10.1785/gssrl.76.3.299y

Bryant, R. A., & Njenga, F. G. (2006). Cultural sensitivity: Making trauma assessment and treatment plans culturally relevant. *The Journal of Clinical Psychiatry, 67*(Suppl 2), 74–79. PMID: 16602819.

Chakrapani, V., & Bharat, S. (2023). Mental health in India: Sociocultural dimensions, policies and programs—An introduction to the India Series. *SSM—Mental Health, 4*, 100277. https://doi.org/10.1016/j.ssmmh.2023.100277

Chandra, V., Pandav, R., & Bhugra, D. (2006). Mental health and psychosocial support after the tsunami: Observations across affected nations. *International Review of Psychiatry, 18*(3), 205–211. https://doi.org/10.1080/09540260600655805

Dahdouh-Guebas, F., et al. (2005). How effective were mangroves as a defence against the recent tsunami? *Current Biology, 15*(12), R443–R447. https://doi.org/10.1016/j.cub.2005.06.008

Fazan Ahmad, N. D. (2024). The relationship between attitude, subjective norm, sense of community, collective efficacy and trust in agencies on intention to prepare for a tsunami disaster among households in Kudat, Sabah. *Jurnal Pengguna Malaysia, 38*(2), 168–187. https://jpmjurnal.com/jpm/article/view/69

Ghodse, H., & Galea, S. (2006). Tsunami: Understanding mental health consequences and the unprecedented response. *International Review of Psychiatry, 18*(3), 289–297. https://doi.org/10.1080/09540260600709149

Gosney, J., & O'Connell, C. (2016). Rehabilitation of disaster casualties. Koenig and Schultz's Disaster Medicine: Comprehensive Principles & Practices, 377–388.

Government of India. (2009). *National disaster management policy.* Ministry of Home Affairs. https://ndma.gov.in/sites/default/files/PDF/ndm-national-policy.pdf

Government of India, Ministry of Home Affairs. (2005). *Disaster impact assessment report on cyclones and tsunamis in Tamil Nadu.* National Disaster Management Authority. https://ndmindia.mha.gov.in/ndmi/images/pdf/Strategy-Papern-Tsunami.pdf

Gupta, A., & Sharma, K. (2006). *Tsunami recovery in India: Lessons for the future.* Oxford University Press.

International Federation of Red Cross and Red Crescent Societies. (2007). *Capturing coordination learning in the tsunami disaster.* https://www.rcrc-resilience-southeastasia.org/wp-content/uploads/2016/08/CAPTURING-COORDINATION-LEARNING-IN-THE-TSUNAMI-DISASTER_IFRC_Movement_Coordination.pdf

James, L. E., et al. (2020). Integrating mental health and disaster preparedness in intervention. *Psychological Medicine, 50*(2), 342–352. https://doi.org/10.1017/S0033291719000163

Kar, N., Krishnaraaj, R., & Rameshraj, K. (2013). Long-term mental health outcomes following the 2004 Asian tsunami disaster. *Disaster Health, 2*(1), 35–45. https://doi.org/10.4161/dish.24705

Kasi, S., Bhadra, S., & Dyer, A. (2007). A decade of disasters: Lessons from the Indian experience. *Southern Medical Journal, 100*(9), 929–931.

Khan, A. A. (2012). Seismogenic sources in the Bay of Bengal. *Natural Hazards, 61*, 1127–1141. https://doi.org/10.1007/s11069-011-9970-x

Lay, T., et al. (2005). The great Sumatra–Andaman earthquake of 26 December 2004. *Science, 308*(5725), 1127–1133. https://doi.org/10.1126/science.1112250

Math, S. B., et al. (2008). Psychological impact of the tsunami on children and adolescents. *Primary Care Companion to the Journal of Clinical Psychiatry, 10*(1), 31–37. https://doi.org/10.4088/pcc.v10n0106

McAdoo, B. G., et al. (2006). Smong: How an oral history saved thousands on Indonesia's Simeulue Island. *Earthquake Spectra, 22*(3 Suppl), 661–669. https://doi.org/10.1193/1.2204966

Millar, R., Mannion, R., Freeman, T., & Davies, H. T. O. (2013). Hospital board oversight of quality and patient safety: A narrative review and synthesis of recent empirical research. *The Milbank Quarterly, 91*(4), 738–770. https://doi.org/10.1111/1468-0009.12032. pmc.ncbi.nlm.nih.gov.

Ministry of Finance, Government of India. (2001, 2004, 2013, & 2020). *Economic survey of India.* https://www.indiabudget.gov.in/economicsurvey/

Murthy, R. S., & Lakshminarayana, R. (2006). Mental health consequences of war. *World Psychiatry, 5*(1), 25–30. https://www.ncbi.nlm.nih.gov/pmc/articles/PMC1472271/

Narayan, J. P., et al. (2006). Tsunami intensity mapping. *Pure and Applied Geophysics, 163*, 1279–1304. https://doi.org/10.1007/s00024-006-0074-6

National Disaster Management Guidelines: Psycho-Social Support and Mental Health Services in Disasters. (2009). A publication of the National Disaster Management Authority, Government of India. ISBN 978-93-80440-00-2, December 2009, New Delhi. https://nidm.gov.in/PDF/pubs/NDMA/8.pdf

Norris, F. H., & Wind, L. H. (2009). The experience of disaster. In Y. Neria, S. Galea, & F. H. Norris (Eds.), *Mental health and disasters* (pp. 29–44). Cambridge University Press. https://doi.org/10.1017/CBO9780511730030.003

Officer, S., & Gianniri, A. (2005). United Nations Office for Disaster Risk Reduction (UNDRR). United Nations Office for Disaster Risk Reduction.

Okal, E. A. (2015). The quest for wisdom: Lessons from 17 tsunamis. *Philosophical Transactions of the Royal Society A, 373*(2053), 20140370. https://doi.org/10.1098/rsta.2014.0370

Padmavati, R., et al. (2020). Learnings from conducting mental health research during 2004 tsunami in Tamil Nadu. *BMC Public Health, 20*, 1627. https://doi.org/10.1186/s12889-020-09733-y

Patel, P., et al. (2015). PHP227—A systematic literature review to assess the impact of social networks on healthcare in India. *Value in Health, 18*(7), A640. https://doi.org/10.1016/j.jval.2015.09.1782

Paton, D. (2006). Disaster resilience. *Disaster Prevention and Management, 15*(3), 337–350.

Ranjan, R. K., et al. (2008). Evaluation of geochemical impact of tsunami on mangroves. *Environmental Geology, 55*, 687–697. https://doi.org/10.1007/s00254-007-1019-9

Raphael, B., & Maguire, P. (2012). Disaster mental health research. In Y. Neria, S. Galea, & F. H. Norris (Eds.), *Mental health and disasters* (pp. 7–28). Cambridge University Press.

Sabri, I. L. M., Sabrina, M. H. F., Sakkeera, I. L. H. F., Faisal, I. L. M., & Thahyeena, A. N. F. (2024). Influence of Mangrove forests in mitigating the tsunami risk in coastal areas of Sri Lanka. *Tsunami Science in Sri Lanka*, 46.

Sphere Project. (2011). *The Sphere Handbook: Humanitarian charter and minimum standards in humanitarian response.* Practical Action Publishing. https://spherestandards.org/handbook-2018/

Tata Institute of Social Sciences. (2006). *Capacity building and training in mental health: Enhancing local professional skills.* Tata Institute of Social Sciences. https://www.tiss.edu

Tharoor, H., & Thara, R. (2020). Evolution of community telepsychiatry in India showcasing the SCARF model. *Indian Journal of Psychiatry, 42*(5 Suppl), 69S–74S. https://doi.org/10.1177/0253717620958161

Tsuji, Y., et al. (2006). Damage due to the 2004 Indian Ocean tsunami. *Journal of Natural Disaster Science, 28*(1), 13–27.

Tsunami Evaluation Coalition (TEC). (2006). *Joint evaluation of the international response to the Indian Ocean tsunami: Synthesis report.* Overseas Development Institute. https://www.preventionweb.net/files/4144_SYNTHESISREPORTfinal.pdf

United Nations Development Programme. (2005). The post-tsunami recovery in the Indian Ocean: Lessons learned, successes, challenges and future action. UNDP Bureau for Crisis Prevention and Recovery.

UNICEF. (2006). *Psychosocial interventions in emergencies.* https://www.unicef.org/emergencies/files/Psychosocial_Interventions.pdf

Van der Velden, P. G., Grievink, L., Kleber, R. J., et al. (2006). Post-disaster mental health problems and the utilization of mental health services: A four-year longitudinal comparative study. *Administration and Policy in Mental Health, 33*, 279–288. https://doi.org/10.1007/s10488-005-0027-x

Wilkinson, C., Souter, D., & Goldberg, J. (2005). *Status of coral reefs in tsunami-affected countries: 2005.* Australian Institute of Marine Science. https://www.icriforum.org/wp-content/uploads/2021/09/Status-of-coral-reefs-in-tsunami-affected-countries-2005.pdf

World Bank. (2006). Rebuilding lives after the 2004 tsunami: Economic and social impacts in affected areas (Report No. 31381). The World Bank. https://documents1.worldbank.org/curated/en/493591468771648239/pdf/313810IND0reconstruction1notes01public1.pdf

World Health Organization. (2005). *Mental health and psychosocial support after the tsunami.* https://iris.who.int/bitstream/handle/10665/205698/B0761.pdf

World Health Organization & World Organization of Family Doctors. (2008). *Integrating mental health into primary care: A global perspective.* World Health Organization. https://www.who.int/publications/i/item/9789241563680

13

Navigating and Mapping Crisis: Rapid Psychosocial Needs Assessment Strategies During the Karnataka Flood Response

Urmila Bamney, Sanjeev Kumar Manikappa, and Kasi Sekar

Introduction

A disaster is an abrupt, devastating occurrence that causes significant harm, destruction, loss, and desolation to individuals and assets. Such events are an inescapable part of life and a complicated worldwide issue. The United Nations Office for Disaster Risk Reduction (UNIDSR) defines disaster as a serious disruption of the functioning of a community or a society causing widespread human, material, economic, or environmental losses that exceed the ability of the affected community or society to cope using its resources (UNDRR, 2023). In recent years, there has been an enormous rise in the rate of catastrophic occurrences. Catastrophes both created by humans and caused by

U. Bamney • S. K. Manikappa (✉) • K. Sekar
Department of Psychosocial Support in Disaster Management, NIMHANS, Bengaluru, Karnataka, India

S. Bhadra et al. (eds.), *Psychosocial and Mental Health Support for Disaster Management in India*, Palgrave Studies in Disaster Science and Emergency Management,
https://doi.org/10.1007/978-3-032-02511-1_13

nature fall under this category; the first category includes situations like wars, military conflicts, and terrorist attacks including explosives, chemical, biological, and radioactive weapons while the latter category includes events like earthquakes, floods, and cyclones (Srivastava, 2010).

Natural disasters are widespread in developing nations, and there is rising concern that they might grow increasingly prevalent due to climate change (United Nations Environment Programme, n.d.). Natural disasters have claimed millions of lives over the past two decades or so, negatively impacted the lives of at least 1 billion additional people, and caused significant financial losses (Deshpande, 2022). Because of this, in 1989, the United Nations General Assembly designated 1990–2000 as the International Decade for Natural Disaster Reduction. The goal is to minimize the loss of human life, and property, and economic and social problems destruction through international action and suitable management strategies, particularly in developing countries (Kaur, 2006). The Indian subcontinent stands out from other regions in that it has one of the highest rates of natural disasters, with over 85% of the landmass of India being vulnerable to numerous kinds of hazards. Approximately 60% of the Indian landmass is vulnerable to earthquakes of varying magnitudes; more than 40 million hectares are at risk of flooding; cyclones can affect 8% of the entire area; and 68% of the country is vulnerable to drought (Stephen, 2012; Rajesh et al., 2020). Flooding is an ongoing obstacle in India, resulting in significant damage to human lives, resources, living conditions, amenities, and public services (Mohanty et al., 2020; Vajiram & Ravi, 2024).

Floods indicate a major natural hazard with profound social and economic consequences, specifically for agricultural societies dependent on cultivating for survival and earnings (Bubeck et al., 2017; Gunadal et al., 2024). The biggest contributors to flooding in India include prolonged monsoon rains, diminished river basin capacity to bear large flows, degradation of riverbanks and channel bed siltation, inadequate water drainage in places vulnerable to flooding, cloudbursts, and several other climatic phenomena (Mohanty et al., 2020; Gupta, 2025). Thirteen Indian states experienced floods in July and August of 2019 due to continuous rains. There were 200 deaths and one million displaced persons. Maharashtra and Karnataka were most affected by the greatest monsoon in twenty-five years. June to October 2019 saw the deaths of around 1600 people (ActionAid India, 2019).

Types of Flooding

River Floods

A river flood, also known as fluvial flooding, which happens when a river overflows its shores, or when its flow cannot be managed inside its channel (Shaw, 2022). River floods have also provided life-sustaining energies to human cultures that rely on their flow for cultivation and soil health (The Many Effects of Flooding, n.d.). Climate change could lead river floods to evolve into greater volumes or to become more common in certain areas while decreasing in size and frequency in others (Climate Change Indicators: River Flooding | US EPA, 2025). Higher degrees of humidity allow more water to evaporate from land and sea, and shifts in the magnitude and frequency of excessive precipitation may affect the size and frequency of river flooding (United Nations, n.d.).

Flash Floods

Flash floods are typically characterized by destructive floods that breach the banks of rivers, urban areas, or mountainside rivers, wiping away everything in their path (Flash Flood, 2023). Densely settled places are particularly vulnerable to flash floods. The construction of buildings, roadways, roadways, and parking areas raises flow by limiting the quantity of rain absorbed by the soil. This discharge increases the risk of a flash flood. Flash floods represent roughly 85% of flooding incidents and have the greatest mortality rate (measured as the number of deaths per number of people impacted) of any type of flooding (e.g., riverine or coastal) (Toppr, 2020).

Coastal Floods

Flooding on the coast is unexpected and rapid flooding of a coastal environment produced by a short-term rise in the sea level induced by a storm wave or excessive tides (United Nations Office for Disaster Risk Reduction [UNDRR] & International Science Council [ISC], 2025). Coastal flooding is mostly a natural phenomenon; nevertheless, the impact of humans on the coastal environment can worsen coastal flooding. Coastal flooding can cause substantial financial losses and deaths (Canada WaterPortal, 2025). Furthermore, coastal flooding can have many environmental consequences at many levels of time and space (Bubeck et al., 2017). Approximately two million people have been killed in floods over the past 200 years, mostly in South Asia (Watson et al., 2007). As sea levels rise and populations living along the coast develop, the likelihood of coastal flood disasters is expected to increase globally (United Nations Environment Programme, n.d.; United Nations, n.d.).

Pluvial Floods

Severe rainfall-induced flooding is referred to as pluvial flooding. Flooding of this type happens when the land cannot withstand sufficient rainfall, or when excess water overwhelms drainage systems in urban areas (Floods - Definition and Different Causes of Floods | Toppr, 2020). Pluvial flooding is becoming a bigger issue for communities worldwide, resulting in significant financial losses and even endangering human life in the worst situations (Climate Change Indicators: River Flooding | US EPA, 2025b). Additionally, pluvial flooding happens when snowmelt saturates the earth, resulting in limited porosity (Heavy Rain | DKKV, n.d.).

Urban Floods

Urban flooding is a natural disaster that occurs annually and is a significant problem in many regions of the world (Urbanization - Understanding Global Change, 2022). An overflowing of land in a developed environment, especially in heavily settled places, is known as urban flooding

(Unacademy, 2022). It occurs when rainfall or related events exceed the capacity of drainage systems (Mohanty et al., 2020). Major Indian cities have been adversely impacted by the recent rise in urban flooding (Deshpande, 2022; Vajiram & Ravi, 2024). The 2005 Mumbai floods, the 2007 Kolkata floods, the 2009 Delhi floods, the 2015 Bangalore floods, and the 2020 Hyderabad floods are just a few of the most notable instances of urban flooding. Urban flooding is caused due to faster flow, defective drainage systems, global warming, and lack of waste management (Feng et al., 2021).

Groundwater Floods

Groundwater flooding takes place when the natural under-the-ground drainage system is unable to remove rainwater adequately, leading the water levels to rise above ground level. Groundwater flood risk management presents a distinct set of technological and ecological difficulties that distinguish it from other flood types (e.g., rivers, and coastal) (Coastal Flood, 2023; UNDRR, 2023).

Causes of Flooding

Floods are mainly caused by natural phenomena. It could also be a result of human forces. It causes significant harm to life as well as assets (Toppr, n.d.; UNDRR, 2023). Flooding can result from a variety of factors. Among the most significant of them are:

Natural Causes of Flooding

Flooding can be triggered by excessive rainfall, quick snowmelt, or a storm tide from a tropical cyclone or tsunami in coastal locations.

Heavy rainfall Heavy rainfall is characterized as an enormous quantity of rainfall in a brief amount of time, typically falling in a small area and with short warning periods because of its conduction origin (Heavy Rain | DKKV, n.d.). Flooding may result from extremely high rainfall levels that quickly raise water levels in small streams and rivers (Francis & Gadgil, 2006; Mohanty et al., 2020). Chikkamagaluru and Madikeri in Karnataka are repeatedly affected by persistent rainfall, leading to severe flooding on bridges and roads (Gouda et al., 2023).

Cloud burst A cloudburst is an unexpected, intense downpour that often occurs locally and lasts only for a short time. Mountainous regions are particularly prone to cloudbursts. This is most likely due to a thunderstorm's warm air currents' propensity to follow a mountain's higher slope. These occurrences are becoming more frequent and intense because of climate change and global warming (Gupta, 2024; United Nations Environment Programme, n.d.). Heavy rains brought on by a violent cloudburst in 2024 produced landslides and flash floods in Manali. Numerous people lost their lives because of the tragedy, which also severely damaged infrastructure and disrupted transportation, particularly the Chandigarh–Manali National Highway. At least ten people have died because of Kedarnath's heavy rains, which has also seriously damaged bridges and buildings (ReliefWeb, 2013).

Cyclone Cyclones are created by atmospheric variations that surround a region of low pressure, characterized by rapid and frequently damaging airflow. Serious storms and unfavourable weather often accompany cyclones. The powerful rains and strong winds of tropical cyclones can result in significant property damage, fatalities, soil erosion, and flooding when they hit land. Cyclone Dana in the states of Odisha and West Bengal caused flooding (Coastal Flood, 2023; UNDRR, 2023).

Global warming Climate change and water are closely related. Water around the world is impacted by climate change in a variety of aspects. Most of the effects of climate change effects are related to water, including fluctuating rainfall patterns, melting glaciers, increasing sea levels, floods, and droughts (United Nations, n.d.; United Nations Environment Programme, n.d.). Climate change is making prolonged rainfall occurrences more often and severe in many parts of the world, like other hazardous weather occurrences (Climate Change Indicators: River Flooding | US EPA, 2024). Flood danger is increased by climate change and changes in the landscape, such as the loss of vegetation (Boyle, 2024).

Earthquakes and landslides When there is a high water level and sandy ground, earthquake shaking can cause liquefaction of the soil, which could flood the region with sand and groundwater that is expelled to the surface (Floods - Definition and Different Causes of Floods | Toppr, 2020). Landslides, on the other hand, also make floods more likely. The reason for this is that the debris causes the river's sediment to rise. Floods are the outcome of rivers with erratic courses becoming more common (Udayashankara et al., 2016; Mohanty et al., 2020).

Human-Induced Causes of Flooding

Floods, which were historically attributed entirely to natural causes, have experienced tremendous modification as a result of human activity (UNDRR, 2023; United Nations Environment Programme, n.d.). As the world continues to urbanize, industrialize, and extract natural resources, the frequency and severity of flood occurrences increase (Urbanization - Understanding Global Change, 2022; Mohanty et al., 2020). Among the human-induced causes of flooding are the following:

Deforestation Deforestation is the deliberate destruction of forest areas. The more frequently deforestation occurs, the more severe its consequences on close neighborhoods, which endure frequent flooding (Boyle, 2024). These disastrous floods have the potential to relocate individuals, destroy assets, and, in the most extreme case, claim lives (Boyle, 2024).

Urbanization Urbanization is the process of turning vacant or poorly settled land into cities with a high population. Urbanization frequently leads to habitat degradation, forest clearing, and groundwater extraction; all of these can change the geographic distribution of species and reduce ecological diversity (Urbanization - Understanding Global Change, 2022). Urbanization elevates the region's impervious surface area, which slows hydrological reactions and hence raises flood risks (Mohanty et al., 2020; Feng et al., 2021).

Dam construction Floods created by dams are unforeseen, and, because of their severity and lack of preparedness of individuals living nearby, their impact on human life and property is more devastating (Floods in Indian Rivers: Are Dams and Embankments the Solution or the Problem?, 2025). Although dams are made to safely handle floodwater, when floods surpass the spillways' design capacity, water is released uncontrollably over the dam peak, increasing the likelihood of failure (Udayashankara et al., 2016). Flooding in reservoirs can result in death, damage to ecological systems, loss of cultural assets, and financial damage (Environmental Impacts of Flooding - Alberta WaterPortal, 2023; United Nations, n.d.).

Impact of Floods

Flooding has both beneficial and harmful effects. Although floods are extremely vital to ecosystems, the maintenance of riverbank vegetation can stimulate the growth of new plants. On the other hand, when floods strike human surroundings, they possess a chance to generate a variety of adverse effects.

Physical impacts Flooding has a severe physiological impact, including drowning in water, injury, hypothermia, and bites by animals. Health concerns are also related to individual evacuation, loss of healthcare workers, and impairment of health facilities, including critical pharmaceuticals and supplies. Floods can impact human health both immediately and over time, directly or indirectly. Other significant health risks in the event of flooding are diseases and epidemics. Water-borne illnesses like cholera and hepatitis A are more likely to spread after flooding incidents. Static pools of water created by flooding can serve as the ideal habitat for mosquitoes, which are known to spread diseases like malaria.

Mental health Flooding can have long-lasting, significant impacts on people's mental health and overall well-being. In the early phases of a flood, many individuals are shocked and distressed. Longer-term psychological consequences for those who survived may include social breakdown, pain, anxiety, sadness, and discomfort. In severe circumstances, these distresses can develop into mental disorders, often known as psychopathologies. The probability of dealing with negative mental health effects after flooding is known to be linked to several aspects. These comprise sociodemographic traits, including age, gender, socioeconomic status, level of education, and elements associated with the type of flooding (e.g., depth and length), and elements about the actual hazard that define the severity of floods for humans, such as water depth, flood type, and length, as well as elements related to the detrimental effects of floods, such as injuries, death threats, the destruction of property, monetary losses, and relocation.

Economic impacts Persistent floods can lead to mass relocation or displacement of communities by causing loss of employment and production, and also other long-term financial consequences and different kinds of distress. The enormous expense of relief and recovery could harm local infrastructure investments and other development initiatives, and, in some situations, it could destroy the region's already fragile economy.

Social impacts Social impacts are those that influence our social structures and the interactions between them. These effects arise from harm to homes, vital services, and public infrastructure during a flood. Floods can have a wide-ranging social influence which can seriously undermine the quality of life of individuals and affected communities. Among these effects are physical damage to buildings and infrastructural components. The most visible consequence of flooding involves the direct damage produced by physical contact between floodwaters and economic possessions, cultural properties, or individuals, which results in fatalities and injury. It also results in increasing levels of social marginalization. Disasters exacerbate poverty, leading to emotions of susceptibility and despair.

Environmental impacts Flooding can harm the ecosystem by causing soil and bank erosion, bed erosion, sedimentation, and landslides. It can damage plants, and the contaminants transported by floodwater can influence water quality, ecosystems, flora, and animals. However, flooding can also have a positive impact on natural environments. Floodwater does frequently carry garbage and contaminants. Floodwater contaminants such as germs and pesticides can travel considerable distances. Flooding in metropolitan settings may be exceedingly devastating and expensive, affecting structures, residences, and businesses.

Floods in India

India is extremely susceptible to flooding, because of India's distinct topographical placement and socioeconomic contexts. It accounts for one-fifth of all flood-related deaths globally, making it the most flood-affected country after Bangladesh. India's geo-climatic factors have resulted in devastating flood casualties and destruction. In recent years, the nation has experienced numerous devastating floods that have caused devastating harm to human lives, assets, livelihoods, and structures. Among the most devastating floods that occurred in India are:

Maharashtra floods, 2005 The 2005 Maharashtra floods affected multiple areas of its capital city, Mumbai, causing roughly 1094 fatalities and destroying 14,000 homes. In 24 hours, the city received 944 mm of rain, the most recorded for a century. Ten thousand trucks and Tempo Traveller were grounded, 900 buses, 4000 taxis, and 37,000 autorickshaws suffered damage, and the city bore a direct loss of almost ₹ 5.5 billion. The accumulation of water on the tracks caused local trains to stop, and 52 local trains sustained damage.

Assam floods, 2012 In the northeastern Indian state of Assam, flooding began in numerous areas on June 26, 2012, due to severe rainfall during the monsoon season. Approximately six million people were displaced, and 126 individuals lost their lives because of landslides and flooding. In total, it has impacted 2,391,369 individuals as well as 9.35 million hectares of land over 4540 villages, with 19 persons reported as having been disappeared. The situation is extremely concerning because it has expanded to multiple regions that are typically not impacted by Brahmaputra River floods, with 43 breaches in the river's riverbank solely and water levels over the danger zone. Numerous settlements throughout the state became trapped by the floodwaters, and many more were inundated for days. Approximately 3829 communities experienced flooding as of July 2, 2012.

Uttarakhand floods, 2013 In June 2013, the religious town of Kedarnath, which is perched at a height of 3438 meters among the Himalayan hills, saw enormous destruction due to heavy rainfall, flash floods, and landslides. The four districts that suffered the most were Pithoragarh, Uttarkashi, Chamoli, and Rudraprayag. More than 73,000 people were stranded in different locations due to damaged or obstructed highways, and more than 500 people were been killed in the destruction.

Jammu and Kashmir floods, 2014 Major parts of the districts of Anantnag, Kulgam, Pulwama, Baramulla, Bandipora, and Srinagar were submerged by the devastating floods that occurred in Jammu and Kashmir in September 2014 because of heavy and continuous rainfall that persisted for more than a week. A major flood trapped many people inside their flooded homes. By the evening of the first day of the massive flooding, 227 people had been killed, scores of buildings had been demolished, and 2500 villages throughout Kashmir had been impacted.

Chennai floods, 2015 Due to the development of a storm surge over the southwest Bay of Bengal, South India saw torrential rainfall in November and December of 2015. Flood-like conditions were caused by rivers and lakes overflowing as a result of heavy rainfall in portions of Tamil Nadu, Puducherry, and coastal Andhra Pradesh. The flood that struck Tamil Nadu in November and December 2015, particularly in Chennai, devastated the state, killing more than 400 people and causing massive financial and domestic devastation. The areas most impacted were primarily those close to Chennai's coast, including Tiruvallur and Kanchipuram.

Kerala floods, 2018 An exceptionally high amount of rainfall occurred in Kerala between June 1 and August 19, 2018. Approximately 500 people lost their lives, 19,000 homes were demolished, 1.1 million people were temporarily displaced, and 5.5 million people were impacted by the flooding and landslides brought on by the rainfall. The UN system assessed recovery expenses at 3.7 billion USD, while the World Bank calculated a total economic loss of 3.4 billion USD. People were forced to evacuate their homes in Edanad, Pandanad, and Chengannur.

Karnataka floods, 2019 Flooding occurred in several areas of Karnataka in early August 2019 because of excessive rains and an enormous reservoir of release of water from the adjoining state of Maharashtra.

Overview of Karnataka State

Karnataka, a state in south India, has a rich historical, cultural, and anthropological legacy. It was formerly a part of several renowned kingdoms and princely republics in the Deccan peninsula [11]. Karnataka, the eighth-largest state in the nation, is divided into ten Agro-Climatic Zones and spans 1.91 lakh square kilometres. Its climatological zones include semi-arid, desert, sub-humid, and humid. A semi-arid to arid climate prevails over around two-thirds of the land area [12]. Karnataka, located on the southwest coast, has a substantial variance in its terrain, which is primarily separated into three zones based on physical features: inland, coastal, and Western Ghats [13]. This variance in topography results in significant variations in weather factors, such as temperature and rainfall intensity across the state. Because of the orographic influence of the western ghats, moist air from the adjacent Arabian Sea is obstructed, resulting in significant rain on the windward side of the Western Ghats and coastal plain, while the leeward side receives less rainfall [14]. In the state of Karnataka, rainfall during the southwest monsoon contributes to approximately 73% of the total annual rainfall [15].

Topography of Karnataka

The state of Karnataka is situated where the Eastern and Western Ghats meet to form the Nilgiris Hills. Karnataka's geography is characterized by a wide range of geographical variances. The state features an appealing combination of peaks, terrain coastlines, and high mountains. The topographical regions in Karnataka are categorized into: the Coastal Plains, the Sahyadri, and the Deccan Plateau.

The Coastal Plains The coastal region of Karnataka is roughly 320 km long and is divided into the districts of Uttara Kannada (160 km), Udupi (98 km), and Dakshina Kannada (62 km). The average breadth of the coastal belt is between 50 and 80 kilometers. From north to south, it covers about 267 kilometers.

The Sahyadri The Sahyadri, another name for the Western Ghats, is a mountain range that runs 1600 kilometers (990 miles) along the Indian peninsula's western coast. The western hills of India begin in the Satpura Mountain Range in the north and run south via Goa, Karnataka, and into Kerala and Tamil Nadu until ending at Kanyakumari, which embraces the Indian Ocean. The mountains span 1600 kilometers and occupy around 140,000 km^2.

River basins Karnataka is home to seven significant river basins. The Krishna and Cauvery River basins account for about 60% and 20% of the state's drainage area, respectively. The seven river basins are Cauvery, Krishna, Godavari, North Pennar, South Pennar, Palar, and the west-flowing rivers of Karnataka. In Karnataka, the rivers provide water for irrigation, drinking, and power production. The majority of rivers start in the Western Ghats and typically travel west until meeting the Arabian Sea after a brief journey that can range from 50 to 300 kilometers.

Context of the Karnataka Floods

There have also been significant floods in Karnataka in 2005, 2009, and 2018. An atmospheric depression in the Bay of Bengal and the ensuing rainfall in neighboring Karnataka, Andhra, and Maharashtra regions caused devastating floods in the North Interior Karnataka districts in October 2009, severely damaging the lives of individuals, assets, and vital structures in seven districts. In the Malnad territory, Kodagu and the nearby jurisdictions of Chikkamagaluru, Hassan, and Shivamogga, as well as the coastal districts of Dakshina Kannada, Udupi, and Uttara Kannada, all suffered major catastrophic flooding throughout the 2018 Southwest Monsoon Season. These floods were accompanied by mud-flows and landslides, which caused substantial damages and death tolls.

The state received 224 mm of rain, having a total variation of +279% between August 3 and August 10, 2019, which was record-breaking for Karnataka in the previous 118 years for the same time frame. Throughout that time, some districts experienced deviations of almost 700% from the usual pattern. The record-breaking flow of water of up to 9 lakh cubic feet per sec over several days from the dams in Maharashtra's Upper Krishna and Bhima basins further exacerbated the circumstances. For the state at this time, the cumulative inflows, and outflows of the main reservoirs—KRS and Kabini in the Cauvery Basin and Almatti and Narayanapura in the Krishna Basin—were unparalleled.

Impact of the Karnataka Floods

The coastal, northern, and Malnad regions were the most severely affected of the 21 districts. 91 fatalities, more than 700,000 people were relocated because of the terrible floods and landslides, destroying numerous towns, which have also severely damaged essential structures and agriculture. Approximately 1.79 lakh of the 2.47 lakh wrecked houses are classified as badly ruined. The loss of shelter has been a terrible experience, even if the residents of the impacted districts have endured great suffering. Massive flooding severely damaged both private and public properties, crops, livestock, agricultural land, as well as essential infrastructure such as roads, bridges, power, and transportation.

Approximately 13,663.51 hectares of agricultural and horticultural land have been damaged by mudslides and landslides in various regions. An estimated Rs. 15,230.00 crores in crops have been lost because of landslides and flooding. Floods wiped out essential facilities, including schools, hospitals, roadways and culverts, power lines, and Anganwadi centers, among many more. In addition to leaving thousands of affected individuals homeless, the extensive damage caused by the calamity has resulted in a loss of livelihood because both public and private properties have been extensively destroyed.

Relief Efforts by Local and Governmental Agencies

In the aftermath of landslides and flooding the Central Government offered full support to the State Governments by mobilizing/providing appropriate transportation and financial backing to help the State Governments' attempts to successfully handle the crisis. Along with the required rescue gear, the logistics assistance offered consists of sufficient numbers of National Disaster Response Force teams, Indian Air Force and Coast Guard helicopters, Army columns, and Navy and Coast Guard troops. The Karnataka floods led to the opening of 1465 relief camps, which, at one point, housed 4.61 lakh people. Relief camps offered food, potable water, medical attention, and other essential supplies. For emergency relief and the restoration or rebuilding of essential facilities, areas impacted by flooding have received the amount of Rs. 914 crores. In addition, 2.02 lakh impacted families have received additional charity assistance of Rs. 10,000.00 per affected family (Rs. 6200 from the State fund).

The Vandhe Bharatham team gathered and delivered three truckloads of vital commodities totalling Rs. 45 lakhs to flood survivors in Dakshina Kannada District, Gadag, and Mudhol. Annapoorna Trust volunteers fed about 330 flood victims in Old Hubli. One non-governmental organization (NGO), based at Athani, Karnataka, organized and provided relief supplies, primarily food, to help them start again. Many impacted households have received relief material kits from us. An NGO at Belagavi arranged a cleanup initiative to remove the trash collected on Peeranwadi's streets and the surrounding area.

Psychosocial Support Before, During, and After Disasters

Psychosocial well-being is crucial for individuals, household members, interpersonal relationships, and neighborhoods recovering from disasters. Strategies to lessen the impact on mental health are essential in regions vulnerable to natural disasters, and they should encourage support before, during, and following an incident. Flooding can either aggravate or trigger psychosocial distress due to the associated socioeconomic losses experienced by affected individuals. Flooding can pose a significant psychological challenge to certain populations like children, elderly people, persons with disabilities and people with mental health conditions. Therefore, there is a need to provide psychosocial support before, during, and after any emergencies.

Preparedness (Before a Flood)

Although some floods evolve gradually, others do happen in a matter of minutes. Being prepared and implementing mitigation strategies, such as raising houses and constructing outside of floodplains, can lessen the likelihood of flooding-related damage and casualties. Disaster preparedness can be characterized as personal precautionary conduct that can be shaped to protect against unexpected conditions that may have a detrimental effect on an individual's life and possessions.

- Engage individuals, families, social networks, and communities in conversation about possible hazards and identify obstacles to minimizing or preventing their effects.

- One important strategy for reducing the risks and surviving during times of flooding is to assemble a preparedness kit.
- Maps of the community ought to contain information about organizations and resource people that can set up activities for psychosocial assistance.
- Communicating risks to people, families, communities, and social networks and including them in the creation of disaster and evacuation plans.
- Implementing disaster preparedness plans in schools. In an age-appropriate manner, teach students about floods, local flood risk, and flood warning systems. Develop their comprehension of the psychological and practical effects of flooding. Activities like geography could be incorporated into normal classes or curricula.

Responding (During a Flood)

The response phase follows the onset of a major disaster or calamity. It comprises acts designed to save lives, reduce financial losses, and relieve suffering. Psychosocial support during a disaster includes:

Psychological First Aid (PFA) Psychological first aid (PFA) aims to minimize the possibility of post-traumatic stress disorder. The National Centre for Post-Traumatic Stress Disorder (NC-PTSD), part of the US Department of Veterans Affairs, created it in 2006. It is critical to provide support in the immediate aftermath of violent incidents. Responding to people's emotional needs during difficult times boosts resilience and aids in the healing process. Five fundamental components of psychological first aid have been identified from field experience, professional consensus, and research on risk and resilience. They are: safety, calm, connectedness, self-efficacy, and hope. Three action principles make up the framework that the World Health Organization (WHO) has created to help provide psychological first aid.

To comprehend the demands of those impacted (LISTEN), and connect them with the knowledge and useful assistance they require (LINK), these principles offer direction on how to perceive and securely approach an emergency (LOOK).

Safe spaces/evacuation center An "evacuation center" is a temporary living option for people who have been relocated by a disaster. They offer emergency shelter from the worst effects of the calamity and crucial information to emergency planners about internally displaced people (IDPs) who are completely homeless or whose shelter is seriously damaged, necessitating a transitional shelter or long-term solution. Families, women, children, and other vulnerable individuals at evacuation camps require more protection than ever before. In living and sleeping areas, flexible barriers should be included whenever feasible. Residents, especially women and girls, must, at the very least, be allowed to shower, use the lavatory, and take care of their sanitation needs, including their menstrual cycle, in a private, safe, and respectable manner.

Emotional support A devastating occurrence or disaster can cause people to feel various emotions both before and after. There are many different reactions that disaster survivors may have; however, they are all conventional methods of dealing with challenging circumstances. The reactions such as physiological and psychological exhaustion, having trouble focusing or making decisions, irritation, feeling worn out, depressed, dull, isolated, or anxious, and noticing alterations in sleep or appetite. A crucial first step in providing emotional support to disaster victims is to comprehend the usual and common reactions they could experience following a disaster. Listening to and understanding the survivors is one of the most crucial ways to offer them emotional assistance. Respectfully paying close attention, and refraining from passing judgment or offering advice are all components of listening, encouraging healthy coping mechanisms that can lessen stress and increase resilience. These can include: practising calming techniques like yoga, meditation, or breathing exercises; keeping up healthy routines like eating right, getting enough sleep, or exercising; remaining in touch with encouraging people like family, friends, or the community; and discovering meaning and purpose through volunteer work, self-help, or being thankful.

Rapid Need Assessment (RNA)

The state must have a mechanism in place that can rapidly assess the extent of reaction needed and transfer the necessary resources when a disaster strikes. The requirements of the impacted people must be evaluated immediately after a disaster. An evaluation of such a situation will reveal gaps that need to be filled, as well as the most pressing needs that call for assistance from the outside. A rapid needs assessment entails conducting primary and secondary research as soon as possible to comprehend important data that can guide the planning and execution of the course of action. To deliver the right sort of assistance, it is essential to accurately assess the needs and impacts of survivors of disasters. Rapid need assessment (RNA) is a collaborative tool which offers a quick overview of the immediate requirements at the community level of a specific population as the consequence of either a significant number of recently arrived refugees, secondary displacement of refugees within Lebanon, or internal displacement of Lebanese people due to a natural disaster or conflict. Rapid need assessment may be carried out by state RNA teams with specialized training, local officials, or combined federal/state RNA or disaster assessment teams, based on the extent of the incident.

Significance of Rapid Need Assessment A rapid need assessment can help in evaluating the impacted population's needs and creating a prioritized action plan by their demands to provide an efficient response. Significant gaps or overlaps in support could arise in the absence of a prompt evaluation, wasting valuable resources during a time of extreme need and possibly adding to the load being placed on the impacted people.

Features of Rapid Need Assessment

Rapidity Rapid need assessments can significantly cut down on the amount of time needed to carry out trustworthy and thorough investigations. This velocity is attained using creative planning, management, and data analysis techniques.

Iterative Data Collection Rapid assessments are continuous and use a dynamic approach that uses direct observations and semi-structured interviews to uncover the unforeseen.

Teamwork Teams comprising "insiders," who possess a thorough understanding of the language of the region, practices, and members of the community, and "outsiders," who possess prior technical knowledge and expertise of the process, are always involved in conducting rapid assessments.

Feasibility Rapid assessment is intended to do just that by focusing on a limited number of subjects that immediately impact the intervention. Rapid need assessments do not concentrate on broad, generic inquiries. Rather, the issues are changed to tackle certain programmatic problems.

Local participation Proactive and significant community involvement is a key component of quick inspection and assessment. This aids in the assessment's resolution of the problem of the absence of community engagement and contribution in the formulation, execution, and review of local development initiatives.

Rapid Need Assessment in Different Disaster Situations

Drought situation in Maharashtra, 2015–16 A rapid need assessment was conducted to determine the most susceptible population's current requirements in the affected area. Its goal was to determine interventions that would provide immediate assistance to the economically disadvantaged and marginalized while attempting to find a long-lasting solution to vulnerabilities brought on by unpredictable weather.

Flood situation in Bihar, 2017 In August 2017, Bihar had one of the most severe flooding events in a decade due to continuous rainfall, which affected 1.22 crore people across 17 districts. A rapid need assessment was conducted and the evaluation suggested emergency water, sanitation, hygiene, and health interventions for short- and medium-term requirements, followed by measures for housing and employment. Additionally, an extended rehabilitative and vocational recovery approach was suggested.

Rohingya refugee camp's response to the monsoon hit Rohingya refugees in Bangladesh had to endure severe climate change that endangered their lives and shelters after escaping Myanmar due to the acts of violence and humiliation they experienced. In the second week of June 2018, a rapid assessment was carried out in four camps. The evaluation took into consideration multiple issues, such as children, gender, disability, the elderly, HIV/AIDS, and the environment while adhering to the Sphere and Core Humanitarian Standards.

Odisha's Cyclone Fani, 2019 Cyclone Fani struck the Indian state of Odisha on May 3, 2019. An 'extremely severe storm' caused devastation in Odisha before moving on to West Bengal, Bangladesh, and Assam. An RNA was conducted in Puri and Khorda, Odisha's two most severely affected districts. In both districts, the RNA was carried out over two days. This assessment's goals were to quickly and comprehensively identify the multisectoral requirements in the regions that were most affected, and to comprehend the effect on social sector services. According to the evaluation, the infrastructure used for service delivery (such as schools, health centers, and anganwadis) sustained extensive damage, and these facilities lost materials and supplies.

Maharashtra floods, 2019 Upon reviewing the data, we confirm that the 802.70 mm of rainfall during the 2019 monsoon in Maharashtra represents 109.43% of the average rainfall for the same period (June to August). This figure is supported by the India Meteorological Department's (IMD) state-wise rainfall statistics for 2019. The RNA team investigated the consequences of flooding on public health, nutrition, Water, Sanitation and Hygiene (WASH), child safety, livelihoods, food security, and education, to enhance the abilities, mentality, competencies, and social assets in dealing with the stress caused by the floods.

NIMHANS Initiatives During the Karnataka Floods

During the relief phase from August 10 to 18, 2019, the Department of Psychosocial Support in Disaster Management (DPSSDM), within the National Institute of Mental Health and Neurosciences (NIMHANS), conducted a rapid psychosocial need assessment in the districts of Shivamogga, Hassan, Dakshina Kannada, Uttara Kannada, Belagavi, Dharwad, Gadag, and Bagalkot of the state to identify and tackle these problems among the flood survivors. According to the reports of the RNA, the socio-demography of the affected population in the Karnataka flood survivors 2019 was as follows:

Geographical patterns The RNA was conducted in the eight most affected districts of Karnataka state: Shivamogga, Hasan, Dakshina Kannada, Uttra Kannada, Belagavi, Dharwad, Gadag, and Bagalkote.

Demographic groups The vast majority of those impacted were farmers who made their living primarily from farming and raising livestock. In addition to losing their crops and fertile land, these farmers also lost their animals, which they saw as essential parts of their families, causing them great emotional and financial hardship. The impacted demographic consisted of vulnerable groups such as women, children, the elderly, and people with disabilities, all of whom had difficulties adapting to living in the relief camps. The absence of regular routines and facilities caused difficulties for children and the elderly, while a dearth of supplies and assistance created additional obstacles for people with disabilities. It was especially challenging for women, who frequently assumed responsibility for attending to emotional and familial demands, to guarantee their families' welfare amid the crowded surroundings of the camps. Adolescent girls were particularly vulnerable during disasters, as evidenced by the fact that they were often transported to their relatives' houses for safety because the relief camps lacked privacy and other security precautions.

Population in relief camps A total of 1160 relief camps were set up throughout the flood-affected areas to house about 396,617 people. These camps served as temporary shelters for families evacuated by the disaster, offering only what was necessary, but frequently lacking the means to properly meet the wide range of demands of the affected population. Most camp members were adults and older people who stayed behind to take care of their close families and necessities. The incident indicated how important it is to implement comprehensive planning and resources to meet the diverse demographic needs of disaster relief efforts.

Socioeconomic characteristics The impacted groups had a strong agricultural heritage as well as strong familial connections, both of which were essential to their way of life. Several households had an emotional bond with their cattle, seeing them as important members of their homes as well as financial possessions. As a result, losing animals caused them not only financial hardship but also psychological pain, which made their suffering even worse. Those most affected were farmers and poor families, who were already struggling financially before the disaster.

Community reaction The impacted population's different responses to evacuation were suggestive of concerns that were distinct depending on gender and generation. Because they felt a strong emotional connection to their ancestral lands and a sense of belonging, elderly people frequently opposed leaving their homes. Many exhibited a stubborn attitude, declaring that they were prepared to stay despite the dangers because they saw their homes as priceless representations of their identities and lives. Younger people, on the other hand, were more practical and put their families' safety above sentimental attachments to their belongings. Recognizing the need to adjust to future uncertainty, they showed a willingness to move to safer places with the assistance of the government and assistance organizations.

Methodologies Used in Rapid Need Assessment

Individual interviews Individual interviews usually involve speaking with a single individual at a time in person, over the phone, via instant messaging, or through other computer-assisted methods. Survivors were interviewed one-on-one to acquire a deeper understanding of their own personal experiences, difficulties, and coping strategies. By using this approach, the assessment team was able to collect in-depth, first-hand reports of how the tragedy affected people's daily lives, physical health, and mental health.

Focus group discussions Focus groups bring together individuals with comparable experiences or backgrounds to talk about a particular topic of interest. Focus groups were conducted with demographic groups, including women, children, and men. These conversations gave participants a forum to explore shared experiences, discover shared problems, and address their concerns and requirements in a safe and encouraging environment.

Key informant interviews Key informant interviews are in-depth, qualitative interviews conducted with individuals who are aware of community events. Key informant interviews are used to gather data from a variety of individuals who have direct experience with the neighborhood, such as citizens, professionals, and community leaders. Doctors, nurses, Asha workers, educators, and community leaders were among the professionals and stakeholders who were the primary subjects of key informant interviews. These interviews provided professional viewpoints on the effects of the disaster, emphasizing community strengths, structural problems, and available resources. Important details regarding the local reactions and possible interventions were also supplied by them.

The primary information was supplemented by secondary data sources, such as government documents, local newspapers, and previously published articles. The investigation supported results from other approaches by providing additional details, including the magnitude of relief efforts, demographic information, and the level of destruction.

Field Observation in the Context of Disaster Response

Field observation is a type of field study that involves observing to obtain views about their conduct, actions, and procedures. As per the rapid need assessment report of the Karnataka floods 2019, the government and local organizations were engaged in evacuation and rescue efforts as part of rescue activities. Based on governmental action, community readiness, and the availability of resources, the quality of humanitarian assistance differed greatly between regions. Camp dynamics depicted that, in shelters, women and children were left unoccupied much of the time, which aggravated their emotional despair. Stress could have been reduced by engaging in activities. Due to anticipation about their safety in the camps, adolescent girls were frequently transported to reside with relatives. Lack of personal space and services for children, the elderly, and those with disabilities were all problems for families.

From a psychosocial point of view, emergency workers and individuals who survived were unaware of the need to attend to emotional and mental health requirements and psychological first aid. Psychosocial treatment was subordinated to fundamental needs. As survivors themselves, Asha workers complained about the lack of assistance for their suffering while providing aid to others. Community members also expressed their grievances, farmers expressed regret for losing livestock and crops, highlighting their emotional attachment and dependency on livestock for their sustenance. Individuals mentioned delaying alerts about flooding and management as evidence of a lack of communication and collaboration across governments. It was also noted that the communities that experienced flooding frequently showed more coping strategies and readiness than places that experienced flooding for the first time. Apart from various issues, it was also observed that the submersion of school buildings resulted in prolonged closures. The loss of educational resources caused disruptions to the education of students.

Identified Needs and Concerns of the Survivors

Insufficient information was given to survivors in temporary shelters concerning their existing circumstances, forthcoming strategies, and government efforts about rehabilitation, benefits, and assistance. Uncertainty and stress have been made worse by this lack of clarity. The elderly, women, children, and people with disabilities have a challenging time adjusting to camp life. Their requirements are frequently disregarded. Although medical care was available, survivors of several camps indicated that medical staff sometimes failed to provide adequate attention. Basic requirements like food and shelter were taken care of during the rescue phase, but longer-term rehabilitation and emotional care are more important.

The knowledge and application of psychosocial care for flooding survivors are severely lacking. Emergency workers must have training in psychological first aid and related interventions. To lessen the consequences of floods and landslides in the future, extensive disaster planning and mitigation programs that include psychosocial components are required. Local, national, and international NGOs provided little or no assistance, regardless the fact that survivors, family members, contributors, and government agencies actively participate in relief efforts. For quicker recovery and rehabilitation, all stakeholders must work together in a coordinated effort.

Psychosocial Intervention and Recommendations

The massive destruction brought about by the 2019 Karnataka floods influenced survivors' physical, social, and mental health. An analysis of the disaster response reveals an enormous gap in meeting the impacted population's emotional needs.

Capacity building for mental health support Capacity refers to the ability's characteristics, and facilities accessible within a community, organization, or society that allow them to handle disaster risks and build resilience effectively. Building capacity is a continuous process that prepares officials, stakeholders, and the community to carry out their duties more effectively after a crisis or disaster. As a part of capacity-building training programs, it is important to provide the capabilities that emergency personnel, government professionals, and volunteers need to meet the psychological needs of people who have survived a disaster. Emergency workers should receive training to learn how they can identify symptoms of severe emotional distress that call for a referral to professional mental health services. Organizing psychological first aid (PFA) training sessions to assist responders in efficiently managing serious psychological issues.

Involving survivors in recreational and relaxation activities Recreation is crucial to rebuilding survivors' capacity to handle the difficulties of the crisis and its subsequent aftermath. Recreation offers habitual routines and activities that aid survivors in returning to normalcy. Recreation can help communities evolve and become more resilient over time as they rebuild and recover. Activities like sports, games, fitness, walking, dancing, spending time with other members in the shelter, and engaging in arts and crafts activities are some forms of recreational activities that can help survivors lower stress levels and provide a feeling of routine and mutual support. Relaxation methods can enhance general well-being and aid with stress management. Relaxation techniques such as mindfulness, meditation, breathing techniques, relaxing music, and self-talk could help the survivors cope better with stressful circumstances. Relaxation techniques typically include focus and awareness, which helps in minimizing monotony, stress, and feelings of sadness in camps. It also helps camp residents form stronger social relationships and encourage sharing experiences.

Improving Community-Based Support Networks Community-orientated initiatives enable families the ability to access important assets and services in favorable settings that improve protective factors. Community-Based Support Networks prepare community-based disaster response teams to organize emergency actions, carry out rescue efforts, and administer first aid in the aftermath of disasters. Community support minimizes difficulties throughout an entire community by utilizing the theorized structures of community resilience and community cohesion. To enhance community-based support networks, it is significant to determine and engage community leaders to coordinate support groups and restoration initiatives and promote indigenous customs and cultural habits to foster a shared feeling of recovery and resilience.

Psychosocial preparedness for future disasters The long-term effects of a disaster or emergency can cause psychosocial problems that may exceed the capacity of individuals to control or cope. Preparedness is a collaborative effort by various stakeholders to allow individuals and communities to predict, respond, and rebuild from the effects of an impending disaster by improving their physical and emotional capacities. Psychosocial preparedness is designed to assist individuals to deal with, and recover from, disasters. Psychosocial preparedness can help in implementing disaster preparedness training that incorporates psychological resilience strategies like mindfulness and stress management. Psychosocial preparedness includes developing hazard-specific teaching materials to increase knowledge of impending calamities and psychological coping techniques. Psychosocial preparedness can help minimize psychological trauma during future calamities because of specified coping strategies.

Conclusion

Disaster Survivors' physical requirements receive timely care; however, their psychosocial needs are typically overlooked. Failure to address these needs can lead to dysfunction and disability. Providing timely psychosocial care can avert long-term difficulties and speed up rehabilitation for survivors.

References

5 Phases of Emergency Management | Organizational Resilience. (n.d.). University of Nevada, Reno. https://www.unr.edu/organizational-resilience/phases

5.4. Mental health and psychosocial support. (n.d.). http://www.saludydesastres.info/index.php?option=com_content&view=article&id=17

5:5-4-atencion-de-la-salud-mental-y-apoyo-psicosocial&catid=160:5-4--atencion-de-la-salud-mental-y-apoyo-psicosocial&Itemid=492&lang=en

About—OPW Flood Risk Management. (n.d.). https://www.floodinfo.ie/about_frm/impacts_of_flooding/#:~:text=Detrimental%20environmental%20effects%20of%20flooding,beneficial%20role%20in%20natural%20habitats

ActionAid India. (2019, September 17). *Jammu and Kashmir flood 2014—Relief response.* Thefansworld. https://www.actionaidindia.org/emergency/jammu-and-kashmir-floods-2014/

Admin. (2022, July 5). *Urban flooding: Overview, factors and steps for mitigation in India.* BYJUS. https://byjus.com/free-ias-prep/urban-flooding-india/

AJEM July 2023—Australian Red Cross psychosocial approach to disaster preparedness | Australian Disaster Resilience Knowledge Hub. (n.d.). https://knowledge.aidr.org.au/resources/ajem-july-2023-australian-red-cross-psychosocial-approach-to-disaster-preparedness/

ApAnnapoorna. (2019, September 1). Flood relief activities by Annapoorna Trust volunteers—August 2019—annapoorna. *annapoorna.* https://annapoorna.org.in/2019/09/01/flood-relief-activities-by-annapoorna-trust-volunteers-august-2019/

Assam floods 2012—India. (2012, July 23). ReliefWeb. https://reliefweb.int/report/india/assam-floods-2012

Bharatham, V. (n.d.). *Flood Relief | Vandhe Bharatham.* https://vb.foundation/flood-relief.html

Bird, M., International Federation of Red Cross and Red Crescent Societies, Reference Centre for Psychosocial Support (PS Centre) C/O Danish Red Cross, Hungarian Red Cross, British Red Cross, Northern Ireland, Danish Red Cross, Akasha, E. S., Berendt, S., Devaney, L., Dinesen, C., Hansen, L. J., Juen, B., Lassen, N., Meyer, A. M., Perera, C., Rice, S., Simpson, K., Vinther-Larsen, L., & Wiedemann, N. (2016). *Key actions for psychosocial support in flooding: Creating resilience in urban areas.* International Federation of Red Cross and Red Crescent Societies Reference Centre for Psychosocial Support (PS Centre). https://pscentre.org/wp-content/uploads/2018/02/Key_Actions-for-PSS-in-Flooding.pdf

Boyle, R. (2024, September 12). How can deforestation cause flooding? *Emission Index.* https://www.emission-index.com/deforestation/flooding

Bubeck, P., Otto, A., & Weichselgartner, J. (2017, June 28). Societal impacts of flood hazards. In *Oxford research encyclopedia of natural hazard science.* Retrieved November 29, 2024, from https://oxfordre.com/

naturalhazardscience/view/10.1093/acrefore/9780199389407.001.0001/acrefore-9780199389407-e-281
Choudhary, V., Sharma, P., & Dhingra, A. (2016). Be equipped psychologically: The psychological first aid. *The International Journal of Indian Psychology, 4*(1), 1–3. https://ijip.in/wp-content/uploads/ArticlesPDF/article_7a93387f9b318ebc341b5abfecbcf6f8.pdf
Climate Change Indicators: River Flooding | US EPA. (2024, October 21). US EPA. https://www.epa.gov/climate-indicators/climate-change-indicators-river-flooding
Claretian Missionaries Fathers. (2019, August 29). Flood relief interventions—Province of Bangalore. *Claretian Missionaries*. https://www.claret.org/flood-relief-interventions-province-bangalore/
Coastal Flood. (2023, June 7). UNDRR. https://www.undrr.org/understanding-disaster-risk/terminology/hips/mh0004
Coastal Hazard Wheel. (n.d.). https://www.coastalhazardwheel.org/coastal-flooding/
Coping After Disaster. (n.d.). https://www.psychiatry.org/patients-families/coping-after-disaster-trauma
Datar, A., Liu, J., Linnemayr, S., & Stecher, C. (2013). The impact of natural disasters on child health and investments in rural India. *Social Science & Medicine (1982), 76*(1), 83–91. https://doi.org/10.1016/j.socscimed.2012.10.008
Deshpande, R. S. (2022). Disaster management in India: Are we fully equipped? *Journal of Social and Economic Development, 24*(Suppl 1), 242–281. https://doi.org/10.1007/s40847-022-00225-w
Disaster preparedness: Floods and flash floods | Habitat for Humanity. (n.d.). Habitat for Humanity. https://www.habitat.org/our-work/disaster-response/disaster-preparedness-homeowners/floods
Disaster Rapid Needs Assessment Methods, Techniques, Tools and Purpose | Monitoring and Evaluation Studies. (n.d.). http://www.mnestudies.com/disaster-management/rapid-needs-assessment
Environmental Impacts of Flooding—Alberta WaterPortal. (2023, September 8). Alberta WaterPortal. https://albertawater.com/what-are-the-consequences-of-flooding/environmental/
Federal Emergency Management Agency. (n.d.). *State Disaster Management Course—IS 208*. https://training.fema.gov/emiweb/downloads/is208sdmunit4.pdf

Feng, B., Zhang, Y., & Bourke, R. (2021). Urbanization impacts on flood risks based on urban growth data and coupled flood models. *Natural Hazards, 106*(1), 613–627. https://doi.org/10.1007/s11069-020-04480-0

Flash Flood. (2023, June 7). UNDRR. https://www.undrr.org/understanding-disaster-risk/terminology/hips/mh0006

Floods in Indian Rivers: Are Dams and Embankments the Solution or the Problem? (2021, February 21). Economic and Political Weekly. https://www.epw.in/engage/article/floods-indian-rivers-are-dams-and-embankments

Floods—Definition and Different Causes of Floods | Toppr. (2020, April 2). Toppr-guides. https://www.toppr.com/guides/chemistry/environmental-chemistry/floods/

Foudi, S., Osés-Eraso, N., & Galarraga, I. (2017). The effect of flooding on mental health: Lessons learned for building resilience. *Water Resources Research, 53*(7), 5831–5844. https://doi.org/10.1002/2017wr020435

Francis, P. A., & Gadgil, S. (2006). Intense rainfall events over the west coast of India. *Meteorology and Atmospheric Physics, 94*(1–4), 27–42. https://doi.org/10.1007/s00703-005-0167-2

French, C. E., Waite, T. D., Armstrong, B., Rubin, G. J., Beck, C. R., & Oliver, I. (2019). Impact of repeat flooding on mental health and health-related quality of life: A cross-sectional analysis of the English National Study of Flooding and Health. *BMJ Open, 9*(11), e031562. https://doi.org/10.1136/bmjopen-2019-031562

fundsforNGOs. (2024, September 24). Building Resilience: Community-Based Strategies for Disaster Preparedness and Recovery—fundsforNGOs—Grants and Resources for Sustainability. fundsforNGOs—Grants and Resources for Sustainability—Grants and Resources for Sustainability. https://www.fundsforngos.org/proposals/building-resilience-community-based-strategies-for-disaster-preparedness-and-recovery/

Gouda, K. C., Nikhilasuma, P., Benke, M., & Agnihotri, G. (2023). Assessment of rainfall variability over Karnataka state in India. *Natural Hazards Research.* https://doi.org/10.1016/j.nhres.2023.08.004

Greening Recovery: The Case of Kerala Floods 2018 | GFDRR. (n.d.). https://www.gfdrr.org/en/events/WRC4/session4b

Health effects of flooding, explained | News | Wellcome. (2022, May 18). Wellcome. https://wellcome.org/news/how-flooding-can-impact-our-health

Healthdirect Australia. (n.d.). *Relaxation techniques for stress relief.* https://www.healthdirect.gov.au/relaxation-techniques-for-stress-relief

Heavy Rain | DKKV. (n.d.). https://dkkv.org/en/topics/heavy-rain/

HERD. (2016). A HERD Publication. https://www.herd.org.np/uploads/frontend/Publications/PublicationsAttachments1/1485497050-Focus%20Group%20Discussion_0.pdf

https://ksdma.karnataka.gov.in/storage/pdf-files/FLOOD%20MEMORANDUM%20August%202022_compressed-1-244.pdf

India: Monsoon Rains and Floods Final Report DREF n° MDRIN024—India. (2020, July 23). ReliefWeb. https://reliefweb.int/report/india/india-monsoon-rains-and-floods-final-report-dref-n-mdrin024

Information on Kerala Floods 2018. (2022, July 29). Unacademy. https://unacademy.com/content/upsc/study-material/general-awareness/kerala-floods-2018/

Kaur, J. (2006). Administrative issues involved in disaster management in India. *International Review of Psychiatry, 18*(6), 553–557. https://doi.org/10.1080/09540260601038449

Krishnamurti, T. (2024, November 19). *Monsoon | meteorology, climate & effects*. Encyclopedia Britannica. https://www.britannica.com/science/monsoon

Madur, & Madur. (2023, November 6). *Topography of Karnataka*. Karnataka.com. https://www.karnataka.com/profile/topography/#:~:text=Karnataka%20boasts%20of%20a%20geography,converge%20into%20the%20Nilgiri%20Hills

Makwana, N. (2019). Disaster and its impact on mental health: A narrative review. *Journal of Family Medicine and Primary Care, 8*(10), 3090–3095. https://doi.org/10.4103/jfmpc.jfmpc_893_19

Mohanty, M. P., Mudgil, S., & Karmakar, S. (2020). Flood management in India: A focused review on the current status and future challenges. *International Journal of Disaster Risk Reduction, 49*, 101660. https://doi.org/10.1016/j.ijdrr.2020.101660

NOAA's National Weather Service. (n.d.). *Flood and flash flood definitions*. https://www.weather.gov/mrx/flood_and_flash

Oluka, E. M., Dossen, S. B., & Ebuenyi, I. D. (2022). Flooding in Nigeria, towards prioritizing mental health and psychosocial support. *Pan African Medical Journal, 43*. https://doi.org/10.11604/pamj.2022.43.199.38251

Parida, Y., Chowdhury, J. R., Saini, S., & Dash, D. P. (2022). Role of income and government responsiveness in reducing the death toll from floods in Indian states. *Scientific Reports, 12*(1). https://doi.org/10.1038/s41598-022-21334-w

Patnaik, I., Sane, R., Shah, A., & National Institute of Public Finance and Policy. (2019). Chennai 2015: A novel approach to measuring the impact of a natural disaster. In *NIPFP working paper series* (Report No. 285). National Institute of Public Finance and Policy. https://www.nipfp.org.in/media/medialibrary/2019/12/WP_285_2019.pdf

Piyush, & Piyush. (2024, August 3). *What is cloudburst? Its causes, effects, and forecasting*. StudyIQ. https://www.studyiq.com/articles/cloudburst/?srsltid=AfmBOop9NWV41565Wi8ut_wAsM1F88q6hRpKaF-mUQUEgd4D5wXAyKW7e

Rabalao, R. T., 2006108977. (2010). The social, *psychological and economic impact of flooding in Ga-Motla and Ga-Moeka communities of Moretele district in north west province, South Africa* (By Disaster Management Training and Education Centre for Africa, University of the Free State, & A. J. Jordaan). https://www.ufs.ac.za/docs/librariesprovider22/disaster-management-training-and-education-centre-for-africa-(dimtec)-documents/dissertations/2274.pdf?sfvrsn=2

Rajesh, G., Binnal, A., Pai, M. B. H., Nayak, S. V., Shenoy, R., & Rao, A. (2020). Insights into disaster management scenario among various healthcare students in India: A multi-institutional, multi-professional study. *Indian Journal of Community Medicine: Official Publication of Indian Association of Preventive & Social Medicine, 45*(2), 220–224. https://doi.org/10.4103/ijcm.IJCM_104_19

Rapid Needs Assessment—RedR India. (n.d.). https://www.redr.org.in/projects/assessments-and-evaluations/assessments/rapid-needs-assessment/

Vajiram & Ravi. (2024, November 18). *Floods in India, causes, impacts, mitigation, measures, UPSC notes*. In Vajiram & Ravi. https://vajiramandravi.com/quest-upsc-notes/floods/

Recovering Emotionally. (n.d.). https://www.redcross.org/get-help/disaster-relief-and-recovery-services/recovering-emotionally.html?srsltid=AfmBOoqnJttH5YsMD-Tfwd4hcD_xFPfPgsyovWz3ZEEclSIadamQE00q

Research Guides: Usability: Individual Interviews. (n.d.). https://libguides.memphis.edu/c.php?g=587193&p=4065797#:~:text=Individual%20interviews%20typically%20refer%20to,to%20use%20for%20follow%2Dup

Roy, S., Hegde, H. V., Bhattacharya, D., Upadhya, V., & Kholkute, S. D. (2015). Tribes in Karnataka: Status of health research. *The Indian Journal of Medical Research, 141*(5), 673–687. https://doi.org/10.4103/0971-5916.159586

Seenirajan, M., Natarajan, M., Thangaraj, R., & Bagyaraj, M. (2017). Study and analysis of Chennai Flood 2015 using GIS and multicriteria technique.

Journal of Geographic Information System, 09(02), 126–140. https://doi.org/10.4236/jgis.2017.92009

Shaw, E. (2022, August 30). *What is a river flood?* Sciencing. https://www.sciencing.com/about-6310709-river-flood-/

Srivastava, K. (2010). Disaster: Challenges and perspectives. *Industrial Psychiatry Journal, 19*(1), 1–4. https://doi.org/10.4103/0972-6748.77623

Stephen, A. (2012). Natural disasters in India with special reference to Tamil Nadu. *Journal of Academia and Industrial Research, 1*(2), 59–66.

Suhaimi, A. W. (2016). The importance of psychological preparedness among flood victims. *The European Proceedings of Social & Behavioural Sciences*, 157–162. https://doi.org/10.15405/epsbs.2016.08.23

t2informatik GmbH (EN). (2024, November 22). *What is a field observation?—Smartpedia—t2informatik*. T2informatik GmbH (EN). https://t2informatik.de/en/smartpedia/field-observation/

The Many Effects of Flooding. (n.d.). https://education.nationalgeographic.org/resource/many-effects-flooding/

Udayashankara, T. H., Murthy, B. S., & Madhukar, M. (2016). Impact of climate change on rainfall pattern and reservoir level. *Journal of Water Resource Engineering and Management, 3*(1), 10–14.

United Nations. (n.d.). *Water—At the center of the climate crisis | United Nations*. https://www.un.org/en/climatechange/science/climate-issues/water

United Nations Environment Programme. (n.d.). *How climate change is making record-breaking floods the new normal*. UNEP. https://www.unep.org/news-and-stories/story/how-climate-change-making-record-breaking-floods-new-normal

Unknown. (n.d.). *Social impact methodology*. https://riversgroup.org.nz/wp-content/uploads/2018/06/3.2.5_GW-Social-impact-of-floods.pdf

Urban Flooding and Causes. (2022, March 23). Unacademy. https://unacademy.com/content/upsc/study-material/disaster-management/urban-flooding-and-causes/

Urbanization—Understanding Global Change. (2022, March 8). Understanding global change. https://ugc.berkeley.edu/background-content/urbanization/

User, S. (2024, July 31). Heavy rainfall causes flooding in Chikkamagaluru, Madikeri | Tap to know more | Inshorts. *Inshorts—Stay Informed*. https://inshorts.com/en/news/heavy-rainfall-causes-flooding-in-chikkamagaluru%2D%2Dmadikeri-1722404093189

Uttarakhand flash floods—A report—India. (2013, June 27). ReliefWeb. https://reliefweb.int/report/india/uttarakhand-flash-floods-%E2%80%93-report

View of the impact of floods on livelihoods of farmers in Bagalkot district of Karnataka, India. (n.d.). https://journalijecc.com/index.php/IJECC/article/view/4121/8117

Vithalani, K. R., & Bansal, N. (2017). Causes and effect of Kashmir flood. *International Journal of Advance Research, Ideas and Innovations in Technology, 3–3*(6), 863–866. https://www.ijariit.com/manuscripts/v3i6/V3I6-1301.pdf

Watson, J. T., Gayer, M., & Connolly, M. A. (2007). Epidemics after natural disasters. *Emerging Infectious Diseases, 13*(1), 1–5. https://doi.org/10.3201/eid1301.060779

West, J. S., Price, M., Gros, K. S., & Ruggiero, K. J. (2013). Community support as a moderator of postdisaster mental health symptoms in urban and nonurban communities. *Disaster Medicine and Public Health Preparedness, 7*(5), 443–451. https://doi.org/10.1017/dmp.2013.74

What are the best ways to support disaster victims emotionally? (2023, September 25). www.linkedin.com. https://www.linkedin.com/advice/1/what-best-ways-support-disaster-victims-emotionally

What are the negative social impacts of flooding?—Associated Programme on Flood Management. (2013, May 19). https://www.floodmanagement.info/what-are-the-negative-social-impacts-of-flooding/#:~:text=Displacement%20from%20one's%20home%2C%20loss,and%20produce%20lasting%20psychological%20impacts

What is groundwater flooding. (n.d.). https://www.gsi.ie/en-ie/programmes-and-projects/groundwater/activities/groundwater-flooding/Pages/What-is-groundwater-flooding.aspx

14

Surviving a Deluge: Insights into Psychosocial Impacts and Lessons Learned from Urban Floods

S. Harshavardhini and Sanjeev Kumar Manikappa

Introduction

With progressing climate change, nations around the world are experiencing increasing natural disasters, with flooding being one of the most prevalent (Thomas & Lopez, 2015; Mohd et al., 2022). Although the phenomenon of flooding is long-standing, and the prevention and mitigation strategies have been practiced and evolved over time, the contemporary context necessitates a renewed focus on the evolving nature and impacts of flooding. In recent decades, urban areas globally have become susceptible to floodings, significantly disrupting and damaging the functioning of the urban populace. While the consequences of rural flooding are undoubtedly severe, urban flooding has emerged as a critical area of concern due to its heightened frequency and the severe impact it has on densely populated areas. The ramifications of urban floods extend beyond

S. Harshavardhini • S. K. Manikappa (✉)
Department of Psychosocial Support in Disaster Management, NIMHANS, Bengaluru, Karnataka, India

S. Bhadra et al. (eds.), *Psychosocial and Mental Health Support for Disaster Management in India*, Palgrave Studies in Disaster Science and Emergency Management,
https://doi.org/10.1007/978-3-032-02511-1_14

just the affected communities, impacting the operation of institutions, governmental bodies, and vital services concentrated in the urban areas (National Disaster Management Authority, 2010; Jha, 2023).

To understand these challenges better, it is important to define urban flooding and distinguish it from rural flooding. Urban flooding refers to the inundation of parts or entire cities due to excessive water levels compounded by the inadequacy of city infrastructure to manage drainage effectively (Singh et al., 2023). This phenomenon of urban flooding is starkly different from the rural flooding due to geological, structural, and sociological processes, including urbanization and urban planning. The impact of urbanization in flooding is significant. It is estimated that due to catchments constructed as a part urbanization, the flood peaks increase from 1.8 to 8 times, and the flood volume increases sixfold in urban areas (National Disaster Management Authority, 2010). Furthermore, climate change-induced factors, such as intensified river overflow, storm surges, and heavy rainfall, exacerbate urban flooding. Thus, urban floods and their impact can be understood as a phenomenon arising from the interaction of various natural and anthropogenic factors.

This issue has particularly gained prominence due to the high stakes involved. Urban flooding not only poses threats to human life through drownings, vehicular mishaps, and structural collapse, but also has a substantial economic toll, with transportation networks and businesses suffering damage and disruption (Agonafir et al., 2023; Singh et al., 2023). Individuals often lose assets, personal items of sentimental value, homes, livelihoods, and even loved ones as a result of urban floods (Jha, 2023; Singh et al., 2023). Widespread relocations, both permanent and temporary, are common, accompanied by their own psychological burdens (Bird, 2016). These relocations are also often marked by a notable lack of choice and autonomy for those affected. Additionally, the diverse and heterogenous nature of urban populations can lead to disproportionate impacts on certain groups.

This issue has been evident in India where numerous cities, spanning from major metropolises to smaller urban centers, have struggled with recurrent flood occurrences over the past few decades. Notable incidents include the Hyderabad floods in 2000 and 2020, the Ahmedabad floods in 2001, the Delhi floods in 2002 and 2003, the Chennai floods in 2004 and

2015, the Mumbai floods in 2005, the Surat flood in 2006, the Kolkata floods in 2007, the floods in Guwahati in 2010, and the 2017 Bangalore floods (National Disaster Management Authority, 2010). However, cities like Mumbai, Hyderabad, Chennai, and Bengaluru, among others, find themselves facing floods almost annually (Narain et al., 2016).

In response to these challenges, urban flooding management was introduced and implemented. Examining the history of urban flood management in India, we find that urban flooding was only recognized as a distinct category only after the 2005 Mumbai Floods (National Disaster Management Authority, 2010). Subsequently, the National Disaster Management Authority, India, published guidelines for Management of Urban Flooding in September 2010.

Despite the annual recurrence of these floods, and the huge urban populations affected, an effective solution to make these cities resilient to urban floods is yet to be found. This discussion becomes essential to initiate conversations about building flood-resilient cities and urban communities, and prioritizing flood-resilient urban planning and infrastructure development. While the issue is a complex one, and its solutions are challenged by various social, political, and economic obstacles, the need to highlight the psychosocial problems faced by urban populations as a result of flooding becomes essential in shaping mitigation and intervention strategies. This chapter aims to explore the various factors contributing to urban flooding, provide a brief case study of selected incidents to understand the impact, and engage in a focused discussion on the psychosocial impacts of urban flooding. Additionally, the chapter will examine past and current responses and interventions addressing the impacts of urban flooding, concluding with a section on future directions.

The Science Behind Urban Flooding

This section aims to provide a theoretical understanding to urban floods, exploring various factors associated with it to develop a nuanced perspective on their consequences. It examines key natural and human-induced causes of urban flooding, including weather systems, urbanization, and climate change.

Weather Systems and Climate Change

The Indian subcontinent, naturally, receives its rainfall from two weather systems—the southwest monsoon and the northeast monsoon. Most urban floods occur during, and result from, these two weather systems. The Southwest Monsoon, known as the Summer Monsoon, and occurring between June and September, contributes about 70 to 75 percent of the annual rainfall received in India (National Disaster Management Authority, 2010). The western coast and the northeastern region, West Bengal and Orissa receive their rainfall from the Southwest Monsoon. The Northeast Monsoon, known as the Winter Monsoon, appears in the month of October, showering rainfall over the southern regions of India. States like Kerala, Tamil Nadu, southern parts of Andra Pradesh, and Karnataka, and Andaman and Nicobar, and Lakshwadeep Islands receive their rains from this monsoon. During the monsoon, various other weather disturbances and phenomena, including the low-pressure areas, cyclones, depressions, thunderstorms, and cloudbursts, all impact rainfall activity (National Disaster Management Authority, 2010). While these weather systems are natural occurrences, they are becoming increasingly unpredictable due to the impacts of global climate change, further exacerbating the challenges urban centers face.

Climate Change

Climate change affects natural patterns of weather events, exacerbating the intensity of these natural weather phenomena, and making it hard for urban centers to cope with the intensity (US Environmental Protection Agency, 2016; Kumar, 2021). As evidence of the influence of climate change grows, studies are showing a marked increase in urban flooding due to more intense and unpredictable weather patterns (Sun et al., 2021; Agonafir et al., 2023).

For instance, a recent study done in China to understand the impact of climate change on urban flooding showed that the volume of urban flood increases with increasing rainfall intensity due to climate change (Sun et al., 2021). While it is difficult to attribute a particular disaster directly to climate change, evidence suggests that human-induced climate change has altered the features of many separate extreme events, and that the frequency and severity of these extreme events have been influenced by human activity (Seneviratne et al., 2021). These changes in weather patterns are not localized but are part of a broader global trend. Since the pre-industrial era, from around 1850, the average global temperature has increased by 0.11 degrees Fahrenheit each decade, to a total increase of about 2 degrees Fahrenheit since 1850 (Lindsey & Dalhman, 2024). This rise in temperature comes with consequences, as observed from the increasing temperature extremes, reducing snow cover, intensifying rainfall, and changes in habitats for plants and animals. In fact, 2023 has been recorded as the warmest year since global records began in 1850 (Lindsey & Dalhman, 2024). A small increase in temperature can lead to a disproportionate increase in extreme weather events. It has been discovered that the frequency of severe storms increases by 21% for every 1.8 degrees Fahrenheit increase in temperature and an examination of climate change estimates indicates that by the year 2100, the frequency of severe precipitation storms is expected to increase by 60% (Agonafir et al., 2023). Urban flooding has been the most frequent and recurring natural disaster, with catastrophic effects globally since the 1990s (Singh, 2022).

Along with climate change, there is another important factor to be discussed: Urbanization, which also acts as a driver for climate change. Since urban activities are significant producers of greenhouse gas emissions, cities play a vital role in climate change. According to estimates, 70% of the world's CO2 emissions originate from urban areas, with buildings and transit accounting for the majority of these emissions (IPCC, 2022).

Urbanization

The Process of Urbanization

Urbanization is the process by which individuals move from rural areas to urban areas, leading to an increase in population in towns and cities. This shift from rural to urban areas primarily occurs in the hope of better economic opportunities. In November 2022, the population of Planet Earth finally reached 8 billion people. According to the United Nations, more than half (55%) of the global population lived in cities, a percentage that is expected to increase to 70% by the year 2050. Similarly, according to the UN HABITAT, urbanization has accelerated to the point where, by 2030, 6 out of 10 people are expected to live in cities, and more than 90% of this rise is expected to happen in Asia, Latin America, the Caribbean and Africa. While individuals move into cities in hopes of better opportunities, the sudden flow of population into urban areas have left cities dealing with a range of issues (Patel & Burke, 2009). As cities grow rapidly, the influx of population often outpaces the capacity of infrastructure, leading to a range of social and environmental challenges. The influx of population, along with the lack of adequate urban planning, has led to a lack of adequate housing and the expansion of slums, along with increased pressure on the antiquated and inadequate infrastructure for public transportation, roads, water, sanitation, and electricity, rising rates of poverty and unemployment, and concerns about health and pollution (UN HABITAT, 2021).

As per the 2011 census, 17.4% of the urban population lived in slums across different states and union territories (Ramudu et al., 2023). However, the overall number of people living in slums is rising with increasing urbanization. In 2020, an estimated 1.1 billion urban dwellers were either living in slums or in situations resembling slums. An additional 2 billion people are anticipated to reside in these settlements during the course of the next 30 years (United Nations, 2023). The expansion of slums not only reflects the strain urbanization places on housing, but also amplifies health risks. While the process of urbanization increases health risks such as injuries, pollution, and chronic diseases, and also diabetes and hypertension, slum dwelling in urban areas comes with additional health hazards due to poor living conditions, and water and sanitation issues, leaving opportunities for infections and the more rapid spread of diseases (McMichael, 2000; Kuddus et al., 2020; Luo & Wang, 2022; Rahaman et al., 2023). This pre-existing hazard is only exacerbated during events of urban flooding, increasing the incidences of water-borne diseases and infections.

Urbanization, Land Use, and Climate Change

In addition to population pressures, urbanization brings significant changes in land use. Urbanization is closely associated with the process of industrialization (Jaysawal & Saha, 2014). The process of urbanization and industrialization often comes at the cost of green cover and environment. This shift in land use patterns often translates to reduced green cover (Sharma et al., 2024; Yu et al., 2024). These changes, particularly deforestation and the reduction of green cover, have far-reaching effects in terms of flood risk and disaster resilience (Feng et al., 2021; Özer & Ercoşkun, 2024; Louis et al., 2024). Evidence shows that increasing urbanization increases fatalities due to natural disasters. Furthermore, there is a negative relationship between forest cover and deaths due to floods and other natural calamities, with states that have higher forest cover experiencing lower levels of death and damage (Agarwal et al., 2023).

However, the impacts of urbanization extend beyond land cover reduction. Rapid urbanization and industrialization places an immense strain on land resources, leading to the development of habitations in natural drains and floodplains (Rentschler et al., 2022). In Indian cities, extensive housing developments are emerging in low-lying regions, often encroaching upon drainage channels. It is also noted that, in the absence of proper sewer systems, many urban settlements discharge sewage into storm water drains, narrowing natural drainage channels and drastically reducing their capacity to manage rainwater flow (National Disaster Management Authority, 2010). Additionally, urbanization increases impervious surfaces, causing higher runoff rates that exceed the capacity of storm water drainage systems (McGrane, 2016; Feng et al., 2021). Consequently, even moderate rainfall can lead to urban flooding.

Beyond these direct effects on drainage systems, urbanization also alters atmospheric conditions, contributing to more frequent and intense rainfall events, a phenomenon known as the Urban Heat Island Effect.

Urban Heat Island Effect

Urbanization has been found to contribute to increased rainfall, a phenomenon observed as early as 1921 when scientists noticed thunderstorms forming over cities but not in rural areas (Shepherd, 2005). This phenomenon was explained by the Urban Heat Island Effect, where increasing heat in urban areas prompts cloud formation, and wind patterns interact with urban-induced convection to produce rainfall. The Urban Heat Island Effect intensifies rainfall over cities, leading to more frequent heavy rain showers, particularly during the day. In India, urban heat islands have been reported in cities like Pune, Chennai, and Hyderabad (National Disaster Management Authority, 2010). This shows that not only naturally existing weather systems but also urban development-induced weather phenomena increase rainfall, leaving urban areas more vulnerable to flooding.

Urbanization and Urban Planning

As cities expand, the importance of urban planning becomes increasingly evident. Unplanned development and infrastructure inadequacies leave urban areas particularly vulnerable to natural disasters like flooding. Urbanization happens when private and public initiatives cut down on travel time and costs while expanding access to employment, housing, transportation, and educational possibilities (Jaysawal & Saha, 2014). However, with the uncontrolled influx of population into urban areas, problems arise related to pollution, inadequate social infrastructure, water and sanitation, inadequate housing leading to the expansion of slums. City infrastructure and facilities get overwhelmed, sometimes leading to saturation in employment generation, which further contributes to poverty and unemployment (Jaysawal & Saha, 2014). These nuances and intricacies of challenges that urbanization brings is important to understand the urban demography, and thus the unique challenges these populations face in times of extreme weather events.

Studies also show that urbanization and unplanned urban sprawl, i.e. the expansion of the cities on undeveloped lands surrounding the urban development, can significantly reduce the coping ability of the drainage system. In various cities around the country, such as Bengaluru and Kochi, unplanned urban development and improper maintenance of the drainage system overwhelm the capacity of the drainage system (Singh et al., 2023). This lack of urban planning is particularly problematic in megacities such as Dhaka, Kolkata, and Mumbai, where populations exceed 50 million. These cities are at heightened risk of severe flood damage, as noted by the World Bank (Singh, 2022). As cities develop without taking into account the gradual changes in climate, their ability to withstand extreme weather events diminishes, leaving a lasting impact on both the urban environment and residents' quality of life.

Case Studies of Urban Flooding

To contextualize the theoretical discussion on urban flooding, urbanization, and climate change, the following case studies explore the real-life implications of these dynamics. The Mumbai floods of 2005 and the Chennai floods of 2015 exemplify how urban planning failures, inadequate infrastructure, and the mismanagement of drainage systems can exacerbate the impact of extreme weather events. These cases provide a closer look at how unprepared urban environments increase vulnerability to flooding, highlighting the severe socioeconomic and psychosocial consequences for affected populations.

Mumbai Floods, 2005

The 2005 Mumbai floods marked a watershed moment in India's approach to disaster management, with the city witnessing one of the heaviest rainfalls in recorded history. The rainfall reached up to 944 mm within 24 hours. According to data available, it was strongest rain recorded in India, with a 100-year high. The rainfall experienced at Santa Cruz observatory, Mumbai, exceeded the rainfall record of Cherrapunji, the wettest place in the world. Along with the heavy rainfall, an inadequate drainage system, the failure on part of the Indian Meteorological Department (IMD) in issuing early warning, encroachment, and the presence of slums, and a lack of sufficient disaster planning and response, parts of the Mumbai city were inundated (Rafiq et al., 2016). The city became paralyzed as transportation, telecommunication, power and financial services were disrupted (Stecko & Barber, 2007), with automobiles and trains being damaged and grounded. More than 1000 people lost their lives, and more than 14,000 buildings and houses suffered damages due to the rain.

In the aftermath, a Fact-Finding Committee set up by the state government investigated the underlying vulnerabilities that exacerbated the disaster. The final report of this committee highlighted the vulnerability factors such as poor sanitation and water drainage systems, crumbling buildings, and the large slum population. It also highlighted the need for a deeper investigation into other factors, including the socioeconomic root causes of poverty, corrupt real estate policies and practices and weaknesses in urban governance. The report focused on the growing concern of slums and informal settlements, highlighting the difficulty state and municipal governments face in housing and providing services for the growing population. The urban poor are commonly forced to live in informal settlements or urban slums. A majority of these slums are located on hill slopes, nallahs, low-lying areas, coastal locations, and pavements alongside water mains and open drainage systems, making them the most prone to flooding during heavy rainfall and high tides. According the report, at the time, more than half of Mumbai's 12 million people were living in slums. Thus, the unique context of Mumbai, and the presence of these large slums, introduced unique challenges, in addition to the challenges that already exist as a consequence of floods, such as disruption in social functioning, transportation, livelihoods of the residents being affected, etc.

These informal settlements, already vulnerable to flooding, also faced serious health hazards. The unsanitary conditions in which slum dwellers lived, combined with poor infrastructure and lack of accessibility, compounded their risk for health-related problems (Fact Finding Committee, 2006).

Further illustrating the devastation, the Conservation Action Trust's report, 'Mumbai Marooned—An Enquiry into Mumbai's Floods 2005,' details the profound loss of life and property. Some low-lying areas were reported to be 10 to 15 feet under water. Thousands of homes in the

Mumbai slums were either washed away or damaged beyond repair. The floodwaters also submerged the ground floors of apartments in many areas. In some areas, the floodwaters did not recede for days, and this situation was further worsened by the outbreak of diseases such as leptospirosis, diarrhoea, malaria, dengue etc.

In light of these severe impacts, it is crucial to examine the historical context of disaster management in Mumbai. In the late 1990s the Government of Maharashtra developed India's first urban disaster management plan for Mumbai. This urban disaster management plan (DMP) was developed to accompany the Maharashtra state Disaster Management Plan. While the State DMP focused primarily on creating and coordinating institutional networks, the Mumbai DMP focused on many of the chronic problems and risks. The plan also identified and emphasized areas with large numbers of slum dwellers, and additional areas within the city that are at the highest risk from flooding during the monsoon season. However, it was reported at the time that, despite the presence of the DMP, no action had been taken to alleviate the identified risks and problems.

Chennai Floods, 2015

Chennai has been facing catastrophic flooding for decades—in 1943, 1976, 1985, 1998, 2002, and 2005—due to heavy rains associated with cyclonic activity. While Chennai had experienced significant flooding in the past, the 2015 floods highlighted a new level of severity, revealing underlying issues in urban planning and flood management. November of 2015 saw another catastrophic flooding as a result of multiple factors coming into play. In November–December 2015, Chennai and its suburban areas received multiple torrential rain spells. The floods resulting from the downpour resulted in the deaths of 289 lives due to drowning, electrocution, wall collapse, etc. (Government of Tamil Nadu, 2017). The floods submerged and damaged lakhs of houses and disrupted the daily functioning and livelihood for many for a number of days.

The extent of the devastation in 2015 was further compounded by significant infrastructural deficiencies and urban planning failures.

Chennai has three major rivers flowing through it, namely Adyar, Cooum and Kosasthalaiyar. The Chennai Metropolitan Area (CMA) has three major tanks, namely, Cholavaram (capacity 1.005 TMC2), Redhills (3.300 TMC) and Chembarambakkam (3.645 TMC). These tanks play a significant role in controlling the floodwater flow in the rivers, thereby impacting the extent of flooding in the CMA (Rafiq et al., 2016). During the Northeast Monsoon of 2015, Chennai experienced torrential rainfall from November 15 to 17; this was followed by a second heavy downpour, on November 23, 2015. A third wave of intense rainfall on December 1, 2015, submerged large portions of the city. These floods brought to light the unchecked urban development in watershed regions, encroachments on water bodies, and shortcomings in flood prevention infrastructure, maintenance, and preparedness. The events also underscored the gaps in flood management and response mechanisms.

The Comptroller and Auditor General of India's report on Performance Audit of Flood Management and Response in Chennai and its Suburban Areas provides a detailed account of the systemic lapses that aggravated the impact of the 2015 floods, highlighting the lapses in the functioning of various bodies and critical areas for improvement in flood management. The audit revealed issues in planning, the management of waterbodies, encroachments, drainage systems, disaster management, and monitoring. Among the issues identified were unauthorized land use conversion, illegal residential colonies, legislative and administrative failures in prevention of, and preparation for, floods, construction activities along waterbodies, non-adherence to land use planning, the non-preservation of non-urban zones and catchment areas, structural concerns and deficiencies in dams, the non-implementation of projects for restoration and protection, and encroachments. All of these contributed to the floods. The encroachments and illegal constructions, coupled with an inadequate drainage system, significantly contributed to the severity of the floods (Government of Tamil Nadu, 2017). The findings also underscored deficiencies in the functioning of the state disaster management authority, further exacerbating the impact of the floods.

As evidenced by the case studies discussed, urban floods share a recurring pattern of systemic failures in relation to infrastructure, urban planning and disaster management. Unchecked and rapid urbanization has led to the encroachment of water bodies and drainage systems, restricting their capacity to cope with excess rainfall. The inadequate and outdated drainage infrastructure, compounded by insufficient disaster preparedness, exacerbates the damage caused by urban floods. Vulnerable populations, including those who live in informal settlements situated in high-risk flood-prone areas, bear the brunt of these disasters. In addition to the physical damage, urban floods also trigger significant psychosocial impacts by displacing communities, disrupting livelihoods, and contributing to long-term mental health issues. The inequities revealed by urban floods highlight deeper socioeconomic challenges, as marginalized groups often face heightened risks with limited access to relief and rehabilitation.

Psychosocial Impact of Urban Flooding

While the physical damage caused by urban flooding is immediately apparent, the psychosocial repercussions often have far-reaching effects that persist long after the waters recede. The disruption of daily life, displacement of communities, and long-term health issues associated with floods contribute to a complex array of psychosocial challenges. This section delves into the psychosocial impacts of urban flooding, exploring how such disasters affect individuals and communities on emotional, psychological, social, and economic levels. Examining these impacts, will enable a holistic understanding of the consequences of urban flooding and help identify ways to mitigate its effects on urban populations.

Physical Impact

Urban floods, similarly to other disasters, inflict severe damage on human lives and property. A systematic review of urban floods in India revealed a plethora of both direct and indirect impacts of urban floods (Singh et al., 2023). Direct impacts include damages to informal settlements and human causalities, damage to houses and buildings, damage to power infrastructures, damage to transportation systems and roadways, damage to water, sanitation and drainage systems, loss of household items and properties. For instance, the Chennai floods in 2015 resulted in the deaths of more than 350 people, with 17.64 lakh people also becoming homeless as the worst rain in nearly a century battered Tamil Nadu (Stalin, 2015). Human causalities during urban floods occur as a result of injuries, drownings, vehicular accidents, collapsed buildings, being swept away by floods are observed. Flooding of basements can lead to individuals being trapped and drowned (Agonafir et al., 2023; Mollan & Jajware, 2024; Das, 2024).

Urban flooding also heightens the risk of water-borne and vector-borne diseases, and the development of long-term illnesses. Following the 2015 Chennai floods, affected populations faced a rise in respiratory tract infections, acute gastroenteritis, fever, and skin problems (Angeline et al., 2017). Vulnerable groups, such as the elderly, injured, and those with pre-existing medical conditions, are especially at risk due to limited access to essential health services and prolonged homelessness (Singh et al., 2023).

Additionally, research indicates that living in a coastal city that experienced severe flooding significantly increased the likelihood of acquiring a disability compared to those in inland cities. Factors such as being older, female, unmarried, living in a single-generation household, and having chronic health conditions also contributed to disability risk, but advanced age had an even stronger association than living through a major flood event (Rendall, 2024).

Urban flooding also significantly disrupts supply chains, causing delays in accessing raw materials, replacement machinery, and food provisions. It also affects communication systems, halts local industries, and results in traffic jams and inaccessibility to cultural places, further compounding the socioeconomic strain on the affected regions (Singh et al., 2023).

Psychological Impact

While several studies have examined the mental health consequences of floods in India, there remains a gap in research that focuses on urban flood events and their psychological impacts. In the Indian context, in the population afflicted by floods, post-traumatic stress disorder (PTSD) is the most commonly diagnosed psychological condition (Asim et al., 2019). Similar results have also been identified in the context of urban flooding (Crabtree, 2013; Bandla et al., 2019; Rahana et al., 2021; Asim et al., 2022). In the aftermath of the Bihar floods in 2008, researchers noted an increase in symptoms associated with PTSD, particularly re-experiencing traumatic events, alongside rising levels of depression and a diminished sense of hope for the future (Crabtree, 2013).

Gender differences in mental health outcomes have also been observed. A study following the Kerala floods in 2018 found that stress, PTSD, anxiety, and depression were prevalent among affected populations, with women reporting significantly higher levels of severity than men (Asim et al., 2022; Rahana et al., 2021). This highlights the differential vulnerability of women in flood-affected regions. Flooding can also trigger coping mechanisms like substance abuse, as demonstrated after the 2015 Chennai Floods, where a spike in alcohol use was observed among affected populations (Bandla et al., 2019). These findings underscore the need for targeted post-disaster mental health interventions that address both the immediate and long-term effects of trauma.

Research outside India presents similar concerns. A study done in the UK to understand the impact of flooding after 2007 floods, revealed that about 28% of the sample met criteria for PTSD, 24.5% for anxiety and 35.2% for depression, with women reporting higher levels of all three conditions compared to men (Mason et al., 2010). Factors like having to leave home due to flooding, prior flood experiences, and poor health were linked to increased psychological distress. The authors do highlight that while causality between the flooding event and mental health are not established, distress remains a significant concern in communities impacted by environmental events. This underscores the importance of taking into account pre-existing vulnerabilities, including chronic health conditions and displacement, when designing psychosocial interventions post-flooding.

Social Impact

Relocation

The unique challenge posed by the urban floods is that essential services and care that are centered in the urban areas get trapped, being unable to provide immediate relief and care to those affected. As urban populations struggle to access essential services during floods, another challenge they face is the need for temporary or permanent relocation. The Intergovernmental Panel on Climate Change (IPCC) stated that since 2008 more than 20 million people per year have been displaced by extreme weather events such as storms and floods. Displacement due to flooding also has been seen as a contributor to poor mental health outcomes due to the chaos and uncertainty that accompanies it (Glenn & Myre, 2022).

This brings into focus the emotional and social consequences of displacement, particularly the loss of sense of place. A sense of place refers to the personal and collective experiences that individuals, families, social networks, and communities associate with the location they live in (Bird, 2016). This encompasses the meanings, beliefs, symbols, memories, values, and emotions tied to their surroundings. People may feel a loss of sense of place due to loss of social networks, disruption in the community norms, damage to their houses, neighbourhood or community (Bird, 2016). Individuals grieve the destruction of their places.

A related, but distinct concept is place attachment, which refers to the emotional connections individuals or groups develop with their physical and social environments, often through behavioural, cognitive, and emotional ties, especially in locations like homes and neighborhoods (Low & Altman, 1992). While the concept of place attachment is often discussed in the context of migration, it also applies to decisions surrounding disaster-induced displacement. Economic and social factors often drive decisions to move from rural to urban regions, but the strength of place attachment can significantly influence whether people choose to stay or relocate, as it shapes their sense of belonging (Riethmuller et al., 2021; Adhikari et al., 2022). It plays an important role in mobility decision-making (Bukvic et al., 2022).

This interplay between place attachment and displacement becomes crucial in understanding the emotional experience of those facing forced relocation due to floods. Although place attachment has been explored in relation to coastal flooding—floods caused by rising sea levels or storm surges—the role it plays in urban flood contexts is less studied (Bukvic et al., 2022). Various urban areas in the country, including Mumbai, Chennai, Kolkata, and Surat, are coastal cities that experience urban floods almost annually. In the context of urban floods, place attachment may play an important role in the decision-making of relocating, especially if the individual is a native to the city. Furthermore, factors like education, past experience, and indigeneity which influence the flood-risk perception, further impacting decisions on relocation (Twerefou et al., 2024). However, a high flood-risk perception and planned relocation may not cause as much psychological stress as a forced relocation.

In urban centers, population that are situated in low-lying and flood-prone areas are the urban poor, often housed in slums (National Disaster Management Authority, 2010). They often constitute the working class who have moved from rural areas in search for better employment opportunities. Interestingly, studies have shown that urban slum dwellers develop place attachment, despite the often-unhealthy environmental conditions they endure (Adewale et al., 2020; Setiawan et al., 2023). However, in addition to place attachment, socioeconomic factors such as financial conditions and lack of adequate housing may inhibit them from moving towards safer areas.

Disruption in Social Cohesion

Urbanization comes with its social issues. Social fragmentation, inequality, and marginalization are a few of the challenges that come with cities that are growing more diverse, heterogenous, and transient in nature. As more individuals move from rural to urban regions in hopes of better opportunities, there is a notable shift in the dynamics of identities and community structures (Chaudhari, 2018). With urban population being socioeconomically diverse, and culturally heterogenous, it disrupts the close-knit social networks and support systems that exist in rural communities. This often leads to a sense of alienation and disconnection in urban populations. With urbanization, there is also the growing shift towards individualism and autonomy, leaving urban dwellers vulnerable to social isolation and exclusion, especially in their neighborhood community. This becomes a vulnerability in coping with flooding events. Urban dwellers may lack the social ties needed for mutual support, with neighbors often remaining strangers, unaware or unwilling to help in times of need. Furthermore, relocation due to urban flooding also disrupts established social networks and community bonds, making it harder to access support and services. Offers of assistance from organizations or local governments may also be overlooked due to people not being part of regular community networks. Vulnerable individuals, even when recognized, are sometimes neglected as they are seen as someone else's responsibility, leaving individuals with a discernible lack of support (Bird, 2016).

Education

Urban floods can severely disrupt education, leading to prolonged school closures that affect the continuity of students' learning. In flood-affected areas, schools may remain shut for several days or even weeks, interrupting the usual academic schedule. Educational institutions often suffer physical damage to buildings, and essential resources like books, uniforms, and learning materials may be destroyed (Krishna et al., 2018). In addition, examinations may be postponed, adding further uncertainty and stress to students and educators alike. Schools are also used as shelters, prolonging the resumption of education for children (Krishna et al., 2018). This disruption hampers academic progress and can exacerbate educational inequalities, particularly for vulnerable students who rely heavily on school infrastructure for learning. Reports following floods have highlighted issues like absenteeism and poor concentration among affected students (PV & Subudhi, 2020). During the 2015 Chennai floods, schools and colleges were closed for at least a month before they were reopened. The school closures began and extended as a precautionary measure during the heavy rainfall and flood. About 29 schools that were damaged by the floods had to reopen later (Stalin, 2015).

Overall, the social impacts of urban floods are wide-ranging, affecting everything from relocation and disruption of community ties to significant interruptions in education. These challenges, compounded by the vulnerabilities of already marginalized populations, underscore the critical need for improved urban planning and disaster preparedness to mitigate the profound social consequences of urban floods.

Economic Impact

Urban floods leave the affected city with a huge economic toll. It disrupts income and employment, leads to labor shortages, and halts commercial, trading, transport, and industrial activities, such as textile production (Singh et al., 2023). There is a loss to the agricultural sector, such as damage to crops, and loss of livestock. Urban flood especially affects the livelihood for small businesses and street vendors (Singh et al., 2023). Not only are individuals affected, but so also is the state economy at large. Cities are economic centers, and any interruption in operations will cause huge losses in terms of money (Jha, 2023). The 2015 floods in Chennai, India, caused $2.2 billion in economic losses, while the 2005 floods in Mumbai caused an estimated loss of US$109 million in local business earnings and thousands of displaced residents who were dependent on insurance claim returns totalling more than US$436 million (Devi et al., 2019; Stecko & Barber, 2007).

Psychosocial Impact on Vulnerable Populations

Urban floods severely impact vulnerable populations, including children, the elderly, the urban poor, and slum dwellers. These groups face heightened psychosocial challenges due to their pre-existing vulnerabilities and the additional stressors introduced by the disaster. Understanding their specific needs is essential for effective support and recovery.

Children

Children affected by urban floods are also likely to experience psychological distress, including symptoms of PTSD (Hassan et al., 2018; Krishna et al., 2018). Furthermore, a lack of appropriate mental health interventions can impact the school attendance and performance of the children following the flood (PV & Subudhi, 2020; Krishna et al., 2018). Children are also vulnerable to health risks, such as skin diseases, coughs, colds, and fever (Krishna et al., 2018). Children returning to schools come from a changed context after experiencing loss of loved ones, houses, and academic materials, hindering their ability to return back to normal (Krishna et al., 2018). The specific needs of these children, particularly in terms of mental health support and educational adjustments, must be considered in order to facilitate their smooth transition back to school. Moreover, children belonging to the urban poor families may leave schools to help contribute to the livelihood of the family and help rebuild their damaged or lost homes (Krishna et al., 2018).

Elderly Population

Older adults who have experienced natural or human-made disasters are reported to face significantly greater health challenges compared to those who have not. They are more likely to rate their health poorly, struggle with daily and instrumental activities, and suffer from both communicable and non-communicable diseases. Mental health issues, including depressive symptoms and psychiatric disorders, are also notably higher among this group. Even after accounting for various factors, older individuals with disaster experience have significantly elevated odds of poor physical and mental health, underscoring the long-lasting impact of such events on their overall well-being (Muhammad et al., 2024). During urban disasters, older adults encounter significant psychosocial challenges due to unmet needs in several critical areas: healthcare, socioeconomic support, evacuation, communication, and cultural considerations (Phraknoi et al., 2023). The lack of coordination in disaster response often results in fragmented aid that fails to address their interconnected needs, leaving many older individuals feeling overlooked and undignified. Additionally, a gap between policy intentions and on-the-ground efforts further exacerbates this issue, while the voices of older adults are frequently unheard, with their needs being filtered through caregivers and responders rather than expressed directly (Phraknoi et al., 2023).

Urban Poor and Slum Dwellers

Urban populations are extremely diverse when it comes to their vulnerability to flooding, with the poor being disproportionately affected. Flood risk management is particularly challenging in areas with informal developments, often exacerbating existing social inequalities and poverty (Moulds et al., 2021). Economically vulnerable populations are at risk of poor mental health after experiencing urban floods (Sehra, 2021). Even in non-disaster situations, slum dwellers at risk of experiencing common mental health disorders, with psychological distress contributing to their functional impairment (Subbaraman et al., 2014).

The psychological burden faced by slum dwellers is intricately linked to their living conditions. Poverty, lack of resources, and constant uncertainty amplify their mental distress. Residing in non-notified slums adds further strain, as residents face deprivations, feel criminalized for meeting basic needs, and experience a sense of isolation from the rest of the city, all of which contribute to a heightened feeling of social exclusion and chronic stress (Subbaraman et al., 2014). A study done in Indonesia examining the psychosocial consequences experienced by the urban poor after floods revealed that urban poor populations show an increase in acute morbidities and depressive symptoms. The study also revealed that while the urban wealthy population showed no health consequences from the floods, the urban poor's negative mental health consequences lasted longer (Escobar et al., 2022). Further research suggests that this can partially be attributed to the less favourable economic results. When floods impact the urban poor, they often endure severe economic and health repercussions, including damage to their homes, loss of livelihoods, and heightened risk of injuries and diseases (Ezeh et al., 2017; Escobar et al., 2022). In the absence of adequate social safety nets, many resort to coping strategies such as selling essential assets, cutting back on food, or pulling children out of school to join the workforce (Escobar et al., 2022).

Systemic barriers and insensitivity further complicate relief and rehabilitation efforts for marginalized communities, including the urban poor. The UN HABITAT report on the Mumbai floods of 2005 highlighted that it was impossible to determine who was eligible for relief, where to access it, or how much was owed. People who had lost family members, faced serious illnesses such as depression or hydrophobia, or had their cherished belongings washed away were further burdened when they sought medical or other forms of aid (Stecko & Barber, 2007). The report also noted that rehabilitation efforts were insufficient, indicating a significant shortfall in support for affected populations.

Responses and Interventions

Institutional Framework

The Urban Flood Management Guidelines released by the National Disaster Management Authority outlines some key action points that are to be implemented. It anointed the Ministry of Urban Development to be the nodal ministry for urban flooding. It also called for the establishment of the Urban Flooding Cell in Ministry of Urban Development and State Nodal Departments and ULBs (National Disaster Management Authority, 2010). Subsequently, the Ministry of Urban Development published the standard operating procedure (SOP) for urban flooding, detailing the SOP of various departments and responsibilities of public agencies. However, in common with most other disasters, the management of urban flooding falls under the purview of state governments and urban local bodies (Press Information Bureau, 2024). The SOP calls for the mandatory establishment of Emergency Support Functions, which include communication, Public Safety and Law & Order, Fire Fighting, Search and Rescue, Mass Care—Housing and Human Services, Relief essential supplies—Food and beverages, Public Health and Sanitation, etc. (Ministry of Urban Development, 2017). The response and management of the urban floods relies on the efficiency of coordination and action of the emergency support functions.

The Fifteenth Finance Commission has recommended an allocation of a portion of the National Disaster Mitigation Fund (NDMF) to prepare integrated solutions for flood management for Chennai, Mumbai, and

Kolkata, and to prevent urban flooding in Bengaluru, Hyderabad, Ahmedabad and Pune (Press Information Bureau, 2024). While significant focus is placed on the prevention and mitigation of urban floods, response and recovery efforts for ongoing flood events often receive inadequate attention. Thus, a lack of streamlined effort or guidelines in addressing the issues and challenges faced by those affected by urban floods in noticed.

Psychosocial Interventions

Psychosocial interventions across the country for urban flooding are not streamlined and standardized. However, based on need, the local or state governments, non-governmental organizations, or mental health institutes, may take initiatives to address the needs. One such initiative, named "Project PARIRAKSHA," was initiated by the Government of Kerala following the catastrophic floods in 2018, to address long-term mental health effects with the aid of mental health professionals from other states and also the assistance of the National Institute of Mental Health and Neurosciences (NIMHANS), Bengaluru. The initiative aimed to benefit around 2 million people across 93 severely affected panchayats. It integrated newly appointed counsellors in primary health centers, with Accredited Social Health Activists (ASHAs) conducting home visits for the early detection of mental health issues. Medical officers received additional training in managing these conditions, and multidisciplinary mobile mental health teams were deployed to ensure specialized care. Lay volunteers were trained by NIMHANS to provide Psychological First Aid (PFA), focusing on reducing distress and promoting recovery. The project strengthened the existing healthcare system by enhancing capacity for post-disaster mental healthcare (Kiran et al., 2021). NIMHANS was also involved in providing psychosocial support following the 2014 Kashmir floods. A multidisciplinary team was sent to the Kashmir Valley to assess the psychosocial issues faced by the affected population and deliver immediate interventions and support (Hassan et al., 2018).

While the response in terms of proving psychosocial intervention of urban flood-affected individuals has not yet been established and practiced in a systematic manner in India, studies show that the psychosocial well-being of the communities is linked with the resource and external support available. The psychosocial preparedness of communities through various awareness programs on urban floods, mental health, and equipping them with the knowledge of resources available is a starting point to building the resilience of the communities. Research also highlighted the positive impact of community collaboration and engagement during disasters; thus, encouraging community cohesiveness and support can help prevent negative mental health impacts through community coping (Glenn & Myre, 2022).

Lessons Learned and Future Directions

- Urban flooding is a complex issue that has received increasing attention in recent years, as demonstrated by the gradual rise in research articles on the subject (Singh et al., 2023). However, despite this growing interest, significant gaps remain, particularly in understanding the human experiences and psychosocial impacts on residents and vulnerable populations, especially in India. This lack of research focusing on nuanced experiences of marginalized communities, highlights the need for more in-depth studies to inform policy responses and interventions tailored to the specific needs of affected people (Nadimpalli et al., 2024). Developing this evidence base is crucial for creating more effective and inclusive policies.
- A key lesson from urban flood risk management is the importance of addressing social inequalities and vulnerability. Informal settlements and economically disadvantaged populations are disproportionately affected by floods, facing not only physical damage but also lasting mental health consequences (Sehra, 2021; Moulds et al., 2021). Researchers argue that reducing their vulnerability through inclusive urban planning and pro-poor governance is essential to mitigating these impacts (Moulds et al., 2021). Urban flood risk management must be rooted in policies that recognize the legitimacy and perma-

nence of informal communities in cities. This approach not only reduces social inequality but also fosters sustainable economic growth, even in areas with high flood exposure (Moulds et al., 2021).

- Urban flooding presents one of the most preventable disasters, as many contributing factors—such as inadequate drainage systems, encroachments, and poor urban planning—can be effectively managed. A comprehensive and coordinated effort between urban management and civil bodies is necessary to ensure timely and appropriate responses to floods. However, current efforts tend to be disjointed, with little integration between key stakeholders (Nadimpalli et al., 2024). Enhancing collaboration among local institutions and ensuring a more unified response can significantly improve flood preparedness and disaster resilience.
- Moreover, resilient and sustainable urban planning must prioritize inclusive policies that foster social cohesion and integrate the voices of marginalized groups. Community collaboration and cohesiveness are vital to making urban populations more resilient to disasters (Glenn & Myre, 2022). Programs that promote social integration can play a critical role in disaster recovery, while also leveraging the diversity of urban communities to contribute to sustainable development (Chaudhari, 2018).
- In terms of psychosocial recovery, research indicates that stress and self-efficacy are positively correlated with post-traumatic growth following urban flooding (Sehra & Mishra, 2022). This suggests that fostering environments that support self-efficacy and positive mental health outcomes is critical in the disaster recovery process. Many policy-makers and practitioners lack action-oriented guidance to promote both immediate and long-term psychosocial recovery after floods, much like in the case of Canadian decision-makers (Escobar et al., 2022). Developing structured, culturally sensitive, and human-centered recovery strategies must become a priority in flood management policies worldwide.
- Sustainable Development Goal 11 focuses on making cities and human settlements inclusive, safe, resilient, and sustainable. With over half of the global population living in urban areas—projected to reach 70% by 2050—addressing the challenges of urban sprawl, slum conditions,

and disaster risks is crucial (United Nations, 2023). Urban flooding, a growing concern, threatens both human and environmental well-being. To achieve SDG 11, implementing inclusive, disaster-resilient urban policies and planning is critical, ensuring cities can withstand and adapt to these increasing risks.

Conclusion

Urban flooding is an increasingly critical issue, driven by rapid urbanization, inadequate infrastructure, and the escalating impacts of climate change. As this chapter has highlighted, the consequences of urban flooding are far-reaching, affecting not only physical landscapes but also the social, economic, and psychological well-being of urban populations, particularly vulnerable groups like the urban poor and slum dwellers. The interconnectedness of these issues highlights the need for comprehensive, inclusive, and resilient urban planning strategies. While significant progress has been made in terms of disaster risk reduction policies, gaps persist in implementing a successful management of urban flooding, particularly in terms of psychosocial recovery and the needs of marginalized populations. Effective flood management requires moving beyond technical solutions to integrate social justice, community resilience, and pro-poor urban governance (Moulds et al., 2021; Sehra & Mishra, 2022; Chaudhari, 2018). As cities continue to expand and climate change intensifies flood risks, achieving Sustainable Development Goal 11—making cities inclusive, safe, resilient, and sustainable—will demand collaborative efforts between governments, local communities, and international organizations. The lessons learned from past urban floods demonstrate the need for stronger coordination between stakeholders, better infrastructure, and an emphasis on human-centered solutions. Only through such an integrated approach can urban areas truly become resilient to the increasingly frequent and severe flooding events of the future.

References

Adewale, B. A., Ibem, E. O., Amole, S. A., & Adeboye, A. B. (2020). Place attachment in Nigerian urban slums: Evidence from inner-city Ibadan. *Cities, 107*, 102902. https://doi.org/10.1016/j.cities.2020.102902

Adhikari, S., Mandal, A., Kujur, F., & Guha, S. (2022). Place attachment, migratory behaviour and its impact on economic activity: A study with special reference to Eastern India. *Rajagiri Management Journal, 17*(3), 202–220.

Agarwal, P., Sahoo, D., Parida, Y., Paltasingh, K. R., & Chowdhury, J. R. (2023). Land use changes and natural disaster fatalities: Empirical analysis for India. *Ecological Indicators, 154*, 110525. https://doi.org/10.1016/j.ecolind.2023.110525

Agonafir, C., Lakhankar, T., Khanbilvardi, R., Krakauer, N., Radell, D., & Devineni, N. (2023). A review of recent advances in urban flood research. *Water Security, 19*, 100141–100141. https://doi.org/10.1016/j.wasec.2023.100141

Angeline, N., Anbazhagan, S., Surekha, A., Joseph, S., & Kiran, P. R. (2017). Health impact of Chennai floods 2015: Observations in a medical relief camp. *International Journal of Health System and Disaster Management, 5*(2), 46. https://doi.org/10.4103/ijhsdm.ijhsdm_5_17

Asim, M., Mekkodathil, A., Sathian, B., Elayedath, R., Rajeev Kumar, N., Simkhada, P., & Van Teijlingen, E. (2019). Post-traumatic stress disorder among the flood affected population in Indian subcontinent. *Deleted Journal, 9*(1), 755–758. https://doi.org/10.3126/nje.v9i1.24003

Asim, M., Sathian, B., Van Teijlingen, E., Mekkodathil, A. A., Babu, M. G. R., Rajesh, E., Kumar, R. N., Simkhada, P., & Banerjee, I. (2022). A survey of post-traumatic stress disorder, anxiety and depression among flood affected populations in Kerala, India. *Deleted Journal, 12*(2), 1203–1214. https://doi.org/10.3126/nje.v12i2.46334

Bandla, S., Nappinnai, N., & Gopalasamy, S. (2019). Psychiatric morbidity in December 2015 flood-affected population in Tamil Nadu, India. *International Journal of Social Psychiatry, 65*(4), 338–344. https://doi.org/10.1177/0020764019846166

Bird, M. (2016). Key actions for psychosocial support in flooding: Creating resilience in urban areas. International Federation of Red Cross and Red Crescent Societies Reference Centre for Psychosocial Support (PS Centre), . https://pscentre.org/wp-content/uploads/2018/02/Key_Actions-for-PSS-in-Flooding.pdf

Bukvic, A., Whittemore, A., Gonzales, J., & Wilhelmi, O. (2022). Understanding relocation in flood-prone coastal communities through the lens of place attachment. *Applied Geography, 146*, 102758. https://doi.org/10.1016/j.apgeog.2022.102758

Chaudhari, K. (2018). Urbanization and social change in India: Impact on community structures and identities. *International Journal of Social Impact, 3*, 2455–2670. https://doi.org/10.25215/2455/0303010

Conservation Action Trust. (2005). *Mumbai marooned: An enquiry into Mumbai floods 2005*. Conservation Action Trust. http://www.indiaenvironmentportal.org.in/files/Mumbai-Marooned.pdf

Crabtree, A. (2013). Questioning psychosocial resilience after flooding and the consequences for disaster risk reduction. *Social Indicators Research, 113*(2), 711–728. https://doi.org/10.1007/s11205-013-0297-8

Das, M. (2024, July 7). Locals blame lack of planning for deaths in urban floods. *The Times of India; Times of India*. https://timesofindia.indiatimes.com/city/guwahati/urban-floods-in-guwahati-lack-of-planning-blamed-for-tragic-deaths/articleshow/111563587.cms

Devi, N. N., Sridharan, B., & Kuiry, S. N. (2019). Impact of urban sprawl on future flooding in Chennai city, India. *Journal of Hydrology, 574*, 486–496. https://doi.org/10.1016/j.jhydrol.2019.04.041

Escobar, M. S., Johnston, D. W., Knott, R., & Sweeney, R. (2022). Flood disasters and health among the urban poor. *Health Economics, 31*(9), 2072–2089. https://doi.org/10.1002/hec.4566

Ezeh, A., Oyebode, O., Satterthwaite, D., Chen, Y. F., Ndugwa, R., Sartori, J., Mberu, B., Melendez-Torres, G. J., Haregu, T., Watson, S. I., Caiaffa, W., Capon, A., & Lilford, R. J. (2017). The history, geography, and sociology of slums and the health problems of people who live in slums. *Lancet (London, England), 389*(10068), 547–558. https://doi.org/10.1016/S0140-6736(16)31650-6

Fact Finding Committee. (2006). *Fact finding committee on Mumbai floods: Final report volume 1*. Government of Maharashtra. https://questionofcities.org/fact-finding-committee-on-mumbai-floods-final-report/

Feng, B., Zhang, Y., & Bourke, R. (2021). Urbanization impacts on flood risks based on urban growth data and coupled flood models. *Natural Hazards, 106*, 613–627. https://doi.org/10.1007/s11069-020-04480-0

Glenn, N., & Myre, M. (2022). *Post-flooding community-level psychosocial impacts and priorities in Canada: A preliminary report*. https://ncceh.ca/sites/

default/files/Post%20flooding%20community%20level%20psychosoical%20impacts%20Nov%2021%202022_0.pdf

Government of Tamil Nadu. (2017). *Report of the Comptroller and Auditor General of India on performance audit of flood management and response in Chennai and its suburban areas*. Government of Tamil Nadu. https://cag.gov.in/webroot/uploads/download_audit_report/2017/Report_No_4_of_2017_-_Performance_Audit_of_Flood_Management_and_Response_in_Chennai_and_its_Suburban_Area.pdf

Hassan, F. U., Singh, G., & Sekar, K. (2018). Children's reactions to flood disaster in Kashmir. *Indian Journal of Psychological Medicine, 40*(5), 414–419. https://doi.org/10.4103/ijpsym.ijpsym_571_17

Intergovernmental Panel on Climate Change. (2022). Climate change 2022 impacts, adaptation and vulnerability. Summary for policymakers, technical summary and frequently asked questions. https://www.ipcc.ch/report/ar6/wg2/downloads/report/IPCC_AR6_WGII_SummaryVolume.pdf

Jaysawal, N., & Saha, S. (2014). Urbanization in India: An impact assessment. *International Journal of Applied Sociology, 4*(2), 60–65. http://article.sapub.org/pdf/10.5923.j.ijas.20140402.04.pdf

Jha, R. (2023, December 30). *Understanding and tackling urban floods in India*. Orfonline.org; Observer Research Foundation (ORF). https://www.orfonline.org/research/understanding-and-tackling-urban-floods-in-india#_edn50

Kiran, P., Mohan, B., Abhijith, V., Abraham, A., Anoop, G., Dinesh, R., Krishnan, H., Mahadevan, K., Peethambaran, M., Kunheen, M., Sidharthan, M., Prathibha, S., Sukesh, G., Thomas, K., Jayaprakashan, K., & Jaisoorya, T. (2021). Framework for strengthening primary health care and community networks to mitigate the long-term psychosocial impact of floods in Kerala. *International Journal of Disaster Risk Reduction, 52*, 101947. https://doi.org/10.1016/j.ijdrr.2020.101947

Krishna, R. N., Ronan, K. R., & Alisic, E. (2018). Children in the 2015 South Indian floods: Community members' views. *European Journal of Psychotraumatology, 9*(Suppl 2). https://doi.org/10.1080/20008198.2018.1486122

Kuddus, M. A., Tynan, E., & McBryde, E. (2020). Urbanization: A problem for the rich and the poor? *Public Health Reviews, 41*(1). https://doi.org/10.1186/s40985-019-0116-0

Kumar, P. (2021). Climate change and cities: Challenges ahead. *Frontiers in Sustainable Cities, 3*. https://doi.org/10.3389/frsc.2021.645613

Lindsey, R., & Dalhman, L. (2024, January 18). *Climate change: Global temperature*. NOAA; Climate.gov. https://www.climate.gov/news-features/understanding-climate/climate-change-global-temperature

Louis, M. J., Crosato, A., Mosselman, E., & Maskey, S. (2024). Effects of urbanization and deforestation on flooding: Case study of Cap-Haïtien City, Haiti. *Journal of Flood Risk Management*. https://doi.org/10.1111/jfr3.13020

Low, S. M., & Altman, I. (1992). Place attachment. In I. Altman & S. M. Low (Eds.), *Place attachment. Human behavior and environment* (Vol. 12). Springer. https://doi.org/10.1007/978-1-4684-8753-4_1

Luo, Y., & Wang, S. (2022). Urban living and chronic diseases in the presence of economic growth: Evidence from a long-term study in southeastern China. *Frontiers in Public Health, 10*. https://doi.org/10.3389/fpubh.2022.1042413

Mason, V., Andrews, H., & Upton, D. (2010). The psychological impact of exposure to floods. *Psychology Health & Medicine, 15*(1), 61–73. https://doi.org/10.1080/13548500903483478

McGrane, S. J. (2016). Impacts of urbanisation on hydrological and water quality dynamics, and urban water management: A review. *Hydrological Sciences Journal, 61*(13), 2295–2311. https://doi.org/10.1080/02626667.2015.1128084

McMichael, A. J. (2000). The urban environment and health in a world of increasing globalization: Issues for developing countries. *PubMed, 78*(9), 1117–1126. https://pubmed.ncbi.nlm.nih.gov/11019460

Ministry of Urban Development. (2017). *Urban flooding standard operating procedures*. Ministry of Housing and Urban Affairs. https://mohua.gov.in/upload/uploadfiles/files/SOP%20Urban%20flooding_5%20May%202017.pdf

Mohd, Shahar, H. K., Baharudin, M. R., Syed, N., Manaf, R. A., Said, S. M., Ahmad, J., & Muthiah, S. G. (2022). Facing flood disaster: A cluster randomized trial assessing communities' knowledge, skills and preparedness utilizing a health model intervention. *PLoS One, 17*(11), e0271258. https://doi.org/10.1371/journal.pone.0271258

Mollan, C., & Jajware, C. (2024, July 29). Delhi: Protests after students drown in Rau's IAS Study Circle building. Bbc.com; *BBC News*. https://www.bbc.com/news/articles/c0xjlll8l24o

Moulds, S., Buytaert, W., Templeton, M. R., & Kanu, I. (2021). Modeling the impacts of urban flood risk management on social inequality. *Water Resources Research, 57*(6). https://doi.org/10.1029/2020wr029024

Muhammad, T., Pai, M., Maurya, C., Srivastava, S., & Kumar, M. (2024). Natural and human-made disaster and associated health outcomes among community-dwelling older adults in India: Findings from LASI, 2017–18. *PLoS One, 19*(7), e0307371. https://doi.org/10.1371/journal.pone.0307371

Nadimpalli, S., Mathew, S., & Cheranda, T. M. (2024). (Re)envisioning inclusive futures: Applying narrative foresight to deconstruct the problem of urban flooding in the slums of Bengaluru, India. *Development Policy Review, 42*(S1). https://doi.org/10.1111/dpr.12786

Narain, S., Sengupta, S., Chakravartty, A., Venkatesh, S., Pandey, K., & Basu, S. (2016, July 28). *Reality of floods*. Down to Earth; Down to Earth. https://www.downtoearth.org.in/natural-disasters/reeling-under-floods-55089#:~:text=Every%20year%20floods%20are%20reported,of%20natural%20water%20storage%20areas

National Disaster Management Authority. (2010). *National disaster management guidelines management of urban flooding*. National Disaster Management Authority, Government of India. https://nidm.gov.in/pdf/guidelines/new/management_urban_flooding.pdf

Özer, B., & Ercoşkun, Ö. (2024). Assessing the impact of urbanization on flood risk by RS and GIS: A case study on Istanbul-Esenyurt. *Journal of Contemporary Urban Affairs, 8*, 57–78. https://doi.org/10.25034/ijcua.2024.v8n1-4

Patel, R. B., & Burke, T. F. (2009). Urbanization — an emerging humanitarian disaster. *New England Journal of Medicine, 361*(8), 741–743. https://doi.org/10.1056/nejmp0810878

Phraknoi, N., Sutanto, J., Hu, Y., Goh, Y. S., & Lee, C. E. C. (2023). Older people's needs in urban disaster response: A systematic literature review. *International Journal of Disaster Risk Reduction, 96*, 103809. https://doi.org/10.1016/j.ijdrr.2023.103809

Press Information Bureau. (2024). *Threat of urban floods*. Pib.gov.in. https://pib.gov.in/PressReleaseIframePage.aspx?PRID=2003165

Pv, G., & Subudhi, C. (2020). Psycho-social and educational impact of flood among school going children. *Journal of Social Welfare and Management, 12*(1), 15–24. https://doi.org/10.21088/jswm.0975.0231.12120.2

Rafiq, F., Ahmed, S., Ahmad, S., Amir, A., Khan, & Arabia, S. (2016). Urban floods in India. *International Journal of Scientific & Engineering Research, 7*(1). https://www.ijser.org/researchpaper/Urban-Floods-in-India.pdf

Rahaman, M. A., Kalam, A., & Al-Mamun, M. (2023). Unplanned urbanization and health risks of Dhaka City in Bangladesh: Uncovering the associations between urban environment and public health. *Frontiers in Public Health, 11*. https://doi.org/10.3389/fpubh.2023.1269362

Rahana, S. R., Sam, J. M., & Udhayakumar, P. (2021). Depression, anxiety, stress, and resilience among the primary survivors of natural disaster: A study with special reference to Kerala flood. *Indian Journal of Social Psychiatry, 37*(4), 388–393. https://doi.org/10.4103/ijsp.ijsp_238_20

Ramudu, Y. J., Lakshmi, N. T., Balakotaiah, C., & Rambabu, M. (2023). State wise status of urban slums in India: Census data. *International Journal of Applied Research, 9*(1), 315–319. https://doi.org/10.22271/allresearch.2023.v9.i1e.10511

Rendall, M. S. (2024). Acquisition of disability after age 50 following extreme urban coastal flooding events in India. *Population and Environment, 46*(1). https://doi.org/10.1007/s11111-024-00447-6

Rentschler, J., Avner, P., Su, R., & Hallegatte, S. (2022, May 23). *Rapid urban growth in flood zones: Global trends in exposure since 1985*. World Bank Blogs. https://blogs.worldbank.org/en/developmenttalk/rapid-urban-growth-flood-zones-global-trends-exposure-1985

Riethmuller, M. L., Dzidic, P. L., & Newnham, E. A. (2021). Going rural: Qualitative perspectives on the role of place attachment in young people's intentions to return to the country. *Journal of Environmental Psychology, 73*, 101542. https://doi.org/10.1016/j.jenvp.2020.101542

Sehra, V. (2021). A study to assess the effect of socio-economic vulnerability to urban flooding and self-efficacy on mental health at Hyderabad city, India. In A. K. Gupta, A. Barwal, A. Madan, A. Sood, & M. K. Bindal (Eds.), *Health adaptation and resilience to climate change and related disasters: A compendium of case studies* (pp. 9–23). National Institute of Disaster Management.

Sehra, V., & Mishra, A. K. (2022). Stress and self-efficacy as predictors of positive growth in aftermath of urban flooding in Hyderabad, India. *International Journal of Disaster Risk Reduction, 83*, 103349. https://doi.org/10.1016/j.ijdrr.2022.103349

Seneviratne, S. I., Zhang, X., Adnan, M., Badi, W., Dereczynski, C., Di Luca, A., Ghosh, S., Iskandar, I., Kossin, J., Lewis, S., Otto, F., Pinto, I., Satoh, M., Vicente-Serrano, S. M., Wehner, M., & Zhou, B. (2021). Weather and climate extreme events in a changing climate. In V. Masson-Delmotte, P. Zhai, A. Pirani, S. L. Connors, C. Péan, S. Berger, N. Caud, Y. Chen, L. Goldfarb, M. I. Gomis, M. Huang, K. Leitzell, E. Lonnoy, J. B. R. Matthews, T. K. Maycock, T. Waterfield, O. Yelekçi, R. Yu, & B. Zhou (Eds.), *Climate change 2021: The physical science basis. Contribution of working group I to the sixth assessment report of the intergovernmental panel on climate change* (pp. 1513–1766). Cambridge University Press. https://doi.org/10.1017/9781009157896.013

Setiawan, T., Riasnugrahani, M., & De Jong, E. (2023). Psychometric properties of Indonesian slums dwellers' place attachment. *Heliyon, 9*(9), e19704. https://doi.org/10.1016/j.heliyon.2023.e19704

Sharma, M., Kumar, V., & Kumar, S. (2024). A systematic review of urban sprawl and land use/land cover change studies in India. *Sustainable Environment, 10*(1). https://doi.org/10.1080/27658511.2024.2331269

Shepherd, J. M. (2005). A review of current investigations of urban-induced rainfall and recommendations for the future. *Earth Interactions, 9*(12), 1–27. https://doi.org/10.1175/ei156.1

Singh, D. (2022). *Causes, impacts, risk and mitigation of Urban Flood Management in India COMPENDIUM REPORT 2022 Occasional Research Paper Series # 2 International Centre for Environment Audit and Sustainable Development (ICED), Jaipur, India.* https://iced.cag.gov.in/wp-content/uploads/Series2.pdf

Singh, H., Nielsen, M., & Greatrex, H. (2023). Causes, impacts, and mitigation strategies of urban pluvial floods in India: A systematic review. *International Journal of Disaster Risk Reduction, 93*, 103751. https://doi.org/10.1016/j.ijdrr.2023.103751

Stalin, J. S. D. (2015, December 14). *Chennai schools, colleges re-open after month-long holiday.* NDTV. https://www.ndtv.com/chennai-news/chennai-schools-colleges-re-open-after-month-long-holiday-1254566

Stecko, S., & Barber, N. (2007). *Exposing vulnerabilities: Monsoon floods in Mumbai, India case study prepared for revisiting urban planning: Global report on human settlements 2007.* https://unhabitat.org/sites/default/files/2008/07/GRHS.2007.CaseStudy.Mumbai.pdf

Subbaraman, R., Nolan, L., Shitole, T., Sawant, K., Shitole, S., Sood, K., Nanarkar, M., Ghannam, J., Betancourt, T. S., Bloom, D. E., & Patil-Deshmukh, A. (2014). The psychological toll of slum living in Mumbai, India: A mixed methods study. *Social Science & Medicine, 119*, 155–169. https://doi.org/10.1016/j.socscimed.2014.08.021

Sun, X., Li, R., Shan, X., Xu, H., & Wang, J. (2021). Assessment of climate change impacts and urban flood management schemes in central Shanghai. *International Journal of Disaster Risk Reduction, 65*, 102563–102563. https://doi.org/10.1016/j.ijdrr.2021.102563

Thomas, V., & Lopez, R. (2015). Global increase in climate-related disasters. *ADB economics working paper series.* Asian Development Bank. https://www.adb.org/sites/default/files/publication/176899/ewp-466.pdf

Twerefou, D. K., Abeney, J. O., Larbi, R. T., & Dovie, D. B. K. (2024). To live with floods or not: Intersectionality of drivers of urban households' adaptation and relocation intentions. *Journal of Flood Risk Management.* https://doi.org/10.1111/jfr3.13015

United Nations. (2023). *The sustainable development goals report 2023: Special Edition*. United Nations. https://unstats.un.org/sdgs/report/2023/

US Environmental Protection Agency. (2016, June 27). *Climate change indicators: Weather and climate | US EPA*. US EPA. https://www.epa.gov/climate-indicators/weather-climate

What is Urbanisation? | UN-HABITAT Regional Office for Asia and the Pacific (Fukuoka). (2021). UN-HABITAT Regional Office for Asia and the Pacific (Fukuoka). https://fukuoka.unhabitat.org/en/urbanisation/

Yu, P., Wei, Y., Ma, L., Wang, B., Yung, E. H., & Chen, Y. (2024). Urbanization and the urban critical zone. *Deleted Journal, 1*(1), 100011. https://doi.org/10.1016/j.ecz.2024.100011

15

Psychosocial Support and Mental Health Services Post Major Landslides During the Last 15 Years in India

Chaitali Mendon and Ajay Kumar Goyal

Introduction

In the middle of the night, a man woke to the sound of a loud rumble. Panicked, he saw his home flooding, and before he could react, the strong current swept him away. He struggled, but the force of the water and other debris was too much, and he lost consciousness.

When he woke up, he found himself injured in a field about one and a half kilometers from his house. He was disoriented and exhausted. Later, his wife was also found near the same farm.

A few years before, a similar disaster had struck in a different state. A man, working far from his village, had returned to find an unspeakable tragedy awaiting him. His entire village, once bustling with life, had been wiped out in an instant. He learned that eight members of his own family had been lost; some were dead, others missing, swept away by the force of mud, rocks and boulders. The tragedy had claimed not only his family but also the families of many others in his village.

C. Mendon • A. K. Goyal (✉)
Department of Psychosocial Support in Disaster Management, NIMHANS, Bengaluru, Karnataka, India

S. Bhadra et al. (eds.), *Psychosocial and Mental Health Support for Disaster Management in India*, Palgrave Studies in Disaster Science and Emergency Management,
https://doi.org/10.1007/978-3-032-02511-1_15

These two stories have been taken from reports on landslides that have struck India in recent decades (India Today, 2024; Barnagarwala, 2024). As the above excerpts illustrate, landslides can have devastating mental health impacts due to the catastrophic nature of the disaster and the extensive damage they cause. Landslides involves the downward movement of rock, soil or debris along a slope (Jain et al., 2023). These mass movements of earth can range in size from small rockfalls to massive, devastating flows of mud and debris. When a landslide occurs, the force of the descending materials can overwhelm everything in its path, including homes, roads, and entire villages. It can destroy infrastructure, disrupt lives, and cause significant loss of life. In many cases, landslides are unpredictable and can strike without warning, leaving little time for communities to react.

The movement of landmasses in landslides can be triggered by various factors, including heavy rainfall, earthquakes, snowmelt, and the weakening of slopes caused by floods or excavation. Overgrazing by livestock and excessive development on slopes can also contribute to the occurrence of landslides. The type of soil, rock, geological structure, and the steepness of the slope also play significant roles in determining the likelihood of a landslide (Jain et al., 2023).

In India, approximately 12.6% of the land area is susceptible to landslide hazards (Jain et al., 2023). It is one of the four countries with the highest risk for landslides (Jain et al., 2023). The Himalayas are the most vulnerable, with 76.19% of the region at risk, followed by the Western Ghats (21.43%) and the Eastern Ghats (2.38%) (Jain et al., 2023). The high susceptibility of the Himalayas and Western Ghats to landslides is primarily due to their steep topographies and the heavy rainfalls these regions receive (Jain et al., 2023). The Himalayan region states and union territories, including Jammu and Kashmir, Ladakh, Himachal Pradesh, Uttarakhand, Sikkim, West Bengal, Arunachal Pradesh, Nagaland, Manipur, Mizoram, Tripura, Assam, and Meghalaya, are particularly vulnerable to landslides. Similarly, the Western Ghats and the Konkan Hill regions, spanning across Maharashtra, Goa, Karnataka, Kerala, and Tamil Nadu, face significant landslide risks due to their steep terrain and heavy rainfall.

Over the past 15 years, the National Disaster Management Authority (NDMA) has adapted to the increasing frequency of landslides in India. In June 2009, NDMA released the National Guidelines for Landslide Management, which had been developed in consultation with various agencies. However, progress was limited in affected regions (NDMA, n.d.). In December 2014, NDMA introduced the *Landslide Risk Mitigation Scheme* (LRMS) to engage state governments and stakeholders in landslide risk reduction (NDMA, n.d.). To address knowledge gaps, NDMA began training programs on landslide mitigation and disaster preparedness and response (DPR) preparation in 2018, in collaboration with leading institutes like Indian Institute of Technology (IIT) and Indian Institute of Science (IISc) (NDMA, n.d.). In 2017, NDMA, in collaboration with IIT Mandi and the Defence Research and Development Organisation (DRDO), also initiated a low-cost landslide monitoring and early warning system, which uses (AI) to predict soil movements and issue warnings. This system was tested and refined, with the potential to be deployed at multiple landslide sites across India (NDMA, n.d.). In 2019, NDMA released the *National Landslide Risk Management Strategy*, which outlined a comprehensive approach to landslide risk reduction, including hazard mapping, monitoring, early warning systems, and public awareness (NDMA, n.d.).

While significant progress has been made in the technical aspects of landslide mitigation, including innovative engineering solutions and collaborative efforts, comparable strides have not yet been made in addressing the human dimension of landslides. The focus has largely been on physical infrastructure, with far less attention given to how people are impacted by such disasters, both before and after they occur.

Before a landslide, community preparedness and awareness are often insufficient, leaving individuals vulnerable to the emotional and psychological toll that comes with such events. Once the disaster strikes, the psychosocial impacts, such as trauma, grief and anxiety, can be overwhelming. Yet, the interventions to support affected individuals in these areas are still developing. This gap in care extends to the mourning process, where the grieving of lost loved ones and missing persons is often either overlooked or insufficiently supported.

Furthermore, when it comes to rehabilitation or planned relocation, there is a critical need to consider the deep-rooted connection individuals have to the land they occupy. For many, their sense of identity is inextricably linked to their ancestral homes, cultural practices and occupations that have been passed down through generations. The emotional and psychological complexities of asking people to leave these spaces, often for their own safety, are profound, as the land that has been their lifeblood is now a threat to their survival.

While there is a growing recognition of the need to address these psychosocial aspects, this area is still evolving and much work remains to be done. In the face of these challenges, it is essential that we begin to treat the people, not just the land, as central to the solutions we develop. By integrating human well-being into the discourse surrounding landslides and their impacts, we can ensure that both the land and its people are protected in a more holistic and compassionate way.

Major Landslides in India in the Past 15 Years

The following are major landslides that have occurred in the country over the past 15 years, all of which have taken place in the Himalayan region or the Western Ghats (The Hindu, 2024).

Kedarnath, Uttarakhand: June 16, 2013

During the devastating Uttarakhand floods, massive landslides occurred in the town of Kedarnath, claiming the lives of over 5700 individuals. Additionally, more than 4200 villages were severely impacted by the flooding and the subsequent landslides. The scale of destruction was immense, affecting not only human lives but also infrastructure and the local environment.

Malin, Maharashtra: July 30, 2014

A catastrophic landslide struck the village of Malin in Pune district, Maharashtra, following a burst of heavy rainfall. The landslide occurred in the early hours of the morning, catching residents off-guard while they were asleep. As a result, at least 151 people lost their lives and more than

100 individuals were reported missing. The incident drew national attention to the vulnerability of rural settlements in areas prone to landslides.

Pettimudi, Kerala: August 6, 2020

In Idukki district of Kerala, relentless rainfall led to a massive landslide that struck a labor camp and a tree plantation estate near the Pettimudi river. The boulder that fell from the Iravikulam National Park, accompanied by a loud noise, caused widespread destruction. Tragically, more than 65 workers perished, as many of them were asleep when the landslide occurred, leaving little time for escape.

Mumbai, Maharashtra: July 18, 2021

A series of landslides, triggered by heavy rains, occurred in the suburbs of Chembur and Vikhroli in Mumbai. The disaster resulted in the deaths of at least 32 individuals, with several others injured. Many victims were trapped under the debris of collapsed houses, highlighting the vulnerabilities of urban areas with poor drainage systems and inadequate infrastructure to withstand extreme weather conditions.

Tupul, Manipur: June 30, 2022

A large landslide struck Noney district in Manipur, near the Tupul railway construction site, burying a group of workers and civilians. The landslide claimed the lives of 58 people, including 29 Indian Army personnel, while three individuals were reported missing and 18 others were injured. The debris from the landslide blocked the Ijai River, creating a risk of flooding for the nearby villages.

Raigad, Maharashtra: July 19, 2023

A deadly landslide occurred in the Raigad district of Maharashtra due to incessant rainfall. The disaster resulted in at least 26 deaths, with more than 100 people feared trapped under the debris. The region had been under an "orange" weather alert for two days prior to the incident.

Aizawl, Mizoram: May 28, 2024

Following the heavy rainfall of Cyclone Remal, a massive landslide struck Aizawl district in Mizoram. The collapse of a stone quarry led to the deaths of at least 14 people, including two minors, while around eight others were reported missing. The event marked a significant loss for the region and highlighted the impact of cyclonic storms in causing secondary disasters, such as landslides in hilly terrains.

Shirur, Karnataka: July 16, 2024

A landslide occurred in Shirur, Ankola in the Uttara Kannada district of Karnataka, following torrential rains. The incident resulted in the deaths of at least eight individuals, with more than three others feared trapped under debris or in the nearby Gangavalli River.

Wayanad, Kerala: July 30, 2024

Heavy rains in the Wayanad district of Kerala triggered multiple massive landslides, particularly affecting the hamlets of Mundakkai, Chooramala, Attamala, and Noolpuzha. Hundreds of people were trapped and the situation prompted urgent rescue operations. This event brought attention to the vulnerability of Kerala's hilly terrains, which are prone to landslides during the monsoon season.

In addition to the landslides in recent years, the Himalayan town of Joshimath faced a severe crisis when torrents of water poured down its lower slopes on the night of January 2, 2023 (Chopra, 2023). Situated at an elevation of 6150 feet (1875 meters), parts of the town experienced significant subsidence, with cracks appearing in buildings, roads, and fields and structures tilting dangerously (Chopra, 2023). On

January 13, the Indian Space Research Organisation (ISRO) released an initial report indicating that Joshimath had subsided by about 9 cm between April and November 2022, with an alarming 5.4 cm drop occurring in just 12 days—from December 27 to January 8 (Chopra, 2023).

The primary cause of this rapid subsidence was the surge in tourism and migration, which had led to the rapid expansion of the hotel and tourism industries, as well as the construction of multi-story hostels and guesthouses. This development had far exceeded the load-bearing capacity of the unstable debris beneath the town (Awasthi et al., 2024). Additionally, the region's ongoing urbanization, coupled with severe erosion and toe-cutting caused by the Alaknanda River, as well as large-scale infrastructure projects, had all contributed to the ground deformation (Awasthi et al., 2024). Experts had stressed the urgent need for immediate intervention and highlighted the importance of adopting a cautious, sustainable approach to development in this fragile region (Awasthi et al., 2024).

Landslides and other natural disasters are often reported like this in the media, with headlines that focus solely on immediate statistics, such as death tolls, the number of missing persons, and homes destroyed. However, these reports fail to convey the broader, long-term consequences of such tragedies. The impacts of natural disasters extend far beyond the immediate loss of life, affecting local economies and infrastructure, and hindering long-term recovery efforts. For each individual affected, entire families and communities are deeply impacted.

Therefore, a more comprehensive approach to disaster mitigation and response must include a focus on the psychosocial consequences for those impacted. Mental health is directly linked to physical health and the psychosocial functioning of individuals. It is crucial to address the emotional, mental, and social toll these events take on individuals and communities, ensuring that responses not only meet physical needs but also support the healing and recovery of people's mental and emotional well-being. Holistic efforts must prioritize both the material and psychosocial aspects of disaster recovery in order to truly support the affected populations.

Changing Frequencies of Landslides in India

Leading experts have claimed that anthropogenically triggered landslides in India have been on the rise due to a combination of factors. G.M. Bhat, a geologist and rector at the University of Jammu's Bhaderwah campus, noted that landslides in Jammu and Kashmir had nearly doubled over the past 20 years (Sharma, 2016). He attributed this increase to deforestation, poorly planned development, and climate change, which has led to longer rainfall periods that destabilize slopes (Sharma, 2016). Additionally, the region's high level of seismic activity also contributes, as frequent earthquakes often trigger landslides (Sharma, 2016).

A study by Risk Management Solutions India (RMSI), a geospatial company focused on disaster assessment, also raised concerns about the growing frequency and severity of landslides in India, particularly following the deadly landslide in Kerala's Wayanad, which killed more than 200 people. This report highlighted that nearly 30% of India's land area, including 22 states, parts of Puducherry, and the Andaman & Nicobar Islands, are vulnerable to landslides. States like Arunachal Pradesh, Sikkim, Kerala, and Uttarakhand are particularly at risk (Tripathi, 2024). The report confirmed that climate change is intensifying the risk, with increased rainfall contributing to slope instability. However, human activities like deforestation and infrastructure development were also identified as key contributors. Regions with slopes between 25 and 45 degrees were found to be especially prone to landslides, suggesting that construction in these areas needs more careful planning. The report called for sustainable development practices to mitigate risks, urging the preservation of natural environments to reduce vulnerability (Tripathi, 2024).

These findings echo the concerns raised in the Madhav Gadgil Report (Western Ghats Ecology Expert Panel [WGEEP] Report) of 2011, which highlighted the increasing frequency of landslides in the Western Ghats due to deforestation, construction, and climate change. The report stressed that infrastructure projects, like roads and dams, disturbed the landscape, exacerbating soil erosion and making the region more prone to landslides. It recommended regulated development, dividing the region into Ecologically Sensitive Zones (ESZs) to protect the environment (*Report of the Western Ghats Ecology Expert Panel*, 2011). It also called for the promotion of sustainable agriculture, eco-friendly tourism, and community-based conservation, while urging a reduction in harmful infrastructure projects and stronger climate change adaptation strategies (*Report of the Western Ghats Ecology Expert Panel*, 2011). The report emphasized the need for a balanced development model that both supported local communities and preserved the ecology of the Western Ghats, warning that unsustainable development would lead to further environmental degradation (*Report of the Western Ghats Ecology Expert Panel*, 2011).

This further highlights the urgent need to address the psychosocial impacts of landslides, while also gaining a deeper understanding of the psychological and social dynamics involved in planned relocations due to the growing frequency of such events. As communities are displaced, it becomes crucial to recognize and mitigate the emotional and social challenges they face. This includes understanding how the loss of homes, disruption of social networks, and upheaval of familiar environments affect both individual and collective well-being. Developing strategies that incorporate mental health support and foster social resilience is essential.

General Consequences of Landslides

Landslides have a wide range of devastating consequences on the lives of the people and communities that are affected. One of the most immediate impacts is on healthcare infrastructure. In Guatemala, for example, a series of landslides completely destroyed a local hospital, burying it along with the surrounding town, and leaving the community without essential medical services (Kennedy et al., 2015). In addition to this, landslides can significantly amplify the effects of other natural disasters. For instance, they can obstruct critical access routes such as roads, hindering rescue and recovery efforts and delaying medical assistance for earthquake survivors, which can lead to increased fatalities. Furthermore, landslides can result in severe economic losses and put individuals at grave risk. Those trapped under debris face life-threatening injuries, including blunt force trauma, crushing, suffocation, and drowning (Kennedy et al., 2015). The intense pressure from the landslide debris can lead to crush injuries or crush syndrome, putting survivors at heightened risk of severe physical harm (Kennedy et al., 2015).

A study conducted in 2002 in Chuuk, Micronesia, investigated mortality risks during landslides and found that suffocation from being trapped under debris was the primary cause of death among the 43 victims (Kennedy et al., 2015). The study also highlighted key risk factors for mortality, such as being under the age of 15, which was statistically significant. While factors like gender and being inside a building during a landslide were also associated with increased mortality, these were not statistically significant. On a more positive note, the study found that individuals who were aware of recent landslides or recognized natural warning signs had a lower risk of death. Other research, including work by Kariya et al. (2005) reported that injuries were also linked to being struck by rocks or debris, even if the individuals were not buried by the landslide (Kennedy et al., 2015).

Landslides are also associated with outbreaks of infectious diseases. Following the 1991 earthquake and floods in Costa Rica, there was a significant surge in malaria cases, largely due to disrupted access to clean water and poor hygiene practices. Many people returned to contaminated river sources, exacerbating the problem. While diarrheal diseases were relatively low (8.8% of households reported cases), malaria (47.7%) and respiratory infections (58.3%) were notably more prevalent. Landslides can also directly contaminate water sources by introducing debris into rivers, increasing turbidity and disrupting waste management. For instance, after a landslide in May 2007 in the Karnaphuli Estuary, Bangladesh, there was a tenfold rise in faecal coliforms and increased levels of *Vibrio cholerae*, although not as significantly as after a cyclone the previous month (Kennedy et al., 2015).

Landslides can have severe impacts on indigenous communities, many of whom reside in remote, mountainous regions along slopes due to their deep-rooted connection to nature. These locations, while culturally and spiritually significant, are often highly vulnerable to landslides. In many cases, the livelihoods and cultural heritage of indigenous peoples are closely tied to these ancestral lands, leading them to remain in place and rely on traditional, indigenous methods for resilience. However, climate change and shifting weather patterns have made such environmental events increasingly unpredictable and intense. A study highlighted that marginalization remains a major challenge for indigenous populations pertaining to local interventions in landslide disaster management in Uganda (Turyasingura et al., 2023). Additionally, indigenous communities are generally more vulnerable to natural hazards and the threat of displacement (Miranda et al., 2020). When displacement does occur, they often face unique challenges, such as limited access to aid and resources (Miranda et al., 2020). Furthermore, legal complexities related to indigenous land rights and local reserves can complicate jurisdiction and response efforts in times of crisis (Miranda et al., 2020).

It is crucial to recognize that the consequences of landslides go beyond physical harm; they take a psychological toll on the affected communities. Being trapped under debris, waiting for help due to blocked routes, or feeling helpless when local hospitals are destroyed can all have profound emotional effects. These traumatic experiences are not limited to the victims but extend to the rescue workers as well. The complexities and stressors of landslide rescue operations, such as rescuing individuals trapped under debris, locating missing persons, reporting deaths, and coordinating complicated relief efforts, can take a significant emotional toll on those involved. The psychological strain on both survivors and responders needs to be considered in disaster management and recovery efforts.

Mental Health Consequences of Landslides

Psychological Impact of Landslides on Survivors

Survivors of landslides are significantly more prone to severe mental health disorders, such as post-traumatic stress disorder (PTSD), panic disorder and major depressive episodes (Kennedy et al., 2015). Studies indicate that PTSD rates among landslide survivors may even exceed those of individuals affected by other types of natural disasters, potentially due to the violent and traumatic nature of landslides. The fear of being buried alive, often experienced during landslides, may contribute to heightened psychological challenges (Kennedy et al., 2015). Furthermore, PTSD and major depressive disorder tend to overlap in survivors of such disasters, a trend commonly observed in various disaster scenarios (Kennedy et al., 2015).

The mental health impact of landslides extends long beyond the event itself. Even years after the disaster, PTSD remains prevalent among survivors, with nearly 47% (n = 276) of those surveyed still suffering from the disorder (Kabunga et al., 2022). Interestingly, the duration of time since the landslide significantly influences the likelihood of developing PTSD. Survivors who experienced the landslide more than two years ago had a 65% reduced likelihood of developing PTSD compared to those who faced the disaster more recently (Kabunga et al., 2022). This suggests that PTSD is often most severe in the immediate aftermath of the disaster, with untreated cases representing a major risk factor for long-term mental health complications.

Risk Factors for PTSD and Mental Health Issues

Several sociodemographic and life factors contribute to a heightened risk of developing PTSD among landslide survivors. Female gender, widowhood, lack of counselling, and secondary education were all found to be significantly associated with PTSD (Kabunga et al., 2022). Additionally, survivors over the age of 60, those who had experienced divorce, or those with a history of mental illness (personal or familial), also exhibited higher PTSD rates (Asnakew et al., 2019). Childhood trauma or neglect, witnessing the injury or death of loved ones, physical injury, and destruction of property further exacerbate mental health symptoms. The emotional toll of fearing for one's life during the landslide was another significant risk factor for PTSD, alongside poor social support (Asnakew et al., 2019). A history of mental illness, whether personal or familial, also emerged as a notable risk factor for PTSD (Asnakew et al., 2019). A study highlighted the strong link between poor social support and higher

PTSD risk, with survivors lacking emotional or social backing being twice as likely to develop PTSD compared to those with strong support systems (Kabunga et al., 2022). The study further suggested that social support acted as a key protective factor in preventing the onset of PTSD, with inadequate support contributing to more severe mental health symptoms (Kabunga et al., 2022).

Socioeconomic Factors and Mental Health

Economic vulnerabilities significantly contribute to the mental health outcomes of disaster survivors. Poverty, particularly among those living below the poverty line or in substandard housing prior to the disaster, significantly raises the risk of developing common mental health disorders (CMDs) following a disaster like a landslide (Kunnathepeedikayil, 2020). Survivors who required medical treatment or hospitalization due to injuries sustained during the landslide or flood events were also at a higher risk of experiencing CMDs (Kunnathepeedikayil, 2020). These socioeconomic factors underline the need for targeted interventions that address the underlying vulnerabilities of disaster survivors. In addition to economic factors, the psychological toll of displacement, loss of property, and disruption of social networks exacerbates mental health challenges. Many victims, particularly those who lost loved ones, experience significantly heightened stress levels and report a strong need for assistance not only in meeting basic survival needs but also in receiving emotional and social support (Kennedy et al., 2015). These broader psychological impacts underscore the complex interplay of economic insecurity, loss, and the lasting emotional burden of such traumatic events.

Long-Term Consequences of Landslides

The long-term mental health consequences of landslides are evident in the persistent impact of PTSD on survivors. In a study that followed survivors of the 1966 Aberfan disaster, a 33-year follow-up revealed that a significant proportion of survivors met the diagnostic criteria for PTSD, with an odds ratio of 3.38 compared to controls (Kennedy et al., 2015). This indicates that the psychological effects of such disasters can persist for decades, underlining the importance of long-term mental health support and monitoring for survivors of landslides. Similarly, recurrent exposure to landslides over the past two decades may have contributed to the high rates of PTSD observed in some communities (Kabunga et al., 2022).

Impact on Emergency Responders and Families

The mental health of rescue workers and their families is also a significant concern during and after disasters. The intense and hazardous nature of emergency response work, combined with factors such as fatigue, fear for personal safety, personal connections to victims, and media exposure, can severely affect the psychological well-being of those involved in rescue efforts (Kennedy et al., 2015). The mental toll on emergency responders is compounded by the pressure of responding to traumatic events while managing their own emotions and stress levels. This underscores the importance of providing adequate psychological support to not only survivors but also the professionals working to save lives during and after such catastrophic events.

Social Support and Its Protective Role

The role of social support is critical in mitigating the mental health effects of landslides and similar disasters. Survivors with strong social networks and family support are less likely to develop PTSD, and family support is shown to reduce suicide risk among disaster survivors (Kabunga et al., 2022). In contrast, survivors who have poor social support are at significantly higher risk for PTSD, with some studies indicating they are twice as likely to develop the disorder compared to those with support systems (Kabunga et al., 2022). Additionally, landslide survivors face a slower recovery of social support compared to those affected by other disasters like floods (Kabunga et al., 2022). This delayed recovery can further aggravate mental health issues, including depression and PTSD. Moreover, emotional support from families plays a vital role in the mental well-being of survivors. Studies following the 1985 landslides in Puerto Rico revealed that lower emotional support was linked to higher rates of alcohol abuse, depression, and other psychiatric symptoms (Kabunga et al., 2022). Social support, therefore, is not only a protective factor but also a crucial resource for the emotional healing of landslide survivors.

While much has been written about the mental health consequences following landslides, there are less often discussed aspects such as the initial shock, the emotional turmoil of being trapped, the stress of navigating government claims, and the long-term process of coming to terms with the immense losses. These challenges continue to affect survivors long after the immediate aftermath.

Displacements Due to Landslides

Displacement refers to the forced relocation of individuals from their homes, often as a result of both natural and human-induced hazards. Among these, natural disasters are increasingly driving higher rates of displacement each year. Landslides, in particular, are a frequent cause of displacement due to their unpredictable and devastating nature, often leaving individuals without shelter. In 2023, the Internal Displacement Monitoring Centre reported that around 120,000 people were displaced by wet mass movements, while 13,000 were affected by dry mass movements (Global Report on internal displacement (GRID), 2024).

Research by Burrows et al. (2021) examined the mental health and well-being impacts of landslide displacement in Banjarnegara, Indonesia, highlighting profound consequences that extend beyond material loss. The study found that landslides not only destroyed homes and livelihoods but also disrupted economic stability, family structures, and community ties. For many participants, their livelihoods were intricately linked to their sense of mental well-being and displacement severely affected their identity and sense of belonging.

The displacement process unfolded in three distinct, though interconnected, phases: the immediate shock and loss (Period 1), temporary housing and the liminality of being unsettled (Period 2), and the rebuilding phase, either in new homes or repaired structures (Period 3). Throughout these stages, participants struggled with grief, shifting social dynamics, and challenges to their sense of self and place. Even in cases where communities relocated together, the disruption of their previous social fabric led to feelings of strain and disconnection.

The loss of livelihoods proved to be both an economic and emotional setback, eroding participants' sense of purpose and stability. Rebuilding livelihoods and establishing new routines played a crucial role in recovery, providing not only financial stability but also the psychological benefits of restored normalcy. These findings align with broader research on the importance of stable employment in post-disaster recovery, underscoring the mental health benefits of returning to routine beyond mere economic recovery.

A similar study in Jammu and Kashmir found that individuals displaced by landslides or those relocated to avoid high-risk areas faced significant challenges in starting anew (Sharma, 2016). In addition to battling poverty, lack of farmland, and limited access to essential services, many were deeply affected by mental health issues, largely stemming from the trauma of losing their homes and livelihoods (Sharma, 2016). Hence, the secondary consequences of landslides are far-reaching, affecting not only the physical environment but also the psychological and social fabric of displaced communities.

This issue closely aligns with the growing discourse around climate refugees. A major challenge in protecting those displaced by climate change is the lack of a clear definition, especially within the framework of the 1951 Refugee Convention (European Parliamentary Research Service, 2023). Climate change, through rising temperatures, is increasing the frequency and severity of disasters like landslides, which often force people to move (European Parliamentary Research Service, 2023). While many are displaced internally and may return home, some areas are becoming permanently uninhabitable, especially during disasters like landslides. Although exact numbers are hard to track, climate-related cross-border migration is expected to rise, straining already burdened refugee systems. Displacement can fuel conflict over resources and deepen existing social tensions (European Parliamentary Research Service, 2023).

Theories on Mental Health and Psychological Effects of Landslides

Place Identity Theory

Place identity theory, rooted in environmental psychology, emphasizes that locations are key factors in shaping personal and social identities. The term was coined by environmental psychologist Harold M. Proshansky in the late 1970s and he stated that place identity is a mix of memories, feelings, and interpretations of physical environments, which evolve as both individuals and their environments change. The link between place and identity is built through interactions with environments, shaping individuals' sense of self (Wolfe, 2024). Key aspects include symbolic meanings of places (e.g., childhood homes), emotional attachment, and social interactions that contribute to identity formation (Twigger-Ross & Uzzell, 1996; Hidalgo & Hernandez, 2001 as cited in Wolfe, 2024). The three main aspects of place identity are: (1) Self-identity reflection, where frequent spaces become part of one's self-definition; (2) Emotional attachment, driven by personal memories and security; and (3) Social relations, facilitated by community venues that foster connection (Wolfe, 2024). Place attachment, beyond sentiment, plays a crucial role in mental health, with stronger attachments linked to greater happiness and reduced stress (Wolfe, 2024). Fig. 15.1 explains the main aspects of place identity:

Landslides dramatically disrupt the very places that shape individuals' identities. Entire villages can be wiped out, erasing not only physical structures but also the emotional and symbolic connections people have with those places. In the context of place identity theory, this loss represents more than the destruction of homes—it is the erasure of memories, feelings, and personal histories tied to those environments. For many, the place they call home is an integral part of their self-definition and when it is destroyed or they are permanently displaced, it can lead to a profound crisis of identity. The displacement disrupts the continuity of self, leaving individuals to cope with the emotional and psychological aftermath of losing a place that once symbolized security, belonging and

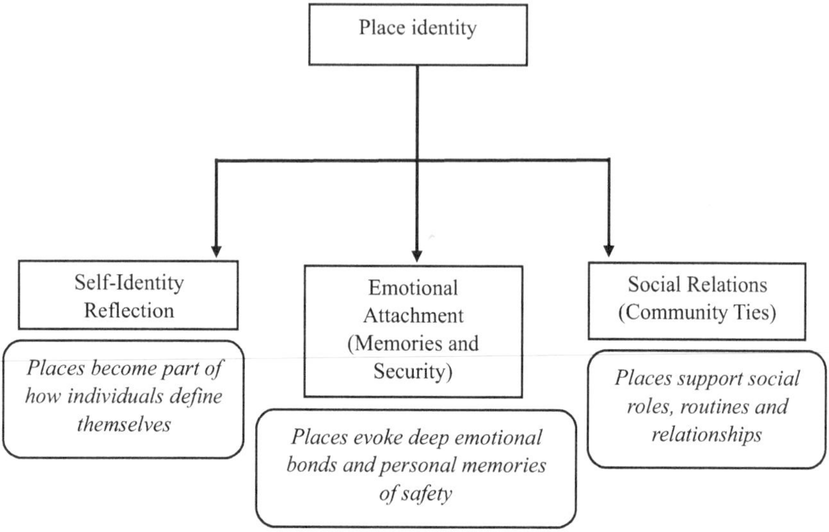

Fig. 15.1 Aspects of place identity theory

community. Place identity theory helps to understand the deep sense of loss people face in such situations, highlighting the psychological impact of losing a place that was central to both their personal and social identity.

Kubler-Ross's Stages of Dying

Dr. Elizabeth Kubler-Ross introduced the five stages of dying in her 1969 book *On Death and Dying*, based on interviews with terminally ill patients. The stages—denial, anger, bargaining, depression and acceptance—serve as a model for understanding emotional responses to imminent death (Tyrrell et al., 2025). This model was later applied to losses experienced in many other contexts. Kubler-Ross emphasized that these stages are not necessarily experienced in order and that not everyone goes through all of them (Tyrrell et al., 2025). Denial involves rejecting the terminal diagnosis, often due to emotional shock, and while it can hinder understanding, it can also serve as an important coping mechanism. Anger arises as patients confront their illness, often directed at medical staff, family or even a higher power. Bargaining occurs when patients try

Individuals may move back and forth, skip stages or experience them uniquely

Denial	Anger	Bargaining	Depression	Acceptance
- Shock and disbelief *- Initial emotional defence mechanism*	*- Frustration and blame* *- Directed at others or higher powers*	*- Making deals for more time* *- Seeking control*	*- Sadness and grief* *- Facing reality* *- Fatigue*	*- Peaceful resolution* *- Acceptance of mortality*

Fig. 15.2 Kubler-Ross's stages of dying

to regain control by making promises or offering exchanges, whether rational or based on magical thinking. Depression is marked by deep sadness and fatigue as patients process the impending loss. Finally, acceptance happens when patients come to terms with their diagnosis, focusing on making the most of their time and preparing for death. Kubler-Ross wrote about the stages to help understand the emotional journey rather than prescribe a rigid sequence (Tyrrell et al., 2025).

Fig. 15.2 displays Kubler-Ross's stages of dying.

This model is also crucial for understanding individuals' reactions and emotional states following traumatic events, such as landslides. Much like terminal illness, a landslide can force survivors to confront the sudden, devastating loss of life and property, leading them through similar stages of emotional turmoil. By recognizing these stages in the aftermath of such disasters, more empathetic and supportive responses can be provided to individuals, to help them navigate their grief and adjust to their new reality.

Psychosocial and Mental Health Services for Landslides

The National Institute of Mental Health and Neurosciences (NIMHANS) situated in Bengaluru has been responding to the mental health consequences of various disasters since the Bangalore circus tragedy in 1981. A similar approach has been adopted for landslides across the country over the past 15 years. NIMHANS's responses to disasters, including landslides, have evolved over time, shaped by lessons learned from its past experiences and the shifting landscape of disaster management. This evolution has seen a transition from a reactive response model to one emphasizing preparedness, alongside the decentralization of mental health treatment and the integration of mental health into public health frameworks.

Following the Malin landslide in 2014, an assessment was conducted to evaluate the psychological and social impacts on survivors, along with their need for long-term rehabilitation. The primary aim was to understand the immediate psychological consequences and identify the support required by affected populations. This assessment highlighted the critical importance of psychosocial care during the initial phase to restore psychological well-being (Mandal et al., 2015).

In the aftermath of the Uttarakhand disaster in 2013, the Government of India designated NIMHANS as the nodal agency to assess and coordinate psychosocial relief efforts (Channaveerachari et al., 2015). A multidisciplinary team was dispatched to the affected Himalayan regions to identify individuals in need of immediate intervention and evaluate psychiatric and psychosocial morbidity (Channaveerachari et al., 2015). The team conducted a comprehensive assessment during emergency relief work across the four worst-hit districts—Rudraprayag, Chamoli, Uttarkashi and Pithoragarh—, providing mental health care over a three-week period (Channaveerachari et al., 2015). They assessed populations through visits to district hospitals, Community Health Centers (CHCs), Primary Health Centers (PHCs), evacuation centers, relief camps, schools, and even remote villages (Channaveerachari et al., 2015). Community leaders played a crucial role in facilitating access to survivors, announcing the availability of mental health professionals in relief camps and villages (Channaveerachari et al., 2015). The team utilized the snowball technique to identify additional people in need through referrals (Channaveerachari et al., 2015). Diagnoses were made according to the International Classification of Diseases-10 (ICD-10) criteria, and informed oral consent was obtained from all participants (Channaveerachari et al., 2015). The assessment revealed that minor mental disorders formed the majority of the diagnoses (Channaveerachari et al., 2015). Additionally, only 2% of individuals developed disaster-induced psychiatric conditions, while the majority had pre-existing mental health conditions (Channaveerachari et al., 2015). The report underscored the critical shortage of mental health professionals and emphasized the need to implement the National Mental Health Program (NMHP) in every district (Channaveerachari et al., 2015).

The 2018 landslides in Idukki District, Kerala, resulted in 51 fatalities and an estimated destruction of ₹2.1 billion ($30 million). The following year saw a significant rise in mental health cases within the Idukki District Mental Health Program, with a 25% increase in patients compared to the previous year. Depression and anxiety were the most commonly reported conditions (Rajendran, 2019).

These experiences reflect a shift in approach from merely diagnosing the mental health consequences of disasters like landslides to actively providing basic mental health interventions. Thanks to the decentralization of mental health care, district mental health services under the National Mental Health Program are now able to provide timely treatment to those in need, which is a significant step forward in disaster-related mental health care as well.

In the recent past, on July 30, 2024, heavy rains triggered devastating landslides in Wayanad, Kerala, resulting in significant destruction and loss of life. In response to this disaster, NIMHANS, as the designated nodal centre for providing psychosocial support (PSS) during disasters, quickly mobilized efforts to aid the affected communities. The director of NIMHANS appointed two faculty members as the focal points for communication and coordination. The team from the Department of Psychosocial Support in Disaster Management (DPSSDM) from NIMHANS promptly developed and distributed Information, Education, and Communication (IEC) materials in Malayalam to provide guidance on mental health and psychosocial care.

On August 6, 2024, a webinar on "Management of Post-Traumatic Stress Disorder (PTSD)" was conducted at the request of the Ayurveda Medical Association of India (AMAI), Muvattupuzha, to help practitioners gain insights into managing PTSD. The session, which was attended by approximately 130 participants, covered effective strategies for identifying and managing PTSD symptoms in disaster survivors.

In collaboration with the Kudumbashree Mission, NIMHANS organized a two-day training workshop on psychosocial support for community counsellors in Wayanad. Held on September 24–25, 2024, in Kalpetta, the workshop was attended by 37 female professionals, including Kudumbashree Mission community counsellors, Snehitha counsellors, Snehitha service providers and Food, Nutrition and Health Worker (FNHW) resource people. These participants had direct experiences in disaster response. The topics covered in the session included, "Sharing of Experiences," "Impact of Disaster," "Stress Reactions," "Breath Retraining," and "Basic Counselling Techniques." The workshop aimed to enhance their capacity to deliver effective psychosocial care, ensuring they could provide structured and ethical mental health interventions while also focusing on self-care and resilience for the counsellors.

Meanwhile, another team from DPSSDM, NIMHANS conducted a series of field visits to the affected areas to assess the needs of the local population and propose a long-term engagement plan. Recognizing the urgent need for psychosocial care, the team worked to integrate mental health support into the broader relief efforts.

From August 4 to 6, 2024, the DPSSDM team visited relief camps across Wayanad to evaluate the immediate needs of affected communities. On August 7, 2024, a sensitization program and meeting were held at the Wayanad Collectorate. The discussions centered on the coordination and execution of relief and rehabilitation efforts, with an emphasis on psychosocial support (PSS) for the disaster-affected population.

On August 8, 2024, the team visited Meppadi, a region at the epicenter of the landslide disaster. On the same day, a crucial meeting was held at the Wayanad Collectorate to discuss both short-term and long-term psychosocial support plans. Representatives from the Kerala State Disaster Management Authority (KSDMA), the District Medical Officer, and nodal officers from various government departments collaborated to design a comprehensive mental health support strategy for the affected population. This was followed by a review meeting, where NIMHANS presented its psychosocial strategies and stressed the importance of interdepartmental collaboration for a coordinated recovery effort.

Earlier in the week, on August 6, coordination meetings with various stakeholders, including the Tribal Mental Health Project team, the District Mental Health Project team, NGOs like Sphere India, Reliance and HIS, as well as KSDMA officials and the Kudumbashree Mission team, were held to finalize the psychosocial support plans. These meetings ensured a smooth integration of mental health services into the relief operations.

As part of the training efforts, a series of orientation programs on psychosocial support were conducted. On August 8, an online session reached 265 participants; this was followed by additional training on August 12 (25 participants) and August 16 (40 participants). These sessions, in collaboration with the Kerala Association of Professional Social Workers and the Department of Psychiatry at Calicut Medical College, aimed to build the capacity of social workers, students, and faculty to address the mental health challenges posed by disasters.

The recovery process continued with full-day Stress Management Programs for community workers. On September 6, 2024, a session for 40 participants from Sreyas NGO was conducted in Wayanad, equipping psychosocial counsellors, school counsellors, *Anganwadi* workers, and supervisors with practical skills to support the mental well-being of the community. A similar program was held on September 7 for 50 participants at Harithagiri, Wayanad, reinforcing the importance of psychosocial care during disaster recovery.

Further enhancing professional capacity, NIMHANS hosted a three-day orientation program at IMHANS, Calicut, from September 9 to 11. It was attended by 35 participants and focused on psychosocial support in disaster management. Additionally, a three-day training workshop was organized from October 9 to 11, 2024, for MPhil trainees from IMHANS and social work students from Holy Cross College, Calicut. The workshop focused on psychosocial support, disaster management and mental health care, aimed at strengthening the skills of future professionals in addressing post-disaster mental health needs.

On September 12, 2024, a specialized orientation session was conducted for the Department of Psychiatry at Government Medical College,

Kozhikode. This session provided medical professionals with essential knowledge and strategies to tackle the mental health challenges faced by disaster-affected communities.

Through these extensive efforts, NIMHANS' DPSSDM team played a vital role in the immediate and long-term psychosocial care efforts in Wayanad, helping to ensure that mental health support was integrated into the overall disaster response. The team's early intervention, training programs and continuous liaison with government agencies and local organizations significantly contributed to the well-being and recovery of those affected by the 2024 Wayanad landslides.

Assessment of psychological and social impacts, long-term needs assessment, identification of individuals needing immediate intervention, evaluation of psychiatric and psychosocial morbidity, provision of mental health care, and training of local service providers were key actions taken by various NIMHANS teams post-disaster.

The National Mental Health Program and District Mental Health Program have been crucial in responding to landslides. These programs are effective as they enable local professionals to provide immediate support. They also ensure a steady presence of mental health professionals in districts and states, creating a valuable resource base, especially during disasters like landslides.

Over the years, the approach to psychosocial support post-landslides has evolved. Initially, the focus was on assessing impacts and needs. Now, specific interventions are delivered at different stages of recovery, either directly or through training local staff to provide continued support to affected communities.

Conclusion

Landslides have profound and lasting psychological impacts on survivors, leading to high rates of PTSD, depression, and anxiety. These mental health challenges are often more severe than those from other natural disasters, partly due to the traumatic nature of landslides. Vulnerability is heightened by risk factors such as gender, age, pre-existing mental health conditions, and a lack of social support. Additionally, socioeconomic factors like poverty and housing instability further complicate recovery, underscoring the need for targeted mental health interventions. The long-term effects of landslides can persist for decades, highlighting the necessity for ongoing psychological support. Social support plays a crucial protective role, as survivors with strong networks tend to experience better mental health outcomes. Therefore, effective disaster recovery must prioritize mental health services, strengthen community support, and address socioeconomic vulnerabilities to help survivors heal emotionally and rebuild their lives.

While significant efforts are being made to identify disaster-prone areas, assess landslide risks, and understand the causes behind the increasing frequency of landslides, equal priority must be given to addressing the mental health impacts on affected communities. Just as much attention is needed to ensure psychological support and intervention strategies are integrated into disaster preparedness and recovery plans.

As landslides become more frequent in India, special attention is needed to address the mental health challenges faced by survivors. Mental health initiatives post-disaster have evolved from simply assessing impacts to providing interventions and integrating mental health programs into broader public health efforts. However, there is still much progress to be made in ensuring these programs reach all affected districts across the country.

In the context of mitigation efforts, particularly planned relocations, place identity theory offers valuable insights into the psychological consequences of such interventions. While relocations may be necessary for safety, they can also disrupt survivors' sense of identity and belonging, making them harder to accept. Place identity theory highlights the emotional attachment people have to their homes and communities and understanding this attachment can help make mitigation strategies more acceptable and effective. By integrating these insights, future interventions can be better tailored to the needs and preferences of affected communities, ensuring both safety and psychological well-being.

Hence, it is crucial to integrate mental health expertise into landslide mitigation and recovery efforts. Just as we prioritize assessing risks and understanding the causes of landslides, equal emphasis must be placed on addressing the psychological impact on survivors. Mental health support should be a key component of disaster preparedness and recovery, ensuring that emotional well-being is prioritized alongside physical safety. Integrating psychological interventions into recovery plans, strengthening social support networks and addressing socioeconomic vulnerabilities are essential for helping survivors heal and rebuild their lives. By doing so, we can create more comprehensive and effective disaster response strategies that promote both physical and mental recovery.

References

Asnakew, S., Shumet, S., Ginbare, W., Legas, G., & Haile, K. (2019). Prevalence of post-traumatic stress disorder and associated factors among Koshe landslide survivors, Addis Ababa, Ethiopia: A community-based, cross-sectional study. *BMJ Open, 9*(6), e028550. https://doi.org/10.1136/bmjopen-2018-028550

Awasthi, S., Jain, K., Sahoo, S., Kumar, R., Goswami, A., Joshi, G. C., Kulkarni, A. V., & Srivastava, D. C. (2024). Analyzing Joshimath's sinking: Causes, consequences, and future prospects with remote sensing techniques. *Scientific Reports, 14*(1), 10876. https://doi.org/10.1038/s41598-024-60276-3

Barnagarwala, T. (2024, July 30). *Life in the shadow of deadly landslides.* Scroll.in. https://scroll.in/article/1055057/maharashtra-cant-stop-landslides-but-can-it-prevent-loss-of-life

Burrows, K., Desai, M. U., Pelupessy, D. C., & Bell, M. L. (2021). Mental wellbeing following landslides and residential displacement in Indonesia. *SSM—Mental Health, 1*, 100016. https://doi.org/10.1016/j.ssmmh.2021.100016

Caritas India. (2013, July 13). *Rapid assessment report of landslide and flash flood in Uttarakhand—India.* ReliefWeb. https://reliefweb.int/report/india/rapid-assessment-report-landslide-and-flash-flood-uttarakhand

Channaveerachari, N. K., Raj, A., Joshi, S., Paramita, P., Somanathan, R., Chandran, D., Kasi, S., Bangalore, N. R., & Math, S. B. (2015). Psychiatric and medical disorders in the after math of the Uttarakhand disaster: Assessment, approach, and future challenges. *Indian Journal of Psychological Medicine, 37*(2), 138–143. https://doi.org/10.4103/0253-7176.155610

Chopra, R. (2023, March 9). *Joshimath: An avoidable disaster.* The India Forum. https://www.theindiaforum.in/environment/joshimath-avoidable-disaster#:~:text=Calamity%20struck%20the%20Himalayan%20town,fields%20and%20buildings%20tilted%20dangerously

Global Report on internal displacement (GRID). (2024). IDMC—Internal Displacement Monitoring Centre. https://www.internal-displacement.org/publications/2024-global-report-on-internal-displacement-grid/

India Today. (2024, August 8). *Was attending to my sick children when I was swept away: Survivor recalls tragedy*. India Today. https://www.indiatoday.in/india/story/wayanad-landslide-survivor-recalls-tragedy-attending-sick-children-fever-swept-away-2579083-2024-08-08

Jain, N., Roy, P., Martha, T., Jalan, P., & Nanda, A. (2023). *Landslide atlas of India (mapping, monitoring and R&D studies using remote sensing data)*. NRSC special publication. NRSC/ISRO. Document number: NRSC-RSA-GSG-GMED-FEB2023-TR-0002167-V1.0.

Kabunga, A., Okalo, P., Nalwoga, V., & Apili, B. (2022). Landslide disasters in eastern Uganda: Post-traumatic stress disorder and its correlates among survivors in Bududa district. *BMC Psychology, 10*(1), 287. https://doi.org/10.1186/s40359-022-01001-5

Kennedy, I. T. R., Petley, D. N., Williams, R., & Murray, V. (2015). A systematic review of the health impacts of mass earth movements (landslides). *PLOS Currents Disasters*. https://doi.org/10.1371/currents.dis.1d49e84c8bbe678b0e70cf7fc35d0b77

Kunnathepeedikayil, S. (2020). *The long-term mental health consequences of floods and landslides in Thrissur District, Kerala, India*. Master's thesis, Harvard Medical School.

Mandal, P., Vigneshvaran, K., Kumar, S., & Sekar, K. (2015). Psychosocial impact on survivors of Pune landslide disaster: A qualitative study. *Indian Journal of Health and Wellbeing, 6*(7), 747–748.

Miranda, Á. S., du Parc, E., Benet, J., Kurkaa, M., & Fung, V. (2020, August 7). *Inclusive data on disaster displacement must include indigenous people*. IDMC—Internal Displacement Monitoring Centre. https://www.internal-displacement.org/expert-analysis/inclusive-data-on-disaster-displacement-must-include-indigenous-people/

National Disaster Management Authority (NDMA). (n.d.). *Getting a grip on landslides reducing the risk of landslides in India*. https://ndma.gov.in/sites/default/files/IEC/Booklets/LandslideRisk Reduction NDMA A5 BOOK.pdf

Rajendran, K. (2019, August 16). *In Kerala, doctors are helping survivors deal with the aftermath of disasters*. World Economic Forum. https://www.weforum.org/stories/2019/08/mental-health-support-natural-disasters/

Report of the Western Ghats Ecology Expert Panel. (2011, August 31). https://www.cppr.in/wp-content/uploads/2013/03/Gadgil-report.pdf

Sharma, A. (2016, June 23). *Risk of landslides drives migration—And mental health worries | Reuters*. https://www.reuters.com/article/us-india-disaster-health/risk-of-landslides-drives-migration-and-mental-health-worries-idUSKCN0Z917W/

The concept of "climate refugee"—Towards a possible definition. (2023, October). EPRS | European Parliamentary Research Service. https://www.europarl.europa.eu/RegData/etudes/BRIE/2021/698753/EPRS_BRI(2021)698753_EN.pdf

The Hindu. (2024, July 30). *Major landslides in India—A timeline*. https://www.thehindu.com/news/national/major-landslides-in-india-timeline/article68463802.ece

Tripathi, S. K. (2024, September 12). *Climate change, rapid infra growth behind rising landslide frequency in India*. India Today. https://www.indiatoday.in/environment/story/climate-change-rapid-infra-growth-behind-rising-landslide-frequency-in-india-2597760-2024-09-11

Turyasingura, B., Ayiga, N., Benzougagh, B., Kader, S., Singh, S. K., Bosco, N. J., Gweyi-Onyango, J. P., & Bojago, E. (2023). The complementary role of indigenous knowledge systems in landslide disaster management in Kanungu District, Uganda. *Nova Geodesia, 3*(4), 157. https://doi.org/10.55779/ng34157

Tyrrell, P., Harberger, S., Schoo, C., & Siddiqui, W. (2025). Kubler-Ross stages of dying and subsequent models of grief. In *StatPearls*. StatPearls Publishing. http://www.ncbi.nlm.nih.gov/books/NBK507885/

Wolfe, T. (2024, April 25). *Place identity theory—Examples and explanations*. Emotion Nest. https://emotionnest.com/place-identitytheory/

16

Community-Focussed and Digitally-Delivered Psychosocial Support Services During the COVID Pandemic: Experiences from a Tertiary Hospital

Ateev Sudhir Chandna
and Dinakaran Damodharan

Introduction

The COVID-19 pandemic emerged as a global medical disaster characterized by its sudden onset, unpredictability, and extensive impact on public health (Haileamlak, 2021, p. 19). The mental health repercussions of the COVID-19 pandemic were profound, marked by a significant increase in mental illnesses among the general population. Simultaneously, traditional in-person mental health services were severely disrupted due to lockdowns and social distancing measures. This created an immense challenge for tertiary hospitals, which had to address the growing demand

A. S. Chandna • D. Damodharan (✉)
Department of Psychosocial Support in Disaster Management, NIMHANS, Bengaluru, Karnataka, India

S. Bhadra et al. (eds.), *Psychosocial and Mental Health Support for Disaster Management in India*, Palgrave Studies in Disaster Science and Emergency Management,
https://doi.org/10.1007/978-3-032-02511-1_16

for psychosocial support despite stringent restrictions and limited resources (Byrne et al., 2021).

This chapter outlines the innovative strategies employed at a tertiary neuropsychiatry care hospital NIMHANS in the southern Indian state of Karnataka to meet the escalating psychosocial needs during the pandemic, with a focus on the development and implementation of telehealth services, outreach initiatives, and capacity-building programs.

The Impact of COVID-19 on Mental Health

The massive impact which the pandemic had on the mental health of the general populace has been well documented. Factors such as quarantine, isolation, physical distancing, job losses, and fear of infection contributed to a heightened vulnerability to mental health issues. Additionally, there was a significant disruption of daily life which cumulatively lead to increase in various mental health disorders like anxiety, depression, panic disorders, and substance abuse (Deng et al., 2021; Kshirsagar et al., 2021). The same was also observed in our tertiary care hospital where there was a significant rise in cases presenting with new-onset mental illness, subsyndromal psychiatric symptoms, and exacerbation of pre-existing conditions, necessitating the rapid expansion of mental health services (*Managing COVID-19 Patients with Mental Illness in a Specialized Neuropsychiatric Setting: An Experience from a Tertiary Care Hospital in India—PubMed*, n.d.).

Challenges Faced by the Hospital During the Pandemic

The hospital confronted several challenges, which plagued service delivery worldwide:

- Resource Constraints: With most resources diverted to manage COVID-19 cases, mental health services experienced limited availability, compounded by the nationwide shortage of mental health professionals, with their only being approximately 0.4 psychiatrists per 100,000 people (Garg et al., 2019).

- Access Barriers: Lockdowns and movement restrictions prevented patients from accessing in-person consultations, and there was a complete shutdown of Outpatient department (OPD) services, which requiring a urgent shift to telehealth services (Vyas et al., 2021).
- Increased Demand: The need for mental health services grew not only among the general public but also among healthcare workers who faced increased stress and burnout, which further compounded the problem of resource constraints (Menon et al., 2022).
- Technological Limitations: Many patients lacked access to digital devices and the internet, posing a barrier to effective telehealth adoption (Malathesh et al., 2021).

Development of Psychosocial Support Services

Assessment of Needs

Key areas of need were identified, and these included:

- Continuity of Care: For existing patients with mental health conditions.
- Emergency Mental Health Support: To address acute psychological distress, including conditions like severe depression, suicidality and acute agitation/aggression.
- Targeted Outreach: For vulnerable groups, such as quarantined individuals and healthcare workers.

Strategic Planning

The hospital's multidisciplinary team developed a strategic plan that focused on:

1. Shifting to Digital Platforms: To continue service provision, overcome access barriers and ensure infection prevention.
2. Strengthening Capacity: Through training programs for healthcare providers, as well as lay personnel.
3. Collaborations: NIMHANS collaborated with other tertiary centers, such as the Central Institute of Psychiatry, Ranchi, and LGBRIMH, Tezpur, to manage the national psychosocial support helpline. It also partnered with non-governmental organizations (NGOs), including Aapta Salaha Kendra and USAID, to conduct community outreach programs. Additionally, NIMHANS worked with government agencies and District Mental Health Programs (DMHPs) to ensure the consistent supply of psychotropic medications at the primary care level.

Establishment of the 24x7 Psychosocial Support Helpline (Sadh et al., 2023)

Infrastructure and Logistics

The hospital, alongside other stakeholders, launched a 24x7 helpline (080-4611-0007) for psychosocial support. It aimed to address psychological distress through a structured, multi-tiered model of care. Additionally, the helpline was structured to accommodate regional language preferences, ensuring accessibility across India.

Volunteer Training and Deployment

The NIMHANS tele-outreach helpline's success relied on a rigorous online training program for volunteers, who included mental health professionals, social workers, and lay counselors. Training emphasized Psychological First Aid (PFA) techniques, active listening, crisis intervention skills, and ethical considerations for telephonic interactions. Volunteers practiced delivering empathetic, culturally sensitive support, managing psychological concerns like anxiety and distress, and using referral protocols for cases needing specialized care. This training ensured consistency and quality in responses, enhancing the helpline's impact and caller satisfaction during the pandemic (Ibrahim et al., 2023).

Service Delivery Model

The helpline's structure included an Interactive Voice Response System (IVRS), which guided callers in multiple languages to connect them with available mental health professionals.

The helpline employed a tiered approach:

1. First-Level Support: Volunteers, including psychiatrists, psychologists, and social workers, initially assessed callers' concerns, providing empathetic listening and Psychological First Aid (PFA).
2. Second-Level Interventions: Cases requiring more intensive support were referred to specialists or local facilities, ensuring continuity of care.
3. Emergency Contacts: Connected callers with the nearest District Mental Health Programs (DMHP) for further care.

Implementation of Telepsychiatry Clinical Services

Transition from In-Person to Remote Consultations

As the OPDs were shut during the lockdown and there was difficulty in accessing the face-to-face services, telepsychiatry services became essential for ensuring continuity of care for patients who were consulting in NIMHANS. The hospital implemented telephonic and video consultations to manage follow-ups and new cases, with explicit consent obtained during prior in-person visits where possible. Efforts were made to use low-bandwidth platforms for teleconsultations and offer telephonic support as an alternative for those without internet access. To facilitate remote consultations, videoconferencing was employed for most of the consultations, while telephonic consultations were used when internet access was limited.

During the COVID-19 pandemic, the Telepsychiatric Aftercare Clinic (TAC) at NIMHANS played a crucial role in ensuring continuity of care for patients with psychiatric disorders. Established in 2017, the clinic significantly scaled its operations post-pandemic to address challenges such as travel restrictions and social distancing. Between December 2017 and December 2021, 1634 teleconsultations were conducted, with a sharp increase in sessions post-COVID (507 consultations from April 2020 to December 2021 compared to 213 pre-COVID). The average duration of consultations increased post-pandemic, reflecting the growing complexity of cases, with more patients presenting with psychiatric comorbidities like anxiety, depression, and psychosis.

The Telepsychiatric Extended Assessment (TEA) program at NIMHANS also emerged as a specialized initiative to provide detailed evaluations for new patients using live video-conferencing technology. Launched in December 2020, the Telepsychiatric Extended Assessment (TEA) program addressed the challenges of in-person consultations by facilitating comprehensive remote assessments. It also served as a valuable training tool for residents in digital psychiatry. Through this initiative, a total of 195 patients received care (Suchandra et al., 2021).

The use of teleconsultations not only improved accessibility for diverse socio-demographic groups, but also reduced cancellations, indicating higher patient satisfaction and acceptance (Paul et al., 2023).

Additionally, the hospital collaborated with DMHPs to provide medicines after tele-follow-ups, enabling patients to access necessary medications and local services without traveling long distances (Rahul et al., 2021).

Tele-Rehabilitation Services (Jayarajan et al., 2020)

During the COVID-19 pandemic, the hospital's community rehabilitation centre, the 'Sakalwara Community Rehabilitation Centre,' faced temporary closure due to safety concerns and restrictions on in-person services. To continue supporting patients, NIMHANS implemented tele-rehabilitation services, enabling remote consultations and online therapy sessions. Additionally, families were trained online to participate in rehabilitation exercises at home, promoting a holistic approach to patient recovery.

The nursing staff/Community Mental Health team conducted health education and recreational activities daily for 40 minutes/day on the online platform. More than 50% of previous inpatients of Sakalwara were contacted, with 747 classes successfully conducted, and a total of 2049 participants in the sessions.

Capacity-Building Initiatives

During the COVID pandemic, NIMHANS used the unique approach of leveraging digital technology to train Primary Care Doctors (PCDs) and Rural Medical Assistants (RMAs) in managing psychiatric disorders at the primary healthcare level.

For theoretical training, NIMHANS developed the 'Clinical Schedules for Primary Care Psychiatry' (Kulkarni et al., 2019), a seven-page tool designed exclusively for PCDs to provide first-line treatment for outpatients at PHCs, covering six illnesses using the TAPSAD (Tobacco Use Disorder, Alcohol Use Disorder, Psychotic Disorder, Anxiety Disorder, Depressive Disorder) approach and offering comprehensive A-to-Z guidelines, including diagnosis, investigation, treatment, referral, counselling, and follow-up.

Two unique practical approaches were also used:

Tele On-Consultation Training (T-OCT) and Collaborative Video Consultations (CVCs).

T-OCT focused on the real-time training of PCDs while they conducted consultations in their outpatient clinics (Manjunatha et al., 2021). Each session lasted between one and two hours, during which 15–20 patients were evaluated under the guidance of tele-psychiatrists. This hands-on approach enabled PCDs to gain practical skills in diagnosing and managing mental illnesses, thereby empowering them to deliver quality mental health care at the primary care level.

Collaborative Video Consultations (CVCs), on the other hand, provided immediate access to specialist advice for PCDs dealing with complex or challenging cases (Pahuja et al., 2020a). Available during working hours and for emergencies, tele-psychiatrists offered second opinions to the PCDs in real time through videoconferencing, ensuring accurate diagnosis and treatment. CVCs supported two key patient groups: those whose conditions required a more nuanced understanding for diagnosis and those whose management plans needed expert validation. This collaborative model significantly improved patient outcomes while reducing the need for referrals and travel.

There was a three-month certificate course which was exemplified by the training carried out with the Government of Chhattisgarh:

Chhattisgarh Community Mental Healthcare Telementoring Program (CHaMP) (Ibrahim et al., 2021)

The Chhattisgarh Community Mental Healthcare Tele-Mentoring Program (CHaMP) was an innovative initiative by NIMHANS, in partnership with the Government of Chhattisgarh, which aimed to bridge the significant mental health treatment gap in underserved areas. The program addressed the severe shortage of mental health professionals in the state by training PCDs and RMAs to identify and manage common psychiatric disorders. Using a structured, blended learning approach, CHaMP included two-day onsite training sessions and an eight-week digital mentoring phase through eLearning and skill development modules. It also featured Collaborative Video Consultations (CVC), where primary care providers sought expert guidance for complex cases. Between August 2019 and May 2020, the program trained 501 healthcare providers, enabling them to deliver mental health services to over 15,000 patients, significantly improving service delivery in remote and tribal regions (Fig. 16.1).

Incorporating principles of adult learning and community-driven approaches, CHaMP exemplified the potential of technology in healthcare capacity building.

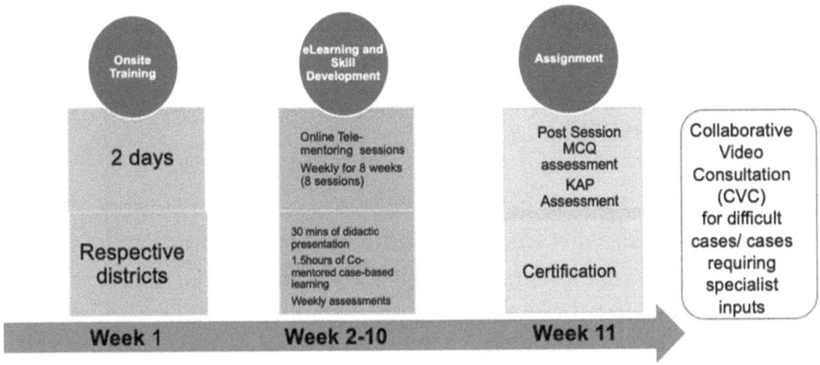

Fig. 16.1 CHaMP training

Beyond financial efficiency, CHaMP established itself as a replicable framework for integrating mental health into primary care, enhancing accessibility, and addressing the critical treatment gap in low-resource settings. Its success highlighted the potential for scaling this model to other states in India to ensure broader mental health service coverage (*Transforming Mental Healthcare*, n.d.).

There was also a more intensive one-year program in association with the governments of Uttarakhand and Bihar:

Diploma in Primary Care Psychiatry (DPCP) (Pahuja et al., 2020b)

This program similarly aimed to upskill primary care physicians in diagnosing and managing psychiatric conditions, bridging the gap in mental health services delivery.

There were similar teaching methods to the three-month course; however, there was a greater number of training hours, with each doctor on average undergoing 125 hours of training and more stringent requirements for accreditation at the end of the course.

A total of 40 doctors were trained through this program during this period.

Community Outreach Programs

Support for Quarantined Individuals and Migrant Workers (Ritish et al., 2020)

During the initial period of lockdown, there was a large number of international travellers who were stranded at special holding facilities. The hospital reached out to approximately 2200 quarantined air travellers in Bangalore, assessing them for common mental health issues and providing necessary interventions.

Upskilling Laypersons in Psychosocial Support (Philip et al., 2022)

The hospital, in collaboration with local counseling centers, aimed to equip volunteer laypeople with basic counselling skills to support communities during the pandemic.

This was an online training program designed for training lay counsellors in providing psychological first aid for the mentally distressed in the community. The program covered topics related to recognizing common psychiatric and mental health in the community, providing counselling and identifying potential cases for referrals to specialists.

During the pandemic, NIMHANS trained over 500 such lay counsellors.

Other Online Webinars and Workshops

NIMHANS also organized many other online webinars and workshops through the NIMHANS Digital Academy (NDA) to sensitize the general public, as well as to offer mental health support and wellness measures to special vulnerable groups during COVID. There were a total of 30,000 participants overall benefited from these training programs.

Advocacy and Contribution to National Guidelines

NIMHANS played a crucial role in shaping national mental health policies and guidelines in India. Recognizing the urgent need for structured and scalable mental healthcare delivery, NIMHANS collaborated with the Indian Psychiatric Society and the Telemedicine Society of India to develop the Telepsychiatry Operational Guidelines 2020 (Rina et al., 2021). These guidelines provided a comprehensive framework for remote mental healthcare, addressing essential aspects such as patient consent, privacy, data security, and the ethical responsibilities of mental health professionals. In addition to telepsychiatry, NIMHANS also developed guidelines for telepsychotherapy, telenursing, and telepsychiatric social work, thereby encompassing a holistic approach to mental health care delivery. These specialized guidelines ensured that diverse aspects of mental health services, including counseling, nursing interventions, and social work, could be delivered effectively and ethically via digital platforms.

Beyond guideline formulation, NIMHANS actively advocated for mental health awareness and capacity building during the pandemic. The institute organized nationwide webinars and training sessions for healthcare professionals to ensure the effective implementation of these guidelines. Additionally, it collaborated with governmental and non-governmental organizations to disseminate information on managing stress, coping with isolation, and addressing pandemic-related psychological issues. These efforts not only facilitated the seamless integration of telemedicine into India's mental health care framework but also ensured that mental health care remained accessible and prioritized during the crisis.

Outcomes and Impact of Interventions

Analysis of Helpline Usage and Feedback

The helpline addressed diverse mental health concerns, including stress, anxiety, and substance use disorders. The services were well-received, with callers expressing satisfaction and reduced distress after receiving support.

Statistics from the initial month demonstrated substantial usage, with 20,475 calls handled, including 7639 calls related to adults, 6991 concerning children, and 3288 from women. Specific groups, such as healthcare workers and the elderly, also used the helpline extensively, highlighting its accessibility and relevance across demographics. Feedback revealed over 90% caller satisfaction, affirming the helpline's efficacy in providing crisis support during the pandemic (Sadh et al., 2021, 2023).

Effectiveness of Telepsychiatry

Remote services effectively stabilized patients' symptoms and prevented relapses, reaching even those in remote and underserved areas.

The use of teleconsultations not only improved accessibility for diverse socio-demographic groups but also reduced cancellations, indicating higher patient satisfaction and acceptance.

The impact of TAC extended beyond clinical outcomes to significant logistical and financial benefits for patients. The program saved approximately 1,55,769 hours of travel time and over 8,300,000 kilometers in travel distance, translating into an estimated out-of-pocket expense saving of ₹14.5 crores (Das et al., 2020).

Capacity-Building Results

The CHaMP initiative significantly enhanced the accessibility and quality of mental health care in Chhattisgarh by training PCDs and RMAs to identify and manage psychiatric disorders at the primary care level. As of July 2021, all 28 districts in the state were covered, with more than 2300 hours of training delivered. Over 49,985 psychiatric consultations were self-reported from primary health centers (PHCs) following the training, demonstrating a substantial increase in mental health service delivery. CHaMP not only addressed the critical shortage of trained mental health professionals but also empowered local healthcare providers through innovative telementoring and collaborative models. Moreover, its cost-effective model demonstrated substantial economic benefits, with a return on investment of 386% (Ibrahim et al., 2021).

The Diploma in Primary Care Psychiatry (DPCP) implemented in collaboration with various state governments, aimed to upskill medical officers in diagnosing and managing psychiatric conditions at the primary care level. In Uttarakhand, the DPCP program trained two batches of medical officers, benefitting over 1529 patients through teleconsultation and collaborative video sessions. In Bihar, where mental health resources were critically limited, the DPCP program trained medical officers across 11 districts, resulting in 8037 patients receiving psychiatric care over the course of two years. By providing structured training and follow-up support, DPCP strengthened the capacity of District Mental Health Programs (DMHPs), ensuring sustained mental healthcare delivery in resource-constrained regions.

Studies also showed high skill uptake by doctors in both CHaMP and DPCP, highlighting the transformative potential of capacity-building initiatives in addressing the treatment gap for mental illnesses in India (Gajera et al., 2021; Jayasankar et al., 2022; Pahuja et al., 2020b).

Challenges Encountered and Lessons Learned (Malathesh et al., 2021)

During the COVID-19 pandemic, integrating technology into mental health capacity-building initiatives faced several challenges, particularly in our resource-constrained setting.

A significant issue was the digital divide, which restricted access to the internet and technological infrastructure, especially in rural areas. This limitation reduced the ability of healthcare providers to participate effectively in telementoring and online training programs, thereby hindering the reach and efficacy of these initiatives. Additionally, resistance to adopting new technologies among some healthcare professionals emerged as a major barrier. This resistance was often due to a lack of familiarity or confidence in using digital tools, which slowed the implementation of technology-driven mental health services (Suchandra et al., 2021).

Ensuring the quality and consistency of training delivered through digital platforms also proved challenging. Virtual environments struggled to maintain engagement and interaction, leading to concerns about the effectiveness of training outcomes. Data privacy and security issues further complicated the situation, as the rapid adoption of digital platforms raised questions about protecting patient confidentiality. These challenges underscored the need for robust infrastructure, comprehensive training of trainers, and ethical safeguards to ensure the success of technology-driven mental health initiatives during the pandemic.

Several administrative challenges also compounded the difficulties in integrating technology into mental health capacity-building efforts. Rapid implementation of telepsychiatry and digital training programs often lacked a coordinated strategy, leading to inconsistencies in execution. Many healthcare providers reported inadequate administrative support for scheduling, monitoring, and evaluating teleconsultations and training sessions, which affected the overall efficiency of these programs. Additionally, there was a lack of streamlined policies and protocols for telemedicine operations, resulting in confusion among providers about regulatory compliance and best practices (Choudhary et al., 2024).

Resource allocation also became a significant issue, as many healthcare systems prioritized immediate COVID-19-related needs over mental health services. This led to delays in funding, staffing, and logistical support for telepsychiatry initiatives. Moreover, ensuring timely supply of psychotropic medications at primary health centers was often disrupted due to administrative bottlenecks and supply chain interruptions (Rahul et al., 2021). These administrative hurdles highlighted the need for better planning, inter-agency coordination, and robust policies to sustain mental health services during public health crises.

Future Directions and Recommendations

The lessons learned from the COVID-19 pandemic have brought about transformative changes in mental healthcare practices and policies at our tertiary care hospital and at a national level.

During the pandemic, the rapid adoption of tele-mental health services ensured continuity of care for patients despite restrictions on movement and physical consultations. This innovative shift has continued post-pandemic, with teleconsultations becoming a regular part of care delivery. Supported by ongoing training programs and investments in digital infrastructure, NIMHANS has integrated telepsychiatry as a core component of its mental health services. This has led to a sustained increase in consultations over the years, far surpassing pre-pandemic numbers, demonstrating the scalability and long-term viability of telepsychiatry as a model of care (Paul et al., 2023).

In addition to maintaining these services, significant efforts have been directed toward capacity building and the development of contingency plans to prepare for future public health emergencies. These efforts have expanded beyond the hospital, encompassing all states in India through collaborations with state governments, the central government and NGOs like Goldman Sachs, and the Infosys Foundation (*Https://Ndanimhans.In/*, n.d.)

One of the most notable outcomes of the learnings from this pandemic has been the launch of the National Tele-Mental Health Program of India (Tele-MANAS). Building on the foundation of the psychosocial helpline established during the pandemic, Tele-MANAS has adopted a structured, tiered structure of 24x7 system of care that enhances accessibility and ensures free comprehensive mental health support for the population throughout the country (Sagar & Singh, 2022) (Fig. 16.2).

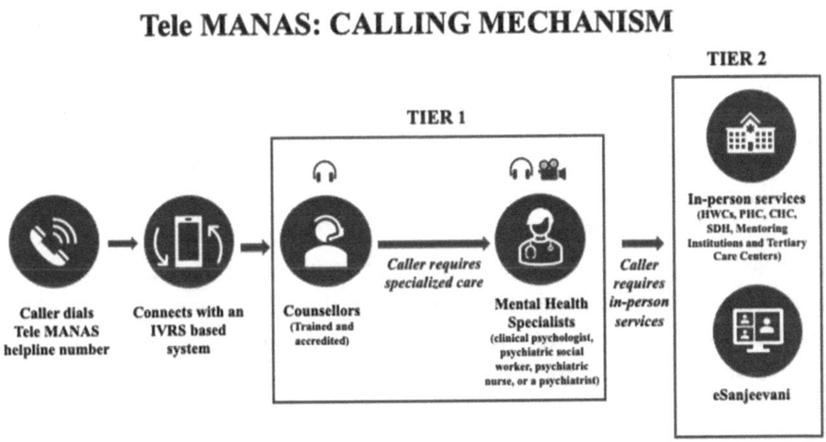

Fig. 16.2 Tele MANAS

Moreover, NIMHANS has engaged in extensive research programs that have validated the efficacy of digital training models and tele-mental health services in the community (Kumar et al., 2020; Nirisha et al., 2023). These studies have provided crucial insights into the effectiveness of telementoring in diverse settings and informed evidence-based enhancements to capacity building through online technologies.

Alongside these developments, the refinement of telemedicine guidelines has provided clear frameworks for specialists, enabling them to deliver high-quality care remotely while ensuring ethical and professional standards.

Collectively, these advancements represent a paradigm shift in mental healthcare delivery, positioning India as a leader in leveraging technology to address mental health challenges in response to large-scale disasters.

Conclusion

The COVID-19 pandemic underscored the necessity for innovative mental healthcare delivery methods, particularly during crises. At a tertiary care neuropsychiatry hospital like NIMHANS, this period catalyzed transformative changes in psychosocial support services, policies, and practices. Recognizing the rising demand for mental health interventions, compounded by resource constraints and access barriers, the hospital adopted a multifaceted approach to address these challenges. By shifting to digital platforms for telepsychiatry services, launching the 24x7 psychosocial support helpline, and liaising for medicine distribution with the district mental health programs, NIMHANS ensured continuity of care for diverse populations, particularly from vulnerable groups Collaborative efforts with other institutions, NGOs, and governmental agencies enabled the institute to mentor primary care practitioners in peripheral regions through innovative digital technologies. This initiative significantly enhanced capacity building and improved mental health accessibility in the most underserved areas.

The long-term impact of these measures has been profound, leading to the integration of tele-mental health services as a regular feature of care delivery. Initiatives like the National Tele-Mental Health Program

(Tele-MANAS), refined telemedicine guidelines, and capacity-building programs for healthcare professionals exemplify the scalability of these innovations. Moreover, the hospital's emphasis on research and feedback-driven improvements has validated the efficacy of telehealth models, paving the way for a more inclusive, accessible, and resilient mental health care system. These lessons have set the foundation for robust preparedness in future public health emergencies, highlighting the importance of adaptability and collaboration in overcoming unprecedented challenges.

References

Byrne, A., Barber, R., & Lim, C. H. (2021). Impact of the COVID-19 pandemic—A mental health service perspective. *Progress in Neurology and Psychiatry, 25*(2), 27–33b. https://doi.org/10.1002/pnp.708

Choudhary, S., Dutt, S., Torous, J., & Mehta, U. M. (2024). Bridging the mental health gap: The scope, challenges, and future of digital psychiatry in India. *Asian Journal of Psychiatry, 101*, 104215. https://doi.org/10.1016/j.ajp.2024.104215

Das, S., Manjunatha, N., Kumar, C. N., Math, S. B., & Thirthalli, J. (2020). Tele-psychiatric after care clinic for the continuity of care: A pilot study from an academic hospital. *Asian Journal of Psychiatry, 48*, 101886. https://doi.org/10.1016/j.ajp.2019.101886

Deng, J., Zhou, F., Hou, W., Silver, Z., Wong, C. Y., Chang, O., Huang, E., & Zuo, Q. K. (2021). The prevalence of depression, anxiety, and sleep disturbances in COVID-19 patients: A meta-analysis. *Annals of the New York Academy of Sciences, 1486*(1), 90–111. https://doi.org/10.1111/nyas.14506

Gajera, G., Malathesh, B. C., Nirisha, P. L., Kumar, C. N., Manjunatha, N., Suchandra, H. H., Ramachandraiah, S., Basavarajappa, C., Gowda, K. M. R., & Bada Math, S. (2021). Tele-mentoring and monitoring of the national mental health program: A bird's-eye view of initiatives from India. *Telehealth and Medicine Today*. https://doi.org/10.30953/tmt.v6.262

Garg, K., Kumar, C. N., & Chandra, P. S. (2019). Number of psychiatrists in India: Baby steps forward, but a long way to go. *Indian Journal of Psychiatry, 61*(1), 104. https://doi.org/10.4103/psychiatry.IndianJPsychiatry_7_18

Haileamlak, A. (2021). The impact of COVID-19 on health and health systems. *Ethiopian Journal of Health Sciences, 31*(6), 1073–1074. https://doi.org/10.4314/ejhs.v31i6.1

Https://ndanimhans.in/. (n.d.).

Ibrahim, F. A., Malathesh, B. C., Gajera, G., Pandey, P., Nirisha, P. L., Jyrwa, S., Kumar, C. N., Manjunatha, N., Jain, S., Bairy, B. K., & Bada Math, S. (2021). Chhattisgarh community mental healthcare tele-mentoring program (CHaMP): Digitally driven initiative to reach the unreached. *The International Journal of Social Psychiatry, 68*(5), 954–957. https://doi.org/10.1177/00207640211011191

Ibrahim, F. A., Sadh, K., Ravindran, S., Barikar, M. C., Nirisha, P. L., Reddy, P. B., George, S., Christopher, A. D., Damodharan, D., Manikappa, S. K., Roopesh, B. N., Kumar, C. N., & Sekar, K. (2023). Mental health concerns and their management among individuals reaching out to the national psychosocial helpline in India during COVID-19. *Indian Journal of Social Psychiatry, 39*(2), 178. https://doi.org/10.4103/ijsp.ijsp_83_21

Jayarajan, D., Sivakumar, T., Torous, J. B., & Thirthalli, J. (2020). Telerehabilitation in psychiatry. *Indian Journal of Psychological Medicine, 42*(5 Suppl), 57S–62S. https://doi.org/10.1177/0253717620963202

Jayasankar, P., Nirisha, P. L., Manjunatha, N., Kumar, C. N., Gajera, G. V., Malathesh, B. C., Pandey, P., Suhas, S., Ohri, U., Kumar, R., Bajpai, P., Kumar, R., & Math, S. B. (2022). Are the collaborative video consultations module in diploma in primary care psychiatry helpful. *Indian Journal of Psychiatry, 64*(Suppl 3), S516. https://doi.org/10.4103/0019-5545.341490

Kshirsagar, M. M., Dodamani, A. S., Dodamani, G. A., Khobragade, V. R., & Deokar, R. N. (2021). Impact of Covid-19 on mental health: An overview. *Reviews on Recent Clinical Trials, 16*(3), 227–231. https://doi.org/10.2174/1574887115666210105122324

Kulkarni, K., Adarsha, A. M., Parthasarathy, R., Philip, M., Shashidhara, H. N., Vinay, B., Manjunatha, N., Kumar, C. N., Math, S. B., & Thirthalli, J. (2019). Concurrent validity and interrater reliability of the "clinical schedules for primary care psychiatry". *Journal of Neurosciences in Rural Practice, 10*(3), 483–488. https://doi.org/10.1055/s-0039-1697878

Kumar, C. N., Chand, P. K., Manjunatha, N., Math, S. B., Shashidhara, H. N., Basavaraju, V., Thirthalli, J., Manjappa, A. A., Parthasarathy, R., Murthy, P., Ibrahim, F. A., Jagtap, N., Jyrwa, S., Reddy, S., Arora, S., Hawk, M., Kumar, S., Egan, J., & Mcdonald, M. (2020). Impact evaluation of VKN–NIMHANS–ECHO model of capacity building for mental health and addiction: Methodology of two randomized controlled trials. *Indian Journal of Psychological Medicine, 42*(6_suppl), S80–S86. https://doi.org/10.1177/0253717620969066

Malathesh, B. C., Ibrahim, F. A., Nirisha, P. L., Kumar, C. N., Chand, P. K., Manjunatha, N., Math, S. B., Thirthalli, J., Manjappa, A. A., Parthasarathy, R., Reddy, S., & Arora, S. (2021). Embracing technology for capacity building in mental health: New path, newer challenges. *Psychiatric Quarterly, 92*(3), 843–850. https://doi.org/10.1007/s11126-020-09859-7

Managing COVID-19 patients with mental illness in a specialized neuropsychiatric setting: An experience from a tertiary care hospital in India—PubMed. (n.d.). Retrieved November 22, 2024, from https://pubmed.ncbi.nlm.nih.gov/39387273/

Manjunatha, N., Sadh, K., Shashidhara, H., Manjunatha, B., Shashank, H., Ashwatha, K., Parthasarathy, R., Kumar, C., Bada Math, S., & Thirthalli, J. (2021). Establishing performance indicators of telemedicine-based "on-consultation training" of primary care doctors: An innovation to integrate psychiatry at primary care. *Indian Journal of Community Medicine, 46*, 75. https://doi.org/10.4103/ijcm.IJCM_223_20

Menon, G. R., Yadav, J., Aggarwal, S., Singh, R., Kaur, S., Chakma, T., Periyasamy, M., Venkateswaran, C., Singh, P. K., Balachandar, R., Kulkarni, R., Grover, A., Mishra, B. K., Viray, M., Devi, K. R., Singh, K. H. J., Saha, K. B., Barde, P. V., Thomas, B., et al. (2022). Psychological distress and burnout among healthcare worker during COVID-19 pandemic in India-A cross-sectional study. *PLoS One, 17*(3), e0264956. https://doi.org/10.1371/journal.pone.0264956

Nirisha, P. L., Malathesh, B. C., Kulal, N., Harshithaa, N. R., Ibrahim, F. A., Suhas, S., Manjunatha, N., Kumar, C. N., Parthasarathy, R., Manjappa, A. A., Thirthalli, J., Chand, P. K., Arora, S., & Math, S. B. (2023). Impact of technology driven mental health task-shifting for accredited social health activists (ASHAs): Results from a randomised controlled trial of two methods of training. *Community Mental Health Journal, 59*(1), 175–184. https://doi.org/10.1007/s10597-022-00996-w

Pahuja, E., Kumar, S., Kumar, A., Uzzafar, F., Sarkar, S., Manjunatha, N., Balhara, Y. P. S., Kumar, C. N., & Math, S. B. (2020a). Collaborative video consultations from tertiary care based telepsychiatrist to a remote primary care doctor to manage opioid substitution therapy clinic. *Journal of Neurosciences in Rural Practice, 11*(3), 498–501. https://doi.org/10.1055/s-0040-1713293

Pahuja, E., Santosh, K. T., Harshitha, N., Fareeduzaffer, Manjunatha, N., Gupta, R., Kumar, C. N., Math, S. B., & Chandra, P. S. (2020b). Diploma in primary care psychiatry: An innovative digitally driven course for primary care doctors to integrate psychiatry in their general practice. *Asian Journal of Psychiatry, 52*, 102129. https://doi.org/10.1016/j.ajp.2020.102129

Paul, J., Govindan, R., Vijayalakshmi, P., Kathyayani, B. V., Gandhi, S., Madegowda, R. K., Basavarajappa, C., Manjunatha, N., Kumar, C. N., & Math, S. B. (2023). An audit of initial six years of 5885 telepsychiatric direct video consultations: Findings from "benefits of savings" analysis and the effect of COVID-19 pandemic. *Indian Journal of Psychiatry, 65*(6), 611–616. https://doi.org/10.4103/indianjpsychiatry.indianjpsychiatry_131_23

Philip, S., Chander, K. R., Varshney, P., Patley, R., Pandey, P., Suhas, S., Nirisha, P. L., Suchandra, Vinay, B., Manjunatha, N., Kumar, C. N., & Math, S. B. (2022). The legality and ethical issues of certifying laypersons as mental health counselors in India. *Indian Journal of Psychological Medicine, 44*(6), 537–543. https://doi.org/10.1177/02537176221074253

Rahul, P., Chander, K. R., Murugesan, M., Anjappa, A. A., Parthasarathy, R., Manjunatha, N., Kumar, C. N., & Math, S. B. (2021). Accredited social health activist (ASHA) and her role in district mental health program: Learnings from the COVID 19 pandemic. *Community Mental Health Journal, 57*(3), 442–445. https://doi.org/10.1007/s10597-021-00773-1

Rina, K., Padhy, S. K., & Chadda, R. K. (2021). The Telepsychiatry Operational Guidelines 2020 in India: A welcome step. *BJPsych International, 18*, 1–3. https://doi.org/10.1192/bji.2021.20

Ritish, D., Dinakaran, D., Chander, R., Murugesan, M., Ibrahim, F. A., Parthasarathy, R., Pandey, P. K., Sharma, M. K., Pandian, D., Manjunatha, N., Reddi, S. K., Moirangthem, S., Kumar, C. N., Suresh, B. M., & Gangadhar, B. N. (2020). Mental health concerns in quarantined international air passengers during COVID-19 pandemic—An experiential account. *Asian Journal of Psychiatry, 53*, 102364. https://doi.org/10.1016/j.ajp.2020.102364

Sadh, K., Bhasker Reddy, P., George, S., Christopher, A. D., Mosale, A., Gupta, N., Raghunath, M., Devaki, N. S., Ravindran, S., Ibrahim, F. A., Nirisha, P. L., Malathesh, B. C., Dinakaran, D., Goyal, A. K., Manikappa, S. K., Christy, J., Roopesh, B. N., Sekar, K., & Kumar, C. N. (2021). Samaashraya: An initiative to address the COVID-19 and pandemic-related psychosocial and mental health concerns in India. *Indian Journal of Psychological Medicine, 43*(2), 181–183. https://doi.org/10.1177/0253717621988995

Sadh, K., Ravindran, S., Mosale, A., Christopher, A. D., Reddy, P. B., George, S., Gupta, N., Raghunath, M., Devaki, N. S., Ibrahim, F. A., Nirisha, P. L., Malathesh, B. C., Dinakaran, D., Goyal, A. K., Manikappa, S. K., Christy,

J., Roopesh, B. N., Sekar, K., & Kumar, C. N. (2023). National tele-helpline for psychosocial support and mental health services during COVID-19: An analysis of the feedback from the callers. *Indian Journal of Social Psychiatry, 39*(3), 303. https://doi.org/10.4103/ijsp.ijsp_8_21

Sagar, R., & Singh, S. (2022). National Tele-Mental Health Program in India: A step towards mental health care for all? *Indian Journal of Psychiatry, 64*(2), 117–119. https://doi.org/10.4103/indianjpsychiatry.indianjpsychiatry_145_22

Suchandra, H., Damodaran, D., Malathesh, B. C., Nirisha, P. L., Manjunatha, N., Kumar, C. N., Gajera, G., Ramachandraiah, S., Basavarajappa, C., Gowda, K. M. R., & Math, S. B. (2021). Telepsychiatry during the COVID pandemic: Reflection from India. *Telehealth and Medicine Today, 6*(2), 2. https://doi.org/10.30953/tmt.v6.263

Transforming Mental Healthcare: A Crude Return-on-Investment Analysis of the Chhattisgarh Community Mental Healthcare T…. (n.d.). Retrieved November 22, 2024, from http://ouci.dntb.gov.ua/en/works/7WAOpYrl/

Vyas, S., Sharma, N., Archisman, Roy, P., & Kumar, R. (2021). Repercussions of lockdown on primary health care in India during COVID 19. *Journal of Family Medicine and Primary Care, 10*(7), 2436–2440. https://doi.org/10.4103/jfmpc.jfmpc_1991_20

17

Raising Resilience: Empowering and Preparing Children in Times of Disaster through Psychosocial Support and a Preparedness Approach

Urmila Bamney, Sanjeev Kumar Manikappa, K. A. Tansa, Anil Hemanna Doddamani, and Kasi Sekar

Background

Disasters have occurred throughout human history. The term "disaster" is a broad one, encompassing a wide range of events, from natural events like earthquakes to intentional human acts of terrorism. A disaster is a rapid nd devastating occurrence that causes substantial harm, destruction, impairment, and havoc to both people and property. Disasters wreak unbearable harm and have an impact on the mental, financial, political, and cultural well-being of the impacted region. According to the definition by the World Health Organization (WHO), disasters are events that disrupt the

U. Bamney • S. K. Manikappa (✉) • K. A. Tansa • A. H. Doddamani • K. Sekar
Department of Psychosocial Support in Disaster Management, NIMHANS, Bengaluru, Karnataka, India

S. Bhadra et al. (eds.), *Psychosocial and Mental Health Support for Disaster Management in India*, Palgrave Studies in Disaster Science and Emergency Management,
https://doi.org/10.1007/978-3-032-02511-1_17

daily functioning of a community or society causing material, economic or environmental losses, and overwhelming the local capacity to cope. There are three types of disasters: natural disasters, man-made disasters, and hybrid disasters. Climatic and geophysical phenomena, such as high or low temperatures, floods, storms, earthquakes, tsunamis, volcanic eruptions, landslides, and drought, are typically linked to natural calamities. On the other hand, disasters caused by humans or technology are usually linked to a more difficult and drawn-out recovery process, particularly if those disasters are perceive as being foreseeable or controllable. A hybrid disaster is caused by human and natural forces, such as the eradication of a forest, resulting in a landslip. All forms of catastrophes may culminate in humanitarian emergencies because they typically affect large numbers of people.

In the past two decades or so, India has experienced several disasters, both natural and man-made. A National Portal of India study states that natural disasters continue to be a threat in 27 out of 36 states and union territories. Approximately 60% of the Indian landmass is vulnerable to earthquakes of varying magnitudes; more than 40 million hectares are at risk of flooding; cyclones can affect 8% of the entire area; and 68% of the country is vulnerable to drought. Natural disasters cause major loss of lives and ongoing incapacity as the result of serious injuries. Depending on the nature and magnitude of crises, their effect on human population, health, and facilities might vary, but the results may be significantly comparable. Over the period of the study, natural disasters have killed approximately 60,000 people per year. Developing countries suffer disproportionately due to poor finances and structures, and a lack of disaster-preparedness mechanisms. In numerous instances, financial operations cease, and the government must invest additional money to recover the losses and restore economic activity to normalcy.

Impact of Disasters

Physical Impact

Natural disasters have an impact on humans, whether direct or indirect, and can result in health problems, property destruction, and losses of human lives. They also carry certain intrinsic risks, such as damage to structures and the collapse of vegetation, which enhance the chances of injury for anyone directly exposed. Natural disasters can have an impact on the spread of already existing infectious illnesses.

Psychological Impact

The psychological consequences of an incident are felt by people before, during, and following the actual disaster event. According to the Global Burden of Disease survey, the prevalence of mental health issues is more than 10% throughout all continents. Disasters enhance the chance of adverse psychological outcomes, such as extensive post-traumatic psychopathologies.

Social Impact

Disasters contribute to the disruption of social networks, livelihoods, and social infrastructure. Disasters' social effects are also predicted to worsen, disrupting long-standing social, economic, and cultural norms because of relocation, resettling, and migration. The disturbances to social networks, their livelihoods, and the social structures can all be crucial components in this context.

Economic Impact

Disasters also affect the economy, both directly and indirectly. Direct consequences happen when a natural disaster immediately damages resources (like property), with damages happening at the scene of the disaster or soon after. The loss of homes, enterprises, infrastructure, productive capital, crops, animals, and (monetized) effects on physical and mental health are a few instances of direct economic losses. Indirect effects, or shifts in the economy after the accident, might result from the direct effects. This involves disruptions in financial activity as well as any favorable repercussions brought on by production substitution and reconstruction requirements.

Understanding Vulnerabilities in Disasters

Vulnerability is the characteristic of a person or group and their situation that influences their capacity to anticipate, cope with, resist, and recover from the impact of a natural hazard (Wisner et al., 2003). Vulnerability is the degree to which a population is susceptible to negative consequences because of being exposed to dangerous circumstances. It has an immediate effect on disaster response, recovery, and preparedness. Disaster vulnerability is significantly associated with property damage and human losses, and high levels of vulnerability might result in higher destruction or a longer period of recovery. Vulnerability is generally regarded as a condition that can be reduced via preparedness. This entails learning to recognize dangers, developing coping mechanisms, and obtaining the material resources needed for survival. People are perceived as being significantly less vulnerable if they have made the required disaster planning, either on their own or in collaboration with their communities.

Vulnerability is determined by historical, political, cultural, institutional, and natural resource processes that impact the lives of individuals which can result in various kinds of underlying vulnerabilities. This includes living in disaster-prone areas or substandard housing, as well as illness, political conflicts, and a lack of local institutions or emergency preparedness. Vulnerable populations include women, children, youth, senior citizens, individuals with impairments or chronic medical conditions, migrants, ethnic minorities, Indigenous peoples, and sexual minorities. Fig. 17.1.

Children's Vulnerability in Disasters

Natural disasters, such as floods, cyclones, droughts, heatwaves, severe storms, and earthquakes, are estimated to impact 175 million children worldwide per year. Children, especially the younger ones who rely on adults either completely or to some extent, are highly vulnerable and comprise a major portion of those who suffer devastating long-term impacts of disasters. Children and adolescents are more

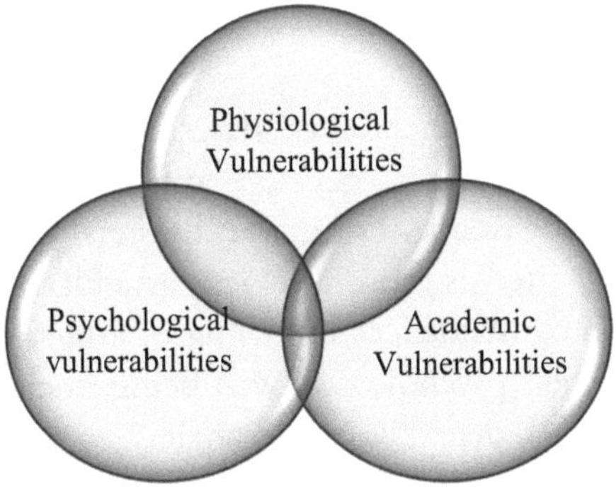

Fig. 17.1 Vulnerability factors among children

likely to be traumatized by a disaster because they are more prone to be seriously injured, possess a limited awareness of safety practices, and have lesser comprehension of the situation. They are more vulnerable to emergencies and face additional challenges with their physical and mental well-being, and schooling after stress.

Physiological Vulnerabilities

Children may be particularly vulnerable to disasters as a result of physiological factors. Their immune systems are fragile, their breathing patterns are faster, and their bodies are still growing and developing. They are more likely to be killed or harmed than adults and are often more sensitive to health issues, infections, and starvation. Children may also acquire hunger, thirst, and weariness faster than adults, and they are more susceptible to infectious infections. For instance, in the aftermath of floods, people might develop physical health issues such as colds, influenza, sore throats, skin rashes, gastrointestinal illnesses, chest disease, hypertension, and asthma, leading to mental stress.

Psychological Vulnerabilities

The term "psychological vulnerability" describes how vulnerable individuals and communities are to negative psychological and emotional impacts brought on by frequent or major disasters. Children and adolescents are frequently cited as those who are particularly vulnerable and at risk of unfavorable consequences following disasters, with indicators of adverse effects on their psychological well-being, such as post-traumatic stress disorder (PTSD), depression, and anxiety.

Academic Vulnerabilities

A vital human right and a major factor in determining one's quality of life is having access to high-quality education. Natural disasters have a detrimental effect on the educational system through interfering with regular operations. Disasters can disrupt the education of children by demolishing schools, relocating families, demolishing schools, and forcing them into the workforce to support their families during difficult times. Sometimes children may not go to school as frequently or may do worse academically if they are injured, ill, or undernourished because of disasters. In countries like India, families might often choose to take their children out of school and direct them into the workforce to increase family income in the aftermath of an adverse event or disaster.

Developmental Stages of Children and Their Response to Disasters

Infants and Toddlers

From birth, human infants are highly dependent on their parents. Toddlerhood, which lasts roughly from 15 to 36 months, is a time of transition and change that connects infancy to early childhood. Due to their cognitive limitations, at this age children do not comprehend the concept of disasters and their causes. In addition, they are extremely sensitive to modifications in their surroundings and caregivers' behavior, which can cause discomfort among infants and toddlers. A sense of security is based on the relationship with primary caregivers. Disruptions to this bond due to the death or relocation of parents or caregivers can cause profound distress. Therefore, these development phases make infants and toddlers more vulnerable during disasters and emergencies because they rely primarily on parents or caregivers for safety, emotional stability, and fundamental needs.

Early Childhood

A child's cognitive abilities, and their social, physiological, and emotional growth, is most crucial during the initial eight years of life. During the period of early childhood, the children's mental abilities rapidly increase as they learn to analyse, solve problems, and communicate. The ability to regulate emotions is still evolving. Children rely on caregivers to help them manage and understand their emotions. Motor abilities are growing, allowing for greater independence in activities such as running, sketching, and construction. During calamities, they remain physically vulnerable to injury or sickness. During disasters, children of pre-school age depict behavioral changes like thumb-sucking, bed-wetting, temper tantrums, and irritability. There are also somatic symptoms like headache or stomach ache.

Middle Childhood

Middle childhood is the stage of development which starts when children enter school and continue until they reach adolescence. According to Piaget, children in middle childhood begin a new phase of cognitive development in which they are enhancing their logical abilities. During middle childhood, children enhance both their short-term and their long-term memory. Children can use reasoning to overcome issues based on their personal knowledge, but they struggle with hypothetical challenges and abstract concepts. Children during middle childhood can understand the causal relationships and connections, which may help in grasping the fundamental concepts of disasters, even if the understandings remain basic or real. They also depict higher levels of curiosity and ask various questions about the emergency event. Although their emotional regulations is improved in comparison with early childhood, children may continue to have trouble with complicated emotions like fear, grief, and anxiety. From a social development point of view, children develop peer relationships, which become significant because they offer comfort and a means of processing common experiences.

Adolescence

Adolescence is a phase of transformation between childhood and adulthood. Children approaching adolescence have numerous physiological and cognitive changes. Adolescents surpass boundaries and can consider whatever might be real, rather than what they see as real. They can work with abstract concepts, test theories, and visualize endless possibilities. Adolescents also grow socially during this period. The most crucial aspect of adolescent social development is a need for individuality. Adolescents' experiences in disasters are typically ones of widespread loss. The death of family members, destruction of homes, loss of valuable things, and displacement from society are all linked to a loss of opportunity, order, and learning. During calamities, adolescents frequently demonstrate a combination of adult resiliency and juvenile vulnerability. Their reactions are determined by their surroundings, the assistance they receive, and their coping techniques. Adolescents depict emotional responses such as high sensations of fear, rage, or grief that are frequently accompanied by a loss of control. Disasters can also significantly disrupt the behavior of adolescents by increasing resistance, especially when there is no formal direction, as well as disengagement from social networks and peer interactions. Stress-induced headaches, exhaustion or irregular sleep patterns, alterations in appetite, and injuries are the somatic responses to disasters.

Understanding Children's Need During Disasters: A Comparison with Maslow's Hierarchy of Needs

Most citizens in regions in developing countries are children, who are frequently the first casualties of disasters. During disasters, they may experience fear and exhibit transient behavioral changes. They could be afraid of things they do not comprehend, and their misunderstandings could result in incorrect responses and judgments. Children may be put in danger if their special requirements are not met before a crisis strikes, which could lead to morbidity and physical and emotional stress for both the children and their carers. The needs of children during the disaster can be well understood from the viewpoint of Maslow's hierarchy of needs. This was initially presented by Abraham Maslow in his 1943 paper "A Theory of Human Motivation," as well as in his later book *Motivation and Personality*. Maslow's hierarchy of needs is a psychological theory of motivation that consists of a five-level representation of human needs, which is sometimes represented as a pyramid with layers. The hierarchy has five levels: self-actualization, esteem, safety, love/belonging, and physiological. Before meeting higher demands, lower-level necessities such as food, water, and safety are required to be satisfied, as shown in Fig. 17.2.

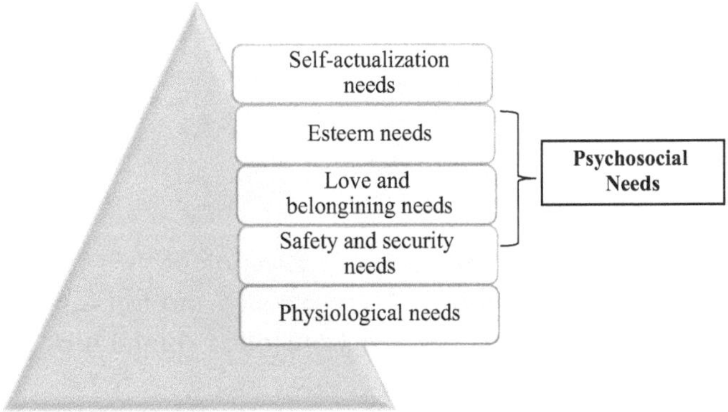

Fig. 17.2 Needs of children during disasters

Physiological Needs

Children are more vulnerable to disease or injury in an emergency because their bodies are smaller and less developed. Disasters can disrupt food supplies, access to clean and safe drinking water, weather-appropriate clothing, medical care, sanitation, and hygiene. Children require adequate nutrition, which is necessary for their growth and vitality. Dehydration and water-borne illnesses like diarrhoea, which can be devastating for children during emergencies, can be avoided with access to clean and safe drinking water. Disasters can lead to injuries, which should be treated appropriately by trained healthcare providers in order to prevent problems and encourage healing. In disaster-affected communities, having adequate restrooms and laundry facilities is essential for preserving cleanliness and stopping the spread of illnesses among children. Post-disasters, the children should be encouraged to get back to their routine and they require quiet locations to get enough sleep and recover from the strain of the calamity.

Safety and Security Needs

Throughout disasters, children confront a variety of security and safety challenges. Their susceptibility, reliance on adults, and the unpredictability of crisis circumstances are the causes of these difficulties. During disasters, children are vulnerable in terms of displacement, exploitation, abuse, or trafficking. The children should be placed in evacuation centers with safe infrastructures.

Love and Belonging

Disasters adversely impact the care and affection of their parents, teachers, and peers. Feelings of uncertainty, anxiety, and fear can result from losing one's home, being uprooted from one's community, and being separated from loved ones.

Self-Esteem Needs

According to the Maslow model, a person's esteem requirements might involve feeling empowered, assured, and competent, as well as feeling deserving of respect and appreciation. For a while after experiencing trauma, people frequently must put their physical existence needs—the lowest levels of the hierarchy—above their emotional health and esteem. Survivors frequently experience emotions of insignificance or neglect and the responsibilities that survivors play as workers, carers, or community leaders might be taken away by disasters.

Psychosocial Needs of Children During Disasters

Children need urgent care for their physical, mental, and emotional health since they are among the most vulnerable groups during emergencies. Prioritizing their fundamental needs—food, clean water, shelter, and medical attention—will help them survive and avoid becoming ill from malnutrition, dehydration, and other conditions. In displacement situations, it is also essential to provide safe spaces or reunite them with carers to ensure their safety. Initial intervention is crucial because a lack of these basic needs can result in higher trauma and adverse health outcomes over time. Children need more than just physical assistance; they also need mental and behavioral help to deal with the fear, unpredictability, and distress that come with emergencies. They frequently experience increased anxiety, fear, bewilderment, and sadness because of abrupt life changes, the death of a family member, being uprooted, or being exposed to stressful circumstances. Children require secure environments in which they can process what they have experienced, vent their emotions, and get comfort from trustworthy adults and carers. To help children rebound from the effects of disasters and avoid long-term psychological distress, these needs must be addressed.

Psychosocial Support and Resilience During Disaster

When emergencies strike, they may aggravate mental health problems by adding the cost of relocation, grief, and limited availability of resources, ultimately resulting in emotional distress and increasing the likelihood of mental health conditions over time. The capacity of the disaster survivors to sustain themselves is overburdened by the loss and stress that come with the crises, resulting in feelings of sadness, regret, humiliation, worry and grief. Prolonged social structures, and local societal networks, may fail to function properly, destroying the psychological and social issues of the individuals, families, and communities. Early detection of problems and the rapid recovery for those impacted are made possible by prompt mental health intervention or psychosocial support programs Mental Health and Psychosocial Support (MHPSS) | Epidemic Control Toolkit, n.d.).

The concept of "psychosocial" implies an interrelationship between an individual's psychological and social aspects, which influence each other, as depicted in Fig. 17.3. Psychosocial support helps recovery from a crisis. The Psychosocial Framework of 2005–2007 of the International Federation defines psychosocial support as "a process of facilitating resilience within individuals, families and communities." The spectrum of psychosocial support includes fostering regular, supportive relationships with caregivers, peers, teachers, healthcare providers, community

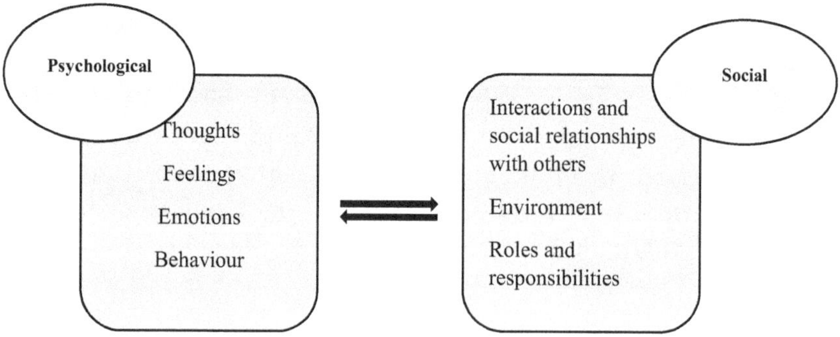

Fig. 17.3 The concept of psychosocial support

members, and access to specialized psychological and social services, all of which help individuals, families, and communities build resilience and cope with challenges.

Disaster resilience refers to a community's potential to withstand calamities, minimize destruction, and maintain physical, social, and psychological capacity. Resilience is a psychosocial concept typically defined as an individual's adaptive qualities which enable them to deal with and overcome difficult circumstances. According to resilience studies, the degree of exposure to a negative incident can affect both immediate and long-term physical and mental health effects. Resilience is frequently thought of consisting of two aspects: (1) going through adversity, which may be operationalized in various ways, including floods and wars; and (2) emerging on top despite the risks mentioned. Resilience is influenced by a variety of socioeconomic (social justice, fairness of opportunity), familial (parenting relationships, support from outside the family), and individual (e.g., personality, adaptability skills) factors. On the other hand, resilience is attained by perseverance, self-improvement, effective coping, and positive emotions and moods. Resilient children are more inclined to bounce back and thrive in healthy, fulfilling lives because they can better manage the psychological and physical strain that disasters can cause. Children and adolescents are not just the survivors of disasters; rather, they contribute and play an active role in disaster risk reduction, by collaborating with various governmental and non-governmental activities, offering unique abilities, and personal experiences, and focusing on solving problems and ideas.

Children in Disaster Risk Reduction

The United Nations organizations are placing a greater emphasis on disaster risk reduction, or disaster risk reduction (DRR). DRR is a strategy that is distinct from standard disaster management strategies since it attempts to mitigate the related risk by anticipating the potential consequences of disasters and planning for, or responding to, them. The Sendai Framework for Disaster Risk Reduction 2015–2030, offers a global roadmap of action for minimizing the risk of disaster and boosting resilience, which is directly related to DRR (Admin, 2022). Disaster risk reduction

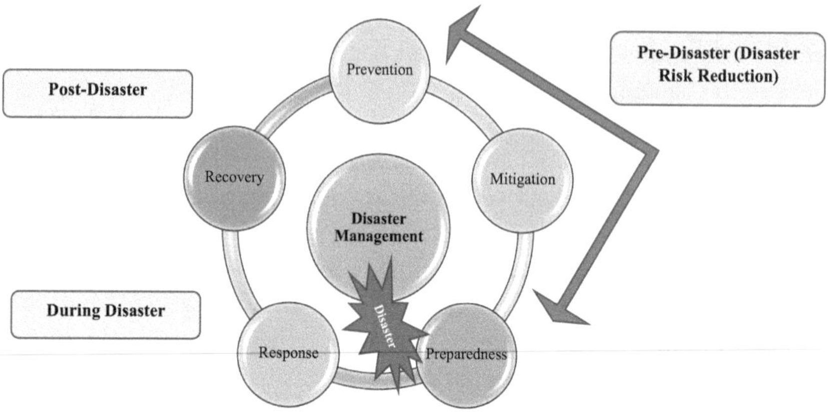

Fig. 17.4 Phases of disaster with DRR

aims to prevent future disasters, reduce existing disasters, and manage residual risk, all of which help to increase resilience and so achieve sustainable development, as presented in Fig. 17.4.

Key Phases of Disaster Management

Pre-Disaster Pre-disaster actions include preparedness, prevention, and mitigation. The goal of prevention is to protect people from impending natural disasters or terrorist attacks (both physical and biological). Planning, organizing, training, equipping, exercising, assessing, and corrective action are all ongoing cycles of preparedness.

During disasters The most crucial tasks during a disaster are response and relief. These activities, carried out immediately after a disaster, are known as the disaster-response phase." To provide essential services to those impacted, response efforts should be started as soon as possible; otherwise, people's suffering would worsen. A response strategy should be created before the disaster strikes to prevent delays.

Post-Disaster The three main post-disaster efforts are recovery, reconstruction, and rehabilitation. Restoring a certain level of normalcy in the impacted area is the goal of the post-disaster phase of disaster management. After the response phase, the goal of recovery is to rebuild and strengthen resilience. It is when restoration attempts coexist with normal operations and activities.

Role of Children in Disaster Risk Reduction

Children and youth are more than just disaster victims. They can actively contribute to risk reduction by working with authorities and humanitarian organizations. The involvement of children contributes to the systematic addressing of the threats to their survival and welfare.

Spreading awareness A key component of social and economic development, disaster risk reduction is necessary for long-term, sustainable development. Effective risk communication, as well as education, are crucial for achieving the Sustainable Development Goals. Children who get empowerment, especially through education, might be better able to safeguard themselves and, by passing on whatever they have acquired in the classroom, they become catalysts for change in their homes and neighborhoods. Disaster Risk Reduction Knowledge is valuable for all age groups, in addition to throughout the school years. Engagement can lead to long-term benefits such as thinking critically, problem-solving, empowerment, and responsible governance.

Practical school-based disaster risk reduction programs Disaster risk reduction and resilience education (DRRRE) for children is an important undertaking related to their existence; children must first comprehend the potential threats in their community. Engaging in experiential learning may assist children in comprehending local dangers by letting them explore how the social and natural features of their community might result in different levels of hazard exposure. Performing frequent emergency drills is a crucial approach for schools to build emergency response skills and increase knowledge of the importance of assessment, preparation, and minimizing risk.

Community-based disaster risk reduction A participatory strategy called community-based disaster risk reduction (CBDRR) aims to tackle the factors that influence disaster risk reduction and the development of societal resilience locally. It is an approach to risk analysis and management that comes from, and is coordinated by, local communities. Children's understandings and skills are developed through instruction and practical hazard vulnerability and capacity analysis (HVCA) approaches, empowering them to evaluate and track their communities' risks, hazards, vulnerabilities, and capacities. Children and adolescents may assist with organizing and implementing initiatives by taking part in HVCA.

Children's participation in disaster preparedness The United Nations International Strategy for Disaster Reduction stated in 2011 that children are "the group most affected by disasters each year." This encouraged them to get involved in disaster risk reduction initiatives. Although children experience various emotional and behavioral effects because of disasters, children are also catalysts for bringing out creative changes and play a crucial role in reducing the risks of disasters. The first step in disaster risk reduction is to increase children's involvement in disaster response. Children will be more equipped to handle disasters if they are explicitly taught disaster information and skills. It is important to involve children in disaster risk reduction at a young age. Developing children's disaster-reduction readiness takes time and involves progressive development. Teachers and child-care professionals can involve children in creating a disaster kit and creating a school evacuation route to teach them the fundamentals of remaining protected in an emergency. Parents may additionally assist by adjusting the activity and discussion to the age and development stage of the child. This involves strengthening practices that help children feel safe and involved.

Psychosocial Preparedness for Children

Emotional regulation The human experience is incomplete without emotions, which influence our responses, choices, and general well-being. As a result of their experiences during a crisis, children and adolescents are particularly susceptible to emotional distress. Children require the assistance of adults in "co-regulating" their feelings through their interactions with secure and caring adults. Yet the way in which children react to a disaster can vary greatly based on several factors, including: (1) the degree to which they were exposed to the event; (2) the level of support received simultaneously with and after the disaster; and (3) the degree of social upheaval as well as private loss. Children frequently use their actions to express when they need assistance with emotional management.

Coping skills Coping skills are methods individuals use to deal with dangerous or stressful circumstances. It is a phrase used specifically to describe the conscious and deliberate mobilization of actions, as opposed to "defence strategies," which are responsive automatic or unintentional reactions that both seek to lessen or accept stress. Children who have direct experience with loss and devastation may find it distressing and require reassurance that grieving is acceptable, as well as encouragement to express about their emotions. Children may have worries that are difficult to articulate. As discussed above, the age of the children may affect how they behave, but there are certain typical ways in which they deal with stress. The ideal method for parents and other adults to support children is when they have learnt coping mechanisms and are aware of their own emotions. Forming and utilizing networks of friends, family, community organizations, religious institutions, and other resources, offering comfort, upholding a schedule, promoting candid dialog, and restricting media exposure can help children learn effective coping mechanisms throughout as well as following disasters.

Impact of COVID-19 Pandemic on Underprivileged Children

The COVID-19 pandemic has had a worldwide effect on many aspects of life, with socioeconomic implications in addition to its immense effect on medicine and healthcare, further contributed to a significant loss of life on a global scale and poses an unparalleled public health problem in addition to causing economic and social upheaval. COVID-19 affected family life in various ways, including occupations, unstable finances, psychological wellness, children's schooling, family well-being, and interpersonal resilience. However, children and adolescents are not at a significant risk of spreading infection, and, if children do get ill, the effects will probably be minor. Yet there were significant concerns about the pandemic's biopsychosocial impacts.

The implementation of the quarantine policy worldwide was to stop the spread of the contagious virus, but this created a blockage in the daily routine of the children. The children encountered unexpected situations because of the epidemic, including the shutdown of schools, the relocation of classes to internet-based venues, and the lack of opportunities to contact their peers. Scholastic activities were conducted via the internet mediums, so the children had to thrive on smartphones, tablets, and PCs. Following initiatives by governments and schools to replace classroom instruction with online learning methods, the United Nations International Children's Emergency Fund (UNICEF) reports that over 1.6 billion children have lost their education because of school closures. The school modifications not only increased hours spent indoors but also had a detrimental effect on children's physical activity rates, and influenced both children's and their parents' mental health. Depression, anxiety, ambiguity, loneliness, excessive screen time, and parental exhaustion have all damaged children's emotional well-being.

The survey showed that the COVID-19 pandemic has had a disproportionately negative impact on children and adolescents from lower socioeconomic backgrounds, most disadvantaged groups of children, primarily children with disabilities, children from relocated families, children from impoverished homes, children in larger family units, and children in households with only female carers. The closure of schools worsened malnutrition. Many students with low incomes consider schools not only an opportunity to acquire knowledge but also a chance to consume foods healthily. Additionally, the school closure enabled children to attend classes from home and the living circumstances that children face in low-income families make this difficult. Typically, computers and reliable access to the internet are needed in virtual classroom situations during such situations. Due to a lack of digital equipment and internet connection, many disadvantaged children are unable to participate in online learning.

Children from impoverished backgrounds are more susceptible to abuse and mental health problems because of their parents' or their guardians' lack of income or loss of employment during the COVID-19 lockdown, as well as dealing with adverse socioeconomic and environmental factors. The volume of child abuse instances recorded worldwide has increased alarmingly amid the pandemic when the standard precautions for children were seriously undermined. Furthermore, because they were confined to their abusive homes, children from violent or dysfunctional families were more likely to experience maltreatment because of school closures. Children who were orphaned were especially susceptible to human trafficking and other forms of abuse, such as forceful extortion, sexual assault, and other forms of child labor. To help their younger siblings, older children frequently drop out of school. Child labor and child marriage rates were probably going to rise because of the COVID-19 crisis's worldwide economic collapse, which included a significant loss of jobs worldwide.

NIMHANS Interventions for Children After the COVID-19 Pandemic

The COVID-19 pandemic posed significant problems to mental health and well-being, especially for children and communities with vulnerabilities. Recognizing the critical need for psychosocial assistance, the Department of Psychosocial Support in Disaster Management (DPSSDM) at NIMHANS contributed significantly to pandemic recovery initiatives by recognizing the core psychosocial issues among the children and designed interventions centered on student enrichment, mental health awareness, and resilience building. SOS Children's Village is a global non-governmental organization dedicated to supporting children without parental care and also those at risk of losing it. It provides a family-like environment where children receive education, healthcare, and emotional support to ensure their overall well-being. Recognizing the impact of the COVID-19 pandemic on children's mental health and education, SOS Children's Village partnered with DPSSDM and NIMHANS to implement the Student Enrichment Programme (SEP) and Life Skills Education (LSE) for children belonging to vulnerable communities in Bengaluru and other districts of Karnataka.

Life Skills Education (LSE)

Life skills is a term used to describe a set of basic skills acquired through learning and/or direct life experience that enable individuals and groups to effectively handle issues and problems commonly encountered in daily life. Life skills are a collection of cognitive, psychosocial, and decision-making skills that enable children to effectively communicate, control their emotions, and make wise decisions. There are many different types of life skills, and their definitions and characteristics will probably vary depending on the culture and context. Ten fundamental life skills that assist individuals with overcoming obstacles in life have been recognized by the World Health Organization (WHO). The life skills education offered by the WHO includes problem-solving, decision-making, critical thinking, creative thinking, effective communication, interpersonal relationships, empathy, coping with stress, and coping with emotions.

Life Skills Education in Disaster Context

Education in life skills is crucial in crises because it gives people—children and adolescents in particular—the skills they need to cope with stress, make wise decisions, and adjust to changing conditions both during and after disasters. To improve resilience and readiness, it incorporates critical thinking, emotional control, problem-solving, and interpersonal skills.

Problem-Solving

Problem-solving is frequently referred to as "the ability to understand the environment, identify complex problems, review related information to develop, evaluate strategies and implement solutions to build the desired outcome." Children's problem-solving abilities are essential because they offer a framework for successfully addressing and resolving difficulties. Children with problem-solving abilities may find suitable answers to issues and accomplish their goals because they foster critical thinking and reasoning. Studies have indicated that children who participate in individual or group problem-solving activities gain resilience and get an innovative perspective on issues. Children's ability to solve problems is essential during disasters because it enables them to react appropriately to unforeseen obstacles, make wise decisions, and remain safe. In times of emergencies, children can use their problem-solving abilities by identifying possible threats and responding immediately to protect themselves and their community. The first step in problem-solving is to identify potential dangers in their immediate environment, such as regions that are prone to flooding, unstable structures, or fire threats. Children can have a greater comprehension of their surroundings and be better equipped to make decisions in the event of a disaster by participating in activities such as risk assessment exercises and hazard mapping.

Decision-Making

Every human action is centered on making decisions or choices. Making decisions involves choosing a certain course of action from a range of options to accomplish a set of predetermined objectives. The process of selecting a course of action, obtaining data, and evaluating potential solutions is known as decision-making. The ability to identify risk, create action plans, and collaborate with others are all necessary for making decisions effectively in difficult situations. By critically evaluating circumstances, putting safety first, and acting appropriately, children can use their decision-making abilities in an emergency. In such a situation, individuals must immediately assess their surroundings, recognize dangers, and make wise decisions. Through disaster-preparedness decision-making, children can help their community be ready for disasters. They can take part in making emergency kits, determining safe areas, and talking about emergency plans as a family. Their decision-making skills are improved and a sense of responsibility is fostered when they are encouraged to express their ideas and participate in readiness exercises.

Critical Thinking

Critical thinking is the capacity to comprehend, assess, and analyse the information at hand to decide or determine whether something is correct or incorrect. Critical thinking abilities are a potent collection of mental tools that help us solve difficult problems, assess evidence, analyse complex information, and make well-reasoned decisions. In disaster situations, children can use critical thinking abilities by assessing possible risks and coming to well-informed conclusions to protect themselves and others. Children who use critical thinking skills are better able to weigh risks, analyse various information sources, and foresee potential outcomes. Their ability to think critically enables children to come up with alternate solutions, including setting up temporary classrooms during school closures or making emergency shelters out of resources on hand. Additionally, during an emergency, critical thinking enables children to distinguish between trustworthy and untrustworthy information. Misinformation can spread swiftly in this age of social media and immediate communication.

Creative Thinking

The term "creative thinking" describes the application of aptitudes and soft skills to provide novel solutions to issues. Creative thinking abilities are methods for approaching the problem from many innovative perspectives, utilizing the appropriate instruments to evaluate it and formulate a strategy. Children can use their creative thinking abilities in disaster situations by coming up with original answers to problems they encounter before, during, and following disasters. They can tackle issues from a variety of angles due to creative thinking, which also helps them come up with ingenious solutions to aid others, stay safe, and rebuild their communities. Children who can think quickly and creatively are better able to cope with stress and uncertainty during emergencies. Creative thinking helps in recovery and reconstruction after a disaster. Children can offer suggestions for improving the resilience of their communities or schools, such as creating safer school buildings or coming up with innovative ways to conduct emergency drills.

Effective Communication

Good communication is essential in many facets of life. All crises are inherently unpredictable and extremely dynamic, resulting in social, emotional, and physiological disorders. During a disaster, effective communication entails employing simple language, conveying timely, clear, and simple information to the public through reliable channels, modifying messages for various audiences, and demonstrating empathy and recognition of the event's emotional impact. Children need to be able to communicate well to securely and effectively handle adverse scenarios. In an emergency, being able to communicate concisely and clearly guarantees that they can properly follow instructions, ask for assistance, and convey their requirements. In times of disaster, nonverbal communication is just as crucial. When noise, fear, or language problems prevent children from communicating verbally, they might utilize gestures, facial expressions, or even written communications. Children can become more mindful of the requirements and emotions of others around them if they are taught to identify and decipher nonverbal clues from others.

Interpersonal Relationships

Interpersonal skills include the capacity to interact with others and establish connections. Children's interpersonal interaction skills are essential in disaster situations because they promote collaboration, emotional support, and efficient communication both during and after a crisis. Children must cooperate, communicate their emotions, and support one another during disasters because they frequently cause uncertainty, worry, and stress. Effective communication is one method children can use to practise interpersonal skills. Another important interpersonal skill children can use in a catastrophe situation is empathy. In an emergency scenario, teamwork and collaboration are also essential interpersonal skills. Children who function well in groups can contribute more successfully, whether they are taking part in a school evacuation practice or assisting with the distribution of goods in a shelter. To make sure that everyone is secure and supported, they can collaborate, divide duties, and take shifts.

Empathy

The word "empathy" can refer to a variety of situations. Empathy, according to psychologists, is the capacity to imagine what another person could be thinking or experiencing as well as to detect their emotions. Children who possess empathy are better able to comprehend and assist others in times of need, especially during emergencies. Children who advance in empathy are more perceptive of the feelings and hardships of others impacted by disasters, whether they are friends, family, or neighbors. They can handle situations with love and compassion because of their emotional awareness, which fortifies social ties and promotes togetherness in trying times. Children can put their empathy skills to use practically by actively assisting others in need. By taking part in neighborhood clean-ups, distributing supplies, or organizing shelters, they can support relief efforts.

Coping with Stress

Stress is a normal response to some situations and expectations, but persistent stress can negatively affect one's health and well-being. Stress does not necessarily affect children the same way it does adults. Disasters are difficult circumstances that can seriously damage families and communities. Children who experience a disaster may exhibit signs of post-traumatic stress disorder, anxiety, and despair. By identifying and expressing their feelings in appropriate ways, children can use stress-coping techniques in an emergency situation. Another crucial coping mechanism in crisis scenarios is the development of a sense of routine. The breakdowns resulting from disastrous events can create uncertainty, thus it is critical for children to maintain a daily routine, even in temporary shelters. Participating in routine activities such as schoolwork, games, and domestic tasks can provide a sense of security and control. Schools and community initiatives can help by developing scheduled activities that allow youngsters to re-establish a sense of normalcy. Social support is critical in helping children cope with stress in emergency scenarios. Children should be taught to ask friends, family, and teachers for help when they are feeling stressed. Emotional well-being and resilience can be enhanced by constructive social connections.

Coping with Emotions

Humans react emotionally to things that happen to them or to circumstances. Neurophysiological alterations cause emotions, which are mental and physical states that are varyingly linked to sensations, thoughts, behavioral reactions, and a level of pleasure or dissatisfaction. A child's emotional reaction to an emergency will differ from that of an adult. Because their worldview is limited, individuals may struggle in placing events into context. Children who are conscious of their emotions can better handle stress since disasters might cause feelings of fear, grief, rage, or confusion. Encourage children to communicate about their observations with an adult they trust, write or draw to express their emotions, or engage in group conversations to help them process their emotions rather than suppress them. Children can benefit from learning relaxation skills like deep breathing, mindfulness, or physical exercise to help them relax both mentally and physically in stressful situations. Children may more effectively regulate their emotions and adjust to the difficulties presented by disasters by using these coping mechanisms.

The SEP was a key initiative implemented by DPSSDM, and NIMHANS to support children in vulnerable communities. The program aimed to promote students' social, emotional, and cognitive growth through interactive and immersive learning techniques. SEP sessions helped students overcome learning gaps and adjust to the learning atmosphere during the pandemic by emphasizing academic skill development, emotional control, and personal development. The objectives of the program were to increase students' resilience, self-awareness, critical thinking, and problem-solving skills. Free listening, group discussions, role-playing, and games were among the activities used to make sure that the learning process was interesting and productive. In addition to meeting children's scholastic demands, the SEP gave them vital life skills that will help them deal with future obstacles.

The Importance of Integrating Life Skills Education (LSE) and Student Enrichment Programme (SEP) into Disaster Risk Reduction (DRR)

Disasters of every kind are major risks to populations around the world. The information, skills, and perspectives that students need to be prepared for, respond to, and bounce back from emergencies are mostly provided by schools, which serve as centers of learning and social development. As pillars of society, schools must prepare students for such situations. Life Skills Education (LSE) and Student Enrichment Programme (SEP) seek to offer prospects for practical education that develop students into well-rounded individuals who can manage a range of life circumstances. Children who participate in LSE gain vital problem-solving, decision-making, handling emotions, and coping skills that help them confront emergencies. By fostering the adaptive behaviors and stress-reduction strategies necessary for disaster preparedness and recovery, it promotes resilience. In a similar vein, SEP allows students to utilize life skills in actual crises by offering an organized framework for experiential learning. Children actively participate in risk assessment, disaster planning, and community preparedness measures when these programs are integrated into DRR projects. This method guarantees that children not only comprehend possible risks but also acquire the skills required to defend themselves and assist others in times of need.

Conclusion

Natural or man-made disasters have an extensive influence on children, affecting their social development, education, and psychological health. Children are particularly vulnerable in catastrophe situations, so it is important to incorporate psychosocial support systems that address both short-term trauma and long-term emotional and cognitive resilience. The Department of Psychosocial Support in Disaster Management (DPSSDM), NIMHANS has been crucial in initiatives to recover from the pandemic. Their programs, such as the Student Enrichment Programme (SEP) and Life Skills Education (LSE), have been crucial in helping children develop critical thinking, emotional control, and problem-solving abilities. These initiatives have improved children's capacity to overcome obstacles in the future while also lessening the psychological effects of disasters. Through the integration of psychological preparedness into disaster risk reduction measures, DPSSDM and NIMHANS have exhibited a multi-sectoral strategy that encompasses community stakeholders, educators, and mental health professionals. The focus on social connectivity, resilience building, and adaptive coping strategies has created a culture of readiness in children, empowering them to take an active role in their own safety and healing.

References

19. Psychosocial support | Epidemic Control Toolkit. (n.d.). https://epidemics.ifrc.org/volunteer/action/19-psychosocial-support

7.A-7-Coping with the emotional response to disaster. (n.d.). Anthem. https://www.anthem.com/mental-health/emotional-impact-of-disaster

Admin. (2022, December 7). *Sendai framework for disaster risk reduction—An overview.* BYJUS. https://byjus.com/free-ias-prep/sendai-framework-disaster-risk-reduction/

Ahmed, G. K., Elbeh, K., Gomaa, H. M., et al. (2021). Does COVID-19 infection have an impact on children's psychological problems? *Middle East Current Psychiatry, 28*, 77. https://doi.org/10.1186/s43045-021-00155-z

Algorani, E. B., & Gupta, V. (2025, January–). Coping mechanisms. [Updated 2023 Apr 24]. In *StatPearls* [Internet]. StatPearls Publishing. Retrieved from https://www.ncbi.nlm.nih.gov/books/NBK559031/

Amatya, B., & Khan, F. (2023). Disaster response and management: The integral role of rehabilitation. *Annals of Rehabilitation Medicine, 47*(4), 237–260. https://doi.org/10.5535/arm.23071

Arshad, M., Mughal, M. K., Giallo, R., & Kingston, D. (2020). Predictors of child resilience in a community-based cohort facing flood as natural disaster. *BMC Psychiatry, 20*(1). https://doi.org/10.1186/s12888-020-02944-y

Before, during, and after an emergency. (2024, October 24). *Children and school preparedness.* https://www.cdc.gov/children-and-school-preparedness/before-during-after/index.html

Blogger, G. (n.d.). *The importance of including children in emergency preparedness planning.* https://info.childcareaware.org/blog/importance-including-children-emergency-preparedness-planning

Central Square Foundation, Singh, B. D., Jr., & Menon, R. (2015). Life skills education in India. In *Life skills in India.* https://medha.org.in/user-content/uploads/2020/10/Life-Skills-in-India-CSF.pdf

Children and Disasters. (n.d.). SAMHSA. https://www.samhsa.gov/dtac/disaster-survivors/children-and-disaster

Choo, M., & Yoon, D. (2024). A meta-analysis of the relationship between disaster vulnerability and disaster damage. *International Journal of Disaster Risk Reduction, 102*, 104302. https://doi.org/10.1016/j.ijdrr.2024.104302

Cianconi, P., Hanife, B., Grillo, F., Zhang, K., & Janiri, L. (2021). Human responses and adaptation in a changing climate: A framework integrating biological, psychological, and behavioural aspects. *Life (Basel, Switzerland), 11*(9), 895. https://doi.org/10.3390/life11090895

Comfort, L. K., & Wukich, C. (2013). Developing decision-making skills for uncertain conditions: The challenge of educating effective emergency managers. *Journal of Public Affairs Education, 19*(1), 53–71. https://doi.org/10.1080/15236803.2013.12001720

Considering the impact of COVID-19 on children. (2025, February 5). https://www.who.int/europe/activities/considering-the-impact-of-covid-19-on-children

COVID-19's devastating impact on children. (2020, October 28). *Human Rights Watch.* https://www.hrw.org/news/2020/04/09/covid-19s-devastating-impact-children

Dannen, R., & Dannen, R. (2024, April 28). *Esteem | YWCA Spokane*. YWCA Spokane |. https://ywcaspokane.org/survivetothrive-esteem/

De Rubeis, V., Lee, J., Anwer, M. S., Yoshida-Montezuma, Y., Andreacchi, A. T., Stone, E., Iftikhar, S., Morgenstern, J. D., Rebinsky, R., Neil-Sztramko, S. E., Alvarez, E., Apatu, E., & Anderson, L. N. (2021). Impact of disasters, including pandemics, on cardiometabolic outcomes across the life-course: A systematic review. *BMJ Open, 11*(5), e047152. https://doi.org/10.1136/bmjopen-2020-047152

De Ville De Goyet, C., Marti, R. Z., & Osorio, C. (2006). *Natural disaster mitigation and relief.* Disease Control Priorities in Developing Countries—NCBI Bookshelf. https://www.ncbi.nlm.nih.gov/books/NBK11792/

Definition: Disaster risk reduction. (2007, August 30). UNDRR. https://www.undrr.org/terminology/disaster-risk-reduction#:~:text=Disaster%20risk%20reduction%20is%20aimed,the%20achievement%20of%20sustainable%20development

Deshpande, R. S. (2022). Disaster management in India: Are we fully equipped? *Journal of Social and Economic Development, 24*(Suppl. 1), 242–281. https://doi.org/10.1007/s40847-022-00225-w

Dimitrova, M., & Snair, M. (2024). Classifying disaster risk reduction strategies: Conceptualizing and testing a novel integrated approach. *Globalization and Health, 20*(1). https://doi.org/10.1186/s12992-023-01006-8

Disaster response and relief. (2022, November 22). Unacademy. https://unacademy.com/content/upsc/disaster-management-notes/disaster-response-and-relief/

Doma, H., Tran, T., Romero, L., Makleff, S., Krishna, R. N., Varshney, K., & Fisher, J. (2023). Effects of natural hazards on early childhood development: A systematic review protocol. *BMJ Open, 13*(6), e070068. https://doi.org/10.1136/bmjopen-2022-070068

Du, Y., Ding, Y., Li, Z., & Cao, G. (2015). The role of hazard vulnerability assessments in disaster preparedness and prevention in China. *Military Medical Research, 2*(1). https://doi.org/10.1186/s40779-015-0059-9

Dutta, K. K., & Talegaonkar, V. (2022). Impact of prolonged Covid-19 pandemic lockdown on residential Institute of Underprivileged children and its functionaries, managed by an NGO—A case study. *Interwoven: An Interdisciplinary Journal of Navrachana University, 5*(1). Navrachana University. https://nuv.ac.in/wp-content/uploads/pdf/interwoven/issue/Volume5_50.pdf

Emerging minds—Browser unsupported. (n.d.). https://emergingminds.com.au/resources/emotional-regulation/

Empathy Definition | What is empathy. (n.d.). *Greater good*. https://greater-good.berkeley.edu/topic/empathy/definition

Felman, A. (2023, October 27). *Why stress happens and how to manage it*. https://www.medicalnewstoday.com/articles/145855#physical-effects

Gayatri, M., & Puspitasari, M. D. (2022). The impact of COVID-19 pandemic on family well-being: A literature review. *Family Journal (Alexandria, VA), 31*, 10664807221131006. https://doi.org/10.1177/10664807221131006

GBD 2017 Disease and Injury Incidence and Prevalence Collaborators. (2018). Global, regional, and national incidence, prevalence, and years lived with disability for 354 diseases and injuries for 195 countries and territories, 1990–2017: A systematic analysis for the Global Burden of Disease Study 2017. *Lancet (London, England), 392*(10159), 1789–1858. https://doi.org/10.1016/S0140-6736(18)32279-7

Guariso, A., & Nyqvist, M. B. (2023). The impact of the COVID-19 pandemic on children's learning and wellbeing: Evidence from India. *Journal of Development Economics, 164*, 103133. https://doi.org/10.1016/j.jdeveco.2023.103133

Guglani, B. (2023, December 2). The impact of COVID-19 on underprivileged children's education. *Medium*. https://medium.com/@bharat.guglani15/the-impact-of-covid-19-on-underprivileged-childrens-education-85798c248b85

Guha-Sapir, D., & Vanderveken, A. (2016, December). *CRED CRUNCH: 2016 preliminary data: Human impact of natural disasters* (Issue No. 45). Centre for Research on the Epidemiology of Disasters (CRED).

Ha, K. M. (2021). Mitigating psychological impact: The experience of Korean disaster management. *Community Mental Health Journal, 57*(3), 416–423. https://doi.org/10.1007/s10597-020-00671-y

Handbook, U. E. (2024, January 16). Mental Health and Psychosocial Support (MHPSS). *UNHCR*. https://emergency.unhcr.org/emergency-assistance/health-and-nutrition/mental-health-and-psychosocial-support-mhpss

Harville, E. W., Beitsch, L., Uejio, C. K., Sherchan, S., & Lichtveld, M. Y. (2021). Assessing the effects of disasters and their aftermath on pregnancy and infant outcomes: A conceptual model. *International Journal of Disaster Risk Reduction: IJDRR, 62*, 102415. https://doi.org/10.1016/j.ijdrr.2021.102415

Helping Children Cope with Disaster. (2023, May 2). FEMA.gov. https://www.fema.gov/fact-sheet/helping-children-cope-disaster#:~:text=Here%20are%20some%20tips%20to,provide%20a%20sense%20of%20familiarity

http://www.saludydesastres.info/index.php?option=com_content&view=article&id=175:5-4-atencion-de-la-salud-mental-y-apoyo-

psicosocial&catid=160:5-4-atencion-de-la-salud-mental-y-apoyo-psicosocial &Itemid=492&lang=en
https://dergipark.org.tr/en/download/article-file/1980120
https://doi.org/10.1093/reep/rez004
https://nidm.gov.in/PDF/Disaster_about.pdf
https://socialwelfare.vikaspedia.in/viewcontent/social-welfare/disaster-management-1/national-disaster-management-disaster-mental-health-services/introduction-to-mental-health-and-psychosocial-support?lgn=en
https://www.physiopedia.com/Protecting_the_Vulnerable_in_Disasters_and_Conflicts
https://www.researchgate.net/publication/383241976_Maslow's_Hierarchy_of_Needs#:~:text=Maslow's%20hierarchy%20of%20needs%20is,esteem%2C%20and%20self%2Dactualization
https://www.unesco.org/en/disaster-risk-reduction
https://www.unhcr.org/sites/default/files/legacy-pdf/4c98a5169.pdf
https://www.unicef.org/disaster-risk-reduction-and-recovery
https://www.unicef.org/disaster-risk-reduction-and-recovery?utm_source=chatgpt.com
https://www.unicef.org/india/impact-covid-19-childrens-mental-health#:~:text=Grief%2C%20fear%2C%20uncertainty%2C%20social,the%20mental%20health%20of%20children
https://www.unicef.org/malaysia/stories/building-childrens-resilience-towards-disaster-through-education
https://www.who.int/news/item/13-10-2020-impact-of-covid-19-on-people's-livelihoods-their-health-and-our-food-systems
Hyams, J., Save the Children, Child Protection Working Group, & International Federation of Red Cross and Red Crescent Societies. (n.d.). Child protection in disasters and emergencies. In *International Federation of Red Cross and Red Crescent Societies public awareness and public education for disaster risk reduction* (pp. 123–126). https://www.ifrc.org/sites/default/files/2021-06/22-PART-B3-HR-1.pdf
Iacoviello, B. M., & Charney, D. S. (2014). Psychosocial facets of resilience: Implications for preventing posttrauma psychopathology, treating trauma survivors, and enhancing community resilience. *European Journal of Psychotraumatology, 5*(1). https://doi.org/10.3402/ejpt.v5.23970
International Federation of Red Cross and Red Crescent Societies. (2005–2007). Psychosocial framework. International Federation of Red Cross and Red Crescent Societies.

International Federation of Red Cross and Red Crescent Societies. (2018). *Public awareness and public education for disaster risk reduction: Action-oriented key messages for households and schools* (Second). https://www.ifrc.org/sites/default/files/PAPE-2.0-English.pdf

Introduction to Disaster Management cycle. (2022, November 22). Unacademy. https://unacademy.com/content/upsc/disaster-management-notes/introduction-to-disaster-management-cycle/

Kar, N. (2010). Indian research on disaster and mental health. *Indian Journal of Psychiatry, 52*(Suppl. 1), S286–S290. https://doi.org/10.4103/0019-5545.69254

Keya, T. A., Leela, A., Habib, N., Rashid, M., & Bakthavatchalam, P. (2023). Mental health disorders due to disaster exposure: A systematic review and meta-analysis. *Cureus, 15*(4), e37031. https://doi.org/10.7759/cureus.37031

Kousky, C. (n.d.). Impacts of natural disasters on children. In Emilia Simeonova, Johns Hopkins University, Resources for the Future, & Save the Children (Eds.), *The future of children* (pp. 73–75). https://files.eric.ed.gov/fulltext/EJ1101425.pdf

Krishna, R. N., Spencer, C., Ronan, K., & Alisic, E. (2022). Child participation in disaster resilience education: Potential impact on child mental well-being. *Disaster Prevention and Management an International Journal, 31*(2), 134–143. https://doi.org/10.1108/dpm-03-2021-0110

Lazzara, J. (2020, June 26). *Middle childhood*. Pressbooks. https://open.maricopa.edu/devpsych/chapter/chapter-6-middle-childhood/

Math, S. B., Nirmala, M. C., Moirangthem, S., & Kumar, N. C. (2015). Disaster management: Mental health perspective. *Indian Journal of Psychological Medicine, 37*(3), 261–271. https://doi.org/10.4103/0253-7176.162915

Mental Health & Psychosocial Support (MHPSS). (2024, December 12). https://wkc.who.int/our-work/health-emergencies/knowledge-hub/mental-health-psychosocial-support-(mhpss)

Mohammadinia, L., Ardalan, A., Khorasani-Zavareh, D., Ebadi, A., Malek-Afzali, H., & Fazel, M. (2017). The resilient child indicators in natural disasters: A systematic review protocol. *Health in Emergencies & Disasters Quarterly, 2*(2), 95–100. https://doi.org/10.18869/nrip.hdq.2.2.95

MSEd, K. C. (2023, June 29). Emotions and types of emotional responses. *Verywell Mind*. https://www.verywellmind.com/what-are-emotions-2795178

Mudavanhu, C., Manyena, S. B., Collins, A. E., Bongo, P., Mavhura, E., & Manatsa, D. (2015). Taking children's voices in disaster risk reduction a step forward. *International Journal of Disaster Risk Science, 6*(3), 267–281. https://doi.org/10.1007/s13753-015-0060-7

National Portal of India. (n.d.). https://www.india.gov.in/

New School: A modern approach to disaster risk reduction and resilience education for children. (n.d.). https://hazards.colorado.edu/news/research-counts/new-school-a-modern-approach-to-disaster-risk-reduction-and-resilience-education-for-children

Newnham, E. A., Tearne, J., Gao, X., Guragain, B., Jiao, F., Ghimire, L., Balsari, S., Chan, E., & Leaning, J. (2018). Tailoring disaster risk reduction for adolescents: Qualitative perspectives from China and Nepal. *International Journal of Disaster Risk Reduction, 34*, 337–345. https://doi.org/10.1016/j.ijdrr.2018.12.020

News-Medical. (2024, February 12). *Long COVID in children: A closer look reveals lasting impacts.* https://www.news-medical.net/news/20240211/Long-COVID-in-children-A-closer-look-reveals-lasting-impacts.aspx

Orru, K., Hansson, S., Gabel, F., Tammpuu, P., Krüger, M., Savadori, L., Meyer, S. F., Torpan, S., Jukarainen, P., Schieffelers, A., Lovasz, G., & Rhinard, M. (2021). Approaches to 'vulnerability' in eight European disaster management systems. *Disasters, 46*(3), 742–767. https://doi.org/10.1111/disa.12481

Pal, A., Tsusaka, T. W., Nguyen, T. P. L., & Ahmad, M. M. (2023). Assessment of vulnerability and resilience of school education to climate-induced hazards: A review. *Development Studies Research, 10*(1). https://doi.org/10.1080/21665095.2023.2202826

Pfefferbaum, B., Pfefferbaum, R. L., & Van Horn, R. L. (2018). Involving children in disaster risk reduction: The importance of participation. *European Journal of Psychotraumatology, 9*(Suppl. 2). https://doi.org/10.1080/20008198.2018.1425577

Professional, C. C. M. (2024, September 20). *Adolescent development.* Cleveland Clinic. https://my.clevelandclinic.org/health/articles/7060-adolescent-development

Proulx, K., & Aboud, F. (2019). Disaster risk reduction in early childhood education: Effects on preschool quality and child outcomes. *International Journal of Educational Development, 66*, 1–7. https://doi.org/10.1016/j.ijedudev.2019.01.007

Psychosocial impact of the COVID-19 pandemic on the pediatric population: An implication for clinical practice. (n.d.). https://www.jpmer.com/abstractArticleContentBrowse/JPMER/26843/JPJ/fullText

Rana, I. A., Niazi, I. U. H. K., Khalid, Z., Nawaz, A., & Najam, F. A. (2023). A novel framework to assess multidimensional disaster resilience of children:

From conceptualization to quantification. *International Journal of Disaster Risk Reduction, 96*, 103914. https://doi.org/10.1016/j.ijdrr.2023.103914

Rao, K. (2006). Lessons learnt in mental health and psychosocial care in India after disasters. *International Review of Psychiatry, 18*(6), 547–552. https://doi.org/10.1080/09540260601037961

Scapini, V. (2020). Disaster, infrastructure damage, and health. *International Journal of Safety and Security Engineering, 10*(2), 219–225. https://doi.org/10.18280/ijsse.100208

Severin, P. N., & Jacobson, P. A. (2020). Types of disasters. In *Nursing management of pediatric disaster* (pp. 85–197). https://doi.org/10.1007/978-3-030-43428-1_5

Shah, S., & Plan International. (2013). Investing in the youngest: Early childhood care and development in emergencies. In Plan Australia, *Plan International*. https://iecah.org/wp-content/uploads/2013/04/Informe_ingles_Invertir_en_los_mas_jovenes.pdf

Shaluf, I. M. (2007). An overview of disasters. *Disaster Prevention and Management an International Journal, 16*(5), 687–703. https://doi.org/10.1108/09653560710837000

Sipabacus. (2024, July 30). *Why problem solving skills are essential for a child's development?* SIP Abacus. https://sipabacus.com/in/blog/why-problem-solving-skills-are-essential-for-a-childs-development/

Speaker Agency. (2024, April 25). *Effective communication: Essential skills for work, school, and life*. Speaker Agency. https://www.speakeragency.co.uk/blog/effective-communication-essential-skills-for-work-school-and-life

Srivastava, K. (2010). Disaster: Challenges and perspectives. *Industrial Psychiatry Journal, 19*(1), 1. https://doi.org/10.4103/0972-6748.77623

Stone, G., Witzig, T., & McIntosh, C. (2022). The impact of COVID-19 on school-age children. *Psychology in the Schools*. Advance online publication. https://doi.org/10.1002/pits.22831

Support, P. (n.d.). *Module five: Psychosocial support*. https://www.indianredcross.org/fmr/Module5.pdf

Teaching Problem-Solving Skills | Centre for Teaching Excellence | University of Waterloo. (n.d.). https://uwaterloo.ca/centre-for-teaching-excellence/catalogs/tip-sheets/teaching-problem-solving-skills

The Five Phases of Emergency Management | Bexar County, TX—Official website. (n.d.). https://www.bexar.org/694/Five-Phases

The hidden impact of COVID-19 on children's education | Health and Education Resource Centre. (n.d.). https://healtheducationresources.unesco.org/library/documents/hidden-impact-covid-19-childrens-education

United Nations. (n.d.). *International Day for Disaster Risk Reduction | United Nations*. https://www.un.org/en/observances/disaster-reduction-day
Van Lancker, W., & Parolin, Z. (2020). COVID-19, school closures, and child poverty: A social crisis in the making. *The Lancet. Public Health, 5*(5), e243–e244. https://doi.org/10.1016/S2468-2667(20)30084-0
Vincent, J., Santhakumari, R. M., Nair, A. N. K., Sharahudeen, A., Asvini, K. P., Suresh, M. M., Valamparampil, M. J., Gayathri, A. V., Sujatha, C., & Surendran, A. T. (2024). What our children lost and gained at the time of school closure during the Covid-19 pandemic: A study on psychological distress, behavioural concerns and protective factors of resilience among preschool children in Kerala, India. *International Journal for Equity in Health, 23*(1). https://doi.org/10.1186/s12939-023-02090-3
Vulnerability and Vulnerable Populations. (2024, October 24). https://wkc.who.int/our-work/health-emergencies/knowledge-hub/community-disaster-risk-management/vulnerability-and-vulnerable-populations
Vulnerable groups in emergencies—Humanitarian Global. (2021, September 28). https://humanitarianglobal.com/vulnerable-groups-in-emergencies/
Wahyuni, D. (2022). A brief study of actual and strategic issues field of people's welfare. In *Building children's participation in disaster risk reduction*. https://berkas.dpr.go.id/pusaka/files/info_singkat/Info%20Singkat-XIV-23-I-P3DI-Desember-2022-218-EN.pdf
Watson, J. T., Gayer, M., & Connolly, M. A. (2007). Epidemics after natural disasters. *Emerging Infectious Diseases, 13*(1), 1–5. https://doi.org/10.3201/eid1301.060779
What are life skills and why teach them? | British Council Greece. (n.d.). https://www.britishcouncil.gr/en/life-skills/about/what-are-life-skills
Winston, R., & Chicot, R. (2016). The importance of early bonding on the long-term mental health and resilience of children. *London Journal of Primary Care, 8*(1), 12–14. https://doi.org/10.1080/17571472.2015.1133012
Wisner, B., Blaikie, P., Cannon, T., & Davis, I. (2003). At risk: Natural hazards, people's vulnerability and disasters (2nd ed.). Routledge.
Wisner, B., Blaikie, P., Cannon, T., & Davis, I. (2007). At risk: Natural hazards, people's vulnerability and disasters. *The Geographical Journal, 173*(2), 189–190.
World Health Organization. (1994). Life skills education for children and adolescents in schools. Pt. 1, Introduction to life skills for psychosocial competence. Pt. 2, Guidelines to facilitate the development and implementation of life skills programmes. https://iris.who.int/handle/10665/63552

World Health Organization. (2020). *WHO | definitions: Emergencies [Internet].* WHO. World Health Organization.

Writer, R. C. (2023, October 16). Creative thinking skills: Definition and examples. *Rock Content.* https://rockcontent.com/blog/creative-thinking-skills/

Zar, H. J., Dawa, J., Fischer, G. B., & Castro-Rodriguez, J. A. (2020). Challenges of COVID-19 in children in low- and middle-income countries. *Paediatric Respiratory Reviews, 35*, 70–74. https://doi.org/10.1016/j.prrv.2020.06.016

18

Psychosocial Support for Harmony and Peacebuilding: Rebuilding Communities After Communal Conflict

Subhasis Bhadra, Kasi Sekar, and Allen R. Dyer

Introduction

Conflicts in human society are common, and many of these conflicts have deadly consequences that extend over years, decades, and generations. The country or region affected by conflict faces multiple developmental challenges. The causes of conflict are sometimes religion, ethnicity, or any other identity that has deep-rooted connection with the basic interest of controlling and gaining power. The Indian state of Gujarat had witnessed a terrible riot in 2002, following an incident of burning a train compartment on 27 February (Yagnik & Sheth, 2002), that led to a religious conflict between the majority and minority communities, which left about 1000 people dead and more than a million people displaced, striking at the very roots of human emotions orchestrated (Engineer,

S. Bhadra (✉) • K. Sekar
Department of Psychosocial Support in Disaster Management, NIMHANS, Bengaluru, Karnataka, India

A. R. Dyer
Psychiatry and Behavioral Sciences and Education, George Washington University, Washington, DC, USA

S. Bhadra et al. (eds.), *Psychosocial and Mental Health Support for Disaster Management in India*, Palgrave Studies in Disaster Science and Emergency Management,
https://doi.org/10.1007/978-3-032-02511-1_18

2003a, 2003b; Mander, 2004; Kothari, 2002). The disaster also caused a large number of secondary traumas like loss of habitat, resource base, and livelihood. Physical harassment, sexual violence, and injuries leading to disability were widespread. This not only resulted in acute stress for the individuals but also broke the social fabric of the community, rendering the struggle for survival even more difficult. Many relief and rehabilitation programs were initiated by local organizations and national organizations. From the first day, as the people battered by violence reached the community camps, the psychological needs surfaced prominently. Unfortunately, the violence, curfew, and displacement spread over many areas and continued for more than three months. Though the majority of the displaced people were from the minority community, people from the majority community belonging to the lower socioeconomic strata still faced a severe problem of earning as violence and curfew halted all the normal activities. As in other areas of India, also in the state of Gujarat, the Hindu and Muslim communities have traditionally lived alongside each other; this has not necessarily always been a completely peace coexistence, but there had never been such escalations of violence (Ahmed, 2004). Considering such a volatile situation, the approach that was adopted by the non-governmental organizations (NGOs) was to develop a forum and work for the support of the survivors. The first major forum was named 'AmanSmudaya' (Community for peace), and another major program, launched by CARE India, was 'Gujarat Harmony Project (GHP).'

Community-Based Peace-Building Project

'AmanSamudaya' (a campaign for peace and justice) was principally driven by Action Aid India, with support from other professionals and NGOs. This forum started in the aftermath of communal violence. *AmanSamudaya* addressed the issues in the different fronts like providing basic supplies, legal support to survivors of violence, a campaign against human rights violations, rehabilitating the vulnerable families, and providing psychosocial support to the survivors, traumatized women, children, and men. Under the banner of *'AmanSamudaya'*, peace and justice, psychosocial

support started immediately by identifying and training local community-level workers (CLW) through the NGOs. These CLWs were trained on the basic seven skills to provide psychosocial care and involve people in the community with multiple activities and subsequently in various peace-building efforts through community engagements (Chachra, 2004). In this programme, the CLWs called '*AmanPathiks*' (peace volunteers) were the backbone, spending time with the survivors and providing support.

The Gujarat Harmony Project (GHP) was funded by CARE India with a strong commitment to promote peace and harmony at a moment when the communities were torn apart with tension, mistrust and misleading information, worries, and insecurity. GHP, with the aim of promoting the value of idealistic pluralism, compassionate tolerance, and mutual acceptance, ensured that every program it funds has to be directed to ensure communal harmony by engaging people in the community through common dialogue, sharing ideas, exchanging support, and mutual cooperation. GHP evolved as a consortium of ten organizations with psychosocial support as an important component of all programs, where every worker could reach out to the survivors with an empathetic attitude and work hand in hand to rebuild individual psyches, family unity, and community commitments to harmony. GHP had a specific program focused on livelihood restoration, psychosocial support, social reconciliation, community education, and advocacy to promote social harmony (Ahmed, 2004).

Process of Moving from Relief Camp to Community

Immediately after the riots, the survivors, running for their lives, gathered in the core minority areas. These camps were organized in common community facilities such as school buildings and mosque campuses, and also in a burial ground. The survivors were immediately supported by the local organizations, businessmen, and other people, who stepped up before the arrival of organized support from the NGOs and the government. Coincident with the provision of basic relief supplies, psychosocial support was instituted to ensure basic healing in the lives of battered survivors. During this time in the relief camps, activities were initiated with children (play centers, recreational centers, etc.) and with women (engaging in community kitchen and in sewing, stitching, and craft work). Subsequently, in some camps, mobile libraries were organized, mass prayers were held, and there were regular discussions with the volunteers about making plans for the future. Men and youths took the biggest roles in managing the camp and also looking for compensation, rebuilding homes, and livelihoods. Gradually, people moved to the temporary shelters and to permanent housing. At this stage, people from the neighboring areas belonging to the majority community became increasingly involved. Various activity centers were initiated, and a series of community meetings, discussions, and community events were organized to engage people from both communities.

Psychosocial Support Program in Communities

Within the psychosocial support program, four basic strategies were adopted to facilitate communal harmony and peace building: first, capacity building of the staffs, then the volunteers through the training of trainers (TOT), cascade training by the TOTs to the volunteers, and regular follow-up workshops; second, providing supportive supervision in the field; third, development, and the use of psychosocial support manuals, pamphlets, posters; and fourth, identifying a strength area that could be supported to develop a specific peace-building programme for an NGO.

Capacity Building

Capacity building is the key pillar to the success of any program. In India, mental health is less recognized, and stress reactions are commonly understood as physical symptoms. In the situation of the riots, however, the rampage was so high that the psychological needs were very visible and openly expressed by the survivors in their inability to sleep, continuous nightmares, inability to control anger, unexplainable headaches, body aches and, specifically, the problems of the children who had witnessed the horrific events and the women who faced the threat of severe sexual assault. Hence, there was a need for training that encourages skill building among the community-level workers (CLW) to be with the survivors and provide support to facilitate normalization by reducing suffering and identifying a process to initiate mutual understanding among the community people belonging to both the Hindu and the Muslim communities. The design of a capacity-building module was a combination of multiple skill-building modules and basic skills for providing psychosocial support (namely, ventilation, active listening, empathy, social support, externalization of interest, relaxation and recreation, and spirituality) (Fig. 18.1). Also, specific methodologies for working with the children and women survivors, promoting communal harmony through various community engagement programs, challenging the stereotypes and prejudices to promote rational thinking, and, finally, a balanced emphasis on self-care strategies for the disaster intervention workers, were part of the module. This capacity-building program was a combination of

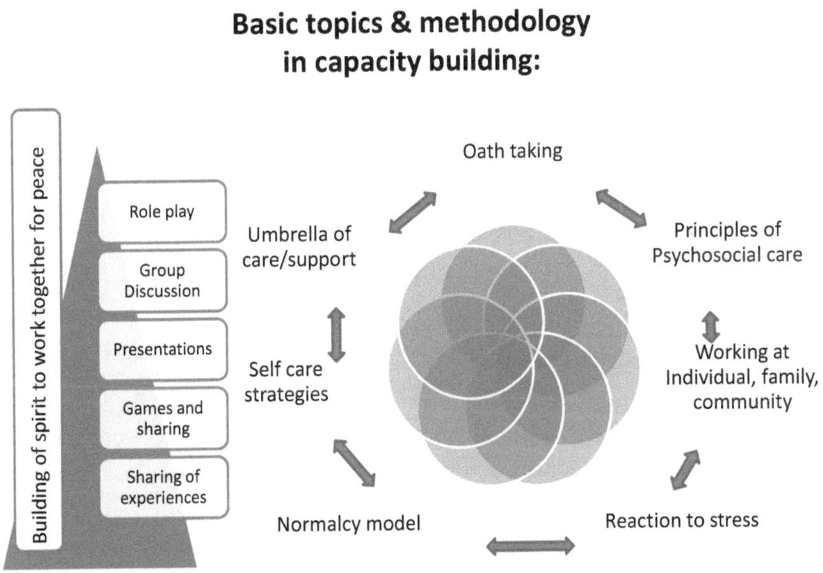

Fig. 18.1 Capacity building for psychosocial support

methodologies that encouraged experiential learning through various self-reflections of experiences during the riots, role-play, a number of group discussions with reflections, psychomotor-oriented games for learning concepts, and presentations by the facilitators. Initial capacity building was for a period of three days, and at times, evening or half-day sessions were conducted depending on the situation and context. But there was continuous support and follow-up by the mental health workers to work with the survivors. Subsequently, master trainer training was conducted by selecting some of the CLWs, coordinators of the program, to provide higher-level intensive training. The master trainer programme was conducted to develop a clear cascading model that the master trainer could supervise and support a group of about six or seven CLWs. Each of these could be in close contact with 25 families. As the situation was very demanding considering the perceived threat and prevailing sociopolitical tension, it was ensured that between three ans five CLWs could work together as a team (Fig. 18.1).

Supportive supervision was an essential step in ensuring the actual implementation of the training skills by the CLWs. Through supervisory visits, it was ensured that, in any situation, the CLWs would encourage the survivors to talk about their issues, feelings, and build a sense of support and trust with the group members and the surrounding environment. At this stage, a strong emphasis was made to integrate psychosocial support with all other interventions as an umbrella of support that every individual is taken care, families are supported to resume their function, and communities are intervened to re-establish their networks and relationships that a "sense of place" can be rejuvenated (Fullilove, 1996).

Peacebuilding Initiatives

Among the important vulnerable groups were: women who were sexually abused; children who witnessed violence, families that lost close relatives, and the youths who were used as muscle power in rioting. With each of these groups, specific program interventions were developed that were introduced as models of psychosocial support and peacebuilding. From the very initiation of the psychosocial program, promoting harmony was at its core; therefore, a few simple steps toward peacebuilding were considered for every intervention. All the organizations encouraged their Hindu workers to visit and work in the camp and in the minority areas so that a basic trust and empathy could be developed between the conflicting communities. In every program, the participation of both communities was mandatory. For example, in respect of livelihood promotion, the beneficiaries were from both the communities, and micro financing/self-help/saving-credit groups were developed with the participation of both Hindu and Muslim members (Bhadra, 2011). Peace committees were developed by the trained CLWs through the mobilization of the community leaders, both men and women, thereby ensuring equal participation. A number of activity centers, library, women groups, and youth groups were organized for peacebuilding, where interdependency and interaction between the communities were made mandatory by design. The supportive supervision, which was also known as a hand-holding exercise, was a process of continuous interaction with the CLWs. At the same time, the CLWs were allowed to reflect their challenges from the field so that they could be provided with adequate support by master trainers and the other programme experts in order to bring about improvements in the operation of the program.

Information Education Communication (IEC) Materials for Psychosocial Support

In this entire process of promoting communal harmony, the need for appropriate IEC materials for capacity building, and to disseminate information effectively to the survivors was a priority. Different psychosocial support materials were produced from time to time in the form of manuals, posters, pamphlets, handouts, etc. A numbers of songs, street plays, and poems were organized, written, and presented by the survivors, literary communities, and professionals in an attempt to promote peacebuilding. Various religious festivals, such as 'Ramzan' (the Muslim Holy month), 'Diwali' (the Hindu festival of light), and national days of importance (Republic Day, India's Independence Day, and the birthdays of national leaders such as Gandhi-ji, Baba SahebAmdebkar), were celebrated by members of both communities where songs on communal harmony, dramas, lectures, and interfaith religious prayers were organized to enhance mutual understanding. Material development was achieved through multiple examples of field-testing and follow-up to ensure that appropriate, intended messages were communicated and practiced by the target group. The materials that were produced differed in nature, including informational manuals for survivors (Dave et al., 2002; Sekar et al., 2002), community-level workers, and specifically for working with children and women. Another set of materials was developed for capacity-building purposes (e.g. workbook, handouts etc.). Finally, some IEC materials, such as posters and leaflets, were intended to promote mass community awareness.

Community Engagements for Peace

The overall structure of GHP incorporated eight NGOs with different specialized areas of focus. The purpose of GHP was to create a synergy between these NGOs and their programming so that each of their specialized skills could be shared and pooled together. Each of these organizations was supported by psychosocial support training and capacity-building activities. It was emphasized that every organization should ensure the implementation of the psychosocial support program's activities in an integrated manner. This included working with individuals, specifically with the vulnerable groups, families and developing groups of survivors, and conducting regular meetings to discuss their feelings and experiences. Sharing positive changes became a source of support for the members, rather than them continuing to function as simply as a micro-credit or livelihood group. At an individual level, through continuous psychosocial support the purpose was to reduce stress reactions and develop positive coping routines through participating in the family and community activities and developing better adjustments to the present situation. The intention behind working with the families was to strengthen their capacity to function as a cohesive unit by providing opportunities to resolve the issues and re-establish the family practices and rituals and to bring about better neighborhood relationships through group participation and community engagements. In turn, psychosocial support at community level was intended to enhance community participation at every level so that people develop their capacity to plan, design, and implement activities for rehabilitation and promotion of harmony. Through community participation, peacebuilding was made a reality, as physical proximity between the communities after the riots had raised the level of wariness; therefore, it was crucial to create a common platform for sharing and discussion, and to remove mental, social, and political barriers. Towards this goal, the model of peacebuilding through psychosocial support activities that was developed was structured as follows:

- Peacebuilding through activity centers for children, women, and youths.
- Community cultural events and peacebuilding.
- Women's collectives for peace.
- Youths for reconciliation.
- Life skills education to promote harmony and resiliency.

Peacebuilding through activity centers Activity centers were begun in the camps and continued in the temporary shelters as well as in the permanent housing, and in those affected areas where people were able to return to their reconstructed houses. The essential purpose of these centers was to provide a common platform in a most non-threatening, safe, and comfortable atmosphere to people from the communities. Strategically, these activity centers were established in the areas where the minority and majority communities lived in close proximity. These centers staged regular activities for the children, women, youths, as well as holding specific community events. To support the needs of the children, there were hobby centers, and pre-school centers where children from both communities could come together and spend time. For school-going children, there were supportive coaching and tuition classes to help them catch up on their studies following their absence from schools during the stay in camps. In addition, there were activity centers for the women, where classes for training in various skills was organized. This included activities such as sewing, stitching, the tailoring of simple clothing, and small-scale production of bags, folders, various food items etc. Through the activity centers, as the women came together, they were also supported in developing self-help groups, women for peace committees, etc. In all these community centers, the trained workers used to hold discussions about their reactions to stress, daily acts of religion, the value of humanity etc. In all these topics, free discussion among the participants from both communities emerged as the key factor in removing mental barriers and the drawing of the conclusion that acceptance, pluralism, justice, equality and rights are common to all human beings.

Community cultural events for peacebuilding Community-based participatory programs were initiated as people became settled in the areas, after a period of three to six months. At this time various community cultural events were organized through engaging very large numbers of people in common platforms through mass events, such as interfaith religious prayers, children's days, women's days, and celebrations which drew together people from many different communities in a common hall or on a community ground. Most of these mass gathering events were organized in communally sensitive areas so as to reduce stigma and to enhance a greater degree of trust between members of different communities. In these mass events, it was ensured that local leaders, religious leaders, and eminent figures from the nearby areas could join and give a message of peace, leading to the creation of a safe and harmonious habitat for everyone. These community events were seen as a major public forum which people could join after overcoming their concerns. The NGOs and the local volunteers also came into the limelight for their efforts in promoting harmony, which could have a wider impact on the wider civil society.

Women's collectives for peace 'Binding bonds of harmony' (Pathak, 2004) through initiating a trusting relationship between Muslim and Hindu women was one of the unique aspects of this program. The process of making the peace chain was initiated from individual contact and continued through group efforts, and then extended to the future generation (i.e., adolescent girls). The overall aim was to get all women together to generate and sustain the initiative for peace in different areas. Women who had received the training carried out individual contacts with women in different areas, both the Hindu and Muslim. Mostly, they continued the contacts that were established during the days spent in the relief camp. Further, they demonstrated, through discussion, that their problems are common for any woman without a job, livelihood, proper health, and housing facilities, irrespective of her religious faith. In the next phase, women from different religions were put together in a common forum of discussion to challenge each other's preconceptions and reach conclusions relating to their common problems and sufferings as a result of the riots. This phase of discussion was the most intensive, and resulted in the women developing essential bonds of trust and a shared commitment to maintain peace. At this stage, women had clearly understood that peace is essential for all, and that pain is equal for all if someone loses her house, husband, or family. Hence, the maintenance of peace is everyone's responsibility. In the next stage, those women send their adolescent daughters or young daughters-in-law to interact closely with the CLWs and learn about maintaining peace. These young girls were also supported with skill training through the organization of classes for sewing and stitching in order to increase their livelihood options. Further, these groups continued periodic inter-phase meetings in different areas and celebrated various mass events to promote peace and harmony.

Youths for reconciliation During the riots, the youth from the camps were motivated to help in the relief work and to support others who were in trouble. At the same time, they were engaged in the psychosocial support training session, which provided an opportunity was created to talk about their feelings of anger. This resulted in the expression of a great deal of hatred towards the people of other communities and also the leadership of political parties. During this phase, a number of the youths from the Hindu community, who had lost their jobs, were also mobilized. As they began to work together, their frustration and anger, and their desire for revenge, withered away gradually, and they felt good about their service to the affected people. Helping the affected people provided a great deal of satisfaction to the youth, helping them to overcome their feelings of inferiority and shame at not being able to save their families during the crisis. These initial contacts and various sessions helped to establish the commonality in the problems among the youths (e.g., unemployment, poverty, and lack of education among all the youths from both communities who belonged to the lower socioeconomic strata) beyond the religious boundary. With the help of these youth, some common places were identified in the community, and libraries were set up with a few books and materials for games. It was the young people who played the main part in developing these libraries, which eventually became a place for gathering and the sharing of information. At this time, youth groups played a major role in helping young people to withstand the pressure from religious groups to promote divisions in the community (Bhadra & Malik, Working paper series, 2008). As peace volunteers, these youths also developed various youth groups, called 'Micro Level Youth Groups,' in other areas and worked to ensure peace and tranquillity.

Life skills education Reconciliation and conflict resolution is a long-running process. Working to alleviate the immediate problems is one step. Young people must also be prepared to restore and maintain peace. Therefore, it was decided to promote psychosocial competencies among the children and adolescents in order to promote sustainable peace. Life skills education is one such approach. Recognized worldwide in various preventative and promotive activities, life skills enhance the coping capacities of young adolescents (Bharath et al., 2002; WHO, 1997, 2005). Life skills education was also essential in promoting higher self-worth and positive attitudes towards other community members, thereby helping to promote better psychosocial adjustment (Kovacev & Shute, 2004). Therefore, a life skills education program was initiated as a model in a few schools, with its focus on health promotion coupled with conflict resolution. Ten schools were selected from the middle economic background (both government-aided and trust-managed) from different areas of the violence-affected city. During the selection process, it was regarded as important to ensure a good mixture of religious backgrounds. Therefore, four Muslim-trust managed institutions, two Christian organization-managed schools and four Hindu-majority schools were selected. In a three-tier approach, the teachers were trained up during a two-day workshop on ten basic life skills: decision-making, problem solving, creative thinking, critical thinking, effective communication, inter-

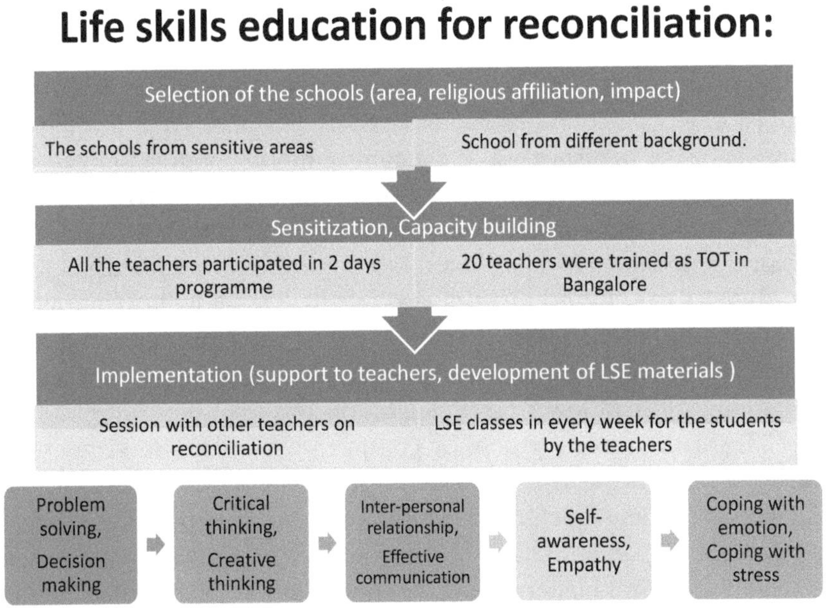

Fig. 18.2 Life skills education for peacebuilding and reconciliation

personal relationships, empathy, self-awareness, coping with emotions, and coping with stress (WHO, 1997). Additionally, a second group of teachers was selected as master trainers and trained through a weeklong residential program. These master trainers were given the main responsibility of coordinating the life skills sessions with other teachers. Various sessions were developed and practiced to promote the value of humanity, acceptance, and pluralism (Fig. 18.2).

Impact Assessment of Psychosocial Support

The positive impact of the psychosocial support program was quite evident from the response of the organizations, community-level workers, and the involvement of the survivors in the programme activities. Therefore, a rigorous research exercise was undertaken during the third year of intervention to evaluate the impact of the psychosocial support interventions. This study follows the quasi-experimental design, with both an experimental group and a control group. The experimental group consists of a population that had received psychosocial support interventions following the riots, while the control group's population had not received any such psychosocial care intervention (Sekar, Jayakumar, & Bhadra, An Evidence Based Research on Impact of Psychosocial Care for Disaster Ssurvivors in India (Draft), 2007). Different standardized tools were used to measure the psychological distress, disability, impact of events, quality of life, and economic burden. The result showed a clear difference between the experimental and control groups. The experimental group (7.8) had lower psychological distress than the control group (11.73). In the control group, by contrast, 77% of the survivors were regarded as probable cases for mental health problems, whereas 40% of the survivors of the experimental group were seen as probable cases, when a self-reporting questionnaire (SRQ) was used. The mean psychosocial disability score was higher among the control group (30.44) than among the experimental group (16.6) following the disability assessment schedule (WHO-DAS). In all domains of quality of life, i.e. physical, psychological, social and environmental aspects, the control group had a significantly lower score than the experimental group denoted low quality of life among the survivors who did not receive psychosocial support. The conclusion of this study was that the survivors who received psychosocial support experienced lower stress reactions and disabilities and enjoyed better health status and quality of life. It was also concluded that they had optimistic views about the future, had developed strong bonds with their neighbors, showed higher levels of participation in various community events, and spent more time in volunteering.

Sustainable Efforts of Peacebuilding

While the funded intervention of the Gujarat Harmony Project for peacebuilding ended in 2004, the local organizations continued their work of promoting peace and harmony. The International Medical Corps (IMC) conducted a needs assessment on November 2009 to investigate the long-term impact of the peacebuilding effort through the psychosocial support activities and the possibilities of working in India. It was seen that communal tension exists in the state for a variety of sociopolitical reasons, but the CLWs are very active in pursuing peace, and people have developed strong and trusting relationships with their neighbors in the intervention areas. All of the organizations have recalled that the psychosocial support training and work was one of the major skills and knowledge that helped them to establish rapport and initiate other interventions. In every activity which they have carried out the psychosocial support skills have been used to organize groups, to make field visits, and also to initiate events in the community for peacebuilding. At present, all the organizations have various programs and are continuing some of the psychosocial work that has been initiated, namely working with youths, women, and working with Self Help Groups (SHG), working with the teachers in schools, and facilitating life skills education etc. In their programs, he organizations still maintain the approach of bringing in people from different religious groups as beneficiaries and providing a continuous platform of sharing and discussion.

Throughout this whole approach of psychosocial support and peacebuilding, the major barrier was the power motive of casing rifts in society in order to gain power (Engineer, 2003a, 2003b; OOmmen, 2008).There were some other interventions for peacebuilding carried out by a number of organizations ensure justice for the survivors and strengthen the human rights perspective in the peacebuilding process. However, in a situation like this, where delivering justice was causing more worries in the immediate environment and sometimes further victimizing the minority community, it was essential to reinforce an unbiased image of the serving organizations working to re-establish peace and tranquility. Hence, throughout this process of psychosocial support and peacebuilding, the organizations had to be very careful about the political situation of the state and act rationally to involve the government systems in the peacebuilding process. In this respect, through the psychosocial support program, the organizations were engaged and developed close relationships with the government hospitals and government schools. Their involvement with the local self-government and the education department representatives showed that the approach of peacebuilding can be a long-term, non-threatening solution for everyone. Ultimately, in the long term the psychosocial support program for peacebuilding was part of the developmental program of the organizations where the psychosocial components of community participation, working with individuals, families, and groups, and facilitating of appropriate information through IEC materials are being practiced, developed, and modified according to need.

Restorative Justice and Peace

In the case of human-made disasters, such as riots, where human intention to cause harm is involved, more disturbances are created. Therefore, the peacebuilding process should be grounded in historical realities rather than looking only at present events. Ultimately, the focus of the program for establishing peace has to be in a continuum and merged with developmental needs so that social inequalities can be addressed and resolved in the process of ensuring a redistributive system of justice. This three-year intervention showed that removing mental barriers and promoting a common identity, along with acceptance, pluralism, and tolerance beyond religious or other identities that divides people is crucial for peacebuilding. Though time-bound programs can't change every causative factor of conflict, they can help establish a foundation for peace by ensuring individual responsibility and community support.

Complex emergencies, such as the turmoil witnessed in Gujarat in 2002, involve many levels of response, from local, state, and humanitarian communities, from immediate shelter and security to food and medical services, mental health and psychosocial support, and, ultimately, attempts at peacebuilding and community rehabilitation. The work of peacebuilding through psychosocial support was restored in accordance with models of restorative justice, depicted in the following diagram (Fig. 18.3).

Incidents of communal conflicts are complex in part because of the complexities of the power politics situation in which they occur, so ultimately, basic human rights must be recognized and justice restored. It is

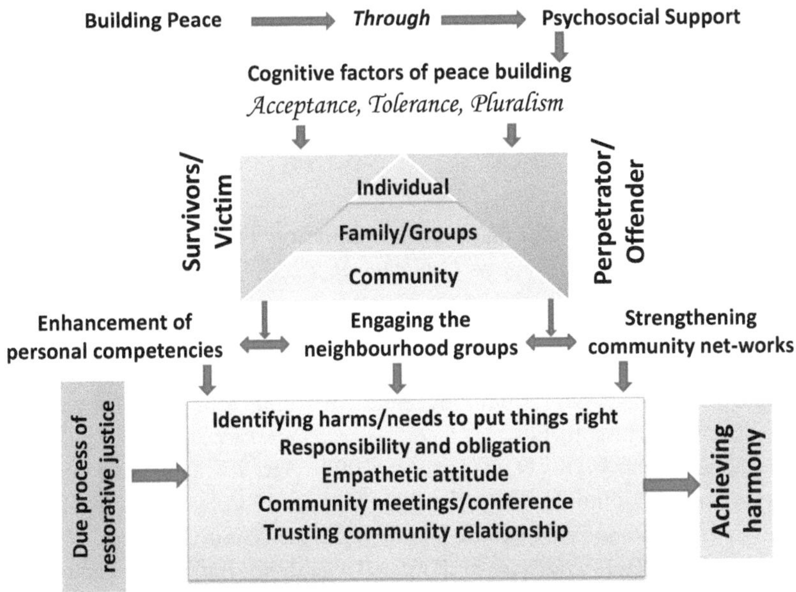

Fig. 18.3 Model of restorative justice through psychosocial support in peacebuilding

ironic in a sense that divisive forces pitted Hindu and Muslim communities against each other, when neither religion condones such violent and unjustified intolerance. Justice operates or fails to operate at many levels: spiritual, legal, and personal. The efforts of the humanitarian organizations working in Gujarat have attempted to go beyond justice as vengeance or retribution to inculcating a sense of restorative justice. Globally, restorative justice has been undertaken in many complex emergencies, where violence has occurred or might have been expected. Notable examples have been South Africa after apartheid, Rwanda after the genocide, Greensboro, North Carolina, USA, after a labor demonstration turned violent, and even in schools to address bullying, thievery, and fights. Restorative justice operates at a personal level where the involved parties come together in a community setting to acknowledge what has happened and to try to find a way to move forward together (Ikpa, 2007). Seldom is the process easy, as feelings can run high, but, as demonstrated in the case of Gujarat, careful humanitarian response can support healing over time.

References

Ahmed, S. (2004). Sustaining peace, re-building livelihoods: The Gujarat Harmony Project. *Gender and Development, 12*(3), 94–102.

Bhadra, S. (2011). Livelihood promotion for peace building in communities affected by human-made disasters. *Jharkhan Journal of Development and Management Studies, 9*(1), 4291–4301.

Bhadra, S., & Malik, M. (2008, November). Working with youth for peace. In S. Jaswal & J. Joseph (Eds.), *JTCDM working paper series* (pp. 33–34).

Bharath, S., Kumar, K. K., & Vranda, M. (2002). Activity manual for the teachers on health promotion using life skills approach: 8th Standard. In *Life skills manuals*. National Institute of Mental Health and Neuro Sciences.

Chachra, S. (2004). Disasters and mental health in India: An institutional response: Action Aid India. In J. O. Diaz, S. Murthy, & R. Lakshminarayana (Eds.), *Disaster mental health in India* (pp. 151–160). Indian Red Cross Society.

Dave, A. S., Sekar, K., Bhadra, S., Rajsekar, G. P., Kumar, K. K., & Murthy, S. (2002). Psychosocial care for individuals. In *Informational manual-1*. Books for Change.

Engineer, A. A. (2003a). *Communal challenge and secular response*. Shipra Publication.

Engineer, A. A. (2003b, January 25). Communal riots in 2002: A survey. *Economic and Political Weekly, 38*(4), 280–282.

Fullilove, M. T. (1996). Psychiatric implications of displacement: Contributions from the psychology of place. *American Journal of Psychiatry, 153*(12), 1516–1523.

Ikpa, T. S. (2007). Balancing restorative justice principles and due process rights in order to reform the criminal justice system. *Journal of Law & Policy, 24*, 301–325.

Kothari, R. (2002, November 30). Culture of communalism in Gujarat. *Economic and Political Weekly, 37*(48), 4823–4825.

Kovacev, L., & Shute, R. (2004). Acculturation and social support in relation to psychosocial adjustment of adolescent refugees resettled in Australia. *International Journal of Behavioral Development, 28*(3), 259–267.

Mander, H. (2004). People's action in disasters. In P. O. Diaz, S. Murthy, & R. Lakshminarayana (Eds.), *Disaster mental health in India* (pp. 231–237). Indian Red Cross Society.

Oommen, T. K. (2008). *Reconciliation in post-Godhra Gujarat: The role of civil society*. Pearson Education India.

Pathak, I. (2004). *Binding bonds of harmony*. AWAG.

Sekar, K., Dave, A. S., Bhadra, S., Rajsekar, G. P., Kumar, K. K., & Murthy, S. (2002). Psychosocial care by community level helper for survivors. In *Informational manual-2*. Books for Change.

Sekar, K., Jayakumar, C., & Bhadra, S. (2007). *An evidence based research on impact of psychosocial care for disaster survivors in India (Draft)*. Department of Psychiatric Social Work, NIMHANS.

WHO. (1997). *Life skills education for children and adolescent in schools; Program on Mental Health*. World Health Organization, Mental Health Division.

WHO. (2005). *The physical school environment, as essential component of health—Promoting school*. World Health Organization.

Yagnik, A., & Sheth, S. (2002, March 16). Whither Gujarat? Violence and after. *Economic and Political Weekly, 37*(11), 1009–1011.

19

Psychosocial Support After The Fukushima Triple Disaster, 2011: An Example of Cascading Disaster

Shubham Tiwari, Ateev Sudhir Chandna, and Dinakaran Damodharan

Introduction

According to the United Nations Office for Disaster Risk Reduction, a disaster constitutes a severe disruption in the functioning of a community or society due to hazardous events interacting with conditions of exposure, vulnerability, and capacity, leading to significant human, material, economic, and environmental losses.

Traditionally, disasters have been conceptualized linearly: hazards acting upon vulnerable populations result in risk and, subsequently, disasters.

S. Tiwari
Geriatric Psychiatry, NIMHANS, Bengaluru, Karnataka, India

A. S. Chandna • D. Damodharan (✉)
Department of Psychosocial Support in Disaster Management, NIMHANS, Bengaluru, Karnataka, India

S. Bhadra et al. (eds.), *Psychosocial and Mental Health Support for Disaster Management in India*, Palgrave Studies in Disaster Science and Emergency Management,
https://doi.org/10.1007/978-3-032-02511-1_19

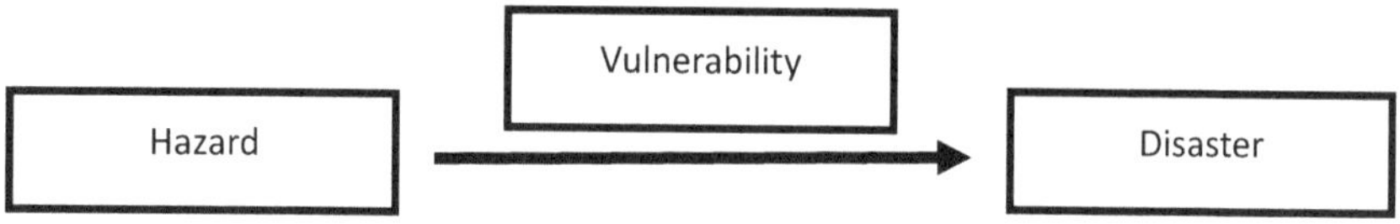

The concept of the magnitude–frequency relationship for natural hazards states that larger events occur less frequently. Modern understandings emphasize that hazards and vulnerabilities evolve and interact dynamically. Vulnerability manifests through various dimensions—physical, environmental, social, psychological, and institutional—that are deeply interconnected and mutually reinforcing.

$$\textbf{Hazard} \rightarrow \textbf{Vulnerability} \times \textbf{Vulnerability}\ldots\ldots\left[\textbf{/multiple exposures}\right] \rightarrow \textbf{Extended impact}$$

Overview of the Fukushima Tragedy

On March 11, 2011, Japan experienced an unprecedented chain of disasters: a magnitude 9.0 earthquake, a resulting tsunami, and the subsequent nuclear crisis at the Fukushima Daiichi Nuclear Power Plant. The failure of cooling systems at the plant led to reactor meltdowns and substantial releases of radioactive materials (Gauntt et al., 2012).

Key points of the disaster include:

- **Earthquakes and tsunamis:** Natural disasters cause extensive damage to plants' infrastructures, knocking out power, and turning off cooling systems.
- **Nuclear Meltdowns:** Overheating of the reactors led to core meltdowns, hydrogen explosions, and the release of radioactive materials.

Major releases into the atmosphere of radionuclides, including long-lived cesium-137, occurred, mainly in mid-March. The population within a 20 km radius had been evacuated three days earlier. The primary source of radioactive releases was the apparent hydrogen explosion in the suppression chamber of Unit 2 on March 15.

Impact of the Disaster

- **Humanitarian impact:** More than 19,000 people died, and approximately 154,000 residents were evacuated from the surrounding areas due to radiation risks.
- **Environmental Impact:** Contamination affected land, water, and food supplies, leading to long-term environmental and health concerns.
- **Economic Impact:** The local economy suffered from the destruction of businesses, agriculture, and fisheries. Rebuilding efforts have been substantial but costly.

The official investigation of the National Diet of Japan (2012) deemed the nuclear accident to be a man-made disaster, highlighting regulatory failures and lapses in safety standards by both government and private actors.

Mental health consequences after the Fukushima disaster The aftermath of the triple disaster left a lasting impact on mental health. Witnesses to the plant explosion and tsunami reported symptoms consistent with post-traumatic stress. Survivors faced unique dual trauma—natural disaster shock compounded by nuclear anxiety. Social dislocation, economic instability, and fear of radiation exposure—especially among mothers—fueled ongoing anxiety and depression.

Key Findings

- **PTSD Prevalence**: 25% of evacuees met the diagnostic criteria, **twice the rate of non-nuclear disasters** (Leppold & Reifels, 2024).
- **Radiation Stigma**: Evacuees reported **discrimination in housing and employment**, worsening self-stigma (Leppold et al., 2022).

Community fragmentation led to a rise in suicide rates and intensified psychological distress, particularly among evacuees, who also experienced stigma, both from others and internally. Notably, individuals living outside Fukushima showed elevated distress levels, which diminished when controlling for factors like job loss and diminished social networks. This underlines the importance of comprehensive support systems for evacuees, including job assistance and social reintegration efforts.

Multiple Disasters: Concept

Consecutive disasters	Consecutive disasters refer to two or more events that occur sequentially, with overlapping impacts that strain recovery capacities. A notable example is Haiti, which suffered multiple hurricanes in 2008, followed by a devastating earthquake in 2010, and a subsequent cholera outbreak. These overlapping crises intensified human suffering and delayed recovery processes
	One key feature of consecutive disasters is the gap—or lack thereof—between events. When recovery from the first event is incomplete before the next occurs, residual vulnerabilities persist or deepen. Damaged infrastructure, exhausted emergency resources, and unresolved trauma contribute to greater fragility, making communities more susceptible to subsequent shocks. Understanding and addressing these recovery gaps is essential to strengthening resilience and reducing cumulative disaster impacts
Compound disasters	Compound disasters involve simultaneous or closely timed events that interact to intensify their combined effects (Liu & Huang, 2014). These events often stem from distinct, yet converging hazards, amplifying challenges in response and recovery. A notable example is Hurricane Sandy in 2012, where a convergence of meteorological systems across North America and the North Atlantic influenced the storm's unusual trajectory and intensity. This interaction led to severe flooding and widespread damage across the New York metropolitan area
	Such events present particular difficulties because the compounding hazards may be individually manageable but become overwhelming in combination

Cascading disasters	Cascading disasters are characterized by an initial event setting off a chain of subsequent disruptions, each intensifying the severity and scope of impact. Unlike compound events, which occur in tandem, cascading effects unfold over time as interconnected systems fail one after another **Fukushima Case**: Earthquake → Tsunami → Nuclear meltdown → socioeconomic collapse, demonstrating critical infrastructure interdependencies
Recurring or recurrent disasters	Recurring disasters refer to the repeated occurrence of the same type of hazard in a specific geographic region over a period of time. These events may not always be linked causally, but their frequency amplifies cumulative impacts on infrastructure, public health, and social systems A prominent example is Pakistan's experience with severe flooding over three consecutive years—2010, 2011, and 2012. Each flood season brought renewed destruction to homes, agricultural land, and essential services. The repetition of similar disasters within short intervals hindered recovery, deepened vulnerabilities, and stretched the capacity of humanitarian and government agencies Persistent exposure to recurring disasters can erode resilience, especially in communities lacking adequate resources for preparedness and recovery

Cascading Disaster Cascades are events governed by cause-and-effect relationships. According to Pescaroli and Alexander (2016)

> "Cascading effects are the impact of a physical event or the development of an initial technological or human failure that generates a sequence of events in human sub-systems that result in physical, social, or economic disruption. Thus, cascading effects are complex and multi-dimensional and evolve constantly over time. They are associated more with the magnitude of vulnerability than with hazards. Low-level hazards can generate broad chain effects if vulnerabilities are widespread or not addressed properly in sub-systems."

Cascading effects are initiated when an initial hazard or failure sets off a chain of interrelated events, often magnified by systemic vulnerabilities. These effects depend more on societal and infrastructural fragility than the magnitude of the initiating hazard. **Escalation points**—moments when vulnerabilities align to exacerbate outcomes—are critical in understanding such disasters.

Key features of cascading disasters can be listed as follows:

Key features of cascading disasters can be listed as –

The primary event
↓
A chain or network of effects
↓
Secondary events
↓
A complex interaction of **vulnerabilities** that acts as **escalation points** and complex effects on **critical infrastructures**

Critical infrastructure refers to the systems, facilities, and assets vital for the functioning of society and the economy. They are interconnected, interdependent, and susceptible to the domino effect, leading to widespread consequences.

Examples—energy sector, water and wastewater system, chemical sector, healthcare, emergency, food and agriculture sector, etc.

Complex adaptive systems (CAS) Complex adaptive systems (CAS) theory views critical infrastructures as interconnected components that evolve and adapt but are prone to collapse when rigidities or failures cascade through the system.

The concept of "panarchy" illustrates how interactions within nested adaptive cycles influence overall system behavior. Holling (2001) emphasized that ecosystems—and, by extension, societal systems—go through repeated resource accumulation and renewal phases. These cycles involve the gradual build-up of potential, followed by periods of rapid transformation, often triggered by crises. The ability of a system to withstand or adapt to shocks—its "adaptive capacity"—reflects its level of vulnerability and resilience.

Panarchical Collapse A phenomenon known as "creative destruction"—where transformative events at one scale instigate breakdowns at others—can expose underlying vulnerabilities across systems. This dynamic highlights how the failure of one component or system can ripple outward, destabilizing other parts of a larger interconnected network. For example, a localized infrastructure failure, such as the breakdown of a power grid during a natural disaster, can escalate into a broader crisis affecting healthcare, communication, and emergency response systems. When this interplay is magnified across different sectors, the outcome can lead to a cumulative weakening of societal resilience, and even system-wide collapse.

This process may culminate in broader systemic crises with compounding consequences, particularly when rigid structures cannot adapt or absorb the shock. These cascading failures do not occur in isolation; instead, they emerge from the interactions among various sub-systems, each with vulnerabilities and thresholds for failure. Rinaldi et al. (2001) emphasize that critical infrastructure—encompassing utilities, transportation, finance, and communication—acts as the connective tissue of modern society. These infrastructures are intricately tied together, functioning as nodes where local disruptions can trigger wide-ranging national or global repercussions. Within this complex web, panarchies serve as the framework through which these systems interact across different spatial and temporal scales, linking global risks with local dynamics. Combining micro- and macro-level dynamics creates conditions where even low-impact triggers can initiate severe and far-reaching outcomes.

The Cascading Disasters Magnitude Scale

Planning for cascading disasters poses unique difficulties, primarily because many disruptions, interdependencies, and vulnerabilities are not immediately visible, as intricate and often-hidden connections shape them. Accurately mapping these linkages is essential to comprehend their influence and to formulate effective contingency strategies to manage their effects.

In this context, several key operational definitions are important. A crisis is "a threatening condition that requires urgent action." An incident is "a sudden event, typically resulting in an emergency, that necessitates intervention from one or more agencies. Incidents tend to be narrower in scope and impact compared to disasters." A disaster is "a major disruption to the functioning of a community or society that results in widespread human, economic, material, or environmental losses, exceeding the capacity of the affected population to manage using their resources."

This classification system introduces a structured framework for assessing cascading incidents, crises, and disasters. One of its most valuable features is comparability, which allows for evaluating different events by analyzing their cascading characteristics, particularly the emergence and impact of escalation points. However, it is important to note that cascading events are inherently dynamic, and their scale and intensity can shift over time, often growing more severe as they unfold.

Level 0 [Simple Incident or Major Incident]

There is no evidence of significant cascades or escalation points. Simple, direct, linear cause-and-effect relationships between the primary impact driver and its consequences. This level will mainly apply to geographically localized incidents of brief duration with no significant side effects or knock-on consequences.

Level 1 [Major Incident, of Limited Complexity]

At this stage, cascading effects are minimal and short-lived. Any secondary consequences are directly linked to the original incident, with no substantial interdependencies or escalation points. The relationship between the triggering event and its immediate outcomes is straightforward and isolated, lacking any significant ripple effects across systems.

Level 2 [Major Incident or Small Disaster, with Some Complex Consequences]

The initial event may trigger a limited sequence of effects that extend to a tertiary level. In such scenarios, secondary emergencies or complications that are nearly as critical as the primary event may arise. New vulnerabilities may be exposed, and escalation points may surface as the impact spreads into new domains.

Level 3 [Disaster, with Complex Consequences]

This level marks the emergence of more developed cascade chains, typically involving at least one escalation point. Various sectors—such as economic, social, environmental, and institutional—are simultaneously affected, creating interconnections between sub-systems. These interactions result in layered consequences, some of which may intensify the overall emergency.

Level 4 [Disaster, with Substantially Complex Consequences]

Here, cascading impacts are pronounced and easily observable. Vulnerability intersections become escalation points, extending and complicating the emergency. The fallout of the disaster permeates numerous aspects of daily life, significantly altering routines and conditions for extended periods. The original event may become secondary to its cascading effects regarding overall disruption.

Level 5 [Catastrophe, with Overwhelmingly Complex Consequences]

A high-impact event initiates long, branching chains of cascading consequences. Multiple escalation points generate parallel disruptions, infiltrating most or all aspects of regular societal function. The result is massive upheaval, often involving multiple concurrent crises triggered by systemic interdependencies. The disruption spans vast geographic areas and can have global repercussions, affecting international transport, trade networks, or communications. Notable examples include the 2004 Indian Ocean tsunami and the 2011 Fukushima disaster.

Determinants of Inter-Event Linkages

While identifying the scale of inter-event connections is essential, gaining insight into the underlying factors that govern their formation and intensity is even more critical. Effective mitigation strategies must be grounded in a thorough understanding of these influencing elements. These determinants are broadly categorized into **physical and human-related factors**. Depending on the characteristics of the initial event, physical causes may include **hydrological or geological** phenomena—such as earthquakes that result in tsunamis or prolonged rainfall triggering landslides.

On the other hand, human-related factors encompass a broad spectrum of macro- and micro-level dynamics. At the macro level, policies governing urban growth, energy use, and environmental management can significantly shape the trajectory and impact of disasters. At the community level, preparedness initiatives, risk-reduction efforts, and timely post-disaster response—such as rescue, relief, and reconstruction—can either buffer or amplify the cascading effects.

While separating these determinants into physical and human categories is helpful, the boundary between them is often blurred. For instance, extensive rainfall may trigger landslides due to deforestation or unsustainable land use—both human-induced alterations to the ecosystem. Moreover, changes in global climate patterns, increasingly influenced by anthropogenic activities, are transforming what were once considered natural and uncontrollable hazards. Thus, the long-held belief that natural hazards occur independently of human actions is being reevaluated in light of mounting evidence linking climate change to disaster frequency and severity.

Even when physical events lie beyond direct human control, proactive intervention is possible—and necessary—at the levels of exposure and vulnerability. This includes anticipating failures in interconnected systems, investing in resilient infrastructure, and building adaptive capacity within communities. By addressing these modifiable determinants, societies can significantly reduce the likelihood of one disaster leading to another and mitigate the ripple effects of cascading linkages.

One critical dimension of these inter-event linkages lies in the human-made systems upon which modern life depends. Over centuries, technological advancement has created intricate, high-efficiency infrastructures that support transportation, communication, energy, healthcare, and finance. However, these systems are often highly interdependent, with tightly coupled components that leave little room for error. As a result, a failure in one sub-system—especially during a natural hazard—can rapidly cascade across others, amplifying the overall impact.

The deeper our reliance on such complex systems, the more vulnerable we become to their disruption. A power outage during a flood, for example, might disable hospital operations, hinder emergency services, or interrupt supply chains—all within a short period. Therefore, while developing more robust and fail-safe technologies is essential, equal emphasis must be placed on fostering preparedness within communities. Populations must be equipped with knowledge, protocols, and resources to withstand the failure of these systems, particularly when natural hazards compromise the environments upon which those systems depend. Bridging this preparedness gap is critical to enhancing resilience in the face of cascading disasters.

Public Health Implications

Extensive research highlights the mental health burden faced by individuals exposed to multiple disaster events (Agyapong et al, 2023). High rates of psychological conditions—including acute stress reactions, post-traumatic stress disorder (PTSD), depression, panic disorder, and increased suicide risk—have been documented in such populations (Mitchell et al., 2024). Repeated exposure often results in cumulative psychological effects, with each additional event compounding the stress response. Contrary to some assumptions, experiencing one disaster does not appear to build psychological immunity against subsequent ones. Instead, the mental health impact varies with the intensity of exposure, which may include factors such as the level of destruction, personal injury, displacement, difficulty accessing essential resources, or perceived threat to life. Several protective and risk-modifying factors influence mental health outcomes after multiple disasters. These include individual traits like optimism, the will to live, psychological resilience, and external supports such as religiosity, strong social networks, and communal coping strategies. A sense of collective efficacy—believing that a community can recover and adapt—also contributes to psychological well-being (Grineski et al., 2022).

Significantly, the toll of recurrent disasters extends beyond mental health (Stough and North 2018). People affected by repeated events have shown a higher prevalence of physical conditions, such as hypertension, asthma, and chronic illness. Children, in particular, may suffer from delayed growth or development, while communities face spikes in water-borne and food-borne illnesses due to compromised infrastructure and sanitation. These findings underscore the need for integrated public health responses that address both psychological and physical dimensions of disaster impact.

In addition, systemic limitations such as understaffed healthcare facilities can severely impair disaster response efforts. When medical personnel are insufficient to meet surging demands, especially in crisis scenarios, the capacity to deliver timely care diminishes drastically. This challenge is further exacerbated by heightened **public complacency**—a phenomenon where individuals underestimate or dismiss potential threats, often failing to prepare despite clear warnings. Such attitudes may stem from prior false alarms, misinformation, or a sense of fatalism. Together, these factors delay emergency interventions, elevate the risk of preventable illness and death, and significantly prolong recovery in communities already strained by disaster.

Learnings from the Disaster from an Indian Perspective

India has faced several catastrophic events that illustrate the nature of cascading and compound disasters. One such example occurred on 26 January 2001, when a powerful earthquake measuring 7.9 on the Richter scale struck the Kutch region in Gujarat. The earthquake's epicenter was located northeast of Bhuj, and the tremors caused extensive destruction of homes, schools, infrastructure, and utilities, affecting more than 37 million people. In the wake of this natural disaster, another crisis emerged in February 2002, when communal riots erupted in Gujarat, displacing thousands and compounding the trauma of the earthquake's survivors. This sequence of events exemplifies how one disaster can set the stage for further human-induced crises.

Another critical example is the Indian Ocean tsunami of December 2004. While the immediate impact of the massive tidal waves was catastrophic, it also triggered a cascade of challenges related to displacement, loss of livelihoods, health emergencies, and long-term rehabilitation.

More recently, during the COVID-19 pandemic, India experienced numerous concurrent natural disasters, including cyclones, floods, droughts, flash floods, and landslides. These events placed immense pressure on an already overburdened health system and emergency services, highlighting the compounded nature of vulnerabilities during prolonged crises. The co-occurrence of these disasters during a global health emergency magnified social, economic, and infrastructural stresses, reinforcing the need for integrated and adaptive disaster risk management strategies tailored to multi-hazard environments.

References

Agyapong, B., Shalaby, R., Eboreime, E., Obuobi-Donkor, G., Owusu, E., Adu, M., et al. (2023). Effects of cumulative trauma from multiple natural disasters. *European Psychiatry, 66*, S949.

Gauntt, R. O., Kalinich, D. A., Cardoni, J. N., Phillips, J., Goldmann, A. S., Pickering, S. Y., et al. (2012). *Fukushima Daiichi accident study: Status as of April 2012* (No. SAND2012-6173). Sandia National Laboratories (SNL), Albuquerque, NM, and Livermore, CA (United States).

Grineski, S. E., Collins, T. W., & Chakraborty, J. (2022). Cascading disasters and mental health inequities: Winter Storm Uri, COVID-19 and post-traumatic stress in Texas. *Social Science & Medicine, 315*, 115523.

Leppold, C., & Reifels, L. (2024). Mental health in the context of multiple exposures to disasters. In *Major incidents, pandemics and mental health: The psychosocial aspects of health emergencies, incidents, disasters and disease outbreaks* (Vol. 7, p. 58).

Leppold, C., Gibbs, L., Block, K., Reifels, L., & Quinn, P. (2022). Public health implications of multiple disaster exposures. *The Lancet Public Health, 7*(3), e274–e286.

Liu, M., & Huang, M. C. (2014). *Compound disasters and compounding processes.* The United Nations Office for Disaster Risk Reduction.

Mitchell, A., Maheen, H., & Bowen, K. (2024). Mental health impacts from repeated climate disasters: An Australian longitudinal analysis. *The Lancet Regional Health–Western Pacific, 47*.

Pescaroli, G., & Alexander, D. (2016). Critical infrastructure, panarchies, and the vulnerability paths of cascading disasters. *Natural Hazards, 82*, 175–192.

Stough, L. M., & North, C. S. (2018). The association of adverse mental health effects with repeated exposure to disasters. *Annals of Clinical Psychiatry, 30*(1), 17–24.

Index

S. Bhadra et al. (eds.), *Psychosocial and Mental Health Support for Disaster Management in India*, Palgrave Studies in Disaster Science and Emergency Management,
https://doi.org/10.1007/978-3-032-02511-1

H

I

K

L

M

S

Kolibri 360 GmbH
Ferdinand-Jühlke-Straße 7
99095 Erfurt, Deutschland
produktsicherheit@kolibri360.de